THE ROUTLEDGE HANDBOOK OF THE HISTORY OF WOMEN'S ECONOMIC THOUGHT

The marginalization of women in economics has a history as long as the discipline itself. Throughout the history of economics, women contributed substantial novel ideas, methods of inquiry, and analytical insights, with much of this discounted, ignored, or shifted into alternative disciplines and writing outlets.

This handbook presents new and much-needed analytical research of women's contributions in the history of economic thought, focusing primarily on the period from the 1770s into the beginning of the 21st century. Chapters address the institutional, sociological and historical factors that have influenced women economists' thinking, and explore women's contributions to economic analysis, method, policies and debates. Coverage is international, moving beyond Europe and the US into the Arab world, China, India, Japan, Latin America, Russia and the Soviet Union, and sub-Saharan Africa. This new global perspective adds depth as well as scope to our understanding of women's contribution to the history of economic thought.

The book offers crucial new insights into previously underexplored work by women in the history of economic thought, and will prove to be a seminal volume with relevance beyond that field, into women's studies, sociology, and history.

Kirsten Madden is Associate Professor of Economics at Millersville University, USA.

Robert W. Dimand is a Professor of Economics at Brock University, Canada.

CONTRIBUTORS

Giandomenica Becchio (B.A./M.A. Philosophy, University of Torino; Ph.D. Economics, University of Florence) is Assistant Professor of Economics (University of Torino). Her research fields are: history of economic thought, economic methodology, gender and feminist studies, and Austrian School of economics. She is the author of many publications on Menger, Hayek, Polanyi, Einaudi, as well as of a recent monograph (with Giovanni Leghissa) on *The Origins of Neoliberalism: Insights from Economics and Philosophy* (Routledge, 2017). She is currently working on a book on the history of feminist economics within both the classical liberalism tradition as well as the socialist tradition.

Sheetal Bharat has been at the Bengaluru Dr B. R. Ambedkar School of Economics, Bengaluru, India since 2017. Before that she was at Christ University, where most of the work for this paper was carried out. She completed her doctoral studies from the University of California at Riverside in 2012. Her research interests lie in the areas of history of economic thought, Indian economic history, and development economics. She enjoys time spent in classrooms – on either side.

Lucy Brillant is Assistant Professor at the University of Bourgogne-Franche-Comte (France). She is also permanent fellow at the research center of Dijon (LEDi), and associate member at the research center PHARE (Paris 1 Panthéon-Sorbonne), where she completed a Ph.D. thesis in 2015. Her research interests include the Great Depression, and the role of finance in developing countries. Her works dealing with the origins of the theory of the term structure of interest rates in the 1930s were published in the *European Journal for the History of Economic Thought* (2014), and in the *Journal of the History of Economic Thought* (2018). She received the Gilles Dostaler Prize (2016) and the Young Scholar Awards for the History of Economic Thought Society (2015) and for the European Society for the History of Economic Thought (2014).

Cléo Chassonnery-Zaïgouche is a postdoctoral researcher in history of economic thought at the Centre Walras-Pareto (University of Lausanne, Switzerland). She received a Ph.D. in Economics from the University Paris 1 Panthéon-Sorbonne (France). Her research interests are the history of the economics of discrimination in the USA and the history of the 'equal pay for equal work' controversy in the UK. In 2017, she published "From warfare to welfare: contextualising Arrow and Schelling's models of racial inequalities (1968–1972)" with Larrouy Lauren in *The European Journal of the History of Economic Thought*. She received the STOREP Young Scholar Prize for a chapter in *Scientific Imperialism: Exploring the Boundaries of Interdisciplinarity* entitled "Crossing boundaries, displacing previous knowledge and claiming superiority: is the economics of discrimination a conquest of economics imperialism?" She is also conducting research on the representation of women in economics in the USA and in Switzerland.

Marcella Corsi has been Professor of Economics at the Sapienza University of Rome since 2005. She holds a Ph.D. in Economics from the University of Manchester (UK) and a degree in Statistics/Economics from University of Rome "La Sapienza". She has worked as consultant for the European Commission, European Parliament and OECD, and for several Italian institutions. She is among the founders of the association Economia Civile (www.economiacivile.it). Her research activity mainly focuses on issues related to social inclusion, social protection and income distribution (often in a gender perspective). In these fields of study, she is the author of several articles published in English and Italian, and she has been one of the scientific coordinators of the European Network of Gender Equality Experts. Since March 2017, she is the editor of the *International Review of Sociology*.

Robert W. Dimand is a Professor of Economics at Brock University, in Canada, and received his Ph.D. at Yale University. An historian of economic thought specializing in the history of macroeconomics, of game theory and of women in economics, he is the author or co-author of three books and 95 journal articles, and the editor or co-editor of a dozen books, including co-editorship of *Women of Value: Feminist Essays in the History of Economics* (Elgar, 1995), *A Biographical Dictionary of Women Economists* (Elgar, 2000), and *The Status of Women in Classical Economic Thought* (Elgar, 2003). In 2016, he received the Thomas Divine Award of the Association for Social Economics and Brock University's Distinguished Research and Creative Activity Award.

Mary Ann Dzuback is an Associate Professor of Women, Gender, and Sexuality Studies, Education, and History (courtesy) at Washington University in St. Louis, and chair of the Women, Gender, and Sexuality Studies Department. She received her Ph.D. in History and Education from Columbia University. Her current work uses gender analysis to explore women academic social science scholars in the period between 1890 and 1940, and their influence on college and university institutional cultures, on local and national social policy making, and on the development of knowledge in the social sciences. Her publications include *Robert M. Hutchins: Portrait of an Educator* (University of Chicago Press, 1991) and a number of articles and book chapters on women social science scholars in academic institutions. Her research has been supported by the Rockefeller Archives Center, Oberlin College, Center for Studies in Higher Education at the University of California, Berkeley, Washington University, and the Spencer Foundation.

Lola Fowler is a Brock University alumnus with bachelor degrees in Economics and Business and a postgraduate degree in Business Economics. She is of African ancestry and commenced the project, "African Female Economists" during her postgraduate studies as a means to highlight the accomplishment of African women – many of whom remain faceless or unknown – who have contributed to economics. A Social Sciences and Humanities Research Council (SSHRC) winner, she has also written on female labor participation and tightness and is interested in economic history and social economics.

Rebeca Gómez Betancourt is Professor of Economics at the University of Lyon 2 and Researcher at Triangle, UMR-CNRS. She earned her Ph.D. in economics in 2008 at University of Sorbonne, Paris. She has held appointments as Visiting Professor at Universidad of los Andes, Bogota-Colombia, at Universidade Federal Minas Gerais, Belo Horizonte-Brazil, and at De Paul University, Chicago. She served as President of the French Association for the History of Economic Thought and remains currently as the Vice-president. She is also director of the Master's program in Theories and History of Economics at the University of Lyon 2. Her work focuses on the history of monetary thought (in particular in the US), but also on women and economics, Latin American economic thought, US monetary history, and classical political economy. She has published on the history of the Federal Reserve System, the quantity theory of money, and monetary regimes in Latin America and India. She is currently working on the history of the International Association for Feminist Economics. She lives in Lyon, France.

Virginie Gouverneur is currently an Assistant Professor of Economics at the University of Haute-Alsace (France). She received her Ph.D. from the University of Vincennes Saint-Denis in 2013. She is also permanent fellow at BETA-University of Strasbourg and associate member at PHARE-University Panthéon-Sorbonne, where she worked as a postdoctoral fellow. Her main field of research is the history of economic thought on inequalities between men and women. She has written articles on issues related to the traditional sexual division of labor and the inclusion of unpaid domestic work within the production boundary that were published in *The European Journal of the History of Economic Thought* and *History of Political Economy*.

Shoshana Grossbard is a Professor of Economics at San Diego State University and a fellow at the IZA Institute in Bonn, Germany. She is founding editor of the *Review of Economics of the Household* and President of the Society of Economics of the Household. Her publications include seven books and over 80 journal articles and book chapters. Her two sole-authored books are *On the Economics of Marriage: A Theory of Marriage, Labor and Divorce* (Westview Press,1993) and *The Marriage Motive* (Springer, 2015). She teaches on the economics of households, work, marriage, and family, and tweets @econoflove.

Aiko Ikeo has been a professor at Waseda University, Japan since April 2000. She was trained in economics and the history of modern economics at Hitotsubashi University. She taught at Kokugakuin University from 1985 to 2000 and she was a research professor in its Institute for the Study of Japanese Culture and Classics from 1996 to 1999. She edited *Economic Development in Twentieth Century East Asia* (Routledge, 1997) and *Japanese Economics and Economists since 1945* (Routledge, 2000). She published *Globalization Reconsidered* (in Japanese, Soseisha, 2017) and *A History of Economic Science in Japan* (Routledge, 2014). She has been working on the history of international economic policy in East Asia for more than a decade.

Marianne Johnson is a Professor of Economics at the University of Wisconsin Oshkosh. She received her Ph.D. in Economics from Michigan State University in the history of economic thought and in public finance. Dr. Johnson's research focuses on evolution and legacy of the Wisconsin Institutional School, and this work has been published in *History of Political Economy*, the *Journal of Economic Issues*, and *Research in the History of Economic Thought and Methodology*. Her paper on Harold Groves and Wisconsin Institutionalism won the Editor's Choice award in 2015 from the Association for Evolutionary Economics (AFEE) for its publication in the *Journal of Economic Issues*. Dr. Johnson is currently the secretary for the History of Economics Society and on the editorial board for the *Journal for the History of Economic Thought* and for *Oeconomia*.

Farida Chowdhury Khan is Associate Professor and Chair at University of Colorado, Colorado Springs. She is retired as Professor of Economics at University of Wisconsin-Parkside where she recently received the Faculty Research and Creative Activity Award and the Distinguished Faculty Service Award. Her research focuses on developing countries, primarily in South Asia, and covers a range of topics such as trade policy, gender, micro-finance, and labor. Her recent co-edited volumes include *Money and Macroeconomics* and *The Bangladesh Economy in the 21st Century*. She has held office in professional organizations such as Bangladesh Development Initiative, the Association for Economic Development Studies on Bangladesh, International Association for Feminist Economics, Association for Social Economics, and Bangladesh Environmental Network. She serves on the editorial board of *The Journal for Bangladesh Studies*.

Anna Klimina is Associate Professor in the Economics Department at St. Thomas More College, University of Saskatchewan, Canada. She earned her Ph.D. in Economics in 2004 from the University of Manitoba (Canada), her Ph.D. (candidate of sciences degree, a Ph.D. equivalent) in History of Economic Thought from the Institute of Economics of the Ukrainian Academy of Sciences in 1992 (Ukraine), and her M.A. in Political Economy from Kiev State University in 1987 (USSR). Anna's research interests include economics of post-Soviet transition, seen through institutionalist and post-Keynesian perspectives, and history of Russian economic thought. Her papers are primarily published in the *Journal of Economic Issues*; her most recent publication is a 2017 chapter entitled "Rethinking the Role of the State" in *The Routledge Handbook of Heterodox Economics*.

Kirsten Madden earned her Ph.D. in Economics in 1995 at the University of North Carolina at Chapel Hill with fields in the history of economic thought and economic development. Since 1996, she has served as a faculty member at Millersville University of Pennsylvania. Her research publications center on three main topics: economic methodology in the history of econometrics, the history of women's economic thought, and economics pedagogy.

Clara Elisabetta Mattei is Assistant Professor of Economics at The New School for Social Research. She holds a Ph.D. jointly from the Sant' Anna School of Advanced Studies (SSSUP) in Pisa, Italy, and Université de Strasbourg, École Doctorale Augustine Cournot in Strasbourg, France, an M.A. in Philosophy from Pavia, and a B.A. in Philosophy from Cambridge University. Clara mainly teaches Methodology and History of Economic Thought. Her research contributes to the history of capitalism, exploring the relation between economic ideas and technocratic policy making. She is currently working on her book project called: *Economic Crisis and Technocratic Repression: On the Origins and Rationality of Austerity*. Among her recent articles are: "Treasury view and post-WWI British austerity: Basil Blackett, Otto Niemeyer, and Ralph Hawtrey" (*Cambridge Journal of Economics*, 2017), "Austerity and repressive politics: Italian economists in the first years of the Fascist government" (*European Journal of the History of Economic Thought*, 2017), and "The guardians of capitalism: international consensus and the technocratic implementation of austerity" (*Journal of Law and Society*, 2017).

Camila Orozco Espinel is an interdisciplinary scholar. She has an Economics degree with an emphasis in mathematics from the National University of Colombia, and a Master's degree in history of economic thought and philosophy of economics from the University of Paris 1 Panthéon-Sorbonne. Camila is currently a doctoral candidate in sociology at the EHESS (École des Hautes Études en Sciences Sociales, School of Advanced Studies in the Social Sciences). Her research focuses on 20th-century history of economics, primarily the post-World War II quest of economics for scientific authority. She recently published "Homogenize the profession to do science? Economics in the United States after World War II" in the *Revue d'Histoire des Sciences Humaines*. She also pursues research on women economists in Latin America and careers determinants of undergraduate and graduate female students of economics.

Joseph Persky is Professor of Economics at the University of Illinois at Chicago. Persky has published extensively in both history of economic thought and urban economic policy. In both sub-disciplines his research centers on distributional questions. Persky's writings on the history of economic thought include *The Burden of Dependency*, an exploration of economic thought in the Southern U.S., and most recently, *The Political Economy of Progress*, on John Stuart Mill and the origins of modern radicalism. On the policy side Persky is co-author of *Does "Trickle Down" Work?* (Upjohn Institute for Employment Research, 2004) which is concerned with the distributional implications of metropolitan economic development strategies. Persky received his Ph.D. in Economics from Harvard University in 1971. He has previously taught at Fisk University, Yale University, and the University of Alabama in Birmingham.

Joanna Rostek is Professor of Anglophone Literature, Culture and Media Studies at the University of Giessen, Germany, and was a visiting scholar at universities in Scotland, Poland, and the USA. She holds a degree in International Cultural and Business Studies and a Ph.D. in English Literature from the University of Passau, Germany. Her research interests include women's and gender studies as well as interrelations between economics, literature, and culture. She has published articles on Jane Marcet and Harriet Martineau, the implementation of feminist economics for the study of literature, and 21st-century fictions of capitalism. Her current book project is entitled *Women's Economic Thought in the Age of Romanticism: Towards a Transdisciplinary Herstory of Economic Thought* (forthcoming with Routledge). Her full academic profile is available at www.uni-giessen.de/rostek.

Janet Seiz received her Ph.D. in Economics from Duke University in 1986. She has been a member of the Economics Department at Grinnell College since 1990, teaching courses including economic development, Marxian economics, and the distribution of income and wealth in the US. She was one of the founding members of the International Association for Feminist Economics (IAFFE), and she served on the editorial board for its scholarly journal *Feminist Economics*. She has written articles on the history of economic thought, feminist economics, and (most recently) popular resistance to globalization in Costa Rica. She was a co-editor, with Kirsten Madden and the late Michele Pujol, of *A Bibliography of Female Economic Thought to 1940* (Routledge, 2004).

Zoe Sherman is Assistant Professor of Economics at Merrimack College and holds a Ph.D. from University of Massachusetts Amherst. Her main research interest is in the political economy of communications and she has published in *Review of Radical Political Economy* and *Rethinking Marxism*. She is also a member of the editorial collective and a regular contributor to *Dollars & Sense* magazine. She was a co-editor of *Our Economic Well-Being: A Popular Economics Collective Responds to Questions About the Economy from a United Methodist Congregation*, published by *Dollars & Sense* in 2017. She was awarded a 2016 William Waters Summer Research Grant from the Association for Social Economics to support her research on the modernization of advertising and the commodification of audience attention in the United States at the turn of the 20th century.

Yue Xiao earned her Ph.D. in 2018 at Zhongnan University of Economics and Law (ZUEL), China. Her dissertation on "The Foreign Trade Thought of Chinese Overseas Students in Modern China" is a subproject sponsored by the National Social Science Foundation of China. She received her Master's degree in English Literature at ZUEL, and was a visiting doctoral student at the University of Illinois at Chicago during the 2016–2017 academic year. Her research interests include history of economic thought, China's modern history, international trade, and political economics. Her research is published in *Researches in Chinese Economic History* (a journal of the Institute of Economics, Chinese Academy of Social Sciences) and *Journal of Zhongnan University of Economics and Law*.

Talia Yousef holds an Honours BA in Applied Economic Analysis from Brock University, St. Catharines, Ontario, where she began the research published in this book. She is now a graduate student completing her M.A. in Political Economy and a Teaching Assistant in Economics at Carleton University, Ottawa. Talia has worked in social economic policy within non-profit organizations in the Niagara region, and previously held a position as an economic analyst for the Ministry of Transportation of Canada, in Ottawa.

Giulia Zacchia is a research fellow in Economics at Sapienza University of Rome. She holds a Ph.D. in History of Economic Thought from the University of Macerata (Italy). Her research interests extend to social and financial inclusion in a gender perspective, but also cover gender gaps in academia, in particular in economics. She has worked, as practitioner, on women's empowerment, financial literacy, and micro-finance. She is one of the coordinators of the working group on Gender economics for the Young Scholars Initiative of the Institute of New Economic Thinking (INET). She is also a member of the Gender Equality Committee of the Italian Economic Association (SIE) and of Minerva laboratory on gender diversity and gender inequality at Sapienza University of Rome.

ACKNOWLEDGMENTS

Thanks to Millersville University of Pennsylvania for supporting completion of this project by funding a full year sabbatical and a course release for one semester.

INTRODUCTION

Kirsten Madden

By design this Routledge handbook is about women and about time and about economics. By design this handbook is global. Otherwise, this handbook is not easy to capture, condense, or consolidate into leading archetypes and primary themes.

The women are diverse. They include a Soviet game theorist and a Liberian president; wives of noted 19th-century economists and Buddhist nuns from millennia past; many a Ph.D. and some self-educated at home; revolutionaries, terrorists, even an assassin; caretakers of extended family and founders of political parties; many an activist, a few academic award winners and a merchant adventurer-explorer; an undercover factory worker, a formal factory inspector, and a handful of journalists; statisticians and heads of ministries; academicians creating new fields of inquiry and "invisibles" undertaking research in global institutions.

Geographic coverage is extensive. Many of the women documented in these pages situate in the U.S. and England. There are women of Austria and Italy and Spain. Three are of Chinese heritage, ten of Japanese. Many more of Russia and the Soviet Union, of sub-Saharan Africa and the Arab Homeland, of Latin America, and of India.

The timeframe is predominantly the 19th and 20th centuries. But there is also brief commentary regarding women reaching centuries into the past, and one chapter works substantially through a selection of thoughts preserved for over 2,000 years.

This handbook covers both thoughts and experiences of women contributing to economics. Some chapters more heavily emphasize thought, others experience, and some chapters emphasize both. The economic thoughts of women covered in these pages include those from Austria, Britain, China, Italy, India, Japan, Russia and the Soviet Union, a number of countries in sub-Saharan Africa, and the U.S.

The economic topics addressed in this handbook are extensive and diverse. Historically, many women contribute to the understanding of gender and economy. This requires a broad definition of economy inclusive of household, marriage, and the informal sector. Eleven chapters[1] emphasize women's analysis of gender and/or the household. Women explain the crowding hypothesis and analyze pay gaps, advocate minimum wages, affirmative action, co-operation, write textbooks and create academic departments for the efficient discharge of housework, and model the coordination of individual decision making within the household.

Some of the other topics include colonialism, trade, development, and finance; contributions to Soviet political economy and Soviet reform; and economic statistics. The women of these pages contribute substantial and vast economic insight, for example: an historical analysis of Chinese agriculture; an explanation of Italian economic dualism; analysis of free banking, the crafting of a new structure of ownership for Soviet reform; the creation of an input-output model for Italy, critical analysis of international aid to Africa, and quadratic programming of the Egyptian cotton market. Some of the women in these pages consolidate into established schools of economic thought: the Institutionalists, the Austrians, and at least three variants of socialists—the Soviets, the applied Marxists, and the co-operative movement. Classical political economy makes its appearance in four chapters.[2]

Chapters analyzing experiences of women economists as contributors to economic thought[3] address a variety of circumstances: conditions of entry, ability to contribute, treatment and progress, and livelihood outcomes. Whether it be the Americas, Africa, the Middle East, Europe or Asia, cultural constraints and stereotyped biases against women as women affect these economists' pursuit of their intelli-craft. The women economists of these pages are not passive recipients toward the constraints they face: some of these stories explore women economists' creative agency to open opportunities for intellectual participation. And then there are also noteworthy state interventions toward affirmative action across continents, the earliest in the Soviet Union.

Beyond the intended themes (women, time, economics, global coverage) perhaps one other concept crosses all the chapters: exclusion, though even this theme is variegated in form. The women economists in these chapters either experience exclusion in pursuit of their interests (with most pushing through) and/or construct economic artifacts in support of those excluded in economy.

Across time and geographic location, as these pages document, societies deny girls access to formal education, reducing their options as women in economy and in construction of knowledge about economics. And even women earning substantial credentials face exclusion from formal participation in economics. Many chapters document barriers to women's participation in constructing economics knowledge, and the efforts to surmount barriers.[4]

Though the theme of exclusion persists, careful reading across chapters suggests that, relative to the past, there is some increasing opportunity afforded women to construct knowledge about economics. Both basic and advanced education open to women across continents. Work positions open, allowing formal participation in knowledge creation. Many of these positions are independent, many are subordinate, and a smaller number of women advance in positions of leadership, particularly as time draws nearer to the present day.

Where women do contribute to the construction of knowledge, they often write about exclusionary economy: whether based on gender, class, race, economic sector or entire economy. The women in these pages write about economic dependence arising from enforced custom, about women's isolation, equal wages for equal work, and minimum pay, particularly in the literature through the early 20th century. These women write about the household across time (the 1790s to the 1970s) and place (U.S., Britain, Japan). These women address the issue of race in 19th-century colonial empire, write against apartheid in 1950s South Africa, and for racial justice in the 1960s.[5] These women write of exclusion from the formal economy, whether it be about the realities of working in the "informal sector" or entire nations left out of "development."

Across these pages are examples of agency and activism by women contributing to economic thought, opening doors for themselves and for excluded others. The formally trained women economists energizing economics departments in women's colleges and creating opportunities for popular education of women workers. The women co-operators organizing housewives against household isolation, and academicians building arguments supporting a minimum wage standard. The Buddhist nun challenging a Brahman and the Perestroika-era Soviet reformers visualizing economic institutions to invigorate alienated workers. The first woman of China to earn a U.S. Ph.D. in Economics leaving academia for mission work in New York City and the woman of India developing a statistical institution to uncover facts in support of workers informally employed. Barriers rise and with them the forces of dissolution, embodied in so many women with persevering determination.

Though many women in these pages open doors, it is false to suggest that as a universal outcome across all these pages. There are also instances of women colluding with oppression.[6]

The research resulting in this volume is complex and multi-faceted. There is no perfect partitioning scheme of the chapters in this handbook. Of the possibilities, temporal partitioning is a sensible approach,[7] though even this scheme has its peculiarities. Review of the years of the source material for each chapter returns (a) the first year in which substantial coverage begins, whether or not that coverage is *the* primary focus of the chapter; (b) the primary period of coverage; and (c) the last date through which coverage extends. The first year in which coverage begins is the primary guiding factor for chapter placement, even if the initial source material is not the temporal centerpiece of the chapter. In most chapters, there is relatively small time differential between first primary source and the primary period covered in a chapter. Where judgment calls come into play, the primary period of coverage as well as timing of the last substantial source covered shapes final placement decisions. The descriptions of the parts below identify cases of discrepancy.

There are five parts in this handbook based on time delineation. Each part holds four or more chapters. Parts I and II, "Beginning prior to 1850" and "Beginning in the late 19th century," each contain five chapters. Five chapters appear in Part III, "Beginning in the early 20th century," with initial main sources for each chapter falling somewhere in the 1900–1921 timeframe and each primary period of coverage extending only into mid-century. Part IV, "Spanning the mid-20th century," presents four chapters, and Part V presents five chapters "Beginning mid-20th, extending into the 21st century."

Part I: beginning prior to 1850

There is still substantial work to be done in the history of women's economic thought before 1850, but this handbook provides an impressive pass through minimally charted territory. There are three new early studies of the relatively more frequently researched women of Great Britain. Part I presents new and novel scholarship on women of Japan and of India.

The only account in this handbook to delve into ancient literature is the study of women of India. The preserved texts of Buddhist nuns' poetry circa 5th century BC and the Bhakti literature of the 8th–19th centuries are two primary sources from India. This chapter also analyzes selected popular literary and political writings in the late 19th and early 20th centuries. Bharat dissects this expansive literature for women's insights derived from experiences with ever-prevalent patriarchy and women's agency in response to patriarchy.

This early period includes three studies on the economic thoughts of women of Great Britain. Rostek's theme of "contestation and conformity to gender norms" is central to her circa 1800 analysis. Institutionalized constraints on women's options leave marriage and the household as key economic considerations for women of this time-space. Hester Mulso Chapone, Maria Edgeworth, and Priscilla Wakefield exhibit conformity to social norms in elaborating woman's household duty and its efficacious discharge. Contestation arises against women's economic dependence in marriage and in advocacy for access to the professions—two of the thinkers covered here are Mary Wollstonecraft and Mary Hays. Four economic concepts surface in Rostek's analysis of this early literature: the crowding hypothesis, occupational segregation, the gender pay gap, and a precursor to the idea of affirmative action.

Seiz undertakes comparative analysis of the thoughts about British Empire from three women influencing public opinion through writing and speeches between 1837 and 1911. Influenced by Classical political economy and its promotion of trade and markets, all three support 19th-century British imperial efforts to varying degrees. Unlike the "truly orthodox imperialist" Flora Shaw Lugard, Harriet Martineau and Mary Kingsley raise negative implications; Kingsley is unique of the three in promoting the participation of native populations in colonial administration.

Like Rostek, Gouverneur identifies marriage as a fundamental economic reality in women's experiences of this early period. But Gouverneur's focus lies in analyzing the implications for three women of *being* married to British economists circa 1848–1921. This chapter compares the career outcomes for the women and analyzes the women's contributions to one overlapping topic addressed by all three: gender inequality. Harriet Taylor Mill only receives posthumous recognition for her contributions to the economic thought attributed to her husband, John Stuart Mill. Interestingly, Gouverneur identifies in the economic thought of Harriet the idea that the social gains of freedom from gender-centered unpaid domestic servitude outweigh the potential decline in individual wages that might arise from the increased supply of women's paid labor. As a long time intellectual partner of John, Harriet makes noteworthy (albeit surreptitious) contributions to economics. The turn of Alfred Marshall's opinion against the intellectual capability of women coupled with her willing compliance limit the contributions of Mary Paley Marshall after marriage, but Beatrice Potter Webb operates in a true partnership, providing substantial contributions both in her own right and with husband Sidney throughout her married life.

For Ikeo, over two centuries of coverage, the ability for women of Japan to contribute to economic thought correlates with Japan's "changing international relations." The only woman of Japan making a substantial contribution to political economy before Japan's economic opening is Makuzu Tadano with her publication, *Solitary Thoughts* in 1812. Nearly a century passes until the next women of Japan publish economic insight. With the *Meiji* restoration, two groups are particularly relevant: women activists (including a factory inspector) and the household economists of Japan. After World War II, Japan's universities open more generally to women. Ikeo ends the chapter profiling some of the first women academicians contributing to Japan's economic thought in the late 20th century.

Part II: beginning in the late 19th century

The first three chapters in Part II cover the four decades surrounding the turn of the 20th century, and the last two chapters pass beyond mid-20th century. Klimina analyzes the contributions of Russian women activists as Russia moves toward revolutionary upheaval. These Russian women span the political spectrum: a populist, variants of socialism, and a woman predisposed toward Classical liberal thinking. Klimina finds these women are "organizers, promoters, and even terrorists, but also wrote letters, asked important questions." Common to each of these women across the political spectrum is their promotion of a democratic Russia.

The next two chapters emphasize women's welfare in Great Britain. Chassonnery-Zaïgouche addresses the changing arguments of three women concerning the "equal pay for equal work" debate. All three initially argue against equal pay but then support it from "altogether different intellectual, social and political arguments *and* public images." Chassonnery-Zaïgouche analyzes the change of mind of the Classical liberal Millicent Garrett Fawcett, the Fabian socialist Beatrice Potter Webb, and the "welfare feminist" Eleanor Rathbone.

The methodology of the Women's Co-operative Guild is the subject of analysis for Madden and Persky. Guild strategy centers on participatory fact-gathering and common sense theorizing to generate reform for women that aligns with co-operative and socialist values. This chapter analyzes the effectiveness of the women co-operators' reform movement strategy. The strategy is effective in three cases: most effectively in raising awareness and change associated with women's household isolation; in a minimum wage campaign for co-operatively employed women; and also somewhat effective in an anti-credit campaign at co-operative stores. The strategy does not come to fruition in the call for producer co-operatives.

The next chapter organizes women's documented allegations of discriminatory treatment in their efforts contributing to economic thought. These accounts span the late 1800s through the 1960s in the U.S. and Western Europe. Perceived as intellectual inferiors, many highly educated women identify less access to resources and opportunities in a variety of contexts. The negative implications include limitations for the growth of knowledge.

The timeframe of the final chapter is the most extensive in Part II, from the end of the 19th through the end of the 20th centuries. Sherman weaves a theme of "the complex entanglement of revolutionary consciousness, human agency, and institutional structures" to analyze the economic contributions of: Eleanor Marx (daughter of Karl), the revolutionary Marxist, Rosa Luxemburg, and the Trotsky-Marxist turned humanist, Raya Dunayevskaya. All three provide insight into multiple dimensions of exploitation and advocate emancipation, whether the exploitation is based in class, race, or gender. All three are outspoken communicators in political venues with theoretically sophisticated insights into Marxian socialist ideology impelling them to act for the interests of the oppressed.

Part III: beginning in the early 20th century

The five chapters that begin in the early 20th century focus on academic women economists with advanced degrees (almost all Ph.D.s) earned in the U.S. The first three chapters analyze the experiences of women economists in academia. The last two chapters emphasize the economic ideas of the women economists.

Dzuback identifies the limited opportunities and resource constraints for academic participation by women economists in the construction of knowledge during the first few decades of the 20th century. Her agency story identifies how women economists create localized nodes of power within women's colleges to construct and disseminate knowledge, including for the benefit of local communities. Dzuback highlights the following women economists and women's colleges beginning in the 1920s: Emilie Hutchinson at Barnard and Susan Kingsbury at Bryn Mawr; Esther Lowenthal at Smith and Mabel Newcomer at Vassar; Amy Hewes at Mount Holyoke and Elinor Pancoast at Goucher. Strategies include taking leadership roles within their departments, locating local sources of funding for research and running research projects that address regional issues. These women professors integrate students in research, facilitate the placement of students in employment that can apply their training, and provide employment outlets for women academicians.

The Institutionalist school under John R. Commons at the University of Wisconsin is an example of an early 20th-century university program integrating a multitude of women into academic inquiry. Johnson covers the "branding" of Wisconsin Institutionalism, emphasizing the role Commons' women students play. Many of these women do relatively atheoretical, statistical, and multi-disciplinary analysis in line with their Institutionalist training. But as "sociologists, social workers, government researchers and administrators of nonprofit organizations, lobbying groups, and government" workers their efforts diffuse Institutionalism while diluting the "brand" in the economics discipline.

Six U.S. women win a coveted award for their theses between 1915 and 1930. Of the six award winners, Madden finds diverse career outcomes: one disappears from the discipline, three are "separatists", with careers in non-economics departments, government, or women's colleges, one has a "status quo" life-long appointment at a major state university, and one is a "subordinate" from an academic career perspective, contributing part-time to economics and academia, focusing on her primary social contribution as a mother. Two of the separatists have "superperforming" careers making major contributions in tangentially related academic disciplines. As a result, these six are unknown to most in the history of economic thought.

Mattei analyzes the minimum wage arguments of two Columbia University women economists, Emilie Josephine Hutchinson and Elizabeth Faulkner Baker. These women's views run against prevailing U.S. policy trends of the early 20th century, making way for more liberal legislation in the future. Baker and Hutchinson argue for the extension of minimum wage legislation for all workers, rather than limiting this policy to women and children. Working with other women at Columbia University to infuse economic education among the working class, Hutchinson is also in part responsible for the establishment of the Barnard Summer School for Women Workers.

Xiao begins her study of women economists of China by tracing two 19th-century educational trends: the increase in educational opportunities for girls in China and the development of study abroad programs out of China. Three women of China take advantage of both opportunities to earn economics Ph.D.s in the U.S.: Mabel Ping-hua Lee (Columbia University, 1921), Chung-ying Kuo (University of Wisconsin, 1947), and Yu-pu Pan (University of Illinois, 1948). This chapter analyzes the economic content of the three Ph.D. theses. Xiao finds a combination of influences from Confucian philosophy and Western economic thought in the earlier dissertation by Lee. Western economic thought is the foundation of the two later dissertations in international trade.

Part IV: spanning the mid-20th century

The four chapters of the mid-20th century primarily associate with Western Europe and the Soviet Union. The first women Austrian School economists received training in Austria in the early 20th century, with later Austrian generations from Britain and the U.S. The other three chapters focus on: women economists of the Soviet Union over its 70-year history; two women of the London School of Economics; and women of Italy.

The chapter by Becchio highlights the intellectual contributions of 14 women of the Austrian School during the 20th century. Becchio breaks these women into four generations: the first study under Eugene Böhm-Bawerk and Friedrich Wieser at the University of Vienna; the second study under Ludwig Mises in his extramural seminars of the 1920s and 1930s; the third are students of Friedrich Hayek at the London School of Economics in the 1930s and 1940s and students of Mises at New York University in the 1940s and 1950s; and the fourth generation is part of the Austrian revival associated with Hayek's receipt of the Nobel Prize. Becchio provides insight into the Austrian economics contributions of these women. For example, Lionel Robbins identifies an "'acute analytical intelligence'" in second generation Austrian Martha Braun's (1929) theoretical work to develop micro-foundations for an apolitical monetary policy. And Marjorie Grice-Hutchinson receives critical acclaim for her analysis of the 16th-century Spanish School of Salamanca's contribution to subjective value theory. Grice-Hutchinson makes the case that Salamanca substantially pre-dates subjective value theory of Stanley Jevons, Leon Walras, and Carl Menger.

Klimina's second contribution to the handbook is "a concise history of women's economic thought in the Soviet Union." Women lack education to participate in the formal construction of Soviet economic thought in the 1920s. By the 1930s, Soviet policy of equal access to education brings highly educated women into USSR political economy. But in a repressive political climate, their abilities to add to knowledge depend upon "their willingness to parrot the Party line" into the 1960s. Only in non-ideologically driven game theoretical applications of mathematical science is the work of a Soviet woman "on par with Western scholarship." A handful of Soviet women stand out in the era of Perestroika (a term coined by Tatiana Zaslavskaia). Zaslavskaia and Rosalina Ryvkina address worker incentives in association with Soviet ownership structures. These two and two more, Natalia Figurnova and Irina Starodubrovskaya, propose "three co-dependent, co-existing levels of ownership: the state level, the enterprise (firm) level, and the worker (employee) level." It is in this era of reform thinking that Klimina finds the most creative contributions with potential to move the Soviet Union toward participatory democracy.

Brillant analyzes the insights for development finance from two women trained at the London School of Economics, Vera Lutz and Ursula Hicks. A student of the Austrian economist, Friedrich Hayek, Lutz's Ph.D. thesis is about the development of a free banking system. After World War II and addressing the dualist development of South and North Italy, Lutz's views moderate; she advocates a conservative monetary policy by Italy's Central Bank. In contrast, underlying Hicks' views are Keynesian tendencies. By the mid-20th century, Hicks is an economic advisor to numerous governments of developing economies. In that work she advocates a strong central bank to promote growth-enhancing, stabilizing banking services, including banking system participation in public securities markets.

The chapter by Corsi and Zacchia provides the first temporal analysis of women's participation in the universities of Italy and women's contributions to the economics journals of Italy. From 1956 until 1979, women are authors of as few as 1.4% and always less than 10% of Italian economics journal articles. The chapter focuses on a comparative analysis of the careers, affiliation with schools of macroeconomic thought, and empirical techniques of two Italian women economists, Vera Cao Pinna and Almerina Ipsevich during the 1950s–1970s. Vera Cao Pinna is the "mother" of input-output modeling for Italy in the 1960s, supporting the statistical realization of economic planning. Almerina Ipsevich undertakes short-term forecasting of market trends to gain statistical knowledge that aligns with her free market-based philosophy, and ultimately rises to Director-General of the Italian Institute for Economic Planning.

Part V: beginning mid-20th, extending into the 21st century

The final part of this handbook is noteworthy for its global nature. It is in this later 21st-century timeframe that openings in opportunity for some educated women overlap with rising opportunity for more people of developing economies. Women become economists in sub-Saharan Africa and in the Arab Homeland. Highly educated women of Latin America publish through their employment with the United Nations Economic Commission for Latin America and the Caribbean. Raised on different continents (Asia and Europe), two women make substantial progress in understanding the informal sector of developing economies. And coverage of two women of the U.S. returns the reader of this handbook to studies of the household.

Fowler and Dimand provide nearly a century overview of some leading women economists of sub-Saharan Africa. Three women of South Africa with European ancestry are the first formally trained and/or publishing women economists of Africa during the height of the colonial era and before 1941. The chapter introduces ten prominent women economists with African ancestry who work in Africa. These women are from Ghana, Liberia, Namibia, Nigeria, Tanzania, and Zambia. Seven have degrees in economics: two with Ph.D.s (including Ngozi Okonjo-Iweala of Nigeria, earning her Ph.D. from MIT in 1981); two with Master's degrees (the earliest earned in 1979) and three with Bachelor's degrees. The "mother of statistics" in Africa, Tinuke

Johnson of Nigeria, holds a Master's degree in statistics from the London School of Economics, earned in 1966. With academic positions in economics departments of Africa held by men, these women forge career trajectories through high levels of their national governments and with international economic agencies such as the World Bank and African Development Bank. Both the first woman President of Liberia, Ellen Johnson Sirleaf, and the first woman Prime Minister of Namibia, Saara Kuugongelwa-Amadhila, have Bachelor's degrees in economics.

Yousef and Dimand introduce the women economists of the Arab Homeland. This chapter identifies two women economics instructors working as early as the mid-1940s at the American University of Beirut in Lebanon. Salwa Ali Soliman Farghali is likely the first Arab woman to earn a Ph.D. in economics in 1966 from the University of Southern California; her dissertation considers risk in the context of planned socialist economies with an emphasis on the United Arab Emirates (UAE). Hanaa A. Kheir-El-Din earns her economics Ph.D. from MIT in 1967 with a dissertation concerning the quadratic programming of the Egyptian cotton market. Both of these Ph.D.s receive faculty appointments at the University of Cairo. This chapter identifies other women economists in universities of the following countries: Egypt, Iraq, Jordan, Lebanon, and Saudi Arabia. The paper also identifies 13 women economists working in various government ministries of Egypt, Jordan, Lebanon, Morocco, Palestine, Syria, Tunisia, and UAE. A few of these ministerial appointments occur in the 1990s, the rest after the turn of the 21st century.

Gómez Betancourt and Orozco Espinel present a gender-based bibliometric analysis of the publications at the United Nations Economic Commission for Latin America and the Caribbean (CEPAL). The results return a list of the most prolific men and women of CEPAL. The chapter presents a bibliographic profile of the ten most prolific women: three formally trained economists, one biologist, and six sociologists. The women of Latin America are from: Argentina, Bolivia, Brazil, Chile, and Mexico; and one more from North America. From their bibliographic review, the authors find these women tend to publish on "social issues and more specifically on gender studies and affirmative action, poverty, education, and demographics;" their publications tend to be applied. Analysis of online visibility of the most prolific men and women finds the men more visible than the women.

Khan covers the contributions from two women concerning the informal sector in developing economies after the 1980s: Lourdes Beneria in Latin America and Marty Chen in South Asia. Originally from Spain and settling in the U.S., Beneria's contributions are noteworthy in providing a theoretical analysis of the growth of the informal sector in developing economies from a feminist perspective. Both Beneria and Chen make detailed contributions toward the collection of empirical facts about this sector. Both emphasize the circumstances of women in this sector. Aligning her activism with her academic interests, Marty Chen is a founder of Women in Informal Employment: Globalizing and Organizing in 1997. WIEGO consolidates statistical information on the informal sector of developing economies to support labor organization and policy initiatives on behalf of informal sector workers.

Grossbard discovers in a 1972 *American Economic Review* article by Charlotte Phelps an economic theory of marriage receiving no attention in the household economics literature. Phelps pre-dates Gary Becker's highly referenced piece on economics of marriage by one year. Grossbard's contributions to the analysis of household decision making are also the subject of this chapter. Unique to the approach of both women is that they model decision making within the household at the individual level. Grossbard formalizes Phelps, compares and contrasts Phelps' work to her own contributions through the second decade of the 21st century, and compares the works with Becker. The chapter argues that Phelps "deserves credit for being a pioneer in modeling household production as an individual decision in need of coordination with other household members' decisions."

Notes

1 Bharat, Rostek, Gouverneur, Ikeo, Chassonnery-Zaïgouche, Madden & Persky, Sherman, Mattei, Fowler & Dimand, Khan, and Grossbard.

2 See chapters by Rostek, Seiz, Klimina (pre-revolutionary Russia), and Chassonnery-Zaïgouche.

3 Chapters emphasizing women's experiences as a predominant theme include Gouverneur, both chapters by Madden, Dzuback, Johnson, Corsi & Zacchia, Fowler & Dimand, and Gómez Betancourt & Orozco Espinel. Chapters covering women's abilities to contribute to economics as a non-primary issue include Ikeo, Klimina, and Xiao.

4 See Gouverneur, Ikeo, both Madden chapters, Dzuback, Corsi & Zacchia, Fowler & Dimand, Yousef & Dimand, and Gómez Betancourt & Orozco Espinel.

5 See Sherman's coverage on Raya Dunayevskaya in the section "Class and its intersections with race and gender."

6 See Bharat, Seiz, and Madden (Discrimination). Also different levels of "conformity" to narrowed roles and opportunities appear in Rostek, Gouverneur, Chassonnery-Zaïgouche, and Gómez Betancourt & Orozco Espinel.

7 Thanks to Joanna Rostek for encouraging the timeline partitioning strategy among the alternatives under consideration.

PART I

Beginning prior to 1850

1

INDIAN WOMEN'S AGENCY THROUGH INDIAN WOMEN'S LITERATURE

Sheetal Bharat[1]

Patriarchy has been a dominant institution influencing the structure of society through recorded human history. In this chapter, I bring out the various ways in which Indian women have engaged with this institution from the fifth century BCE till colonial times. I use Amartya Sen's construct to identify the well- (or ill-) being of women as it is represented in their own writings, and go further to identify their exercises of agency in effecting welfare.

Welfare, according to Sen (1985), is determined by more than a certain state of wellbeing of the individual concerned. It must also include agency in choosing among a range of aims, including those unrelated to personal wellbeing.[2] Freedom is the central idea in Sen's notion of wellbeing and is incorporated in the analysis through agency, a related and wider concept (Sen 1985, p. 203).

> A person's "agency freedom" refers to what the person is free to do and achieve in pursuit of whatever goals or values he or she regards as important. A person's agency aspect cannot be understood without taking note of his or her aims, objectives, allegiances, obligations.

The historical source material must be suitably broad-based to afford an understanding of women's "aims, objectives, allegiances, obligations", a task critical to understanding agency. I look at a sample of the surviving and accessible literature produced by Indian women through recorded history. For reasons of economy, I restrict the sample to works for which an English translation is accessible. This reduces the sample size to a few dozen works spread over two millennia. Tharu and Lalita's exhaustive two-volume anthology of Indian women's writings is a primary resource, supplemented by other works, as available.

The oldest anthology consulted is the *Therigatha* (*Theri*: nun; *gatha*: songs), by Buddhist nuns who lived and composed verses about their religious experience in the time of the Buddha around the fifth century BCE. This is the earliest surviving literature by women anywhere in the world (Tharu and Lalita Vol. I 2015, p. 65). Around the time that these verses were composed, script was not in common use. This meant that if these experiences of realisation were to be shared, they had best be in poetic form that is easy to commit to memory (Murcott 1991, p. 5).

The *Bhakti* (meaning devotion) movement produced rich literature in several languages across the subcontinent from the eighth till the nineteenth century CE. The aspect that ties this vast body of literature together is that it was composed by people who formed a wave of revolt against *brahmanical* supremacy (Nadkarni 2013, pp. 67, 97). The idea was that salvation is not the sole prerogative of the elite male. Anyone can achieve the highest religious goal by unconditional devotion to their chosen idol.

Two *Mughal*[3] women's works are included in this study: Empress Nur Jahan (1577–1645) did not leave any written works, but the train of her thoughts and actions is available to the modern scholar through travellers' records. Princess Zeb-un-Nissa (1638–1702), daughter of the last powerful *Mughal* emperor, Aurangzeb, composed poetry for her pleasure.

Literary and political works from the nineteenth century, when India was under colonial rule are innumerable. The range of works includes poetry, novels, speeches, newspaper contributions, journal articles and official communication with the government, covering themes of politics, social issues, religion and science.

Since literary composition demands use of higher mental faculties, the women who composed poetry, wrote novels and made speeches may be considered intellectually abler than the average woman in each age. There is no reason to believe that the lived experience of an intellectually abler woman would be any worse than average. Judging by the content of their writings, these literary women write of troubles that reflect the experience of the masses, and so their descriptions can be considered representative of the women of the age, even though these women themselves might not have been representative. Appendix 1 has a list of women named through this chapter with some details for quick reference.

In the following section titled *Lack of wellbeing achievement and the vicious cycle of gender discrimination*, literature from across the ages is cited to illustrate instances of women's ill-being. Chronological continuity is unnecessary as women's lived experiences from across two millennia are strikingly similar in respect of their lack of wellbeing, and the material is rather presented to reveal the elements of a vicious cycle. The latter section titled *Agency in effecting wellbeing* highlights instances of women exercising their agency in expanding freedoms for themselves and other women.

Lack of wellbeing achievement and the vicious cycle of gender discrimination

One starting point in a cycle is as good as another (see Figure 1.1). I begin a description of this vicious cycle with girls not being given opportunities to learn skills that would be valuable outside the house. A word of justification is due for the expression – skills valuable outside the house. It is valid to argue that women who work in the house develop skills related to the house and provide a valuable service in sustaining the family. Members of a family working outside rely, for their sustenance, on those staying in. Sen explains that "the activities that produce or support that sustenance, survival or reproduction [of earning members] are typically not regarded as *contributing* to output, and are often classified as 'unproductive' labour" (1987, p. 11, emphasis in original). Boserup (1970) and Papanek (1979) have written extensively on the supporting role played by women in creating family status. Given the acknowledgement that both men and women do productive work, the unequal status appears to be due to valuation. Work done outside the house is valued more than that performed within. Sen (1987, p. 25) points out that it is a person's 'perceived contribution' to household income that determines their status. "The impact of '*perceived* contribution response' may have been primitively associated with acquiring food from *outside*" (Sen 1987, p. 29, emphasis in original), and this perception lingers to the modern day. Gender disparities tend to be strikingly unfavourable to women, and even sex ratios (number of women to number of men) tend to be lower in northern India where women work more indoors, compared with the south (Sen 1987, p. 31).

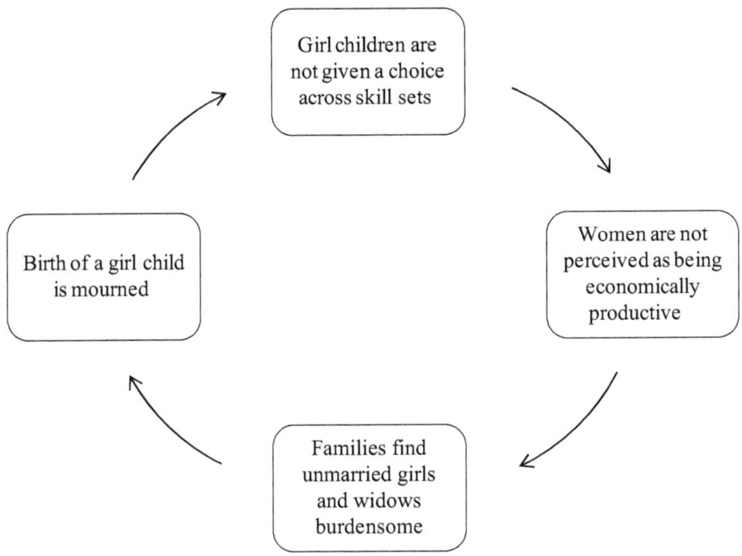

Figure 1.1 Vicious cycle of gender discrimination

Women staying at home results in them not being perceived as economically productive. Historically, property was handed down through sons, while daughters commanded ownership only over movable property such as jewellery and clothes gifted at the wedding (Altekar 1956, pp. 217–20). This meant that parents had to spend a lot for their daughter's wedding. They were not sent to school or made to feel a valued member of the family, and so the cycle continued. King and Hill (1997, p. vi) mention a vicious cycle vaguely in the form discussed above. The details of the elements are substantiated with reference to the human capital literature (Schultz 1990; Becker 1994).

In the remainder of this section, I cite women's literature from across the ages to illustrate each element in the vicious cycle.

Mutta, the fifth-century BCE Buddhist nun, celebrates the freedom she won from domesticity: "O free indeed! O gloriously free / Am I in freedom from three crooked things:-- / From quern, from mortar, from my crookback'd lord!" (Rhys Davids 2007, p. 15). She is clearly overjoyed with the new opportunity she found in Buddhism, while being relieved of her domestic responsibilities involving hand-milling and cooking for her husband. Similarly, Sumangala's mother, the rush-weaver's wife (her own name unknown[4]) expresses complete frustration with her domestic chores and even her husband (Rhys Davids 2007, p. 25): "Me stained and squalid 'mong my cooking-pots / My brutal husband ranked as even less / Than the sunshades he sits and weaves alway". These women's alienation is evident in the use of the words "crookback'd" and "brutal".

This gendered occupational segregation begs justification for this early age. Rhys Davids (1901, pp. 310, 313; 1923, pp. 205–6[5]) and Altekar (1956, p. 179) confirm that there was division of labour in the early Buddhist period not just at the level of a household, but also at the level of the community. Men engaged in occupations that took them outside, while women tended to stay at home. The economic background to the sentiment in these quotes is therefore consistent with current knowledge about the economy of the age.

Newer-age evidence of the occupational segregation of women is revealed in Bahinabai's life story (1628–1700, *Bhakti* poet, Marathi language). After a series of supernatural occurrences involving a calf and a travelling preacher,[6] Bahinabai at age eleven, had to decide whether or not to continue with her deep devotion of Lord Vitthal, while simultaneously performing her responsibilities at home. Her husband had a foul temper and "[w]hen it came to his mind to do so he beat [Bahinabai] violently. He tied [her] (hand and foot) into a bundle and threw [her] aside" (Tharu and Lalita Vol. I 2015, p. 113). The preacher, after gauging the devotion that the girl was capable of, advised the husband:

> [T]he manner of life she must adopt is of a very austere kind. Now do not distress her any more. By her special wifely duties she will do you service; and you will save your soul . . . [T]he calf is her guru . . . and all who live in association with her, will joyfully drink the sweet juice of *bhakti*.

Nonetheless, her husband vowed to leave home, because he did not want a wife who was more interested in prayers than in him – he took it as a personal insult. "Perhaps out of sagacity, perhaps out of timidity" (Tharu and Lalita Vol. I 2015, p. 109), Bahinabai says (pp. 114–15):

> [H]olding to my own special duties, I will give my mind to listening to the Scriptures, and the winning of God. My duty is to serve my husband, for he is God to me. My husband himself is the Supreme Brahma. . . . This is then the determination, and the desire of my heart. I want my thought concentrated on my husband.

The composition of these lines follows an advanced level of religious attainment. This is a decision that Bahinabai arrives at after a thorough consideration of her choices. One interpretation is that she exercised her agency and chose to serve her husband with all her attention. Alternatively, her decision could be a result of internalising and rationalising harsh patriarchal social relations. Any agency, then, is rendered meaningless. Being part of multiple generations of the vicious cycle, Indian women typically came to internalise the inferiority society imposed upon them and made choices that benefited the socially valued men, even to their own detriment.

Rassundari Devi's (1810–?, Bangla[7] language) autobiography is among the most fascinating works in Indian literature. She has no meaningful choices in her life. Married at the age of twelve, mother of eleven, she was caught in an unending stream of domestic responsibilities. She describes her pitiful emotions at her wedding. Though she was happy through the festivities, Rassundari Devi cried through most of the journey to her new home which lasted a few days (Tharu and Lalita Vol. I 2015, pp. 192–4):

> "Don't give me over to them, Mother!" . . . I was trembling all over with fear . . . I clung to whomever came to pick me up and went on weeping incessantly. . . . I sank into a deep depression. . . . Very soon I felt too parched to cry. . . . Sorrow engulfed me like a raging forest fire. Those who have had such experiences perhaps know how useless words seem in times of sorrow.

Girls even younger were married and sent off to distant villages, and the trauma of separation was assumed to be something a girl had to go through unquestioningly. At her new home, though she accepts that her family were kind to her, Rassundari Devi led a far from contented life (p. 196).

> There were eight maidservants in the house, but . . . [a]s was the custom, I had to do all the work and look after the children as well. . . . Suffice it to say that I had no time to think about my own health. So much so that I often did not eat either of the two meals.

The above instances of women speaking out against their social experiences and of being buttonholed to the house, are not petulant complaints of mildly difficult circumstances, and neither are they anachronistic projections of modern sensibilities. These women made specific comparisons with men to highlight a *relative* deprivation. The fifth-century BCE Buddhist nun Patacara says (Rhys Davids 2007, pp. 72–3):

> With ploughshares ploughing up the fields, with seed
> Sown in the breast of earth, men with their crops,
> Enjoy their grains and nourish wife and child.
> Why cannot I, whose life is pure, who seek
> To do the Master's will, no sluggard am,
> Nor puffed up, win to Nibbana's bliss?[8]

Other nuns make similar comparisons (pp. 73, 94). Patacara feels that she was being kept out of an opportunity by the force of tradition. That she managed to attain *Nibbana* shows the strength of her agency in the face of constraining tradition.

The sentiment is echoed almost identically in an early twentieth-century female contributor to the journal *Navabharat* [New India]: "In terms of brain power there is no difference between men and women. . . . The artificial demarcation of their spheres is, therefore, totally illogical. In fact, both should be able to participate in the same kind of activities" (Ray 1991, p. 11). The educationist Abala Bose (1855–1951) argued in 1907 that women needed an education (Ray 1991, p. 8):

> not because we may make better matches for our girls . . . not even that the services of the daughter-in-law may be more valuable in the home of her adoption, but because woman like man is first of all a mind, and only in the second place physical and a body.

The comparisons were incisive, but answers in these respective ages were not forthcoming. Insults were. The omnipresence of discrimination is illustrated in the language used. The fifth-century BCE nun Soma includes in her verses, words that were spoken by Mara, the demon "invisible and in the air" (Rhys Davids 2007, p. 45):

> That vantage-ground the sages may attain is hard
> To reach. With her two-finger consciousness
> *That* is no woman competent to gain! [emphasis in original]

The phrase "two-finger consciousness" is in reference to the practice of checking with two fingers if rice is cooked. The suggestion was that the only work that women did was to cook, and so the only skill that they needed to have was to check if rice was cooked. Women were incompetent outside the house and it was acceptable for them to stay indoors. If this indeed was a widespread attitude, it would have greatly undermined the ability of women to develop their potential.

Along similar lines, Sulekha Sanyal (1928–1962, Bangla language novelist) presents the contours of a common argument in the following tirade by Punasashi when her granddaughter, Chobi, a school-going girl, asks for a second helping of dessert (Tharu and Lalita Vol. II 2006, p. 293, *Nabankur* [Seedling]):

> Teach her to read and write, and look what happens next! The girl imagines she's as good as these darling boys of mine! Ridiculous! Will you be earning like the boys? All you'll ever be is a shackle on your father's neck. Yes, those days are coming, and pretty soon, when we won't be able to get food down his throat for worrying over how to get you married off.

Later, Chobi's mother pulls her by her hair to discipline her for her impertinent demand. Chobi's behaviour was born more out of ignorance of custom rather than a desire to rebel against it. She was unaware that custom expected her to be submissive, and was being "socialised for inequality" by her grandmother and mother (Papanek 1990, pp. 176, 179). As the older women in the family harshly impose restrictions on the younger girls, they themselves go through a secondary phase of socialisation for women's inferiority, accepting it as necessary to maintain harmony over generations. Every member of the family, young and old, was made to realise that unmarried girls were a burden.

As an instance of how widowed women were seen as burdensome as well, an anonymous woman wrote in 1889 about the typical life of a widow from the *kayastha* caste, known for being particularly dogmatic about ritual pollution (Tharu and Lalita Vol. I 2015, pp. 358–63). "[W]omen from the barber caste" were hired to tear off the jewellery from a woman's body as soon as her husband passed away. It is instructive to quote her at length (pp. 359–61).

> [N]o one comes near her to console her. . . . [T]hose who had loved her from her childhood, and had brought her up tenderly, even they shower curses on her. . . . There has to be a distance of two hundred feet between her and the rest of the women [in the funeral procession] because it is believed . . . that if her shadow falls over a married woman, she too will become a widow. . . . A woman whose husband is dead is like a living corpse. She has no rights in the home. . . . Her mother-in-law says, "This horrible snake bit my son and killed him. He died, but why is this worthless woman still alive?" . . . [T]here is nothing in our fate but suffering from birth to death. When our husbands are alive, we are their slaves; when they die, our fate is even worse.

Since women did not have the rights to any property, male relatives grudgingly spent for their maintenance. They would often need to find an alternative source of income using the only skills society allowed them to develop – by working as a servant – and so being brought down to the lowest social stratum, regardless of their earlier position.

Further household behaviours resulting from this discrimination are illustrated in this conversation overheard by the narrator in Sarat Kumari Chaudhurani's (1861–1920, Bangla language) story, *Adorer na Anadorer?* [Beloved, or Unloved?]. At the river bank for a bath, a woman reveals that her sister-in-law had had a third daughter (Tharu and Lalita Vol. I 2015, pp. 263–4):

> When my brother heard it was a girl, he said to me, "Keshto, I can't get up. I feel drained of all my strength." . . . His wife wouldn't pick the baby up; she took it in her arms only after a lot of coaxing, and even then she said she'd throttle it. . . . Sorrow hangs over the whole house.

A sympathetic listener responds (p. 264):

> [T]hree girls, no less, to be married off to *kayastha* families – a tough job it's going to be. It's hard on the wretched woman too – giving birth to a lump of earth, having carried it in her womb for ten months!

The vicious cycle of gender discrimination is here illustrated through women's reports of their lived experiences. The *Therigatha* verses, and *Bhakti* poetry show women as being constrained to domestic responsibilities and as not having, or not being perceived as having, the skills required to survive outside the house. Women report that they are systematically excluded from the opportunity of engaging in an occupation that is perceived as valuable. Modern literature is cited to show how the birth of a girl child is considered a burden on the family – specifically on the father who has to pay heavily for the wedding. Sending a girl to school is presented as a grave mistake that can only result in her nursing unrealistic expectations regarding her worth. The suggestion that "efficiency criteria alone would predispose a family to invest differentially in the human capital of their children, depending on their *perception* of the ability and opportunities of each child" (Schultz 1990, p. 3, emphasis added) seems true, not just in a modern utilitarian economy, but in ancient times as well. The morbid sorrow that accompanies the birth of the girl child in Keshto's brother's home completes the illustration of the vicious cycle of gender discrimination.

The above instances are from specific points in time separated by centuries. An explanation for them still justifiably forming part of a single cycle is provided by Sen (1987, p. 28): the asymmetries in the status of men and women are "stable and sustained", regardless of how they might have started. A "feedback transmission" effect causes asymmetries in access to opportunities and benefits to be perpetuated "from one generation to the next, indeed from one historical epoch to the next" (Sen 1987, pp. 26–7).

Agency in effecting wellbeing

Most women, presumably those who did not rebel or compose poetry or talk publicly about their woes, had accepted tradition. Many might have recognised their relative status but might have been timid to speak out. Only a few agitated and took measures to correct the inequality. Still fewer left a record of their attempts. This section gleans from the literature the attempts at improvement of those women who were conscious of their inferior status adversely affecting their health, community participation and livelihood options.

The inclusiveness that Buddhism promised to all persons regardless of caste or social status caused it to spread far from its place of origin in eastern India. But this inclusiveness, for women, neither came easily, nor was it unconditional. After the establishment of the Buddhist monks' monastery, Gautam Buddha's aunt and foster mother, Mahapajapati Gautami begged his permission for women to enter the order. The Buddha declined. A disciple argued on behalf of women with the question: are women as capable as men of religious attainment? Answering in the affirmative, the Buddha laid out eight rules that the women's monastery was to follow, all of which explicitly granted the monks superiority (Rhys Davids 2007, p. 7; Murcott 1991, pp. 15–16).

This attitude toward women in a system that prided itself on individual agency in religious attainment was probably due to the culture that it nonetheless was part of. Williamson (2000, p. 597) identifies institutions related to religion or custom as deeply "embedded". They "display a great deal of inertia – some because they are functional; others take on symbolic value with a coterie of true believers; many are pervasively linked with complementary institutions".

The institution of patriarchy derived its legitimacy from religion, and dictated the way the economy functioned, ensured the preservation of tradition, and the mode of social interactions. So deeply embedded does patriarchy turn out to be, and so pervasively is it linked with complementary institutions, that it continues to display inertia to the present.

When Mara, the demon, insulted Soma in the forest by suggesting that women were only suited to see to the cooking, it was a clear representation of this tradition. Soma responds with calm confidence (Murcott 1991, p. 159):

> What harm is it
> to be a woman
> when the mind is concentrated
> and the insight is clear?

Soma's interlocutor, whether demon or man, was avowedly a member of the above-mentioned 'coterie'. He adhered to the general norms of behaviour with regard to women in non-traditional roles – in this case, a woman who was in a forest, alone, aiming to something that was considered the male prerogative. These nuns were doing something radical, denying the social worldview of the age to free themselves of domestic drudgery and fulfil their aspirations.

The following conversation in the fifth century BCE between Punnika, a slave-turned-nun, and a *brahman* named Udakasuddhika, is another instance of a woman asserting an influence that the times did not afford her (Murcott 1991, p. 175):

> [Punnika:]
> [W]hat are you afraid of, brahman,
> that makes you go down to the water?
> Your limbs shake with the bitter cold.
> [Udakasuddhika:]
> But you know why, Punnika.
> I am doing good to prevent evil.
> Anyone young or old who has done something bad
> is freed by washing in water.
> [Punnika:]
> Whoever told you
> you are freed from evil by washing?
> The blind leading the blind!
> In that case all frogs and turtles
> would go to heaven,
> and water snakes and crocodiles
> and the rest of the water creatures.
> Butchers of sheep, butchers of pigs,
> fishers and trappers,
> thieves, executioners,
> and other wrongdoers
> would be freed from their bad karma
> by washing in water.
> If these streams carried away all your old evil
> they would carry away your virtue too.
> You would be separated from both.

This verse is striking for two reasons. First, it presents a conversation between a former slave and a *brahman*, itself a social aberration. Further, the dynamics in this conversation are such that it is both a *slave* and a *woman* admonishing a *brahman*, thus causing religious instruction to flow *to* the *brahman* instead of *from* him. Punnika throws a direct challenge to the prevailing *brahmanical* monopoly of religious practice. She argues that if indeed religious goals could be attained through the ritual involving water, then anyone with access to water could wash away their sins; where was the need for the *brahman* class? Rituals were complex and expensive, and therefore exclusive. Buddhism stressed self-discipline, which did not require wealth or high birth.

Mutta, Mahapajapati Gautami, Soma and Punnika are only a few women among several in the fifth century BCE who broke the social mould and chose a path that afforded them self-actualisation. They composed verses to share their experiences with others and encourage them to follow. The *Therigatha* is composed by nuns who meditated and roamed through settlements begging for alms. This is the price they paid for being nonconformist: they were not part of society. That said, their interactions with members of society caused these members to reflect on their actions and on what they wanted in their own lives. Mahapajapati Gautami brought "five hundred women"[9] with her, many recently widowed due to a war, to join the order (Murcott 1991, pp. 14–15). The *brahman* Punnika spoke with went on to become a Buddhist himself (p. 177). These nuns achieved their aims of freeing themselves from oppressive domesticity and achieving the highest spiritual state, and also presenting their own lives as a viable and satisfying livelihood option to other oppressed women.

The *Bhakti* movement poet-saints played a similar role in the communities that they travelled through and interacted with, but unlike the Buddhist nuns, renouncing the world was not a necessary condition to be a *bhakt* or *bhaktin* (a male or female devotee). While formally entering the Buddhist order entailed a strictly adhered to initiation process, being a *bhakt* or *bhaktin* only required devotion. This implies that their interactions with, and influence on, lay society is likely to have been more powerful.

An important characteristic that all *Bhakti* poets share is that they composed in the vernacular with the explicit aim of reaching the most people, intending to demonstrate that the language of the Gods was not exclusive. Atukuri Molla (sixteenth century, Telugu language; Tharu and Lalita Vol. I 2015, p. 97) writes:

> As honey sweetens
> the mouth readily
> a poem should make sense
> right away.
> Obscure sounds and sense
> are no better than
> the dumb and the deaf conversing.

Legend has it that she, being a lower caste woman, took it up as a challenge to compose her own version of the *Ramayana* in the local language in just five days when a minister in the royal court insulted her village. Not only did she keep her word, but Molla's *Ramayana* is considered a classic of Telugu literature – a significant personal achievement, and a boost to Telugu literature (p. 95).

Janabai (1298–1350, Marathi language) worked as a maid and wrote about the difficult and mundane lives of other women (Tharu and Lalita Vol. I 2015, p. 82). She encourages women to be independent, even if it means breaking norms (p. 83):

Cast off all shame,
and sell yourself
in the marketplace;
then alone
can you hope
to reach the Lord.

The general perception of women out in the open as being of easy virtue lends Janabai her choice of words, but the above verse is to be interpreted as Janabai encouraging women to step out of home and set up a trade (p. 83).

Akkamahadevi's (twelfth century, Kannada language) verses are said to possess a "mystic complexity" and "her many-hued images . . . shift and glow into life" (Tharu and Lalita Vol. I 2015, p. 78). She stands out as an exemplar of *Bhakti* poets in her use of the "metaphor of illicit love" (p. 79) for her devotion to Lord Shiva. Her verses contain erotic descriptions of her intimacy with Lord Shiva, which, coming from a woman, were a startling contrast to what was considered appropriate for the times (p. 79).

> For women, her work embodies a radical illegitimacy as she . . . include[s in her poetry] the struggles of her body, struggles against the pettiness of roles she is forced into as a woman, . . . and against the social expectations that restrain her.

The following verse (Swamy 2012, verse 1232) reflects her disgust with the society that made demands on her, in which she also points out that her shunning of society should not suggest that she is in any way intimidated by it. In fact, having dismissed the romantic advances of a local king, she travelled naked in search of her ideal, carrying out public debates with religious and secular scholars and mendicants, and composing verses that remain popular to the present day.

If a swine were to meet an elephant on its way
if the elephant were to move aside in disgust
would the swine become a lion?

Akka's confidence in her dealings with society are also seen in Muktabai's life and verses (thirteenth-century poet-saint who attained *samadhi*[10] at the age of eighteen, Marathi language). Muktabai spoke lucidly about the non-duality of Lord Shiva and Goddess Shakti, his wife. The worldly extension of this doctrine was gender equality, which she demonstrated by offering instruction in public to learned men. Muktabai's brother, Jnaneshwar, was a great saint as well, and often received instruction from Muktabai on appropriate conduct. With the famous saint Changdev, she held prolonged discussions and preached to him on the nature of knowledge and ascetic temperament before accepting him as her guru (Irlekar and Jahagirdar 1999, p. 187). In Indian tradition, the guru is held as being superior to God.[11] Yet here was Muktabai teaching her teacher, more by dint of her confidence in the quality of her spirituality than arrogance (Deshpande 1999, p. 196).

Except Hari, none can liberate your soul for ever
Only He can redeem you from misfortunes of the mundane world . . .
Not only is Muktai redeemed from the mundane world ever and anon
Herself indivisible, she has already sundered dissimilitude

The didactic element in her poetry is obvious in the first couplet above where she exhorts her listeners to focus their meditation on Hari (Lord Krishna), while distancing themselves from "the mundane world". She then confidently presents herself as an example.

Lal Ded or Lalla (fourteenth-century *Bhakti* poet-saint[12] from Kashmir) too had a didactic vein running through her verses. She composed in the vernacular, and made references to the daily concerns of the masses, and so giving hope (Ded and Hoskote 2013, p. 102):

> Does the sun not warm every country he visits
> or does he touch only the richest ones?
> Does water not flow in every house?
> But Shiva can play hard to get: hold on to that message.

Lalla suggests that while salvation is not easy to attain, its attainment is certainly not determined by ritual sacrifice, an option open only to the rich. Her verses are replete with insults for those who followed rituals blindly, and reserved severe chastisement for those who sacrificed animals (pp. 43, 61, 64, 82, 83, 125) because these practices eliminated participation of those who could not afford to perform them. Lalla celebrated simplicity (p. 82):

> Wear just enough to keep the cold out,
> eat just enough to keep hunger from your door.

Her prescription for religious attainment is that lives shorn of meaningless ritual practices *can* attain the highest religious goals – the key is knowledge of the Self and service to others (p. 141):

> Don't torture this body with thirst and hunger, . . .
> just help others through life, there's no truer worship.

Chandrabati (sixteenth-century *Bhakti* poet, Bangla language) composed poetry for the first time about socio-political issues through fiction. Her epic poem *Sundari Malua* (Beautiful Malua) is most explicit in its concern for religious and gender biases, and political improprieties that accentuated the crisis. The *Mughal* administration, under Emperor Akbar (1542–1605) imposed certain taxes, but details were often left for local officers to decide. Taking advantage of this leeway, a local Muslim landlord demanded that Malua, a Hindu lady, live with him for a time, because her family was unable to pay an unreasonable tax imposed in an *ad hoc* fashion. To preclude violence, Malua went, but lied that a vow prevented her from sharing a bed with a man for three months. In the meanwhile, the villagers managed to extricate her. But doubting her chastity with a man outside her religion, the villagers wanted to excommunicate her: "[f]or three long months/ She lived between Muslim walls. The shame of it/ Would shatter a tiger! Who can save a doe/ Caught in the wild beast's claws? We can do/ nothing once chastity and caste are gone" (Tharu and Lalita Vol. I 2015, p. 106).

Chandrabati represents in her work the worst of the political corruption and social stigmatisation that she observed in her world. Yet, in response, the eponymous woman and her mother-in-law display a surreal strength of character (p. 104).

> Indian literature of all kinds is full of the enmity between daughter-in-law and mother-in-law. But in this story, when Malua is released, . . . her mother-in-law stands up for her and argues, in a remarkable passage, against the elders of the village, who want to exile her.

As the earliest known piece of Bangla fiction, Chandrabati creates a stunning piece of literature that is taught in modern curricula in West Bengal state in India and in Bangladesh (Sen 1997, p. 164).

Bhakti poet-saints travelled extensively within their respective linguistic zones, and composed verses that became immensely popular in their time and remain so to the present day.[13] These interactions afforded them a wider ambit for acquiring knowledge, for sharpening their religious and social arguments. Importantly, they generated awareness of the restrictions imposed on some and privileges endowed on others by the orthodox Hindu system of social organisation. Tharu and Lalita (Vol. I 2015, p. 58) point out that there was a surprisingly large number of *bhaktins*, and this was no accident. The very idea of the movement was inclusivity, and so several women and lower caste members chose the path of *Bhakti*, which was difficult and liberating. In comparison, the lives hitherto of these marginalised groups were difficult and constraining.

The *Mughal* princess, Zeb-un-Nissa (1638–1702, Urdu language) though from a completely different religion and cultural background, echoes *Bhakti* voices in her verses. She was the daughter of the last powerful Mughal emperor, Augangzeb, unlike the *Bhakti* women who were often either lower caste or poor or both. Not being burdened by the conviction that her religion was the only true one, she accepts the right of all people to find their religious ideals in their own ways (Lal and Westbrook 1913, p. 28).

> Whether it be in Mecca's holiest shrine,
> Or in the Temple pilgrim feet have trod,
> Still Thou art mine,
> Wherever God is worshipped is my God.

Her outright rejection of labels, yet simultaneous adoption of metaphors from two rival religions, reveals her broadmindedness (p. 23).

> No Muslim I,
> But an idolater,
> I bow before the image of my Love,
> And worship her:
> No Brahman I,
> My sacred thread[14]
> I cast away, for round my neck I wear
> Her plaited hair instead.

She also deftly mixes up conventionally assigned gender roles, by referring to either her God or her lover as a woman; in both respects, crossing the boundaries of custom.

Empress Nur Jahan (1577–1645) distinguished herself for a different set of reasons. She was the only *Mughal* woman to be honoured with the title of Empress because she held the reins of empire (1611–1627) while her husband, Emperor Jahangir (1605–1627)[15] was incapacitated, by his own admission, by opium and alcohol abuse. She was the head of a junta rule (Findly 1993, p. 43) and had complete power over all decisions of the palace: so absolute was her power that any order had to carry her seal to be taken seriously (p. 122). Agency, in this case is about political power and the benefits it afforded. The Empress took advantage of her position to enhance her treasury through the abundant trade that flowed through the commercial centre, Agra (p. 151). She also used her wealth to assist women in need. But her most important contribution might have been that she brought about a major change in the social movements that women were permitted. Earlier, women travelled only with their men on hunting missions or pilgrimages. Under Nur Jahan's influence, "women became confident sensualists whose open attire and epicurean habits were fully accepted in the growing cult of material luxury at court" (p. 245). This was a perceptible improvement from a millennium and a half earlier, when women who went on a "pleasure trip with other women" were to be fined[16] (Chakravarti 1993, p. 584), according to the *Arthashastra*.[17]

Though Zeb-un-Nissa, two generations later, was an obvious beneficiary of this change, this benefit was not afforded to common women even two centuries later. Rassundari Devi, the child bride constrained by housework, did not have a say in her marriage at age twelve. Rassundari's agency becomes apparent in her later years. The expectation of her age was that women should remain illiterate. But so strong was her desire to read the scripture that she covertly stole pages from her son's book and matched the letters with her memory of what she learned in her school days to teach herself to recognise letters and decipher words. This she did while nursing agonising guilt and hiding her reading materials in the cooking quarters: they had the least chance of being discovered there, since no one other than herself normally went in.

Regarding her domestic responsibilities she writes, "[p]eople never realize these things unless they go through similar pressures . . . Every human being should know this. Most people do not have any knowledge about the matter" (Tharu and Lalita Vol. I 2015, p. 198). These lines indicate a desperate attempt by the author to inform men of the deprivations that women go through in the most mundane sense – food and resources might have been abundant, but the time and freedom to benefit from them were not. She felt inhibited to speak out, so she waited to teach herself to read and then wrote her autobiography. Rassundari was not a scholar or saint, but she developed a consciousness of inappropriate constraints imposed on her and broadcast this experience to society to support the awakening of consciousness and agency of others. There is reason to infer that this work was widely read, being the first autobiography in Bangla, and being well received by leading thinkers of the age (p. 190).

Women during colonial India with a lot more exposure than Rassundari Devi made similar observations. They represented truth in fiction to raise public awareness of the potential role that women could play in society, if they could think beyond tradition and exert their identity.

Hannah Catherine Mullens[18] (1826–1861) wrote the first piece of Bangla fiction in prose in 1852 (Tharu and Lalita Vol. I 2015, p. 203). Her protagonist seems, and probably Mullens herself was, desperately impatient with the superstitions that negatively influenced local practices at times as critical-for-life as childbirth. "I have seen myself how very often Bengali women lose their babies in the womb because of the ignorance of these midwives" (p. 208). Mullens' stated aim in having written this novel was "to show the practical influence of Christianity on the various details of domestic life" (p. 204). Nonetheless, her writing had the effect of bringing about an awareness of physically and socially healthy practices so that women questioned tradition when it went counter to their personal wellbeing.

Razia Sajjad Zaheer (1917–1979, Urdu language) with her Marxist leanings (Tharu and Lalita Vol. II 2006, p. 144) aimed for social awakening. Her protagonist in the short story *Neech* (Lowborn) is a fiercely independent woman, Shyamali, who claims that her husband is dead, though she has actually left him. She displays a cool confidence when confronted (pp. 148, 153):

> He thought he could order me around just because he gave me food and clothing. Am I a prostitute to be bought with money? My limbs are sound. I can work. I have the courage to feed ten like him. . . . [W]hat is this fuss about making a living?

Rokeya Sakhawat Hossain (1880–1932, English language), in her feminist utopian fiction *Sultana's Dream*, imagines a world where the men are cloistered in the *mardana* (a male equivalent word for *zenana*, where women were cloistered) and women run the world with aplomb. Science is used in the service of humanity rather than to gather power or profits, and crime and war are unheard of (Tharu and Lalita Vol. I 2015, p. 340).

In all the above examples women have set examples, either personally, or through fictional characters, questioned tradition, goaded women to exert themselves, to aim higher, or shown a mirror to society to reflect its treatment of women. These were their conscious aims. It is not possible to even begin to answer the question of whether these efforts bore fruit, but the fact of women's agency in countering patriarchy is firmly established.

There were others who tried a more direct approach – they wrote, spoke and overtly acted to bring about institutional changes in the position of women in Indian society through direct or indirect engagement with the government.

Tahzib un-Niswan (Culture and Education for Women) was an Urdu language magazine launched in 1898 by a couple, Sayyid Mumtaz Ali and Muhammadi Begam (Minault 1988, p. 2). It aimed to provide *parda*-observing women[19] with reading material to help them think for themselves and broaden their horizons. Articles identify the need to eliminate spending on rituals and dowry and, instead, spend on education. Ladies who completed courses of higher education are warmly congratulated; "[b]y the 1930s, the readers of *Tahzib* had come a long way" (p. 4). Waheed Jahan Begam, co-editor of the magazine, *Khatun* (Woman) writes (p. 6):

> Uneducated women, who do not go out, think that respectability is confined to the four walls of their houses. . . . But God has ordained education for both men and women, so that such useless ideas can be gotten rid of.

These publications and their readership played an important role in educating women and impacting the way the Muslim population reacted to the child marriage discussions of the 1920s and 1930s. Formal education was the most important channel of change chosen by women. Hannah Catherine Mullens (Tharu and Lalita Vol. I 2015, p. 203) and Krupa Sattianadan (p. 275), among several others, established schools for orphans, lower caste girls and Muslim women. Savitribai Phule was a courageous woman who broke all customs that threatened the rights of women to life and an education. She writes, in her collection of poetry, *Kavyphule* (NCERT 2008, p. 2):

> If you have no knowledge, have no education,
> And you yearn not for the same,
> You possess intellect but work not on the same,
> How then can you be called a human being?

She sheltered destitute women at personal cost, both in terms of money and ostracism (Verghese *et al.* 2014). Several other women too were actively writing and talking about the oppressiveness of customs such as child marriage and *sati*.[20] A woman at an All India Women's Conference branch meeting said that child marriage "crushed [girls'] individuality and denied them opportunities for education and development of mind and body". Another, in 1929, places the responsibility for change on women themselves by suggesting that it is the "outlook of women [that] should undergo a radical change" and that the "inferiority complex" must be eliminated (Forbes 1998, p. 87).

The Hindu Child Marriage Bill[21] was proposed in 1927 and it was enacted as the Child Marriage Restraint Act in 1930. It set the minimum marriageable age for all women regardless of caste or religion as fourteen and for men as eighteen. Muslim leaders demanded an amendment to exclude Muslims from the purview of the Act, but the Muslim members of the All India Women's Congress wrote to the Viceroy (Forbes 1998, p. 89):

> We, speaking also on behalf of the Muslim women of India, assert that it is only a small section of [Muslim] men who have been approaching your excellency and demanding exemption from the Act. This Act affects girls and women far more than it affects men and *we deny their right to speak on our behalf* [emphasis added].

These women were, for the first time, politically voicing their dissatisfaction with men making decisions on issues that concerned women. It was also the first learning opportunity for women as organised groups to formulate their strategies and negotiate at the policy level (p. 83). This was a major event in the history of the struggle against patriarchy in India, and a telling example of women's agency in ensuring the most fundamental human rights of women. The aim of the women quoted above was to ensure to all women that they would not be married earlier than their bodies were ready to engage in intercourse and childbirth.

Mrinalini Sen, a suffragette from the early twentieth century argued that though women were subject "to all the laws and rules of the land exercised by the British Government", they did not have the right to vote. It seemed as if women were expected to get their justice at home (Forbes 1998, p. 103). This attitude is represented by Darisi Annapurnamma (1907–1931) in her Kannada-language short story. A police inspector hears noises at night and says to his wife: "It must be Keshavaiya thrashing his daughter-in-law. That is a family matter and it is *not just to interfere*. If you can't sleep here, let us move to another room" (Tharu and Lalita Vol. I 2015, p. 458, emphasis added). In the real world, this tendency to resist positive change again showed up in relation with the Child Marriage Restraint Act, which the British government refused to amend in favour of the Muslim men, not because an amendment would have been detrimental to Muslim women, but because "there was general agreement that the [Child Marriage Restraint] Act was a dead letter [anyway]. Enforcement for the Act was practically non-existent" (Forbes 1998, p. 89). The institution of patriarchy was resilient even in the face of formal institutional changes, and any perceptible change in the lived experience of women demanded great effort.

The gifted orator Sarojini Naidu did more than anyone toward reminding women of their responsibilities. She claimed to be spreading Mahatma Gandhi's message of *swadeshi* (of one's own country, meaning preferring local production and consumption over importing) as an economic policy move at the level of individual households, and her primary justification was that it would help women (Naidu 1925, pp. 294–5).

> [E]very inch spun of this stuff (pointing to her *saree* [made from course hand-spun, hand-woven fabric, *khadi*]) there is the benediction of a women who knows that her hands are buying bread for her little children . . . [T]he women behind the *Purdah*, who cannot go out as their Hindu sisters do, have blessed the spinning wheel because it has saved them from the reproach that they are idlers hanging on the one solitary wage earner.

Naidu went to London to present the case for universal franchise in India, an effort that bore fruit in 1947. In the meanwhile, Saraladevi Chaudhurani continued the fight for women to have equal access to all manner of opportunities. In what is cited as "certainly the most forceful feminist speech of the 1930s" (Forbes 1998, p. 143) she listed ten fundamental rights that should be accorded to women: "equal inheritance, equal rights to guardianship, no sex discrimination, fair wages, punishment for sex-related crimes, closing brothels, compulsory primary education, adult education, female teachers in co-educational institutions, and adult franchise" (Forbes 2005, p. 57). These incredibly liberal demands were part of Saraladevi's proposal for creating a separate women's Congress because "woman's feeling has never been the man's, neither the woman's point of view his". Eventually most of these demands were rejected and the separate women's Congress was not formed (Forbes 1998, p. 143).

Concluding remarks

Patriarchy has had a resilient presence for at least two millennia, though its manifestation has been changing. Correspondingly, the way women have exercised their agency roles in fighting patriarchy has also changed.

Chakravarti (1993, p. 580) infers that "the first large group to be enslaved in early Indian history [was] women as there are more frequent references to 'dasis' [female slaves] than 'dasas' [male slaves]" in the Rig Vedic literature. The Rig Vedic period ended around 600 BCE, when the Buddhist period began. Punnika, the slave-turned-nun who reproached the *brahman*, was a victim of this most severe manifestation of patriarchy – women were bought and sold for their utility as bearers of children and as sex objects. This was a denial to women of their most fundamental *human* right, because they were valued as commodities. Punnika escaped her reality by entering the Buddhist order, and so gained the confidence to exercise her agency role. She rebuked a *brahman*, a man who enjoyed the highest standing in the community that enslaved her. It was only by exiting society, so to speak, that Punnika and others like her were able to have their voices heard and fight patriarchy.

Later, instead of being treated as commodities, women were treated as members of the family whose movements had to be strictly controlled. Since women bore children, their sexual alliances determined the caste purity of a family line, and caste purity has been of supreme importance to all castes according to the *brahmanical* texts (Chakravarti 1993, p. 579) through the Buddhist period all the way till present times. These constraints imposed on women's options in all areas of their lives were contested by Buddhist nuns, *Bhakti* poets and writers of the colonial period.

Literacy was a sign of the elite in pre-independent India. Two per cent of the adult female population and ten per cent of the adult male population were literate in India in 1910 (Census of India 1911, Vol. I, Part I, p. 293). These numbers were lower still in earlier years. So throughout this entire stretch of history considered in this chapter, anyone desirous of communicating with large groups of people used poetry, maybe set to music. Often this poetry passed down several generations orally before being committed to script. The oral tradition of a community is both a reflection of, and has an influence on, its guiding beliefs and ideals. Singing or hearing folk songs in which women are represented as being capable of the same religious attainment as men, or where women are encouraged to be assertive and independent, would have diminished the force and influence of the patriarchy ordained by tradition. Given that having their voices heard and seeing women's lives change for the better were some of the aims of several of the women discussed in this chapter, their agency role took shape in their poetry and lyrical compositions that were repeated and imbibed by the masses.

It is only during the late nineteenth century that women could expect to communicate through writing. The publication, circulation and readership of newspapers and magazines showed a sharp increase near the end of the nineteenth and early twentieth centuries (Annual Reports of the Post Office of India). This gave a boost to the struggle for national independence. Reach of the written word was certainly limited; but not as limited as the literacy numbers would suggest, because there was a village culture of reading the news and other information aloud in community spaces, and sharing stories (Ahmed 1995, p. 303). Discussion of political issues has long been an Indian hobby. Women's role in the independence movement is linked in an important way with their fight against patriarchy (discussed in Bharat forthcoming, and Forbes 1998, 2005). The urgent need to fight British rule drew women outside their homes and, importantly, legitimised their social and political presence in the eyes of society. Women's agency gained a great deal of force in this period. They were negotiating directly with the foreign government to ban child marriage and to grant women the vote. They were making public speeches to encourage women to exert themselves. They set up schools and shelters for destitute women to afford them the life of respect that tradition denied them.

Without these varied exhortations, the faith in women's agency would be misplaced. Urvashi Butalia (1993, WS13) questions the assumption that agency is a force for good. She points out that "women's loyalties could have shifted, that they were not undifferentiated and homogeneous, that their interests could tie in with those of their men and their class". These are references to women who encouraged their men to slaughter the girls in the family to preclude religious conversion during the communal riots of the 1940s, they resisted offering water to a dying person of a different religion, they assisted their husbands in looting during social tensions. These women were "acting upon some kind of a *perceived* notion of the good of their community [emphasis added]" (WS15), so reinforcing Sen's suggestion that women supported events or persons they perceived as valuable, even to their own detriment.

The only way to then distinguish true agency that might foster gender equality, from reactions born out of internalised oppression that might only sustain inequalities, is education and informed debate. To restore some faith in women's agency, all the women's writing presented in this chapter exemplifies a positive kind of agency that is a force for overcoming oppression.

This understanding of women's status in society and their agency in the fight against patriarchy afforded by looking into literature produced by women is not possible by looking at the more abundant literature produced by men. For the modern scholar, ancient Hindu religious and secular texts, written presumably by (*brahman*) men, paint a picture of precisely the patriarchal norms that women were struggling against.[22] The *Therigatha* is the first Indian text to bring up the concern of patriarchy and to demand gender equality. *Bhakti* literature produced by men was not so closed to the concerns of women and other oppressed groups. The literature produced by men during the nationalist period is more varied in its concern for women. There were reformers who worked unstintingly to diminish the horrors of patriarchy, and several others (reformers and obscurantists) who upheld patriarchy as essential to maintain social order. Many simply ignored the issue. For women, patriarchy pervaded every aspect of their lives and livelihoods and they could not possibly ignore it, whether they produced poetry or prose, whether they wrote of reality or created fiction, whether their subject was religious or political or social.

The thoughts of artists of all persuasions and activists in all areas of public life are often at the forefront of social change. Given that it has been mostly women who have written about and against patriarchy, it can be concluded that it is women's writings and activities that have been responsible for any expansion of women's freedoms through history.

Notes

1 Assistant Professor, Bengaluru Dr B. R. Ambedkar School of Economics, India. I am extremely grateful to Kirsten for her patience with my several drafts. Her unbelievable sincerity in reviewing my work has only helped it improve. Any shortcomings are my responsibility. I am thankful to Susan for putting me in touch with challenging research opportunities. I thank former colleagues at Christ University, specifically Divya, Gerard Sir and Adaina. I thank Ritu, Nadkarni Sir, Susan, Mary Ma'm, Asha and Deshpande Sir for comments on drafts. I relied heavily on the library resources at Christ. I thank my family.

2 The additional distinction Sen makes between achievement and freedom in each of the notions of wellbeing and agency is key to being able to measure welfare. As measurement is not the focus in the current work, this distinction is brushed aside.

3 Babar from central Asia established the *Mughal* Empire in India in the early sixteenth century CE. His grandson, Akbar was the most popular *Mughal* emperor and ruled for half a century. The eighteenth-century emperors were reduced to nominal heads by the East India Company.

4 In Buddhist literature, the only occupations attributed to women were courtesan and prostitute because these were the only women who were financially independent. Other women were identified as being related to a man. Significantly, when the first elections were being planned in Independent India in 1950 (Guha 2007, p. 144), a problem faced by Sukumar Sen, the first Chief Election Commissioner, was that women refused to give their own names to be registered as voters, but insisted on being put down as related to a man.

5 Robert W. Dimand identified in email correspondence that Rhys Davids is the original translator into English of the ancient Buddhist nuns' poetry. As is apparent in Dimand (2000), Rhys Davids was a Pali scholar from Great Britain in the early 1900s and brought a feminist lens to her work which might influence the analysis in this chapter.

6 Bahinabai and the calf were deeply attached to each other. At a crowded sermon by Jayaram Swami, the calf was dragged outside the seating area. Bahinabai and the calf both wept. The Swami, "discerner of the soul", had the calf brought back in and the sermon continued with the calf "showing intense attention". Later as Bahinabai prostrated herself at the Swami's feet, the calf did the same. "When the [sermon] was ended, the people went away, remarking to themselves on the event, such as had never occurred before" (Tharu and Lalita Vol. I 2015, pp. 111–12).

7 The more commonly used anglicised adjective is Bengali.

8 *Nibbana* is the highest level of religious attainment in Buddhism.

9 A term used multiple times in the Pali language texts of the age, probably to be loosely interpreted as "many."

10 Muktabai attained the highest state of realisation, when the body ceases to have an independent existence and is united with the Divine, at eighteen and she then chose to become one with nature and die.

11 A fifteenth-century male poet Kabir is credited with the famous couplet which says that a teacher should be respected more than God, because it is the teacher who teaches one about God.

12 Hoskote (Ded and Hoskote 2013, pp. xxvii–xxviii) chooses to diverge from the traditional classification. He claims that Lal Ded was not a *Bhakti* poet-saint, because her method was more focused on attaining divine realisation through knowledge rather than purely through devotion.

13 The idea of worship through *bhakti* has been incorporated into the fold of formal Hinduism in modern times.

14 Hindu *brahman* men, after an initiation process, wear a sacred white thread over one shoulder and across their chest.

15 The grandfather of Emperor Augungzeb.

16 The fine was set at "three to six panas". Five panas was the monthly salary for the lowest paid (Rangarajan 1992, p. 110).

17 There is no consensus on when the Arthashastra was written. Dates range from fourth century BCE to second century CE (Habib and Jha 2004, p. 48).

18 There seems to be some doubt about whether Hannah Catherine Mullens was Indian or British, though it is certain that she was born in Calcutta, married a Christian missionary, and spent almost all her life in Calcutta (Tharu and Lalita Vol. I 2015, p. 203). This is reason enough for me to include her in this paper on *Indian* women's economic thought.

19 The *pardah* is a veil that women in many traditional societies must use. They are expected to not appear in public, especially in front of distantly related and unrelated males.

20 A custom that required a widow to immolate herself on the funeral pyre with her husband.

21 The Hindu Child Marriage Bill was proposed by a teacher, judge and politician Harbilas Sarda. The Act continued to be known by his name, Sarda Act.

22 With the notable exception of the *Upanishads*, which discuss spirituality, regardless of the gender identity or social standing of the seeker.

References

Ahmed, N. H. (1995). *India Post through the Ages: A Saga of Communications*. Kurnool: Postal History Society of India.

Altekar, A. S. (1956). *The Position of Women in Hindu Civilization, from Prehistoric Times to the Present Day*. Delhi: Motilal Banarsidass.

Becker, G. S. (1994). Human capital revisited. In *Human Capital: A Theoretical and Empirical Analysis with Special Reference to Education* (3rd edition) (pp. 15–28). Chicago: University of Chicago Press.

Bharat, S. (forthcoming, 2019). Two sides of the colonial coin: British and Indian women's engagements with colonialism and patriarchy. In Ajit Sinha & Alex Thomas (eds) *Economics and its History*. New Delhi: Routledge.

Boserup, E. (1970). *Woman's Role in Economic Development*. Abingdon: Earthscan.

Butalia, U. (1993). Community, state and gender: on women's agency during partition. *Economic and Political Weekly*, WS12–WS24.

Chakravarti, U. (1993). Conceptualising brahmanical patriarchy in early India: Gender, caste, class and state. *Economic and Political Weekly*, 28(14), 579–85.

Ded, L., & Hoskote, R. (2013). *I, Lalla: The Poems of Lal Ded*. Trans. Ranjit Hoskote. New Delhi: Penguin.

Deshpande, P. G. (1999). Muktabai. *Indian Literature*, 43(1) (189), 196–9.

Dimand, Robert W. (2000). Caroline Augusta Foley Rhys Davids. In Robert W. Dimand, Mary Ann Dimand & Evelyn L. Forget (eds) *A Biographical Dictionary of Women Economists*. Cheltenham, UK: Edward Elgar, pp. 129–31.

Findly, E. B. (1993). *Nur Jahan, Empress of Mughal India*. Oxford: Oxford University Press on Demand.

Forbes, G. (1998). *Women in Modern India* (Vol. 2). Cambridge: Cambridge University Press.

—— (2005). *Women in Colonial India: Essays on Politics, Medicine, and Historiography*. New Delhi: Orient Blackswan.

Guha, R. (2007). *India after Gandhi: The History of the World's Largest Democracy*. New York: Harper Perennial.

Habib, I., & Jha, V. (2004). *A People's History of India, 4, Mauryan India*. New Delhi: Tulika Books.

Irlekar, S., & Jahagirdar, C. (1999). From freedom to salvation: The poetry of Saint Muktabai. *Indian Literature*, 43(1) (189), 178–95.

King, E. M., & Hill, M. A. (eds). (1997). *Women's Education in Developing Countries: Barriers, Benefits, and Policies*. Baltimore, MD: Johns Hopkins University Press for World Bank.

Lal, M., & Westbrook, J. D. (1913). The Diwan of Zeb-un-Nissa, sacred-texts.com (accessed on 24 May 2016).

Minault, G. (1988). Urdu women's magazines in the early twentieth century. *Manushi*, 48, 2–9.

Murcott, S. (1991). *The First Buddhist Women: Translations and Commentaries on the Therigatha*. Berkeley, CA: Parallax Press.

Nadkarni, M. V. (2013). *Handbook of Hinduism*. New Delhi: Ane Books Pvt. Ltd.

Naidu, S. (1925). *Speeches and Writings of Sarojini Naidu*. Madras: GA Natesan & Company.

NCERT. National Council for Educational Research and Training. (2008). Savitribai Phule First Memorial Lecture.

Papanek, H. (1979). Family status production: The "work" and "non-work" of women. *Signs: Journal of Women in Culture and Society*, 4(4), 775–81.

—— (1990). To each less than she needs, from each more than she can do: Allocations entitlements and value. In Irene Tinker (ed.) *Persistent Inequalities: Women and World Development*. New York: Oxford University Press, pp. 162–82.

Rangarajan, L. N. (ed.). (1992). *The Arthashastra*. New Delhi: Penguin Books India.

Ray, B. (1991). Women of Bengal: Transformation in ideas and ideals, 1900–1947. *Social Scientist*, 19(5), 3–23.

Rhys Davids, C. A. F. (1901). Economic conditions in Ancient India. *The Economic Journal*, 11(43), 305–20.

—— (1923). Economic conditions according to early Buddhist literature. *Cambridge Ancient History of India*. New York.

—— (2007). Psalms of the early Buddhists. 1—Psalms of the Sisters. Elibron Classics.

Schultz, T. P. (1990). Returns to women's education. *Centre Discussion Paper No. 603*. Yale – Economic Growth Center.
Sen, A. (1985). Well-being, agency and freedom: The Dewey lectures 1984. *The Journal of Philosophy*, 82(4), 169–221.
—— (1987). *Gender and Cooperative Conflicts* (No. 1342). Helsinki: WIDER.
Sen, N. D. (1997). Rewriting the Ramayana: Chandrabati and Molla. *India International Centre Quarterly*, 24(2/3), 163–77.
Swamy, N. O. L. (ed.). (2012). *Vachana*. Bengaluru: Basava Samiti.
Tharu, S. J., & Lalita, K. (eds). (2006). *Women Writing in India: The Twentieth Century* (Vol. II). New Delhi: Oxford University Press.
—— (eds). (2015). *Women Writing in India: 600 BC to the Early Twentieth Century* (Vol. I). New Delhi: Oxford University Press.
Verghese, Leah, Ranjana, & Sundar, M. (2014). *People and Ideas: Savitribai, Journey of a Trailblazer*. Bengaluru: Azim Premji University.
Williamson, O. E. (2000). The new institutional economics: Taking stock, looking ahead. *Journal of Economic Literature*, 38(3), 595–613.

Appendix 1.1 List of women writers cited, with some details

Name	*Period*	*Category*
Abala Bose	1865–1951	Colonial
Akkamahadevi	Twelfth century CE	Bhakti
Atukuri Molla	Sixteenth century CE	Bhakti
Bahinabai	1628–1700	Bhakti
Chandrabati	ca. 1550–1600	Bhakti
Darisi Annapurnamma	1907–1931	Colonial
Hannah Catherine Mullens	1826–1861	Colonial
Krupa Sattianadan	1862–1894	Colonial
Lal Ded (Lalla)	Fourteenth century CE	Bhakti
Mahapajapati Gautami	Fifth century BCE	Buddhist
Mrinalini Sen	?	Colonial
Muhammadi Begam	1878–1908	Colonial
Muktabai	Thirteenth century CE	Bhakti
Mutta	Fifth century BCE	Buddhist
Nur Jahan	1577–1645	Mughal
Patacara	Fifth century BCE	Buddhist
Punnika	Fifth century BCE	Buddhist
Rassundari Devi	1810–?	Colonial
Razia Sajjad Zaheed	1917–1979	Colonial/Independent India
Rokeya Sakhawat Hossain	1880–1932	Colonial
Saraladevi Chaudhurani	1872–1945	Colonial
Sarat Kumari Chaudhurani	1861–1920	Colonial
Sarojini Naidu	1879–1949	Colonial
Savitribai Phule	1831–1897	Colonial
Soma	Fifth century BCE	Buddhist
Sulekha Sanyal	1928–1962	Colonial/Independent India
Sumangala's mother	Fifth century BCE	Buddhist
Waheed Jahan Begam	?	Colonial
Zeb-un-Nissa	1638–1702	Mughal

2

ENGLISH WOMEN'S ECONOMIC THOUGHT IN THE 1790s

Domestic economy, married women's economic dependence, and access to professions

Joanna Rostek

Preliminary remarks and historical contextualization

In 1798, Priscilla Wakefield, author and philanthropist with "a claim to be seen as the founder of the earliest savings bank in England" ("Priscilla Wakefield: Life"), notes at the outset of her *Reflections on the Present Condition of the Female Sex*:

> It is asserted by Doctor Adam Smith, that every individual is a burden upon the society to which he belongs, who does not contribute his share of productive labour for the good of the whole. [. . .] [Smith] does not absolutely specify, that both sexes [. . .] are equally required to comply with these terms; but since the female sex is included in the idea of the species, and as women possess the same qualities as men, though perhaps in a different degree, their sex cannot free them from the claim of the public for their proportion of usefulness.
>
> *1798, p. 2*

Wakefield's reference to Smith calls to mind that in the second half of the eighteenth century, Britain saw what is frequently termed the beginning of modern economics. Smith's *An Inquiry into the Nature and Causes of the Wealth of Nations* was published in 1776 and the following decades brought the gradual institutionalization of political economy as an academic discipline (see Schabas 2003, pp. 178–9). Standard histories of economic thought reiterate the male-centered view that Wakefield saw in Smith: they create the impression that women did not participate in these developments and failed to contribute to the economic discourse of their times. The reception of Priscilla Wakefield's *Reflections* is a case in point in that regard: as Robert Dimand notes in a rare economic analysis of her text, Wakefield "is familiar to historians of economics, if at all, as the mother of Edward Wakefield [. . .] and as the grandmother and anxious guardian of Edward Gibbon Wakefield" (2003, pp. 194–5). Posterity is hence more likely to associate

Priscilla Wakefield with putatively 'feminine' roles – that of mother, grandmother, and anxious guardian – than with her achievements as an economic writer and founder of a savings bank.

Such relative sidelining of women's economic contributions from the late eighteenth and early nineteenth centuries is partially attributable to the difficulty in handling the terms 'economy' and 'economics', the meanings of which have shifted over time. The *Oxford English Dictionary* gives several possible usages of the terms for the period around 1800, and in perusing texts by English women, it becomes obvious that depending on the context, the terms could refer to different aspects of social organization and individual activity. The most frequent usage in women's writing at that time seems to be in the sense of domestic economy, i.e. "the art or science of household management, esp. with regard to expenditure" ("economy" I.2a, *OED*). Limiting the investigation into women's economic thought around 1800 to texts that explicitly mention the word 'economy' or 'economics' can therefore create the wrong impression that household management was their principal economic concern. A more thorough glance reveals, however, that texts by women also contain observations approaching the understanding of the term as "[t]he management or administration of the material resources of a community, discipline, or other organized body; the art or science of managing such resources" ("economy" I.1a, *OED*). Yet female authors do not subsume their reflections on such topics under the heading of 'the economy' or 'economics'. This is due, among others, to the fact that these terms had not yet become as recognizable and common for denoting a specific form of enquiry, as is the case today. Besides, gender norms narrowed down the realms of knowledge formation and social analysis women could lay claim to.

Bearing in mind the consequent necessity of properly contextualizing economic writing by women around 1800, this chapter puts forward the following claims:

1 English women wrote about and analyzed the economy around 1800, despite cultural and institutional obstacles to their participation in the economic discourse.
2 English women's economic thought around 1800 is almost invariably connected to issues of gender. It is marked by a tension between contestation of and conformity to gender norms. This tension reflects the period's restrictive ideals of femininity on the one hand, and progressive, liberal tendencies of the 1790s on the other.
3 The economics of marriage forms an important focus within English women's economic thought around 1800, with sub-strands examining domestic economy, the economic dependence of married women, and women's access to professions.
4 English women writers around 1800 formulate ideas that would (re)emerge in twentieth-century social sciences (e.g. crowding hypothesis, gender pay gap, positive discrimination/ affirmative action).

Women around 1800 had to face and overcome gender-specific challenges in order to participate in the economic discourse of their times. These challenges help to explain why their economic analyses occurred in different genres and emphasized different topics from economic thought by men. One major obstacle was unequal access to education. Women were barred from universities, clubs, and scholarly societies involved in the formation of political economy. Their education – if they received any, that is – frequently focused on so-called female accomplishments, which lay an emphasis on foreign languages and literature, writing, basic arithmetic, singing, dancing, playing the piano, drawing, and embroidering. Within the upper and middle classes, these skills were seen as a suitable preparation for a woman's desirable economic and social position, namely that of a wife. But given its limited scope, such education prevented women from shaping the public discourse on a par with men. Instruction, moreover, substantially depended on social class and religious background, with Unitarian women from the middle classes, for example, being more likely to acquire competences necessary to partake in political or social controversies. As a result, the surviving economic texts by women display a certain bias and should not be deemed representative of the experience or ideas of all women. To borrow a phrase from Laura E. Thomason, it is impossible to write "a history of Everywoman" or "to account for every possible permutation of a matter that is both complicated (thus resistant to generalization) and personal (thus resistant to analysis)" (2014, p. 14). This is also true for a history of women's economic thought.

Another factor upholding the epistemological inequality between women and men was the by then already operating ideology of separate spheres, which relegated women to the private and domestic realm, thus creating cultural barriers to the engagement with public topics explored by political economists. Ideology, moreover, limited women's access to authorship, as assuming the public role of an author constituted a trespass on male territory and a potential threat to the ideal of femininity. Women who took up the pen could not choose freely from the available range of genres, the 'higher' ones in particular. Since literature and pedagogy counted among the areas where women could acquire "some public presence" (Benjamin 2001, p. 415), the bulk of writing by English women around 1800 occurred in genres that, from today's perspective, would not qualify as academic or theoretical: conduct books, novels, poems, plays, moral tales, religious tracts, pamphlets, travelogues, diaries, or letters. In such texts, women could present a female perspective on phenomena that men could explore through more 'respectable' genres. As Edith Kuiper points out in the introduction to her invaluable anthology of *Women's Economic Thought in the Eighteenth Century* (2014) – which includes excerpts from many of the texts discussed in the following – women moreover tended to write for different addressees than men:

> where early political economists wrote predominantly for those in positions of power in the emerging industrial society (e.g. legislators, merchants, and entrepreneurs), women economic writers mostly addressed audiences economists hardly considered relevant such as women, girls, and occasionally a queen.
>
> *pp. xvii–xviii*

To retrieve women's historical contributions to economic thought, then, it is indispensable to move beyond generic constrictions and to acknowledge the epistemological worth of texts that do not necessarily adhere to standards of academic composition developed by male scholars. In addition, it must be borne in mind that female authors frequently wrote not only in different genres and for different audiences, but also on different economic topics from men. Kuiper observes that

> [a]s gender distinctions in Europe sharpened over the course of the eighteenth century, women's economic position in society, their life experiences and their topics of interest became more and more differentiated from those of men. This is reflected in their writings on economic experiences, insights and perspectives on the eighteenth century economy.
>
> *2014, p. xiv*

Consequently, it is nearly impossible to separate an analysis of economic writing by English women around 1800 from discussions of gender.

Despite the manifold obstacles to knowledge formation and authorship, female writers entered the literary market in remarkable numbers toward the end of the eighteenth century, making the period a – hitherto largely under-researched – treasure trove of economic writing by British women. William Stafford quotes figures according to which "[b]etween three hundred and four hundred women published during the decade of the 1790s alone" (2002, p. 51). Their increased publishing activity was related to trenchant social, political, cultural, and economic shifts. In the words of Gary Kelly, "[t]he period of the late eighteenth and early nineteenth centuries was one of radical and rapid change – too radical and rapid for some and not enough for others" (1996, p. ix). Decisive events include the American and French Revolutions, the Napoleonic Wars, the rise of capitalist forms of investment and management, the shift to wage economy, the rise of the banking system in Britain, national debt, inflation, and the related restriction period, during which the Bank of England was not required to convert banknotes into gold. Crucially, these developments coincided with heated and consequential debates about individual rights, citizenship, nationhood, political participation, and social organization, with the 'rights of man' becoming a central, if disputed, concept. In the process, authors of both sexes began to inquire into the status of the rights of women. In Britain of the 1790s, this led to what today is referred to as a wave of feminism. Authors from differing political, religious, and ideological backgrounds explored the questions of the rights a woman should enjoy, what her role in society should be, what her particular duties consist in, how she should position herself vis-à-vis men, etc.

While the social climate of the 1790s fostered new channels of female articulation, the lingering ideology of separate spheres still meant for women that as soon as they entered the public discourse, they had to conform to ideals of femininity or else justify their deviance from them. Conflicting patterns of conformity-versus-contestation thus permeate much of the writing analyzed in this chapter, with women's economic status and pursuits nearly always being explored in relation to men. What I have illustrated elsewhere with regard to nineteenth-century popularizers of political economy Jane Marcet and Harriet Martineau also holds true for earlier economic writers: "because women at that time were largely denied scientific and economic authority, [. . .] female authors [. . .] chose a contradictory strategy [. . .] that both confirmed and challenged the traditional and restrictive gender norms" (Rostek 2014, p. 21). Dimand makes a similar observation with regard to Priscilla Wakefield, who in *Reflections* uses "the conservative language of the duties and obligations of women to argue for a radical alteration of women's education and opportunities" (Dimand 2003, p. 201).

The proto-feminist debate – which abated in the course of the Napoleonic Wars – touched upon economic concerns. Stafford concludes in his study of (anti-)feminist controversies in the 1790s that they stressed "the importance of women's access to resources" (2002, p. 216). For women of that period, access to resources mostly depended on marriage. Elizabeth Bergen Brophy confirms that marriage was "[i]n theory [. . .] a condition ordained by God that provided them the widest opportunities for practicing and promoting virtue. In practice marriage was usually the only way that women could achieve some measure of economic security" (1991, p. 139). Thomason equally stresses that "[m]arriage was the most important practical decision affecting a woman's life: the means of fulfilling an accepted social role and ensuring financial security" (2014, p. 7).

As a result, marriage is arguably *the* key economic topic in English women's writing around 1800, yielding several interrelated sub-strands of economic analysis:

1 Domestic economy

Texts within this strand concentrate on household production and expenditure, with a particular emphasis on those aspects of domestic economy that should be managed by wives and daughters in accordance with prevalent gender norms. They often take the form of conduct books and pedagogical treatises, and aim at young women and/or their parents.

2 Economic dependence of married women

Several novels and plays, but also pamphlets and polemical treatises explore the situation of married women. Some of them combine economic with legal analyses, especially when they take issue with the common-law regulations of coverture, which stipulated that a man acquired the right to dispose of nearly all of his wife's property upon marriage. The authors illustrate and criticize the consequences of the economic dependence of married women.

3 Access to professions for women

This strand of analysis relates to the preceding one and concentrates on the question of how women can attain more economic independence, in particular when marriage as the standard source of maintenance fails, be it through spinsterhood, widowhood, or the husband's inability to provide for his family. The texts indict cultural obstacles to women's access to paid labor and recommend concrete professions suitable for women.

It is important to stress that these strands do not reflect a distinct school of economic thought that would have been recognized as such by the authors in question. Used in the singular, 'economic thought' implies the notion of one or several coherent bodies of ideas and axioms. Yet with regard to women's early writings, it seems more appropriate to use the plural and speak of 'economic thoughts'. For reasons explained above, economic observations by women are scattered across various texts, genres, audiences, and topics, and do not take the form of an academic dispute between advocates and opponents of specific economic measures. Women's cultural and institutional exclusion from scholarly practices as well as "[t]he wide variety of backgrounds, perspectives, and interests, prevented these women from developing one vision and one voice, something the political economists of their day were successful in achieving" (Kuiper 2014, p. xix). It is possible to identify strands within English women's economic thought(s) in the 1790s; but it bears emphasizing that this thematic grouping is imposed retrospectively on what was a dynamic, controversial, and multifaceted discourse.

The following three sections of this chapter consecutively present selected examples of English women's writing on domestic economy, the economic dependence of married women, and women's access to paid professions. They illustrate that women around 1800 produced a gender-sensitive form of economic enquiry and developed ideas that would resurface again in twentieth-century social sciences.

Domestic economy

Within the conformity-versus-contestation spectrum, texts concerned with domestic economy lean toward the former: for the most part, they do not question the sexual division of labor within households, but lay down instead what the particular duties of women consist in and how to discharge them most effectively and appropriately. They combine descriptive with prescriptive elements. This is true, for example, of Hester Mulso Chapone's letter "On Economy", which forms part of her widely read *Letters on the Improvement of the Mind Addressed to a Young Lady* (1773) – a conduct book predating the 1790s. Chapone (1727–1802), a writer associated with the Bluestocking circle, which united a group of intellectual women in the second half of the eighteenth century, begins her letter by stating that

> Economy is so important a part of a woman's character, so necessary to her own happiness, and so essential to her performing properly the duties of a wife and of a mother, that it ought to have the precedence of all other accomplishments, and take its rank next to the first duties of life. It is, nevertheless, an *art* as well as a *virtue* – and many

> well-meaning persons, from ignorance, or from inconsideration, are strangely deficient in it. Indeed it is too often wholly neglected in a young woman's education – and, she is sent from her father's house to govern a family, without the least degree of that knowledge, which should qualify her for it: this is the source of much inconvenience: – for though experience and attention may supply, by degrees, the want of instruction, yet this requires time – the family in the mean time may get into habits, which are very difficult to alter; and, what is worse, the husband's opinion of his wife's incapacity may be fixed too strongly to suffer him ever to think justly of her gradual improvements.
>
> *Chapone 1773, p. 316*

In this passage, Chapone does not challenge the association of women with the domestic sphere: female economic activity has to comply with patriarchal standards and includes deference to the husband's needs. Yet in terming economy "an *art* as well as a *virtue*", Chapone emphasizes that managing a household requires particular skills a woman should be taught to promote the welfare of her family as well as herself. Accordingly, her letter contains advice for young female readers on household expenditure, saving, time management, and the managing of servants. Such general counsel usually appears within a clearly gendered context: expertise in domestic economy accords with notions of ideal femininity. In managing their households, women should "aim at *propriety* and *neatness*" (p. 318), pay attention to their "appearance and character" (p. 320), and avoid becoming "excessively troublesome to every body, [. . .] particularly to her husband" (p. 320).

"On Economy" also contains interspersed references to price, although they seem too short to deduce an underlying theory from them. Chapone instructs her readers that they

> must endeavour to acquire skill in purchasing; and, in order to [achieve] this, you should begin now to attend to the prices of things – you should take every proper opportunity of learning the real value of every thing, as well as the marks whereby you are to distinguish the good from the bad.
>
> *p. 318*

Here, Chapone appears to suggest that price does not necessarily reflect the "real value" of goods, which is why women should take into consideration additional (albeit unspecified) "marks" to measure the value of a good. By underlining public consequences of private economic behavior, Chapone also admonishes middle-class readers not to ruin the working classes through excessive credit-based spending:

> Regularity of payments and accounts is essential to Economy: – your house-keeping should be settled at least once a week, and all the bills paid: – all other tradesmen should be paid, at farthest, once a year. Indeed I think it more advantageous to pay oftener: but, if you make them trust you longer, they must either charge proportionably higher, or be losers by your custom. Numbers of them fail, every year, from the cruel cause of being obliged to give their customers so much longer credit than the dealers, from whom they take their goods, will allow to them. If people of fortune considered this, they would not defer their payments, from mere negligence, as they often do, to the ruin of whole families.
>
> *p. 318*

This passage, like many others, combines an economic analysis with moral deliberations. Elsewhere, Chapone discourages young women from "ever keep[ing] a domestic, however expert in business, whom they know to be guilty of immorality" (p. 321); she recommends "family prayers" (p. 324), and promotes "[t]he prudent distribution of [. . .] charitable gifts" (p. 324). A moral(ist) perspective on economic behavior is in fact typical of both men's and women's writing of that period, calling into mind that classical political economy emerged out of moral philosophy.

A similar amalgamation of domestic economy and feminine virtues with didactic and moral guidance permeates the pedagogical treatise *Practical Education* (1798), jointly penned by the popular Anglo-Irish novelist and educationist Maria Edgeworth (1768–1849) and her father Richard Lovell Edgeworth (1744–1817). The book contains a chapter "On Prudence and Economy", in which the authors assert that "[e]conomy is in women an essential domestic virtue" (p. 274). Like Chapone's text, *Practical Education* presents the task of educating girls and young women in the realm of household economy as compatible with culturally prescribed notions of femininity. In many respects, it echoes the advice given by Chapone:

> Young women should be accustomed to keep the family accounts, and their arithmetic should not be merely a speculative science; they should learn the price of all necessaries, and of all luxuries; they should learn what luxuries are suited to their fortune and rank, what degree of expence in dress is essential to a regularly neat appearance, and what must be the increased expence and temptations of fashion in different situations; they should not be suffered to imagine that they can resist these temptations more than others, if they get into company above their rank, or should they have any indistinct idea, that by some wonderfully economical operations they can make a given sum of money go farther than others can do. The steadiness of calculations will prevent all these vain notions.
>
> *Edgeworth and Edgeworth 1798 pp. 279–80*

The Edgeworths thus promote prudence, modesty, and risk-aversion in women, and they implicitly discourage social mobility.

The chapter "On Prudence and Economy" also refers to money, but the brevity of the comments makes it difficult to ascertain the authors' theoretical understanding of money. Rather, in the context of the didactic treatise that *Practical Education* undoubtedly is, it emerges that economic observations on money go hand in hand with an emphasis on morals, virtue, and education. The Edgeworths claim that money

> should be represented to our pupils as what it really is, the conventional sign of the value of commodities; before children are acquainted with the real and comparative value of any of these commodities, it is surely imprudent to trust them with money.
>
> *p. 277*

What seems important to the Edgeworths is that children should not be trusted with money until they understand the concept of value and are capable of judicious and responsible spending.

Although the passage on money quoted above does not distinguish between girls and boys, but speaks of "our pupils", other passages contain gender-specific advice on dealing with money. Tellingly, the Edgeworths entrust fathers with their sons' financial education:

> Before a young man goes into the world, it will be a great advantage to him to have some share in the management of his father's affairs; by laying out money for another person he will acquire habits of care, which will be useful to him afterwards in his own affairs.
>
> *p. 283*

These stipulations reflect gendered notions of men's and women's specific economic tasks: while boys are to obtain expertise in management before they go "into the world" and thus enter the public realm, girls' economic education focuses on the family and their appearance (dress, fashion, etc.). The Edgeworths' recommendations for mothers/girls and fathers/sons thus adopt and reinforce the ideology of separate spheres.

At the same time, advice for girls and boys seems to be fueled by the rich version of utilitarianism as developed by Jeremy Bentham, whom Maria Edgeworth knew personally. Throughout, the Edgeworths caution their readers to act responsibly in financial affairs and to bear in mind that "real pleasures" have more than just a narrowly defined material dimension:

> The worth of money is to be estimated by the number of real pleasures which it can procure: there are many which are not to be bought by gold; these will never lose their pre-eminent value with persons who have been educated both to reason and to feel.
>
> *p. 290*

Clearly, the Edgeworths view knowledgeability in economic affairs as forming only one aspect among many within the overarching goal of promoting moral perfection and social usefulness in their pupils.

Domestic economy also plays a vital role in Priscilla Wakefield's less-known treatise, *Reflections on the Present Condition of the Female Sex; with Suggestions for Its Improvement* (1798). Wakefield (1751–1832) was a writer, philanthropist, and founder of a penny bank for children as well as a frugality bank for laborers and servants. Her treatise follows Chapone and the Edgeworths in taking for granted that "[t]he indispensable duties of wives, mothers, and heads of families, are incumbent upon all ranks" (p. 81) of women. Wakefield's text is noteworthy for postulating the existence of four different socio-economic classes. The observations on domestic economy are thus embedded within political economy. The author posits that

> [s]ociety may be resolved into four classes or degrees; the first comprehends the nobility, and all those who, either by the influence of high offices, or extensive hereditary possessions, rival them in power; the second contains those, who by the application of their talents to learning, commerce, manufactures or agriculture, procure a respectable subsistence approaching to opulence; to the third may be referred those, whose honest and useful industry raises them above want, without procuring for them the means of splendid or luxurious gratification: The fourth is composed of the labouring poor.
>
> *p. 63*

Like most contemporaries, Wakefield sees this gradation as God-given, and consequently does not ponder, let alone encourage, social mobility. Instead, *Reflections* contains a chapter dedicated to each rank, with class-specific instructions as to the domestic duties incumbent on women.

In Wakefield's analysis, the amount of bodily labor to be performed by women at home is inversely proportional to their family income: the lower the class, the more menial tasks women have to undertake. Female members of the nobility have above all supervising and managing duties:

> to inspect the whole; to regulate the plan of action; and to examine whether their substitutes discharge their respective engagements properly. As wives, the disposal of that part of their husband's revenue, which is consumed by the family, falls under their direction, and they are required to prevent either the profusion of waste, or the unbecoming parsimony of want.
>
> *p. 81*

Women from the second class cannot afford to delegate as many tasks to servants: their "moderate situation requires that they should be discharged in person" (p. 100). The practical advice given to young women from the second class resembles that formulated by Chapone and the Edgeworths, thus confirming that their texts aim mostly at women from the middle ranks. Wakefield writes:

> The art of œconomising and rendering all kinds of food as palatable and nourishing as possible, by different modes of cookery, will repay the mistress of a household for the trouble of investigation, and should indisputably form a part of the regular instruction of girls of the middle rank, to which, as they advance towards maturity, may profitably be added a knowledge of the value of all necessary articles consumed in a family, whether for the table or the wardrobe, as well as the quantities of each which are requisite for respective uses. As theory is of little avail, unless exemplified by practice, they should be habituated to exercise the department of house-keeper under the inspection of their mother, not only by purchasing the different commodities wanted for the use of the family, but likewise by keeping an exact account of the domestic expences, which will afford opportunities of teaching them a judicious application of money, and giving them distinct ideas, where frugality may most properly be exerted, and where greater latitude may be allowed.
>
> *pp. 100–2*

Observations on the type of household management to be practiced by the third class are less specific, because the latter "includes several gradations, including the daughters of every species of tradesmen below the merchant, and above the meaner mechanic: consequently, very different degrees of refinement befit the individuals who form the extreme links" and "[t]he peculiar duties of each, will vary according to their respective situations" (p. 141). The chapter on the fourth class begins by stating that "[t]he manner in which the labouring poor should pass their time, requires but few observations; for their lot dooms them, even in those countries where their situation is most favourable, to incessant toil, as a necessary means of subsistence" (p 176). Wakefield nevertheless stresses that "the rigour of the labour of the female poor should be moderated, by the consideration of their inferiority of strength" (p. 176). She exhorts women of this class to remember that "œconomy, cleanliness, industry, and, above all these, good temper, are the attractions which draw the husband to his own fire-side, after the labour of the day is over" (p. 177). The phrasing emphasizes that 'the husband' remains a focal point of women's domestic activities.

That treatises on domestic economy teach women how to 'draw' the husband back to his home reflects not only the period's ideals of submissive femininity, but is also an implicit economic strategy: given that for women around 1800, a husband was the major source of financial maintenance, caring for his needs becomes synonymous with investing into a wife's economic security. Texts on domestic economy seem to take this arrangement for granted and largely conform to established gender norms; radical women writers, by contrast, protest against the economic dependence of married women.

Radical critiques of married women's economic dependence

Marriage had significant and ambivalent economic consequences for English women: on the one hand, a wife obtained a legal claim to maintenance from her husband; on the other, the right to own and dispose of her property devolved almost entirely on him. This mechanism was secured by the English laws of coverture, which remained in place from the Middle Ages into the late nineteenth century (Stretton and Kesselring 2013, p. 7). Jurist William Blackstone described the eighteenth-century understanding of coverture in his monumental *Commentaries on the Laws of England* (1765–1769):

> By marriage, the husband and wife are one person in law: that is, the very being or legal existence of the woman is suspended during marriage, or at least is incorporated and consolidated into that of the husband: under whose wing, protection, and *cover*, she performs every thing; and is therefore called in our law-french a *feme-covert*; is said to be *covert-baron*, or under the protection and influence of her husband, her *baron*, or lord; and her condition during her marriage is called her *coverture*.
>
> *Blackstone 1765, p. 430*

This conception of marriage translated into a remarkably constrained economic agency of married women in the eyes of the common law. The limitations were not necessarily enforced in the daily lives of most women and men: Nicola Phillips, among others, claims that there is "strong evidence to show that significant numbers of women could and did remain in business throughout the years from 1700 to 1850, and that even married women could *de facto* and *de jure* continue to trade" (2006, p. 259). Nevertheless, the legal regulations became consequential in times of disagreement between spouses and had, as Tim Stretton and Krista J. Kesselring (2013, p. 9) underscore, ideological and normative power. Coverture meant that

> [u]pon marriage a wife lost the ability to own or control property, enter into contracts, make a will, or bring or defend a lawsuit without her husband. A married woman's real property – her lands – fell under her husband's control. [. . .] A woman's movable property – her money, livestock, and personal possessions – became her husband's outright. He had total control over any cash she brought to marriage or inherited or earned thereafter. He could sell her possessions, including her clothes and personal effects, or make bequests of them in his will without her permission. This extraordinary power of ownership set England apart from most other European countries and territories, where spouses held personal property separately or shared in a 'community of goods'.
>
> *Stretton and Kesselring 2013, p. 8*

Women of higher ranks could secure some of their property through costly marriage settlements or the establishment of trusts. Besides, English women also profited from coverture regulations, for instance by not being held answerable for debts and certain criminal offences. Yet female writers of the 1790s explicitly addressing coverture appear to emphasize its drawbacks, rather than the benefits. Arguably, for them, "the written word became a means by which to exercise the power that they otherwise lacked" (Thomason 2014, p. 1).

Because of the longevity of coverture in England, discussions of married women's property are not exclusive to female economic thought in the 1790s, but form a strand of analysis spanning centuries and genres. A noteworthy pamphlet raising the issue in the early eighteenth century is, for example, *The Hardships of the English Laws. In Relation to Wives* (1735) by Sarah Chapone (1699–1764; mother-in-law of the abovementioned Hester Mulso Chapone). In the mid-nineteenth century, Caroline Norton (1808–1877) challenged the economic discrimination of married women in her *Letter to the Queen on Lord Chancellor Cranworth's Marriage and Divorce*

Bill (1855). Around 1800, discussions of property regulations also feature in English women's writing, especially in novels. Edward Copeland has demonstrated that in Gothic tales in particular, "it is the economy, as it is represented by unpredictable, feckless, improvident, destructive, and tyrannical males, that provides the active source of terror for women" (2004, p. 41). It should be noted, however, that many of these fictional texts focus more on the emotional consequences of female financial vulnerability than on an analysis of the legal and economic mechanisms as such.

Against this background, Mary Wollstonecraft's posthumously published *The Wrongs of Woman: Or, Maria. A Fragment* (1798) stands out for combining a fictional investigation into the psychological effects of coverture with a description of its legal and economic workings. A vociferous advocate of women's rights and a prolific commentator on social and political questions, Wollstonecraft (1759–1797) is today probably the best known of the authors mentioned in this chapter. *The Wrongs of Woman* recounts the story of the eponymous heroine, who is kidnapped and imprisoned in a madhouse by her avaricious husband. Maria's unjust incarceration provides a metaphor for "the dependent state of a woman in the grand question of the comforts arising from the possession of property" (*Wrongs*, p. 137). The narrative makes plain that Maria's husband views his marriage solely as a means of getting at his wife's money, which he spends on gambling and risky speculations. He frustrates Maria's attempts to provide financially for herself, her sisters, and her daughter, which repeatedly makes her indict coverture regulations:

> [A] wife being as much a man's property as his horse, or his ass, she has nothing she can call her own. He may use any means to get at what the law considers as his, the moment his wife is in possession of it, [. . .] and all this is done with a show of equity, because, forsooth, he is responsible for her maintenance. The tender mother cannot *lawfully* snatch from the gripe of the gambling spendthrift, or beastly drunkard, unmindful of his offspring, the fortune which falls to her by chance; or (so flagrant is the injustice) what she earns by her own exertions. No; he can rob her with impunity, even to waste publicly on a courtezan; and the laws of her country – if women have a country – afford her no protection or redress from the oppressor, unless she have the plea of bodily fear.
>
> *Wrongs, p. 140*

Such summarizing descriptions of the deficient legal and economic status quo are enhanced through interspersed testimonies of fictional women of various social classes, who had been sexually and economically exploited by their husbands and other men. The novel does not stop short at describing the problems; it also advocates a radical solution by the standards of its time, namely the possibility of obtaining a divorce, so that women can regain control of their financial resources and find a more suitable partner. Accordingly, Maria asserts before a judge: "I claim then a divorce, and the liberty of enjoying, free from molestation, the fortune left to me by a relation" (p. 173).

The notion that, from an economic vantage point, marriage is a form of contract in which maintenance by the husband is exchanged for domestic labor performed by the wife was fairly accepted around 1800. Wollstonecraft is exceptional in suggesting that women deserve a bigger share of 'profits' within this exchange. In her texts, she argues that the economy of marriage encompasses emotional and sexual exchanges, and avers that women are as much at a disadvantage in this respect as in financial matters:

> Besides, how many women of this description pass their days; or, at least, their evenings, discontentedly. Their husbands acknowledge that they are good managers, and chaste wives; but leave home to seek for more agreeable, may I be allowed to use a significant French word, *piquant* society; and the patient drudge, who fulfils her task, like a blind horse in a mill, is defrauded of her just reward; for the wages due to her are the caresses of her husband; and women who have so few resources in themselves, do not very patiently bear this privation of a natural right.
>
> *Vindication, p. 86*

In *The Wrongs of Woman*, Wollstonecraft similarly implies that reducing wives merely to the performance of their domestic duties can constitute a form of exploitation that is sufficient ground for claiming a divorce:

> The magnitude of a sacrifice ought always to bear some proportion to the utility in view; and for a woman to live with a man, for whom she can cherish neither affection nor esteem, or even be of any use to him, excepting in the light of a house-keeper, is an abjectness of condition, the enduring of which no concurrence of circumstances can ever make a duty in the sight of God or just men.
>
> *p. 139*

Wollstonecraft's radical observations on marriage tie in with her less controversial suggestions for reforming female education. Like many of her contemporaries (e.g. Priscilla Wakefield; see Dimand 2003, p. 199), she establishes explicit and implicit links between women's education and their economic wellbeing. In her canonical *Vindication of the Rights of Woman* (1792), Wollstonecraft claims that training young girls in the art of attracting and pleasing a potential husband is only a short-term, narrow economic strategy. She deplores that girls

> spend many of the first years of their lives in acquiring a smattering of accomplishments; meanwhile strength of body and mind are sacrificed to libertine notions of beauty, to the desire of establishing themselves, – the only way women can rise in the world, – by marriage.
>
> *p. 15*

She points out that "[g]irls who have been thus weakly educated, are often cruelly left by their parents without any provision; and, of course, are dependent on, not only the reason, but the bounty of their brothers" (p. 84). Like many other middle-class authors, Wollstonecraft argues that in order to achieve a long-term happy marriage – and, by extension, to secure sustained financial provisioning – women must be educated to be rational and competent companions to their husbands. Such training is also recommended as making women economically more independent in case they cannot fall back on the financial support of a man.

Even if she does not contemplate the possibility of a divorce, Mary Hays (1759–1843) pursues a similarly polemical line of thought as her friend Mary Wollstonecraft in *An Appeal to the Men of Great Britain in Behalf of Women* (1798). Hays, a social commentator and novelist, begins a passage devoted to the economic dependence of married women with the observation that "it were much to be wished that women were somewhat more attended to, in the distribution of fortune", especially since they are "debarred [. . .] from availing themselves of their talents and industry, to promote their interest and independence" (p. 278). She argues that "fortune being in the present state of things, that which procures every comfort, conveniency, elegance and honour, which this world affords; [women] cannot be accused of being too palpably interested, in wishing to share in it, in a reasonable degree" (p. 280). *An Appeal to the Men of Great Britain* consequently criticizes that men have, "by the most ample and exclusive privileges, secured [money] chiefly in their own hands" (p. 281). The justification men usually provide for the economic disparities between the sexes is

> that it is of little consequence whether women have fortunes or not, as in the course of human events it circulates among them; and that the equilibrium is restored by marriage, which raises women to a participation and communion of fortune.
>
> *p. 281*

Hays refutes this argument with the observation that

> *all* men do not marry. *All* women are not married. And even those who *are*, find that this participation and community of fortune is often merely verbal; – words without any meaning whatever; – and that they are in this respect, as well as in most others, as completely dependent upon their husbands, as it is possible for any one human being to be upon another.
>
> *p. 281*

The solutions envisaged by Hays are less radical in the context of the prevalent norms than Wollstonecraft's. For women of the upper classes, Hays merely defends the right to so-called *paraphernalia*, which gave wives free use of personal items such as clothes or jewelry, even if the latter technically remained the husband's legal possession for the duration of the marriage (p. 284). With regard to women from the middle and lower ranks of society, Hays is more outspoken and advocates their admission to paid professions as a means of fostering their economic independence.

Reflecting the extent to which liberal ideas pervaded English intellectual circles in the 1790s, Wollstonecraft and Hays' claims were radical and controversial, and drew censure from numerous contemporaries. The more conservative writer Hannah More (1745–1833), for example, averred in her bestselling *Strictures on the Modern System of Female Education* (1799) that Wollstonecraft belonged to a "most destructive class in the whole wide range of modern corruptors" (Vol. 1, p. 48) for attacking the sanctity of marriage, and thus both religious doctrine and social stability. It appears, however, that within debates on matrimony, female advocates of women's subordinate status did not draw as explicitly on economic analyses as did feminist thinkers in the 1790s. One reason for this is perhaps that conservative writers often built their foundations on the authority of the Bible, which traced women's inferior position to Eve's responsibility for the original sin. Those who could cite the word of God in their favor were possibly less in need of secular arguments of the kind brought forward by Wollstonecraft or Hays. Radical critics of married women's financial dependence, by contrast, mobilized economic analyses in their fight for female emancipation.

Access to professions

While discussions of coverture address legal impediments to female economic autonomy, demands for women's access to paid professions challenge obstacles grounded in cultural norms. In her *Appeal to the Men of Great Britain*, Mary Hays describes a problem raised by several of her contemporaries:

> However high the sphere of life in which a man is born, if his fortune be not equal to his birth or his ambitions, there are a thousand different ways by which he may advance himself with honour in the world; whereas women of a certain rank, are totally excluded from a possibility, even of supporting that stile of life to which they have been accustomed, if they are left without competent fortunes. But what is infinitely worse – because it leads to want, or infamy, or both – few, very few are the employments left open even for women of the inferior classes, by which they can secure independence; and to which without a doubt may be greatly attributed, the ruin of most of the sex, in the lower ranks.
>
> *pp. 278–9*

Hays' observations tie in with remarks on women's waged labor by Mary Wollstonecraft, Priscilla Wakefield, and Mary Anne Radcliffe, who explore the economic vulnerability of women from different social strata.

Wollstonecraft and Hays' remarks on the difficult position of middle-class women contain an early variant of the crowding hypothesis. The authors posit that middle-class women, due to their education and constrictive ideals of femininity, run the risk of not being able to support themselves except by marriage. Only an insufficient number of professions are adequate to their skills and can be pursued without forfeiting public esteem and self-respect; as a result, these professions are difficult to secure and yield a low income. Hays notes in *Appeal*: "Indeed the business appropriated by custom for women, are so very few in proportion to the number of candidates, that they are soon monopolized" (pp. 279–80). Wollstonecraft focuses particularly on the profession of the governess:

> The few employments open to women, so far from being liberal, are menial; and when a superiour education enables them to take charge of the education of children as governesses, they are not treated like the tutors of sons [. . .]. But as women educated like gentlewomen, are never designed for the humiliating situation which necessity sometimes forces them to fill; these situations are considered in the light of a degradation.
>
> *Vindication, p. 184*

The profession of a governess, briefly undertaken by Wollstonecraft and Radcliffe, indeed counted among the few income-earning and respectable occupations for educated, middle-class women. This resulted, among others, in oversupply and low wages, as Wollstonecraft's Maria exemplifies by relating to her daughter the case of her sisters:

> They were accomplished, yet you can (may you never be reduced to the same destitute state!) scarcely conceive the trouble I had to place them in the situation of governesses, the only one in which even a well-educated woman, with more than ordinary talents, can struggle for a subsistence; and even this is a dependence next to menial.
>
> *Wrongs, p. 131*

The plight of governesses continued to preoccupy Victorian writers and is explored in some, partially autobiographic, detail by mid-nineteenth-century English novelists, for instance by Anne and Charlotte Brontë (see Gilbert 2015).

As solutions to the diagnosed problem, authors of the 1790s propose a more practically oriented education of middle-class women and changes to the extant system of occupational segregation. Wollstonecraft suggests that women could work as physicians, nurses, midwives, and conduct "[b]usiness of various kinds" (*Vindication*, p. 184). Wakefield is more specific in a chapter of *Reflections* entirely devoted to "lucrative employments for the first and second classes [. . .], recommend[ed] as agreeable means of procuring a respectable support" (p. 123). For Wakefield, the difficulty faced by this group of women is that their employments "must be such as are neither laborious nor servile, and they must of course be productive, without requiring a capital. For these reasons, pursuits which require the exercise of intellectual, rather than bodily powers, are generally the most eligible" (p. 125). Building on this premise, Wakefield indicates occupations within the realms of literature, painting, engraving, music, landscape design, gardening, and school management. She hence suggests only professions that are both profitable *and* congruent with prevalent gender (and class) norms.

This, in fact, is true of all authors addressing the question of women's professions: while on the one hand, they challenge what they often term 'false custom' and 'prejudice' regarding women and work, on the other they maintain a clearly gendered notion of economic pursuits. Their argument is not an egalitarian and integrative one, in the sense that women ought to be allowed to choose the same professions as men. Instead, they promote vertical segregation and urge men to drop 'feminine' professions. As Wakefield explains:

> Men monopolize not only the most advantageous employments, and such as exclude women from the exercise of them, by the publicity of their nature, or the extensive knowledge they require, but even many of those, which are consistent with the female character.
>
> *pp. 150–1*

The doctrine of separate spheres is hence transferred onto the labor market and leads to the identification of putatively 'feminine' occupations.

This logic is particularly evident in passages devoted to women from the lower-middle and lower classes, for whom gender-based work restrictions were less severe, but nevertheless present. Mary Anne Radcliffe (1746?–1810?), a less-known writer and novelist with a turbulent economic biography, attacks certain male artisans in her pamphlet-cum-fictional-tale with the suggestive title *The Female Advocate: Or, an Attempt to Recover the Rights of Women from Male Usurpation* (1799). She censures men who earn a living with 'feminine' tasks, such as making hats, dresses, and corsets: "What can be said in favour of men-milliners, men-mantua-makers, and men stay-makers? besides all the numerous train of other professions, such as hair-dressers, &c. &c.; all of which occupations are much more calculated for women than men." (p. 20) Hays argues in a similar vein: "women of the inferior classes might be taylors, hair-dressers, &c. &c." (*Appeal*, p. 200).

Hays, moreover, exposes how internalized ideals of gender and propriety translate into economic discrimination. While it is deemed unseemly for women of the lower ranks to be outfitters of men, which effectively deprives them of income-earning opportunities, it is acceptable for lower-class men to serve upper-class women:

> it is an unaccountable peculiarity, that women of those [lower] ranks, should from motives of delicacy [. . .] abstain from making clothes to men, dressing their hair, and doing other offices for them, by which they might gain their living without hard labour; yet that women of the higher ranks [. . .] admit without scruple – men hair-dressers – men milliners – men mantua-makers. Nay worse than all these, – I blush to write it, – men stay-makers. This is an abuse of privileges indeed.
>
> *pp. 200–1*

Hays criticizes that lower-class men end up having a larger choice of professions than lower-class women, but she also censures women for colluding in this form of segregation.

Wakefield mentions the same fashion-related professions as Radcliffe and Hays, but additionally indicts what in modern parlance would qualify as the gender pay gap: "Another heavy discouragement to the industry of women, is the inequality of the reward of their labour, compared with that of men, an injustice which pervades every species of employment performed by both sexes" (*Reflections*, p. 151). She substantiates her claim with a footnote quoting the respective annual wages of male and female domestic servants: a footman earns 2.5 times as much as a cook-maid, "though her office is laborious, unwholesome, and requires a much greater degree of skill than that of a valet" (p. 151).

The stress on physical labor involved in the cook-maid's work implies that Wakefield might subscribe to a variant of the labor theory of value. She justifies higher wages where more bodily exertion is required. On the basis of differences in corporeal strength, she also seems to accept gender-related differences in income, as men can generally perform more physical labor (and are hence more productive) than women: "In employments which depend upon bodily strength the distinction [in wages] is just, for it cannot be pretended that the generality of women can earn as much as men, where the produce of their labour is the result of corporeal exertion" (p. 152). Wakefield argues that women taken together ("the generality of women") cannot earn as much as the collective of men, because wages reflect "corporeal exertion", which in the case of women will in sum be always lesser than that of men's total bodily exertion. Yet while women's lower *aggregate* pay is justified, paying women less on an *individual* basis is not, if she performs the same amount of bodily labor as a man:

> [I]t is a subject of great regret, that this inequality [in wages] should prevail, even where an equal share of application are exerted. Male-stay-makers, mantua-makers, and hair dressers are better paid than female artists of the same professions; but surely it will never be urged as an apology for this disproportion, that women are not as capable of making stays, gowns, dressing hair, and similar arts, as men.
>
> *p. 152*

As a means of setting right what she deems an unjust situation, Wakefield encourages women of rank to resort to positive discrimination:

> [T]hey should determine to employ women only, wherever they can be employed; they should procure female instructors for their children; they should frequent no shops that are not served by women; they should wear no clothes that are not made by them.
>
> *p. 154*

Radcliffe, in *The Female Advocate*, half-seriously contemplates a similar boycott:

> Suppose no lady would suffer herself to be served, in the shops of these effeminate traders, by any of the short clothed gentry, would it not be a means of compelling all those who chuse to carry on the tragi-comic farce, to effect the business under the disguise of gown and petticoat?
>
> *p. 59*

Hays, somewhat in passing, recommends imposing a tax on premises where men engage in 'feminine' occupations: "Why does not the legislature tax such she-he gentry to the teeth?" (*Appeal*, p. 201).

The authors unanimously assert that the scarcity of respectable income-earning opportunities for women frequently leaves them with but two options for making a living: beggary or prostitution. Socially, both activities tended to be seen as, at least to some degree, resulting from moral depravity, thus locating the problem on the level of individuals. Hays, Radcliffe, Wakefield, and Wollstonecraft, by contrast, conceive of beggary and prostitution as stemming from systemic, socio-economic discrimination. This allows them to frame their demands for women as serving not just a particular clientele, but the common good. Wakefield, for example, postulates, in *Reflections*, that

> [w]ere it easier for women to find employment, or were they brought up more capable of earning a maintenance, the good effects of such a practice would not be confined to themselves alone, but would extend to the whole community, as it would be a powerful means of reducing the number of those miserable women, who support a precarious existence by the wages of prostitution, and who, in their turn, become the seducers of the inexperienced youth of the other sex.
>
> *p. 166*

Radcliffe concurs by claiming in *The Female Advocate* that

> until the grievous precedent of men usurping females' occupations is entirely done away, *or some proper substitute provided*, so as to enable women to share the common necessaries along with their fellow-creatures: till then, we need not wonder at the vast number of pickpockets and housebreakers which, at all times, infest the streets, to the disturbance of all civil society.
>
> *p. 45*

The writers present income-earning opportunities for women as a means of stabilizing public – and thus also male – safety, morals, and prosperity. Such reasoning arguably serves economic, but also strategic purposes: all four authors at some point appeal to men, as the group vested with political power, to help amend the situation of women. They were in all likelihood conscious of the fact that their appeals had a higher chance of success if they could be shown to contribute to the wellbeing of male readers and decision-makers.

Conclusions

Despite cultural and institutional obstacles, English women writers around 1800 conducted economic analyses. Marriage and its economic and legal consequences loom large in their writing, as does the question of women's financial (in)dependence. Undoubtedly, debates on women's access to education, their employment opportunities, or the economic rights of wives are not exclusive to the 1790s, but recur in women's writing throughout the centuries. The period around 1800, however, marks a noteworthy stage within the more prolonged, contested, and intermittent process of women's economic emancipation, because while on the one hand, women faced traditional and restrictive notions of femininity, on the other, the 1790s nurtured a social climate in which those notions could be questioned. This led to a remarkable engagement with gender-related economic topics, covering a wide spectrum of traditional, conservative views and progressive, radical ideas.

Treatises on domestic economy (e.g. by Hester Chapone or Maria and Richard Lovell Edgeworth) tend to focus on female economic activities congruent with the cultural ideal of a wife and a mother. Assuming that it is women's quasi-natural duty to manage their father's and/or husband's households, the texts emphasize that women must be taught the necessary moral and practical skills to perform their economic functions well. According to Hannah More, "[t]hat kind of knowledge which is rather fitted for home consumption than foreign exportation, is peculiarly adapted to women" (*Strictures* Vol. 2, p. 3). With the family considered the bedrock of society, the (economic) education of women in domestic affairs acquires social significance. Since the texts themselves partake in this educational endeavor, their observations on the economy are virtually inseparable from moral overtones, producing a mixture of positivist and normative claims. Because of their frequent adherence to the generic conventions of the conduct book, texts on domestic economy tend to be descriptive and prescriptive rather than analytical. They moreover provide a female perspective on that realm of the economy that was most readily associated with and attributed to women around 1800.

The novels and pamphlets of Mary Wollstonecraft and Mary Hays lean toward the radical range. They contest (albeit not fully) the gender norms of their times and probe alternatives to women's economic status quo. The financial dependence of wives enshrined in the common-law practice of coverture is one of their chief objections. Wollstonecraft and Hays challenge the established view of marriage on several levels: they argue that it is economically irresponsible to make marriage the sole source of maintenance for women, because not all women will marry and not all husbands live up to their role of providing for the family. They moreover censure the limited property rights of married women. Wollstonecraft condemns the subordinate status of wives as "the slavery of marriage" (*Vindication*, p. 193) and makes a case for divorce as a means of regaining financial and emotional independence. Historically, it was not until the Matrimonial Causes Act of 1857, and the Married Women's Property Acts of 1870, 1874, and 1882 that some of Wollstonecraft and Hays' farsighted observations were implemented in English law.

Mary Wollstonecraft, Mary Hays, but also Priscilla Wakefield and Mary Anne Radcliffe identify women's limited access to paid professions as another crucial economic problem. Reflections on this topic arguably fall into the middle range of the conformity-versus-contestation spectrum, because although, on the one hand, the authors challenge the extant system of occupational segregation and argue in favor of women's economic agency, on the other, they propose solutions that transpose the ideology of separate spheres onto the labor market: men are to withdraw from 'feminine' professions. From today's point of view, the strand of analysis focusing on women's access to paid labor is particularly remarkable for describing economic phenomena and measures that would be taken up and conceptualized in more detail in twentieth-century (feminist) economics: crowding hypothesis, occupational segregation, gender pay gap, and positive discrimination.

The writings by English women authors of the 1790s examined in this chapter illustrate that they produced original, gender-sensitive analyses of the economic and social phenomena of their times. As such, they lived up to the task that Priscilla Wakefield formulated in the quotation cited in the beginning of this chapter: they contributed their "share of productive labour for the good of the whole" (*Reflections*, p. 2).

References

Primary sources

Blackstone, William. *Commentaries on the Laws of England. A Facsimile of the First Edition 1765–1769*. Vol. 1: *Of the Rights of Persons*. 1765. Chicago: The University of Chicago Press, 1979.

Chapone, Hester. *Letters on the Improvement of the Mind Addressed to a Young Lady*. 1773. *Bluestocking Feminism: Writings of the Bluestocking Circle, 1738–1785. Electronic Edition*. Vol. 3: *Catherine Talbot and Hester Chapone*. Ed. Rhoda Zuk. London: Pickering & Chatto, 1999, pp. 261–356. Web. 14 March 2017.

Chapone, Sarah. *The Hardships of the English Laws. In Relation to Wives. With an Explanation of the Original Curse of Subjection Passed upon the Woman. In an Humble Address to the Legislature*. London and Dublin: Faulkner, 1735.

Edgeworth, Maria, and Richard Lovell Edgeworth. *Practical Education*. 1798. Vol. 3. London: J. Johnson, 1801.

Hays, Mary. *Appeal to the Men of Great Britain in Behalf of Women*. 1798. Ed. Gina Luria. New York: Garland, 1974.

Kuiper, Edith, ed. *Women's Economic Thought in the Eighteenth Century*. Vols. 1–4. London: Routledge, 2014.

More, Hannah. *Strictures on the Modern System of Female Education. With a View of the Principles and Conduct Prevalent among Women of Rank and Fortune*. 3rd ed. Vols. 1 and 2. London: printed for T. Cadell Jun. and W. Davies, 1799. *Eighteenth Century Collections Online*. Web. 21 March 2017.

Norton, Caroline. *A Letter to the Queen on Lord Chancellor Cranworth's Marriage and Divorce Bill*. London: Wertheimer, 1855.

Radcliffe, Mary Anne. *The Female Advocate: Or, an Attempt to Recover the Rights of Women from Male Usurpation*. London: Vernor and Hood, 1799.

Wakefield, Priscilla. *Reflections on the Present Condition of the Female Sex*. 1798. Ed. Gina Luria. New York: Garland, 1974.

Wollstonecraft, Mary. *A Vindication of the Rights of Woman*. 1792. Ed. Miriam Brody. London: Penguin, 2004.

Wollstonecraft, Mary. *The Wrongs of Woman: Or, Maria. A Fragment in Two Volumes*. 1798. Ed. Gary Kelly. Oxford: Oxford University Press, 2007, pp. 63–178.

Secondary sources

Benjamin, Marina. "Elbow Room: Women Writers on Science, 1790–1840." In *Feminism: Critical Concepts in Literary and Cultural Studies*. Vol. I: *Feminism and the Enlightenment*. Ed. Mary Evans. London: Routledge, 2001, pp. 410–37.

Bergen Brophy, Elizabeth. *Women's Lives and the 18th-Century English Novel*. Tampa: University of South Florida Press, 1991.

Copeland, Edward. *Women Writing about Money: Women's Fiction in England, 1790–1820*. Cambridge: Cambridge University Press, 2004 [1995].

Dimand, Robert. "An Eighteenth-Century English Feminist Response to Political Economy: Priscilla Wakefield's *Reflections* (1798)." In *The Status of Women in Classical Economic Thought*. Ed. Robert Dimand and Chris Nyland. Cheltenham: Edward Elgar, 2003, pp. 194–205.

"economy, n." *OED Online*. Oxford University Press, 2017. Web. 14 March 2017.

Gilbert, Nora. "A Servitude of One's Own: Isolation, Authorship, and the Nineteenth-Century British Governess." *Nineteenth-Century Literature* 69.4 (2015): 455–80. Web. 15 July 2016.

Kelly, Gary. "Introduction." In *British Reform Writers, 1789–1832*. Ed. Gary Kelly and Edd Applegate. Detroit: Bruccoli Clark Layman, 1996, pp. ix–xiii.

Kuiper, Edith. "Introduction." In *Women's Economic Thought in the Eighteenth Century*. Vol. 1: *The Economy of the Household*. Ed. Edith Kuiper. London: Routledge, 2014, pp. xiii–xlii.

Phillips, Nicola. *Women in Business, 1700–1850*. Woodbridge: Boydell, 2006.

"Priscilla Wakefield: Life". *Orlando: Women's Writing in the British Isles from the Beginnings to the Present*. Ed. Susan Brown, Patricia Clements, and Isobel Grundy. Cambridge: Cambridge University Press Online, 2006. Web. 24 May 2017.

Rostek, Joanna. "Female Authority and Political Economy: Jane Marcet and Harriet Martineau's Contradictory Strategy in Disseminating Economic Knowledge." In *Anglistentag 2013: Proceedings*. Ed. Reingard M. Nischik and Silvia Mergenthal. Trier: WVT, 2014, pp. 21–33.

Schabas, Margaret. "British Economic Theory from Locke to Marshall." In *The Cambridge History of Science*. Ed. Theodore M. Porter and Dorothy Ross. Cambridge: Cambridge University Press, 2003, pp. 171–82.

Smith, Adam. *An Inquiry into the Nature and Causes of the Wealth of Nations*. Available online at the McMaster University Archive for the History of Economic Thought (http://socserv2.socsci.mcmaster.ca/econ/ugcm/3ll3/).

Stafford, William. *English Feminists and Their Opponents in the 1790s: Unsex'd and Proper Females*. Manchester: Manchester University Press, 2002.

Stretton, Tim, and Krista J. Kesselring. "Introduction: Coverture and Continuity." *Married Women and the Law: Coverture in England and the Common Law World*. Montreal: McGill-Queen's University Press, 2013, pp. 3–23.

Thomason, Laura E. *The Matrimonial Trap: Eighteenth-Century Women Writers Redefine Marriage*. Lewisburg: Bucknell University Press, 2014.

3

BRITISH WOMEN ON THE BRITISH EMPIRE

Janet Seiz

As the 17th century opened, the British overseas empire consisted mainly of several struggling settlements on the eastern edge of North America and a few trading posts on the Indian subcontinent. Over time, while those territories grew, Britain acquired islands in the Caribbean that it used for highly profitable sugar plantations, and established posts in Africa to facilitate its participation in the slave trade. Colonies were added in Australasia and lost in the American Revolution. After Britain abolished slavery in the empire in 1833, it set out to fight the slave trade that remained; ironically, this entailed enlarging its claims in Africa (Huzzey 2012). By the close of the 19th century, Britain possessed the empire on which "the sun never set," encompassing nearly a quarter of the world's land area and population.

In Britain's intellectual and ruling circles, the empire generated frequent debate. There were arguments about its economic benefits compared with the costs of rule; the roles of religious ambitions, commercial interests, and national rivalries; the moral legitimacy of colonial rule; and the ways in which colonies could best be administered. These discussions drew in government officials, reformers, political economists, clergymen, capitalists, and philosophers; they occurred almost exclusively among men. There were, however, a few British women who managed to play significant roles in this discourse. This chapter will discuss three whose voices were important in the 19th century:

- Harriet Martineau (1802–1876)
- Mary Kingsley (1862–1900)
- Flora Shaw Lugard (1852–1929)

While they were different in many ways, these women had several characteristics in common:

- They received little formal schooling, and mostly educated themselves by reading prodigiously.
- They were born into solidly middle- or upper-class families, but they had to become self-supporting as young women: they did so with their writing.
- They had frequent bouts with illness, sometimes related to overwork. Martineau was also hampered for most of her life by severe hearing loss.

- They traveled quite extensively—extremely rare in their time, especially for women—and wrote about their first-hand observations abroad.
- They believed strongly that the empire could serve the interests of both Britain and the peoples of its colonies.
- They worked hard at shaping public opinion, and they reached large audiences.

The three disagreed considerably about their country's colonial policy, which should not surprise us. As numerous feminist scholars have shown, British women held a wide range of views on, and played varied roles in, the empire (Burton 1994; Chaudhuri and Strobel 1992; Jayawardena 1995; Midgley 1998).

All three of these writers were intensely aware of how anomalous they were as women who had visible influence on public affairs. Privately at least, they all expressed frustration with the restrictions their society imposed on women, but only Martineau championed feminist ideas: she wrote extensively on women's need for better education and wider life opportunities, and she was an early supporter of the campaign for women's suffrage. Mary Kingsley played an ambiguous role: at times she voiced support for traditional gender norms, but the experiences she reported in her books implicitly made a mockery of them. Kingsley opposed admitting women to the Royal Geographic Society (Birkett 1992, pp. 155–57), and both she and Shaw publicly disavowed the suffrage movement. Helly (2012, p. 125) suggests that perhaps Shaw "came to agree with those who were concerned that women's suffrage might pose a threat to vital imperial policies."

Harriet Martineau (June 1802–June 1876)

Harriet Martineau, a "novelist, translator, reviewer, journalist, children's author, personal correspondent, political campaigner, travel writer, pamphleteer, memoirist and historian" (Dzelzainis and Kaplan 2010, p. 1), was one of the first women in Britain to become a successful professional writer and a major public intellectual. Born in 1802 into a business family in Norwich, she began her writing career in the 1820s when an economic downturn caused her father's business to fail. Her writing focused mainly on religious themes until she became interested in the emerging "science" of political economy and read the works of Adam Smith, David Ricardo, Jeremy Bentham, Thomas Robert Malthus, and James Mill. In 1832 she secured a contract to write a monthly series of fictional tales that she called *Illustrations of Political Economy* (1832–34), aimed at popularizing the ideas of the new political economy. The series, which grew to 25 volumes, was a surprise bestseller, and brought Martineau both fame and financial independence.[1]

Martineau sought to help the British public understand the core ideas of Smith *et al.* about the liberatory power of laissez-faire capitalism. The institutions of secure property rights, market competition, and free trade would stimulate individual effort and spur technological progress, bringing about widespread improvement in living standards. The *Illustrations* covered a variety of situations and locations, including colonies, to demonstrate the broad applicability of the principles. At the urging of her publisher, Martineau went on to write two more series of tales, *Poor Laws and Paupers, Illustrated* (1833–34) and *Illustrations of Taxation* (1834).

After the years of intense work on those economic writings, Martineau decided to visit—and study—the U.S. She stayed for two years, and was fêted, hosted, and lobbied by many prominent citizens, including both abolitionists and slave owners. She wrote two books about her visit: *Society in America* (1837) and *Retrospect of Western Travel* (1838a). *Society* combined engaging descriptions of places and activities with strongly critical observations on slavery, the situation of women, and other weaknesses in American democracy; the book created controversy in both Britain and the U.S. *Retrospect* was a more conventional travelogue. During this period Martineau also produced *How to Observe Morals and Manners* (1838b), now considered the first treatise to outline a method for systematically studying a society. Because of this, Martineau is said by some to have been among the creators of sociology (Hill and Hoecker-Drysdale 2001). Some years later she produced a two-volume abridged translation of Auguste Comte's *Positive Philosophy*, the book's first edition in English (Martineau 1853); Comte was the originator of the term "sociology."

Writings on empire

In her Preface to *Illustrations of Political Economy*, Martineau told readers they could expect a variety of settings: "As society is in widely different states of advancement in various parts of the world, we have resolved to introduce as wide a diversity of scenery and characters as it might suit our object to employ" (1834a, vol. 1, p. xvi). She set several of the narratives in colonies, conveying in them what she then thought of empire. In "Life in the Wilds," the first tale in the series, British settlers in southern Africa have all their material resources stolen or destroyed in a raid by hostile natives. The natives, Martineau explained, had earlier been dispossessed of their land by the colonists and "hunted down like so many wild beasts," which "naturally made them fierce and active in their revenge" (Martineau 1834, vol. 1, Tale 1, p. 4). The story centers on the colonists' recreation of their prosperous society through diligent work and application of Smith's principle of the division of labor. One reviewer called the tale a synthesis of *Robinson Crusoe* and *The Wealth of Nations* (cited in Logan 2009, p. 225). In "Demerara," a young brother and sister return from England to their family's sugar plantation in the West Indies, where they try to teach their father about the moral evil and economic inefficiency of slavery. This narrative made Martineau famous among opponents and defenders of slavery on both sides of the Atlantic. "Cinnamon and Pearls" was set in Ceylon, and offered an extremely harsh portrayal of the East India Company's conduct there. In granting the Company a trade monopoly, Britain had in effect given merchants permission

> to make what they could of the natives of the land as well as of the sea; – not only to appropriate the natural wealth of the region, but to bring its inhabitants as near to the brink of starvation as they pleased in their methods of employing their toil.
>
> *Martineau 1834, vol. 7, Tale 2, p. 20*

Ceylon could have generated economic betterment for its native population as well as wealth for the British, but instead the Company's exploitation had been ruinous. Britain's claims that its presence helped the Ceylonese are exposed as disingenuous. A friendly clergyman tries to remind a group of angry natives of the benefits colonization has brought them:

> "[Y]ou speak as if the English settlers were thieves. You speak as if it was nothing to have wise and skillful strangers come to teach you the arts of life. You speak as if you forgot the protection afforded to you by the government of the mother country, and the expense incurred by her for your support."
>
> *Martineau 1834, vol. 7, Tale 2, p. 110*

The natives respond that the British are, in fact, robbing them of their valuable pearls and spices, and that they do not require British instruction. As for protection,

> "From what do they protect us? . . . If they will go away, we will protect ourselves against their returning; and our own expenses we can bear as soon as ships from every land may come to trade on our shores."
>
> *Martineau 1834, vol. 7, Tale 2, p. 111*

Continuing, the natives argue

> that slavery could not be said to be abolished while labourers were dependent for daily bread on the arbitrary will of a monopolizing party; and that, excellent as was trial by jury, the prevention of the manifold crimes which spring from oppression would be still better.
>
> *p. 111*

The tale concluded that Britain should abolish the Company monopoly and restore control over Ceylon's resources to the natives, so that they could pursue mutually beneficial trade with whomever they wished.

These early fictional works showed that Martineau was not afraid to voice radical criticism. She would continue to address questions about the empire throughout her long career, in more than a dozen books and hundreds of articles. She wrote most about Ireland and India.

Ireland

In 1852 Martineau made a three-month visit to Ireland as a correspondent for the London *Daily News*, beginning a career as a newspaper journalist that would last for 16 years. Her dispatches, which appeared in the newspaper unsigned, were collected and published under her name a few months after her return as *Letters from Ireland* (1852).

Ireland was, in a sense, England's oldest colony, having been subjugated repeatedly from the 12th century on, with large tracts of its land being awarded to men from England and Scotland. In 1800, an Act of Union had dissolved Ireland's parliament and put the country fully under British rule. Half a century later, it was still an almost entirely agricultural society, mostly Catholic and mostly poor.

When Martineau toured, the country was still recovering from the Great Famine of 1845–49, in which close to a million people (almost an eighth of the population) had perished of starvation or epidemic disease. Most of the Irish were agricultural wage laborers or tenant farmers, renting from British landowners. Martineau was appalled by the poverty she saw. "A few days of observation of how the people live," she said, "merely by our going to see them, are sad enough to incline one to turn away, and never come again" (Martineau 1852, p. 150).

English observers had long tended to blame "Irish culture" for the people's plight: centuries-old stereotypes held the Irish to be undisciplined, averse to work, duplicitous, violent, and slovenly (Curtis 1968). Martineau forcefully refuted those assertions, insisting that the problem lay not in the country's people, but in its economic institutions. The complex and rigid land tenure system made it difficult to sell land or to lease it long-term. Tenants' plots were often too small to provide a family subsistence. The lack of secure property rights discouraged land improvements, keeping productivity low. "A tenant," Martineau explained, "is not very likely to lock up his capital in buildings, and sow it in the soil, when he cannot reckon on remaining long enough to recover it" (Martineau 1852, p. 38).

She denied that laziness was an innate Irish trait. "There seems to be no room," she wrote, "for a theory of constitutional indolence here" (Martineau 1852, p. 58). In Ireland as elsewhere, people worked hard when their returns were decent, but could be seen "dawdling over their business when hungry and discouraged" (1852, p. 58). The landowner, she noted, "talks of the lazy nature of the labourer, and pays him so little that he has not strength for severe toil, and needs to lie down in the sun as soon as his employer's back is turned" (1852, p. 208).

While Martineau recognized that Ireland's problems were deep, she was not pessimistic. If the constraints on disposal of land could be eased,

> we shall see a common ground provided, on which owners and tenants can traffic. We shall see long leases, landlords' improvements in loving company with those of the tenant, rich fields, full barns, and rising plantations, with no smoke of the assassin's blunderbuss curling among the trees.
>
> *Martineau 1852, pp. 47–8*

In the near term, emigration would continue to reduce the labor supply, enabling wages to rise for those left behind. In the longer run, the country needed educational reform, agricultural modernization, industrialization, and the spread of wage labor. Although she understood Irish nationalist agitation, Martineau insisted that Ireland should not demand independence. Its underdevelopment was due most of all to lack of capital and entrepreneurship, and those could best be supplied from Britain. The country needed to upgrade its institutions, with British guidance and British investment. Independence would only mean that Ireland's agricultural stagnation would be perpetuated.

India

Although she never had the benefit of first-hand observation, Martineau also wrote a good deal about Britain's most prominent colony, India. Colonization there had been almost accidental, according to the conventional story: The East India Company, created in 1600 to trade with the subcontinent, over time acquired territory in the interest of protecting and expanding trade and entered into security agreements with many local political authorities. By the 1800s, the Company was the *de facto* ruler of much of India, subject to rather loose parliamentary supervision. The Company was deprived of most of its trade monopoly in 1813 to make room for more British firms; its largest remaining product was opium, which it exported quite profitably to China, in violation of Chinese law. In 1833 the Company saw all of its monopoly privileges abolished, but it retained its administrative authority; the peculiar hybrid became less "company" and more "state."

In 1857–58, a rebellion against British rule called this arrangement into question. Sensational stories of Indian "savagery" appeared in Britain, and there was talk of punishment. During this tense period, Martineau wrote two books: first a concise history titled *British Rule in India* (1857), then a contribution to the policy debate, *Suggestions toward the Future Government of India* (1858).

The "Mutiny" had come as a shock in Britain, and Martineau again sought to play the role of public educator.

> Our footing in India began and extended without the national cognizance, as it were; and when the region became ours, it was not ruled by the British Government; and to this hour it has never ostensibly been so. It is no colony of ours. It has never been national territory, peopled from home, and organized under the English constitution and laws. The question now—and a tremendous problem it is—is whether India shall be a colony of ours; whether it shall be ruled by the British Government as a colony.
>
> *Martineau 1858, p. 4*

The territory called India, she explained, was populated by many separate peoples, divided by language, religion, governance, and history. "The inhabitants never were a people; and they have not become so under our rule" (Martineau 1858, p. 29). The rule of the East India Company had had largely positive results, Martineau argued: certainly there had at times been rapaciousness, ill-treatment, cultural insensitivity, and corruption, but these had diminished, and the most important thing was that the Company had rescued India from "anarchy" and constant war. Indians, she said, "are evidently more content under our rule than any other—because we have saved them from other conquerors, and have made their lives easier than they ever were before" (Martineau 1858, p. 30). The potential now existed for vast economic gains, which could be widely shared.

> As Macaulay has observed, the people of India were clothed in fine muslins and shawls of Epicurean beauty when our ancestors dyed their skins with woad; and their great men lived in the splendour of a fairy tale before our kings lived in palaces: and yet the resources of their territory had scarcely begun to be attended to. . . . If well governed, India must yield occupation and subsistence to hundreds of millions of human beings, at home and abroad.
>
> *Martineau 1858, p. 11*

> We need India as a source of occupation and wealth; as answering most of the purposes of a colony, and others that no colony ever aspired to. We want it as an ever-expanding market for our manufactures, and as a mine of natural wealth, in the form of raw materials for those manufactures. We desire it as a territory, thickly peopled in comparison with any of our colonies, but admitting and requiring a far larger population to make the most of its resources. We want to clear its jungles, to open its mines, to thin its forests, to till its wastes, to make use of its rivers; and thereby to call into existence tens of millions of human beings who would not otherwise be born. We want to call millions into existence at home by the same means, and to improve the lot in life of millions more.
>
> *Martineau 1858, p. 114*

This did not mean, however, that India should be brought under stronger government control. Martineau insisted that continued Company rule was preferable to making India a Crown Colony.

> If we hastily decide that India shall be a Crown colony, ruled directly and entirely from England, according to existing British notions and habits of colonial government, we shall lose India, speedily, disgracefully, and so disastrously that the event will be one of the most conspicuous calamities in the history of nations.
>
> *Martineau 1858, p. 1*

She was scornful of the government's competence to administer a distant colony. Members of Parliament clearly knew almost nothing about India. Political considerations would shape their decisions, and policy would be erratic as governments changed.

> A parliamentary Government of India, with its political oscillations, its inevitable ignorance and rashness, its adverse chances, where it is improbable that any measure should be good, and thorough soundness would be a matter of miracle, can never be assented to by any man, inside or outside of the Company's pale, who has even the necessary preliminary knowledge of the conditions of the case.
>
> *Martineau 1858, p. 131*

Britain's government would never be able to match "the public-spirit, the generosity, the liberal appreciation of improvements and of merits which have always—and never more than now—distinguished the rule, spirit, and temper of the East India Company" (Martineau 1858, pp. 137–38). "India has long been, and now is, governed on behalf of the Indians; whereas, from the hour when so-called parliamentary government should be instituted, that aim could never more be steadily maintained and fulfilled" (Martineau, p. 145).

These assertions of the Company's benevolence and wisdom strike the reader as both exaggerated and naive (Logan 2009, pp. 133–38). Ultimately, however, her argument appeared to rest on the need for expertise.

> We should not hastily extinguish the power (too singular to be ever replaced) by which our Asiatic empire was acquired and has been sustained, without cost to the British people, while supporting millions of them by a commerce capable of comprehending tens of millions more. We should not throw away the vast stores, or crush the prodigious apparatus of Indian knowledge which exists in the midst of us, combined in the form of a government unparalleled in the history of the world for civic success and social progression.
>
> *Martineau 1858, pp. 146–47*

Similar arguments were made at the time by John Stuart Mill, who had been an employee of the East India Company for most of his adult life. The campaign did not succeed, however: in 1858 Parliament dissolved the Company and declared India a Crown Colony.

During the 1860s Martineau continued to write about the empire, commenting on British policies toward India, Ireland, China, Africa, and Egypt. She also wrote about slavery, the U.S. civil war, women's education, and other subjects. Tallies of her published works vary, but it is safe to say that she authored at least 70 books and close to 2,000 newspaper and magazine articles. She died in June 1876, aged 74.

Mary Kingsley (Oct. 1862–June 1900)

Mary Henrietta Kingsley liked to describe herself as an outsider who felt more at home in West Africa than in England. Her father was from a family that produced several celebrated writers. A physician and amateur anthropologist, he spent much of his time accompanying rich patients on long journeys abroad. Her mother had been a servant in his household, and became his wife only a few days before Mary was born; she was in perpetual poor health, and young Mary served as her nurse. Kingsley obtained most of her education by exploring her father's library and sometimes helping him with his research. When both parents succumbed to illnesses in 1892, when she was 30, Mary dutifully moved in with her brother. She managed his house for him, along with doing her own work, for the rest of her short life.

Kingsley first traveled to West Africa in 1893, ostensibly in order to continue her father's study of indigenous religions (then referred to as "fetish"). She stayed for five months. Her second trip lasted almost a year, from late 1894 to late 1895. This time she was commissioned to collect specimens of fish for the British Museum as she pursued her own ethnographic research.

On her journeys Kingsley traveled by boat along the West African coast from Sierra Leone to Angola, with some incursions inland by river and extended stays in towns. She saw territories claimed by Britain, Spain, France, Germany, and Portugal. Kingsley usually stayed in the homes of other foreigners, either traders or officials or missionaries; but she took some excursions on her own, traveling with small crews of Africans. To meet her expenses, she would trade, exchanging items such as fishhooks, wire, tobacco and cloth for services rendered or for rubber and ivory that she could later sell; her trader guise, she explained, allowed her invaluable face-to-face contact with local people (Frank 1986, p. 63).

Returning to Britain in late 1895, Kingsley immediately became a celebrity: she was the intrepid lady explorer, the naturalist, the expert on West African native societies. Over the next four years she gave public lectures to a variety of audiences, from meetings of scholarly societies to ticketed gatherings of the general public that numbered as high as 2,000. She created an amusingly eccentric persona for her public lectures, looking stern in old-fashioned long black dresses, and she often disarmed her audience with self-mockery (Frank 1986, pp. 257–58).

Her use of humor did not obscure the seriousness of her work. Kingsley's expertise and dedication won her access to prominent people both in and out of government. She wrote articles on West Africa for leading newspapers and journals. She knew well the individuals who were most involved in shaping colonial policy in Africa, and behind the scenes she engaged in extensive letter-writing, networking, and face-to-face lobbying (Birkett 1992).

Kingsley wrote two important books, *Travels in West Africa* (1897) and *West African Studies* (1899). The first was primarily a narrative of her travels, intended for a popular audience, and it was a huge success. The second was more scholarly and less cohesive, containing chapters on native religion and culture and on Britain's political and economic relationship to the West African territories it claimed. This book too was widely read and mostly well-reviewed (Birkett 1992, ch. 7).

In parts of her books, Kingsley employed a self-deprecating, ironic voice, often mocking the conventions of adventurer writing and seeming to skewer imperialist pretensions (Blunt 1994; Mills 1991). An example is this passage from the second book:

> My reputation as a navigator was great before I left Gaboon. I had a record of having once driven my bowsprit through a conservatory, and once taken all the paint off one side of a smallpox hospital, to say nothing of repeatedly having made attempts to climb trees in boats I commanded, but when I returned, I had surpassed these things by having successfully got my main-mast jammed up a tap, and I had done sufficient work in discovering new sandbanks, rock shoals, &c., in Corisco Bay, and round Cape Esterias, to necessitate, or call for, a new edition of *The West African Pilot.*
>
> *Kingsley 1899, p. 89*

The books vividly described the landscapes she saw, the challenges of travel, and the interactions she had with both Europeans and native Africans. The travel stories were to some (unknown) degree exaggerated, in part to make them more entertaining (Birkett 1992). Kingsley wrote frankly about the colonial system she observed. She found herself in strong sympathy with the British traders she met in Africa, whom England's elites generally viewed as an uncouth and unsavory group, and she often defended the trading companies' interests in policy discussions. She had extremely low regard for the work of most missionaries, and she was frustrated by government officials' lack of knowledge about African societies.

Kingsley did not strictly oppose British colonialism in Africa, but she held strong views on how it ought to function. She accepted the economic argument for colonization:

> [The tropical African] markets are of enormous value to us; they are, especially the West African ones, regions of great natural riches in rubber, oil, timber, ivory, and minerals from gold to coal. They are in most places densely populated with customers for England's manufactured goods. The advantages of such a region to a manufacturing nation like ourselves are enormous; for not only do we get rid there of our

> manufactured goods, but we get, what is of equal value to our manufacturing classes, raw material at a cheap enough rate to enable the English manufacturers to turn out into the markets of the civilized world articles sufficiently cheap themselves to compete with those of other manufacturing nations. The importance to us of such markets as Africa affords us seems to me to give us one sufficient reason for taking over these tropical African regions. I do not use the word justification in the matter, it is a word one has no right to use until we have demonstrated that our interference with the native population and our endeavours for our own population have ended in unmixed good; but it is a sound reason, as good a reason as we had in overrunning Australia and America.
>
> *Kingsley 1899, pp. 296–97*

British domination had so far not led to "unmixed good," of course, and Kingsley worked diligently to make colonial policy more humane. Two particular debates occupied her: British traders' sales of liquor in West Africa, and the "hut tax" that the British imposed in Sierra Leone in 1898.

The liquor trade was the subject of a significant public controversy. "Trade spirits" had been widely used in the days of the trans-Atlantic slave trade, even functioning at times as a medium of exchange. By the 1890s, alcohol was still a trade staple: the liquor was largely manufactured in Germany and sold by British traders to African middlemen who then sold it further inland. Colonial administrations depended heavily on liquor duties for revenue. Temperance organizations, whose influence in Britain was growing, began waging a vigorous campaign against the trade, in company with British cotton manufacturers who apparently hoped that the less Africans spent on liquor, the more they would spend on cotton cloth (Olorunfemi 1984).

Kingsley took on this powerful coalition. Observant readers of the prestigious *Times* newspaper, she said in one article, would have seen "how the contemplation of the liquor traffic with Africa gives rise to a feeling of great personal moral elevation, combined with a conviction of the iniquity and absence of high moral ideal in other nations and in persons" (Kingsley 1898b, p. 537).

Speaking from personal observation, she testified that, contrary to some assertions, West Africans rarely drank to excess, so the trade did not present a danger to them.

> I have no hesitation in saying that in the whole of West Africa, in one week, there is not one-quarter the amount of drunkenness you can see any Saturday night you choose in a couple of hours in the Vauxhall Road [in London].
>
> *Kingsley 1897, p. 633*

Further, liquor was vital to expanding Britain's commerce in the region. Restricting the trade in spirits would

> check the expansion of trade in other goods, for spirit is the introducer of other trade—the West African wants it more than he wants your other things, except only guns and gunpowder. He has native equivalents for those other things.
>
> *Kingsley 1898b, p. 551*

To an opponent's declaration that liquor was an indulgence that did not "promote habits of thrift and industry," Kingsley retorted that "your West African native is not the man to wear himself to a thread-paper to buy what he don't want" (1898b, p. 551).

Kingsley's arguments may have carried weight, or perhaps the Colonial Office simply could not figure out a better source of revenue. In any case, the government did not prohibit the liquor trade in West Africa until the First World War.

Kingsley's battle over the Hut Tax was not so successful. Early in 1898, the British imposed a substantial tax on native dwellings in Sierra Leone, as it had done in other colonies. Local chiefs objected that the tax was both onerous and offensive, but they were not heeded. Many people refused to pay, and efforts to force them to do so provoked rebellions. Kingsley urged British officials not to continue pursuing a military solution, but to simply revoke the tax, because it was both unjust and counterproductive. In "African law," she explained, an article that a person had to pay for regularly belonged not to the payer but the payee. To the natives, therefore, imposing the tax was akin to the government's declaring it was confiscating their houses (Kingsley 1898a). British Colonial Office officials did consider her advice, but in the end they retained the tax.

In *West African Studies*, Kingsley also sought to intervene in the broader debate over how Britain's West African territories could best be governed. At the time, Britain held Lagos as a Crown Colony and had established a Niger Coast Protectorate, while other territory was administered by the Royal Niger Company. The government was considering enlarging the area ruled as a colony. Kingsley argued forcefully that this would be a serious error.

> I have attempted to state that the Crown Colony system is unsuited for governing Western Africa, and have attributed its malign influence to its being a system which primarily expresses the opinions of well-intentioned but ill-informed officials at home, instead of being, according to the usual English type of institution, representative of the interests of the people who are governed, and of those who have the largest stake in the countries controlled by it—the merchants and manufacturing classes of England.
>
> *Kingsley 1899, p. 314*

West Africa's harsh climate and the prevalence of tropical diseases ensured that mortality rates were high for Europeans, so postings to West Africa were not seen as desirable. Officials who did venture there tended to serve short tours of duty interrupted by long furloughs, so the colonies had little continuity of administration. Each new governor came in with his own tastes and schemes, resulting in much wasteful expenditure.

> One Governor is truly great on drains; he spends lots of money on them. Another Governor thinks education and a cathedral more important; during his reign drains languish . . . and so it goes on, and of course leads to an immense waste of money. And this waste of money is a far more serious thing than it looks; for it is from it that the policy has arisen, of increasing customs dues to a point that seriously hampers trade development, and the far more serious evil of attempting directly as well as indirectly to tax the native population.
>
> *Kingsley 1899, p. 330*

Kingsley maintained that British traders were far better suited than the state to look after British interests in West Africa. Unlike the short-term colonial official, the traders knew the local people and had an economic interest in promoting their well-being:

> To that [British colonist] family man the native is a nuisance, sometimes a dangerous one, at the best an indifferent servant, who does not do his work half so well as in a decent climate he can do it himself. To the trader the native is quite a different thing, a customer. A dense native population is what the trader wants; and on their wealth, prosperity, peace and industry, the success of his endeavours depends.
>
> *Kingsley 1899, p. 295*

The system Kingsley proposed was a highly original variant of trading-company rule. The Chambers of Commerce of Liverpool and four other major commercial cities would nominate an African Council, which would select a Governor General for West Africa, subject to government approval. There would be two advisory subcouncils: one would include British legal and medical experts, and the other would be an elected group of African chiefs. A relatively small number of Britons would be needed to reside in Africa and administer the system. Revenue would come from taxes on private trading firms and the proceeds from government monopolies on tobacco imports and timber exports. The local population would not be taxed directly. This system, Kingsley argued, would be far less oppressive than Crown rule. Those in charge would be knowledgable about the people and uninterested in saving their souls or otherwise transforming their cultures; Africans would have a formal voice in policy discussions; and the merchants' self-interest would push them to promote native prosperity.

Kingsley was no doubt over-optimistic about how Africans would fare under her scheme, but her prime objective was to protect the people from British interference and appropriation of their land. She wanted economic development to be a voluntary process rather than a forced and exploitative one. Predictably, her proposal made little impression in policy circles. Britain's Colonial Office under Joseph Chamberlain had a vision for the economic transformation of West Africa, and so a new Crown Colony of Northern Nigeria was created in 1900.

Britain was also seeking to increase its control elsewhere on the continent at this time, and in 1899 the British went to war against the two Afrikaner (or Boer) republics of South Africa. Kingsley volunteered to serve there as a nurse early in 1900. She arranged to report on the war for British newspapers while in South Africa, and planned to resume her travels in West Africa afterward. On her arrival she was assigned to care for wounded and sick Boer prisoners of war, which meant working long hours under terrible conditions. Within less than two months she contracted typhoid fever, and she died there—and was buried at sea—at the age of 37 (Frank 1986).

Although Kingsley did not always win the policy battles she fought, she had a considerable impact on Britain's relations with Africa. Her work helped shape perceptions of Africa among both specialists and the general public. For years she pressed for the formation of an organization for Africa experts, arguing that Europeans could not competently or responsibly govern peoples whom they did not understand. Shortly after her death, her historian friend Alice Stepford Green led the creation of the Royal African Society to honor Kingsley's life and work (Birkett 1992). That organization (still active) has played a significant role in promoting inquiry and improving British knowledge about Africa.

Flora Shaw (Dec. 1852–Jan. 1929)

Flora Louise Shaw was born into an upper-class family, the fourth of 14 children. Her father was an Anglo-Irish military officer, and her mother was the daughter of the last French Governor of Mauritius. She received no formal schooling, but read extensively in the library of the Royal

Military Academy, which her father commanded. John Ruskin, the renowned art critic and social thinker, served as a mentor, helping to guide her reading. When Flora was 18 her mother died, and for a year she took over the care of her younger siblings. In her 20s, like many young women of means, she spent two years doing social work in the East London slums. In hope of earning money to live independently and support her sisters' education, she began writing novels for children, one of which was quite successful (Helly 2012).

On a visit to Egypt with family friends in 1888–89, Shaw became interested in colonial policy. She began to write for W.T. Stead's *Pall Mall Gazette* and the *Manchester Guardian* and decided to attempt a career as a journalist, though she knew she would encounter obstacles. When the *Guardian* sent her to Brussels in 1889 to cover the International Anti-Slavery Conference, she was the only woman reporter present. In 1890 she was hired by the *Times* of London to write a regular (unsigned) column on Colonies. The paper's owner was not told until two years later that Shaw was a woman (Helly 2012, p. 119).

As a correspondent for the *Times*, Shaw traveled to South Africa, Australia, New Zealand, and Canada in 1892 and 1893. The articles she sent back touched on many topics, but she focused especially on the colonies' potential for economic development. She favored the idea of a grand confederation of Britain's white settler colonies, and was disappointed to find that the colonists had little interest in forming closer economic and political ties with each other. Australia, she reported, was a social and cultural extension of England, with an industrious settler population thriving on a physically diverse continent. The visit that most impressed her was the one to South Africa, where British and Afrikaner colonists were coexisting uneasily with each other and with native Africans in a territory of extraordinary economic promise. British diamond mining and gold mining operations were beginning to flourish and generate fortunes, and the agricultural possibilities seemed enormous: "Everything that is written of the material resources of this astonishing country must read like exaggeration, and yet exaggeration is hardly possible. The fertility of the soil is no less amazing than the mineral wealth" (Shaw 1893a, p. 36).

The challenge was to find enough labor. The climate would likely prevent large-scale settlement by whites, and so the country's potential could be realized only if some "system or process could be devised by which the average raw native could be converted into an effective labourer" (Shaw 1893a, p. 93). Colonists often said "that the native is inherently lazy and that nothing but force will compel him to work," but in many cases, employers' "real trouble is not that they cannot get labour but that they cannot get it at their own price" (Shaw 1893a, p. 99). Most natives had access to land that assured them of subsistence. Working for wages was not necessary for survival, so natives had to be induced to it. This would be no easy task.

> [T]he ordinary native is like his ordinary fellow-man in this—that he does not care to work after his most pressing wants have been satisfied. A wife is soon bought, a hut is soon built, and when these objects have been accomplished, he defies white energy by preferring a pipe in the sun to all the luxuries which continued labour could accumulate.
>
> *Shaw 1893a, p. 20*

Shaw had observed in the diamond and gold mining areas that "the native has shown not only that he can work, but that he will work, if for any reason it becomes worth his while. Up to this point there is not one of us who is not essentially lazy" (Shaw 1893a, p. 99). The colonists, she urged, must not try to force people to work, using taxes or other coercive means; such schemes were merely "slavery in disguise." Instead, employers must attract labor by offering sufficiently high wages. In the longer run, she proposed that native land tenure systems could be reformed so that land was owned by individuals rather than in common. Those who parted with their land would then be "of necessity labourers," and more natives would migrate to the areas of high labor demand (Shaw 1893a, p. 101).

Shaw's African dispatches, having been extremely well-received, were republished (still without her name) as *Letters from South Africa* (1893a); the Australia writings followed, titled *Letters from Queensland* (1893b). That year, the *Times* promoted her to Colonial Editor, making her, at 41, the highest-paid woman journalist in Britain (Helly and Callaway 2000, p. 53). Her authority was soon recognized in another setting as well: in 1894 she presented papers on "The Australian Outlook" and "Colonial Expansion" to the Royal Colonial Institute, being the first woman to speak before that all-male learned society (Helly 2012, p. 122).

Shaw's writing on the colonies was engaging, well-researched, thoughtful, and flattering to British sensibilities. Her power of persuasion probably also benefited from the fact that she was beautiful and tremendously charming, a prominent presence in both intellectual and social circles (Perham 1956, p. 647). No other woman had comparable influence on colonial matters. She was personally close to the men who set Britain's colonial policy in Africa, including Joseph Chamberlain (the Colonial Secretary), Cecil Rhodes, and George Goldie (head of the Royal Niger Company). Her position at the *Times* gave her an ideal audience for her purposes: that paper, as one author put it, was "the daily issue of authoritative print that all the people of education and influence in the country . . . certainly the 'top people of the day'—had been reading" (Perham 1960, p. 64).

One tribute to Shaw's influence is a name: in a January 1897 column in the *Times*, she suggested that the area referred to as the Royal Niger Company Territories be renamed "Nigeria." The government did exactly that in 1900, when it took over control from the Company and created the Crown Colony of Northern Nigeria (Perham 1960).

Shaw became deeply involved in the complicated politics of South Africa. In *Letters from South Africa*, she suggested that British and Afrikaner settlers could all prosper there, the Afrikaners as farmers and the British as industrialists. Tensions between the two communities increased, however, and Shaw strongly supported the British side. In 1895 she was involved in the planning of what turned out to be a disastrous military action by British soldiers, and she had to devote considerable energy to defending herself, the *Times*, and the man who had financed the operation, Cecil Rhodes (Helly and Callaway 2000). Later she would be an eloquent supporter of Britain's 1899–1902 Boer War.

After ten years at the *Times*, Shaw resigned as Colonial Editor in 1900, citing poor health. She had written "over five hundred articles on economic and political issues in the colonies, vigorously supporting British expansion, by military force if necessary" (Callaway and Helly 1992, p. 79). She would continue to write on colonial affairs for another decade. In 1902, at almost 50, Shaw married her friend Sir Frederick Lugard, a military officer celebrated for his successful campaigns in Central Africa, Uganda, and Nigeria. He was High Commissioner for Northern Nigeria from 1900 to 1907, and would serve as the first Governor General of the consolidated Colony of Nigeria from 1914 to 1919. Flora found living in Africa with him was too difficult, in part because of her delicate health, so she returned to England, where Lugard joined her for a few months a year until he retired from colonial service in 1919 (Perham 1960).

As Lady Lugard, Flora continued her work as a scholar-advocate, writing primarily about West Africa. In a 1904 paper titled "Nigeria," she declared that while public interest in Britain's empire had so far focused mainly on the white settler colonies of America, Australasia, and South Africa, she was certain that "our next colonial chapter will be a tropical chapter" (Shaw 1904a, p. 370). The tropical colonies presented special challenges: how to find and exploit new economic opportunities, and how small white populations might govern large non-white ones who had very different modes of living.

Nigeria, she said, showed what was possible: the slave trade had been suppressed, and Lord Lugard was establishing a system of "indirect rule" that worked through pre-existing political structures, similar to that developed in British India. Those were "but the first steps by means of which we, as it were, reclaim a waste from history for cultivation." Once order was established, "we naturally hope that some material advantage shall result" (Shaw 1904a, p. 380). In particular, she foresaw a vast expansion of cotton cultivation in Nigeria that would benefit Britain's textile industry.

In another 1904 paper, "West African Negroland" (i.e., the Nigerian interior), she summarized the history of western Africa, noting that in some periods there had been African civilizations far more advanced than those in Europe. She incorporated this glorious past into her own formulation of Britain's "civilizing mission."

> Our hope is now that, in . . . carrying British administration for the first time into the fine uplands of higher Negroland, it may be our happy fortune to initiate a new era of prosperity, and to introduce into those countries blessings of peace and justice under which the qualities these peoples showed themselves to be possessed of in the past may ripen to a finer fruit.
>
> *Shaw 1904b, p. 321*

She further elaborated this theme in her 1905 book, *A Tropical Dependency*, which provided a prodigiously researched (though not entirely accurate) history of western Africa, from ancient times to the present, and closed by articulating her imperialist vision for the future.

> The administration of Northern Nigeria is but five years old. Its duty has been to bring under control a congeries of states, of which the internal disorders necessitated, in the first instance, a resort to the plain argument of military conquest. The administration has not in the short period of its existence been able to do more than to affirm the conquest of the country, and to create a skeleton of the machinery of government which it will be for time to bring to its full perfection. But a beginning has been made. . . . A territory which we found in chaos has been brought to order. The slave trade has been abolished within its frontiers. Its subject races have been secured in the possession of their lives and property. Its rulers have been converted with their own consent into officials of the British Crown, and are working sympathetically to promote an order of things that shall render a return to old abuse impossible. There has been no great shock and no convulsion, only into the veins of a decadent civilisation new blood has been introduced, which has brought with it the promise of a new era of life.
>
> *Shaw 1905, pp. 499–500*

The natural resources of the tropical colonies, just beginning to be explored, offered inestimable riches—if people could be found to do the work of cultivation and extraction. She expressed optimism about the prospects.

> Tropical labour is coloured labour, and we have not yet faced the question of organising free coloured labour. But that this question has not yet been faced is not a reason why the difficulties attending it should be regarded as insurmountable.
>
> *Shaw 1905, p. 3*

After 1905 Shaw's public visibility declined, though as Lugard's wife she continued to be involved in policy discussions. In recognition of her authority in colonial matters, she was asked to write the 1911 *Encyclopaedia Britannica* entries on the "British Empire," "Nigeria," "Cecil Rhodes," and several other topics. During the First World War, Lady Lugard led successful efforts to organize relief for refugees from Belgium. After the war her health problems worsened, and she died in England in 1929, aged 76 (Perham 1960).

Assessing Flora Shaw's achievement, one scholar commends her

> sweep of mind which embraced both the colonies of white settlement and the tropical colonies in one span of thought. She was the first in the literary world—and outside Parliament and the Colonial Office—to unite a vast range of experience in both the temperate and the tropical Empire. Others knew well some colonial territories, but her travels—first alone, and then in company with her husband—brought her a range of first-hand acquaintance which few outside the official world had had before that time, and none had had the opportunity to bring to a wide audience.
>
> *Cumpston 1959, p. 74*

Concluding reflections

What were these writers' contributions? Where did they agree and disagree? How did their ideas compare to the received wisdoms of their times regarding racial hierarchy and the morality of empire? We will conclude with some reflections on these questions.

One would not say that any of these writers made original contributions to political-economic theory on empire. Their many discussions of economic policy issues—public finance, colonial trade, infrastructure investment, land tenure, work incentives, labor relations—were informed by current economic thinking, but their aim was to help policymakers and the public choose sides in existing debates, not to argue with economists.

Their disagreements were deep. Harriet Martineau, writing in the 1850s, looked forward to economic and social progress in Ireland and India with British assistance, but she was wary of increasing British government control over distant territories. Her work conveys ambivalence: she portrayed colonial authorities sometimes as thoroughly benevolent and other times as essentially exploitative, and she never satisfactorily resolved this inconsistency. Decades later, in the 1890s, Flora Shaw endeavored to build public support for empire, so that Britain would devote more resources to territorial expansion, political consolidation, and economic development, especially in Africa. Mary Kingsley, perhaps a reluctant imperialist and certainly a skeptical one, saw much potential for economic benefit but sought to protect Africans from British domination.

Racial hierarchy

Ideas about empire have always been closely entangled with ideas about "race": Europeans used assertions about "race"—in fact, constructed their concepts of race—to justify imperial domination. In the 19th century, the term's meaning was unsettled: the "English race" might be distinguished from the Irish, for example, blurring the lines between the biological and the cultural. In any case, in those times the dominant British view was that Britain was the most advanced and progressive of all societies, and that the colonized peoples of Asia and Africa were backward in comparison. These women writers were, of course, products of their times; but it is worth noting that Martineau and Kingsley energetically contested some of the principal racist ideas then in circulation.

Martineau touched on the subject of racial inequality in many of her writings on colonies and on slavery. She consistently attributed apparent group differences to institutional and environmental factors, rather than to innate biological endowments; in this she followed Adam Smith, John Stuart Mill, and other classical political economists (Pitts 2005).[2]

In 1838 she decided to attack the race question differently. She wanted, she said in an 1838 article, to address the question "whether negroes are constitutionally, and therefore irremediably, inferior to whites in the powers of the mind." Appearances were misleading, since any observed limitations could be due to "the circumstances amidst which negroes have lived, both in their own countries and abroad" (Belasco 2000, p. 165). But if some black individuals were found to have as much "genius" as the most eminent whites, it would prove that being black was compatible with the very highest levels of achievement. Martineau saw such genius in Toussaint l'Ouverture, who led the slave rebellion in Haiti that in 1803 created the hemisphere's first black republic: As she put it, he showed "what the negro race at large can do and become" (Belasco 2000, p. 165). Her fictionalized biography of Toussaint, *The Hour and the Man: A Historical Romance* (1841), was widely read on both sides of the Atlantic, despite its 900-page length.

Mary Kingsley declined to take a stand on whether innate racial differences existed beyond the superficial visible ones, saying that science knew too little about race (Kingsley 1899, p. 385). She did believe that African natives and Britons had very different ways of thinking: the British approached phenomena in a materialist way, while Africans viewed causation in more spiritual terms, and this could help explain the societies' very different relationships to technology (Kingsley 1899, pp. 385–87). It seems unlikely she would have endorsed the period's hierarchical racial taxonomies purporting to identify "natural" differences in capacities.

Kingsley mocked Britons' incoherent and self-serving stereotypes of "the African,"

> the creature that turns up in mission literature as a Simple Child of Nature, our Unsophisticated Brother, &c., and in newspapers as an Incarnate Fiend wallowing in blood, . . . given to cannibalizing round corners whenever the white eye is off him, and a lazy brute when the white eye is on.
>
> *Kingsley 1898a, pp. 538–39*

She sometimes overgeneralized about "Africans," or wrote about them flippantly or condescendingly; but when she was serious, her central message was a plea to her countrymen to try to understand African people's lives and viewpoints, rather than seeing them as savages who had to be either Europeanized or eliminated.

Flora Shaw Lugard expressed far less criticism of the ideology of racial hierarchy. She explicitly approved the racial division of labor she observed in South Africa's mining areas, while leaving some ambiguity about its duration:

> The native is recognized as the motor power by means of which material development is carried out; the white man takes the position of director of this motor power, which is the only position that he can hold with satisfaction to himself in the African climate. Muscle on the one side and brain on the other must, for a long time to come, represent the respective contributions of the two races to the public stock.
>
> *Shaw 1893a, p. 19*

"For a long time to come" might suggest that Shaw saw racial differences as related to education rather than immutable characteristics—but this would be small comfort to the generations of black workers who would be confined to South Africa's worst and most poorly paid jobs.

Some of Shaw's later writings gave considerable attention to race due to her focus on the colonies of tropical Africa. Her 1905 book began by stating "It has become the habit of the British mind to think of the British Empire as a white empire. But, as a matter of fact, we all know that ours is not a white empire." Only an eighth of the empire's inhabitants were white, and unlike the white settler colonies, the non-white territories required governments "more or less in the nature of an autocracy which leaves with the rulers full responsibility for the prosperity of the ruled" (Shaw 1905, p. 1). After governance came the labor question: historically, it was slave labor that had made industrialization possible, and now it would have to be free African labor that developed the tropical colonies. Shaw referred to various "races" throughout the book's historical account, often identifying them as "higher" or "lower," "finer" or "degraded." Similarly, her "British Empire" entry for the *Encyclopaedia Britannica* began with a lengthy inventory of the colonies' populations, classified as white, black, yellow and brown (Shaw 1910–11). One cannot be sure about Shaw's precise understanding of "race"—but she was comfortable using the language of racial hierarchy, and she often expressed a blatantly instrumental view of the empire's people of color.

Morality and empire

Of these authors, only Flora Shaw comes across as a truly orthodox imperialist. Mary Kingsley, whose relationship with Shaw was a frosty one, wrote in an 1899 letter that "She is imbued with the modern form of imperialism. It is her religion" (Helly 2012, p. 110). Shaw herself might not have disagreed. Reflecting on her life in a 1904 letter to her husband, she said she was proud of having "helped to rouse the British public to a sense of Imperial responsibility and an ideal of Imperial greatness." "I never thought of my work exactly as journalism," she wrote, "but rather as active politics without the fame" (Helly and Callaway 2000, p. 50). Writing from Nigeria in 1902, she waxed enthusiastic about "this conception of an Empire which is to secure the ruling of the world by its finest race" (Perham 1960, p. 81).

We can see in Shaw's writings many of the standard justifications of empire:

- Britain liberated the colonies' peoples from oppressive rulers and put an end to the violence that had long plagued them, such as the raiding of villages to capture slaves.
- The natives had been doing very little to develop the rich resources that surrounded them. The British would not leave those resources idle.
- The British sought the betterment (civilization) of their colonial subjects: over time natives' living standards would improve and their ways of life would advance.
- If Britain had not colonized the territories, another European power would have, and the natives would have been much less well-served.

Harriet Martineau voiced some of these same ideas, as we have seen, but she was much more ambivalent about empire. The leading scholar on Martineau calls her "both a cautious advocate and severe critic of British imperialism" (Logan 2009, p. 9). Her hopes for the empire conformed with her period's

> ethnocentrism secure in its assumption that western industrial society is unquestionably superior to pre-industrial cultures, and that the benefits of modern technology, political economy and enlightened social philosophy must be desired by, and bestowed upon, those cultures as the ethical realization of the Civilizing Mission.
>
> *Logan 2009, p. 13*

Although Martineau acknowledged that many injustices and blunders had come with British rule, she believed in the ability of British capital, technological knowledge, and free-market institutions to promote progress and prosperity in the colonies. In time the colonies would become capable of self-government, and then they would (they must) be given their independence.

Mary Kingsley's writing also contained scraps of the conventional language about progress and mutual gain. She was, however, uniquely insistent that change in West Africa must be fully voluntary. She did not trust that the changes brought by colonization would be better for native communities. British rhetoric on the colonies, she said, was mostly "humbug."

> [W]e have proclaimed that we are only in Africa for peaceful reasons of commerce, and religion, and education, not with any desire for the African's land or property: that, of course, it is not possible for us to extend our friendship or our toleration to people who go in for cannibalism, slave-raiding, or human sacrifices, but apart from these matters we have no desire to meddle with African domestic affairs, or take away their land.
>
> *Kingsley 1899, p. 368*

West Africans had begun to see through this pretense, and they were resisting, not out of some irrational hostility but a "reasonable dislike to being dispossessed alike of power and property in what they regard as their own country" (Kingsley 1899, p. 375). The future did not look promising, unless Britain drastically altered its approach.

> The desire to develop our West African possessions is a worthy one in its way, but better leave it totally alone than attempt it with your present machinery . . . You have got a grand rich region there, populated by an uncommon fine sort of human being. You have been trying your present set of ideas on it for over 400 years; they have failed in a heart-breaking drizzling sort of way to perform any single solitary one of the things you say you want done there. West Africa to-day is just a quarry of paving-stones for Hell, and those stones were cemented in place with men's blood mixed with wasted gold.
>
> *Kingsley 1899, pp. 390–91*

We might picture Kingsley as pleading her case from one end of the imperialist spectrum and Shaw campaigning energetically from the other, with Martineau lecturing from somewhere in between. All three women—intellectually gifted, well-informed, prolific, with compelling public personas—helped to shape debate on the empire during Britain's "imperial century." Their skills and dedication made the discussion a richer and more inclusive one.

Notes

1 Martineau's writing on political economy was in part inspired by Jane Marcet's 1816 *Conversations on Political Economy* (see Polkinghorn 1995). Two excellent biographies of Martineau are Logan (2002) and Pichanick (1980). Logan (2004) brings together Martineau's most important works on empire.

2 As John Stuart Mill put it in 1848, "Of all vulgar modes of escaping from the consideration of the effect of social and moral influences on the human mind, the most vulgar is that of attributing the diversities of conduct and character to inherent natural differences" (Mill 1848, p. 319). Pitts (2005) notes that his repudiation of biological racism did not diminish Mill's support for the rule of the East India Company; she suggests that Mill deployed his concept of "national character" as a similarly problematic justification for British domination.

Bibliography

Belasco, S. (2000) Harriet Martineau's Black Hero and the American Antislavery Movement. *Nineteenth Century Literature* 55(2): 157–94.

Birkett, D. (1992) *Mary Kingsley, Imperial Adventuress.* London: Macmillan.

Blunt, A. (1994) *Travel, Gender, and Imperialism: Mary Kingsley and West Africa.* New York: Guilford Press.

Burton, A. (1994) *Burdens of History: British Feminists, Indian Women and Imperial Culture, 1865–1915.* Chapel Hill: University of North Carolina Press.

Callaway, H. and Helly, D. O. (1992) Crusader for Empire: Flora Shaw/Lady Lugard. In Chaudhuri, N. and Strobel, M. (eds) *Western Women and Imperialism: Complicity and Resistance.* Bloomington: Indiana University Press, pp. 79–97.

Chaudhuri, N. and Strobel, M. (eds) (1992). *Western Women and Imperialism: Complicity and Resistance.* Bloomington: Indiana University Press.

Cumpston, M. (1959) The Contribution to Ideas of Empire of Flora Shaw, Lady Lugard. *Australian Journal of Politics and History* 5(1) (May): 64–75.

Curtis, L. P. (1968) *Anglo-Saxons and Celts: A Study of Anti-Irish Prejudice in Victorian England.* New York: New York University Press.

Dzelzainis, E. and Kaplan, C. (eds) (2010) *Harriet Martineau: Authorship, Society and Empire.* Manchester: Manchester University Press.

Frank, K. (1986) *A Voyager Out: The Life of Mary Kingsley.* Boston: Houghton Mifflin.

Helly, D. O. (2012) Flora Shaw and the *Times*: Becoming a Journalist and Advocating Empire. In F. E. Gray (ed.) *Women in Journalism at the Fin de siècle: Making a Name for Herself.* London: Palgrave Macmillan, pp. 110–28.

Helly, D. O. and Callaway, H. (2000) Journalism as Active Politics: Flora Shaw, the *Times* and South Africa. In D. Lowry (ed.) *The South Africa War Reappraised.* Manchester: Manchester University Press, pp. 50–66.

Hill, M. R. and Hoecker-Drysdale, S. (eds) (2001) *Harriet Martineau: Theoretical and Methodological Perspectives.* London: Routledge.

Huzzey, R. (2012) *Freedom Burning: Anti-Slavery and Empire in Victorian Britain.* Ithaca, NY: Cornell University Press.

Jayawardena, K. (1995) *The White Woman's Other Burden: Western Women and South Asia during British Rule.* London: Routledge.

Kingsley, M. H. (1897) *Travels in West Africa, Congo Francais, Corisco and Cameroons.* London: Macmillan.

——. (1898a) The Hut-tax in Africa. *Spectator* 84 (March 19): 407–08.

——. (1898b) Liquor Traffic with West Africa. *Fortnightly Review* 69 (n.s. 63) (April): 537–60.

——. (1899) *West African Studies.* London: Macmillan.

Logan, D. A. (2002) *The Hour and the Woman: Harriet Martineau's "Somewhat Remarkable" Life.* Dekalb, IL: Northern Illinois University Press.

——. (ed.) (2004) *Harriet Martineau's Writings on the British Empire.* 5 vols. London: Pickering & Chatto.

——. (2009) *Harriet Martineau, Victorian Imperialism, and the Civilizing Mission.* Farnham, UK: Ashgate.

Marcet, J. (1816) *Conversations on Political Economy.* London: Longman.

Martineau, H. (1833–34) *Poor Laws and Paupers, Illustrated.* 4 vols bound in 2. London: Charles Fox.

——. (1834a) *Illustrations of Political Economy.* 9 vols (orig. 25 vols, 1832–34). London: Charles Fox.

——. (1834b) *Illustrations of Taxation.* 5 vols bound in 2. London: Charles Fox.

——. (1837) *Society in America.* 3 vols. London: Saunders and Otley.

——. (1838a) *Retrospect of Western Travel.* 3 vols. London: Saunders and Otley.

——. (1838b) *How to Observe Morals and Manners.* London: Charles Knight & Co.

——. (1841) *The Hour and the Man: A Historical Romance.* 3 vols. London: Edward Moxon.

——. (1852) *Letters from Ireland.* London: John Chapman.

——. (tr., ed.); (1853) *The Positive Philosophy of Auguste Comte, freely translated and condensed.* 2 vols. London: John Chapman.

——. (1857) *British Rule in India; A Historical Sketch.* London: Smith, Elder & Co.

——. (1858) *Suggestions Toward the Future Government of India.* London: Smith, Elder & Co.

Midgley, C. (ed.) (1998) *Gender and Imperialism.* Manchester: Manchester University Press.

Mill, J. S. (1848/1965) *Principles of Political Economy with Some of Their Applications to Social Philosophy*, vol. 2 of *Collected Works*, edited by J. M. Robson. Toronto: University of Toronto Press.

Mills, S. (1991) *Discourses of Difference: An Analysis of Women's Travel Writing and Colonialism*. London: Routledge.

Olorunfemi, A. (1984) The Liquor Traffic Dilemma in British West Africa: The Southern Nigerian Example, 1895–1918. *International Journal of African Historical Studies* 17(2): 229–41.

Perham, M. (1956) *Lugard: The Years of Adventure, 1858–1898*. London: Collins.

——. (1960) *Lugard: The Years of Authority, 1898–1945*. London: Collins.

Pichanick, V. (1980) *Harriet Martineau: The Woman and Her Work, 1802–76*. Ann Arbor: University of Michigan Press.

Pitts, J. (2005) *A Turn to Empire: The Rise of Imperial Liberalism in Britain and France*. Princeton: Princeton University Press.

Polkinghorn, B. (1995) Jane Marcet and Harriet Martineau. In Dimand, M., Dimand, R. and Forget, E. (eds) *Women of Value: Feminist Essays on the History of Women in Economics*. Brookfield, VT: Edward Elgar, pp. 71–81.

Shaw (Lugard), F. L. (1893a) *Letters from South Africa, by the Times special correspondent*. London: Macmillan.

——. (1893b). *Letters from Queensland, by the Times special correspondent*. London: Macmillan.

——. (1893–94) The Australian Outlook. *Proceedings of the Royal Colonial Institute* 25: 138–65.

——. (1894–95) Colonial Expansion. *Proceedings of the Royal Colonial Institute* 26: 3–29.

——. (1904a) Nigeria. *Journal of the Royal Society of Arts* 52 (March 18): 370–84.

——. (1904b) West African Negroland. *Journal of the Royal Colonial Institute* 35: 300–26.

——. (1905) *A Tropical Dependency: An Outline of the Ancient History of the Western Soudan with an Account of the Modern Settlement of Northern Nigeria*. London: James Nisbet.

——. (1910–11) British Empire. *Encyclopaedia Britannica*, 11th edition, vol. IV, 606–15. London: Encyclopaedia Britannica Co.

4

HARRIET TAYLOR MILL, MARY PALEY MARSHALL AND BEATRICE POTTER WEBB

Women economists and economists' wives

Virginie Gouverneur

Introduction

The chapter focuses on three English women who lived between the nineteenth century and the beginning of the twentieth century and were married to well-known economists: Harriet Taylor Mill (1807–58), Mary Paley Marshall (1850–1944) and Beatrice Potter Webb (1858–1943). These women evolved in similar social backgrounds and expressed economic ideas, either by producing their own written works or by taking part in the production of works. Nevertheless, their stories diverge on several points.

First, they faced different contexts. Important changes occurred at the society level during the Victorian and Edwardian periods in England, notably regarding women's emancipation. Among these changes, women's access to education became possible as did academic teaching posts for female students.

In parallel with these social circumstances, great differences appear in the three women's personal experiences. After the initial developments of their intellectual circle and interest in Political Economy, they engaged in different types of relationships with eminent economists (John Stuart Mill, Alfred Marshall and Sidney Webb). These relationships took the form of partnerships, which had distinct effects on their "career" as economists, their participation in economic circles and the dissemination of their economic ideas.

The main purpose of the chapter is to compare the implications of these partnerships on the three women's contributions to the development of economic thought. While the role of Harriet Taylor Mill has always been discussed, the role of Mary Paley Marshall has been rediscovered recently (Hayek, 1951; McWilliams Tullberg, 1991, 1995). As for Beatrice Potter Webb, she was quickly reputed as a social researcher and never considered only as the wife of Sidney Webb.

The chapter also reviews, for each of the three women, a particular piece of their contribution, linked with the issue of the inequalities between men and women. These pieces, all distinct in form and in content, reflect great variations in their independence as thinkers and writers.

Harriet Taylor Mill

Born Harriet Hardy on 8 October 1807, Harriet was probably educated at home, no attendance at an outside school appearing in her biography (A. Robson, 2004: 1). This "largely self-educated woman" married John Taylor in 1826, a man noticed by her father (Rossi, 1970: 24). Harriet and John Taylor were active members of the Unitarian parish of William J. Fox, who, in 1827, became the editor of the *Monthly Repository*, the journal of the Unitarian Radicals. Harriet Taylor met John Stuart Mill in 1830. They married two decades later, in April 1851, two years after the death of Harriet's first husband and they lived together until her death in 1858. Their long relationship, defined by Hayek as "friendship and subsequent marriage", was marked by regular discussions and exchanges of views (Peart, 2014: *Editor's introduction*). Moreover, Harriet Taylor's intellectual circle widened through John Mill's connections, even if several members of the *Philosophic Radicals*, the social circle to which Mill belonged in his youth, were rather sceptical about her intellectual capacities and influence on Mill (Rossi, 1970: 37). Her ideas have been expounded by way of her own works, published under Mill's name, and works to which she contributed significantly.

Harriet Taylor's writings

In 1831–32, Mill and Taylor exchanged their *Essays on Marriage*, in which, influenced by Taylor's first marriage, they talked about marriage laws and the problem of divorce[1] (Rossi, 1970: 22–3). In 1851, *Enfranchisement of Women* was published under Mill's name. He explained in the preface of the second edition that the treatise was entirely hers (Taylor, 1851: 91–3). Taylor's authorship has since been confirmed (Rossi, 1970: 41–2; J. Robson, 1984: lxxiii–vii; Forget, 2003: 288, 299–302). A question then immediately comes to mind: why didn't Taylor publish in her own name? Two reasons can explain that. First, it might be due to the long extra-conjugal nature of the Mills' relationship, which was not acceptable at the time (Rossi, 1970: 40–1). Second, it has to be linked to the prevailing circumstances: women's voices were rarely heard or considered equivalent to those of men. Therefore, Taylor and Mill might have chosen, through pragmatism, to publish under Mill's name, to allow the ideas expressed about women's emancipation to receive greater consideration.

Besides these individual productions, Taylor also collaborated with Mill on philosophical and economics books.

Mill's and Taylor's partnership

It is difficult to determine precisely Taylor's contribution to the works presented by Mill as the fruit of their collaboration. In his autobiography, published in 1873, almost 15 years after Taylor's death, Mill undertakes to bring into light her participation to these "joint productions" (Mill, 1873: 251). Then began a controversy about her real contribution to Mill's writings, which has raged for more than a century (Rossi, 1970: 31–9). Several commentators have presented Mill's portrait of Taylor as an exaggeration. Mill was indeed very eulogistic about Taylor's intellectual capacities. Numerous passages describe her as a brilliant woman. However, it cannot be said that these remarks were solely the reflection of Mill's great affection for Taylor. Other elements confirm both the influence that she had on Mill's thought – including a socialist influence[2] – and the existence of a true collaboration (Hayek, 1951; Rossi, 1970; Pujol, 1995). In his autobiography, Mill detailed their complementarities. He affirmed that her mind was more practical than his and bolder in foresight:

> The writings in which this quality [practicality] has been observed, were not the work of one mind, but of the fusion of two, one of them as pre-eminently practical in its judgments and perceptions of things present, as it was high and bold in its anticipations for a remote futurity.
>
> *Mill, 1873: 197–9*

Moreover, he established a precise list of works to which Taylor would have contributed. He mentioned in particular the *Principles of Political Economy*, the first edition of which was published in 1848,[3] and *On Liberty*, published in 1859 (Mill, 1873: 249, 255). The absence of mention of Taylor's name as co-author, or at least as contributor, might be linked to Mill's and Taylor's fear of the detrimental effects of such a mention on the reception of the works and to their belief that Mill's established name would attract a larger readership. A dedication was, however, added in the copies of the first edition of *Principles* given to friends (Hayek, 1951: 121–2).

Several elements indicate that Taylor was deeply involved in the production of the *Principles*. First, Mill, as thinker, was not easily influenced by the ideas of others (Rossi, 1970: 39). Second, in the list that he established of the works to which Taylor would have contributed, he did not include his *System of Logic* (1843), thus separating clearly his own works from the "joint productions" (Rossi, 1970: 39). Third, Taylor's and Mill's correspondence and Taylor's letters to her husband about her work on the *Principles* show that she contributed extensively to the book (ibid.: 39–40). Last, Mill distinguished Taylor's contribution to the *Principles* from his. He asserted in particular that Taylor was the main author of the chapter entitled "On the Probable Futurity of the Labouring Classes" (Mill, 1848: 758–96; 1873: 254–5; Jacobs, 1998: 291). This assertion can be supported by the examination of the chapter in parallel with the argumentation adopted by Taylor in *Enfranchisement of Women*. Many points of convergence appear between both. In particular, Taylor, adept in socialist ideas, offered an interesting comparison of the relations between the poor and rich classes and the relations between the sexes, as they prevailed at the time.

Sex and class in Taylor's economic thought

At the beginning of *Enfranchisement of Women*, Taylor explains that "the division of mankind into two castes, one born to rule over the other, is [. . .] an unqualified mischief; a source of perversion and demoralization [. . .] forming a bar [. . .] to any really vital improvement, either in the character or in the social condition of the human race" (Taylor, 1851: 98). The law and custom by which women are instituted as a dependent class, men as their superiors, must be fought (ibid.: 97, 109, 118). This statement appears in line with the critique of the "theory of dependence and protection" which is contained in the chapter in the *Principles* on the future condition of the labouring classes. In this critique, a direct parallel is made between the social relations between men and women and the relations between rich and poor as they are legitimated by the "theory of dependence" (Mill, 1848: 759, 761):

> The relation between rich and poor*, according to this theory [of dependence] (a theory also applied to the relation between men and women)*[4] should be only partly authoritative; it should be amiable, moral, and sentimental: affectionate tutelage on the one side, respectful and grateful deference on the other.
>
> *Mill, 1848: 759*

The *Principles*' chapter points out the idea of a progressive transformation of the relations between capitalists and hired labourers: "it is not to be expected that the division of the human race into two hereditary classes, employers and employed, can be permanently maintained" (Mill, 1848: 767). Moreover, it expresses a strong belief in the capacity of "self-government" of the individuals and denounces the patriarchy and paternalism implied in the "theory of dependence and protection": "[t]he rich should be in loco parentis to the poor, guiding and restraining them like children" (ibid.: 759, 762, 763–4). Similarly, Taylor explains in *Enfranchisement of Women* that men have not to decide for women their "proper sphere", namely "private and domestic life": "The proper sphere for all human beings is the largest and highest which they are able to attain to. What this is, cannot be ascertained, without complete liberty of choice" (Taylor, 1851: 100).

The enlargement of women's sphere of action requires the opening of all occupations to women. A greater efficiency of work would follow from *laissez-faire*. It would lead to the specialization of each labourer, whatever his or her sex or class, in the paid occupation to which his or her aptitudes are the best adapted:[5]

> Each individual will prove his or her capacities [. . .] by trial; and the world will have the benefit of the best faculties of all its inhabitants. But to interfere beforehand by an arbitrary limit, and declare that whatever be the genius, talent, energy or force of mind of an individual *of a certain sex or class*, those faculties shall not be exerted [. . .] is not only an injustice to the individual, and a detriment to society [. . .] but is also the most effectual mode of providing that, *in the sex or class so fettered*, the qualities which are not permitted to be exercised shall not exist.
>
> *Taylor, 1851: 101; italics added*

Then, Taylor examines the negative effects of the increase of competition which would be induced by women's free participation in the labour market. She admits the idea, often invoked at the time, that women's freedom of occupation, by leading to an increase of the number of competitors, would depress wages in the "employments monopolized by men" (Taylor, 1851: 104). The worst consequence would be that "a man and a woman could not together earn more than is now earned by the man alone" (ibid.: 104). But even in this case, Taylor considers that married women should work to contribute to the family income[6] (ibid.: 105). By this contribution, the wife "would be raised from the position of a servant to that of a partner" (ibid.: 105). The *Principles*' chapter describes the same kind of evolution regarding the relations between employers and employed. With the progress of society, hired labourers would be raised from the position of servants to that of "partners" (Mill, 1848: 766–9).

Finally, to strengthen her argument in favour of women's work, Taylor mentions several forms of compensation for the depression of wages that would be caused by women's massive entry into the labour market. The interdiction of children's work would limit competition: contrary to women, they "are necessarily dependent, and under the power of others; and their labour, being not for themselves but for the gain of their parents, is a proper subject for legislative regulation" (Taylor, 1851: 105). Taylor evokes also two positive ultimate results of the progress of society:

> With respect to the future, we neither believe that improvident multiplication, and the consequent excessive difficulty of gaining a subsistence, will always continue, nor that the division of mankind into capitalists and hired labourers, and the regulation of the reward of labourers mainly by demand and supply, will be for ever, or even much longer, the rule of the world.
>
> *Taylor, 1851: 105*

The decrease of population growth would eliminate progressively the evil of over-population and its negative effects on individual wages. This decrease would be permitted by factors exposed in the *Principles* chapter. A change of habits, in particular through education and mental cultivation, shall be accompanied by "the opening of industrial occupations freely to both sexes"; indeed, "the industrial and social independence of women" would probably lead to "a great diminution of the evil of over-population" (Mill, 1848: 763–6). More generally, women's confinement to maternity and their dependence on men form a bar to human improvement:

> The ideas and institutions by which the accident of sex[7] is made the groundwork of an inequality of legal rights, and a forced dissimilarity of social functions, must ere long be recognised as the greatest hindrance to moral, social, and even intellectual improvement.
>
> *Ibid.: 765*

Therefore, law and custom should not prevent women from gaining a livelihood:

> The same reasons which make it no longer necessary that the poor should depend on the rich, make it equally unnecessary that women should depend on men; and the least which justice requires is that law and custom should not enforce dependence [. . .] by ordaining that a woman, who does not happen to have a provision by inheritance, shall have scarcely any means open to her of gaining a livelihood, except as a wife and mother.
>
> *Mill, 1848: 765*

Taylor, in *Enfranchisement of Women*, refers to the end of the division of mankind into capitalists and hired labourers (Taylor, 1851: 105). This reference echoes the idea, defended in the *Principles* chapter, that the "[t]endency of society towards the disuse of the relation of hiring and service" will induce the replacement of the concurrence by the cooperation between labourers (Mill, 1848: 766). Then, men and women would become partners rather than competitors.

Questions remain about Taylor's capacities as an economist: would she have been able to write her own economics books? Or to write entire parts of the *Principles* without Mill's touch? But also consider a simple inversion of this question: would Mill have been able to produce the *Principles* as they were published in 1848 and modified in subsequent versions without Taylor's influence and comments? With regard to at least one chapter, it was most certainly her ideas, although edited by Mill, that were expounded.

Mary Paley Marshall came into the world in 1850, 43 years after Taylor. Contrary to Taylor, Marshall had access to higher education and revealed the required capacities for becoming an economist; yet her contribution to economic thought was limited, partly because of her marriage to Alfred Marshall.

Mary Paley Marshall

Raised in a broad-minded family, Mary Marshall, supported by her father, was among the first women to be admitted to Cambridge University. There, she discovered an interest in studying Political Economy (M. P. Marshall, 1947: 50). She was the student of her future husband, Alfred Marshall, who encouraged her to study for the Moral Sciences Tripos, which included examination papers in Political Economy (McWilliams Tullberg, 1995: 152–4). Mary Marshall passed her Tripos examinations with distinction in 1874. In 1875, she was invited to return to Newnham College to lecture on Political Economy in place of Alfred Marshall, being thus the first woman economics lecturer at Cambridge. She and Alfred Marshall became engaged in 1876. During their engagement, they began to work together on *The Economics of Industry*. They married in 1877, contracting out of the clause whereby wives vow to obey their husband (ibid.: 155).

From Marshalls' **The Economics of Industry** *(1879) . . .*

Mary Marshall was living proof that women could attain formal qualifications and academic recognition in the field of Political Economy. She had a long career as a teacher in Political Economy and was regarded as a role model by female students.[8] Additionally, she started a career as an economist, which was shortly afterwards interrupted. She collaborated with her husband on *The Economics of Industry*, published under both their names in October 1879. John Maynard Keynes wrote in his biography of Mary Marshall that the book, "which was originally hers", was an excellent text (Keynes, 1944: 333). Her personal contribution is nevertheless difficult to delimit. The production came about through a request from Professor Stuart, who asked Mary Marshall in 1876, two years after her success in the Moral Sciences Tripos, to write a small economics textbook for the University Extension Lectures, which had just started at Newnham (M. P. Marshall, 1947: 22). Mary Marshall, who was soon scared by the work required by such a book, asked help from her fiancé Alfred Marshall (ibid.: 22). Thus, while the first part of the book is mainly hers, the following parts are probably his in great part.

The joint production was a sales success. It was reprinted nine times between 1879 and 1891 and a revised edition was published in 1881. Yet, Alfred Marshall never liked the book, criticizing its elementary nature and brevity (M. P. Marshall, 1947: 22). Despite continuing high demand, the book was allowed to go out of print in the early 1890s (Keynes, 1944: 333–4). It was replaced by an abridged version of Alfred Marshall's *Principles of Economics*, which was published in 1892 under the title *The Economics of Industry*[9] and with Alfred Marshall's sole name.

. . . to Alfred Marshall's **Principles of Economics** *(1890)*

The Marshalls' first experience of co-authorship was never repeated. After the revised edition of *The Economics of Industry* (1881), Mary Marshall put her capacities totally into the service of her husband. She contributed to the production of the *Principles of Economics* through proofreading and suggestions (Keynes, 1944: 336). Alfred Marshall wrote in the preface of the first edition: "My wife has aided and advised me at every stage of the MSS and of the proofs, and it owes a very great deal to her suggestions, her care and her judgement" (A. Marshall, 1890, vol. 2: 37; cited in Groenewegen, 1993: 104). He reiterated these acknowledgements in the fifth and final editions. However, Mary Marshall was not cited as co-author. Her work was one of secretary and subeditor rather than that of a colleague taking part in content and structure (McWilliams Tullberg, 1995: 167). Her help was also recognised by her husband in the preface of *Elements of the Economics of Industry*: a slight compensation for the fact that her name disappeared from the front cover. Mary Marshall accepted without complaint the deletion of the evidence of her contributions. She assisted Alfred Marshall until his death in 1924, notably in the production of his last two works, *Industry and Trade*, published in 1919, and *Money, Credit and Commerce*, published in 1923, when Marshall was more and more unwell. After Marshall's death, she played an important role in the last 20 years of her life in the development of the Marshall Library of Economics in Cambridge.

Keynes described the Marshall partnership in this way:

> This was not a partnership of a Webb kind, as it might have become if the temperaments on both side had been entirely different [. . .] Yet it was an intellectual partnership just the same, based on profound dependence on the one side (he could not live a day without her), and, on the other, deep devotion and admiration, which was increased and not impaired by extreme discernment.
>
> *Keynes, 1944: 335*

Unfortunately, Mary Marshall was married to a man who, "in spite of his early sympathies and what he was gaining all the time from his wife's discernment of mind [. . .] came increasingly to the conclusion that there was nothing useful to be made of women's intellects" (Keynes, 1944: 335). In 1894 for example, Alfred Marshall said: "Economics is like a fine chest of tools, which will not turn out anything of value except in skilful hands. This indicates that economics is a subject generally unsuited for advance by women" (Manuscript note, 28 May 1894, Marshall archives, Box 5, Item 1b; cited in McWilliams Tullberg, 1991: 235).

Apart from *The Economics of Industry*, Mary Marshall's bibliography comes down to two contributions in the *Economic Journal*. In March 1896, she reviewed some of the papers presented at the "Conference of Women Workers" held at Nottingham in October 1895 under the aegis of the National Council of Women. The most substantial section of her review consisted in a critique of Beatrice Webb's plea for "Further restrictions on women's labour" (B. Webb, 1896). She mentioned "more moderate advocates" of such restrictions, among whom her own husband, in his *Principles of Economics*, presented the regulation of women's labour as a necessary condition to enable women to perform properly their maternal and domestic duties (A. Marshall, 1890, vol. 1: 69, 685). Six years later, in 1902, she reviewed Clara Collet's book *Educated Working Women*, a collection of some of Collet's papers. In her review, she agreed wholeheartedly with Collet's idea that there are natural differences between men's and women's intellects which lead them to exercise different and complementary occupations, rather than to be in competition (M. P. Marshall, 1902: 252).

So, Mary Marshall was not inclined to voice her opinions loud and clear. And some of her words were clearly taken from her husband. Nevertheless, her exceptional devotion for Alfred Marshall did not prevent her having personal ideas, in particular on women's education and wages. A paragraph of *The Economics of Industry*, which focused on the inequalities between men's and women's wages, disappeared totally in Alfred Marshall's *Principles of Economics*, although this book was supposed to enrich the previous one. This suggests that the paragraph was largely based on Mary Marshall's ideas.

Mary Paley Marshall on inequalities of wages between the sexes

The object of the paragraph about inequalities between men's and women's wages is to identify the sources of the wage discrimination[10] which affected women on the labour market. No principles-writing economist had addressed the subject since John Stuart Mill, who devoted a chapter of the *Principles of Political Economy* to the study of the causes of women's low wages (Mill, 1848: 337–8).

The main idea defended in the paragraph is that a great part of women's relative low wages comes from custom and general opinion, despite equal productivity:

> In England many women get low wages, not because the value of the work they do is low, but because both they and their employers have been in the habit of taking it for granted that the wages of women must be low. Sometimes even when men and women do the same work in the same factory, not only the Time-wages, but also the Task-wages of the women are lower than those of the men.
>
> *A. and M. P. Marshall, 1879: 175–6*

This departure from a marginal productivity determination of wages is explained by several factors. To the extent in which differences in pay are due to "custom", they would decrease through "the progress of intelligence" and the "habits of competition" (A. and M. P. Marshall, 1879: 176). However, an important part of the differences is due to causes of a permanent character. Employers "say that if a man and a woman are equally good workers, the woman is of less service in the long run" (ibid.: 176). A woman's thoughts are considered more likely to be occupied about her home rather than her work abode and her work is "more liable to be interrupted than that of a man" (ibid.: 176). Moreover, women would have "on the whole less persistence, and less judgment and resource in cases of difficulty" (ibid.: 176). As a result, "the employer often prefers to have men, because he can select from them foremen and overlookers as well as workers in those branches of the business in which discretion is wanted" (ibid.: 176). Women would also be at a disadvantage in many kinds of work which, while generally regarded as light, "occasionally require the use of great physical strength, and perhaps the working overtime in special emergencies" (ibid.: 176). In the end, the occupations for which women are well fitted are few. They therefore are "overcrowded and badly paid", the excess of labour supply inducing a decrease of labour productivity and wages (ibid.: 176). Then, this fact "influences custom and general opinion, and causes women to be underpaid when they are doing difficult work well" (ibid.: 176). While the law of normal wages implies that "[t]rades in the same industrial grade generally required an equally difficult and expensive education and have equal wages", this is not the rule with regard to women's wages (ibid.: 131). In their case, custom and tradition are greater determinants than actual productivity.

The last part of the *Principles*' paragraph shows that the effects of the occupational segregation on women's wages are decreasing with the progress of society. First, "the progress of science and machinery is opening out to women many new occupations", as telegraphy or lighter metal trades, "in which very little physical strength is required" (ibid.: 176). Second,

> the progress of education is fitting women to do more difficult work and is making them more ready to demand, and employers more ready to grant them higher wages for it: and it is much increasing their employment in the higher part of the work of education itself
>
> *Ibid.: 176*

Third, "the progress of enlightenment" is breaking down barriers, as "prejudice, and trades union rules", which limit women's entry in "a very few occupations for which they are well fitted", in particular the "medical treatment of women and children" (ibid.: 176). Last, the paragraph forecasts a gradual increase of women's employment in works of business management (ibid.: 176–7).

Several elements indicate that the ideas expressed in this paragraph are rather those of Mary Marshall. The emphasis on women's access to education and on the increase of their employment in the higher part of the work of education is in line with her proper experience. In contrast, Alfred Marshall's position on these subjects changed rapidly. He refrains totally in his ulterior works from addressing the question of the inequalities between the sexes on the labour market, rather insisting on the fact that women's place is, above all else, at home. The ideas contained in the paragraph contrast clearly with those that Alfred Marshall defends less than ten years after in his *Principles of Economics*. In this book, he affirms that too high wages can lead women "to neglect their duty of building up a true home, and of investing their efforts in the Personal capital of their children's character and abilities" (A. Marshall, 1890, vol. 1: 685). In order to oblige women to stay at home, he preconizes the control of their wages (Pujol, 1992: 128). As for Mary Marshall, she remained all through her life an active champion of women's education and of the increase of their employment, particularly in the domains of teaching and business management. For example, in her review of Collet's book *Educated Working Women*, she agrees with Collet's plea for the introduction of women in business and in factory management (M.P. Marshall, 1902: 256).

To sum up, if Mary Marshall had probably the means to engage in a career as an economist, she used her talents, beyond a successful career as teacher, for contributing to her husband's works as assistant rather than as collaborator. This can be explained by the circumstances of the time – women had only just been introduced into the sphere of high studies and still met great difficulties in being admitted to the same positions as men – by her marriage to a man who quickly adopted a one-way vision of intellectual partnership, and by her own personality, which was discreet and opposed to conflict. A question nevertheless arises: could Alfred Marshall have had the same career without his wife helping him and taking care of him?

Beatrice Potter Webb was only eight years younger than Mary Marshall. However, her character, experience and inclinations were quite different. While a professional career and a happy marriage were thought to be incompatible for women at the time, she had both.

Beatrice Potter Webb

On 8 March 1889, Beatrice Potter, future Beatrice Webb, recounted in her diary a particular piece of advice from Alfred Marshall concerning her research interests:

> There is one thing that you, and only you can do – an inquiry into that unknown field of female labour. You have (unlike most women) a fairly trained intellect, and the courage and capacity for original work, and yet you have an insight into a woman's life. There is no man in England who could undertake with any prospect of success an inquiry into female labour [. . .] A book by you on the Co-operative movement I may get my wife to read to me in the evening to while away the time, but I shan't pay any attention to it.
>
> *B. Webb, 1926: 398–9*

Yet, making choices contrary to Alfred Marshall's advice, Beatrice Webb received the highest recognition as an economist among the three women considered here. Several facts proved her acceptance by academics. She was the first woman to be elected a Fellow of the British Academy in 1930. She was Visitor of the London School of Economics, a high honour, and was also invited by the School from the early years of its foundation to come and speak on various subjects, contributed a standard teaching practice of a series of five lectures on a specialist subject. In 1909, she gained an honorary doctorate from the University of Manchester for the Commission on the Poor Law's Minority Report that she submitted.

Beatrice Webb was born in 1858 in an affluent upper-middle-class family of radical dissenters. She was "educated at home by governesses, by extensive travel on the continent and by a wide and serious range of reading" (Hamilton, 1959: 936). She received her earliest political inspirations through discussions with her father's distinguished visitors, including Herbert Spencer. One of her first contributions was to assist her cousin Charles Booth in carrying out his immense and pioneering survey of the Victorian slums of London, which eventually became the massive 17-volume *Life and Labour of the People in London* (1902–1903). She contributed research into the conditions of labour for homeworkers in the East End garment trade. In 1887, she published an article, entitled "Dock Life in East London". The following year, five of her articles on sweated labour had been published. She began to enjoy a reputation as a knowledgeable social scientist and gave evidence before the House of Lords Select Committee on the Sweating System (Magill *et al.*, 1999: 3905).

Beatrice Webb also participated in philanthropic work carried out by the Charity Organisation Society based in London. She was rapidly critical of the usual modus operandi of charitable work which, according to her, was ineffective to improve the condition of the vast numbers of the poor. She thus started to give priority to the understanding of the causes of poverty in order to use charity "as a means to prevent poverty, not just relieve it" (Cicarelli and Cicarelli, 2003: 217). She visited incognito relatives of her family who lived in the industrial towns of Lancashire and discovered the labouring class and its organisations. Her experiences with workers in sweatshops led her to conclude that "destitution is a disease of society itself" and resulted in the publication of her first book, *The Co-operative Movement in Great Britain*, in 1891 (B. Webb, 1948: x). In this book, she coined the terms "co-operative federalism" and "co-operative individualism". She identified herself as a co-operative federalist, advocating consumer co-operative societies. Her research on co-operative societies led her to study another form of working-class organisation: the trade unions. The task of gathering information about these "democracies of producers" proved more complicated than the job she did for the "democracies of consumers" (S. and B. Webb, 1921: vi). She thus looked for help and was recommended to Sidney Webb in 1890. His name was then moderately well known in circles interested in social reform. Introduced in 1884 to the Fabian Society, which was founded in 1883, he rapidly became a member of its executive committee and started to write and to lecture for the Society. It was through him that Beatrice came into contact with the Fabian Society. Married in June 1892 when Beatrice Webb was 34 years old, they shared from that time on professional and political activities.

The Webb partnership

Contrary to Taylor and Mill, Beatrice and Sidney Webb enjoyed a reputation for truly shared work. Their biographer Mary Agnes Hamilton has described their partnership in the following terms:

> It is not only that they have written, together, books in which no one can detach what belongs to one from what belongs to the other [. . .] They are in fact [. . .] the brightest example of what she has called a "double-star-personality, the light of one being indistinguishable from that of the other".
>
> *Hamilton, 1932: 1–2*

The first product of the Webb partnership was a book in the field of economic history: *The History of Trade Unionism*, published in 1894. It was followed in 1897 by *Industrial Democracy*, which, as a sequel to the preceding study, was devoted to an analysis of the structure, function and theory of trade unionism (Cicarelli and Cicarelli, 2003: 218). The book recommended the transformation of some of the doctrines of British trade unionism to put them in conformity with modern democratic principles. It contained policy proposals addressed to the government, defending the idea of a "national minimum" necessary to prevent poverty (ibid.: 218). Two years after, in 1899, the Webbs began a great study of the history and problems of English local governing bodies, called later "democracies of citizens". This study resulted in ten large volumes published at intervals between 1906 and 1929, in addition to some half-dozen smaller books on specialized local government problems. In 1921, they returned to the study of the associations of consumers and published *The Consumer's Cooperative Movement* (S. and B. Webb, 1921: vi). In 1928, they retired to Hampshire and lived there until their deaths in the 1940s. After the fall of the second minority Labour government, their interest turned to the Soviet Union, where, during travel in 1932, they virtually discovered a Fabian paradise. This led them to their last large-scale book, *Soviet Communism: A New Civilisation?* published in 1935, which was strongly criticized for its reckless glorification of the Soviet economic experiment. In particular, their denial of the famine and defence of Stalin's purges and show trials was a dramatic shift from their long upholding of Fabianism rather than revolution.

The Webb partnership was also effective in the creation of social institutions and political activism. In 1895, they co-founded the London School of Economics and Political Science. Their other major achievements were the co-founding in 1913 of the *New Statesman*, a weekly review of politics, and of the Fabian Research Department, with a view to providing information to support trade union activity and campaigns. In 1914, they became members of the Labour Party. Some years later, Beatrice Webb collaborated with her husband in his writings as Fabian representative on the Executive Committee of the Labour Party, which include the policy statement *Labour and the New Social Order* (1918).

Moreover, Beatrice and Sidney Webb did not neglect questions related to women, whether it be in partnership or independently (Nyland and Ramia, 1994). Beatrice Webb already showed a concern for working-class women's living conditions before she met Sidney Webb[11] (ibid.: 110–11). One year after their meeting, in 1891, Sidney Webb wrote an article upon the "Alleged Differences in Wages Paid to Women and Men for Similar Work". The paper indicated several possible causes of the inferiority of women's wages, namely custom and public opinion, lower standard, lower productivity and lack of protective power (S. Webb, 1891: 660–1). In 1896, Beatrice Webb argued in favour of the legal regulation of wage-earning women's hours and conditions of labour in a plea entitled "Women and the Factory Acts".[12] She then explained that such a regulation induced more advantages than free competition supported by liberal feminists. According to her, it promoted (female) workers' economic independence and industrial efficiency (B. Webb, 1896: 4). The question of sex equality was also directly included in Beatrice and Sidney Webb's preoccupations. Deploring the sweating system, they pointed out the disastrous effect of unrestrained competition on the lives of the many thousands of workers in the sweated trades, especially on women. Between 1905 and 1909, they wrote together a Minority Report of which the purpose, according to Beatrice Webb, was to call for policies designed to "secure a national minimum of civilised life [. . .] open to all alike, of both sexes and all classes" (B. Webb, 1948: 481–2).[13] Then, over the years, Beatrice Webb became somewhat more involved in the women's movement. In 1914, she published five papers about women's "Personal rights and the Woman's Movement". The last two papers dealt with women's rights to unrestricted entry into all occupations and to equal remuneration with men under a national minimum wage. In 1919, she wrote a Minority Report published under the title "The Wages of Men and Women: Should They Be Equal?" Nothing indicates that Sidney Webb contributed to this report. While it contains ideas that Sidney shared with Beatrice, notably on destitution and the need of a national minimum, it conveys also a more personal evolution in Beatrice Webb's ideas.

Beatrice Webb's Minority Report on men's and women's wages

In 1918, the War Cabinet Committee on Women in Industry appointed a Committee "to investigate and report on the relation which should be maintained between the wages of women and men having regard to the interests of both as well as to the value of their work" (B. Webb, 1919: 3). Beatrice Webb was "unable to agree with the Majority Report" which was produced by the Committee, "either in its scope and substance, or in its conclusions and recommendations" (ibid.: 7). She thus wrote the Minority Report in which she proposes her own recommendations about "the relation that should prevail in future between men's and women's wages" (ibid.: 4).

In her report, Beatrice Webb links the problem of the inequality between men's and women's wages to the more general question of the inequality between capitalists' and labourers' incomes:

> The present inequality between men's and women's earnings – an inequality without any relation to their respective efforts and sacrifices – is only part of a larger question, the inequality between the incomes of those who live by owning and organising the instruments of production, and the incomes of those who live by using these instruments.
>
> *B. Webb, 1919: 5*

Challenging "The formula of 'Equal pay for Equal Work'", that she considers too ambiguous and easy to get round by employers, she argues that wages must be determined by the occupational rate (ibid.: 21–4, 46–8).

She first affirms that "[t]he principle of individual bargaining" must be rejected (ibid.: 7–8). According to her,

> experience has demonstrated [. . .] that to leave the determination of wages, in a capitalist organisation of industry, to the unfettered operation of "individual bargaining" in the "higgling of the market" between individual employers and individual wage-earners, is to produce, in the community, a large area of "sweating".
>
> *Ibid.: 9, 27–8*

Instead of payments settled by individual bargaining, an occupational rate must be fixed by collective bargaining "between representative organisations of the employers and the employed" in all occupational grades (ibid.: 31, 72). This "principle of collective bargaining and of the occupational rate" would address the need for "minimum conditions of service" (ibid.: 11). As Beatrice Webb explains, "[t]he argument in favour of a common standard rate as a minimum for each occupational grade [. . .]" is "much the same as that in favour of the national minimum, only stronger" (ibid.: 28, 30).

Other reasons, "applicable both to manual workers and to brainworkers", justify the existence of "an occupational rate" (ibid.: 32). If the employer must pay the standard rate as a minimum to every person engaged, "he will be continually seeking to pick, for the common price, the most efficient worker" (ibid.: 31). The enforcement of standard conditions of employment makes for maximum production in the sense that it affects positively the productivity of industry through "increased efficiency in the selection of the workers and the stimulus to their progressive improvement" (ibid.: 32).

Nevertheless, Beatrice Webb condemns the fact that, "at present", the principle of the occupational rate leads to a female rate and to a male rate:

> The determination of wages by the occupational rate operates [. . .] largely to keep down women's wages in relation to men's. For reasons into which we need not here enter, women have so far been unable to make as much use as men of collective bargaining or political pressure, and they have found the balance of power against them.
>
> *B. Webb, 1919: 13*

She mentions some additional influences that have "tended to lower the occupational rates for women, as compared with those for men" (B. Webb, 1919: 13). First, she explains that "the more or less adjustment of money wages to the cost of living has worked against women" (ibid.: 13). For her, the principle of raising money wages in correspondence with any substantial increase in the cost of living must apply equally to men's and women's wages. Second, she considers that "[t]he principle of determining wages by [the extent of] family obligations" must be rejected (ibid.: 13). She criticizes the assumption that women, contrary to men, have no family obligations, which is used as "an argument in favour of a lower national minimum and lower occupational rates for women than for men" (ibid.: 16, 44). Last, Beatrice Webb objects to the maintenance of "[t]he principle of the vested interest of the male". She disapproves "[t]he long-continued exclusion of women from nearly all the better-paid occupations", which "has been largely the result of the assumption that these occupations were the sacred preserve of men" (ibid.: 17, 20). To prevent women accessing better-paid occupations is not only a restriction of their liberty, but is also damageable from an economic point of view: "any such narrowing of the field of selection, and any such limitation of choice of occupation, necessarily detracts, to an unknown degree, from that utilisation to the fullest extent of every available talent upon which maximum productivity depends" (ibid.: 44). It is necessary to open "all posts and vocations to any individuals who are qualified for the work, irrespective of sex, creed or race" (ibid.: 72). The best utilisation of the available talents in society would be guaranteed by the extension to all kinds of occupations of "the principle of making employment conditional on the possession of a specific technical qualification for the calling" (ibid.: 20). Brain-working as well as manual occupations would become professions requiring "a prescribed minimum of technical efficiency" (ibid., 45).

Beatrice Webb's opposition to the existence of a male rate and a female rate reflects an evolution in her views. It coincides with a reversal of her opinion upon regulation of women's work; she indeed maintains in her report that there is no case for a sex-specific protective labour law (B. Webb, 1919: 10, 40; Nyland and Ramia, 1994: 138). It eliminates also any margin for concession. In *Industrial Democracy*, Beatrice and Sidney Webb accepted the idea that segregation, or the existence of male and female occupations paid at different rates, was justified by women's lesser strength and skill (B. and S. Webb, 1897: 506–7; Nyland and Ramia, 1994: 128, 138). In her 1919 report, Beatrice Webb denounces the fact that the segregation of men and women in industry caused by the First World War, whether it "was influenced by custom and convention, or determined by relative aptitude", has given rise to "markedly different rates of remuneration for what was recognised as a 'man's job' and what as a 'woman's job'" (B. Webb, 1919: 19). In "Personal Rights and the Woman's Movement" (1914), Beatrice Webb conceded, although reluctantly, that it was still necessary to maintain a separate female and male standard rate in many trades in which women could be hired only by taking employment for less than the standard rate (Nyland and Ramia, 1994: 140). In her Minority Report, she advocates the enforcement of identical occupational rates and admits no exception to the rule (B. Webb, 1919: 35–9):

> The existence within any one occupational grade of higher and lower rates of wages, or of special deductions which make it equally profitable to the employer to engage at the lower rate, or with the deductions, workers of relatively inferior efficiency – and, as must inevitably happen, sometimes in the employer's opinion, even more profitable – is accordingly positively inimical to maximum production. The proposal to allow a lower occupational rate, or exceptional deductions from that rate, for women than for men engaged in the same occupational grade must therefore be definitely condemned.
>
> *B. Webb, 1919: 3*

She explains at the end of the report that it is necessary, in order to reduce "the chaos in which the relative earnings of individuals and classes had been left" by the War, to adopt an "additional principle of general application", "on which the relation between [sexes] can be based", namely that of "a closer correspondence of occupational rates to relative efforts and needs" of all grades and sections of the wage-earning population (ibid.: 53–4, 56).

Conclusion

The contributions of Harriet Taylor Mill, Mary Paley Marshall and Beatrice Potter Webb to the development of economic knowledge vary greatly. This is in part linked to the different nature of the marital partnerships that they experienced with prominent male economists. While Taylor and Webb had partners who supported their complete intellectual engagement, Marshall's husband denied her advanced intellectual participation after the initial stage of their relationship.

Taylor's work as a researcher took diverse forms after her encounter with J. S. Mill. Nowadays, she is largely recognised as the author of *Enfranchisement of Women*. She collaborated also in J. S. Mill's philosophical and economics books. Her contribution was in part hidden with a strategic purpose, few men being then ready to recognise women as colleague economists. Mill later affirmed in his autobiography that she contributed greatly to several works published under his name, including the *Principles of Political Economy*. He asserted that the chapter on the futurity of the labouring classes issued from her mind. A close reading of this chapter in parallel with the *Enfranchisement of Women* confirms this statement, while it clarifies Taylor's contribution to socialism and to the question of inequalities between men and women.

Born 43 years after Taylor, Mary Marshall undertook graduate studies at one of the first women's colleges, Newnham College, founded in 1871. She thus was trained to become an economist. However, her contribution to the development of economic thought was limited by her husband's refusal to live with a competitor; he demanded a "true wife". After the young couple's joint production, *The Economics of Industry*, her name disappeared from her husband's works. Although she assumed conscientiously the role of assistant, her help was not fully recognised. So, her major contribution as an economist appears in *The Economics of Industry*. In addition to writing the first chapters, she most likely instigated the paragraph examining the economic and social factors of the inferiority of women's wages.

Contrary to Mary Marshall, who was only eight years her senior, Beatrice Potter Webb did not undertake formal economics studies. During her youth, she met eminent thinkers of her father's circle and early on was involved in the field of social research, contributing notably to Charles Booth's *Life and Labour of the People in London*. After her marriage to Sidney Webb, she co-authored many books with him. Beatrice and Sidney Webb shared socialist ideas and concern for working-class women's condition. They addressed this topic in co-productions and in separate works. Beatrice published several pamphlets on the subject and, in 1919, wrote a Minority

Report about the relation between men's and women's wages. In comparison to her preceding works, this report gives insight into the evolution of her ideas on women. Nevertheless, Beatrice's writings on women were only a small part of a substantial contribution to socialist thought, which put her among the first women economists to be really recognised contributors.

The three women's personal circumstances, including early family environment, individual skills and intellectual stimulation supported their aptitude for economic reasoning. But Webb made more effective contributions than Taylor, and Taylor made greater contributions than Marshall. During the 1800s and early 1900s, women were at the mercy of circumstances. Timing meant Taylor was less able to be recognised as an economist than Webb. Women's romantic involvement also had consequences for their contributions to economics. Women were at the mercy of their partners' inclinations, well illustrated in Marshall's case.

Additional differences might have influenced the nature of the three women's marital relationships and contributions to economic thought. While it is difficult to distinguish differences of intellectual capital, some contrasts are apparent in the women's characters and convictions. First, Taylor and Webb had big personalities and were surely less accommodating than Marshall. Second, Taylor and Webb constructed and defended socialist ideas. While Taylor's contribution in this domain has been recognised with difficulty even by male liberal economists, Webb's fame as a Fabian socialist was almost immediate. It would be interesting to consider in future work whether mutual support for intellectual endeavours is more likely among couples, and whether women were more "easily" accepted as researchers, within socialist rather than liberal spheres.

Notes

1 Before his marriage to Harriet Taylor, Mill wrote a text (*Statement on Marriage*, 6 March, 1851) in which he morally renounced the powers that the law would give him over Taylor in case of marriage (Mill, [1984]: 99):

> [T]he whole character of the marriage relation as constituted by law being such as both she and I entirely and conscientiously disapprove, for this among other reasons, that it confers upon one of the parties to the contract, legal power and control over the person, property, and freedom of action of the other party, independent of her own wishes and will; I, having no means of legally divesting myself of these odious powers (as I most assuredly would do if an engagement to that effect could be made legally binding on me), feel it my duty to put on record a formal protest against the existing law of marriage, in so far as conferring such powers; and a solemn promise never in any case or under any circumstances to use them.
>
> *Mill, 1963–1991, vol. XXI: 99*

2 On Taylor's socialism, see Hayek (1951: 17–18, 117–51), Peart (2014, Editor's introduction), Pujol (1995: 84, 95) and Forget (2003). This socialist influence might explain the scepticism of several members of the *Philosophic Radicals* against her.

3 Four editions of the *Principles* (1848, 1849, 1852, 1857) were published before Taylor's death, while three were published posthumously (1862, 1865, 1871).

4 The passage *–* was added in the 1852 edition of *Principles*, one year after the publication of *Enfranchisement of Women*, and remained in the later editions of 1857, 1862, 1865 and 1871.

5 Mill, in *The Subjection of Women*, written in 1859 and published in 1869, would never treat the categories of class and sex simultaneously.

6 Unlike Taylor, Mill distinguished two states of things. In the unjust conditions which then prevailed, he considered it preferable that wives contribute to the family income, even if "no more is earned by the labour of a man and a woman than would have been earned by the man alone" (Mill, 1848: 394). In a just state of things, where legal equality between spouses would have been established, he recommended the traditional sexual division of labour between husband and wife, by which the man is the sole breadwinner (Mill, 1869: 483–4).

7 An analogous reference to the distinction of sex as "accidental" is made in *Enfranchisement of Women* (Taylor, 1851: 96).
8 On Mary Marshall's career as a teacher, see McWilliams Tullberg, 1995: 155–64.
9 The small book's full designation is *Elements of the Economics of Industry*, but the spine bears the title *Economics of Industry*.
10 The term discrimination refers here to differences in wage rates for equally productive groups of workers.
11 A debate exists on Beatrice Webb's feminism. In 1889, she signed an article opposing women's right to vote. Even if she later publicly retracted this, her act has induced commentators such as Caine and Pujol to call into doubt her feminism (Caine, 1982; Pujol, 1992: 84). Unlike them, Nyland presents her as a socialist feminist (Nyland and Ramia, 1994: 125; Nyland, 1994).
12 This plea was strongly criticized by Mary Marshall (see previous section).
13 In 1905 Beatrice was appointed to the Royal Commission on the Poor Law and Relief of Distress. For four years, she headed the production of the Minority Report, which called for reform of the Poor Law system and established the foundation of the modern Welfare State in Britain. Although Sidney was not a member of the Commission, they co-produced the report (Nyland and Ramia, 1994: 130).

References

Booth, Charles (1902–1903). *Life and Labour of the People in London*. London and New York: Macmillan.

Caine, Barbara (1982). Beatrice Webb and the "Woman Question". *History Workshop Journal*, (14) (Autumn): 23–43.

Cicarelli, James and Cicarelli, Julianne (2003). *Distinguished Women Economists*. Westport, CT: Greenwood Press.

Collet, Clara E. (1902). *Educated Working Women*. London: P. S. King and Son.

Dimand, Mary Ann, Dimand, Robert W. and Forget, Evelyn L. (1995). *Women of Value: Feminist Essays on the History of Women in Economics*. Aldershot: Edward Elgar.

Dimand, Robert W. and Nyland, Chris (2003). *The Status of Women in Classical Economic Thought*. Northampton and Cheltenham: Edward Elgar.

Forget, Evelyn L. (2003). John Stuart Mill, Harriet Taylor and French Social Theory. In Dimand and Nyland (2003), pp. 285–310.

Groenewegen, Peter D. (1993). A Weird and Wonderful Partnership: Mary Paley and Alfred Marshall 1877–1924. *History of Economic Ideas*, 1(1): 71–109.

—— (1994). *Feminism and Political Economy in Victorian England*. Aldershot: Edward Elgar.

Hamilton, Mary Agnes (1932). *Sidney and Beatrice Webb: A Study in Contemporary Biography*. London: Sampson Low, Marston & Co.

—— (1959). WEBB, (Martha) Beatrice (1858–1943) – under "WEBB, Sidney James". In *Oxford Dictionary of National Biography*. Oxford: Oxford University Press, 2004.

Hayek, F. A. (1951). *John Stuart Mill and Harriet Taylor: Their Correspondence and Subsequent Marriage*. Chicago, IL: The University of Chicago Press.

Jacobs, Jo Ellen (1998). *The Complete Works of Harriet Taylor Mill*. Bloomington: Indiana University Press.

Keynes, John Maynard (1944). Mary Paley Marshall. *Economic Journal*, 54(214): 268–84. Reprinted in *Essays in Biography*, edited by Geoffrey Keynes. New York: The Norton Library, 1958, pp. 232–50.

Magill, Frank N., Moose, Christina J., Aves, Alison and Rehn, Mark (1999). *Dictionary of World Biography – Vol. IX: The 20th Century O–Z*. New York and Oxon: Routledge.

Marshall, Alfred (1890). *Principles of Economics*. 9th edition (variorum), edited by C. W. Guillebaud, 2 vols. London and New York: Macmillan, 1961.

—— (1892). *Elements of the Economics of Industry*. London: Macmillan.

—— (1919). *Industry and Trade*. London: Macmillan.

—— (1923). *Money, Credit and Commerce*. London: Macmillan.

Marshall, Alfred and Marshall, Mary Paley (1879). *The Economics of Industry*. London: Macmillan. Reprinted with a new intro. by D. P. O'Brien. Bristol: Thoemmes Press, 1994.

—— and —— (1881). *The Economics of Industry*. Revised edition. London: Macmillan.

Marshall, Mary Paley (1896). Notes and Memoranda: Conference of Women Workers. *The Economic Journal*, 6(21): 107–9.

—— (1902). Book Review of "Educated Working Women" by Clara E. Collet. *The Economic Journal*, 12(46): 252–7.

—— (1947). *What I Remember*. Cambridge: Cambridge University Press.

McWilliams-Tullberg, Rita (1991). Alfred Marshall and the Male Priesthood of Economics. *Quaderni di storia dell'economia politica*, 9(2/3), Vol. 1: Alfred Marshall's "Principles of Economics" 1890–1990: 235–68.
—— (1995). *Mary Paley Marshall, 1850–1944*. In Dimand, Dimand and Forget (1995). Aldershot: Edward Elgar, pp. 150–93.
Mill, John Stuart (1831–1832). *Essay on Marriage*. In Rossi (1970), pp. 65–87.
—— (1843). *A System of Logic, Ratiocinative and Inductive*. In *Collected Works of J. S. Mill*, Vol. VII [1973].
—— (1848). *The Principles of Political Economy, with Some of Their Applications to Social Philosophy*. 7th edition, 1871. In *Collected Works of J. S. Mill*, Vols II & III [1965].
—— (1859). *On Liberty*. In Mill, J. S. [1975], pp. 1–141.
—— (1869). *The Subjection of Women*. In Mill, J. S. [1975], pp. 427–548.
—— (1873). *Autobiography*. In *Collected Works of J. S. Mill*, Vol. I [1963], edited by J. M. Robson and J. Stillinger.
—— [1975]. *John Stuart Mill: Three Essays*. London: Oxford University Press.
—— [1984]. *Essays on Equality, Law and Education*. In *Collected Works of J. S. Mill*, Vol. XXI.
—— [1963–1991]. *The Collected Works of J. S. Mill*. 33 vols. Edited by John M. Robson. Toronto: University of Toronto Press and London: Routledge and Kegan Paul.
Nyland, Chris (1994). Beatrice Webb as feminist. *University of Wollongong (Department of Economics) Working paper series*. WP 94–3: 1–31.
Nyland, Chris and Ramia, Gaby (1994). The Webbs and the Rights of Women. In Groenewegen (1994), pp. 110–46.
Peart, Sandra (2014). *Hayek on Mill: The Mill-Taylor Friendship and Related Writings*. Chicago, IL: Chicago University Press.
Pujol, Michèle A. (1992). *Feminism and Anti-Feminism in Early Economic Thought*. Cheltenham and Northampton: Edward Elgar, 1998.
—— (1995). The Feminist Economic Thought of Harriet Taylor (1807–58). In Dimand, Dimand and Forget (1995), pp. 82–102.
Robson, Ann P. (2004). Mill, Harriet (1807–1858). *Oxford Dictionary of National Biography*. Oxford, UK: Oxford University Press, 2004.
Robson, John M. (1984). Textual Introduction to Mill's *Essays on Equality, Law and Education*. In *Collected Works of J. S. Mill*, Vol. XXI.
Rossi, Alice S. (1970). *Essays on Sex Equality, by John Stuart Mill and Harriet Taylor Mill*. Chicago and London: University of Chicago Press.
Taylor, Harriet (1831–1832). *Essay on Marriage*. In Rossi (1970), pp. 84–7.
—— (1851). *Enfranchisement of Women*. In Rossi (1970), pp. 89–121.
Webb, Beatrice Potter (1887). Dock Life in East London. *Nineteenth Century*, xxii.
—— (1891). *The Co-operative Movement in Great Britain*. London: Swan Sonnenschein & Company, Paternoster Square.
—— (1896). Women and the Factory Acts. *Fabian Tract No. 67*. London: The Fabian Society.
—— (1914). Personal Rights and the Woman's Movement. *The New Statesman*, 1 (August): 525–7.
—— (1919). The Wages of Men and Women: Should They Be Equal? *Minority Report*. London: The Fabian Society.
—— (1926). *My Apprenticeship*. Harmondsworth: Penguin Books Ltd, 1938.
—— (1948). *Our Partnership*. New York: Longmans, Green and Co.
Webb, Sidney James (1891). Alleged Differences in Wages Paid to Women and Men for Similar Work. *The Economic Journal*, 1(4): 635–62.
—— (1918). *Labour and the New Social Order: a Report on Reconstruction*. A Labour Party pamphlet. London: Labour Party.
Webb, Sidney James and Webb, Beatrice Potter (1894). *The History of Trade Unionism*. London and New York: Longmans and Co.
—— (1897). *Industrial Democracy*. London and New York: Longmans and Co.
—— (1921). *The Consumer's Cooperative Movement*. London and New York: Longmans and Co.
—— (1906–1929). *English Local Government*. London: Longmans and Co.
—— (1936). *Soviet Communism: A New Civilisation?* 2 vols. New York: Charles Scribner's Sons.

5

JAPANESE WOMEN'S ECONOMICS, 1818–2005[1]

Aiko Ikeo

Overview

The position of women in Japanese society has been shifting with changing international relations. As an island country, the opportunity of international exchange for the Japanese was extremely limited by the technology of sailing vessels prior to the steam engine. Peaceful cross-border activities were accomplished by a few correspondents (old diplomats), Buddhists, and adventurers. Turning points are witnessed in 1854 (the end of isolationist policy), 1868 (Meiji restoration), and 1945 (the conclusion of WWII).

Only a few documents preserve the thought of women of Japan from earlier millennia, but those contributions are noteworthy. *The Collection of Ten Thousand Leaves* (*Manyoshu*, 20 volumes, seventh–eighth centuries) preserved many *tanka* (short) poems, including works by the genius woman *tanka* poet Nukata-no-okimi (active in the seventh century). It is noteworthy that *tanka* composing and *tanka* rhythm were important parts of noble women's culture in Japan.[2] More than a dozen court ladies are known for their wonderful poems and/or diaries written based on the observation of seasonal connotation and elegant daily life inside the imperial house. The two women writers, Sei Shonagon (*c.*966–*c.*1025), who wrote *Pillow Book* and *Diary* (1008–10), and Murasaki Shikibu (*c.*973–*c.*1014), who authored *Tale of Genji* and *Diary and Poetic Memories*, are well known outside Japan.

Before 1603, both Kyoto and Nara served as the capital city. The imperial house was in Kyoto even during the Tokugawa period (1603–1867) while the Tokugawa shogunate situated its main castle in Edo (now Tokyo). The shogunate implemented an isolationist policy, with one notable exception which allowed for diplomatic relations with the Dutch in Dejima, Nagasaki. Its policies covered a ban on the construction of large sailing boats and bridges over rivers in Honshu (Japan's mainland). During the Tokugawa period, Confucian and Chinese books were imported via Nagasaki and read by Japanese male thinkers. The education for daughters differed from education for sons; women were expected to play the role of mother and wife inside "*ie*" (house/household). Against the isolationist policy and Confucian thought, Makuzu Tadano is the first woman of Japan to write a treatise on political economy, *Solitary Thoughts* (1818).

Japan's open-up policy of 1854 and the Meiji restoration of 1868 brought many changes to the country. Kikue Yamakawa, Koko Sanpei, and Setsu Tanino experienced and observed the changes happening both in women's social status and more generally throughout society. They eventually became leaders for women seeking equal rights after 1945, when Japan lost the Asia-Pacific campaign.

In the Meiji period, many men began to commute to their workplaces. Departing from the old, male-centered "*ie*" (family business) system, the government hoped to form the new "*ie*" system in which a man could work for a company or a public institution. Japanese household economics was innovated by Sumi Oe (the founder of *kaseigaku*, household management) and Tomoko Matsudaira (Ochanomizu University for women), who firmly connected *kaseigaku* and economics. It emphasizes house/household management (including business and assets). The roots of *kaseigaku* trace back into the household management explored by Ekiken Kaibara, a male Confucian scholar of the Tokugawa period. After 1945, Akiko Ito and Eiko Shinotsuka placed the household at the center of economic analysis. Further, Ito examined the standard of living and the weight of housing loan planning. It is noteworthy that parts of the analysis bear some resemblance to Gary Becker's *Human Capital* (1964), which focused on households and education, generating both empirical studies and theoretical discussion.

Political and educational reforms for equal rights for women were brought by the Allied occupation force from September 1945 to April 1952. In 1947 Japanese women finally obtained their right to vote. Also in 1947, many former male-only universities began to take women as regular students.[3] Keio University most attracted capable women, and the university welcomed and trained them to become professionals earlier than any other (formerly male) universities. Keio produced Yoko Sazanami (international economics) and Yoko Sano (human resource management), the first women economists in their respective fields. These formally trained women economists then encouraged younger economists (including Eiko Shinotsuka) to engage in advanced research. Using Gary Becker's phraseology, Shinotsuka became an economist through on-the-job-training at the Japan Center for Economic Research and came to contribute to the field of labor economics.[4]

Tokugawa period: the first woman *samurai*

Makuzu Tadano (1763–1825) and her Solitary Thoughts *(1818)*

Makuzu Tadano was the single powerful woman scholar of the isolationist Tokugawa period. She has received proper attention from several Japanese women historians. Yoneko Suzuki edited *A Collection of Makuzu Tadano* (1994) and included a survey of scholarly articles published before Tadano (1994). Then two excellent biographies, Bettina Gramlich-Oka (2006) and Tamiko Seki (2008) became available.

Makuzu Tadano was born to a daughter of the *samurai* medical practitioner Heisuke Kudo (1734–1800). Her mother was a daughter of a medical doctor in the Edo house of the Date Family of Sendai domain. Heisuke's library contained some books on Western medicine including the Japanese translation (1774) (from the Dutch translation) of Adam Kulmus' *Ontleedkundige Tafelen* (Anatomical Tables, 1722). Heisuke became famous by opening a medical school and publishing a hundred books on medicine. Well-informed people such as Japanese diplomats for the Dutch, and visitors from the Matsumae domain (which traded with Russia) assembled in Heisuke's house. Tadano (1812) wrote that Heisuke was acquainted with a Dutch man. Heisuke submitted his proposal "On the Information of Ezo" (1783) (including his suggestion for an open-up policy) to the Tokugawa shogunate, but it was forgotten due to a change in shogunate. The woman *tanka* poet Aoko taught Makuzu about composing poetry and reading Japanese classics including *Kokinshu* (a collection of *tanka* poetry from the tenth century). Makuzu listened to her brother Genshiro reading *the Analects of Confucius* aloud and thus received instruction in Confucian ethics. This was unusual because historically, Confucianism is substantially the domain of male scholarship.

Makuzu read books in her father's library and listened to the conversations and discussions between her father and other doctors on new medicines imported via Nagasaki from China and other countries. Medical doctors knew the merit of international trade and tended to support a more open policy, particularly for the importation of more medicines and books on medical science. They understood the disadvantages of trade restriction, although it is hard to tell how much they were concerned about higher domestic prices of medicine.

Moreover, Makuzu's economic discussion was heavily indebted to her father Heisuke's exposure to economics. It is noteworthy that Heisuke received lectures on international trade and taxation from Konyo Aoki (1698–1769). Aoki was one of the four shogunate officials who specialized in reading books (in Japanese, Chinese, and Dutch). His lectures seem to be based on Shundai Dazai (1680–1747).[5] Dazai's *On Political Economy* (1729) and its supplement discussed government policies, political economy (managing the economy and saving the people), the efficient utilization of domestic resources (land, talented people, and their skills), and the effect of trade with foreign countries.

In 1797, Makuzu married Iga Tadano, a *samurai* of Sendai, and moved there. After raising the children of Iga and his first wife, Makuzu spent her days writing *Old Stories* (1812) and *Solitary Thoughts* (1818).

Makuzu Tadano's *Solitary Thoughts* (1818) showed her knowledge of Western countries such as Russia and the Netherlands.[6] She confidently argued for the opening-up of Japan and maintained that international trade would bring benefit and enrich Japan. She paid attention to those products that were not produced in Japan and referred to the fact of foreigners carrying a watch because "Tadano recognized time as a crucial element of social conditions. Our idiom 'time is money' is useful in understanding how late Tokugawa society required a restructuring of time due to greater commercialization" (Gramlich-Oka 2006, p. 223). Tadano listed those products exported from Japan (via Nagasaki), namely gold, silver, copper, iron ore, and medicines. She noted that the sugar price was higher than the salt price in Japan whereas the opposite was true in some foreign countries. She wrote about the flow of money, the fluctuation of the prices of goods, and a steep rise in prices right after the event of a big fire. She described the competitive bidding for public construction of a castle and stated that the lowest bidder was to be selected for the project. Observing increasing competition for money among merchants and town people, she repeatedly mentioned that humans were fond of competition by their nature and that their behaviors were motivated to make more money by want. She maintained that if senior councilors and other officials start a business by being "wise men," they would be able to receive "just profit" and that their engagement in international trade would be able to enrich Japan.

Tadano highly valued only "sincerity" in "the way of sages" (Confucian classics), which discriminated against women throughout the literature. She argued that we should not apply Confucianism to Japan, Confucianism was "simply a system made by human beings and borrowed from China" (Gramlich-Oka 2006, p. 211). Her radical statement, "Both the teachings of Buddha and the way of the sages are systems created by human beings; they did not arise of their own accord," was often quoted by scholars (for example, Gramlich-Oka 2006, p. 212). Tadano evaluated the nativist Motoori Norinaga's *Commentary on the Records of Ancient Matters* (1798) and referred to *Tale of Genji, Ise Story*, and *Essays in Idleness*.[7]

Bakin Takizawa (1767–1848), who corresponded with Makuzu Tadano, published his "Commentary of Solitary Thoughts" in 1820. He quoted fully from Tadano's *Solitary Thoughts* (1818) and vehemently criticized her arguments with citations from Confucian literature. Takizawa's quotations tell us correctly that Tadano was opposed to both the caste system and the isolationist policy. Takizawa described her as "a woman thinking like a man," in praise of her.[8]

Women activists and the radical changes for women after 1854 and 1945

Japan abandoned its isolationist policy in 1854 and gradually opened its door to many countries. In 1867 the Tokugawa shogunate returned its power to the Japanese emperor, and in 1868 the new government came into power. This series of events is called the Meiji restoration. Three women (Kikue Yamakawa, Koko Sanpei, and Setsu Tanino) observed the radical changes triggered by the open-up policy of 1854 and later changes brought by the Allied occupation from September 1945 to April 1952. These three women raised concerns about the treatment of women in Japanese industry and were activists promoting better working conditions.

Kikue Yamakawa (1890–1980)

Kikue Yamakawa was a feminist activist, critic, and prolific writer through her whole life (Ikeo 2000c). She was concerned about the working conditions of women and the changing role of women in family life. She joined the women's liberation movement and the socialist movement in the 1920s, undertook a folklorist project around 1940, and became a civil servant at the Bureau of Women and Minors in the Ministry of Labor from 1947 to 1951.

Kikue Yamakawa's *Record of Women in Two Generations* (1956) describes the lives and experiences of her mother Chise Morita (1857–1947) and herself up to the 1940s. Chise Morita's father, Enju Aoyama, and three uncles were scholars of Chinese learning, edited *The Grand History of Japan* (397 volumes, 1657–1906), and taught at the School of Mito. The turbulent changes after 1854 brought civil war to Mito. Yamakawa (1974) tells us how she and her family survived the turmoil (Ikeo 2000c).

Kikue was born in Tokyo in 1890. She was the third child of Ryunosuke and Chise Morita who moved to Tokyo from Mito. From 1908 to 1912, Kikue studied at the Women's School for English Study (now Tsuda University).[9] In 1916 Kikue was married to Hiroshi Yamakawa (1880–1958), who was an intellectual leader of leftwing activists. Kikue suffered from tuberculosis soon after her marriage and recuperated in the suburbs of Tokyo. During WWI, Japan increased its exports of industrial goods to those countries to which the fighting European countries had decreased exports, such as India, and Japanese firms gained large profits. In contrast, the working conditions for Japanese laborers were worsened because their wages did not keep up with rising consumer prices.

During the period of her relatively good health, at the request of economist Tatsuo Morito, Kikue Yamakawa delivered a talk on "The problems of women at work" at a meeting of the Society of Social Policy in 1918. The transcript appeared in *Kokka-gakkai Zasshi*, the journal of the Law Department of the Imperial University of Tokyo (the University of Tokyo after 1947) in 1919. Her speech went as follows:

> "Woman at work" has become an issue since the industrial revolution. Capitalism has emerged in Japan. Now women participate in the workforce in the process of industrialization and continue to do household affairs and rear children. The on-going accumulation of capital and wealth has caused various problems differently among the women of middle and working classes. On one hand, later marriages are not unusual for women of the middle or bourgeois class because they become professional and earn

> enough to secure economic independence. On the other hand, a number of other (young) women together operate machines in a (for example, cotton) mill. Their poor working conditions have a grave influence on their mind and body, and cause various problems such as ill health, sterility, low birthrate, and a bad effect on our future generation as a whole. These women are low paid because they have no family to support.

It is not surprising that the protection of women workers became a topic at the first meeting of the International Labor Organization (ILO) in Washington D.C. However, the male delegates from Japan, representing the government, employers, and laborers, unanimously objected to the article of protection for women workers, by maintaining the uniqueness of Japanese circumstances. Nonetheless, Yamakawa's speech seems to have opened the door to a woman (Tomoko Matsudaira) to audit regular courses at the Imperial University of Tokyo. These special arrangements were necessary because the university did not allow women to enroll as regular students before 1947.

In 1923, the Tokyo metropolitan area was shaken by major earthquakes. Kikue, Hitoshi, and their son Shinsaku survived although their house collapsed. Kikue moved from Tokyo to Kobe to recuperate further when she managed to sell the lumber from her collapsed home.

In 1925 Kikue Yamakawa was back at the forefront of the women's liberation movement. At the time, she criticized the socialist men who were arguing for the abolition of the women's divisions in trade unions and were objecting to the organization of the women's allies. She continued to persuade socialist men of the importance of the particular problems of women in the course of the proletarian movement toward a socialist revolution. From the late 1920s, Kikue began to increase awareness of the situation of women. She translated feminist works by Mary Wollstonecraft, August Bebel, and Edward Carpenter.

Kikue Yamakawa took care of her sick son from 1930 until 1935. Losing the freedom of speech and press, Kikue and Hitoshi Yamakawa could not earn by writing any more. They began to keep quail, and sold their eggs to restaurants. Kikue and her son moved into a rural farming village, Okamura in Kamakura-gun, in 1936.

Encouraged by the folklorist Kunio Yanagita (1875–1962), Yamakawa published *Women of the Mito Domain* (1943a, 1992) and *The Village Where I Live* (1943b). She knew nothing about farming and had no friends when she moved into the village which was filled with native farmers. She learned about farming, conducted hearings with the village people she met, and collected the materials in a facility to which a researcher in the Ministry of Health and Welfare had given her access. Yamakawa (1943b) included both the description of the lives of the village people and the oral history narrated by them to her.

In August 1945, the Pacific campaign ended. In 1947, the Ministry of Labor which included the Bureau of Women and Minors was established. Kikue Yamawaka was appointed the first Director-General of the Bureau, and boldly decided to give the nearly 250 staff positions in prefectural offices only to women, after becoming irritated by receiving the recommendations only for male candidates (Tanino, 1982). In 1952, Yamakawa agreed to resign from the position, when it was "recommended" she do because she did not pass the civil servants' examinations.

After that, Yamakawa participated in many activities supporting women's liberation and continued to publish many books (Yamakawa, 1956, 1974). In 1981 ten volumes of her *Collected Works of Kikue Yamakawa* were published with one supplement.

Koko (Takako) Sanpei (1903–78)

Koko Sanpei was an economic historian. Born in Fukushima in 1903, she graduated from Tokyo Women's Christian University in 1928 and then studied as an auditor in the School of Economics and Political Science of Waseda University from 1928 until 1931. In 1931 she became a researcher in the Takahashi Institute for Economic Research and in 1940 she joined the Japan Institute of Labor Science. She did fieldwork on rural villages and factories with the aim of improving working conditions. After WWII, she became a member of the Employment Security Council at the Tokyo Prefectural Labor Office in 1948, and a member of the Minimum Wage Council at the Ministry of Labor in 1952 (Ikeo 2000a).

Sanpei's first book *The Historical Development of the Cotton Spinning Industry in Japan* (1941) is regarded as the first masterpiece produced by a Japanese woman in the field of economic history. Sanpei uncovered the fact that women were the main workforce in Japan's cotton-spinning industry, which was the key sector in Japan's early capitalist economy. She described the introduction of a modern spinning technique into Japan by the government around 1870. She observed that the gradual diffusion of modern techniques and machines was accompanied by a fall in home manufacturing of cotton handicraft and the decline of hand looms in rural areas. Cotton growing in Japan decreased as imports from India increased. Later Sanpei (1961) included statistical data and a chronological table of the weaving and textile industry in Japan.

Sanpei (1941) discussed in detail the fierce competition between Lancashire (England) and Japan over India's cotton cloth market, especially in the early 1930s (Ikeo 2000a). Sanpei's *Rise and Fall of Home Manufacturing and Industries in Japan* (1944) traced the historical changes in Japan's six major traditional industries (indigo blue dye, Japanese paper, lacquer, green tea, rapeseed oil, and china and porcelain) from the closed-door era (1639–1854) to the modernization period (Ikeo 2000a).

Sanpei's *History of Working Women* (1956) was one of the best books for enlightening women. It was published with the strong encouragement of Kikue and Hiroshi Yamakawa. She traced the process of women's participation as the labor force and their conditions before, during, and after WWII. When Japan started the war against China in 1937 and restricted the production of cotton goods for private use, many women lost their jobs in the textile industry. At the same time, men were drafted and sent off to war. As a result, women had to fill the positions that had been occupied by men. Twenty percent of the jobless women from the textile industry began to engage in farming in their home villages. The remaining 80 percent plus many housewives were forced to work in the munitions factories and in heavy industry. This was work which had previously been believed to be impossible for women to engage in.

Sanpei (1956, p. 134) writes:

> The war brought women from the home to the workplace, and a new variety of workplace at that. The prejudice that women were neither good at nor able to work outside the home had been overcome. Women themselves learned from their experience that they can do many things that men can if only they get the relevant training and the doors are open to them. Women can become liberated by getting themselves jobs and earning a wage. This was the major turning point in the history of Japanese women.

Nonetheless, those women were removed from their jobs after the war concluded and men came back home.

Setsu Tanino (Setsuko Ochiai) (1903–99)

Setsu Tanino (Setsuko Ochiai) was born in Chiba Prefecture in 1903, and graduated from the Department of Social Work in Japan Women's University in 1926. She unexpectedly found a job in the Ministry of Home Affairs, the most powerful ministry in pre-WWII Japan. She became the first woman probationary factory supervisor in 1928. At that time, Japan was regularly criticized internationally (including by the ILO) for the practice of night work and long hours. Inside Japan, the necessity for a female factory supervisor was realized by male factory supervisors and scholars based on their voluntary inspection of textile mills. Men could not observe the real working and living conditions of women workers, especially in the textile industry, because 80 percent of workers were from remote villages and lived in company residences. Tanino was the only woman (probationary) factory supervisor during the 1930s when the function of the factory supervisor increased in importance in Japan's rapidly developing industrial society (Ikeo 2000b).

Tanino wrote reports on the conditions of working women based on documents sent from factories. She also stayed in the residence of a spinning mill (usually overnight and once for a month) to experience night work with women workers. She occasionally conducted "surprise" inspections of mills to investigate the real working conditions of women. Her reports and articles appeared in several governmental journals such as *Industrial Welfare, Social Works*, and *Welfare Japan*. Yet a report on extremely miserable working conditions was not published until 1985 (Tanino *c.*1936).

Tanino and Suzuki's "On the effect of the prohibition of night work" (1931) is a summary of her investigation of the production and the workers' physical conditions in the textile industry during September and December 1929 after women's and minors' night work was legally prohibited in July 1929. The actual results crucially depended on the operating speed of spindles and crankshafts, the dexterity of workers, the quality of raw materials, and the environment of working rooms. On the one hand, the labor productivity actually increased because workers began to handle more spindles than before and the number of ill workers declined. On the other, the injury rate remained unchanged.

Tanino's "The participation of women in the labor force during the past five years" (1933) is a report compiled in response to a request by the ILO. During the severe depression of the early 1930s, it was surmised in many countries that the unemployment of male workers was – at least partially – caused by women's participation in the labor force. Tanino investigated this hypothesis during 1927 and 1932. She found that the respective number of men and women workers decreased, and that the ratio of women to men workers declined during the period. A few more women began to work in the textile industry and machine manufacturing than before, whereas the number of women working in coal mines conspicuously decreased because the legal prohibition of women's underground working was scheduled to come into effect in September 1933. Yet more women were employed than men in the newly developing service sectors (transportation, communications, hotels, and restaurants).

Tanino also compiled three reports for submission to the ILO in order to respond to the severe criticism from many countries of Japan's "poor" working conditions. It was believed that Japan's exports had increased after it abandoned the gold standard in December 1931. Japan was fiercely criticized for "social dumping" at the 1933 general assembly of the ILO and further condemnation was expected at the 1934 assembly. In 1934, Fernand Maurett, the Deputy Secretary-General of the ILO, was sent to Japan to inspect conditions. When he visited a new textile mill, he unexpectedly found good education facilities for the women workers who lived in the company residence. In fact, employers had to provide better welfare facilities and fringe benefits (to make up for low wages) because it was becoming harder for them to secure new women workers as the poor working conditions gradually became known in remote (farming) areas (Kitagawa, 1985, vol. 1, pp. 257–9; Taikakai, 1971, pp. 450–2; Ikeo 2000b).

Tanino's "A note of a woman probationary factory supervisor" (*c.*1936) was first published in 1985. It was the record of the unannounced inspection of small factories, which were the basis for Japan's export industries in the 1930s. In textile mills, Tanino was surprised to see women workers competing fiercely, both at individual and at group levels. She witnessed a girl with flu and a fever forced to work by her team-mate, with the expectation of gaining an award for the team. With regard to the remittances of young workers in large factories to their parents in remote villages, the parents tended to believe that factories which allowed the children to remit the most money were the best. Tanino remarked that the parents did not usually notice how low the children's pocket money was.

Japan's military force began to fight with China in July 1937. Many men in the prime of life were drafted to the battlefields and women had to fill the vacant positions on Japan's mainland. In a series of reports including her "Women's advance into machine shops and their adaptability" (1939a) and "Working women and welfare facilities" (1939b), Tanino called attention to the need for immediate improvement of working environments for women because women were suddenly working in the machine shops and munitions factories which were designed specifically with men in mind.

In September 1947 Tanino became the section chief at the Bureau of Women and Minors in the newly established Ministry of Labor and began to work under Director-General Kikue Yamakawa. Tanino became the third Director-General in the Bureau in 1955 and held the position for a decade. In 1965 she retired from the Ministry of Labor and became a member of the judging Committee of Labor Insurance.

Household economics

While three women became leaders documenting labor problems and advocating change for women workers, a different group of women, who taught at women's universities, innovated the field of household economics in Japan. The Meiji government (established in 1868) abolished the old *han* (feudal domain) system and newly established prefectures in 1871. In 1872 it promulgated the new education system. In 1875 it founded Japan's first institution of higher education for women, Tokyo Women's Normal School (now Ochanomizu University). In 1884 Toyo Eiwa Jogakko (women's school) was opened in Tokyo by Martha J. Cartmell, a missionary sent by the Woman's Missionary Society of the Methodist Church of Canada (currently the United Church of Canada).

'New Japan' needed more highly educated men to adapt to the changes of shifting from a closed, feudal community with little outer communication to an open, modern society with international trade. Some men worked outside of their households (*ie*) for the public sector or for private companies. They commuted to their workplaces while their female family members had to manage the new life at home. Other men kept working in their households (*ie*) and started modern family businesses with relatives.

These women "economists" paid attention to empirical facts and focused on the household (*ie*), rather than the individual, as the unit of decision-making in consumption and life planning. The powerful role of men decreased in the household, while that of women increased. To understand the importance of this household work, we need to understand the "*ie*" system established in the Tokugawa period (1603–1867).

The "ie" system

"*Ie*" translates as house or household. Originally, *ie* was an economic unit for running the (family) business and sharing daily life in the Tokugawa period. When the Confucian philosopher Ekiken Kaibara (1630–1714) said, "Each *samurai* (feudal) warrior, farmer, artisan, or tradesman owns an '*ie*'-household" (Kaibara 1711), he referred to the class system of the four groups which

家

1. house
2. household
3. household members share a house built on a site purified by a ground-breaking ceremony

Figure 5.1 Meaning of the Kanji character "*ie*"

was institutionalized in this hierarchical order from the top to the bottom by the Tokugawa shogunate. Yet, the typical "*ie*" should be found in the house of a merchant or tradesman and the house of a *samurai* warrior.

In the early Meiji period, a selection from Kaibara's *Precepts on Household Management* (1711) and other writings (Kaibara 1710, 1713), which had been originally authored for men, were used as the textbook for women. Kaibara summarized four maxims in household management as follows:

> The discipline of house/household management includes four maxims. First, make a living by working in the family's business. Second, increase the fortune by thriftiness. Third, protect oneself by caution. Fourth, love a person in empathy. Empathy is to do what he likes and not to do what he hates by imagining in your mind how he must feel in his mind. A house or household manager must keep these four maxims.
>
> *Kaibara 1711, quoted in Tsunemi 1971, p. 124*

It gave women the essence of household management. The Meiji edition of Kaibara's *Household Management* included the following conception of lifecycle:[10]

> A man must have a plan to do at each stage of his lifetime, namely from the age of ten to sixty years old. At age 10, he must follow the instructions of his father and mother who support him. It is called the plan of living. At age 20, he must pursue scholarship, master a skill, support the family business, and rise in the world. It is called the plan of advancement. From the age 20 to 40, he must run his household affairs and keep the family business as planned. It is called the plan of household. At age 50, he must make a plan for his offspring. His offspring are too young to know the world. Father must make a plan for his children. It is called the plan of old man. Over the age 60, he must make a plan for those left behind after his death. It is pointless to regret at the moment of his death that he has not done something for his afterlife. [It is called the plan of death.] The people in the world should practice these five plans.
>
> *Kaibara 1711, quoted in Tsunemi 1971, p. 124*

In the Meiji period, a woman (mistress), instead of a man (the eldest son or adopted son), had to make these five plans for her family lifetime. This was an expansion of women's responsibilities from the earlier Tokugawa period, when a woman was expected to be no more than a "good mother" inside "*ie*"-household. It is noteworthy that Confucian literature was widely learned in Japan but women were not formal recipients or contributors to the scholarship (see the former section on Makuzu Tadano in this chapter as well as Zurndorfer (2014)). This idea of "good mother" was not created by women, but it was formed and sophisticated on the basis of the male Confucian scholar Kaibara (1710, 1711, 1713) including precepts on health, joy, and happiness.

The Meiji government promoted the expanded role of "good wife/wise mother" rather than "good mother" to be suitable to the new "*ie*" life of the modern period. Intent on promoting this new role, the government entrusted to women the task of developing a curriculum and educating young women. Women obtained a new opportunity of becoming instructors at normal schools for women's education to train future good wives/wise mothers.

Sumi Oe (1875–1948)

Sumi Oe accepted the policy of promoting the model of "good wife/wise mother" and established Tokyo Kasei Gakuin (Women's School for Domestic Science [*Kaseigaku*]) in 1925. She was born in Nagasaki and her father Moritaro (former farmer, Buddhist of Nichiren sect) worked for the House of Glover (an arms dealer who gave rich information of foreign affairs to aspiring Japanese youth). Reading Yukichi Fukuzawa's *Encouragement of Learning* (1872–76) and looking for a better opportunity in Tokyo for his children, Moritaro took a position at the Ministry of the Navy (and a little later at the Ministry of the Imperial Household); then the rest of the family settled there in 1880. After studying at Toyo Eiwa Jogakko (1889–94), Sumi Oe was christened and taught there for several months. Passing the exam to enter Tokyo Women's Normal School (Ochanomizu University), she became a student in the Department of Domestic Science.

As she was especially good at English, she was sent to England by the government from 1902 to 1906. She studied at the Training School of Domestic Science, Battersea Polytechnic, and then took the hygiene course at Bedford College. She studied various disciplines (chemistry, physiology, physics, etc.). She learned that English workers paid little attention to budgetary constraints and spent most of their weekly wages at once, soon after they were received, without considering putting money aside for savings and for living expenses for the rest of the week. This kind of "observation" by her and others was transmitted to Japanese educators and led them to emphasize the importance of monthly pay (instead of weekly pay) and of keeping household accounts (Shibanuma 1999).

Returning to Japan, Oe established Tokyo Kasei Gakuin, a women's school to train future brilliant housewives to manage their household rationally and to care for their families under the constraints of their husbands' earnings. Her *The Essence of Applied Domestic Science* (1916) provided the blueprint for an efficient and comfortable house. She recommended a house with an inner courtyard so that family members could share an intimate space and natural sunlight. In her model house, a woman could run the household with a maid by taking care of family members and ordering supplies from door-to-door tradesmen.

An additional goal of Oe's *kaseigaku* was to train future wives of businessmen, who ran family businesses or planned to start businesses. The educational courses included asset management operation, such as loan planning and renting a house or property. Oe regarded "borrowing money for the purpose of making more money" or "business loan" as a secret virtue that paved the way to expand a business by way of borrowed capital.[11] Oe (1916) defined *kasei* as "the discipline of governing a house/household," and she believed that the quality of the house/household would affect the welfare and strength of the nation. Oe wrote:

> A nation is nothing but a whole set of houses/households politically unified by the government. Therefore, whether a nation is strong or weak as well as whether it is civilized or primitive must depend on the conditions of houses/households which are members of the nation. The good conditions of *kasei*, namely the good management of a house/household, are naturally related not only with the happiness in the house/household but also welfare and strength of a nation. The house/household manager should pay great attention to this regard.
>
> *Oe 1916, quoted in Tsunemi 1971, pp. 188–9*

For Oe, the aggregation of "*ie*"-households becomes a national economy. A housewife must consider the following points (Tsunemi 1971, p. 189):

1 To promote the health (joy and happiness) of the members in the house or household
2 To increase the wealth of the house or household
3 To educate children to become healthy citizens of the next generation
4 To promote peace and mutual friendship among members of the house or household and their relatives and to enhance the grace (dignity) of the house

Believing that "physical training" was very important, Oe had a kitchen laboratory with attention to hygiene built in her school and gave practical cooking training using thermometers, scales, and other equipment. Her cooking lessons resembled chemical experiments at a science lab. She was eager to introduce the latest home appliances such as refrigerators, ironing tools, and washing machines. In this sense, it can be said that a "good wife/wise mother" is synonymous with a "rational and progressive consumer."[12] Yet we should note that other private women's universities were established with the purpose of promoting the cultivation of woman's sprit of self-reliance (or self-support).

Tomoko Matsudaira (1894–1969)

Tomoko Matsudaira was the first woman economist to teach at an institution of higher education. She was born in Tokyo and studied at Tokyo Women's Normal School from 1913 to 1917. Although the system of higher education was reformed in 1919 and 1920, no national university changed their policy against women. The president of Tokyo Women's Normal School, Genichi Yumoto, came up with a plan to upgrade the curriculum in household economics under the three pillars of "Health (Joy and Happiness)," "Education for Children," and "Household Economy." He decided to send some graduates to men-only universities to take regular courses as special students. Matsudaira was chosen to study at the Economics Department of the Imperial University of Tokyo (the University of Tokyo) for the then regular three-year program (1919–22). She was supervised by Susumu Kawazu (1875–1943) and Kakujiro Yamazaki (1868–1945, specialized in money and banking) (Kurita et al. 2016).

In 1921, she was appointed to the Tokyo Women's Normal School and offered a course on household economics. In 1925, she began publishing many books, indeed three books in a year (Matsudaira 1925a, b, c). Her first book, *Household Economics* (two volumes, 645 and 504 pages, respectively) was indebted to her former supervisor Kawazu's advanced textbook *Economics* (1924) and the then leading economist Tokuzo Fukuda's introductory *Textbook in Economics* (1911). It is interesting to note that Kawazu's *Economics* (1924) eliminated the German and European elements from Fukuda's *A Study of Economics* (1920), the best research monograph on the German historical school in Japan; thus Kawazu had de-Germanized or de-Europeanized Fukuda (1920), which had discussed German history and institutions in detail, to make it more abstract and more fitting for Japanese students (Ikeo 2017).

Matsudaira's writings reflect both contemporary Japanese and Western economics literature through her reading of Kawazu's and Fukuda's books. Therefore, her books are premised on *kaseigaku* and her contribution could be found in her improvement of the form of household accounts more suitable to both weekly or monthly flow management and yearly asset management. Using Knut Wicksell's phraseology, volume one of Matsudaira's *Household Economics* (1925a) took a general approach to economic (household) life, the national economy, public finance, and the supply of public goods. She encouraged women (as consumers) to enjoy the technical progress occurring in the world by purchasing new products and electric appliances. Volume 2 took a monetary approach to economic life. In it, she explained household accounts, savings, and financial goods (stocks, bonds, and bank deposits), and included the maxim "Don't keep all your eggs in one basket" to call attention to the risks in financial trading and family business.

Matsudaira (1925a, volume 1, pp. 649–50) connected early modern thrift or economizing and modern rational thinking to the household as follows:

> Economizing (*setsuyaku*, thrift, savings) means to reduce consumption as much as possible and to satisfy our wants as much as possible, that is the most effective utilization of our goods. Economizing is the most important knowledge in the use of goods.
>
> Economizing is the opposite of extravagance and an application of the first principle of "economics."
>
> We have to take economizing of goods, effort, and time into consideration. For example, in cooking, it is necessary: (1) To decide the menu suitable to our health and family welfare by expending as little as possible; (2) To find better cooking methods in time, nutrition, digestion, and family tastes; (3) To improve kitchen and cooking equipment (gas stove rather than fire wood stove).

Matsudaira (1925a, volume 1, pp. 653–4) discussed rational thinking and scientific knowledge:

> Women should be conscious about advances in consumption style and the rationalization of economic life, and they should make a big contribution to both the household and society. Thanks to the use of modern science and technology, great progress has been made in production methods of the past century. However, the consumption style remains unchanged. Women should learn modern science and make a special study of lifestyle, and then master the science and technology applicable to our lifestyle. Women are truly responsible for developing our lifestyle.

Matsudaira urged women to bring technical progress into the household and improve the standard of living. She also encouraged them to keep household accounts for budgetary efficiency (Matsudaira 1930). Eventually their household accounts became a source of econometric analysis (Ikeo 2014, p. 80). She continued to publish many books in household economics by adding current events and reflecting her new reading (Matsudaira 1948–9, 1953, 1954, 1968).

Akiko Ito (b. 1919)

Akiko Ito was born in Tokyo and graduated from Tokyo Women's Normal School in 1941. She was appointed an assistant at Ochanomizu University in 1952 and promoted to full professor in 1971. She was good at econometric analysis and collaborated with economists linked with Hitotsubashi University. Ito and Koichi Emi (an econometrician at Hitotsubashi University) edited the ambitious advanced textbook *Household Economics* (Emi and Ito 1982). The third edition (1997) covers household planning, occupation and income, income and expenditure, lifestyle and consumption, the choice of savings, family and lifecycle, the connection of households and firms, general prices, public finance, social security and welfare, standard of living, and "household and the world economy."

Ito's *Standard of Living* (1977) came out after Japan's economy enjoyed rapid growth in the 1960s, when the focus on GDP as the index of economic welfare aroused fierce criticism. She painstakingly traced the historical changes in the standard of living and its size from the Meiji period to 1970. She paid attention to the structural changes in occupations (farmers, laborers, and white-collar professions) and the income differentials by occupations. She noticed the differences in the estimations of income and Engel's coefficients calculated by several econometricians. Referring to the United Nations (UN) Research Institute for Social Development's concept of the level of living index, which included "welfare," she discussed the index of nutrition, housing service and health as well as expenditure on education and leisure, and the data on human security (death rate, unemployment rate, rate of those insured for medical services, and rate of pension recipients). She examined Japan's livelihood protection system in detail.

Ito's *Housing Loan and Household Management* (1988) statistically studied the impact of housing loans (the biggest purchase in a household budget) on household asset management. Using the National Survey of Family Income and Expenditure, she unexpectedly uncovered that households with housing loans kept almost the same consumption level as households without, and that the former households had a larger income than the latter households. In 1988, Ito also co-edited *Dictionary of Household Economics* with Shigetake Iizuka, who specialized in small- and medium-sized enterprises.

In a personal communication, Ito's co-author Iizuka said: "Many women economists were working on household economics but household economics is just the economics with emphasis on particular points (household behavior and asset management)". The evolution of Ito's major contributions to economics is a case in point.

It seems that asset management (at an introductory level) started earlier in *kaseigaku* (household economics) than in economics. Household economics has become more technical by using statistical and econometric analysis; it can be said that there is a shift away from "good wife/wise mother" training toward more of a microeconomics emphasis on rationality.

Eiko Shinotsuka (b. 1942)

Eiko Shinotsuka is a labor economist skilled in econometric techniques and served as the first woman member of the Policy Board of the Bank of Japan during 1998–2001. Graduating from Musashi University, she started her career by working for the Japan Center for Economic Research (JCER) in 1965 and became a researcher in 1968. After teaching part-time at three universities, she was appointed an associate professor at Ochanomizu University in 1987, promoted to a professor in 1992, reappointed in 2002, and retired in 2008. She obtained her doctoral degree (in commercial science) based on Shinotsuka (1989) without formal graduate coursework from Keio University in 1990.[13]

Shinotsuka's *Women's Labor in Japan* (1982) found that a woman's labor supply depends on whether she is single or married and on the family age structure when she is married. A woman is supposed to make a spending plan based on her budget (salary) and satisfaction when she is single. However, she makes decisions on her labor supply under consideration of her whole family and life stage when she is married. Shinotsuka referred to Paul Howard Douglas and Hiromi Arisawa's earlier findings.

Shinotsuka's *Employment Adjustment in Japan* (1989) statistically examined the shifting labor market conditions after the oil shocks. It was believed that the lifetime employment system predominated in sizable corporations in Japan instead of employment adjustment responses to changing market conditions. She witnessed that employment adjustment was actually taking place among many companies: reducing extra works and new recruitment and laying off part-timers, temporary employees, and even full-timers (through voluntary retirement). It became clear that immediately after the oil shocks small enterprises increased employment whereas large enterprises decreased employment, and that companies came to regard middle-aged women part-timers as adjusting variables (shock-absorbers) in facing environmental changes. She also noticed the on-going micro-electronics revolution had a significant impact on the labor demand in the 1980s.

In 1986 Shinotsuka ran an annual JCER research project and wrote the report "The Equal Employment Opportunity Law and its impact on management." Twice a month she invited JCER personnel directors from sizable companies in the electronic machinery, textile, steel, chemical, retailing, financial, educational, general trading, and information technology industries, as well as vocational advisors from universities and the editor of a job-hunting magazine. She conducted hearings on their attitudes toward the new law (effective on April 1986) and found their new interest in recruiting women graduates from four-year universities instead of two-year colleges. She assigned chapter authors and co-edited with Tadashi Hanami *Management and Labor in the Age of Equal Employment Opportunity* (1987). This book might have enhanced personnel directors' awareness of the new law. She was a woman *samurai*.

Formally trained academic economists after 1947

After 1947, Keio University attracted excellent women including Marxian economists (according to Kiyoko Imura). Non-Marxian women economists were trained at the Keio Economic Observatory, which was established in 1959 for the promotion of empirical studies and the communications between business leaders and economists. Keio women economists encouraged other women to engage in the economics profession.

Yoko Sazanami (Kawashima) (b. 1932)

Yoko Sazanami is the first Japanese woman economist to work for the UN and the first woman economist to teach at a formerly all-male university in Japan. She is a renowned economist specializing in international trade and trade policy. She graduated from Keio University in 1955. A Fulbright grant brought her to Harvard University itself (not Radcliffe College – the women's college associated with Harvard).[14] J. S. Duesenberry's course on economic growth and business cycles stimulated her to consider the challenges accompanying economic growth. She obtained her master's degree in 1957. She was an economist in the UN Department of Economic and Social Affairs in New York during 1959–1962[15] and she worked with Jacob L. Mosak (who specialized in trade and general equilibrium analysis) on economic problems of Southeast Asia for the annual *World Economic Survey* and on primary goods matters for the annual *Commodity Survey*. She linked existing trade theories with empirical studies in her research.

She was appointed an assistant in 1962 and an associate professor in 1967 at the Keio Economic Observatory. Receiving her doctoral degree from Keio University, she was promoted to associate professor in the Economics Department. Before retiring from the university, she published seven books (in Japanese), 58 papers in Japanese, and 24 papers mostly in English (Sazanami 1998).

Sazanami's *Economic Growth and International Competitiveness* (1968) works toward a theoretical integration of international trade and economic growth under the assumption of technological progress and increasing physical capital. She paid attention to the differences in problems faced by two groups of countries. One group consists of underdeveloped countries exporting primary goods and facing volatility in their prices caused by changes in natural conditions, the international environment, and speculative trading by international investors. Primary goods such as coffee beans, cocoa, and rubber plants grow only in this torrid zone and it is hard to stop producing them in response to declines in price once their cultivation is initiated. Another group consists of the countries exporting industrial goods and importing raw materials. Sazanami argued that international trade leads to more efficient use of resources and higher real income in the world. She confirmed that late-comers need new technology via capital goods imports and that developed countries welcome the expansion of the world market for such goods.[16] She found that after around 1950 Japanese firms increased exports due to increasing labor productivity, which was stimulated by intensive investment and technical progress through the purchase of patents.

Sazanami's *International Division of Labor and the Japanese Economy* (1980) examined the expanding world trade in the 1960s and 70s by using inter-industry relations analysis, and discussed the on-going industrial adjustment initiated by oil shocks and floating exchange rates. She revealed that an impact of tariff reductions by the GATT rounds and the effort of economic integration (such as the formation of the European Economic Community, EEC) caused an increasing trade of intermediate goods (machinery parts). This increasing intermediate goods trade was also promoted by the fragmentation of the production process and the specialization in the production of industrial parts among advanced countries, especially within the expanding EEC economy. She argued that economic integration and its expansion would promote international production, especially intra-industry trade, by the strategic decisions of multinational corporations.

After 1980, Sazanami participated in many international conferences and projects on trade. She contributed her papers "Japanese trade liberalization" (1984), "Japanese trade in the Pacific rim" (1987), "Telecommunication and information services" (1988), "Trade and investment patterns and barriers in the United States, Canada, and Japan" (1989), and "Determinants of Japanese foreign direct investment" (1992). She offered a course on the Japanese economy at University Paris 1 Pantheon-Sorbonne. At that time, she co-organized with J.-L. Mucchielli (who had served the French Embassy to Japan for the research of Japanese multinationals) the French-Japanese conference on "Europe and Japan under the new era of competition and cooperation" in February 1992, which focused on the establishment of the European Union the following year. At the time, France and Europe supported the policy of inviting foreign direct investment as they expected decreasing unemployment and trade deficits as well as technology transfer. At the conference, Sazanami gave the paper entitled "Strategies of Japanese manufacturing firms: Their impact on trade flows between Europe, Asia, and North America." The revised version (Sazanami and Ching 1997) was included in the English version of the proceedings (Buckley and Mucchielli 1997).

Sazanami instinctively grasped the new challenges emerging from a changing international environment and organized effective research projects with several younger economists. For example, because of similar research on the US, Sazanami invited Shujiro Urata and Hiroki Kawai to co-author *Measuring the Cost of Protection in Japan* (1995). They examined the causes of the differentials in the prices of tradable goods inside and outside Japan. Their inter-industry relations analysis showed that Japanese consumers suffered from welfare losses caused by higher domestic prices compared with international prices of these goods. Also in 1995, Sazanami and other leading international economists fully examined the changes to be expected by the establishment of the World Trade Organization (WTO) and shed light on the results of the GATT negotiations, the trade in services (GATS), and dispute settlements (Sazanami and Nakakita 1997). In 1997, Sazanami and Fukunari Kimura organized a research project on the formation of a sub-regional market and the role of Japanese firms in East Asia. They witnessed Hong Kong's absorption by China under the policy of "One Country, Two Systems," and observed the contagion of currency and financial crisis occurring in East Asia in that year. They questioned the dollar-peg policy which had been implemented by several ASEAN countries and their quantitative analysis mainly focused on the regional trade in East Asia including China during the 1990s, namely the pre-crisis period (Sazanami and Kimura 2000).

In 1998 Sazanami served as the chair for the Financial Crisis Management Committee of the Deposit Insurance Corporation in assessing the financial conditions of several sizable banks. The committee judged the possibility of bail-outs to avoid systemic risks under the uncertainty associated with the fallout from the Southeast Asian financial crisis. At the time, some economists expected further financial contagion beyond East Asia and in fact the IMF (2014, p. 30) stated that in hindsight "spillovers from Asia had raised borrowing costs, and precipitated sharp declines in oil and other commodity prices" and that they hit Russia and some Eastern European countries. Sazanami's reputation in international economics might have eased some anxiety felt by international scholars and policy makers outside Japan even though domestic finance was outside of Sazanami's specialty.

Yoko Sano (b. 1931)

Yoko Sano specialized in human resource management. She graduated from the Economics Department, Keio University in 1954. She was appointed an assistant for the Keio Economic Observatory in 1960 and a professor in the Commerce Department in 1972. She obtained her doctoral degree in economics in 1970. She visited the Institute of Labor and Industrial Relations of Illinois University for a year from September 1964. She stayed for a shorter period at the Australian National University, Glasgow University, ESSEC Business School, Cranfield Business School (both in Europe), and Philippine National University. She assumed the presidency of the Japan Society of Human Resource Management in 1987–1989, the Department Chair at Keio in 1989–1991, and the presidency of Kaetsu University in 2001–2005. She skillfully employed her expertise (human resource management) in running the Commerce Department and the university.

With the support of many male colleagues, she co-authored several books, including *Pay Determination of Small and Medium Enterprises* (1971), *Women Labor Economics* (1972), and *A Study of Job Transfer* (1978). Sano and her colleagues occasionally conducted surveys of employers and employees. They found a variety of pay systems and their trends as well as the female ratios at the micro and macro levels and their trends. They sometimes collaborated with the Ministry of Labor (now Ministry of Labor and Welfare) and indirectly with the ILO. Sano paid attention to the Equal Employment Opportunity Law (effective in April 1986) and expected that an increasing number of more highly educated women would find regular positions over part-time work and more opportunity for career development. The findings and analysis, especially in her *Internal Labor Market* (1989), show that the style of both office works and production line operations (in manufacturing) has been dramatically changed by the introduction of new technology such as micro-computers, automated systems, and home working systems. The phrase "internal labor market," which is often used by Japanese business economists, implies high mobility of employees and subsequently high frequency of their turnover within an organization or group of companies. The managers of a sizable company preferred this employment practice rather than lay-offs. However, Sano (1997) noticed the new trend of some employers departing from this practice in facing rapid globalization, which she thought was mainly caused by the accelerating progress in information communication technology.

Conclusions

The historical globalization process is associated with increased opportunities for a few Japanese women to participate in economics. The opportunities involved constructing knowledge concerning women in the Japanese workforce, making policy proposals associated with Japan's integration into the global economy, becoming economic activists for women's liberation and enlightenment, educating young women to become rational and progressive consumers at home, and, in the second half of the twentieth century, becoming professional economists and leaders in Japan's government bureaucracy.

In the early nineteenth century, Tadano became the first woman to contribute to recorded economic thought. In part, this isolated contribution from a woman is due to the opportunities afforded her from the intellectual background of her family and their social status. Apparently, traditional Confucian thinking obstructed women from contributing outside "*ie*" – the household – and deterred changes in men's mentality against women's social participation. Thus, it took roughly another century for opportunities to open for additional contributions to economic thought from Japanese women after Tadano. In part, these opportunities arose because of challenges from the international order about working conditions in Japan. In the early twentieth century, women were needed to study women's working conditions in Japanese industry because of requirements imposed by the ILO. And in the early twentieth century, the first opportunities emerged for women in academia as the notion of "*ie*" evolved from a household-centered economic structure to an industrial- and corporate-centered economic structure. Those opportunities were strictly limited to training women as rational, efficient consumers. It was after Japan's complete opening to the forces of globalization in the second half of the twentieth century that formal opportunities opened for women in economics departments and within the government bureaucracy. The Equal Employment Opportunity Law for Men and Women (effective in 1986 and revised in 1997) might have had a positive impact on the hiring of women economists in Japan.

Notes

1 I thank Shujiro Urata, Bettina Gramlich-Oka, Alisa Freedman, Nobuko Nagase, and Kirsten Madden for their valuable information and comments related with this chapter.
2 *Tanka* is a 31-syllable poem consisting of five lines in the pattern 5–7–5–7–7; the dominant form in classical Japanese poetry (*waka*) from the seventh century to the present (*Encyclopedia of Japan*, August 12, 2017).
3 Prior to 1947, Tohoku Imperial University (now Tohoku University) took the first three women regular students (in 1913) and was followed by Waseda University (in 1939).
4 See Ikeo (2000d) on Japan's academic environment during the period of 1945–1970.
5 Gramlich-Oka (2006, p. 267) called my attention to the importance of Dazai. Aoki authored no economics book but did write a book on the sweet potato.
6 Tadano's writings had Buddhist and Shinto elements, too. Iga had a friend who was a Shinto priest who owned a good library and another friend who was a Rinzai-sect Buddhist priest.
7 *The Records of Ancient Matters* (completed in the eighth century) was a book on the history of Japanese *kami* (deity) and emperors.
8 It is noteworthy that it was legal to publish a criticism against the opposition to the Tokugawa policies, whereas it was illegal to openly criticize the policies.
9 Women's School for English Study (Tsuda University) was established in 1900 by Umeko Tsuda (1864–1929). In 1871, five girls (including her, the youngest) accompanied the Iwakura Mission to the West. They remained in the US and three of them studied there for ten years. In Japan Tsuda taught at the School for Noble Women. Then she revisited the US to study biology and education at Bryn Mawr College from 1889 to 1892 (National Archives of Japan, 2016).
10 Kaibara referred to the Song philosopher Zhu Xin Zhong.

11 Sumi Oe was indebted to her own mother for this idea (Ohama 1978, pp. 17–18).
12 Chapter 2 of Sand's *House and Home in Modern Japan* (2003) includes an illustration of "The Housewife's Laboratory."
13 Shinotsuka (2008) and Japan's National Dietary Search website http://iss.ndl.go.jp/books/R100000002-I000000230495-00 (accesssed January 27, 2018).
14 There is a complicated history of women as degree earners from Harvard University. "It's complicated: 375 years of women at Harvard" (Radcliffe Institute for Advanced Study, Harvard University) www.radcliffe.harvard.edu/schlesinger-library/exhibition/its-complicated-375-years-women-harvard (accessed September 2, 2017).
15 Japan joined the UN in 1956.
16 After the loss in WWII, Japan resumed private exports and imports in August 1947 and the single exchange rate was fixed at $1 = ¥360 in April 1949. Japan exported textile goods to advanced countries and machines to Southeast Asian countries in the 1950s.

Bibliography

Becker, Gary (1964) *Human Capital*. New York: National Bureau of Economic Research. 2nd edition, 1975.
Buckley, P. and J.-L. Mucchielli eds (1997) *Multinational Firms and International Relocation*. Aldershot: Elgar.
Dazai, Shundai (1729) *On Political Economy*. Edo. In *A Collection of Dazai Shundai*, edited by Shiro Yokokawa, Tokyo: Seibundoshinkosha, 1935.
Dimand Robert W., Mary Ann Dimand, and Evelyn L. Forget eds (2000) *A Biographical Dictionary of Women Economists*. Cheltenham: Edward Elgar.
Emi, Koichi and Akiko Ito eds (1982) *Household Economics*. Tokyo: Yuhikaku. Third edition, 1997.
Encyclopedia of Japan. Tokyo: Kodansha. Published as *Japan: An Illustrated Encyclopedia* in 1993. Available at https://archive.org/details/japanillustrated02koda (accessed June 21, 2018).
Fukuda, Tokuzo (1911) *Textbook in Economics*. Tokyo: Dobunkan.
Fukuda, T. (1920) *A Study of Economics*. Tokyo: Dobunkan.
Fukuzawa, Yukichi (1880) *Encouragement of Learning*. Tokyo.
Gramlich-Oka, Bettina (2006) *Thinking Like a Man: Tadano Makuzu (1763–1825)*. Leiden: Brill.
Iizuka, Shigetake and Akiko Ito eds (1988) *Dictionary of Household Economics*. Tokyo: Buren Shuppan.
Ikeo, Aiko. (1997) Three women economists in Japan: Kikue Yamakawa, Koko Sanpei and Setsu Tanino. *Institute for the Study of Japanese Culture and Classics Bulletin*, (79): 98–126.
Ikeo, A. (2000a) Koko (Takako) Sanpei (1903–78). In Dimand et al. eds (2000), pp. 378–81.
Ikeo, A. (2000b) Setsu Tanino (b1903). In Dimand et al. eds (2000), pp. 409–15.
Ikeo, A. (2000c) Kikue Yamakawa (1890–1980). In Dimand et al. eds (2000), pp. 481–9.
Ikeo, A ed. (2000d) *Japanese Economics and Economists since 1945*. London: Routledge.
Ikeo, A. (2014) *A History of Economic Science in Japan: The Internationalization of Economics in the Twentieth Century*. London: Routlege.
Ikeo, A. (2017) Comments on Kurita et al. 2016. Read at the seminar on Women and Economics in Japan, the Institute of Gender Studies of Ochaomizu University, 22 February.
IMF (2014) *25 years of transition: Post-communist Europe and the IMF*. IMF.
Ito, Akiko (1977) *Standard of Living*. Tokyo: Koseikan.
Ito, A. (1988) *Housing Loan and Household Management*. Tokyo: Japan Statistical Association.
Kaibara, Ekiken (1710) *Rakukun* (Precepts on Intellectual Culture and Pleasure). Fukuoka. In Kaibara (1969).
Kaibara, E. (1711) *Kadokun* (Precepts on Household Management). Fukuoka. In Kaibara (1969).
Kaibara, E. (1713) *Yojokun* (Precepts on Health Care). Fukuoka. In Kaibara (1969).
Kaibara, E. (1969) *Ekiken Kaibara*, edited by Michio Matsuda. Tokyo: Chuokoronsha.
Kawazu, Susumu (1924) *Economics*. Tokyo: Shimizu Shoten.
Kitagawa, Nobu (1985) Introduction. In Tanino (1985, pp. 9–40).
Kulmus Adam (1722) *Ontleedkundige Tafelen* (Anatomical Tables).
Kurita, Keiko, Hiroshi Matsunoo, and Kotoe Ikegaki eds (2016) *Women and Economics in Japan*. Sapporo: Hokkaido University Press.
Matsudaira, Tomoko (1925a) *Household Economics: Economic Study of Domestic Life*, 2 volumes. Tokyo: Bunshodo. Reprint, 1982.
Matsudaira, T. (1925b) *Household Economic Reader*. Tokyo: Bunshodo. Revised enlarged edition, 1931.
Matsudaira, T. (1925c) *Manual of Household Economics*. Tokyo: Bunshodo.

Matsudaira, T. (1930) *Household Accounts*. Tokyo: Bunshodo.
Matsudaira, T. (1948–9) *Manual of Family Economics*, 3 volumes. Tokyo: Koryosha Shoten.
Matsudaira, T. (1953) *A Study of Household Economy*. Tokyo: Chukyo Shuppan. Revised in 1958. Third enlarged edition, 1966.
Matsudaira, T. (1954) *Principles of Kaseigaku*. Tokyo: Koryosha Shoten.
Matsudaira, T. (1968) *Principles of Matsudaira Kaseigaku*. Tokyo: Koseikan.
Motoori, Norinaga (1798) *Commentary on the Records of Ancient Matters*. Edo.
National Archives of Japan (2016) *Exhibit on Distinguished Women*. Tokyo: National Archives of Japan.
Oe, Sumi (1916) *The Essence of Applied Domestic Science*. Tokyo: Saibunkan. 15th edition, 1925.
Ohama, Tetsuya (1978) *Oe Sumi Sensei*, edited and distributed by Koen-kai of Tokyo Kasei Gakuin, Tokyo (available in Waseda University Library).
Sand, Jordan (2003) *House and Home in Modern Japan: Architecture, Domestic Space, and Bourgeois Culture, 1880–1930*. Cambridge, MA and London: Harvard University Press.
Sano, Yoko (1987) New technology and job opportunities for women. *Keio Business Review*, 24: 61–72.
Sano, Y. (1989) *Internal Labor Market*. Tokyo: Yuhikaku.
Sano, Y. (1997) Pay for performance: Individuals, groups and companies. *Keio Business Review*, 33: 117–31.
Sano, Y. ed. (1972) *Women Labor Economics*. Tokyo: Nihon Rodo Kyokai.
Sano, Y., Hideo Ishida, and Shozo Inoue (1971) *Pay Determination of Small and Medium Enterprises*. Tokyo: Toyokeizaishinposha.
Sano, Y., H. Ishida, and Toshiaki Izeki eds (1978) *A Study of Job Transfer*. Tokyo: Sogo Rodo Kenkyujo.
Sanpei, Koko (1941) *The Historical Development of the Cotton Spinning Industry in Japan*. Tokyo: Keio Shobo. Reprint, Tokyo: Iwanami Shoten, 1947.
Sanpei, K. (1944) *The Rise and Fall of Home Manufacturing and Industries in Japan*. Tokyo: Ito Shoten.
Sanpei, K. (1956) *The History of Working Women: History and Status Quo*. Tokyo: San-ichi Shobo.
Sanpei, K. (1961) *The History of Weaving in Japan*. Tokyo: Yuzankaku.
Sazanami, Yoko (1968) *Economic Growth and International Competitiveness*. Tokyo: Toyokeizaishinposha.
Sazanami, Y. (1980) *International Division of Labor and the Japanese Economy*. Tokyo: Toyokeizaishinposha.
Sazanami, Y. (1984) Japanese trade liberalization: An assessment of the implications for Southeast Asian countries. In *Western Pacific Trade*, edited by W.F. Gossling, Suffolk, UK: Input-Output Publishing Co.
Sazanami, Y. (1986) Japanese trade in the Pacific rim: Relationship between trade and investment. In *The Pacific Rim: Investment, Development and Trade*, edited by P.N. Nemetz, Vancouver: University of British Columbia Press, pp. 53–73.
Sazanami, Y. (1988) Telecommunication and Information Services. In *Pacific Trade in Services*, edited by L.V. Castle and C. Findlay, Boston: Allen & Unwin. pp. 209–27.
Sazanami, Y. (1989) Trade and investment patterns and barriers in the United States, Canada, and Japan. In *Trade and Investment Relations among the United States, Canada, and Japan*, edited by Robert M. Stern, Chicago: University of Chicago Press, pp. 90–126.
Sazanami, Y. (1992) Determinants of Japanese foreign direct investment: Locational attractiveness of European countries to Japanese multinationals. *Revue Économique*, 43(4): 661–70.
Sazanami, Y. (1998) Professor Yoko Sazanami's personal record and publications. *Keio Journal of Economics*, 90: 951–8.
Sazanami, Y. and Wong Yu Ching (1997) Strategies of Japanese multinationals: Changes in the locational importance of Asia, EC, and North America. In *Multinational Firms and International Relocation*, edited by P. Buckley and J.-L. Mucchielli, Aldershot: Elgar, pp. 103–22.
Sazanami, Y., Shujiro Urata, and Hiroki Kawai (1995) *Measuring the Cost of Protection in Japan*. Washington, DC: Institute for International Economics.
Sazanami, Y. and Toru Nakakita (1997) *The Changes Brought by the WTO*. Tokyo: Nihonhyoronsha.
Sazanami, Y. and Fukunari Kimura (2000) *The Reformation of the Asian Regional Economy*. Tokyo: Keio University Press.
Seki, Tamiko (2008) *Makuzu Tadano*. Tokyo: Yoshikawa Kobunkan.
Shibanuma, Akiko (1999) The formation of educational thought for women by studying in England: The cases of Tetsu Yasui and Sumi Oe. *Keiwa College Research*, 8: 243–67.
Shinotsuka, Eiko (1982) *Women's Labor in Japan*. Tokyo: Toyokeizaishinposha.
Shinotsuka, E. (1989) *Employment Adjustment in Japan: Labor Market after the Oil Shocks*. Tokyo: Toyokeizaishinposha.
Shinotsuka, E. (2008) Eiko Shinotsuka's Homepage. Last updated in 2008 and accessed on August 20, 2017.

Shinotsuka, E. and Tadashi Hanami eds (1987) *Management and Labor in the Age of Equal Employment Opportunity*. Tokyo: Toyokeizaishinposha.

Tadano, Makuzu (1812) *Old Stories*. In Tadano (1994).

Tadano, M. (1818) *Solitary Thought*. In Tadano (1994).

Tadano, M. (1994) *A Collection of Makuzu Tadano*, edited by Yoneko Suzuki. Tokyo: Kokushokankokai.

Taikakai, The Editorial Committee of the History of the Ministry of Home Affairs (1971) *History of the Ministry of Home Affairs*. Vol. 3. Tokyo: Taikakai.

Takizawa, Bakin (1820) *Commentary of Solitary Thoughts*. In Tadano (1994).

Tanino, Setsu (1933) The participation of women in the labor force during the past five years. *Industrial Welfare*. June. In Tanino (1985).

Tanino, S. (*c*.1936) A note of a woman probationary factory supervisor. In Tanino (1985).

Tanino, S. (1939a) Women's advance into machine shops and their adaptability. *Industrial Welfare*. September. In Tanino (1985).

Tanino, S. (1939b) Working women and welfare facilities. *Social Works*. October. In Tanino (1985).

Tanino, S. (1982) Yamakawa Director-General in the Women's and Minor's Bureau, advertisement to vol. 7 of Yamakawa (1982).

Tanino, S. (1985) *The Record of the Woman Factory Supervisor: The Collected Articles of Setsu Tanino*. 2 vols. Edited by Nobu Kitagawa. Tokyo: Domes Shuppan.

Tanino, S. and Ryuji Suzuki (1931) On the effect of the prohibition of night work. *Industrial Welfare*. June. In Tanino (1985).

Tsunemi, Ikuo (1971) *Kaseigaku Seiritsushi* (A History of Kaseigaku or Household Management). Tokyo: Koseikan.

Yamakawa, Kikue (1919) On the problems of women at work. *Kokka-gakkai Zasshi*, 33: 174–83, 334–69.

Yamakawa, K. (1943a) *Women of the Mito Domain*. Tokyo: Mikuni Shobo.

Yamakawa, K. (1943b) *The Village Where I Live*. Tokyo: Mikuni Shobo.

Yamakawa, K. (1956) *The Record of Women in Two Generations: Mother and Daughter*. Tokyo: Nihon Hyoron-shinsha.

Yamakawa, K. (1974) *Notes on Late-Tokugawa Mito*. Tokyo: Iwanami Shoten.

Yamakawa, K. (1981) *The Collected Works of Kikue Yamakawa*, 10 vols, edited by Sumiko Tanaka and Shinsaku Yamakawa. Tokyo: Iwanami Shoten.

Yamakawa, K. (1992) *Women of the Mito Domain: Recollections of Samurai Family Life*, translated into English by Kate Wildman Nakai, Tokyo: University of Tokyo Press.

Zurndorfer, H.T. (2014) Women in Chinese learned culture: Complexities, exclusivities and connecting narratives. *Gender and History* 26(1): 23–35.

PART II

Beginning in the late 19th century

6

CONTEXTUALIZING WOMEN'S ECONOMIC THOUGHT IN LATE IMPERIAL RUSSIA AND IN THE EARLY YEARS OF REVOLUTION

1870–1920

Anna Klimina

Introduction

The particular reality of women's economics in late Imperial Russia was largely determined by Russia's socio-economic backwardness, which resulted in limited participation in Russian economic studies by women before the 1917 Russian Revolution. Russia's backwardness included all the debilitating characteristics of a feudal society: arbitrary autocracy,[1] conservative social values, deep aversion to radical political and social reforms, and perpetual struggle for women's higher education, even in the upper classes. Russian women did not pursue advanced degrees in economics-related fields; consequently, they did not do economics, and left no formal economic writings.

In late Imperial Russia, the best and most historically interesting contributions by women to socio-economic scholarship were always part of the larger political struggle of thoughtful Russians against the autocratic regime, and for political, social and economic freedoms. That direct involvement in political struggle is clearly evident in the political speeches, popular articles and actions of a few educated women[2] – mostly members of the privileged classes – who were either activists like Vera Figner, Vera Zasulich, Catherine Breshko-Breshkovskaya, Maria Spiridonova, and Alexandra Kollontai, or political journalists like Ariadna Tyrkova and Ekaterina Kuskova.

In the late 1860s, as Russia began its move toward modernity, animated debates about the transformation of Russian society took place across the country among the educated and involved. Reviewing these widely diverse and often intensely held opinions as thoughtful educated Russian women acted upon them and wrote out their perspectives reveals a hitherto unwritten chapter in Russian intellectual history. This is the main purpose of this essay.

Contextualizing women's socio-economic thought in pre-1920 Russia

At the boundary of the 19th and 20th centuries, Russia's economy, despite state-led industrialization, remained the least developed of all the major European countries (Gregory 1994: 35). The overriding concern in Russia at the time, because of its very backwardness, was the acceleration of comprehensive modernization. However, in their visions for modern order and, consequently, for the directions of social change, Russian would-be modernizers differed substantially.

These differing views on Russia's liberation from its feudal past this chapter conceptualizes as revolutionary (radical) and moderate; in Russia, as Pavel Milyukov explains, radicals were primarily "socialistic" while moderates have always been known as "liberals" (1906: 222).

The Russian liberal reformers supported pro-Western capitalist development, argued for establishing in Russia a popularly elected legislative parliament, and advocated for solutions to the ills of Russian society through peaceful and constitutional means. They viewed a market order, nurtured and maintained by a constitutional and democratic Russian state, as a viable alternative to revolution and unanimously considered socialism both disastrous and utopian. In contrast, Russian radicals, whose views prevailed in public discussion, wanted to free Russia from "both paternalistic monarchy and capitalist exploitation" (Raeff 1959: 221, 229) through socialist revolution and a subsequent collectivist order. Each of these currents of Russian modernization thought included women writers and activists.

The uniqueness of the Russian situation lay in the surprisingly prominent role that women played in the Russian radical movement. Robert McNeal acknowledges, "Few if any political movements or parties can surpass Russian radicalism before 1917 with respect to female participation", both "in proportionate numerical strength and in leadership" (1971: 143, 145). Several scholars have noted women's high participation in radical activity; Engel, for example, suggests that in backward Russia, left-wing opposition "provided women with unprecedented opportunities for initiative and leadership" (Engel 1977: 101), and McNeal points out that revolution had become one of the few options through which women could achieve "equality with men", and rise to influence and power (McNeal, 1972: 4–5). Vera Zasulich, one of the prominent revolutionaries of the 1870s, confessed in her memoir ([1931] 1975: 69):

> Even before I had revolutionary dreams, I made elaborate plans to escape becoming a governess [the only probable career, given her gender and social position as impoverished gentry[3]]. The specter of revolution . . . made me equal to a boy; I too could dream of "action", of "exploits", and of the "great struggle."

Historians also see a connection between increased educational opportunities for women[4] in 1860s and 1870s Russia and increased scope in their revolutionary involvement (Engel 1977; Knight 1975). However, as Richard Stites argues, that rise in women's radicalism happened not because "education itself generated radical thought and behaviour" (Stites 1977: 44), but because those newly established educational institutions, in addition to becoming training centres for a generation of professional women, also provided fertile ground for radical groups who wished to recruit women to their cause. Given the limited opportunities for professional employment, many educated women were eager to seek fulfilment and meaning through a radical fight against the tsarist regime.

At the same time, there was "very little separate female radicalism", since Russian women were accepted as full-fledged members of mixed revolutionary groups, and "literally fought tsarist autocracy shoulder to shoulder with men" (McNeal 1971: 143). As a matter of fact, most of the female revolutionaries "had been attracted to radicalism by the people's cause, not by the women's" (Stites 1991: 127); politically radical women tended to regard any special women's cause as less important than the common cause of the socialist revolution, which sought to liberate all people and build socialism in Russia.

However, in their understanding of a desirable economic foundation for socialism, revolutionaries differed substantially. Russian Marxists, considering the industrial proletariat the most advanced socio-economic class, advocated first a dictatorship of a proletariat as the new form of post-revolutionary state, and then centralized state control of the economy on behalf of the proletariat as the future economic model (Lenin [1917] 1974: 402–410). In contrast, non-Marxist socialists, wary of replacing the capricious tsarist autocracy with an equally authoritarian proletarian state, began with the assumption that economic democracy had to be the foundation of a new order. These reformers imagined socialism almost exclusively in conjunction with workplace democracy, worker ("toiler") ownership, local governance and economic decentralization. To them, democratizing the economic system of post-capitalist Russia required the freedom of working people to form and control production, and to cooperate voluntarily with other producers (Chayanov 1919: 31).

Since socialist radicalism attracted far more women than did liberal reformism, the larger portion of this essay is devoted to discussing the views and actions of revolutionary women. The next section focuses on economic ideas of non-Marxist women socialists in detail, after which the following sections respectively present the economic views of Russia's women Marxists and liberal reformers.

Non-Marxist socialism in Russia as democratic socialism: Vera Zasulich, Catherine Breshko-Breshkovskaya, and Maria Spiridonova

In late Imperial Russia, non-Marxist socialism was comprised of two successive socio-economic movements: Radical Populism in the 1870s and 1880s, and neo-Populism in the 1900s and 1910s.

Radical Populists, whose clandestine organization "Land and Liberty" was formed in 1876, argued that Russia could skip a development of capitalism and move directly to a democratic socialist order, based on decentralized small-scale farming, situated in the context of village communal governance,[5] known for its "connectedness, selflessness and cooperation" (Zasulich 1884: v). These communes were viewed by Radical Populists as an embryonic form of a socialist organization of production, a form that already epitomized collectivism and primitive democracy (Gerschenkron 1955: 27–28). Since most land in Russia belonged to the landed gentry, the development of an advanced collectivist society from the commune was envisioned through confiscatory land reform. The Populists demanded the requisition of all privately owned land and its subsequent transfer to the rural communes and small landed proprietors for cultivation either individually or collectively, "but only by those who were toiling in it" (Figner [1881] 1964: 411). The federation of independent peasant communes (republics) was imagined as a model of Russia's future democratic governance.

Because of a disagreement over how to speed up the coming of peasant socialism, in 1879, "Land and Liberty" broke up into two factions: the terrorist "People's Will", which advocated political terror as the only historically justified form of action, and the much smaller non-terrorist "Black Repartition", which favoured peaceful propaganda in the countryside.

The majority of women members of "Land and Liberty" joined the terrorist "People's Will", and participated equally with men in violence; in the Executive Committee of the "People's Will", almost 30 per cent were women (Engel 1977: 92). However, as McNeal admits, "the first generation of narodnik [populist] radicals did not produce female theoreticians" (1971: 160); most revolutionary terrorist women simply acted on their beliefs, revealing in that way their views concerning the desirable direction of Russia's socio-economic development.

The "People's Will" plan began with killing the tsar, then Alexander II (1818–1881), and his key officials, which they expected would ignite the peasant revolution. This revolution, in turn, would result in a transfer of land to the peasantry, the first major step in building peasant socialism in Russia. Even before that, in 1878 Vera Zasulich (1849–1919), a beautiful young daughter of gentry, attempted to assassinate the Governor-General of St. Petersburg, Fyodor Trepov, the first act of terrorism in Russia. The dramatic trial and her unjustified acquittal[6] turned her into a revolutionary icon that "helped give [emerging] terrorist groups the . . . pedigree they needed in order to legitimize their existence" (Bergman 1979: 244). It could be argued that pardoning Zasulich's violent action sparked a dramatic increase in political warfare in the country.

Among the most well-known members of the terrorist "People's Will" was one of its leaders Vera Figner (1852–1942), who, being convinced that only killing the tsar could bring socialism to Russia, helped organize several assassination attempts, and maintained a clandestine flat where Executive Committee meetings were held and bombs were assembled. After the successful assassination of the tsar in March 1881, and ensuing arrests of nearly all members of the Executive Committee, Figner held the remnant of the quickly disintegrating "People's Will" together for almost two years, practically singlehandedly, and even coordinated one more successful assassination, this time a high-ranking Russian police official. When she was eventually arrested in 1883, she was given the death penalty, which was later commuted to life imprisonment. Figner spent more than 20 years in solitary incarceration, becoming a symbol of revolutionary martyrdom (Hartnett 2014: 205–219).

Another prominent member of the "People's Will" Sofia Perovskaya (1853–1881) actually directed the final assault on Alexander II. She arranged the locations of the lookouts and bomb-throwers and, from a concealed position, gave the final signal for the bomb that actually killed the tsar. All bomb-throwers were arrested and sentenced to death, but Perovskaya became "the first Russian woman to be executed for a political crime" (Engel 1977: 100).

A more recognizable contribution to socio-economic thought, primarily through correspondence with Karl Marx, was made by Vera Zasulich who, despite having become an inspirational figure for many female radicals, never actually justified the terrorism. In fact, in 1879, she joined the non-terrorist "Black Repartition". Its members originally saw the peasantry as a basic revolutionary force, but in the early 1880s, after reading Marx's general analysis of capitalism and its laws of motion, they realized that capitalist development of large-scale industry in Russia was necessary for a successful revolutionary transition to an advanced collectivist society. They therefore abandoned their Populist stance and converted to orthodox Marxism (as generally understood then and now). A decade later they welcomed the emergence of the Russian proletariat, recognized as the principle agent of revolutionary change in Marxist teaching.[7] In 1883, in Geneva, members of "Black Repartition" established the first Russian Marxist organization, the "Emancipation of Labour" group, led by Georgi Plekhanov (1856–1918).

Zasulich, however, was still not fully persuaded by the Marxist conception of socio-economic development. In March 1881, she wrote to Marx and asked whether the Russian rural commune would be "capable of developing in a socialist direction, that is gradually organizing its production and distribution on a collectivist basis", or would be "expected to perish" in which case Russian socialists would have to reconcile themselves to the inevitability of capitalist industrialization in order to move successfully to industrial socialism (Zasulich [1881] 1983: 98).

What is significant in Zasulich's letter to Marx is what might have motivated her to question, precisely when her fellow Populists from "Black Repartition" began converting to Marxism, its vision of socialism, based on "the most determined centralization of power in the hands of the state authority" (Marx [1850] 1950: 106–107) and state-directed large-scale industrial production. Though no direct statement of opinion is evident in her letter, her very questioning seems to imply that the socialized peasantry organized around democratic institutions of the commune would, in her view, be a better alternative. In essence, Zasulich doubted the democratic promise of centralized socialism.[8] In 1884, in her foreword to the Russian translation of Fredrick Engels' *Socialism: utopian and scientific*, Zasulich emphasized that nurturing democratic institutions of peasant commune, above all its cooperative organization of labour and self-governance, "would be of the greatest service in Russia" (1884: vii).

In his reply to Zasulich, Marx acknowledged that "his special study [of the Russian commune] has convinced [him] that the commune is the fulcrum for social regeneration in Russia", and admitted that "history offered Russia a chance to avoid the full-blown capitalist stage of economic development" (1944: 354–355). However, nowhere in his subsequent writings (from 1881 to 1883, the year of his death) did Marx further elaborate either on the means through which the commune could move backward Russia to an economically advanced society; or, most importantly, on potential negative consequences of centralization under socialism. The newly converted Russian Marxists chose not to focus on this one letter with its unorthodox musing on the commune and accepted as universally applicable his theory of history for Western society (Plekhanov [1885] 1948: 252–253).

To return to Zasulich, it can be argued that, despite her evident economic romanticism, she saw the dangers of supplanting the tsarist's autocracy with the dictatorship of proletariat, and intuitively sensed an inverse correlation between the coercive power of a centralized socialist state and respect for personal freedoms and democratic self-governance. As Isaiah Berlin observes, "the majority of Radical Populists were deeply democratic; they believed that all power tended to be corrupt, that all concentration of authority tended to perpetuate itself, that all centralization was coercive and evil" (1978: 221–222). Small wonder that Zasulich considered the October 1917 Bolshevik Revolution a "coup d'état" that, "from the point of view of socialists who remained faithful to the legacy of socialism", was "worse than no revolution at all" (1918: 286).

This strain of populist or democratic thought was not lost with Zasulich's reluctant acquiescence to Marxist thought. In 1902, the successors of Radical Populists, the neo-Populists, founded the Socialist Revolutionary Party (known as Essers, from the initial letters), the party of the Russian peasantry. Although Essers were aware of the strong communal spirit among peasants, they linked the democratic potential of peasant agriculture more to the development of small-scale independent farming, and believed that democratic socialism would not be feasible without a strong class of small democratic owners and cultivators. Essers were opponents of industrial concentration, as they feared that large-scale production would alienate working people. For this reason, they favoured workers' artels and decentralization in industry (Radkey 1958: 43–45). In agriculture Essers supported socialization of land, most of which belonged to landlords, by democratically elected state authorities, and its subsequent transfer to peasantry under the condition that

> no one was to buy land, or sell it, or rent it, or lease it; it was to belong to all people and was to be used equally by all who wished to cultivate it with their own labour, and only for as long as they worked it themselves.
>
> *Chernov, cited in Radkey 1955: 69*

Instead of the dictatorship of proletariat, Essers favoured the rule of all toiling people, peasants and workers.

The Esser party owes much of its beginnings to its founding mother, Catherine Breshko-Breshkovskaya (1844–1934), a former member of the terrorist "People's Will", who in 1896 returned from prison eager to revive the ideas of Radical Populists. Many historians recognize the crucial role of Breshko-Breshkovskaya in "calling the elder generation of revolutionaries back into service" (Radkey 1958: 52) and recruiting new activists for socialist revolutionary groups through "carrying the written and spoken word to them" (Maxwell 1990: 140–141). Vladimir Zenzinov (1880–1953), one of the oldest party members, attests that "everywhere [Breshko-Breshkovskaya] went she left an organization behind her" (1953: 106). In his obituary for Breshko-Breshkovskaya, Alexander Kerensky (1881–1970)[9] wrote that

> the period from 1896 to 1903 was for Breshko-Breshkovskaya the one of her most active work. While the police followed on her heels, she secretly travelled through literally the whole of Russia, creating the Party of Socialist Revolutionaries, and everywhere inspiring young people to fight for freedom for the whole people and for land for the peasants – under the motto of "land and liberty".
>
> *Kerensky 1935: 429*

Breshko-Breshkovskaya's name is inseparably linked with the propaganda of political terror, which Essers, influenced by the example of the "People's Will", used to speed up revolution during their early years. Vindicating political violence, Breshko-Breshkovskaya, a veteran revolutionist, explained that a "terrorist's self-sacrifice could not help but fire the hearts of thousands of others who also wished to champion the cause of the general good" (quoted in Zenzinov 1953: 106).

Breshko-Breshkovskaya's call for violent struggle and self-sacrifice appealed most to educated, upper-class women, as in the early 1880s. They began actively participating in assassinations of high-ranking members of tsarist bureaucracy; according to Amy Knight, "from 1905 to 1908 alone, eleven individual terrorist acts were committed by Socialist-Revolutionary women" (1979: 139). However, mixed terrorist militant groups, in which men and women participated in political warfare together, were more common (McNeal 1971: 157). Essers' most well-known terrorist exploits were the murders of the Minister of Interior Dimitri Sipyagin in 1902, his successor Vyacheslav von Plehve in 1904, and the Governor-General of Moscow, Grand Duke Sergey Aleksandrovich (uncle of then Tsar Nicolas II) in 1905 (Hilbrenner and Schenk, 2010: 166).

At the same time, as Victor Chernov (1873–1952) has clarified, "[Breshko-Breshkovskaya] was not a theoretician, a strategist or a tactician, but rather a preacher, an apostle with convincing words; even more, an active example" (1953: 316); in her public speeches Breshko-Breshkovskaya primarily propagated economic views of Socialist-Revolutionaries, most eloquently articulated in the works of party members Victor Chernov and Vladimir Kosinskii (1866–1938), and in the publications of non-party socialist Alexander Chayanov (1888–1937). Essers believed that at the base of land socialization small-scale peasant farming in agriculture would be preserved as the main organizational form, income differentiation among peasantry would be avoided, and conditions for decentralization and growth of regional democracies in Russia would be created (Chernov 1919: 45). Socialist-Revolutionaries were convinced that "the death" of numerous "self-governed peasant communities" would mean "death, or at any rate, a vast setback to freedom and equality in Russia" (Berlin 1978: 237).

Most non-Marxist socialists, and not just Essers, acknowledged a strong connection between the existence of thriving peasant family farming and the voluntary development of a cooperative movement. Chayanov explained that "peasant cooperation . . . is a part of peasant economy" and projected that under democratic socialism, small independent cultivators would constitute the basis of the agrarian system, while their various, freely formed cooperative associations would sustain its successful existence (1919: 21, 301). Non-Marxist socialists strongly objected to Bolshevik plans for land nationalization (Chayanov 1919: 42, 301) and argued against "tilling the land by large social groups . . . even within the framework of the socialist state" (Tugan-Baranovsky 1916: 364–365). Needless to say, the majority of Socialist-Revolutionaries did not support the October 1917 Bolshevik Revolution. Catherine Breshko-Breshkovskaya, like Vera Zasulich, considered the Bolshevik Revolution as "the reactionary coup d'état", stressing that "where there is no freedom there is no revolution" (Kerensky 1935: 429).

Yet in April of 1917, a small fraction of the Socialist Revolutionary Party formed a subgroup, known as Left Socialist Revolutionaries. In late October 1917, just prior to the Bolshevik Revolution, they split entirely from the Essers. After establishing their own party in December 1917, the Left Essers joined the Bolsheviks to create the Bolshevik-Left Essers coalition government, "the only coalition government in the history of Soviet Russia" (Häfner 1991: 324). Their fear was that if the Left Essers' representatives did not actively participate in the new Bolshevik government, Lenin would nationalize land and not transfer it to peasants (Boniece 1995: 408–409).

The most prominent woman representative of Left Essers was Maria Spiridonova (1884–1941). Spiridonova, of noble birth, studied to become a teacher, then, in 1905, began a nursing course, but gave up her studies for revolutionary work. On behalf of the Essers in 1906, she shot and killed General Luzhenovskii, an act for which she spent the next 11 years in prison (Steinberg 1971: 3–5). After her liberation by the Provisional Government in the spring of 1917, Spiridonova joined the emerging group of Left Essers and became their leader by election. After October 1917, she served the new Bolshevik government as the Head of the Peasant Section of the Central Executive Committee of the All-Russian Soviet of Workers', Peasants', and Soldiers' Deputies. In her numerous speeches of the time[10] (she wrote little, not even in prison), Spiridonova advocated for what she considered the most important task of the Bolshevik Revolution – the socialization of the land and transfer of property rights to local communities, and not to the centralized state. She believed that "if Soviet Russia is to be saved, it will be saved solely by the peasants, who are working [on their land] to build their new Soviet countryside" (cited in Cinnella 1997: 72). However, in late spring of 1918, the Bolshevik-Left Socialist Revolutionary coalition was broken, primarily due to a food supply crisis. The Peace Treaty of Brest-Litovsk with Germany cost Russia its primary grain supply, to which Lenin responded with compulsory requisitions of grain from Russian peasantry with devastating impact. Shortly thereafter, in July, Spiridonova and her party attempted to organize armed insurrection against Bolsheviks; as typical Essers, they were convinced that a terrorist attack on the German ambassador, Count Mirbach, would spark a popular uprising (Häfner 1991). The uprising failed; Spiridonova (along with many Left Essers) was arrested, and spent the rest of her life in Siberian exile, which ended with her execution in 1941 (Rabinowitch 1995: 425–428). By the mid-1920s, many Socialist-Revolutionaries, not only Leftist, were either imprisoned (Jancen 1982), or already abroad, and the Soviet government stopped publishing their views. With their defeat, a viable democratic socialist alternative to Bolsheviks' Marxism in Russia was lost.

Anna Klimina

Women of importance in Russian Marxist economic thought: Nadezhda Krupskaya, Ekaterina Kuskova and Alexandra Kollontai

The Marxist Party in Russia – the Russian Social Democratic Labour Party (RSDLP) – was established in 1898; most members of Plekhanov's "Emancipation of Labour" group joined it. In 1903 RSDLP split into the Bolshevik faction, headed by Vladimir Lenin (1870–1924) who perceived Russian Marxism as an elitist movement, and the much smaller Menshevik faction, led by Julius Martov (1873–1923) who wanted the party to be organized more democratically. Although Bolshevik and Menshevik views on the party's organizational principles differed, "the economic and political program [up to the early 1920s] was identical for both groups" (Tyrkova 1919: 45). Leninist Bolsheviks, the dominant force in Russian Marxism, argued that the "vanguard", a professional party elite, should assume state power on behalf of the proletariat, and create a single party state that would dictatorially govern the economy and lead society (Plekhanov 1906: 27; Lenin [1895] 1972: 102–118). The Bolshevik Party itself was run on the dictatorial principle of so-called democratic centralism that demanded unanimous compliance to party decisions and forbade the formation of any intra-party factions.

Almost all pre-1917 Marxist women intellectuals in Russia came from privileged classes; they began their revolutionary activities with "the mastery of the literature of Marxism", and then "made their way to the factory courtyard, the barracks, or labour circle" (Stites 1991: 243) to organize the emerging industrial proletariat for socialist revolution. Thus, Nadezhda Krupskaya (1869–1939), a daughter of a democratically minded gentry family, acquired her intimate knowledge of the proletariat while teaching reading, arithmetic, history, and Russian literature to illiterate factory workers in the "Evening-Sunday" School from 1891 to 1896 (McNeal 1972: 32). In 1898, Krupskaya became Lenin's wife.

Overall, the economic views and actions of Bolshevik women were obviously determined by their party's dictatorial politics. Krupskaya, one of the leading women Bolsheviks, seems to epitomize the conduct of most Bolshevik women of the time in her submission to the party with "unlimited moral ardor" (McNeal 1972: 65). She was "only a follower, a devoted technician", not a policy maker or independent critic (ibid.). She always "believed overwhelmingly in exclusive Bolshevik rule" and by 1920 completely accepted Bolshevik authoritarianism (Farnsworth 1973: 325). Yet in one field she dared to disagree with Lenin and the party – the training of the proletariat; she believed that all students should be exposed to the "fullest possible and most comprehensive education", and not merely taught utilitarian skills. Krupskaya strongly argued against "narrow productionism in education" that "suppresses individuality", insisting instead on establishing "socialist schools" that are "schools of freedom" and "creativity" ([1918] 1988: 52–54). She clearly realized that without such liberal education social progress in backward Russia would not be possible (ibid.: 59). Nevertheless, after Stalin destroyed political opposition and consolidated his power at the end of the 1920s, Krupskaya, understandably, did not openly oppose the establishment of the Stalinist model of utilitarianism and productionism in the Soviet educational system.

The most interesting economic ideas in the Bolshevik camp, however, came from those women who were not afraid to fight for establishing truly democratic foundations for the new economic order.

Ekaterina Kuskova (1869–1958) joined Plekhanov's "Emancipation of Labour" group in 1897. She seems to be the first opponent, from within emerging Russian Marxism, who sensed authoritarian danger in Lenin's vision for the Marxist Party as the exclusive shaping force in the Russian proletariat's ambivalent journey to revolution (Lenin [1895] 1972: 102–116).

Kuskova disagreed with Lenin's vision for party monopoly over the labour movement. In her article *Credo*, published in 1899, she explained that in a truly democratic setting, workers should have the freedom to organize themselves spontaneously and work out their independent ideology without being manipulated into political struggle under the guidance of the party (1899: 14). Kuskova considered trade unions to be among the most important of such "spontaneously formed" workers' organizations. She argued that trade unions, while focusing on immediate demands for better wages and working conditions, could nevertheless become an "awakening" that would teach workers how to create the political "organizations" needed to "receive and enjoy political freedoms" (1899: 15–16). Equally important in Kuskova's vision of trade unions was her conviction that the desired improvement in workers' economic conditions did not have to depend exclusively on a socialist revolution. These improvements could also be achieved gradually, through the trade union's non-violent struggle for economic and social reforms (1906: 325). To that end, Kuskova maintained, trade unions should remain politically independent (1906: 325).

Lenin fiercely opposed Kuskova's reformist ideas, arguing that "only socialist revolution could bring serious improvements in the life of workers" ([1902] 1973: 373). For Lenin, his monopolistic Bolshevik Party was necessary to "subordinate [workers'] struggle for reforms . . . to the revolutionary struggle for socialism" (ibid.: 406). Immediately after publishing *Credo*, Kuskova was expelled from the Russian Social Democratic Labour Party.

In 1903, being convinced that only "participation in liberal-oppositional activity" (Kuskova 1899: 17) could help move Russia in a democratic direction, Kuskova joined Russia's Union of Liberation Movement, founded by Peter Struve (1870–1944). In 1905 Struve, together with Pavel Milyukov (1859–1943), created the first liberal party in Russia, the Constitutional Democratic Party (Cadets). Kuskova became a member. However, as a left-wing liberationist, Kuskova disagreed with many pro-capitalist Cadet policies, and left Cadets in 1910. She converted to syndicalism and became actively involved in the cooperative movement, echoing the democratic views of many Russian non-Marxist socialists discussed earlier. Kuskova argued that cooperatives are best situated to "serve as a conduit for democratic ideas" and "a mechanism for preparing Russia for [democratic] self-government" (quoted in Norton 1992: 104). She did not approve of the Bolshevik Revolution and, in 1922, together with other prominent anti-Soviet intellectuals, was exiled from Russia (Finkel 2003: 602).

Another dissident, whose criticism of the Bolsheviks' authoritarian approach to economics had definite consequences, was Alexandra Kollontai (1872–1952), a daughter of military gentry, who became involved in radical politics from the 1890s. Kollontai joined Russian Marxists in 1906, first on the side of Mensheviks, and then, in 1915, she joined the Bolshevik Party. Kollontai expressed open disagreement with increasing centralization of production after the Bolshevik Revolution and the weakening of trade unions. Before the revolution, Bolsheviks gained overwhelming support from Russian workers by promising worker control of industrial property through conversion of existing enterprises into cooperatives, collectively run by worker unions. Immediately after the Bolshevik Revolution, those syndicalist ideas were actually put into practice through establishing worker-run factories (Avrich 1963: 49–52). However, by the end of 1918, that collegial worker control over enterprises was eliminated because Bolsheviks thought it was "sectarian", "chaotic, shattering, primitive, incomplete" (Lenin [1918] 1974: 140), and not congruent with the state's plans to establish a strict industrial hierarchical order.

The elimination of worker-run factories provoked strenuous objection from workers who formed what is known as Workers' Opposition, a movement that Kollontai openly supported. Her self-printed pamphlet, circulated among party members under the title *The Workers' Opposition*, put together workers' demands. She clearly explained that the Bolsheviks' intended move to centralization and autocracy would undermine worker independence, jeopardize natural development of workers' socialism, and further a proliferation of bureaucracy ([1919] 1977: 188–190). Workers' Opposition was heavily criticized by Lenin ([1921] 1973: 210–214), subsequently crushed in the early 1920s, and its leaders imprisoned (Allen 2005). Kollontai was forced to leave active politics.

Kollontai is also internationally renowned as a leading Bolshevik feminist; she wrote extensively on moral and political oppression of women, and argued for their emancipation through gender equality, personal autonomy, and socialization of domestic labour and child care[11] (1916: 571, 576; 1923). From 1918 to 1920, Kollontai was Head of the Commissariat for Social Welfare. From 1920 to 1922, the year she left Russia, she chaired the Women's Bureau[12] within the Central Committee of the Communist Party. Those positions gave her the authority to establish full state funding of maternity care "from conception through the first year of life", to initiate the reform of the marriage code, and to advocate – in her numerous speeches of the time – policies supporting the promotion of women into positions of leadership in the government and in the party (Kollontai 1921: 10–12; 1923; see also Clements 1979: 149–176).

None of these women, despite the thoughtfulness of their convictions or their willingness to risk their safety, were able to affect the Russian Marxists' vision of capitalism as the necessary, but intermediate, step toward centralized, bureaucratic socialism. That left the clearest advocacy for social reformism and liberal democracy in the hands of Russian liberals. The liberals supported the development of capitalism, seeing it as the final stage of Russia's transformation.

Placing liberalism within Russian context: economic views of Ariadna Tyrkova

Russian liberals advocated for a peaceful transformation of Russia's political regime from unlimited autocratic power to a rule-governed constitutional monarchy. They recognized that under Russia's conditions of socio-economic backwardness, "perfect democratic governance cannot be created overnight to replace the existing state" (Shapiro 1986: 76–78). Liberals believed that a modernized autocracy, restricted by a constitution created in the Western fashion, could (and should) be used together with a newly created legislative parliament to institute and nurture capitalism in Russia and find constitutional solutions to Russia's ills. They "were always willing to make peace with the monarchy and would at all times have preferred to have it grant political liberty on its own accord than to have liberty wrestled from it through revolution" (Pipes 1972: 75). However, as Milyukov explains, "Liberalism in Russia connoted the idea of state intervention", and since no Russian "liberal" thought had existed in laissez-faire days, it was free to become "more socially reformist, without being inconsistent with a former tradition" (1906: 224). As a much smaller group than the ones previously discussed, and given their more moderate agenda, liberals seemingly attracted fewer women. Hence this essay presents the Russian liberal perspective through the voice of one woman only. Ariadna Tyrkova (1869–1962) was the sole woman member of the Central Committee of Cadet Party from its beginning in 1906 until the October 1917 Bolshevik Revolution.

Tyrkova, a well-educated woman from landed gentry, worked in the 1890s and 1910s as a journalist, a career opportunity available to her as "most professions were not" (McReynolds 1990: 285). Always keenly interested in politics, she chose to identify with the cause of Russian Liberalism, drawn by its "purpose to secure the basic human and civil rights and to establish a democratic system" (Tyrkova 1951: 8). In 1903, she joined Struve's Union of Liberation and began to write for its main publication, the oppositionist review *Liberation*. In 1904–1905, Tyrkova participated in the formation of the Constitutional Democratic Party, and wrote frequently for the liberal press (Tyrkova 1953: 173–175). After the establishment of the Constitution (1906) and subsequent elections of the people's representatives to the Imperial Duma (the first Russian parliament), Tyrkova covered the Imperial Duma's political debates for various St Petersburg and Moscow newspapers from 1906 to 1912. She also lobbied for women's political rights in feminist newspapers (Stites 1991: 220) and at "all major feminist congresses" (Edmondson 1984: 173). Tyrkova was not a theoretician, but in her public speeches and newspaper articles, she explained and popularized the main ideas of the Russian liberal movement. In 1951, she summarized her vision in the autobiographical article "Russian Liberalism".

Like many Russian liberals, Tyrkova emphasized that Russia, economically and culturally backward, needed evolutionary change, which would include educating the masses for a responsible role, rather than radical revolutionary transformation (1919: 41). She saw the party's role as nurturing pro-democratic attitudes among Russian population through propaganda (1951: 12–13). Cadets opposed both Marxists and Socialist-Revolutionaries, who "denounced the liberals as [backward-looking] traitors and enemies of the people because the Cadet Party stood for constitutional monarchy instead of a republic and for social reform instead of social revolution" (Tyrkova 1951: 11).

Not until after the February 1917 Revolution and the tsar's abdication, did Russian liberals accept "the desirability of a republic in lieu of a constitutional monarchy", but this was "the only one serious alteration of [their] political program" (Tyrkova 1919: 41). Taking advantage of the new right of women to hold political office, in the summer of 1917, Tyrkova won election to the Petrograd City Council (Soviet). In her legislative capacity, she continued to advocate for the Cadets' vision of the country's socio-economic development.

As Tyrkova clearly explained, Cadets (like the Essers) insisted that the core of economic reform lay "in endowing the peasant with land out of state reserves and private holdings" (1919: 40). Although the top leaders of the Cadet Party were landowners, Cadets were convinced that "the land problem could be solved only by means of the compulsory alienation of the landowners' property for distribution among land-poor peasants" (ibid.). However, unlike Essers, who argued for the confiscation of private land without compensating owners, "the liberal program provided for a fair compensation of the landlords for the confiscated land", because liberals "recognized the right of [private] property as a necessary foundation of contemporary Russia's economic order and development" (Tyrkova 1919: 40, 117). They believed that Russian capitalism could mature only if a class of Russian owners of private property was created and protected (ibid.).

The Cadets' societal ideal highlighted both freedom and social justice, which, they believed, were realizable only by the combination of market economy and "state intervention through social legislation" (Milyukov 1906: 224). The purpose of such legislation, Tyrkova wrote, was "improving the lot of the workers within the framework of the capitalist system" (1953: 175), much as had already been done "by the progressives in all advanced Western countries [of the time]" (Tyrkova 1951: 10). Social legislation, advocated by the Cadets, included

> the right to organize in unions, the right to strike, freedom of assembly, participation of labour deputies in factory inspection, an eight-hour working day, strict control of child and female labor, arbitration of labor disputes, insurance against accidents, disease, and old age.
>
> *Tyrkova 1953: 175*

After the Bolshevik Revolution, when Lenin declared the Cadet Party a "party of enemies" and eliminated it, killing many of its leaders (Tyrkova 1953: 185–186), Tyrkova secretly fled

Russia. In 1919, soon after her arrival in England, she published "a volume of over five hundred pages" entitled *From Liberty to Brest-Litovsk*, a work of outstanding historical value as it provided English-speaking readers with the first eyewitness account of Russian Liberalism and its fate in the revolution of 1917 (Norman 1962: 280). Tyrkova articulated her conviction that the Bolshevik Revolution was a coup d'état, being inherently "hostile to all democratic forms of governance" (1919: 261). The revolution led to "a gloomy period of enforced communism" and Russia's subsequent "relapse into the most terrible experiences of the Middle Ages" (ibid.). In fact, Tyrkova's book was the first publication in the West that offered a direct and politically detailed critical narrative of the revolution. Not until after the beginning of the Cold War was a similarly critical assessment of the Bolshevik regime provided, by both right-wing and left-wing opponents of Soviet Communism in the West. Tyrkova anticipated their view by more than thirty years.

In her years abroad, Ariadna Tyrkova became one of the central figures in the Russian anti-Communist emigration, and, until her death in 1962, she "stood in firm opposition to the Soviet dictatorship" (Norman 1962: 281). Summarizing the Cadets' position, which she defended for many years in exile, she said that Cadets had

> stubbornly tried to explain to the public opinion of the free world what a threat to Christian civilization the Soviet regime represented. Hardly anyone listened to them. The Cadet party is no more. But Russian liberalism is not dead. Over there, in Russia, at the price of heartbreaking experience, people have learned to realize what becomes of life when it is stripped of justice, of rights, of human respect and freedom.
>
> *Tyrkova 1951: 14*

Her key message, central to the Cadet's Party political philosophy – that without respect for democracy, pluralism, individual freedom, and the rule of law a democratic Russia can never come into being – is what I consider her most valuable gift to future generations of Russian democrats.

Conclusion

This chapter has discussed the particularities of women's economic thought in late Imperial Russia and in the early years after the 1917 Revolution, years of dramatic changes, both political and social, as Russia sought to overcome its feudal backwardness. The prevailing currents of thought among those who opposed autocracy can be divided into two streams: the evolutionary advance of capitalism, advocated by Russian liberal reformers, and a revolutionary destruction of the existing state to make way for some form of socialism, advocated by both non-Marxists and Marxists. Educated women helped to disseminate both main currents of thought, primarily through action rather than in print. Among the Russian liberal reformers, the sole prominent woman is Ariadna Tyrkova, a political journalist and writer, whose contribution was primarily dissemination of liberal democratic ideas of the time. More women were notable among non-Marxists socialists – Radical Populists and their successors Socialist-Revolutionaries – but their contribution is primarily political activism, not theory or publications. The most representative women have been discussed in this chapter: Vera Figner, Vera Zasulich, Catherine Breshko-Breshkovskaya and Maria Spiridonova. All of them passionately believed that to be democratic, socialism must be decentralized and based on a strong class of small democratic owners and cultivators. Interestingly, among the Leninist Bolsheviks, the dominant force in Russian Marxism, the leading women, whose contributions are theoretically significant, played a role somewhat different from merely disseminating or carrying out the ideas of the party. Ekaterina Kuskova and Alexandra Kollontai were not afraid to disagree with Lenin's vision for socialism in which the single party owns the state, and governs the entire economy through dictatorship. To their own detriment, they argued against party monopoly over the labour movement and advocated industrial democracy under socialism.

In summary, I argue that the crucial point of Russian democratic thought of the time, with which many of the above women would agree, is that without economic empowerment of people, political democracy cannot develop. Post-1917 Russian history has supported the views of these women. In October 1917, Leninist Bolsheviks successfully replaced tsarist autocracy with a more authoritarian state, accomplishing, as Ariadna Tyrkova put it, "the transition from absolute monarchy to absolute Communism – in terms of the historical process – with breathtaking speed" (1951: 4). Sovietologists and Russianists agree that there are few differences between the autocracy of tsarist rule and the autocracy of the Soviet regime (Mullerson 1993: 473). Richard Pipes, in fact, sees this continuity of authoritarianism in the current re-establishment of autocracy in Putin's Russia (2006: A14), which at present is known internationally – again, as pre-1917 Russia was known – as an authoritarian country (Habdank-Kołaczkowska 2015: 4), characterized by the omnipotence of a centralist state and, necessarily, a disempowered society.

Hence, the main message of the women discussed in this essay still stands, as relevant and applicable as ever: only through creating and strengthening the economic power of the public is it possible to democratize and thus civilize Russia. While Russian women did not exclusively create this message, it motivated them to seize a unique opportunity to contribute substantially in the political and economic upheaval of pre-1920s Russia. They acted primarily as organizers, promoters, and even terrorists, but also wrote letters, asked important questions and spoke out for their passionately held vision for a new democratic Russia. It is unfortunate that their voices were not heeded enough to prevent the subsequent descent into autocracy and repression.

Notes

1 Up until 1906 Russia was an autocracy in principle and in fact; from 1906 onwards it had become a constitutional monarchy.

2 Even at the time of the 1917 Russian Revolution, Russia's population was still 80 per cent peasants, mostly illiterate (Pipes 1994: 217); therefore, educated women comprised a very small proportion of society.

3 Cynthia Whittaker explains that "Besides literary work, the only professions traditionally open to educated women at the time were those of governess, school teacher, or midwife" (1976: 44).

4 In 1869 the opening of the Lubianskie evening courses in Moscow (which were modelled on the three-year liberal arts and science courses in the regular Moscow University curricula) and the similar Alarchinskie evening courses in St Petersburg made advanced education available to women for the first time (Johanson 1987: 44–45); in 1876, the first women's university – St Petersburg Higher Women's Courses, popularly known as Bestuzhevskie Courses – was established. Women's higher courses were also founded in Kiev, Moscow and Kazan. In the late 1870s, a medical school was finally opened for women.

5 The communal form of peasant society in Russia has been known since the 16th century. In 1877 some 89 per cent of peasant households were in communes (Mironov 1990: 29).

6 The day after her acquittal, Zasulich was sought by the police and would have been arrested if found, so she fled abroad where she spent 25 years, in total, avoiding arrest (Kucherov 1952).

7 Russia started to industrialize in the late 1880s. Most capital for industrialization came from foreign investors and tended, given the Russian state's interest in the development of its own heavy industry, to "favour heavy industrial branches" and "production of producers' goods" (Gerschenkron 1963: 152–153). This process led, by the end of 1890s, to increasing numbers of industrial workers (proletariat), employed in large-scale capital goods industries.

8 Jay Bergman, the author ofVera Zasulich's biography, appropriately asserts that "Zasulich's Marxism in the 1880s was hardly of an orthodox variety" (1983: 96).
9 Alexander Kerensky, himself a member of the Socialist-Revolutionary Party, was the last chairman of the Russian Provisional Government, which was established during the February 1917 Revolution that dismantled the tsarist autocracy and was itself overturned by Vladimir Lenin during the October 1917 Bolshevik Revolution.
10 Most of them are presented in *The Left Socialist Revolutionary Party: Documents and Materials, Vol. 1: July 1917–May 1918* (in Russian), 2000, Moscow: ROSSPEN.
11 Between April and June 1921 Kollontai delivered fourteen lectures at Sverdlovsk University on *Women's Labour in the Evolution of the Economy* (published in 1923), in which she discussed origins of women's oppression and questioned marriage and traditional sexuality. Kollontai argued that if society takes responsibility for domestic labour, a new morality that "[enables] individuals freely to express their love and sexuality" ([1923] 1977: 291) could be created. Feminist historians agree that Kollontai was the first Russian Marxist scholar to raise "sexuality and sexual relations as a proper topic for political discussion" (Engel 1992: 317).
12 The Women's Bureau was closed in 1929, as the Soviet Government declared that there was no "woman's question" in the USSR (Valkova 2008: 165).

References

Allen, B. 2005. "Alexander Shliapnikov and the Origins of the Workers' Opposition, March 1919–April 1920". *Jahrbücher für Geschichte Osteuropas*, 53 (1): 1–24.

Avrich, P. 1963. "The Bolshevik Revolution and Workers' Control in Russian Industry". *Slavic Review*, 22 (1): 47–63.

Bergman, J. 1979. "The Political Thought of Vera Zasulich". *Slavic Review*, 38 (2): 243–258.

Bergman, J. 1983. *Vera Zasulich: A Biography*. Stanford, CA: Stanford University Press.

Berlin, I. 1978. *Russian Thinkers*. London: The Hogarth Press.

Boniece, S. 1995. *Maria Spiridonova, 1884–1918: Feminine Martyrdom and Revolutionary Mythmaking*. Ph.D. dissertation, Indiana University.

Chayanov, A. 1919. *The Basic Ideas and Organizational Forms of Peasant Cooperation* (in Russian). Moscow: Universal Library.

Chernov, V. 1919. *Land and Law: Collection of Articles* (in Russian). Petrograd: n. p.

Chernov, V. 1953. *Before the Storm* (in Russian). New York: Chekhov Publishing House.

Cinnella, E. 1997. "The Tragedy of the Russian Revolution Promise and Default of the Left Socialist Revolutionaries in 1918". *Cahiers du Monde Russe*, 38 (1/2): 45–82. Available at: www.jstor.org/stable/20171032 (accessed April 20, 2017).

Clements, B. 1979. *Bolshevik Feminist: The Life of Alexandra Kollontai*. Bloomington: Indiana University Press.

Edmondson, L. 1984. *Feminism in Russia: 1900–1917*. Stanford, CA: Stanford University Press.

Engel, B. 1977. "The Emergence of Women Revolutionaries in Russia". *Frontiers: A Journal of Women Studies*, 2 (1): 92–105.

Engel, B. 1992. "Engendering Russia's History: Women in Post-Emancipation Russia and the Soviet Union". *Slavic Review*, 51 (2): 309–321.

Farnsworth, B. 1973. "Review of *Bride of the Revolution: Krupskaya and Lenin* by R. H. McNeal". *Russian Review*, 32 (3): 324–325.

Figner, V. [1881] 1964. "The Demands of the Peoples Will", *in*: Vera Figner, *Documented Works*, Vol. II (in Russian). Moscow: Mysl, 411–412.

Finkel, S. 2003. "Purging the Public Intellectual: The 1922 Expulsions from Soviet Russia". *Russian Review*, 62 (4): 589–613.

Gerschenkron, A. 1955. "The Problem of Economic Development in Russian Intellectual History of the Nineteenth Century", *in*: E. Simmons (ed.), *Continuity and Change in Russian and Soviet Thought*. Cambridge, MA: Harvard University Press, 11–39.

Gerschenkron, A. 1963. "The Early Phases of Industrialization in Russia: Afterthoughts and Counterthoughts", *in*: W. Rostow (ed.), *The Economics of Take-off into Sustained Growth*. New York: Palgrave Macmillan, 151–169.

Gregory, P. 1994. *Before Command: An Economic History of Russia from Emancipation to the First Five-Year Plan*. Princeton, NJ: Princeton University Press.

Habdank-Kołaczkowska, S. 2015. *Nations in Transit: Democracy on the Defensive in Europe and Eurasia.* Washington, DC: Freedom House. Available at www.freedomhouse.org. (accessed October 22, 2015).

Häfner, L. 1991. "The Assassination of Count Mirbach and the 'July Uprising' of the Left Socialist Revolutionaries in Moscow, 1918". *Russian Review* 50 (3): 324–344.

Hartnett, L. 2014. *The Defiant Life of Vera Figner: Surviving the Russian Revolution.* Bloomington, IN: Indiana University Press.

Hilbrenner, A. & Schenk, F. 2010. "Modern Times? Terrorism in Late Tsarist Russia". *Jahrbücher für Geschichte Osteuropas*, 58 (2): 161–171.

Jancen, M. 1982. *A Show Trial under Lenin: The Trial of the Socialist Revolutionaries, Moscow 1922.* The Hague: Martinus Nijhoff Publishers.

Johanson, C. 1987. *Women's Struggle for Higher Education in Russia, 1855–1900.* Montreal: McGill-Queen's University Press.

Kerensky, A. 1935. "Catherine Breshkovsky (1844–1934)". *The Slavonic and East European Review*, 13 (1): 428–431.

Knight, A. 1975. "The Fritschi: A Study of Female Radicals in the Russian Populist Movement". *Canadian-American Slavic Studies*, 9 (1): v–17.

Knight, A. 1979. "Female Terrorists in the Russian Socialist Revolutionary Party". *Russian Review*, 38 (2): 139–159.

Kollontai, A. 1916. *Society and Motherhood* (in Russian). Petrograd: Life and Knowledge.

Kollontai, A. 1921. *The Women Worker and Peasant in Soviet Russia* (in Russian). Moscow: Gosizdat.

Kollontai, A. 1923. *Women's Labour in the Evolution of the Economy* (in Russian). Moscow: Gosizdat.

Kollontai, A. [1919] 1977. "Workers' Opposition", *in*: A. Holt (ed.), *Selected Writings of Alexandra Kollontai.* London: Allison & Busby, 159–200.

Kollontai, A. [1923] 1977. "Make Way for Winged Eros: A Letter to Working Youth", *in*: A. Holt (ed.), *Selected Writings of Alexandra Kollontai.* London: Allison & Busby, 276–292.

Krupskaya, N. [1918] 1988. "Concerning the Question of Socialist Schools", *in: Krupskaya's Selected Works* (in Russian). Moscow: Politizdat, 50–59.

Kucherov, S. 1952. "The Case of Vera Zasulich". *Russian Review*, 11 (2): 86–96.

Kuskova, E. 1899. "Credo" (in Russian). *Rabochee delo*, no. 4–5: 13–18.

Kuskova, E. 1906. "Review of *From History of Labour Movement and Social Democracy in Russia, 1900–1904* by F. Dan" (in Russian). *Byloe*, 10 (1), 325–327.

Lenin, V. [1895] 1972. "Draft and Explanation of a Programme for the Socialist-Democratic Earty", *in: Lenin's Collected Works*, Volume 2. Moscow: Progress Publishers, 93–121.

Lenin, V. [1902] 1973. "What Is to Be Done", *in: Lenin's Collected Works*, Volume 5. Moscow: Progress Publishers, 347–530.

Lenin, V. [1917] 1974. "The State and Revolution", *in: Lenin's Collected Works*, Volume 25. Moscow: Progress Publishers, 387–497.

Lenin, V. [1918] 1974. "Speech at the Extraordinary Sixth All-Russia Congress of Soviets of Workers', Peasants', Cossacks' and Red Army Deputies on November 6, 1918", *in: Lenin's Collected Works*, Volume 28. Moscow: Progress Publishers, 135–164.

Lenin, V. [1921] 1973. "On the Trade-Unions: Speech at the Tenth Party Congress on March 14, 1921", *in: Lenin's Collected Works*, Volume 32. Moscow: Progress Publishers, 210–214.

Marx, K. [1850] 1950. "Address of the Central Committee to the Communist League, March 1850", *in: K. Marx and F. Engels' Selected writings*, Volume 1. Moscow: Foreign Languages Publishing House, 106–107.

Marx, K. 1944. *Selected Correspondence of Karl Marx and Friedrich Engels: A Selection with Commentary and Notes.* London: Lawrence.

Maxwell, M. 1990. *Narodniki Women: Russian Women Who Sacrificed Themselves for the Dream of Freedom.* New York: Pergamon Press.

McNeal, R. 1971. "Women in the Russian Radical Movement". *Journal of Social History*, 5 (2): 143–163.

McNeal, R. 1972. *Bride of the Revolution.* Ann Arbor: The University of Michigan Press.

McReynolds, L. 1990. "Imperial Russia's Newspaper Reporters: Profile of a Society in Transition, 1865–1914". *The Slavonic and East European Review*, 68 (2): 277–293.

Milyukov, P. 1906. *Russia and Its Crisis.* Chicago, IL: The University of Chicago Press.

Mironov, B. 1990. "The Russian Peasant Commune in 1860s", *in*: B. Eklof & S. Frank (eds.), *The World of the Russian Peasant: The Post-Emancipation Culture and Society.* Boston: Unwin Human, 7–43.

Mullerson, R. 1993. "The Continuity and Succession of States, by Reference to the Former USSR and Yugoslavia". *International and Comparative Law Quarterly*, 42 (3): 473–493.

Norman, A. 1962. "Ariadna Tyrkova-Williams, November 26, 1869–January 12, 1962". *Russian Review*, 21 (3): 277–281.
Norton, B. 1992. "Laying the Foundations of Democracy in Russia: E.D. Kuskova's Contribution, February–October 1917", *in*: L. Edmondson (ed.), *Women and Society in Russia and the Soviet Union*. Cambridge: Cambridge University Press, 101–123.
Pipes, R. 1972. "Peter Struve: The Sources of his Liberal Russian Nationalism, *in*: C. Timberlake (ed.), *Essays on Russian Liberalism*. Columbia, MO: University of Missouri Press, 62–77.
Pipes, R. 1994. "Did the Russian Revolution Have to Happen?" *The American Scholar*, 63 (2): 215–238.
Pipes, R. 2006. "Why the Bear Growls". *The Wall Street Journal*, March: A14.
Plekhanov, G. [1885] 1948. *Our Differences* (in Russian). Moscow: Gospolitizdat Publishing House.
Plekhanov, G. 1906. *Anarchism and Socialism*. London: Twentieth Century Press Ltd.
Rabinowitch, A. 1995. "Maria Spiridonova's 'Last Testament'", *Russian Review*, 54 (3): 424–446.
Radkey, O. 1955. "Chernov and Agrarian Socialism before 1918" *in*: E. Simmons (ed.), *Continuity and Change in Russian and Soviet Thought*. Cambridge, MA: Harvard University Press, 63–80.
Radkey, O. 1958. *The Agrarian Foes of Bolshevism*. New York, NY: Columbia University Press.
Raeff, M. 1959. "Some Reflections on Russian Liberalism". *Russian Review* 18 (3): 218–230.
Shapiro, L. 1986. *Russian Studies*. London: Collins Harvill.
Steinberg, I. 1971. *Spiridonova, Revolutionary Terrorist*. Freeport, NY: Books for Libraries Press.
Stites, R. 1977. "Women and the Russian Intelligentsia: Three Perspectives", *in*: D. Atkinson (ed.), *Women in Russia*. Stanford, CA: Stanford University Press, 39–62.
Stites, R. 1991. *The Women's Liberation Movement in Russia: Feminism, Nihilism, and Bolshevism, 1860–1930*. Princeton, NJ: Princeton University Press.
The Left Socialist Revolutionary Party: Documents and Materials, Vol. 1: July 1917–May 1918, compiled by A. Leontiev (in Russian). 2000, Moscow: ROSSPEN.
Tugan-Baranovsky, M. 1916. *The Social Foundations of Cooperation* (in Russian). Moscow: Kushnerev.
Tyrkova, A. 1919. *From Liberty to Brest-Litovsk: The First Year of the Russian Revolution*. London: Macmillan and Co. Ltd.
Tyrkova, A. 1951. "Russian Liberalism". *Russian Review*, 10 (1): 3–14.
Tyrkova, A. 1953. "The Cadet Party". *Russian Review*, 12 (3): 173–186.
Valkova, O. 2008. "The Conquest of Science: Women and Science in Russia, 1860–1940". *Osiris*, 23 (1): 136–165.
Whittaker, C. 1976. "The Women's Movement during the Reign of Alexander II: A Case Study in Russian Liberalism". *The Journal of Modern History*, 48 (2): 35–69.
Zasulich, V. [1881] 1983. "A Letter to Marx, February 16, 1881", *in*: T. Shanin (ed.), *Late Marx and the Russian Road: Marx and "the Peripheries of Capitalism"*. London: Routledge and Keagan Paul plc, 98–99.
Zasulich, V. 1884. "Foreword" in Fredrick Engels *"Socialism: Utopian and Scientific* (in Russian). Geneva: n. p., 2–7.
Zasulich, V. 1918. "Smolnyi's Socialism" (in Russian). *Nasha Zhyzn'*, 4 (2): 280–288.
Zasulich, V. [1931] 1975. "Memoir", *in*: B. Engel & C. Rosenthal (eds.), *Five Sisters: Women against the Tsar*. London: Weidenfeld and Nicolson, 59–94.
Zenzinov, V. 1953. *Living Memories* (in Russian). New York: Chekhov Publishing House.

7

IS EQUAL PAY WORTH IT?

Beatrice Potter Webb's, Millicent Garrett Fawcett's and Eleanor Rathbone's changing arguments

Cléo Chassonnery-Zaïgouche

Introduction[1]

In February 1918, some British women over the age of 30 gained the right to vote. This political move has been interpreted by many as a reward for women's efforts during the First World War.[2] In August of the same year, female tramway and bus conductors in London led a successful strike against unequal war bonuses, claiming the same increase of five shillings a week as their male colleagues. The multiplication of "equal pay strikes" led the War Cabinet to set up a committee to examine the "problem" that "women in industry" constituted; the Atkin Committee was appointed in September 1918 to examine the relations between men's and women's wages in industry. It presented its report the next year. Part of the official inquiry was to determine whether women received a man's rate when occupying a "man's job" following the 1915 "Treasury Agreement" with the trade unions; and if not, why? The formula "equal pay for equal work" refers to fair conditions of work either being equal (hour or piece) rates or equal scales of payment for men and women.[3] In its historical scope, the formula refers to a burning controversy "which touches not only the pocket but the home" (Edgeworth 1922, 431). Can women perform the same jobs as men in times of emergency? Does not equal pay and women's work destroy what was considered one of the main bases of Victorian society – the differentiation of the sexes (Vaid 1985)? Should women be paid the men's rate when they are supposedly not supporting a family? During the First World War, these issues became framed as a question of national (and imperial) survival.

Equal pay had been at the core of many political and intellectual disputes since the mid-19th century. The gradual development of labour legislation and the issue of equal pay in the growing Civil Services administration made it an even more burning issue. Why women were paid less was also a theoretical conundrum for economists, and crystallized methodological debates on the status of empirical inquiry. The rise of the marginalist theory of labour productivity has been far from a unified and linear process. The debates on women's wages encapsulate the difficult transition from a logic of subsistence to a logic of production, a transition from a theoretically based discipline to an observational one. The gallery of the "facts" on women's work – gathering data through large scale surveys in the grey zone between social work and the emerging discipline of sociology – were often opposed to the promotion of traditional moral values.[4] Though absent from textbooks and *Principles* and despite the lack of reliable statistics, unpacking the economic status of women resulted in a flow of articles, reviews, and comments in academic journals (Groenewegen 1994).

The scholarly, intellectual, public and political debate over equal pay was, if not dominated, then at least shaped, by women's contributions. This chapter concentrates on the arguments of three major contributors: Beatrice Potter Webb (1858–1943), Millicent Garrett Fawcett (1847–1929) and Eleanor Rathbone (1872–1946). They were no Oxbridge armchair economists, yet their positions became pre-eminent in the public sphere and in academic debates, in journal publications and in the press, in intellectual circles and parliamentary discussions. In 1915, Beatrice Webb signed a "Women's Appeal to Women" to ask for "equal conditions and equal wages for the same work" (War Emergency Workers' National Committee 1915). That same year, Millicent Garrett Fawcett explained that due to the dramatic increase in women's productivity which the First World War had helped to "discover", women merit equal pay (Fawcett 1917). In 1918, the Family Endowment Committee led by Eleanor Rathbone issued a pamphlet to celebrate the death of the "family wage" as a men-only right.[5]

My purpose is to outline the personal and intellectual trajectories that led these three major public intellectuals to support equal pay at the end of the war. In doing so, I hope to challenge the tendency to isolate the internal coherence of texts and, rather, to weave together different sources to explore the dynamics of individuals' thoughts. That they were women bears, to some extent, a relation to the fact they work on "women's problems",[6] but it does not explain their different and changing argumentative strands. For this apparent consensus on equal pay is underpinned by altogether different intellectual, social and political arguments *and* public images. In the public eye, Fawcett, Webb and Rathbone became epitomes of different political figures: the liberal feminist, the socialist "feminist", and the new or "welfare feminist".[7] My contribution is focused on the dialogue between the intellectuals; on their ambiguities, unease and changes of mind regarding the under-researched problem of equal pay in the history of economic thought.[8]

Remarkably, Webb, Fawcett and Rathbone had *all* initially exhibited a staunch pre-war opposition to the "equal pay for equal work" principle, here too for very different reasons. Webb thought equal pay was a threat to the standard of living of the working class – a standard based primarily on the wage of male breadwinners. Fawcett entered the equal pay discussion from a classical liberal point of view, favouring unrestricted competition in the labour market. She initially opposed equal pay because she thought women would lose the competition game due to their lack of training and education. In the early 1900s, Rathbone saw the formula as a "trap" set by the trade union movement to decrease women's employment. How, then, did these three intellectuals eventually find themselves defending the same "erroneous" (Fawcett 1892, 176), "ambiguous" (Webb 1919, 223), or "vague and ill-defined" (Rathbone 1917, 58) formula of "equal pay for equal work" at the end of the war?

Unpacking the heterogeneous trajectories that lay beneath my protagonists' common social background – the three women came from Victorian middle-upper-class families with high intellectual and political capital – will allow me to highlight how personal motives, political commitments, epistemic stances and intellectual constructions combined into positions that evolved in reaction to events. I concentrate on their public conversation. Though the three intellectuals knew each other and met several times, their "dialogue" is explored through exchanges within the press, academic journals, and reports.

First, I briefly present biographical elements to understand from where Fawcett, Webb and Rathbone entered the debate. I then discuss the early positions of Fawcett and Webb in the 1890s as a frontal opposition of two sets of general principles: Fabianism and classical liberalism. In the third section, I show how changes occurring before the war served as the catalyst of new arguments that challenged the "family wage". The final section analyzes the period during and after the First World War and the emerging fragile consensus in favour of the "equal pay for equal work" principle.

Three public intellectuals

Fawcett, Webb and Rathbone entered this debate from different foundational experiences, but not from different *milieus*.[9] Their eminent families included a wealth of successful business leaders, members of parliament and philanthropists whose commitment was fuelled by Unitarian spirituality and liberal politics for the Rathbones, utilitarianism and a Tory sensibility for the Potters, conservative turned liberal for the Garretts. If they have in common a childhood in a mansion and a difficult relationship to their mothers, they also reflect in their writings a very similar heroic representation of their fathers, successful Victorian businessmen supporting the emancipatory aspirations of their daughters.[10] Despite their shared Victorian middle-upper-class background, the three women had entirely different early intellectual experiences and contrasting domestic environments.

Millicent Garrett Fawcett (1847–1929) is remembered for her early commitment to "the Cause" – the campaign for the enfranchisement of women – and as leader of the National Union of Women's Suffrage Societies (NUWSS) between 1897 and 1914. Fawcett was surrounded by feminists, starting with her role model and sister Elizabeth Garrett Anderson, the first British woman physician, a close friend to Emily Davis and an active member of the Langham Place circle. Fawcett gave her first speech advocating the suffrage for women at the age of 21, two years after marrying Henry Fawcett, the blind Professor of Political Economy from Cambridge University. She continued her public activities after their only child was born.

Her political economy and philosophy were shaped through her interactions with John Stuart Mill, who introduced her to Henry Fawcett. Millicent Fawcett worked with her husband on the revision of his *Manual of Political Economy*. She published two best-selling books: *Political Economy for Beginners*, in 1870, which underwent more than ten editions, and *Tales in Political Economy*, in 1874 (Pujol and Seiz 2000; Henderson 2004). Fawcett was a public figure who fits in the tradition of female knowledge brokers in economic thought (Forget 2016). Sometimes characterized as the "most eminent female political economist", Fawcett was suggested as a possible member of the Political Economy Club by Charles Dilke, but Mill eventually turned down the proposal (Rubinstein 1989, 77).

Beatrice Potter Webb (1858–1943) was introduced to the misery of working-class women when she was a rent collector for the philanthropist London East End Dwellings Company. During her work as social scientist for (her cousin) Charles Booth's *Life and Labour of the People* survey (Webb 1889a, 1889b, 1889c), Beatrice Potter showed herself to be a "born first-hand investigator" (Shaw 1942, 10–11; see also Webb 1886, 1888).

Beatrice Potter decided to meet Sidney Webb after reading his historical chapter in the *Fabian Essays in Socialism*, edited by Shaw. After a passionate but dead-end relationship with (Liberal Unionist and central political figure) Joseph Chamberlain (their main rift was about the role of married women), she found in Sidney Webb, a then promising statesman, an intellectual partner (Davis 2004). They got married in 1892 and became one of the most influential couples in British intellectual and political history, through their common published works and respective political careers. The whole project of the Webbs was to make socialism "constitutional, respectable, and practical" (Shaw 1942, 10).

A graduate from Somerville, Oxford, the very year it became a College, Eleanor Rathbone (1872–1946) followed an intellectual trajectory which had only recently become accessible to women: from a highly selective intellectual circle at Oxford to a subsequent career in British state administration and at the House of Commons. An early suffragist and philanthropist in her hometown of Liverpool, she became her father's successor, both in business and in politics (Pedersen 1996). Her formative experience was her practical encounter with social work while organizing the family allowance administration during the First World War. When she replaced Fawcett as President of the NUWSS in 1919, she was recognized as an experienced social worker with great administrative skills.

Rathbone was more of a stateswoman than a political economist. Concerned with the economic dependence of women, her *The Disinherited Family* (1924) was later heralded by William Beveridge, Hugh Dalton and other economists as one of the most important modern treatises on distributive economics (Pedersen 2004). Her contribution to the scholarly debate was her statistical demonstration of the lack of 'fit' between wages and family needs. Younger, Rathbone entered the debate on equal pay much later – in the 1910s – and in a more practical fashion. Fawcett and Webb, by contrast, were first opposing each other on general principles.

Abstract principles and the "woman question"

Sidney Webb's (1891) is one of the first economic analyses of the gender pay gap. His article provoked the first academic paper by Fawcett (1892) and Beatrice Webb's subsequent indirect attack against "the Cause" (1896). Webb and Fawcett made the women's wage issue a special case within a general creed to defend, respectively, classical liberalism and Fabianism.

Applying the theory of non-competing groups to women

Millicent Fawcett (1892) frontally attacked Sidney Webb's considerations about the major determinant of women's wages. According to Sidney Webb, the lower pay was related to the general inferiority of women's work, in terms of quality and quantity of output, as well as in terms of advantage to the employer. The general inferiority determined wage levels, even in occupations where women were superior in skills (Webb 1891, 657). But, more importantly, men and women rarely worked in the same job, and when they did, they rarely performed the same work: women usually undercut men's wages as "the Chinese men have superseded American women in laundry work" in another context (Webb 1891, 658). Webb enumerated different commonly accepted factors as causing this wage differential: differences in physical strength and differential capacity to react in emergencies, custom and discrimination – that he admitted being unable to weight properly.

According to Fawcett, wages were subject to more unifying economic principles: wages are determined "on the most part" by competition (Fawcett 1874, 111, 113). Influenced by John Stuart Mill and John Elliott Cairnes (Henderson 2004), she applied the theory of non-competing groups to women. "What makes the rate of wages in any particular group?" she asks, to which she answers: "[t]he value of the produce of the labour in the most productive industry of the group" (Fawcett 1892, 174). Women are crowded in the least productive occupations (Fawcett 1892, 175). Denied access is the cause of the lower productivity of women, and not the more common reverse argument of the time that women are not allowed in trades because they are inferior in productivity. Hence, widening women's opportunity in terms of education and opening the profession, rather than "organizing women's labour", would increase women's wages. Fawcett was, at the time, against "equal pay for equal" work. Fawcett's systematized version of the "crowding hypothesis" is directed toward Craft and Trade Unions' policies, which controlled access and training for specific occupations – especially the more skilled professions.[11]

Besides her early work on East London working-class women, Beatrice Webb entered more directly the debate in the context of the Factory Act. The amendment of 1895 aimed at improving safety and sanitation conditions, employer's liability and age limitations (all provisions applied to men and women alike). However, limitation regarding hours of labour were sex-specific and specifically targeted (mainly women-occupied) sweated industries such as textiles.[12] Beatrice Webb's first Fabian Tract – *Women and the Factory Acts* (1896) – is based on two speeches delivered at a meeting of the National Union of Women Workers and before the Fabian Society. It clearly targets feminist arguments against sex-specific legislation. Her tract aimed at unveiling the "real" anti-legislation spirit of the "ladies who have usually led the cause of women's enfranchisement" (Webb 1896, 3). Voicing their concern on women-specific legislation, the "most energetic and prominent opponents of women's Factory legislation [. . .] Mrs. Henry Fawcett and Miss Ada Heather-Bigg" openly "avow" their scepticism over *any* legislation (Webb 1896, 4).[13]

In earlier debates over the extension of the Factory Acts, notably in 1873, Henry Fawcett, at the time a Liberal MP, and Millicent Fawcett campaigned actively against a bill to restrict women's employment (Rubinstein 1989, 79). The couple were clearly identified in public opinion as major figures against sex-specific legislation. In a letter to *The Times*, Millicent Fawcett discerned behind the bill "the old Trade Union spirit to drive women out of certain trades where their competition is inconvenient" (Fawcett in a letter dated June 1873, quoted by Rubinstein 1989, 79). For many feminists, imposing restrictions on women's employment reduces the demand for women's labour, a claim largely shared by economists at the time. In her answer to Sidney Webb, Fawcett made her case in favour of equal opportunity over equal pay. In the teaching profession, equal pay is "an error, both in principle and in tactics" (Fawcett 1892, 176). "The cry 'the same wages for the same work' is very plausible, but it is impossible of achievement when the economic conditions of the two sexes are so widely different" (ibid.). Fawcett's priority was to demand equal job opportunity, regardless of wages. For trade unionists, this demand was equivalent to the promotion of blacklegging (Nyland and Ramia 1994, 119).

Toward a "minimum of civilized existence"

Beatrice Webb was convinced state regulation was the solution to the existence of sweated trades. She added a strategic point: legislation was progressive for all workers but its political implementation was, as a first step, only possible for women (Webb 1896, 4). The independence of working-class women rested on the improvement of the material conditions of work. But, more importantly, protective legislation for women was also a means to protect women's living standard as dependants, obtained from men's breadwinner wage. The distinction between classes of women became central to Webb's thought.

> When we are concerned with the propertied classes – when, for instance, it is sought to open up to women higher education or the learned professions – it is easy to see that freedom is secured by abolishing restrictions. But when we come to the relations between capital and labour an entirely new set of considerations come into play.
>
> *Webb 1896, 5*

Webb's "new set of considerations" referred mainly to differences in bargaining power (Webb 1896, 6). Constitutional struggle for regulation would improve bargaining power for labour to ask for a "minimum of civilized existence". Beatrice Webb challenged the "laissez-faire" views on labour legislation, but also dismissed the common idea that regulation will diminish the demand for women's work. Webb argued that this common idea is based on two *false* assumptions.

> The first assumption is, that in British industry to-day, men and women are actively competing for the same employment; [t]he second assumption is, that in the few cases in which men and women may be supposed really to compete with each other for employment, the effect of any regulation of women's hours is pure loss to them, and wholly in favour of their assumed competitors who are unrestricted.
>
> *Webb 1896, 10–12*

The first assumption is denied based on Sidney Webb's and Clara Collet's empirical work: women and men are segregated in different occupations by means of natural (physiological differences) and artificial barriers (customs). Hence, specific legislation for women concerned trades dominated by women and especially in need of regulation, i.e. the sweated industries.

Webb developed, rather ambiguously, a response to the second claim. If women are equal to men in productive power, equal pay should not have specific effects on women's employment (why would employers prefer men?); but if women are not as productive, the fair treatment is to get rid of them.[14]

> The first necessity is the exclusion of illegitimate competitors. The real enemies of the working women are not the men, who always insist on higher wages, but the unskilled and half-hearted female "amateur" who simultaneously blacklegs both the workshop and the home.
>
> *Webb 1896, 12*

"Blacklegging the home" is an implicit reference to the "family wage". First thought as a privilege and an ideal in the early 19th century, the "family wage" conflated with asking for a "living wage" and became an explicit demand from the labour movement in the 1890s (Clark 2000). The concept rested upon a powerful naturalization of men's role largely shared at the time.[15] Men were breadwinners while women and children were dependants. Women as dependantless and pocket money earners were *temporarily* on the labour market or married women working to complement men's wages. A sufficient "family wage" makes women's work superfluous as women were forced to work in sweated industries *because* men's wages were not sufficient "living wages".[16]

Fighting for higher ideals

Both Millicent Fawcett and Beatrice Webb were fighting for higher ideals rather than only women's hours of labour. Fawcett struggled to secure equal citizenship for women while Webb was fighting for constitutional socialism.

Early in her life, Millicent Fawcett, who was born surrounded by feminist siblings, decided to throw herself into the struggle for suffrage. Fawcett was highly respected first as a dedicated wife who helped her blind husband by reading him books, working on his manuscript and writing his correspondence as well as walking him to the Houses of Parliament, waiting patiently on the bench outside (Caine 1993). Fawcett personified the Victorian lady in her outlook and manner, and her personal image played an important role in making the suffragists a respectable movement. She devoted herself to one single cause for strategic reasons. But on several occasions, her liberal position would be challenged, as she realized her feminist ideas could not mechanically be "contained and expressed within the terms of liberalism" (Caine 1993, 3).

Webb's reluctance to establish a research programme on the "woman question" is to be understood in the context of the pursuit of a "higher ideal" as well as from more personal unease. Contrary to Fawcett, Webb was also fighting for a legitimate status within intellectual affairs, a recognition Fawcett never asked for. Beatrice Webb received advice from several male intellectuals about what she should study. She challenged both Herbert Spencer's suggestion to study the women-suited science of botany, and Alfred Marshall's advice to study women's issues as she, as a woman, had a comparative advantage, even if, as a woman, she was not suited for intellectual activities (Caine 1982, 24).

Since her very first publications, Webb wanted to consider "social problems in their entirety, rather than concentrating on the position of women" (Caine 1982, 32). As a sincere (but bearing the radicalism of a converted) Fabian, Beatrice Webb's early social surveys were instrumental in her rejection of the "philosophic individualism" of her family background:[17] a philosophy she identified in the suffragist movement. In the late 1890s, Beatrice Webb was opposed to the enfranchisement of women. She went as far as to sign the "Anti-suffrage Appeal" in 1889, a "false step" she later regretted (Webb [1926] 1979, 302–303).

The occasion given by the Factory Acts to legally improve women workers' conditions echoes Webb's priorities that made her prefer social improvement to gender equality, *if she had to choose* (Nyland and Ramia 1994, 118). Webb's further change of mind personifies "how difficult, contradictory even, was the bid to win the 'economic independence of women' as part of the 'great fight for the brotherhood of man'" (Lake 1992, 2).

Challenges to the "family wage"

The two decades before the First World War saw changes that would influence the reformulation of the equal pay issue. From an antagonist position at the beginning of the century, Millicent Fawcett's and Beatrice Webb's position on the franchise and labour legislations would converge. The issue of family maintenance emerged as a new point of contention. However, they were still against the principle of "equal pay for equal work".

Sweated industries and equal pay

The problem of equal pay had not only been a problem of lower pay relative to men's wages, but also a problem of low pay in absolute terms. Historically, low wages means women's work. In 1906, an efficient public campaign made the problem of low pay, especially in the sweated industries, a central public issue. It eventually led to the first British attempt to legally control wages.

Directly inspired by the failure of the 1880s Lords' Committee on the sweating system to which Beatrice Potter gave a testimony, the Webbs developed the concept of "national minimum" (Webb and Webb 1897, 774). The idea was to expand the "common rule" of a uniform rate within a trade to the nation as a whole. The minimum wage as a solution to end "parasitic sweated trades" attracted few supporters in the later years. It was dismissed as economically unsound (notably by Alfred Marshall); it was considered impractical to legally control wages, even though such a control had been implemented for hours of work and sanitary conditions.

But in the early 1900s, the first authoritative wages data (the "Earnings and Hours of Labour Enquiry"), the election of a Liberal Government and the creation of an Anti-Sweating League meant that "[t]he problem of sweating, previously the concern of a few interested bodies, emerged as the centre of public conversation" (Blackburn 1991, 55). George Cadbury, owner of the *Daily News*, launched the 1906 campaign against sweated industries. It culminated in a 45-day sensationalist exhibition in the West End, a major event of the London season.[18] Opened by royalty, the event had the direct impact of creating the National Anti-Sweating League (Blackburn 2007, 91–104). Both the League and major women's organizations were instrumental in the passage of the 1909 Trade Board Act. The Act introduced compulsory industry-specific boards (composed of equal numbers of employers' and employees' representatives and members chosen by the government) in charge of pay arbitration. Four sweated industries were covered, all with a women-dominated workforce: domestic chain making, ready-made tailoring, paper-box making and the lace and finishing trade. No feminists spoke against the trade-specific legislation, even if it concerned, in facts and if not nominally, women.

A lesser-known element of the campaign for a minimum wage in other industries was its link to the claim for equal pay. The Webbs lamented the restrictive scope of the Trade Boards Act, which included only four industries. Men-dominated trade unions tended to ignore the women-dominated sweated industries, and focused on large concentrations of labour within factories and mines (Davis s.d.). Trade unions' tactics changed in the 1910s. Despite a diverse labour movement, a strong position in favour of equal pay, especially in skilled industry was formulated in relation to a new commitment to legislation. More and more voices were advocating for a standard rate for each grade with a statutory minimum. This tactic mirrored some of the early arguments in favour of minimum wages and was close to earlier concerns of the Webbs. Many thought a uniform rate for men and women would lead to a labour market segregated by sex (Webb and Webb 1902, 498). This segregation would not need any "express regulation", and was perceived as acceptable, essentially because of physiological differences between men and women as well as preferences of trades suitable for each sex (Webb and Webb 1902, 506). Fawcett identified the trade unions' strategic commitment to equal pay in a review of a book published by James Ramsay Macdonald.[19] In the review, she condemned the "vehement Trades' Unionist bias" and summed up the "whole theory of Trade Unionism" in this way:

> "[T]he women must either be paid at the same rate of the men or got rid of altogether". [. . . It] explains in one sentence its influence in throwing out or keeping out of work all workers, male or female, whose industrial efficiency is not equal to creating the value needed to reproduce the Trades' Union rate of wages.
>
> *Fawcett 1904, 296*

According to Fawcett, the average productivity of women was not equal to the average productivity of men "for various reasons, partly natural, partly artificial" (Fawcett 1904, 296). To insist on equal rates was "to shut women out of the employment all together" (ibid.). Fawcett repeated examples of trade unions' opposition to women's access to technical training, which constituted the main source of women's low wages (overcrowding in low-wage occupations).

There seemed to have been a consensus that equal pay, just like a minimum wage, would have a negative impact on employment. The argument did not follow from rigidities imposed on employers in a labour market that needed flexible prices to adjust, but rather from the impossibility for certain groups of workers to be productive enough. The objective of minimum wage legislation was to enact a minimum rate to cope with employers' power to impose low wages *and* to protect some classes from "unfit" workers (Leonard 2005). In the case of women, legislation also aimed at protecting the "weaker sex"; protections such as safety and improved work conditions that would become a claim for all workers over the 20th century.

Toward a political rapprochement

In 1913, a special supplement of the newly created *New Statesman*[20] was devoted to "The Awakening of Women" (Webb 1913). Coordinated by Beatrice Webb, it included Fawcett's first positive statement on trade unions. Targeting Prime Minister Asquith as well as all "the people who ha[d] not yet found out that women are human beings" (Fawcett 1913, viii), she listed all the "typical facts" in the progress of women's rights and advancement in all sectors of life, including forming trade unions (ibid., ix). In a subsequent issue, Beatrice Webb noted that the suffrage movement no longer reflected "the vested interests and personal prejudices of the existing order" (Webb 1914b, 585). Both Webb and Fawcett moved closer to the Labour Party during the 1910s.

The woman franchise was a major ideological controversy related to strategies of political action – opposing militants and constitutionalists. In 1903, the Pankhursts created the Women's Social and Political Union (WSPU) – better known as the Suffragettes. Their "militant" strategies – setting fire to public and private property, chaining themselves to railways, disrupting political events, destroying paintings at the National Gallery, etc. – were a direct challenge to the wait-and-see, moderate suffragist movement lead by Fawcett. Beatrice Webb decided to publicly change her mind on suffrage at this very moment of division within the women's movement. In 1906, she wrote a pro-suffrage letter (intended for publication) to Fawcett.[21] The "particular obligation of women" – i.e. "[t]he rearing of children, the advancement of learning, and the promotion of the spiritual life" – were becoming the prerogative of the state. The franchise would allow women to fulfil their "function by sharing the control of state action".

Many feminists changed their mind on social welfare legislation at the time, including Millicent Fawcett. Early welfare legislations excluded women, especially concerning medical care and insurance (Thane 1978, 45; Pedersen 1995, 40). Once such legislation existed, feminists fought for equal treatment. In 1908, Beatrice Webb supported the creation of the Fabian Women's Group, which campaigned actively for equal unemployment benefits. Equal opportunity for women became part of the Fabian creed in the 1910s.

Debates on rights to vote also concerned class interests. Many suffragists demanded the franchise on the same terms as men, in opposition to universal adult suffrage, as a politically feasible strategy or, for some, as a class conviction. Originally, the NUWSS lead by Fawcett campaigned for the vote on the same terms as it was *or may be* granted to men. In 1910, property qualifications excluded more than 50 per cent of men aged 21. In her writings, Millicent Fawcett demanded the restricted franchise as a first step. The debate was also a matter of electoral strategy. If the vote was granted to women on the existing property conditions, it was expected to favour the Conservative Party. Up to 1912, the NUWSS did not support any party, but Fawcett, a convinced liberal, was sickened by the Liberal Party politics over suffrage and especially its failure to pass the Conciliation Bill (which would have granted the franchise to women). The Labour Party changed its basis in the 1913 Party conference and made a pledge in favour of suffrage. Fawcett gave the party her full support expressed in *The Common Cause* (Caine 1993, 15). The NUWSS officially supported any suffragist *via* the Election Fighting Fund Committee. In practice, the fund was used to target anti-suffrage Liberals' seats (Smith 2007, 66–71).

This new alliance between constitutional feminists and constitutional socialists also mirrors how the Webbs counselled the labour movement against revolutionary syndicalism and Marxism.[22] The rhetoric of women as the "slaves of the slaves" (developed by Engels, Bebel and Lenin, among others) increasingly influenced the labour movement. The Webbs radically opposed the analysis of the family as a capitalistic institution aiming at preserving private property. Beatrice Webb also voiced her concern against the socialist support for free love (especially against H. G. Wells' philosophy). The family was the moral safeguard of society both for Webb and Fawcett.

Equal pay and the family

Eleanor Rathbone not only opposed Fawcett's strategy to move closer to the Labour Party (Smith 2007, 69), but also radically opposed Fawcett's values on family. The division between the old women's movement and the "New feminists" centred on the role of legislation concerning family. In the first decades of the century, equal pay became framed as a cogent issue of family and, by extension, of the population problem. Between 1870 and 1910, the birth rate fell by 37 per cent in Britain (Allen 2000, 481). Neo-Malthusianism and eugenics put women at the centre of debates regarding birth control, both as "mother of the race" and as dependants.

Eleanore Rathbone was convinced family welfare had to be improved by public intervention. She had long been concerned with one obsession: debunking the rationale for the economic dependence of women as inefficient in terms of family welfare. Her earliest published work (Rathbone 1904) focused on the impact of men's casual work in Liverpool Docks on dockers' wives, who were forced "to plan out the expenditure of a weekly income that zigzags in this bewildering way" (quoted by Pedersen 2004, 103).[23] A later survey of household budgets showed the inadequacies of the wages delivered by the labour market to maintain families (Rathbone 1909). These two published studies confirmed earlier work undertaken for the Liverpool Women's Industrial Council in the 1890s and focused on the irregularity of pay, and its cumulative effect with low pay (Pedersen 2004, 102–104). The lack of "fit" between the wage system and the needs of a family would be central to the family allowance campaign launched in the interwar period, but already before the war, Rathbone advocated for direct state provision for family maintenance (Rathbone 1912).

Millicent Fawcett was infuriated by propositions for state intervention in family affairs, seen as a control of marriage and maternity. In a review of Ethel Snowden's *The Woman Socialist*, she insisted children were the responsibility of parents (Fawcett 1907).

> In the Socialist community, we are told by Mrs. Snowden marriages are to be regulated by the state, the children born will belong more to the state than to the parents [. . .]; a wife who bears children will not look to her husband for support, she will receive a salary from the state.
>
> *Fawcett 1907, 377*[24]

Fawcett implicitly endorsed the "family wage" as an incentive tool for men and women alike: family responsibility was the driver of hard work. In a more personal stance, Fawcett pointed out the majority of the proponents of this "socialist nightmare" were childless (ibid.).[25]

Socialist proposals vary from total control to light proposals for (small) subsidies of motherhood, as Sidney Webb proposed in a letter to *The Times* in 1906.[26] If a separate family allowance contradicts the demand for a "family wage", the usually very small transfer of revenue proposed was not considered as a major threat to wage bargaining, but as a means to alleviate extreme poverty and to encourage parents to have children. More crucially for the Webbs, family allowance met eugenic concerns.[27] In series of texts published just before the war (Webb 1914a, 1914b, 1914c, 1914d), Beatrice Webb provided her updated answer to "certain definite problems [. . .] raised by the feminist movement" (1914d, 397). At the heart of her discussion lay the population problem (Webb 1914d, 428–430). The main cause of the falling birthrate was a voluntary reduction of the number of children by upper- and middle-class women. Beatrice Webb insisted this decline would invariably mean a rise in "bad" immigration, a "disastrous situation" to come for "the British race" (1914d, 429). The whole argument is reinforced by the existence of a "surplus [of] unmarried women", perceived as a middle- and upper-class problem, and the moral problem of maternity outside of "wedlock" (Webb 1914d, 462). Webb also added women's "handicap" on the labour market derived from the *assumption* of fewer needs – women had "less to eat, more to do, fewer opportunities for mental and physical development" (ibid., ii) – that drove "a quite *unconscious* 'blacklegging' of their male workmates" (ibid., my emphasis). She also recognized the "personal right of a woman to earn her living", but asks whether this claim was always consistent with "the right of the consumer to the best available service" (Webb 1914d, 494).

To sum up, all three positions evolved without endorsing equal pay as a principle but all challenged the relation between the maintenance of family and wage determination. According to Fawcett, the market delivers a family wage to individuals which works as an incentive for work effort. Webb's eugenics made her accept the principle of family allowance because it can lead to an increased birthrate. She now wanted to give women the vote to allow them to determine their pay scales for themselves. Rathbone wanted a family allowance to make sure basic needs were met and to give women some control over that pay. In this "perplexing climate of benevolence and backlash" (Allen 2000, 481), feminists diverged on the role of the state, socialists were divided on the role of family, and relatively new discourses enlightened the consequences of a "new motherhood" based on reproductive decision-making, sometimes in relation to the preservation of "the British race". The war amplified these trends that took root in the late Victorian contradictions.

The economic consequences of the war

Beatrice Webb published "Personal Rights and the Woman's Movement" from July 4 to August 1, 1914. The United Kingdom entered the war on August 3. On August 10, the government and the Suffragettes declared a truce; meanwhile feminists as well as socialists were divided over their support for the war. In the midst of radical tension and disruption of families, concrete policies and events transformed the arguments on equal pay.

Unveiling the productive power of women

For many in the interwar period, the First World War was seen as the catalyst for the "awakening of women" because the war "revealed" the capacities of women (Thom 2000, 2005, 2017, 46–50). "It is one of the virtues of war that it puts light which in peacetime is hid under a bushel in such prominence that all can see it" (Randolph Churchill, 1916).[28]

At least one million women were formally added to the British workforce between 1914 and 1918 as part of the war effort (Bean 2015, 4–5). If the representation of *munitionettes* and war nurses came immediately to mind, many different jobs were opened to women. Women entered the work force at much lower wages than men in comparable (unskilled and skilled) work. The temporary and exceptional element in the new arrangement was crucial for the employers, the trade unions and the War Cabinet. Women were a "reserve". After the first five months of high female unemployment at the beginning of the war (Thom 2017, 53–54), the following months were spent negotiating the "system of dilution" to increase (or, at least, to not decrease) the overall national production, especially the output necessary for the war effort. "Dilution" refers to the explicit policy of transformation of the operations of skilled occupations into semi- or unskilled work (division of operation, addition of machine, change of process, etc.). However, "skill" was itself a gendered concept. The war exposed to many "the degree to which 'skill' was socially, rather than technically, defined" (Pedersen 1995, 95). Indeed, women entering a "man's occupation" without any alteration of the process – e.g. driver, tram conductor, gravedigger, ticket collectors, railway porters, postwomen, land-girls, carpenters, policewomen, mechanics, clerks – were also considered dilutees (Thom 2017, 54–57). New occupations were also created to be filled mainly by women, e.g. in the munitions factories. The change in gender ratio was not value-neutral. In many cases, feminization meant "degradation" of the work, a concept that justifies lower pay. "Degradation" referred to changing production processes, but most of the time, it meant the work was done by women.[29]

In the topical case of munitions factories, the "Shells Crisis" of 1915 – a shortage of artillery shells on the front lines due to a change in the military strategy – was responsible for the creation of the Ministry of Munitions and the subsequent organization of dilution.[30] To control this process, what became known as the "Treasury Agreement" was enacted in May 1915, planning to grant "equal pay" for "all dilutees" in 1916, the same year as the conscription of men was decided.[31] In exchange for a guaranteed rate for dilutees, trade unions would relax barriers to entry and industrialists would keep "excess profit" down (Rubin 1977). Strikes were outlawed. "Dilutees" came to refer almost exclusively to women. The unions' objective was to preclude the "undercutting" of wages and avoid "blacklegging", fearing that employers would continue to employ women at a lower wage when the men returned from the war. In this context, arguments in favour of equal pay were justified by the government's willingness to strengthen the war effort by joining forces with trade union representatives, whose primary objective was to protect the post-war "rate for the job". Women's work was seen as a temporary problem that evolved in a national anxiety toward a general "replacement" of men by women.

During the war, along with traditional lady-like war work, Millicent Fawcett participated in the on-going observation of "the replacement of men by women".[32] She eventually changed her position on the demand for equal pay (Fawcett 1917, 191–215). She added the rhetoric of the "discovery" of women's real productive power to her traditional argumentation: "The discovery of the immense reservoir of unused, or only partially used, productive power which this country possesses in its women is one of the economic events of the war" (Fawcett 1917, 189). This productive power included both maternity and domestic work: "[T]he married working woman, while her children are coming, is the hardest worked mortal in existence. It is one of the little jokes of the Census Department to describe her, officially, as 'unoccupied'" (Fawcett 1917, 192).

Fawcett recognized the legitimacy of equal pay as a means to prevent women from being employed as "cheap labour" as well as the necessity of a living wage for women (ibid., 201–202). She became convinced equal pay would not drive women's employment down. In a paper in *The Economic Journal* she asserted "a large proportion of supposed feminine disadvantages exist more in imagination than in reality" (Fawcett 1918a, 4), in contrast to her earlier arguments about the differences in average productivity among men and women. The 1918 chapter goes on to list anecdotes of arbitrary discrimination gathered in reports and in the press. The repeated topical example of a widow replacing her husband and doing equal work, while receiving a lower wage became a constant of all further works (Fawcett 1917, 1918a, 1918b). The difference between Rathbone and Fawcett, who knew each other well, is described by the latter as "a difference of words and not of facts" (Fawcett 1918a, 4). Rather, Rathbone still saw a major problem in the issue of dependants. To definitively break the "family wage" argument, Rathbone argued that the government needed to put in place separate allowances for family, a scheme a liberal Victorian such as Fawcett could not endorse.

The endowment of family as the corollary to equal pay

In the following years, the "service" women provided not only "for their husband" and family but also "to the nation", would become a focus of a large part of the labour and feminist movements. The analogy between the mother and the soldier came into full operation during the war.

Rathbone's first article published in *The Economic Journal* focused exclusively on the consequences of the granting of separate allowances according to family needs during the war. War, dictating necessity, broke the traditional and trade unions barriers "the 'women's movement' had beaten itself for half a century in vain" (Rathbone 1917, 55). These barriers were by no means completely erased, but were weakened

> to such extent that it is plain that if re-erected they [the barriers] will have to be based frankly upon desire of the male to protect himself from competition, and no longer upon the alleged incapacity of the female to compete.
>
> *Rathbone 1917, 55–56*

For Rathbone, wage differences are explained by conventions on family responsibilities, hence, women cannot compete "freely" with men "without undercutting" their own standard of life deriving from male breadwinners' wages (Rathbone 1917, 58). Absolute lower wages of women are explained by the crowding hypothesis and lower bargaining power. Relative low wages of women are explained by the conventional view that their wages are "pocket-money or supplementary wage earning" (Rathbone 1917, 60). Thus far, the financial cost of rearing children had been based on "the indirect and extraordinarily clumsy method of financing the male parent" (Rathbone 1917, 61). The "blind economic forces" accomplish the task "in a very defective and blundering way" (as wages are not always sufficient) and final outcomes depend on men's goodwill to give part of their wage to family maintenance (Rathbone 1917, 61). This "arrangement" implied that women's wages were determined on individual subsistence, because they were considered family-less. One solution could be free entry and equal pay, irrespective of family responsibilities; a solution that is "not less illogical or more unjust" than the actual system of paying bachelors and fathers the same wage, and women with and without dependants considerably lower wages (Rathbone 1917, 63). According to Rathbone however, it was not the more efficient means because the "quantity and quality of children" – a question as "important as the wheat supply" – demanded a *rational* state policy (Rathbone 1917, 65). Hence, her proposal for a separate family allowances scheme paid directly to mothers and controlled by the state.

> [T]he main reason for the differentiation in wages between the two sexes having disappeared, competition between them that was at once free and fair would be for the first time possible, and the service of women – not only in industry, but in the home – would be remunerated on their merits.
>
> *Rathbone 1917, 68*

Her thought emerged after concrete experimentations before the war – part of wages paid directly to seamen's wives in Liverpool (Rathbone and Mahler 1911) – and during the war – in 1916, the Mayor of Liverpool, her cousin Herbert Rathbone, asked her to supervise the granting of family allowance to mothers with a husband on the front (Rathbone 1916). Rathbone became convinced this arrangement would be practical in peacetime and extendable to the nation (Pedersen 1995, 114). In 1918, she formed the Family Endowment Committee – along with other feminists and birth control activists – and published a practical proposal entitled *Equal Pay and the Family*.[33] Family allowances were framed as a corollary to equal pay. In 1919, she was elected to succeed Fawcett as president of the now renamed National Union of Societies for Equal Citizenship (NUSEC).[34] The first of the six points in the manifesto of the new organization was equal pay (Osborne 2001, 23). Rathbone pushed further the case for separate family allowance using the New South Wales experiment (Rathbone 1920).[35]

Contrary to Pujol's account of Rathbone's position (1992, 83–84), she did not simply sacrifice equal pay to family allowance. By the time Rathbone replaced Fawcett as the leader of the NUWSS, she strongly emphasized the argument that family allowance was the correlate to equal pay, a constant of her later discourse (Rathbone 1925, 272). Despite earlier ambiguities, she is the one who introduced equal pay into the mainstream feminist agenda.

Rathbone based her arguments on her own experience and produced statistical data only later (Rathbone 1924). However, data on dependants were already being collected to prove that women did support families (Women's Group Executive 1915, 19). Fawcett relied on this research to debunk the hypothesis that women do not have dependants as mere ideology: "Just as little could 'Charlie Chaplin's' £162,000 a year be explained by attributing to him an extraordinary numerous family" (Fawcett 1917, 194).

Contrary to Fawcett, Rathbone proposed neutralizing this justification by the granting of separate family allowances, not by an extension of competition alone. Beatrice Webb would develop very different arguments.

Toward occupational rates irrespective of sex?

In 1915, Beatrice Webb signed the tract issued by the War Emergency National Committee that urged working women in war industries to join a trade union and to demand equal pay for equal work. Beatrice Webb articulated a more clear-cut view of equal pay while serving in the War Cabinet Committee on Women in Industry (the "Atkin Committee"), producing an 81-page solid Minority Report (Webb 1919). Appointed in August 1917, the Committee had to examine whether equal pay was effectively granted to women engaged in occupations that were considered as men's work before the war, and to elaborate a position on the possibility to extend the principle to other industries. As the only Labour member of the Committee, Beatrice Webb issued a criticism of the Committee's main purpose and results, arguing that the question was one-sided (focusing only on "women's wages"). She specified ten "principles on which [men's and women's] wages have hitherto been determined" (Webb 1919, 8) and defined which principles *should* determine wages.[36] She also gave precise definitions of alternative meanings of equal pay. The definitions of equal pay included "(1) equal pay for equal efforts and sacrifices; (2) equal pay for equal output; (3) equal pay for equal value to the employer" (Webb 1919, 248). The existence of partly overlapping definitions and very different practical systems of fixing wages were part of the problem of equal pay itself (Henderson 1992). Webb insisted, however, that there is "no justification for classifying together all the workers of one sex, and subjecting them to a differential rate" (Webb 1919, 236).

By 1914, Webb favoured increases of women's wages and an improvement in their working conditions through a system of "Wage Boards" and factory inspections, which would enforce a "statutory minimum" by occupation.[37] This policy was now supported by many feminists, including Fawcett in 1916.[38] By 1919, Webb was calling for an "occupational wage" obtained through collective bargaining irrespective of the worker's sex. For the first time, Webb endorsed the principle of equal pay.

> But what, as a matter of fact, has stood in the way of the acceptance of the principle of "Equal Pay for Equal Work," is not the ambiguity of the phrase, but the ease with which its honest application, whatever it may be taken to mean, can be evaded or dodged.
>
> *Webb 1919, 223*

Her Minority Report drew heavily from oral evidence before the Committee. She listed almost every instance of arbitrary treatment of women present in the feminist literature and supported by evidence from the testimonies: from war bonuses to the difference in the adjustment of money wage to real wages, to the enforcement of a "sacred preserve of men", specific situations where "sex disqualification" does not operate to lower men's wages because of their "masculine clumsiness", etc. She also seemed to discover the discriminatory attitude of male trade unions toward women (see e.g. Webb 1919, 217, n.9).

Webb directly addressed the question of dependants, noting the changes that occurred during the war: the granting of separate allowances "has made a deep impression" (Webb 1919, 214). She favoured family allowances on a case-by-case basis:

> [T]he necessity of seeing that adequate provision is made for children [. . .] cannot be done under any system of wages; nor can the adoption of any conceivable principle as to the relation between men's and women's wages achieve this end.
>
> *Webb, 1919, 306*

The assumption according to which "women as a class have no family obligations" is not supported by evidence (ibid., 246). The principle of determining wages by family obligations must then be rejected. Rathbone applauded Webb's Minority Report (Pujol 1992, 93).

Conclusion

This chapter focuses on three public intellectuals' change of minds and the way they articulated their general principles about wage determination and welfare, along with the facts they observed in a specific context. Drawing on Woolf's famous quotation, the history of women's opposition to women's emancipation (and especially here, to equal pay) is as interesting as the story of that emancipation itself.[39] I would not qualify the evolution of their arguments as inconsistencies within their theoretical thoughts but rather as adaptation of their own general principles to what they received as changing facts. Fawcett, Webb and Rathbone relied mainly on qualitative data, especially testimonies, to support their claims, while statistical data were hardly available. As discussed by Barton (1919) at the time, when it comes to the issue of women, the exceptions rather than the average situations were the main focus of both feminists and anti-feminists. Events during the war became the exceptions that shaped Webb's, Fawcett's and Rathbone's changes of mind. The war produced striking experiments such as the "Treasury Agreement" and the granting of family allowance. Millicent Fawcett insisted on the "discovery" of the productive power of women, a fact that overcame her earlier reticence against equal pay. For Beatrice Webb, the war revealed the need for a new way of setting wages *in general* and, for the first time, irrespective of sex. The most important change due to the war, according to Rathbone, was the granting of separate allowance according to family size.

In line with Pujol (1992, 91) and Madden (2002, 25), this chapter has highlighted the diversity of arguments made by women intellectuals: it has described the (sometimes) narrow but important differences that separated the respective "styles" of feminism (Pedersen 1996, 114) of Fawcett, Webb and Rathbone in terms of personal attitudes, theoretical arguments and political strategy. It also stressed moments of convergence over mainly political strategy, rather than agreement on theoretical explanations of wages. In that sense, the word "feminism" conveys a similar variety of (mis)understanding and contortion to that of "liberalism" (Cott 1987). These distortions are striking in the context of the transformation of the "women's movement" into modern feminism, in the view of increasing heterogeneity of loyalties that destroyed the single reference to "the Cause".

Epilogue

Propertied women over 30 voted for the first time in the 1918 General Election that sent the Conservatives to office. It also recorded the irremediable fall of the Liberal Party and the rise of the Labour Party. The 1919 Restoration of Pre-War Practices Bill urged women engaged in the war effort through employment to now "return" to their homes. It was interpreted as the expected follow-up of the "Treasury Agreement" (Rubin 1989, 934). The same year, the Sex Disqualification Removal Act opened the profession of solicitors, barristers and magistrates to women. Despite numerous parliamentary votes since the 1920s (Smith 1996), the principle of equal pay was not implemented in the Civil Services before 1961. The Equal Pay Act prohibiting discrimination in employment was passed in 1970 and implemented in 1976. At the time it became "worth it" for Fawcett, Webb and Rathbone, equal pay was not yet "worth it" for many.

Notes

1 I would like to thank Kirsten Madden for asking me to write this chapter. François Allisson, Maria Bach, Nicolas Chachereau, Béatrice Cherrier, Harro Maas, Keith Tribe, Armelle Weil and the members of the Centre Walras-Pareto helped me considerably to improve this work. All errors remain mine.

2 Only women over 30 who were householders, the wives of householders, occupiers of property or graduates from British universities were granted the right to vote by the Representation of the People Act. The Act also extended the franchise by almost 6 million men, especially those men who lost their right during the war.

3 While more general, the formulation is used almost exclusively in reference to gender discrimination at the time. The debate is also referred to as the "comparable worth controversy".

4 If some authors, e.g. A. Marshall and F.Y. Edgeworth, were arguing for the social necessity of "economic chivalry", the question was increasingly discussed beyond moral arguments; especially within Section F (Statistics and Economic Science) of the British Association for the Advancement of Science, which funded two major series of works on the issue in 1901–1903 and in 1916–1918 (Howarth 1922, 272–273).

5 The "family wage" is a fiction based on a two-parent, three-children family primarily dependent on the father's wage to survive. For a history, see Clark 2000.

6 Family relations also shed some light on why many men decided to work on the "woman question". On Sidgwick, Mill and (Henry) Fawcett, see Caine (1994). On Edgeworth, see Chassonnery-Zaïgouche and Cot (2014).

7 The word feminism was first used in France in the 1830s and spread in the UK in the 1900s. Webb never identifies herself as a feminist. Fawcett used the term suffragist or "women's movement". Rathbone identified with "new feminism".

8 Two exceptions are Henderson (1992) and Pujol (1992).

9 For an intellectual biography of Fawcett, see Caine (1993); on Webb, see Davis (2004); on Rathbone, see Pedersen (2004).

10 All three intellectuals, to different degrees, might fall into the narrative of the "revolt of the daughters", considered the "plague" of the 1890s (Crackanthorpe 1894).

11 The "crowding hypothesis" (occupational segregation in modern terms) refers to the restriction of the range of occupations to some groups by social or institutional barriers, the subsequent oversupply is responsible for lower wages.

12 The sweating conditions refer to "unusually low rates of wages, excessive hours of labo[u]r, and unsanitary work-place" (Webb quoted in Holcombe 1910, 574).
13 Ada Heather-Bigg (1855–1944) was a graduate from University College London (UCL) and a prominent suffragist. She worked for the promotion of women's trade unionism and was part of the Economic Club at UCL.
14 Webb also doubted the equal value of men and women to the employers. For instance, she listed differential rates of absenteeism, sickness, turn-over, and a wide range of conventionally, as well as legally, gendered differences from hours of work to marriage "bars" (the obligation to leave the work force once married).
15 Naturalization refers "to ways of fortifying various social, cultural, political, or economic conventions by presenting them as part of the natural order" (Daston 1992, 209). On the reinforcement of the doctrine of "separate spheres" of men and women in the 1850s–1870s, see Vaid (1985).
16 "Living wage" refers to an individual wage sufficient to survive according to a conventional standard.
17 A *milieu* she shocked by marrying into the lower-middle class (Davis 2004). Spencer cancelled Webb's appointment as his literary executor on the announcement of her engagement to a socialist (Webb [1926] 1979, 29–30).
18 Fabians, Radical Liberals, trade unionists but also social investigators gave daily lectures. More remarkably, actual workers, mainly women, were "featured" in the exhibition. Individual histories of each worker were displayed in pocket-size booklets, featuring family budgets, along with a voluminous exhibitions guide. The guide quoted works by Beatrice Webb including her work in Booth's study.
19 James Ramsay McDonald was a Liberal politician converted to socialism; he became the first Labour prime minister in 1924.
20 The political weekly was used by the Webbs as a platform "to counter propaganda from the Fabian guilds socialists" (Davis 2004).
21 *The Time* (5 November 1906), reproduced in *Diary of Beatrice Webb*, typewritten transcript, vols 21–27.
22 The Webbs barely noticed the creation of the Labour Party in 1900. In the 1910s, however, they decided to take over the party – a strategy that ended the previous Fabian's commitment to political permeation of the existing parties. The Labour Party became "a poor thing but our own" in Beatrice Webb's terms (Davis 2004, 24).
23 The study, started by her father in the 1890s, was thought of as an extension of Beatrice Webb' study "The Docks" (1889a) and was commissioned by Charles Booth.
24 Snowden was a member of the NUWSS's executive committee and a socialist. She favoured the state control of birth and advocated a marriage ban for "mentally ill" individuals (Hannam 2004).
25 She refers to the Snowdens, and the Webbs. Eleanor Rathbone never married and did not have children; she lived with social worker, activist and her life-long partner Elyzabeth Macadam.
26 The letter entitled "Race Suicide" was later published as a Fabian Tract (Webb 1907).
27 On the Webbs and eugenics, see Paul (1984).
28 Lady Randolph Churchill, mother of Winston, edited an oft-forgotten and powerful description of women's work during the war, including "non-conventional" occupations, i.e. outside the munitions factory (Larson 1992).
29 The argument of "degradation" is central to Marshall (Pujol 1992, 122–143) and Edgeworth (Chassonnery-Zaïgouche and Cot, 2014).
30 Lloyd George, then Minister of Munitions made the leading Suffragette Emmeline Pankhurst responsible for organizing a procession in London to recruit women into munitions work in July 1915; the ministry gave £2,000 to the logistics of the "women's right to serve" march.
31 The "pledge" known as the "Treasury Agreement" circulated as a *Memorandum on Acceleration of Output on Government Work*, 19 March 1915 (Webb 1919, 202).
32 "The Replacement of Men by Women in Industry" is a chapter of the BAAS project on the economic effect of war.
33 *Equal Pay and Family*. TUC Library Collections, London Metropolitan University.
34 Rathbone regained her seat in the NUWSS's executive committee when the pacifist members resigned in 1915. She became the dominant figure of the constitutionalist movement from 1919 until 1928. Notably, she managed the negotiation that eventually became the 1918 suffrage bill.
35 The New South Wales government put in place a grading of wage according to family responsibility primarily as a method to reduce costs (total wages paid). See Lake (1992).
36 According to Webb:

> These were: the principle of individual bargaining, the principle of the "national minimum" wage, the "principle of collective bargaining and of the occupational rate leading . . . to a male rate and a female rate", the principle of adjusting money wages to the cost of living, the principle of determining wages by family obligations, "the principle of the vested interest of the male" (by which she meant the enforcement of the concept of "men's work" with high wages and "women's work" with much lower remuneration), "the principle of a definite [technical] qualification for employment", "the principle of limiting wages by foreign competition", the principle of profit-sharing, and finally, "the formula of equal pay for equal work".
>
> *Webb 1919, 8, 9, 11, 13, 15, 17, 20, 24, 25, 31*

37 By the adoption of a minimum wage, Webb also aimed at purging the labour market of the "workshy", the "vagrant" and the "unemployable" (Webb 1919, 203–204). Coupled with the competition mechanism, it would also "eliminate the incompetent or old-fashioned employer" (Webb 1919, 232).

38 Notably in a 1916 letter entitled "The Need for a Minimum Wage", published in *The Common Cause*, and signed also by Beatrice Webb.

39 The original quote:

> The history of men's opposition to women's emancipation is more interesting perhaps than the story of that emancipation itself. An amusing book might be made of it if some young student at Girton or Newnham [two women's Colleges at Cambridge] would collect examples and deduce a theory – but she would need thick gloves on her hands, and bars to protect her of solid gold.
>
> *Woolf, 1929, Chapter 3*

References

Allen, Ann Taylor. 2000. Feminism and Eugenics in Germany and Britain, 1900–1940: A Comparative Perspective. *German Studies Review*, 23(3): 477–505.

Barton, Dorothea. 1919. The Course of Women's Wages. *Journal of the Royal Statistical Society*, 82(4): 508–553.

Bean, Jessica. 2015. Women's Work and Wages during the First World War. *Mimeo*.

Blackburn, Sheila C. 1991. Ideology and Social Policy: The Origins of the Trade Boards Act. *The Historical Journal*, 34(1): 43–64.

Blackburn, Sheila C. 2007. *A Fair Day's Wage for a Fair Day's Work? Sweated Labour and the Origins of Minimum Wage Legislation in Britain*. Aldershot: Ashgate.

Caine, Barbara. 1982. Beatrice Webb and the "Woman Question". *History Workshop*, 14: 23–43.

Caine, Barbara. 1993. Millicent Garrett Fawcett. In Barbara Caine, *Victorian Feminists*. Oxford: Oxford University Press (Oxford Scholarship Online).

Caine, Barbara. 1994. Feminism and Political Economy in Victorian England – or John Stuart Mill, Henry Fawcett and Henry Sidgwick Ponder the "Woman Question". In Peter Groenewegen (ed.), *Feminism and Political Economy in Victorian England*, Aldershot: Edward Elgar, 25–45.

Chassonnery-Zaïgouche, Cléo and Annie L. Cot. 2014. "The Disturbing Effect of Sentiment and Prejudice": Francis Ysidro Edgeworth on Women's Wages. *Mimeo*.

Clark, Anna. 2000. The New Poor Law and the Breadwinner Wage: Contrasting Assumptions. *Journal of Social History*, 34(2): 261–281.

Cott, Nancy F. 1987. *The Grounding of Modern Feminism*. New Haven, CT: Yale University Press.

Crackanthorpe, Blanche A. 1894. The Revolt of the Daughters. *Nineteenth Century*, 35: 23–31.

Daston, Lorraine. 1992. The Naturalized Female Intellect. *Science in Context*, 5(2): 209–235.

Davis, John. 2004. Webb, (Martha) Beatrice (1858–1943). *Oxford Dictionary of National Biography*, Oxford: Oxford University Press (online edition).

Davis, Mary. s.d. An Historical Introduction to the Campaign for Equal Pay. TUC & London Metropolitan University website. [www.unionhistory.info/equalpay/roaddisplay.php?irn=820, accessed 5 May 2017].

Edgeworth, Francis Y. 1922. Equal Pay to Men and Women for Equal Work. *The Economic Journal*, 32(128): 431–457.

Fawcett, Millicent Garrett. 1870. *Political Economy for Beginners*. London: MacMillan.
Fawcett, Millicent Garrett. 1874. *Tales in Political Economy*. London: MacMillan.
Fawcett, Millicent Garrett. 1892. Mr. Sidney Webb's Article on Women's Wages. *The Economic Journal*, 2(5): 173–176.
Fawcett, Millicent Garrett. 1904. Reviewed Work: *Women in the Printing Trades: A Sociological Study*, edited by J. Ramsay MacDonald. *The Economic Journal*, 14 (54): 295–299.
Fawcett, Millicent Garrett. 1907. Reviewed Work: Labour Ideal Series. *The Woman Socialist* by Ethel Snowden. *The Economic Journal*, 17(67): 376–378.
Fawcett, Millicent Garrett. 1913. The Awakening of Women: The Remedy of Political Emancipation. *New Statesman*, November 1: viii–x.
Fawcett, Millicent Garrett. 1917. The Position of Women in Economic Life. In W. H. Dawson (ed.), *After-War Problems*. London: Allen & Unwin, 191–218.
Fawcett, Millicent Garrett. 1918a. Equal Pay for Equal Work. *The Economic Journal*, 28(109): 1–6.
Fawcett, Millicent Garrett. 1918b. Equal Pay for Equal Value. *The Contemporary Review*, 114: 387–390.
Forget, Evelyn L. 2016. Jane Marcet as Knowledge Broker. *History of Economics Review*, 65(1): 15–26.
Groenewegen, Peter. 1994. Women in Political Economy and Women as Political Economists. In Peter Groenewegen (ed.), *Feminism and Political Economy in Victorian England*. London: Edward Elgar, 1–24.
Hannam, June. 2004. Snowden, Ethel (1881–1951). *Oxford Dictionary of National Biography*, Oxford: Oxford University Press (online edition).
Henderson, James P. 1992. Equal Pay vs. Equal Job Opportunity for Women: The Debate in Great Britain from 1891 to 1923. *International Journal of Social Economics*, 19(10/11/12): 298–316.
Henderson, Willie. 2004. Millicent Garrett Fawcett's *Political Economy for Beginners*: An Evaluation. *Paedagogica Historica*, 40(4): 435–453.
Holcombe, A. 1910. The British Minimum Wages Act of 1909. *Quarterly Journal of Economics*, 24(3): 574–577.
Howarth, O. J. R. 1922. *The British Association for the Advancement of Science: A Retrospect 1831–1921*. London: British Association for the Advancement of Science.
Lake, Marilyn. 1992. The Independence of Women and the Brotherhood of Man: Debates in the Labour Movement over Equal Pay and Motherhood Endowment in the 1920s. *Labour History*, 63: 1–24.
Larson, Kay. 1992. Introduction. In Jennie Randolph Churchill, *Women's War Work*. London: C. Arthur Pearson.
Leonard, Thomas C. 2005. Protecting Family and Race: The Progressive Case for Regulating Women's Work. *Journal of Economics and Sociology*, 64(3): 757–791.
Madden, Kirsten K. 2002. Female Contributions to Economic Thought, 1900–1940. *History of Political Economy*, 34(1): 1–30.
Nyland, Chris and Gaby Ramia. 1994. The Webbs and the Right of Women. In Peter Groenewegen (ed.), *Feminism and Political Economy in Victorian England*. London: Edward Elgar, 110–146.
Osborne, Susan. 2001. *Feminism*. Harpenden, UK: Pocket Essentials.
Paul, Diane. 1984. Eugenics and the Left. *Journal of the History of Ideas*, 45(4): 567–590.
Pedersen, Susan. 1995. *Family, Dependence, and the Origins of the Welfare State. Britain and France, 1914–1945*. Cambridge, UK: Cambridge University Press.
Pedersen, Susan 1996. Rathbone and Daughter: Feminism and the Father at the *Fin-de-siècle*. *Journal of Victorian Culture*, 1(1): 98–117.
Pedersen, Susan, 2004. *Eleanor Rathbone and the Politics of Conscience*. New Haven, CT: Yale University Press.
Pujol, Michèle A. 1992. *Feminism and Anti-Feminism in Early Economic Thought*. Cheltenham, UK: Edward Elgar.
Pujol, Michèle A. and Janet A. Seiz. 2000. Millicent Garrett Fawcett. In Robert W. Dimand, Mary Ann Dimand and Evelyn L. Forget (eds), *A Biographical Dictionary of Women Economists*. Northampton, MA: Edward Elgar, 156–162.
Rathbone, Eleanor. 1904. *Report of an Inquiry into the Conditions of Dock Labour at the Liverpool Docks*. Liverpool: Northern Publishing Co.
Rathbone, Eleanor. 1909. *How the Casual Labourer Lives: Report of the Liverpool Joint Committee on the Domestic Condition and Expenditure of the Families of Certain Liverpool Labourers*. Liverpool: Northern Publishing Co.
Rathbone, Eleanor. 1912. *The Problem of Women's Wages: An Inquiry into the Causes of the Inferiority of Women's Wages to Men's*. Liverpool: Northern Publishing Co.

Rathbone, Eleanor. 1916. Separation Allowance: An Experiment in the Endowment of Motherhood. *The Common Cause*, I: 7: 359: 611; II: 7: 362: 648.
Rathbone, Eleanor. 1917. The Remuneration of Women's Services. *The Economic Journal*, 27(105): 55–68.
Rathbone, Eleanor. 1920. The New South Wales Schemes for the Grading of Wages According to Family Needs. *The Economic Journal*, 30(120): 550–553.
Rathbone, Eleanor. 1924. *The Disinherited Family: A Plea for the Endowment of the Family*. London: Edward Arnold.
Rathbone, Eleanor. 1925. Family Endowment in its Bearing on the Question of Population. *The Eugenics Review*, 16(4): 270–275.
Rathbone, Eleanor and Emma Mahler. 1911. *Payments of Seamen: The Present System*. Liverpool: C. Tiling.
Rubin, Gerry R. 1977. The Origins of Industrial Tribunals: Munitions Tribunals during the First World War. *Industrial Law Journal*, 6(1): 149–164.
Rubin, Gerry R. 1989. Law as Bargaining Weapon: British Labour and the Restoration of Pre-War Practices Act 1919. *The Historical Journal*, 32(4): 925–945.
Rubinstein, D. 1989. Victorian Feminists: Henry and Millicent Garrett Fawcett. In Lawrence Goldman (ed.), *The Blind Victorian: Henry Fawcett and British Liberalism*. Cambridge: Cambridge University Press, 71–147.
Shaw, George Bernard. 1942. The Webbs. In Beatrice and Sidney Webb, *The Truth About Soviet Russia*. London: Longman, Green & Co.
Smith, Harold L. 1996. British Feminism and the Equal Pay Issue in the 1930s. *Women's History Review*, 5(1): 97–110.
Smith, Harold L. 2007. *The British Women's Suffrage Campaign 1866–1928*. Harlow, UK: Pearson Longman.
Thane, Pat. 1978. Women and the Poor Law in Victorian and Edwardian England. *History Workshop*, 6: 29–51.
Thom, Deborah. 2000. *Nice Girls and Rude Girls: Women Workers in World War I*. I.B. Tauris Publisher: London and New York. First edition 1998.
Thom, Deborah. 2005. Women and Work in Wartime Britain. In *Women, War and Society, 1914–1918: From the Women's Work Collection at the Imperial War Museum*. London: Gale Digital Collection.
Thom, Deborah. 2017. Gender and Work. In Susan R. Grayzel and Tammy M. Proctor (eds), *Gender and the Great War*. Oxford: Oxford University Press, 46–66.
Vaid, Sudesh. 1985. Ideologies on Women in Nineteenth Century Britain, 1850s–70s. *Economic and Political Weekly*, 20(43): WS63–WS67.
War Emergency Workers' National Committee. 1915. Women's Appeal to Women Who Are Taking Men's Places during this Period of National Crisis. TUC Library Collections, London Metropolitan University.
Webb, Beatrice Potter. 1886. A Lady's View of the Unemployed at the East. *Pall Mall Gazette*, February 18.
Webb, Beatrice Potter. 1888. Pages from a Work-girl's Diary. *Nineteenth Century*, September 24, 301–314.
Webb, Beatrice Potter. 1889a. The Docks. In Charles Booth (ed.), *Life and Labour of the People in London*. London and Edinburgh: Williams & Norgate.
Webb, Beatrice Potter. 1889b. The Jewish Community. In Charles Booth (ed.), *Life and Labour of the People in London*. London and Edinburgh: Williams & Norgate.
Webb, Beatrice Potter. 1889c. The Tailoring Trades. In Charles Booth (ed.) *Life and Labour of the People in London*. London and Edinburgh: Williams & Norgate.
Webb, Beatrice Potter. 1896. Women and the Factory Acts. *Fabian Tract No*. 67. London: The Fabian Society.
Webb, Beatrice Potter. 1913. Introduction to the Special Supplement "The Awakening of Women". *New Statesman*, November 2.
Webb, Beatrice Potter. 1914a. Introduction to the Special Supplement "Women in Industry". *New Statesman*, February 14: i–ii.
Webb, Beatrice Potter. 1914b. Voteless Women and Social Revolution. *New Statesman*, February 14: 584–586.
Webb, Beatrice Potter. 1914c. Motherhood and Citizenship. *New Statesman*, May 16: 10–11.
Webb, Beatrice Potter. 1914d. Personal Rights and the Woman's Movement. I. The Individual, Other Individuals, and the Community, July 4; II. The Falling Birth Rate, July 11; III. Maternity under Free

Conditions, July 18; IV. The Right of the Woman to Free Entry into All Occupations, July 25; V. Equal Remuneration for Men and Women, August 1. *New Statesman*, 395–527.

Webb, Beatrice Potter. 1919. The Wages of Men and Women: Should They Be Equal? A reprint of the Minority Report, with an introduction by Mrs. Webb. Republished in *Historical Studies in Industrial Relations*, 31–32, 2011, 201–282.

Webb, Beatrice Potter. [1926] 1979. *My Apprenticeship*. Cambridge, UK: Cambridge University Press.

Webb, Sidney. 1891. The Alleged Differences in the Wages Paid to Men and Women for Similar Work. *The Economic Journal*, 1(4): 639–658.

Webb, Sidney. 1907. The Decline of the Birth-Rate. *Fabian Tract No.* 131.

Webb, Beatrice and Sidney Webb. 1897. *Industrial Democracy*. London: Longmans, Green.

Webb, Beatrice and Sidney Webb. 1902. *Problems in Modern Industry*, London: Longmans, Green.

Women's Group Executive. 1915. The War, Women and Unemployment. *Fabian Tract No.* 178.

Woolf, Virginia. 1929. *A Room of One's Own*. London: Hogarth Press.

8

THE ECONOMIC THOUGHT OF THE WOMEN'S CO-OPERATIVE GUILD

Kirsten Madden and Joseph Persky

Introduction

The Women's Co-operative Guild emerged in late 19th century Britain as a forum and activist organization devoted to advancing women's influence and concerns within the context of the broader British co-operative movement. From 1883 to well beyond the First World War, the Guild served as a base for a group of talented women, including Amy Sharp, Catherine Webb, Lilian Harris and, most notably, Margaret Llewelyn Davies.[1] All of these women were devoted activists, eager to bring reforms in both the political and economic spheres. They were all doers. They were also thinkers. Through a regular column, the "Women's Corner" in the widely read *Co-operative News*, numerous pamphlets and, occasionally, larger works, Guild writers made significant empirical contributions to the co-operative economics of their day. In several areas, they also generated key theoretical insights that are still relevant to our understanding of the socio-economics of gender.

We argue that the guildswomen emphasized a perspective on co-operation that does not appear anywhere as sharply in other co-operative writing. In particular, we find that (1) they linked co-operative reform ideology with the realities of women working for pay, working in the household, and rearing children. And (2) they attempted to undergird that ideology through an activist empirical methodology, designed to engage their women members in purposeful reform. While historians (Scott 1998; Blaszak 2000) have dealt with the Guild, they have not emphasized the economic coherence of guildswomen's economic work or its sharp contrast from other economic writings on co-operatives. The purpose of this chapter is to reconstruct clearly the Guild's reform ideology and methodology and to demonstrate application in four distinct areas of economic inquiry. The four areas of economic inquiry are the minimum wage for co-operatively employed women, credit and poverty, the debate over producer's co-operatives, and women's isolation in the household sector.

Mary Lawrenson has been credited with the idea of the Women's Co-operative Guild and was General Secretary from 1885 to 1889 (Blaszak 2000, 16). The most productive Guild writers were not drawn from working-class families, but rather from the comfortable middle class. Daughter of a Christian Socialist minister and Unitarian, independent-minded mother, Llewelyn Davies was well off and never married. Davies served as the General Secretary of the Women's Co-operative Guild from 1889 until her retirement in 1921. Lillian Harris, assistant secretary of the Guild who maintained close working and personal ties with Davies, came from a wealthy banking family. Amy Sharp was member of the Guild central committee from 1886 to 1891 including serving as vice president in 1891. Catherine Webb's father had been poor as a child, but had risen to a managerial role in a co-operative society and she had grown up in a middle-class environment. C. Webb was vice president of the Guild Central Committee in the 1880s and again in the early 1890s (Blaszak 2000, Chs 3–4).

These women and others saw themselves as part of a larger reform movement that included the Fabian Women's Group, the Women's Trade Union League and the Women's Industrial Council.[2] While Guild leadership's knowledge of working-class conditions was not based on their immediate family backgrounds, their connection through the Guild to the working-class households of the co-operatives gave them entry and insights other observers would be hard pressed to achieve.

From its start the Guild was closely associated with the Co-operative Union, the Association of Co-operative Societies, as well as the English Co-operative Wholesale Society, which engaged in wholesaling, manufacturing, transportation and finance. The turn of the 20th century was perhaps the most successful period for co-operative enterprises in Britain. Serving a broad market of skilled and semi-skilled working families the movement had grown remarkably from the early days of the Rochdale Pioneers, who had effectively focused on co-operative retail stores promising customers fair prices, solid quality, and a dividend on their purchases. Although many of the Pioneers had been followers of Robert Owen, influenced by his utopian hopes, they had stuck to a pragmatic program oriented to the realities of the market. Piece by piece, the Wholesale Society had used this base and profitably integrated backwards into the various branches of supply.[3] Co-operatives would begin to falter in the post-World War I period, overwhelmed by advances in large-scale retail marketing and advertising. Increasingly co-operatives would appear as dowdy, but at the turn of the century they seemed the wave of the future, the seed of a "co-operative commonwealth."[4]

Early writings, including those by Owen, in support of co-operation caught the imagination of major political economists. Most notably, John Stuart Mill strongly endorsed co-operatives as a solution to the conflicts between workers and capitalists.[5] His writings in turn influenced later work by, among others, William Stanley Jevons and Alfred Marshall. Economists in the late 19th century were engaged in an active debate as to the logic, shortcomings and promises of the co-operative movement. A major contribution to this debate was Beatrice Potter's (later Beatrice Webb) *The Co-operative Movement in Great Britain* (1891). Parallel to this more formal political economy, guildswomen began writing seriously on the economics of co-operation and related topics.

In comparison to other major thinkers about co-operatives, the guildswomen brought to their economics a far deeper understanding of women's place in production and consumption. While both Owen and Mill had been surprisingly egalitarian, even feminist, for their day, their writings on women tend to the abstract. By contrast the guildswomen struggled mightily to understand the realities of working-class women at work, household labor and child rearing. Hence their writings on women and co-operatives have a truer and less visionary ring than the works of Owen and Mill. They have a clearer focus on the practical economics of reform. This combination of values and pragmatism is the hallmark of the Guild contribution. Again, the present chapter considers their perspective in four economic areas: the minimum wage, credit and poverty, producer's co-operatives, and isolation in the household sector.

Two characteristics of Guild writings on co-operatives

Two features characterized written contributions of the Women's Co-operative Guild. First, the writings grew out of an ideologically driven reform movement holding that the institutions of capitalism failed most people; fundamental structural changes were necessary to achieve a range of goals with wide normative appeal. Underlying the reform agenda was a metaphysical vision of social change grounded in the philosophy of Robert Owen. Second, the Women's Co-operative Guild melded their reform vision into social and political campaign strategies aimed at achieving specific goals. The guildswomen's methodology to reach reform objectives includes a distinct set of characteristics. Participant-observation within the British working-class co-operative movement flavored their campaign strategies. The guildswomen shaped a popular empirical approach via fact gathering. Resistance to their reform goals sometimes led the women to apply and construct common sense theories.

A reform ideology

As supporters of the co-operative movement, the Guild writers judged their world as deeply unattractive in many ways. They characterized capitalism at the turn of the 20th century by greed, a lack of decency, waste and inequality. Capitalism corrupted human character. This system they contrasted with one they deemed much more appealing, the "co-operative commonwealth."[6] The co-operative commonwealth would establish conditions in support of deeper human development for the common weal.

In these assessments guildswomen committed to the world-view of Robert Owen. Following Owen they were fundamentally concerned with the development of human character. Owen rooted his approach to co-operation in a deeply value-laden discourse. For Owen the central purpose of co-operatives was to provide a positive environment in which children could develop character free from the competitive pressures of capitalism. Owen's emphasis on values and human development resonated with guildswomen while appreciating that the success of the co-operative movement required attention to business practice. Guildswomen were concerned how best to reinject Owen's broader social values into the movement without sacrificing relevance and pragmatism.

In *A New View of Society*, Robert Owen (1813–1817) held that human character is the product of social customs and institutions. For Owen, "the true and sole origin of evil" generating most human misery is the mistaken view that "each individual man forms his own character, and that therefore he is accountable for all his sentiments and habits, and consequently merits reward for some and punishment for others." The mistakes of one's forefathers shape flawed social systems. Born into flawed social constructs, a person is the product of his environment and will believe what has been impressed on his mind. Thus, any character "may be given to any community . . . by the application of proper means" (Owen 1813–1817, 91).

Women co-operators grounded their ideology in Owen's perspective of social conditioning but were sensitive to the economic complexities of women's realities. For example, writing as a community, the Women's Co-operative Guild briefly touches upon the use of "drugs to procure abortion" by British working-class housewives:

> But here again the cause of the evil lies in the conditions which produce it. Where maternity is only followed by an addition to the daily life of suffering, want, overwork, and poverty, people will continue to adopt even the most dangerous, uncertain, and disastrous methods of avoiding it.
>
> *Women's Co-operative Guild 1915, 15*

The women co-operators identify that drug-induced abortion is an evil falling on women. The social practice results from the social environment, not free human will: social conditions drive human behavior. The next paragraph continues that there are

> certain evils deeply seated in national life. These evils have their origin in social conditions, and they touch life at so many points that they must, if allowed to work unchecked, modify the whole future of the race and the state. There is no sign that society, if left to itself, will secrete some antitoxin to purge its own blood. The industrial and capitalist system tends to become continually more industrial and capitalistic; the gulf between the rich and poor, the fortunate and the unfortunate widens; ideals become higher and broader while the means to satisfy them are narrowed in the possession of a narrow class; only discontent seems to rise while the birth-rate falls. Society cannot cure itself, and the last hope, therefore, is for the State to attempt a cure.
>
> *pp. 15–16*

These passages reflect the reform ideology that characterizes the guildswomen's work. Social practices are embedded in the social system, capitalism—a toxic system which, unchecked, generates morally unacceptable outcomes for the population as a whole and particularly for the Guild's target: women. Leading a social reform movement, the guildswomen chart a policy path to transform socio-economic conditions.

A reform methodology

Reform successes of the Women's Co-operative Guild at the turn of the 20th century built on effective means beyond reform ideology. Through trial-and-error processes the women co-operators melded their reform methodology. Three noteworthy methodological characteristics are: participant-observation, fact gathering for a popular empiricism and common sense theorizing.

The Women's Co-operative Guild writers were participant-observers, members of a popular political movement. Sometimes writing broadly about co-operation, they were often concerned with particular challenges facing that movement. As reformers, they wrote largely to influence the movement's direction. As such their writing was often an integral component of a political campaign on a particular socio-economic issue.

These campaigns typically followed a similar basic strategy. Speeches and pamphlets were used to convince Guild members of the presence of a problem and the need for action. A motivated membership could be enlisted to commit to a course of fact finding and petitioning. The resulting new knowledge could then be incorporated into tracts with a more explicitly empirical view. In the best of circumstances these new writings would play a role in a larger political campaign on the issue in question.[7] Of course, the scenario laid out here is something of an ideal type. Often the various stages would become jumbled. The empirical contributions might be substantial or largely incidental.

Like advocates of other major reform movements, whether the prohibitionists or labor unionists or socialists, the women writing on co-operation necessarily drew on a rough-and-ready empiricism that sought to demonstrate the effectiveness of their favored means for achieving goals. The central question was practical feasibility of goal attainment. Hence, the need for an economics capable of convincing potential co-operators and legislators of the effectiveness of institutional change in achieving larger ends.

The heart of their arguments centered on empirical questions. They sought empirical support of their conviction that market capitalism eroded character, while co-operation built character. These writers needed to demonstrate the short-falls of the present system, and demonstrate the effective promise of the proposed central reform, co-operation.

Guild researches were typically written in journalistic style, sometimes as newspaper articles, often as pamphlets, occasionally as books. These pieces consisted largely of descriptive fact finding. They almost always included extended anecdotes or reports from correspondents. Not infrequently there would also be quantitative data presented in tables. Occasionally, these facts had a sensationalist quality. At their best, these publications were consistent with a range of sociological studies of working-class life at the time, including those of Charles Booth, Sidney and Beatrice Webb, and the later work of the Hammonds.

Objectivity and representativeness of the data can be questioned in Guild writing. The resulting publications were never held up to academic standards of review. Samples were not random, questionnaires were often biased, historical observations were idiosyncratic, and conclusions were readily drawn.[8] At the same time there was a freshness and energy in the approach that allowed the women co-operators to explore major economic problems.

There is only a modest extension of formal economic analysis in the writings of the guildswomen. Like most supporters of co-operation they were committed to free-trade. They generally were sympathetic to the achievement of a "living wage." They were most original with respect to the mechanisms that tended to segment women workers and that generated household debt spirals. Even these original elements are presented in a largely intuitive fashion.

In sum, then, the guildswomen's contributions were shaped by their participation in a major social movement. Their impressive fact gathering aimed to document social failures and institutional possibilities. Motivated by strong values and eager to demonstrate the virtues of co-operation, they made major contributions to the knowledge base of the day. This new knowledge, combined with elements of theory, allowed them to formulate and defend innovative policy positions. Under Margaret Llewelyn Davies' leadership, the Women's Co-operative Guild policy positions were effectively developed and promoted through the Guild's co-operative campaign strategies.

"The minimum wage campaign"[9] for girls and women, 1893–1914

Guild activism regarding co-operatively employed girls and women was part of a bigger British anti-sweatshop campaign (Scott 1998, 100). The 1897 British Women's Industrial Council report, "Home Industries of Women in London," documented low wages and long hours. The response to British sweatshops included social activism: in 1906, the anti-sweatshop movement attracted an estimated crowd of 30,000 to an anti-sweating exhibition.[10]

Following decades of information dissemination and protests against sweatshop industries, Great Britain initiated minimum wage legislation in 1909 under then president of the British Board of Trade, Winston Churchill. The Trade Boards Act of 1909 set up an institutional structure to redress low wages. Results included an increased living standard and a reduction in poverty, especially for women workers, although initially only across the four industries. It was not until after World War I that the Act expanded to cover three million British workers.[11]

Paralleling the British anti-sweating movement during the two decades around the turn of the 20th century, the Guild led a charge for minimum wages within the co-operative movement (C. Webb 1927, 121). The guildswomen's objective was to elicit a majority vote by the Co-operative Wholesale Society supporting a women's minimum wage resolution. A 1911 vote denied their objective. In 1914 a majority vote instituted this minimum wage standard (C. Webb 1927, 119–120). The minimum wage campaign is a fitting example of the Guild's reform ideology and reform methodology.

"A Co-operative Standard for Women Workers" (Women's Co-operative Guild 1908b; hereafter, CSWW) and Harris (1897) are examples of published Guild campaign advocacy. CSWW grounds the minimum wage campaign in reform ideology, disseminates factual information gathered by the Guild, and argues for the minimum wage objective. In a section entitled

"How Guild Women Can Help," CSWW describes actions that guildswomen should take as participants in a popular movement to promote achievement of the minimum wage goal. Harris (1897) reports efforts to collect data on 1,662 women employees' work conditions and wages in 104 co-operative stores. Like CSWW, Harris (1897) opens with co-operative ideals. Most of this publication disseminates factual information with minimal theoretical foundation. Harris's call to action charts co-operative reforms to meet the Guild wage goal.

Reform ideology

CSWW opens with the idea that in the co-operative "world, there is a Co-operative conscience, and we must obey it" (p. 1). Harris (1897) begins with a fundamental principle of the co-operative conscience: "we look to co-operation to remedy the injustices and evils of competition." Specifically, Harris calls for a "minimum living wage" for all co-operative employees (p. 12).

CSWW conveys Robert Owen's principle that social environment shapes human character, with the Guild focused specifically on women's wages. The "supposed inferiority" of women was the primary reason that women received low wages. The learning and the teaching of alleged inferiority derived out of conditioning extending generations into the past (Women's Co-operative Guild 1908b, 15) and instituted economic distortions for women workers.

A reform methodology

Fact finding and reform-oriented political activism were substantial driving forces of the Guild's minimum wage campaign. As the minimum wage campaign progressed and incurred "hostile" push-back, guildswomen developed theoretical responses (C. Webb 1927, 118).

Intensive fact finding about the wages of co-operatively employed women began in the fall of 1895 with formal questionnaires mailed to 170 co-operative societies. Complete returns from about 1,349 women co-operatively employed were "grounds for a vigorous campaign in advocacy of a 'living wage'" (C. Webb 1927, 115–116). CSWW documents a 1903 Co-operative Wholesale Society inquiry providing information on wages of 809 co-operative women employees in England.

The fact-gathering expeditions suggested that women's wages were low relative to men's, and that the co-operatively employed earned higher average wages than Great Britain as a whole, though mostly below the target minimum wage scale. There was wage variation across women workers and wages seemed to be ruled by the "custom of the district" (C. Webb 1927, 117). The Guild recommended a minimum wage scale for women varying by age (Women's Co-operative Guild 1908b, 10; C. Webb 1927, 116).

The Guild disseminated the survey-based data and its analysis, prompting education and discussion through "[v]igorous propaganda." Dissemination mechanisms included co-operative newspaper articles, formal papers, conference speakers, and distributed leaflets (C. Webb 1927, 117).

As reformers, Guild members instituted political strategies to meet their minimum wage scale-adoption objective. The strategies ranged from conferences with managers of co-operative employees to drafting and presenting scale-supporting Co-operative Wholesale Society resolutions to increasing the number of women in unions. The Guild disseminated information on minimum wage scale-adopting co-operative societies in a "Roll of Honour." In 1910, an elaborate petition-signing campaign with 13,337 signatures was presented to Co-operative Wholesale Society directors (C. Webb 1927, 117–118).

Even with factual evidence and a variety of political strategies to shape opinion, guildswomen regularly received arguments opposing a women's minimum wage standard. Guildswomen learned how to respond to their opponents' arguments (C. Webb 1927, 118).

The guildswomen challenged socially accepted norms by stating that the work women do is necessary and "that wages and salaries are not really regulated by 'worth'" (C. Webb 1927, 118). These challenges to accepted social norms opened intellectual space for a dialogue about women's wages. The guildswomen understood the intuition of efficiency wage theory, that "better wages would increase the efficiency of both the workers and the management" (C. Webb 1927, 119). Guildswomen's responses to minimum wage objections are not novel, but the diversity of arguments shows that the guildswomen communicated counterpoints.

The low wage of women workers relative to men was attributed in part to the contemporary view that girls worked for a "mere pocket-money wage." The Guild argued against pocket-wages for girls because it reduced wages for all working women (Women's Co-operative Guild 1908b, 13).

Opponents to minimum wages for women commonly stated that men required higher wages than women since "men have to support a family." CSWW rejected the family support hypothesis with empirically verifiable counterpoints: many men did not support families; many women supported dependents (their own children, parents, or siblings); and single women could not secure themselves from future contingencies because low wages reduce their ability to save (p. 2).

The guildswomen's defense of minimum wages shows applied familiarity with the principles of supply and demand. Harris (1897, 7) sketches an intuitive version of supply and demand to explain the variation in women's wages across English districts: low wages exist where there is no demand for women workers; higher wages exist in areas with greater labor demand. Ethical concerns appear over supply and demand wage determination:

> Why should we [Co-operators] allow our wages to be decided by unrestricted competition—that is, by the action of supply and demand—meaning by this, that we should give no higher a wage than the low one women are willing to take because the supply of women is greater than the demand for their work? We permit humane considerations (which turn out, we may incidentally remark, economically sound) to restrain competition in the matter of hours, why not for wages?
>
> *Women's Co-operative Guild 1908b, 7*

A common minimum wage objection was that it generates higher prices or business losses. CSWW refutes this view, arguing that higher profits result from "better organizing, more efficient business methods, and greater enterprise" when employers cannot offer sub-standard wages (p. 7). CSWW develops the management response in more detail. "A bad Manager may try to make profits by means of low wages." But higher wages cause the co-operative "to insist on first-rate management, and so improve the prosperity of our business. It is really helping to make management more efficient if we prevent bad management being hidden under low wages" (p. 8). This is an interesting positive sum proposition that improved worker wages can set into motion forces generating improved management.

Socio-historic indoctrination into the belief of women's inferiority is offered as a primary reason for low women's wages. "Women, as well as men, are responsible for this view, for they have accepted it and passed it on generation after generation" (Women's Co-operative Guild 1908b, 15). Girls and women are trained to make fewer demands on life. Thus "a woman does not claim money to spend on herself as a husband does . . . she consents to a dependence which is humiliating" (pp. 15–16).

An anecdotal example is provided of deleterious wage effects. In a hosiery business, a woman manager with multiple work tasks including bookkeeping earned 24s. per week. When the business expanded a man was hired with the single task of bookkeeping and received 30s per week. The argument concludes that if "we take a large view we shall see that self-effacement may be as injurious to herself . . . and disastrous to the lives of her sisters, as selfishness" (pp. 15–16). If a culturally engrained attitude of self-effacement exists in wage-negotiating girls, the self-effacing girls accept sub-standard wage offers and might even be the negotiating force generating low wage outcomes. Relevant as a critique of the general applicability of the economic assumption of self-interest from Adam Smith forward, women who internalize a belief of inferiority and exhibit self-effacing behaviors could cause low wages.

Guildswomen's explanations for low women's wages included the pocket wage, the family wage, and the self-effacement hypotheses. Guildswomen explained and challenged all three hypotheses. The Guild's theoretical arguments, their fact gathering and activism, and their ideology established a minimum wage standard for co-operatively employed women.

Credit and poverty

Credit and the Guild ideology

Embedded in the earliest principles of the Rochdale Pioneers was an insistence that co-operative sales be conducted on a cash basis. In the context of the co-operative movement cash sales were seen as a pragmatic business practice and, even more importantly, as a key to independence and character building. The women of the Guild strongly endorsed this position and worked to support it with both statistics and anecdotal empiricism. Margaret Llewelyn Davies observed: "In early Co-operative days, no goods were sold, unless paid for there and then, over the counter." But she went on, "a large amount of credit dealing has gradually crept into the movement" (Davies 1904, 71).[12] Acknowledging that the practice of credit was often "hedged round with various restrictions," Davies still strongly opposed co-op stores selling on credit, "on account of its harmful effects on individuals and on Societies" (Davies 1904, 71).

The case for cash payment was couched by guildswomen in a way to appeal to the realities of women's working-class life. The typical co-operator was from a household with a man employed in a solid job, somewhat above the average. At least in principle such households, with care, were capable of avoiding the worst dangers of credit buying. While the entire co-operative movement emphasized the importance of the ready-cash rule, writings by guildswomen elaborated the point in terms of an ideology that underscored women's responsibilities in their households. For example, Amy Sharp, sometime editor of "The Women's Corner" feature of the *Co-operative News* in her tract, "What Has a Woman to Do with Co-operation?" (1888) made much of the idea that it is primarily the wife's responsibility to keep a household out of debt. In her sociology of the home, husbands would not generally participate in the key consumption decisions, although enlightened ones might recognize the usefulness of the co-operative society. It falls, then, to wives to avoid the mistakes of credit buying and to start actively saving.

Sharp presents her case as a dialogue between Mrs. Morton, a co-operative loyalist, and a friend she is trying to recruit to the co-operative society. Mrs. Morton admits she began her marriage running up substantial debts. Like many new brides of this era, she had never previously handled money or made up a budget. Starting with good intentions, she uses only cash, but finds it easier to let bills run up for a month. Quickly she loses track of her resources and ends deep in debt. Because of the easy availability of credit, Mrs. Morton admits, "I gave up thinking about prices of things when I bought them." As a result much of the household income "got melted away over trifles here and trifles there." She "managed to run [the family] deep into debt in spite of my husband's high wages" (p. 5). Finally, it is her husband who suggests to her the need to join the co-operative society and put things on a cash basis. In any case, it is Mrs. Morton who fully internalizes the message and becomes a staunch advocate of the co-operatives. She asserts it as the wife's duty to manage the household budget and to set up an effective saving plan.

Ever since the first Rochdale stores, consumer co-operatives emphasized the importance of paying dividends as recognition of the common ownership of these enterprises. According to Sharp, the ready-cash purchase system is at least as important as the dividend paid. While the dividend is much appreciated, what is critical is the discipline involved in using the co-ops and avoiding the seductive aspects of credit buying. Her understanding of the potential psychological pitfalls facing working-class women is clearly deeper than the somewhat superficial treatment of such matters in the co-operative political economy of the day.

The Guild argument went further. Not only did women have responsibility for budgeting, but also they had primary responsibility for child rearing. In their expansion of co-operative ideology, consumer debt posed a threat to the character of future generations. Not only might children learn poor consumer habits, but they might be enmeshed directly in the corruption of the debt cycle. Credit in a capitalist market not only corrupted the behavior of women in their roles as consumers, but also had a surprisingly wide range of effects on child rearing.

The argument is elaborated in a Guild paper presented by a "Mrs. Deans." Mrs. Deans starts off with a more or less standard co-operative understanding of the web of debt: "Credit is like a huge spider web, and the more its victims struggle the more they become entangled" (Deans 1898, 3). The mathematics of debt are relentless. The result is not more consumption, but less consumption.

Starting from this typical co-operative position Mrs. Deans develops a much broader argument. The impacts of credit sales, Mrs. Deans claims, extend beyond the creation of a new debtor household. Debt "totally demoralizes" the household, makes both men and women "mean and deceitful, untruthful and dishonest" (p. 4). The co-operative societies are about building independence and character. Extending credit works in just the opposite direction. Most importantly debt can easily corrupt the very core of the household's purposes, child rearing. Mrs. Deans offers a sharply etched anecdote of how the credit system undermines character formation. A young girl of six is instructed by her mother to lie to a baker coming to collect a debt. The child, confused, tells the baker that her mother has instructed her to say that she is not at home. The child gets caught up in the lie, the mother is embarrassed, and as a consequence beats the child for her mistake. In this case credit, the "great evil," results in "marring our better instincts" (p. 4).

The Guild's ideological understanding of credit, while consistent with the theory advanced by political economists sympathetic to the co-operative movement, offered a much broader picture based on the reality of family life in the upper strata of the British working class. They trace the reach of credit beyond the simple mathematics of debt to its influences on the very core of the reproduction of society and character in the family.

Campaigns against credit

Given Davies' interest in the credit question and her political influence in the Women's Guild, it is not surprising that the Guild launched an "Anti-Credit" campaign in 1898. Papers on credit were presented in five Sectional Conferences. Branches were encouraged to propose to their respective societies that they do business only on a "ready-money" system.

The campaign was typical of the Guild's activist, co-operative research method. Some 116 branches (out of 260) participated. At minimum they reported on whether credit was allowed in their stores. Resolutions against credit were then forwarded to Management Committees (Davies 1904, 71).

Closely related to these efforts to broaden knowledge on the practices of co-operative stores, the Guild sought to demonstrate the applicability of cash sales in poorer areas. According to the guildswomen, one of the most dubious defenses of credit was the claim that only credit could attract the poor to the co-operative stores. As Mrs. Deans (1898) had asserted in her paper, "Credit only tends to make the poor poorer" (p. 3). The poor would not benefit from co-operatives offering credit, but they could benefit from association with the movement. Davies argued that co-operatives could have a transformative effect on the overcrowded neighborhoods of the poor with their "usual customs of pawning, drinking, and fighting" (Davies 1904, 90).

The question of how the co-operatives might best approach the poor became a major concern. Again, the Guild undertook to make a report on the matter. Using informal survey techniques, Sheffield, Bury, York, Newcastle, Sunderland, Plymouth and Bristol were investigated. Davies and the Guild excelled at this type of investigative effort. Interestingly, Davies cites Jane Addams's work in Chicago as a model for reaching into poor communities (Davies 1904, 95).

The Guild's report, "The Open Door" made a number of recommendations. Key were proposals to keep prices, entrance fees, and especially dividends low. The problem of balancing competing claims was clear. Somewhat hopefully the Guild Congress of 1897 passed a resolution:

> Co-operators should discourage the payment of a rate of dividend higher than is consistent with a just regard to reasonable charges for goods, liberal treatment of employees, efficient safeguarding of the stability of the Society, and ample provision for the intellectual and social need of its members.
>
> *Davies 1904, 82*[13]

Based largely on experiments with a store targeted to poor households in the Sunderland area, Davies was optimistic that not only might a co-op store in a poor community directly help households meet their consumption needs, but it might also serve as "a foundation and centre for constructive social work" (Davies 1904, 92). Davies looked to such stores serving as means to a broad social end. Building on relationships of "self-help and unspoilt by the demoralizing effects of charity," co-op stores in poor areas had the opportunity to raise the "standard of individual and social life" (p. 95). Ultimately, however, Davies asserts, such an expansion of the co-operative movement must be matched by major local and national reforms.

Producer co-operatives

The question of supporting producer co-operatives, in addition to retail co-operatives, was one that divided Guild leaders. While the call for producer co-operatives was anchored deep in the radical co-operative ideology, there was substantial disagreement in the Guild over whether women workers' interests were well served by producer co-operatives. The topic is interesting in its own right. But more to the immediate point, it provides an example of an important question in which divisions in the Guild leadership short circuited the organization's traditional research campaign machinery.

Ideology, producer co-operatives, and women

At the theoretical level both Robert Owen and J.S. Mill strongly endorsed producer co-operatives.

At the practical level, experience in Great Britain in the last half of the 19th century suggested producer co-operatives were far more difficult to establish and manage than retail co-operatives. By the late 19th century, these difficulties created a major problem for the ideology of the co-operative movement. Writing in 1891 in the "Women's Corner," Llewelyn Davies noted that co-operators were split on whether production should be run by consumers through the organization of co-operative wholesale societies or should be controlled directly by the workforces of productive facilities. Davies observed that on one side were those older idealists such as George Holyoake, who held that worker-managed production was central to the co-operative vision. On the other Davies cited the work of Beatrice Potter, who argued that producer co-operatives were hopelessly utopian.

The Women's Guild generally presented a united front on most issues. But Davies was clear in her article that she was putting forth her personal views and not those of the central committee. That said, Davies' position closely followed that of Potter who, in the same year (1891), had written an important volume entitled *The Co-operative Movement in Great Britain*. Generally supportive of the co-operative efforts in retailing (and of the Women's Guild), Potter was scathing in her treatment of producer co-operatives which she considered utopian and unworkable. The record of producer co-operatives had been a "dismal" one of "repeated failure" (Potter 1891, 149). Potter identified three key reasons for these results: "want of capital, want of custom and absence of administrative discipline."

Producer co-operatives either struggled with limited capital or borrowed at "ruinous rates of interest" which generally meant "rapid shipwreck." Potter's argument on custom emphasized the lack of commercial knowledge among those establishing producer co-operatives. Especially when such shops were set up in hard times they courted disaster. Too often

> these associations were based on the old fallacy of the Labour Exchange; they are formed under the delusion that with industry and skill the worker must create value, whether or not the commodity he manufactures corresponds to any available demand.
>
> *Potter 1891, 151*

This position, of course, ran directly at odds with Owen's commitment to just such exchanges. At the same time it reflected the still relatively new emphasis on demand among the marginalists (Jevons) and neo-classicists (Marshall) with whom Potter was well acquainted. Finally, democratic governance on shop floors went against the entire development of industrial discipline. It was inevitably inefficient if not actually chaotic. Where apparently successful it was simply hypocritical as workers were effectively cheated out of their representation in one way or another (Potter 1891, 149–153).

Potter's take on producers' co-operatives became the accepted position of the Fabian Society in which she and her husband, Sidney Webb, played central roles. Indeed, this position became central to the broader socialist argument in favor of national ownership of industry. Llewelyn Davies, however, did not argue for nationalization. While sympathetic to Potter's arguments against worker management, she advocated as an alternative, not nationalization, but rather ownership and management of production units by the co-operative wholesale societies under the direction of the co-operative movement.

According to Davies, workshops owned by the co-operative stores' wholesale societies, could avoid most of the problems raised by Potter. Most importantly, the "capital supplied by the (co-operative) stores is almost exhaustless," so their workshops could be well financed. Moreover, their wealth made it relatively easy to "secure competent managers," thus addressing Potter's third concern (Davies 1891, 1010). With respect to Potter's fear of lack of "custom," Davies might have added the argument that the wholesale societies, with their strong connections to co-operative stores, were in an excellent position to distribute the goods of their workshops.

Davies went on to consider the relative merits of the two types of production organization from the point of view of the workers themselves. Admittedly in workshops owned and managed by the wholesale societies, workers had no role in governance and took no share of profit. But, by the same token, and perhaps more importantly, they did not risk their wages or savings on the vagaries of the trade cycle. With the wholesale societies acting as employers, "bad times and losses can be stood much more easily; while bad effects are not felt directly by the workers, but are distributed over the whole body of consumers, so that each individual suffers as little as possible" (p. 1011).

Davies acknowledged that profit sharing might carry with it some incentive effects on productivity. But she argued, "There is nothing very exalting in the idea that a man will work harder for himself than for other people." From a moral perspective that included impacts on character development, the upshot might well be worse, not better.[14] She was fearful that workers in profit-sharing enterprises would themselves become "profit grubbing capitalists." Moreover, workers with greater tenure might end up by exploiting new hires, emphasizing exclusivity rather than openness (p. 1011).

All said, Davies is quite aware that the co-operative wholesale societies would not generally identify the interests of the co-operative store movement with those of the workers. But under the circumstances worker ownership was not a solid alternative. Rather than risking ownership, the workers did better to build their trade unions, "the only way of securing a standard wage" (p. 1011).

Writing in response to Davies' article, Mary Lawrenson held to the more traditional co-operator position of Owen and the Christian socialists. Lawrenson starts by pointing out that many women first came to the Guild motivated by the hope that workshops would be established enabling "girls to work for their own profit" (Lawrenson 1891a, 1179).

Lawrenson went on to make an argument that the accumulated capital of the co-operative stores could just as easily be extended to worker-managed firms as to those managed by the wholesale societies. In a subsequent letter (Lawrenson 1891b, 1251), she gave examples of several successful worker-managed firms that deserved co-operative society support.

Lawrenson emphasized the role of women in workplaces, where they might reasonably aspire to less alienating environments. In many cases women workers were subjected to conditions more dispiriting than those of men. Blaszak suggests that Davies and the group around her tended to emphasize the role of women as home-based consumers and this might explain their lack of interest in producer co-operatives (Blaszak 2000, 108–109). Yet it is hard to find this argument convincing in light of Davies' and Catherine Webb's strong support of the campaign for minimum wages for working women. More likely they saw those women's interests as better addressed through reform legislation than through producer co-operatives that were unlikely to empower women workers.

A campaign that did not happen

Mary Lawrenson desired to make the issue of producer co-operatives a Guild project. She proposed that in traditional Guild fashion the question of producer co-operative be made a subject of collective study, at "meetings, lectures and magic lantern views" (Lawrenson

1891a, 1251). She also encouraged women to visit producer co-operatives so that they might gain first-hand experience of the differences between such workshops and those conducted on more traditional lines.

Lawrenson's call for a campaign was very much in line with the customary Guild approach to subjects of interest. But, to the best of our knowledge the Guild did not pick up on the suggestion. Producer co-operatives were not made the center of a Guild reform campaign. The Guild did not add to the data on the subject nor formulate policy proposals. Despite interesting initial points made by both Davies and Lawrenson, the deep disagreements on the issues left the Guild on the sidelines of the larger debate. As a result, its highly effective popular research method was not put in motion in this case.

Isolation of British working-class housewives[15]

The Women's Co-operative Guild mounted telling, if anecdotal, evidence of the problematic domestic circumstances facing many British working-class housewives at the turn of the 20th century. Domestic experiences for housewives included isolation-induced anxiety, drudgery, overwork, melancholia, a longing for "new walls round them, for people to work with"[16] and material deprivation. Guild research also documented a small number of cases of psychological, physical, and sexual abuse of housewives. One of numerous contributory factors identified in the Guild literature included that the housewife "is first without economic [*sic*] independence, and the law therefore gives the man, whether he be good or bad, a terrible power over her" (Women's Co-operative Guild 1915, 8).

Larger in number than the four million British pay-check receiving girls and working women at the turn of the 20th century, were

> the married women, who, as home-makers, contribute by their unpaid labour just as directly as wage-earners to the support of family life. This class is now, through organization, finding its voice, formulating its needs, and taking its part in administrative work as Co-operators and citizens.
>
> *Davies 1904, 162–163*

The social potential of co-operation is well known, not a novel contribution of Davies or the Women's Co-operative Guild. The creative endeavor of guildswomen was the application of their reform ideology and methodology to the problematic domain of British 19th-century housebound working-class wives. The extension of co-operation into a consciousness-expanding educational force for women was a brainchild of Margaret Davies.

The reform ideology in the literature addressing the domestic experiences of British working-class wives manifested primarily in the form of rooting out yet another social "evil" in some working-class English households. Guildswomen argued that formal laws and informal cultural norms fueled an authoritative power structure that worked against the interests of wives. As evidence mounted, it became clear to guildswomen that imbalanced power in the marital relationship was a major issue in need of the agitators' toolkit. Participant-observation exposed the hidden experiential realities of working-class housewives.

Some of the evidence the Guild collected together was haphazardly anecdotal. Referring to a study by Lady Bell on Middlesbrough iron works women, Nash states that likely over half "of the wives have not the health and capacity to manage their homes and children with real success." "Many" of the iron works women fell into inert mental states, "as though they had given up the ideal, if they ever had it, of the possibility of making anything better"

(Nash 1907, 6). Relaying an account of a woman demonstrator yelling at a (wo)manhandling police officer: "'What are you doing, a-hauling me along like that? *I'm not your missis*'," Nash infers it "is only in such glimpses that we can get an idea of what goes on in some homes, for, of course, the privacy of the home is sacred" (p. 12). Chapter 11 of Davies (1904) preserves many anecdotal examples of the typical drudgery of working-class housewives' housework tasks and daily schedules.

Anecdotal examples also relay the restorative effects of co-operative experiences for these working-class housewives. One woman's perspective is quoted across texts: arriving "to Guild many times not knowing how I got there, I was that tired, but I felt stones weight lifted off my shoulders after" (Davies 1904, 155; Nash 1907, 7). A second woman found that Guild participation sequestered her melancholia (Davies 1904, 155).

Working-class women's involvement in branch meetings, educational opportunities, and Guild governance relieved the monotonous, isolating work lives of these housewives. The Guild also offered domestic service courses educating women in more efficient management of their workload.

Abused housewife experiences arising in some isolated household units required greater recourse by the Guild. Domestic abuse formed a primary reason for the Guild's public agitation supporting maternity benefits for women, better divorce laws in Great Britain, and suffrage. Nash (1907) also calls for payment of motherhood allowances by the state to mothers staying home to care for young children.

The maternity benefits campaign included formal fact gathering through the collection of letters documenting women's qualitative experiences of child bearing and rearing. A simple set of leading questions drove this fact-finding initiative: "How many children have you had? How soon after each other were they born? Did any die under five years old, and if so, at what ages and from what causes? Have you had any miscarriages, and if so how many? (Women's Co-operative Guild 1915, 191). This evidence supported the Guild's political activism toward ensuring that a state-paid maternity benefit become the legal property of the mother. The Guild's maternity survey questions also asked about the husband's wages and occupation.

The Guild sent the maternity questionnaire to 600 members; 386 respondents replied covering about 400 maternity cases. The Guild printed 160 letters in its widely acclaimed 1915 publication, *Maternity: Letters from Working Women*. Letters providing evidence of neglect and abuse in four households include: "Men Need Education"; "A Time of Horror"; "A Brutal Husband"; and "Problem of Housework".

The overwhelming majority of these housewife reflections correlate their domestic difficulties with low wages and with uncertain work for husbands. Guild ideology linked inadequate market provisioning of the working class to the capitalist system. Beyond inadequate wages for men, the Guild identified two more factors explaining childbirth and rearing problems: ignorance in pregnancy and childbirth and the personal relationship of a married couple (p. 6).

The housewives' reflections in the maternity letters expose negative maternity and childrearing experiences. Most of the letters relay extremely confined options for the women. The women applied a number of coping strategies in response to their constraints, including (a) succumbing to the limits society and marriage imposed upon them; (b) sparingly managing household resources; (c) abstaining from consumption (especially women denying themselves food, rest, and medical care) to allow meager husbands' wages to nourish him and their children; (d) taking in work to earn small sums; and (e) in some cases, conscious decisions to limit family size. The maternity letters uncovered substantial qualitative empirical evidence to activate Guild agitation.

Economics metaphors and analogies best describe the rudimentary theoretical contributions made by women co-operators on the subject of housewife isolation. Likening marriage to a curtain[17] and applying the workshop[18] concept to the domestic sphere are repeated rhetorical devices. Parallels between domesticity and slavery, between domesticity and servitude[19] and brief references to the non-existence of a labor market[20] in domestic relations re-appear. The institution of the trade union[21] is suggested to undo the harm caused from working-class housewives' isolation.

Davies repeatedly elicits the metaphor of the curtain in her attempts to convey the hidden domestic problems faced by working-class housewives:

> In the past, a heavy curtain had, on marriage, fallen on the woman's life, and the nation felt no responsibility for her personal welfare or for the conditions under which she performed her great tasks. Without money of her own, with no right even to her housekeeping savings, without adequate protection against a husband's possible cruelty, with no legal position as a mother, with the conditions of maternity totally neglected, married women in the home had existed apart, voiceless and unseen.
>
> *Davies in C. Webb 1927, 11*

The isolated working-class household as the woman's workshop is a repeated economic metaphor. Working-class homes "are the workshops of many trades, where overtime abounds, and where an eight hours' day would be a very welcome reform." Davies goes on to note that men do not understand the "drudgery and lonely effort" in housework (Davies 1904, 151).

Building on ideas in J.S. Mill's "The Subjection of Women," Rosalind Nash develops analogies of working-class housewives' marriages with slavery and with servitude. For Nash, slavery is the most appropriate parallel for mid-18th-century working-class housewives' situations. In some senses elevated to the status of servants by the end of the century, Nash describes that these housewives' domestic servitude still rated below servants-for-hire because domesticated housewives lacked access to a labor market. As Nash understood their situation, freedom was constrained more for working-class housewives than for servants because housewives lacked negotiating power in marriages. Nash attributes inexistence of negotiation power to self-effacing related mechanisms and also because the state reinforced the social perception of wives as property of their husbands:

> But wives cannot bargain with their husbands about their own homes and children. Unselfishness, weakness, and custom all combine against their setting a value on themselves, and a wife is still vaguely supposed to be in some sense her husband's property.
>
> *Nash 1907, 5*

At least as early as 1904, Davies refers to unpaid labor contributions by working-class housewives. In 1913, Davies elicits a simple cause-and-effect explanation of housewives' dire life experiences: "the fact that no money value is attached to the services of a woman in her home is also responsible for the position of so many women" (p. 4).

Nash describes in women as well as men the "desire for sensation, excitement and change." Rather than assess this desire as "wickedness," Nash promotes the idea that this "is a force we must direct, not crush." Directing this force toward the Guild as "a kind of trade union . . . we can spread better ideas" (Nash 1907, 8–9). By 1927, Davies suggests this redirection was accomplished:

> It might well have been thought a hopeless task for a class of women who "never knows when their day's work's done," and on whom personal claims are insistent, ceaseless, and irresistible, to organize and educate themselves and undertake public work and responsibilities. But the miracle has been accomplished [via Guild efforts] . . . and . . . a great and hitherto untapped source of strength has . . . been added to national life.
>
> *Davies in C. Webb 1927, 11*

The Women's Co-operative Guild provided working-class housewives with re-directive support. Branch meetings as well as social and political participation reduced household isolation. As a savvy political institution, the Guild shaped legislation enhancing state support for women. Finally, the Guild offered educational opportunities to expand the intellect and the socio-political consciousness of working-class housewives.

Conclusions

The Women's Co-operative Guild focused on reform within the co-operative movement and more broadly across the nation as a whole. The guildswomen certainly deserve recognition for their political efforts on behalf of reform. But they also deserve recognition for their contributions to British economic thought of the late 19th and early 20th centuries. This chapter argues that the Guild brought to its ideological positions a unique methodology. While perhaps no individual guildswoman can be identified as an economist of the first rank, together they expanded the economic thought of their day and added greatly to the accumulation of economic facts.

The British co-operative movement generated a reform ideology that was strongly critical of the capitalist market economy and especially its tendency to erode the best in human character. Like many in the movement, the guildswomen were committed to this ideology. But in their reading, the co-operative commonwealth ultimately rests on homes and families overseen by women freed from the worst corruptions of the marketplace and competent in their housekeeping and child raising. These women must be strong in the moral example they set in their larger community. Guildswomen were convinced of the value of these goals, even if under current conditions, the vast majority of women could not hope to achieve them. The Guild's ideological faith was that nothing inherent in human nature made such a sea change unobtainable. Thus it became their responsibility to identify, research and fight for the key economic reforms necessary to achieve these ends.

Against this background, the guildswomen developed an activist research methodology. Issues were typically brought to Guild congresses and local meetings, where the membership was encouraged to engage in discussion and to contribute to statistical research. The Guild methodology was built on participant-observation, fact gathering and common sense theorizing. While sometimes not rigorous, Guild research was always timely and relevant. Topics ranged widely over issues of concern to women co-operators. Most often the Guild focused on the failures of existing social structures, and especially those of the free market. In turn, the assembled information was most often used in advancing Guild policy proposals.

In previous sections we have attempted to flesh out our understanding of this approach of the Women's Guild to economics by considering four areas of Guild activity: minimum wages, credit and poverty, producer co-operatives, and women's isolation. An excellent example of Guild research in support of advocacy was the campaign around minimum wages within the co-operative movement itself. Documenting the role of women workers in co-operative establishments, the Guild fought for an across the board minimum wage. Not just a fact-finding activity, the campaign generated thoughtful arguments against traditional defenses of women's sub-par wages. The guildswomen questioned common formulations of the pocket wage and the family wage arguments and explored a self-effacement hypothesis. The campaign ultimately was successful with the establishment of a minimum wage in the co-operative movement.

A similar campaign around the dangers of offering consumer credit led guildswomen to research not only the extent and consequences of credit, but also claims that credit was essential to extend co-operative retailing to poorer communities. The guildswomen's approach to fact gathering put the Guild leadership in an excellent position to advocate on these issues within the co-operative movement. At the same time the Guild was less successful in grappling with issues surrounding producer co-operatives. Split on the appeal and practicality of producer co-operatives, a call for a campaign was sidetracked by the leadership. Without such a campaign the Guild added relatively little to the broader topic or the role of women in traditionally managed production facilities supplying co-operative stores.

Guild research was perhaps most creative in considering the economics surrounding the isolation and dependency of working-class housewives. A topic that few traditional economists considered at all, women's isolation became an issue that guildswomen could hardly avoid. While much of the evidence they gathered was anecdotal, it all pointed toward the need for more aggressive organizing, education and political reform. And the Guild pushed to establish state-supported maternity benefits for those women.

Reviewing this record, we find it fair to credit the Women's Co-operative Guild with a unique collective research effort. Over a number of years, working within their ideological world-view, the Guild brought together a wide range of statistics, facts, and cases that offered serious support to the Guild's reform program. The Guild's collective approach to research stands out in the history of economic thought. Guild writers such as Margaret Llewelyn Davies and Catherine Webb made modest contributions to economics in their own right, but as a group the Guild generated a methodology that engaged and educated the guildswomen and, in some cases, re-directed social policy, even as they made meaningful additions to knowledge.

Notes

1 For the early history of the Guild as told by a central participant, see Margaret Llewelyn Davies (1904). The Guild's successor, The Co-operative Women's Guild, disbanded its national organization in 2016.

2 That reform movement included overlapping membership. For example, Catherine Webb was Secretary of the Council early on (Mappen 1986, 237). Like the Guild, several of these other organizations also emphasized an empirical methodology aimed at achieving reform. For example, Clementina Black of the Women's Industrial Council edited investigations into more than 100 trades, publishing the results in *Married Women's Work* in 1915.

3 The history of the 19th-century co-operative movement in Britain is recounted by Bonner (1970).

4 See Peter Gurney (1996).

5 Mill, John Stuart. [1848] 1965. "On the Probable Futurity of the Labouring Classes," Book IV, Ch. 7.

6 The origin of the term "co-operative commonwealth" remains hazy. However, it was in widespread use by 1907 when it appeared throughout Catherine Webb (1907).

7 See the description of methods in the Women's Co-operative Guild (1908a, 144).

8 Of course, the academic standards of the day were themselves somewhat ad-hoc and less than rigorous by modern lights.

9 The title of Chapter IX in C. Webb (1927) explicitly depicts the Women's Co-operative Guild's activism toward a minimum wage standard as a campaign.

10 Both examples on the British sweatshop movement are in Clementina Black (1907).

11 Simon Deakin and Francis Green (2009).

12 A few years earlier, Mrs. Deans reported that 1,113 co-operative societies gave some type of credit, and only 507 did all their business on a cash basis (Deans 1898, 3).
13 More controversial was a suggestion to create "Loan Departments" which could take security "to lend without taking advantage of necessity." These departments would directly challenge the widespread practice of "weekly pawning" (Davies 1904, 77). Presumably, some guildswomen feared that such departments ran the risk of enmeshing borrowers in a debt trap and exposing co-op stores to instability.
14 This argument was also made by Potter.
15 Gillian Scott (1998), Chapter 3, raises and analyzes the isolation issue for the working-class women of the Women's Co-operative Guild. This account draws on Scott's work, and adds to it by using primary source material and emphasizing the underlying economics constructions by the Guild.
16 Nash 1907, p. 6.
17 The curtain metaphor appears in the 5/27/1911 issue of *Co-operative News*, p. 667, as identified by Gillian Scott. It also appears in Women's Co-operative Guild (1915) and in Webb (1927). The metaphor of the curtain is an allusion to the lack of transparency in domestic relations.
18 Gillian Scott attributes the first use of the workshop metaphor in writing of the Women's Co-operative Guild to Miss Amy Sharp in a *Co-operative News* column dated 3/13/1897, p. 268. It also appears in Davies (1904), p. 151.
19 Nash (1907) references J.S. Mill (1869) as a source linking the domestic role of housewives to slavery and also to servitude. The analogy between the domesticity of housewives and slavery appears even earlier in 1792 in Mary Wollstonecraft's *A Vindication of the Rights of Woman*, chapter 4.
20 Non-existence of valuation via labor market processes appears in Davies (1904), pp. 161–162, Nash (1907), p. 5, and Davies (1913), p. 4.
21 Gillian Scott attributes the identification of the Women's Co-operative Guild as a trade union for working-class housewives to Nash (1907).

References

Black, Clementina. 1907. *Sweated Industry and the Minimum Wage*. London: Duckworth & Co.

Black, Clementina. (ed.) 1915. *Married Women's Work*. London: G. Bell and Sons.

Blaszak, Barbara. 2000. *The Matriarchs of England's Cooperative Movement: A Study in Gender Politics and Female Leadership, 1883–1921*. Westport, CT: Greenwood Press.

Bonner, Arnold. 1970. *British Co-operation: The History, Principles and Organization of the British Co-operative Movement*. Manchester: Co-operative Union Ltd.

Davies, Margaret Llewelyn. 1891. Co-operative Workshops. *In the "Women's Corner," The Co-operative News and Journal of Associated Industries*. October 3, 1010–1012.

——. 1904. *The Women's Co-operative Guild 1883–1904*. Kirkby-Lonsdale, Westmoreland, England: Published by the Women's Co-operative Guild.

——. 1913. *The Education of Guildswomen*. London: Co-operative Women's Guild. 1913 Annual Congress.

Deakin, Simon and Francis Green. 2009. "One Hundred Years of British Minimum Wage Legislation". *British Journal of Industrial Relations* (June), 47(2): 205–213.

Deans. 1898. "Credit and High Prices." Manchester: Women's Co-operative Guild.

Gurney, Peter. 1996. *Co-operative Culture and the Politics of Consumption in England, 1870–1930*. Manchester: Manchester University Press.

Harris, Lilian. 1897. "The Treatment of Women Employees in the Co-operative Movement, Being a Report of an Enquiry into the Wages, Hours, and Conditions of Women Working in Co-operative Stores in 1895". Manchester: Co-operative Newspaper Society.

Lawrenson, Mary. 1891a. Comments on Davies. In the "Women's Corner," *The Co-operative News and Journal of Associated Industries*. November 21, 1179.

——. 1891b. Comments on Davies. In the "Women's Corner," *The Co-operative News and Journal of Associated Industries*. December 12, 1251.

Mappen, Ellen. 1986. "Strategists for Change: Social Feminist Approaches to the Problems of Women's Work". In Angela John (ed.), *Unequal Opportunities: Women's Employment in England 1800–1918*. Oxford: Basil Blackwell.

Mill, John Stuart. [1848] 1965. "On the Probable Futurity of the Labouring Classes," Book IV, Ch. 7 In John M. Robson (ed.), *The Principles of Political Economy with Some of Their Applications to Social Philosophy*. Vols. 2–3 of *The Collected Works of John Stuart Mill*. Toronto: University of Toronto Press, pp. 758–796.

Nash, Rosalind. 1907. *The Position of Married Women*. Manchester, England: Consumer Wholesale Society Printing Works.

Owen, Robert. 1813–1817. *A New View of Society, Or, Essays on the Principle of the Formation of the Human Character, and the Application of the Principle to Practice*, third edition. London: Longman et al. https://books.google.com/books?id=P80PAQAAMAAJ

Potter, Beatrice. 1891. *The Cooperative Movement in Great Britain*. London: Swan Sonnenschein.

Scott, Gillian. 1998. *Feminism and the Politics of Working Women: The Women's Co-Operative Guild, 1880s to the Second World War*. London: UCL Press.

Sharp, Amy. 1888. "What Has a Woman to Do with Co-operation?" Manchester: Central Co-operative Board.

Webb, Catherine (ed.) 1907. *Industrial Co-operation: The Story of a Peaceful Revolution*. Manchester: Co-operative Union, Ltd.

——. 1927. *The Woman with the Basket: The History of the Women's Co-operative Guild 1883–1927*. Manchester, England: Co-operative Wholesale Society's Printing Works.

Wollstonecraft, Mary. [1792] 1890. *A Vindication of the Rights of Woman*. New York: Scribner and Welford.

Women's Co-operative Guild. 1908a. "Summarised Report of the Women's Guild," in the *40th Annual Co-operative Congress*. Manchester: Co-operation Union, Ltd.

——. 1908b. "A Co-operative Standard for Women Workers." Pamphlet produced for Annual Congress, June 1908.

——. 1915. *Maternity: Letters from Working Women*. London: G. Bell & Sons, Ltd.

9

ANECDOTES OF DISCRIMINATION

Barriers to women's participation in economic thought during the late nineteenth and early twentieth centuries

Kirsten Madden[1]

Introduction

As a class and historically, women are the recipients of sex discrimination. Sex discrimination is the adverse and unjust treatment of women because of their sex. The adverse treatment includes women being considered inferior, having less access to resources, and finding fewer opportunities.

Between 1861 and 1890 less than three percent of the approximately 1,000 U.S. doctoral degrees were earned by women (25 women in total) (Fitzpatrick, 1990, pp. 74–5). In 70 university catalogues dated 1920, 1921, or 1922, Lonn (1924) identifies 7,499 faculty. Of this total, approximately nine percent were women. Of the women faculty, 488 were instructors, 129 assistants, 35 associates, and 28 were full professors. In comparison, Lonn identifies 2,110 male full professors (p. 5). During the early to mid-twentieth century women earned fewer than eight percent of all doctoral degrees in science and engineering, and although that number grew, it was still disproportionately lower through the twentieth century (Kohlstedt, 2004).

Women have always made up a minority of economics Ph.D.s. According to Libby (1990), women wrote 18.3 percent of economics Ph.D. dissertations in 1918, 15.6 percent in 1919 and 15.0 percent in 1920. In the next decade through 1990, this percentage fell and hovered around 10 percent (p. 121). Moving into the twenty-first century, women earning economics Ph.D.s rebounded. By 2007, the ratio of women earning economics Ph.D.s to the total was at a record high of roughly 33 percent (Broder, 2010, p. 659).

Many sources convey anecdotal examples of sex discrimination. These anecdotal examples turn up in autobiographies penned by women economists, in academic studies rooting out sex discrimination during the twentieth century, and in the secondary literature about women's contributions to the history of economic thought. To date though, there is no single source documenting the variety of evidence that exists of sex discrimination in the history of economic thought.

Who is an economist and what is economics are open questions during the late nineteenth and early twentieth centuries. Madden, Seiz and Pujol (2004) addresses these questions in detail (pp. xx–xxii). For purposes of this study, if a woman contributed to literature that falls within the realm of economics, her experience of sex discrimination is reported.

How did women economists experience sex discrimination during the late nineteenth and early twentieth centuries in the West? This chapter organizes the anecdotal experiences of sex discrimination. Cultural norms expressed in parental attitudes as well as social beliefs about the inferior nature of women affected women economists. Women who wished to pursue higher education received discouragement and discrimination as students. For the women who earned advanced degrees, discrimination in employment, salary, promotion and tenure was problematic. The institution of marriage brought discriminatory barriers to academia in the form of anti-nepotism rules. There is some documentation of student sexism toward women professors and generally in careers requiring Ph.D.s, women economists documented difficulties accessing facilities. Finally, from some of the anecdotal evidence it can be inferred that some women unwittingly colluded in sex discrimination.

Anecdotes about parental attitude and societal beliefs in inferior intellect and abilities of women

Parental opinions toward the role of women in society shape the outcomes for their children. There is not likely to be much evidence of the majority of cases where parents perceive or desire a limited role for women if their daughters succumb to their parents' views. But the case of Jessica Blanche Peixotto is one in which the daughter overcame the prejudices of her father. A high school graduate in 1880, Jessica's wish to attend the University of California at Berkeley was put off by her father's narrow views for women's education. To father Raphael, "'university life was not appropriate for a young girl to whom were available the rich opportunities within a cultured home circle'" and Jessica was further educated with private tutors. Nonetheless, by age 27, Jessica was a student at Berkeley, and by 1900 at the age of 36, she was the second woman to earn her doctorate from this institution (Lobdell, 2000, p. 328; Dzuback, 2006, p. 156). In contrast, the father of Sophonisba Breckinridge was an advocate for women's education, including the education of his daughter (Fitzpatrick, 1990, p. 4). Breckinridge earned both a Ph.D. and a law degree.

A common socially held belief through the early twentieth century is that women were intellectually inferior to men (Clifford, 1983, p. 32). Women economists experienced this prejudiced attitude. Some succumbed to this belief and others transcended it.

Economist Mabel Newcomer documented an account of a sexist belief in intellectual inferiority while she took graduate courses at Columbia University circa 1914. Newcomer wrote:

> A university professor of my acquaintance once told a friend of mine that she should not take his courses because the subject was beyond the comprehension of the female mind. While this did not deter her, and she proved to be the best student in his classes, he was able to recognize and acknowledge the quality of her work, but his conviction remained unshaken. He explained her achievement by the fact that she had a "man's brain."
>
> *Newcomer, 1959, p. 26, as cited in Shackleford, 1995, p. 20*

Married to the neoclassical economist Alfred Marshall, Mary Paley Marshall was an economist in her own right (McWilliams Tullberg, 1995). In 1871, Mary Paley Marshall was one of the first five women to attend "Lectures for Women" at Newnham College in Cambridge at the age of 21. Mary lectured in economics at University College, Bristol as well as Oxford and Newnham. At Newnham she also had administrative responsibilities over students. After her marriage to

Alfred Marshall, she co-authored with him a short book titled *Economics of Industry*. In honor of Mary, John Maynard Keynes wrote a lengthy obituary about her in 1944. Keynes presents his understanding of Alfred Marshall's view of women's minds in Marshall's later years:

> In spite of his early sympathies [for women's academic opportunity] and what he was gaining all the time from his wife's discernment of mind, Marshall came increasingly to the conclusion that there was nothing useful to be made of women's intellects. When the great trial of strength came in 1896 over the proposal to grant women's degrees he abandoned the friends of a lifetime and took, whatever his wife might think or feel, the other side. But Mary Marshall had been brought up to know, and also to respect and accept what men of "strict principles" were like.
>
> *Keynes, 1944, p. 276*

The Fabian socialist and major player in the socio-political structuring of Great Britain during the early twentieth century, Beatrice Potter Webb discussed her intention to shift from studies of women's employment to cooperative industries. Alfred Marshall described as "pernicious" her intention. In response Webb perceived that she was up to the task, as she possessed a "masculine intellect." Arguably, with this gender-ification of intelligence, Webb succumbed to the culturally prevailing notion that feminine characteristics did not include higher order intellectual capability (MacKenzie and MacKenzie, 1977, p. 133).

When the College of Economics and Business Administration was established at the University of Washington in the early twentieth century, the economist Theresa McMahon was the only woman professor in the College. She identifies that she was an outcast because she treated the subject of economics from the perspective of a social scientist with training in sociology. She raised (and challenged) women's alleged intellectual inferiority as a reason that the men of the college considered that she "didn't belong in their school of thought":

> Besides, I was a woman. I think there are still some men who think they are intellectually superior to women working in the same field simply because they are men. This has always amused me, especially when I realize the mediocrity of many of the men; the more mediocre they were the more conceited they were about being males.
>
> *McMahon, 1989, p. 269*

Dean of Women at Berkeley from 1906–1912, Lucy Sprague remembered that "most of the [male] faculty thought of women frankly as inferior beings" (Dzuback, 2006, p. 162). According to Dzuback, this prejudice influenced choices economist Jessica Peixotto made not to attend meetings of the Berkeley economics department even though Peixotto was a department member. Before earning her Ph.D., Berkeley economist Emily Huntington studied for a year during the 1920s at the London School of Economics. According to Dzuback (2006), Huntington recalled Professor Charles J. Bullock openly "criticized women for being 'illogical'" (p. 163).

With a 1926 Ph.D. in economics from Radcliffe College, by 1952 Eleanor Lansing Dulles worked with the U.S. State Department. Her task was to support the reconstruction of Berlin during the Cold War era. Dulles titled a chapter of her autobiography as: "Sex Discrimination in the State Department." Among other factors, she describes attempting to work around the constraint imposed by men who doubted women's professional capacities.

The belief of women's inferiority extended beyond the brain. Some academic women were haunted by fears of not being able to live up to high academic production standards. Women "felt obliged to ensure that their health would not fail while they equaled or exceeded the academic accomplishments of their male counterparts" (Clifford, 1983, p. 32). In her autobiography, the industrial relations expert and University of Chicago economist, Mary Barnett Gilson, wrote specifically about this concern when she spent a few months researching labor relations on Hawaiian sugar plantations. A rupture in her appendix while doing field work tested her resolve "not to disgrace my sex by any physical incapacity to assume any task performed by my [all male] colleagues." Gilson documents that she transformed her health crisis into an opportunity to "investigate plantation hospitals at uncomfortably close range" (Gilson, 1940, p. 236).

Obviously many women transcended specific cases of male gender bias. Ryan and Vaitheswaran (2000) document a high-profile case involving the British international economist, Barbara Ward. According to Lady Bird Johnson, wife of former U.S. President Lyndon B. Johnson, "Lyndon listened to [Barbara Ward] 'which he doesn't always do, especially to women'" (Ryan and Vaitheswaran, 2000, p. 448).

Discouragement from pursuing an economics career

Strober (1975) reports preliminary results of a 1974–75 Committee on the Status of Women in the Economics Profession–American Economic Association Survey of Economists. The study found that the existence of one or more role models during high school was influential toward pursuing a career for 70 percent of the women respondents. In contrast, approximately 30 percent of the women sampled received some form of encouragement to *abandon* aspirations of a professional career while in college (p. 98). An open question concerns how many women might have pursued economics had they not been dissuaded because of their sex.

Evidence on the missing women economists is mostly lacking. But at least one anecdotal example suggests that some men economists discouraged women from pursuing the field. Born in Fall River, Massachusetts in 1911 to an immigrant proprietor of a shoe store, Adelaide Schwartz studied economics at Wellesley College. Completion of her undergraduate thesis titled "The Effects of Business Conditions on Radicalism in the United States Since 1900" earned her an undergraduate degree in 1931 at the age of 20. Shortly after completing her degree, she married the Providence, Rhode Island physician, Henry Weyler, born 1893. Henry encouraged Adelaide to play chess. During the 1930s she was ranked among women chess players. In Providence, Adelaide attended Brown University. From all accounts, she performed well in pursuit of her graduate degree. Adelaide completed her master's degree in economics writing her thesis, "Milk Control with Special Reference to Rhode Island," in 1935. Adelaide seriously considered pursuing a Ph.D. in economics. As recalled by Adelaide to family, Brown University Economics faculty members told her in the 1930s that she would never get an academic job and that she really should look to do something more immediate. Adelaide dropped her goal of a Ph.D. She became a statistician for the Providence Council of Social Agencies, a group of charities in the Providence area. In 1942 she did an innovative report on "Statistics for Census Tracts of Providence," which extensively used correlation analysis, but warned that correlations did not indicate causality. Adelaide kept friendly relations with the Brown economists and their families for the rest of her life. She worked with Teresa Branstetter Taft whose husband was a well-known labor economist at Brown University; the wife of economist Hyman Minsky served as an assistant to Dr. Weyler. After working for a time as a statistician, Adelaide had a child and became a housewife.[2]

Discrimination women economists received as students

Historically, women had limited access to literacy, advanced education, and scholarly credentials in the U.S.A. and Western Europe (Clifford, 1983, p. 6). That sex discrimination excluded women from higher education is not a disputable point. In the U.S.A. up until the mid-eighteenth century, U.S primary education was also not easily available to girls. Clifford (1983) identifies the late eighteenth to early nineteenth centuries as a time when girls saw sharp increases in primary schooling. For example, in this time New England's publicly financed town schools opened to girls; the result increased female literacy in a proportion previously only seen for males (p. 15).

It was not until 1870 that seven public Midwestern universities became coeducational institutions (Clifford, 1983, p. 25). Though it was the second oldest state university, the University of Georgia was the last public university to become coeducational in 1918 (p. 26). The private institutions of higher education were originally closed to women. Opened in 1755, the University of Pennsylvania did not admit women until after the Civil War. By 1900, women could only attend 61 percent of the 389 degree-granting universities and colleges in the U.S.A. (p. 26). Opened in the 1740s, it was not until 1969 that a Princeton University education was available to women, and even then one rationale was to "make Princeton more attractive to men" (p. 29).

According to Dzuback (2003), the men's colleges of Great Britain were emulated in the U.S.A. during the colonial period. Women of the United States had no analogous academic institutions of higher learning until the second half of the nineteenth century. Women's academic options were to find instruction from tutors or to "attend one of the academies or seminaries that offered more than a post primary curriculum" (p. 173). Before 1860, the handful of U.S. colleges that were open to women limited women "to a less rigorous, feminized curriculum or, in the case of Oberlin, [women were] asked to perform domestic chores for their male counterparts" (p. 173). Women's options for training in higher education began more seriously after 1865, including the opening of women's colleges on the east coast.

Women's access to colleges and universities continued to be constrained well into the twentieth century. Rostek (2014) reports, for example, that the 2009 Nobel Prize winner Elinor Ostrom recounts that the UCLA economics department discouraged her from seeking a Ph.D. circa 1960 (p. 22).

In 1959, the Vassar College economist Mabel Newcomer identified with concern the national waste of leaving uneducated the high school girls who were in the top ten percent of academic achievers. Newcomer asks a series of questions which document the level of entrenched sexism in social attitudes about educating women:

> [I]s it as important to our society to have highly educated women as men? And if it is important, how are we going to persuade the women and their families of that importance? Also, if it is important—important for what? Are women to be only transmitters of knowledge, as mothers and teachers? Or are exceptional women to be encouraged, as exceptional men are encouraged to make their contributions to the store of human knowledge and culture as scholars and artists? And if we are going to encourage women in creative thinking, research, and expression, are we going to encourage them to explore any field that catches their fancy, or only those which social usage has designated as of feminist concern?
>
> *Newcomer, 1959, p. 246, as quoted in Shackleford, 1995, p. 22*

Like the U.S.A., European institutions of higher education imposed constraints on women's access. Students of Radcliffe College intent on studying abroad, Emily Greene Balch and Mary Kingsbury had gender-specific barriers to overcome in order to study at the University of Berlin. Because they were women, they were required to obtain permission from the Reich

Cultus Minister, from the University Rector, and from the professors they would study under. Fulfilling these requirements, Kingsbury and Balch were "'curiosities'" at the University of Berlin in 1895–96 (Dimand, 2000a, p. 22). The experience of being barred from a German university was not unique to Balch and Kingsbury. Wobbe (2000) identifies that a closed door policy toward women of Vienna University's doctoral programs between 1910 and 1920 was the reason that the socialist, Käthe Leichter earned a doctorate at Heidelberg instead (p. 254). Becchio (2018, this volume) writes that before 1919, the "first generation" of women of the Austrian economics paradigm earned their degrees in other European countries because Austrian universities were closed to women students. Cambridge University hired women economists such as the American Marjorie Tappan Hollond as early as 1926, but it was not until 1948 that women could study economics and receive degrees from Cambridge (McWilliams Tullberg, 2004).

Beginning in the late 1800s in the U.S. and Europe, a relatively small number of women did find training open at advanced levels in political economy. Where institutions did allow women entry, segregation by sex was the norm. During a year of study at the London School of Economics in the 1920s, Berkeley economist Emily Huntington recalls that Professor Frank W. Taussig segregated women economists in the class room (Dzuback, 2006, p. 163). When the Newnham College-Cambridge "Lectures for Women" opened to five women in 1871, the classes were obviously segregated by sex. Mary Paley Marshall recollects: "We had practically the same lectures as the men, but as mixed classes were improper the lecturers had to give their lectures twice over" (Marshall, 1934, p. 14). The women's classes were chaperoned, as their instructors were men (p. 15). Mary studied political economy under Alfred Marshall. Henry Sidgwick was also one of her instructors. In 1874 Mary informally took the Moral Sciences Tripos. The Tripos were examinations intended for men, so that it "had to be very informal by agreement with the examiners" in order for a woman to take the exam (Keynes, 1944, p. 272).

In 1862, Julie-Victoire Daubié became the first French woman to take and pass a baccalaureate exam from the University of Lyons. In 1861, this exam was open only to male students. When the French Minister of Public Instruction received Daubié's application to take the exam, it was dismissed on account of her gender. The following year Daubié resubmitted her application; it was considered in response to intervention by a French empress (Ivory, 2000, pp. 125–6).

Where women did have formal entry rights into some U.S. universities, they did not always have equal access to courses. Harvard University opened its doors to women via creation of Radcliffe—a women's college—in 1879. The 1915–16 Radcliffe College section of the Harvard University Catalogue states:

> a considerable portion (during the present year 43 courses and 41 half-courses) of the advanced instruction offered by the Faculty of Arts and Sciences of the [Harvard] University which is designed primarily for Graduates is open to properly qualified students of Radcliffe College.
>
> *p. 898*

The 1920–21 Catalogue includes the identical paragraph except that in parentheses the list of openings are 36 courses and 48 half-courses (p. 594). Unstated in the Harvard Catalogues is the portion of the Harvard University graduate courses that were closed to qualified women because of their woman-ness.

Though Harvard established Radcliffe College as its annex for the education of women and Harvard professors were allowed to include Radcliffe women in their classes, a rationale for including women had nothing to do with equal access or educating those most likely to facilitate the growth of knowledge. It was that "some Harvard professors were willing to teach women in order to supplement their incomes" (Clifford, 1983, p. 31).

Mary Barnett Gilson's autobiography, *What's Past is Prologue*, describes her work experiences and research in industrial relations during the first four decades of the twentieth century. She worked 12 years managing employer–employee relations in a clothing manufactory. She studied labor relations in the Hawaiian cane sugar industry and wrote a book on British unemployment insurance. Gilson (1940) expresses with pride that her later academic insights were founded in real world employment experience. Gilson's first choice of academic study was Harvard in the 1920s. She learned that women were unable to sit in the Harvard labor seminars, the only field which made sense for her study based on her work experience (p. 215). Women were also denied the opportunity to work at the Harvard library past 6 p.m., though men could work there until 10. Gilson settled on graduate work in economics at Columbia University where she would expend less energy "kicking against medieval stone walls erected in a dead past when women were not people" (p. 216). By 1940 she had a position with the University of Chicago Economics Department.

According to Fitzpatrick (1990), from its inception the University of Chicago stood out relative to other institutions of higher learning in welcoming women into graduate study. Nearly 23 percent of 110 newly arriving graduate students to Chicago were women in 1894; in 1903 19 percent of 89 were women (p. 29). Though women entered Chicago's graduate programs in a relatively high proportion for the time period, there was a call to segregate women students. Folbre (1998) describes a resolution to segregate classes by sex in 1902 which passed the faculty senate and was approved by the board of trustees. Clifford (1983) suggests this classroom-by-classroom segregation plan was an attempt to prevent "sex repulsion" of men students in higher education as classrooms were filled more and more with women (p. 43). Implementation proved difficult and the issue "seemed to fade away" over a couple years (Folbre, 1998, p. 44).

Dzuback (2006) identifies the unwillingness of male faculty to hire female assistants as a constraint to academic development of the women. Without opportunities for academic work or mentorship, women students would be less likely to develop deep academic skills. In contrast, women faculty members of the Berkeley economics department, such as Jessica Peixotto, asked for and received administrative permission to hire women assistants for teaching support (p. 160).

Gilson documents the constraints women could face doing field research in reflections about her Hawaiian cane sugar study. To collect information field work was necessary but "sugar planters were not accustomed to women in any executive or supervisory capacity," and even lacked women clerical employees (Gilson, 1940, p. 224). Her path to field work was paved by Arthur Young who flew "in the face of custom and tradition when he recommended [Gilson] as a member of the survey staff" (p. 225). She was

> grateful to the men who have been sufficiently scornful of tradition to make gangway for a mere woman . . . it is a man's world and men govern most passages to worthwhile jobs in industry, in universities, and in politics. The attitude of men . . . has much to do with opening opportunities for women.
>
> *p. 225*

Financing a Ph.D. level education has been an issue for the overwhelming majority of graduate students across the twentieth century. Prejudicial issuance of financial support during graduate training might have been an impediment for women. Fitzpatrick reports that from 1894–99 only one of 18 University of Chicago sociology department fellowships went to a woman (1990, p. 80). There is no reported evidence from political economy, though inter-departmental cross-pollination was the norm during this time period. After earning a degree from Stanford University, Mabel Newcomer was accepted into the economics graduate program of Columbia University in 1914. She received a financial package to support her studies, but during "this time university fellowships were offered only to men" so the economics department funded Newcomer out of its departmental allocations (Shackleford, 1995, p. 5).

In the 1970s, respondents to an American Economic Association survey identified fellowships and teaching and research assistantships as important sources of financial support (Strober, 1975). Even in the 1970s, men continued to receive more assistantship aid than women. A primary policy conclusion of this study is that, for those women who dropped out of Ph.D. studies in the 1970s, "better financial aid . . . could have induced them to continue their studies" (Strober, 1975, p. 98).

During graduate training in sociology at the University of Wisconsin in the early 1900s, Theresa McMahon was surprised at receiving a fellowship. In response to her surprise she was told, "'You have been married a number of years and you haven't any children so you probably will stay in a profession and will be a credit to the University of Wisconsin'" (Howe, 1989, pp. 232–3). In her autobiography, McMahon *justifies* decisions to withhold funds and promotions from women. The justification is that women terminated their careers with marriage in order to establish homes and families, "not a very good foundation on which to claim promotions" or funding (McMahon, 1989, p. 258). Sometimes McMahon subsidized student costs of higher education out of her personal income after becoming a professor. McMahon attests that she only provided personal financial support to men students but not to qualified women students. In McMahon's opinion, "[i]t wasn't sex prejudice as much as it was the lack of stability on the part of the good [women] students" (McMahon, 1989, p. 258). In this pronouncement McMahon made no systematic survey to determine how many men dropped out of higher education before earning degrees. Women on the receiving end of logic used to justify sex discrimination sometimes also propagated that logic.

Sophonisba Breckinridge identifies sex discrimination in financial fellowship awards for women when she started her doctoral studies at the University of Chicago in 1897. Though her field was political science, Breckinridge studied under economist J. Laurence Laughlin and her dissertation topic was in monetary history. Writing to her father, Breckinridge doubted she would receive a $500 fellowship to pursue her doctoral degree because women tended to marry:

> I don't believe they will ever give one of them to a woman again, except under extraordinary circumstances, when she has done a large amount of work and is fairly well on in years. A good many of the officers of the University are down on the women fellows for marrying off so, and I don't blame them, and I feel sure that no woman in our department will get a $500 fellowship for years.
>
> *Fitzpatrick, 1990, p. 50*

It is noteworthy that Breckinridge sympathized with the university administrators and not the women students. She gives no additional insight as to what became of the married women fellows. Fitzpatrick identifies the social expectation in the early twentieth century that "a serious woman scholar would forego marriage" (p. 49), a decision Breckinridge made.

Newcomer suggests "that the acquisition of knowledge can be a road to women's own fulfillment and independence" (Newcomer, 1959, p. 247, as quoted in Shackleford, 1995, p. 22). Newcomer lays out her concern that, given the social stereotypes, women would find fewer spots in higher education:

> the overcrowding of the universities and colleges threaten increased discrimination against women students. The fact that women with professional training have not used it as regularly as men for professional ends appears to justify giving preference to men, both in admission and in conferring fellowships.
>
> *Newcomer, 1959, p. 247, as quoted in Shackleford, 1995, p. 22*

Employment discrimination

In the responses of approximately 1,050 university women to a survey, a primary finding summarized by Hutchinson (1928) is: "the discrimination that many women find in appointment, promotion, and salary as they compete with men for positions for which the Ph.D. is required" (p. 592). A federal government Biennial Survey of Education carried out during the second decade of the twentieth century estimated there were four men for every woman employed as teachers at institutions of higher learning and that the gender imbalance had been growing since the 1890s (Fitzpatrick, 1990, p. 72). A 1921 American Association of University Professors report counted only two women out of approximately 2,000 professors at 29 men's universities and colleges. The same report documented 1,600 women out of 13,000 professorial positions in 104 coeducational institutions of higher learning (p. 73). In contrast, women did find employment at 14 women's colleges: 738 of 989 faculty were women in 1921 (p. 74).

Nine women earned doctorates in political economy, political science or sociology at the University of Chicago between 1892 and 1907. Whereas two-thirds of the men with these doctorates became faculty at coeducational universities upon graduation, none of the nine women were so appointed. In a 1901 speech, University of Chicago President William Rainey Harper asked whether this was a result of increased sexual prejudice (Fitzpatrick, 1990, p. 72). In autobiographical notes, the University of Chicago Ph.D., Sophonisba Breckinridge identified this unequal post-graduate placement outcome between her and the male students of political science and economics. Five men with whom she had earned a Ph.D. received academic appointments after 1901. In contrast, Dr. Breckinridge worked as the Assistant Head of a women's residence hall immediately after earning her degree (Hammond, 2000, p. 82).

Mabel Newcomer (1959) depicts discrimination in hiring in her mid-twentieth-century review of higher education job prospects for women:

> [T]he opportunities for women scholars have been greatly restricted. While the women's colleges have taken the position that the best faculty will be one with a good representation from each sex, the men's colleges have for the most part, assumed that women would be out of place on their faculties. And while coeducational institutions have employed some women, the women are a relatively small minority except in the teachers and junior colleges. Research opportunities are also greater for men than for women.
>
> *Newcomer, 1959, pp. 191–2, as quoted in Shackleford, 1995, p. 21*

Clifford notes how difficult it was for women to market advanced degrees (p. 42). Consider an early example in the United States. Ellen Swallow Richards studied astronomy at Vassar and pursued graduate studies at M.I.T. in chemistry circa 1870. Richards "inadvertently founded the field of home economics in order to have scientific work to do" (p. 42). Some of Richards' home economics publications overlapped economics, as in a cost of living study.

The historian and economist Caroline Farrar Ware experienced hiring discrimination before 1940. She had been hired for summer employment at the University of Wyoming. When university officials learned that Ware was married, her appointment "was abruptly canceled." Ware was also informed that women "would not be considered for a post" within the University of Maryland History Department (Scott, 2006, p. 184).

Sadie Tanner Mossell Alexander was the first African American woman to earn a Ph.D. in economics. She did this in 1921 after completing her dissertation, "The Standard of Living among One Hundred Negro Migrant Families in Philadelphia," with the University of Pennsylvania. According to Malveaux (1991), employment opportunities were unavailable to Alexander in economics in the Philadelphia area because of her race, and employment at some African American colleges was unavailable because she was a woman. Her daughter Rae Alexander-Minter stated that "there was no way for her to make a living" in economics in the 1920s (Malveaux, 1991, p. 308). By 1923, Alexander exited the economics profession. She shifted into law.

Walter Beach and Theresa McMahon were two job candidates for a position with the Economics Department at the University of Washington in 1909. Theresa McMahon was not hired: the "very able man" Walter Beach received the appointment (McMahon, 1989, p. 251). McMahon summarizes her impression of this employment outcome:

> I have an idea that [University of Washington] President Kane suggested that they bring Beach in instead of bringing me in, knowing that there would be some opposition to my appointment just because I was a liberal, and secondly, or perhaps primarily, because I was a woman. Women at that time were not appointed to positions in the economics department; they still are rarely found there. Our universities are the most conservative institutions in the country when it comes to the question of recognizing women on the intellectual level with men.
>
> *McMahon, 1989, pp. 251–2*

Though the early twentieth century brought the appointment of four women economists to Berkeley (Jessica Peixotto, Lucy Stebbins, Barbara Nachtrieb Grimes Armstrong and Emily Hungtington), from the 1930s until the 1980s there were no new appointments of women faculty in the Berkeley economics department (Dzuback, 2006, p. 165). It is vaguely feasible that the lack of women appointments was because there were no qualified women applicants, but it seems reasonable to investigate whether sex discrimination in hiring played a role.

In her autobiography, economist Eleanor Lansing Dulles (1980) writes little of her graduate training experiences. She does note that at "Harvard women were treated politely and even in a friendly manner" in the 1920s. This politeness did not extend to job market support. Dulles writes:

> All the graduate economics courses were taught at the main campus by the prestigious Harvard professors, but there was no professional equality. After the men got their doctor's degrees those who had done well were offered a choice of staying at the colleges as instructors or going elsewhere with strong recommendations. For the women, the possibilities were more limited. There were no women faculty members at Radcliffe in those days, I was told.
>
> *p. 117*

Given these limits, Dulles accepted the one offer she received from her undergraduate alma mater, Bryn Mawr, and served with its economics faculty from 1928 to 1930 and 1932 to 1936.

Although women economists with Ph.D.s had substantial intellectual potential, in some cases even when they did hold formal positions of employment, they were "not getting appropriate work" (Dulles, 1980, p. 230). The Bretton Woods conference of 1944, for example, had a highly trained secretarial staff member. Her Radcliffe-Harvard economics Ph.D. earned Dulles a position with the International Secretariat. Her job each night was to prepare that day's minutes for distribution to conference participants the next morning (p. 171). Though the conference probably benefitted from a highly trained economist as the transcriptionist of its minutes, it is likely that Dulles' skill set was underutilized.

When women were in the position to make hiring decisions, some intentionally provided employment outlets for other women. Eveline Mabel Burns was trained at the London School of Economics and the first woman economist to be hired at the rank of lecturer for the Columbia University economics department in 1928. Burns worked for the U.S. National Resources Planning Board in 1939. Reviewing oral history files, Kasper (2012) finds that Burns primarily hired people of Jewish heritage and women for her Planning Board staff because, in Burns's words, "they were the people who had difficulty . . . good people, having difficulty in getting jobs" (p. 333).

Marriage and academic employment

Many women who pursued academic lives in the early twentieth century did not marry, unlike academic men. Clifford unearthed a study in 1930 of all the women who earned doctoral degrees from 1877 to 1924. The study reports that 75 percent of these women Ph.D.s were unmarried (Clifford, 1983, p. 45). Marriageable and married women faced academic job market discrimination. Many social biases limited the academic employment opportunities for these women. First, academic employers feared that young unmarried women would desert their academic posts after finding marriage partners. Second, some women in heterosexual relationships might have received pressure from their partners to give up academic positions. Third, application of anti-nepotism rules constituted a formal institutional barrier to married women's employability.

One consistently applied belief against the hiring of women was: if she is young she will marry and leave her academic post. Dean Marion Talbot of the University of Chicago was approached by President R.H. Jesse of the University of Missouri concerning hiring political economist Katharine Bement Davis for a domestic economy teaching position. Jesse wrote explicitly of his institution's objection to hiring any women, "that if they come young enough to have a future ahead of them they are liable to get married about the time comes when they begin to become really useful" (Fitzpatrick, 1990, p. 76).

Jesse's correspondence with Talbot about potential women job candidates identifies a woman's physical appearance as a screening device for employability in *academia*: "'she is I fear rather young. Further more it seems to appear between the lines that she is pretty. While men never hunt for homely women . . . it is not always an advantage to have them too handsome'" (Fitzpatrick, 1990, p. 76). At least in this case, women were screened out of academic positions if they possessed physical characteristics that men found appealing, beauty interpreted as a signal of future marriage.

Fiancés and husbands could emit pressure on women economists to forego professional opportunities. In 1927 Eleanor Lansing Dulles made plans to marry. Her fiancé urged her to leave her position at Bryn Mawr but Dulles refused. Her fiancé desired "the conventional pattern of expecting a woman to fit her career to the needs of her husband" but Dulles' drive to preserve independence prevailed. They settled into a commuting marriage with Dulles in Philadelphia and her husband in Baltimore (Dulles, 1980, p. 135).

Sarah Scovill Whittelsey completed undergraduate training at Radcliffe College in 1894 and earned a Ph.D. from Yale University in 1898 when she was 26 years old. Her dissertation focused on Massachusetts labor legislation in relationship to economic theory. She served as an instructor at Wellesley College in 1902–3. In 1905 she married a Yale chemistry professor. The marriage correlates with the end of Whittelsey's teaching in higher education. At the turn of the twentieth century, "[e]ven the women's colleges, committed to hiring women, employed a marriage bar against them. Conversely, male professors at women's institutions were expected to be married" (Hammond, 1993, p. 364). After marriage, Whittelsey engaged in independent scholarship (p. 365).

In a letter to a London School of Economics colleague in 1927, Eveline Mabel Burns documented her frustration with the cultural norm of expecting married women to be housewives:

> "I'm going to show these disgusting anti-feminists that there are some women who are keen on their career, who can permanently be interested in those branches hitherto regarded as men's, and that the old view of a woman giving up her job becaus [*sic*] she is married isnt [*sic*] necessarily a true one" (Burns to Morgenstern, November 11, 1927).
>
> *Quote in Kasper, 2012, p. 333*

In her published address to the 1933 Biennial Convention of the American Association of University Women, Dr. Sophonisba Breckinridge identifies formalized institutional constraints for women who wished to pursue both family and an academic career:

> Two great land grant colleges are denying the right of married women to continue in employment or the right of the academic woman to round out her experience by marriage. In one institution the vote on the subject was unanimous, although there was a woman on the board of trustees, and as a result of this vote a dean of women of experience, who happened to be married, was replaced by an unmarried woman. And when an appeal was made to the representative of this organization in the state, because there was no League of Women Voters or Women's Party to whom an appeal could be made, the reply was that after all, "marriage itself was for a woman an adequate career."
>
> *Breckinridge, 1933, p. 198*

In her mature years, Breckinridge understood the importance of women having the freedom to pursue both family and academic career:

> That women should be given an opportunity to equip themselves for practice in these fields and that they should later find opportunity for the practice of their professional skill without denying themselves the privileges and enriching experiences of family life seems to me of immediate and great concern."
>
> *Breckinridge, 1933, p. 195*

Anti-nepotism rules were applied to university faculty hiring processes beginning in the first half of the twentieth century with the intention of preventing political appointments based on patronage. An unintended consequence was that these rules blocked the hiring of qualified Ph.D. women who were married to doctorates employed at institutions of higher learning

(Simon et al., 1966, p. 344). The Great Depression reduced job availability, including within the economics profession. Married women economists were disproportionately displaced from the academic job market during the Depression, positions they might have filled going to men and single women. Anti-nepotism legislation at the federal, state and local levels reinforced this discriminatory hiring trend. "The federal legislation was repealed in 1937 but anti-nepotism rules lingered on in the academic world. These rules forced women" out of desired academic positions (Libby, 1990, p. 126). It was not until 1960 that the American Association of University Women studied anti-nepotism rules to understand the negative effect on women's hiring. Ultimately, the outcome of anti-nepotism studies was to dismantle this employment barrier (Simon et. al., 1966, p. 344), but over most of the decades in the twentieth century, women economists found their employment prospects formally frustrated if they were married.

Documentation exists for a number of women economists with stymied academic careers due to anti-nepotism rules in the first seven decades of the twentieth century. According to Keohane (2003), anti-nepotism at the University of Chicago was a source of employment frustration for Dorothy Wolff Douglas. Married in 1915 to Paul Douglas, the couple intended a two-academic career marriage with numerous children. Dorothy published in 1919 in the *American Economic Review* and in 1920 in the *Quarterly Journal of Economics*. In 1920, Paul received a position at Chicago but Dorothy could not work there because the university applied its anti-nepotism rule to wives. It was not until 1924 that Dorothy became employed at Smith College.

At the University of Washington in the 1930s, President Sieg attempted to impose a nepotism ban on women hires: the university was not to employ the wife if the husband was employed (McMahon, 1989). Theresa Schmid McMahon experienced a threat of job loss due to anti-nepotism. A sociologist by training, McMahon and her husband Edward held academic posts at the University of Washington in 1910. In 1916, Theresa was employed by the economics department after a joint social science department was split. Called into the university president's office, Edward learned that the state governor was pressuring the university to dismiss a family member where two were employed. Specifically, the president signaled that *Theresa's* "resignation would be welcome" though this was not to pass (Dimand, 2000b, p. 304).

Jacobsen (2000, p. 196) identifies anti-nepotism as the reason that Margaret Gordon was not employed by the University of California-Berkeley in the late 1930s due to the tenure track post that her husband Robert held. Mary Jean Bowman was a Ph.D. from Radcliffe in 1938 who taught at Iowa State College and worked for the Bureau of Labor Statistics. Bowman moved to the University of Chicago with her husband C. Arnold Anderson in 1949. Anderson's Chicago appointment in the department of education precluded Bowman's hire at Chicago as recently as 1958 because the university applied its anti-nepotism rules to qualified academic wives. It was in 1969 that Bowman finally received a joint academic appointment in the education and economics departments (Guide to the Mary Jean Bowman Papers).

Alison Comish Thorne's daughter documents nepotism as a leading reason that Alison did not hold a permanent faculty position. Alison Thorne earned her Ph.D. in 1939 from Iowa State College after completing a dissertation in consumer economics. Married in 1937 to Wynne Thorne, the couple moved to Utah around 1940 so Wynne could take a position at Utah State Agricultural College. Daughter Barrie Thorne writes, "Mother used to say that she and Dad were a 'pair-a-docs,' but it was obvious that these docs had quite different opportunities." Specifically, Alison had limited employment options in Logan, Utah because the college applied its anti-nepotism rules to the Thornes (Thorne, 1997, p. 104). Alison was not officially appointed a lecturer until 1965 (in sociology, home economics, and consumer education) (Thorne, 1995, p. 68). She attributes her appointment to the Civil Rights Act of 1964 that illegalized the application of the nepotism rules in academia (p. 70).

Unmarried academic women had caring relationships. Caring responsibilities were not for husbands and birth children, but rather for partners, parents, siblings, foster children, etc. This care-taking role extended to students by voluntary choice for some women faculty and by employment mandate for others. For example, women faculty were expected to live with female students in dormitories in the American South: "Ensuring 'ladylike' behavior and southern women students' virtue were part and parcel of the unmarried women faculty member's responsibility well into the 1940s" (Dzuback, 2003, pp. 192–3). Though northern academic institutions also initially imposed a maternal role on women faculty in their work responsibilities, by the early 1900s northern women faculty members were moving off campus and into "homosocial domestic commitments in which two women lived and cared for their household together." By the second decade of the twentieth century, relationship opportunities also slowly opened for women academics with the option of heterosexual marriage while pursuing careers (Dzuback, 2003, pp. 192–3). As the examples in this chapter suggest though, nepotism barriers continued to be problematic past mid-century.

Salary, promotion and tenure

In the responses of approximately 1,050 university women to a survey, a primary finding summarized by Hutchinson (1928) is: "the discrimination that many women find in appointment, promotion, and salary as they compete with men for positions for which the Ph.D. is required" (p. 592). What follows is the anecdotal evidence available for women economists who documented unequal treatment in salary, tenure and promotion.

Salaries were likely lower for women economists compared to men, but there are only a few anecdotal records documenting discrepancies. A news article in the *Seattle Post-Intelligencer* in 1938 concerned the nepotism rules that the University of Washington attempted to apply to reduce the number of married women working at the institution. In the article, retired, self-described liberal economist Theresa McMahon is quoted about her salary over the course of her career. She said, "I have always been discriminated against in my salary. Whether it was because I was a progressive or because both of us were working I do not know" (Howe, 1989, p. 233). Though it was generous that Theresa offered a non-sex discrimination rationale, her husband, Edward McMahon, was also a liberal and there is no record of his salary being lower. Alison Comish Thorne acknowledges two mentors while she worked on her Ph.D. at Iowa State College: Margaret G. Reid and Elizabeth Hoyt. According to Thorne, both Reid and Hoyt "knew they received less pay than men with comparable training and experience" (Thorne, 1995, p. 65). In a survey of women academicians, Hutchinson (1930) documents an anonymous woman economist who reported: "I work just as hard but get 1/2 pay."

There is some documentation of difficulties women faced in promotion and job security. Lonn (1924) provides a general overview of the situation with regard to rank. Analyzing 70 university catalogues in the 1920 to 1922 timeframe, Lonn identifies 7,499 faculty members, of whom 9 percent were women. Of the 2,138 university full professorships, 28 were women (0.37%), and the absolute "number of women increases, naturally, with the descent in rank" (p. 5). In the Hutchinson (1930) survey of women academicians, an anonymous woman economist documented that "I work just as hard but can't get a tenured position."

A Texas labor economist, Ruth Allen earned a Ph.D. from the University of Chicago in 1931. Allen had a career-long appointment at the University of Texas until her retirement in 1959. After her death in 1979, a university memorial resolution explicitly identified barriers to women's academic promotion during the time of her tenure at Texas: Allen "made her way to the professorship in times when this was close to impossible for a woman" (Bernasek and Kinnear, 2000, p. 8).

At Columbia University, E.R.A. Seligman hired Eveline Mabel Burns as a lecturer in 1928. She was promised "a regular position as soon as obstacles in the form of funding and certain objections to the hiring of a woman were overcome" (Rutherford, 2004, p. 47). The promise never materialized. Burns was still a lecturer when she was let go by Columbia in 1942 (Kasper, 2012, pp. 332–3).

The 1929 promotion of Theresa McMahon to full professor at the University of Washington was slipped through the university system via administrative finagling. The dean of her school said: "We've got to promote that woman" because she was widely respected among the student body. The University President Suzzallo decided, "wait until summer when nobody is paying attention, and we'll promote her then" (McMahon, 1989, pp. 272–3).

In a letter to a colleague, Eveline Mabel Burns provided a simple economic explanation of how marriage interfered with women economists' promotion prospects: "'it is known that even if we dont [*sic*] get the promotions we are unlikely to move because of the problem of "joint supply" . . . Take my warning, and never marry a fellow economist! It ruins your bargaining powers' (Burns to Morgenstern, February 2, 1931)" (quote in Kasper, 2012, p. 333).

Academic women's experiences with sex discrimination in the early twentieth century were highly contingent on circumstance. If colleagues or administrators held sexist views, a woman had difficult circumstances to contend with; if colleagues and administrators believed in equal regard across the sexes, fewer discriminatory experiences were likely. At the University of Washington in the early twentieth century, a president by the last name of Sieg held office. Economist Theresa McMahon

> was prejudiced against him right from the start. Why? Because he didn't have any use for women teachers. It was all right for them to teach home economics, or perhaps music, or physical education, but they had no place in the other departments. These departments were exclusively for the superior sex. All during his administration I don't think a woman ever got a promotion outside of the home economics department.
>
> *McMahon, 1989, p. 270*

After working on post-war Austrian reconstruction, in 1948 Eleanor Lansing Dulles returned to Washington D.C. to work with the State Department. She describes this job as "the worst" in her professional experience, "rooted in sex discrimination" (Dulles, 1980, p. 228). Dulles was told she would not receive promotion "to second place because the chief did not want a woman for his deputy" (p. 230). Dulles summarizes the situation as "hopeless", with her State Department career void of both advancement and pay increases (p. 230).

With turn-of-twentieth-century economics training as doctoral students from the University of Chicago, Edith Abbott and Sophonisba Breckinridge later founded the social work department of the University of Chicago. By 1925, the lack of promotion of these two women to full professor gave partial impetus for formal intervention by Dean Marion Talbot. The University of Chicago was charged "with violating the terms of its charter by failing to provide women with equal 'opportunities'." Fitzpatrick writes of this charge that it was both "accurate and embarrassing" and the board of trustees duly promoted the women (1990, p. 214). Furthermore, Hazel Kyrk used this University of Chicago sensitivity to the issue of gender imbalances as a bargaining chip. Kyrk negotiated a dual appointment in the departments of household administration and economics. She received her post in household administration in 1925 but it took until 1930 for the economics department to honor its commitment (Folbre, 1998, pp. 47–8).

Student sexism toward women professors

Women who served as professors faced additional discriminatory pressure from sexist male students. Annie Marion MacLean (1932) reflects on a sociology course she taught over a 20-year period. She wrote of a German student who lived in Berlin. The German signed up to take her University of Chicago Introduction to Sociology correspondence course in the early twentieth century. The student dropped the course, informing MacLean that "it is not to be supposed . . . that a female can teach me" (p. 465).[3]

After earning her Ph.D. at the University of Chicago with an award-winning thesis, Hazel Kyrk taught at Oberlin College in the 1920s. A dean writing about Kyrk's departure identifies the unwillingness of male students to accept a woman professor as a primary reason for Kyrk's departure. The dean writes that Kyrk was well trained, had an "'agreeable personality'," and was "'of rather unusual natural ability'." Kyrk's teaching is described as clear-headed and applying reasonable standards. But the dean identifies that "'any woman would have enormous difficulty trying to teach subjects as banking and transportation to classes composed almost entirely of men'" [emphasis in the original]. The dean speculates that, "'a man doing exactly the work that Miss Kyrk did and in the same way would have seemed satisfactory in every way'" (Beller and Kiss, 2008, p. 5).

Inaccessible facilities and materials

Segregated facilities undermined the work activities of women economists. Women economists experienced ostracism from receptions, office space, libraries, dining areas, conferences and living quarters. When women could not utilize shared spaces of interaction, they had "little or no chance for the kind of enrichment which comes from unself-conscious and informal contacts with members of their profession" (Gilson, 1940, p. 214). And in one documented instance, a male colleague withheld information that was necessary for a woman economist's work to advance.

Since its inception in 1885, the American Economic Association (AEA) has had women economists as members. Women participated in the annual meetings, including the first one in Philadelphia. But social norms in Philadelphia led to the women participants' exclusion from the first annual meeting reception. The Philadelphia reception was open only to the male members of the AEA. An alternative reception was set up at the last minute for the 15–20 women participants. The women boycotted their segregated reception (Hammond, 1993, 366–7).

Physical segregation by sex of office space occurred in at least one instance. Alison Comish Thorne was the first woman Ph.D. student completing her degree in economics at Iowa State College in 1937 with 14 men degree candidates. Thorne's mentors, Margaret Reid and Elizabeth Hoyt, worked as economists in the economics and sociology department which was chaired by Theodore W. Schultz (Thorne, 1995, p. 60). Hoyt and Reid had offices in Margaret Hall, a building that housed the home economics department. "The remainder of the economics faculty, all male, were in Ag Annex some distance away" (p. 62). Thorne elaborates: "Matters of power were rarely discussed, yet we women sometimes sensed discrimination" (p. 65). She describes the Ag Annex as "overcrowded" and that she did not know if Reid and Hoyt regretted having offices segregated from the male faculty.

The industrial management specialist, Mary Barnett Gilson sensitizes readers of her autobiography to the career effects of seemingly small resource control factors (1940, p. 214). That Harvard University did not permit women in its library after 6 p.m., though men could use the facilities until 10 p.m. in the mid-1920s was one reason that Mary Barnett Gilson decided to study economics at Columbia University instead (p. 216). Gilson describes that women academicians were "on the periphery" in faculty dining facilities in the early twentieth century.

Women faculty members' exclusion from the faculty club also occurred at Berkeley in the early 1900s. The women were relegated "to a corner of one room," restricted "to visits only on special occasions," and admitted "only if they were accompanied by a male member of the club." Perhaps unique to Berkeley, the woman economist Jessica Peixotto helped raise financing to construct a women's faculty club after 1919. This club became an important networking site for women academicians (Dzuback, 2006, p. 162).

Harriet Elliott was the consumer representative to the federal U.S. National Defense Advisory Commission in 1940. Economist and historian Caroline Ware was appointed as Elliott's deputy. The women found

> that the other members of the commission took a dim view of the whole idea of including consumers in the focus of their work as well as a dim view of women commissioners. They made their feelings clear in unkind comments and in such actions as forbidding the women to use the Executive Dining Room, to which the men went for lunch, and failing to include Elliott in policy discussions.
>
> *Scott, 2006, pp. 10–11*

Ware was told by the man who set up the commission: "if you think your [female] commissioner is going to get the same treatment as the head of General Motors [. . .] you have another guess coming" (p. 11).

Eleanor Lansing Dulles, economics Ph.D. from Radcliffe, worked for a stint with the U.S. Social Security Board. After World War II, Dulles was appointed to Austria to support reconstruction. She was assigned official rank of lieutenant colonel and served as a financial attaché; her rank and position was higher than that of 20 women secretaries but she "received from the men the treatment accorded a woman secretary" (Dulles, 1980, p. 190). Dulles attempted to reside in villas where the men were located but was told "This is a boys' club . . . You must stay in town with the women secretaries. We don't want you here" (p. 190). She does not state how much this hampered her work supporting economic reconstruction of Austria. Nonetheless, Dulles managed to make significant contributions. According to her account, Dulles worked to learn about the economic constraints impeding Austrian rebuilding and negotiated with various parties to obtain resources for industry: cotton for idle textile mills, artificial rubber for Austrian tire production, coal for steel mills. Working with others, Dulles wrote a report on the Soviet destruction of their occupation zone in Austria and hypothesized the effects on the rest of the country (p. 209).

Dulles moved from Austria to the State Department in Washington D.C. Her State Department male assistant told her "*he* had been told by the division chief that because [Dulles] was a woman, [the assistant] would not have to take [Dulles] seriously" (Dulles, 1980, p. 229). According to Dulles, one of his regular habits was to hide informative cables from her.

Dulles left and then returned to the State Department in 1952 where sex discrimination continued to be a part of her work experience. She describes as "killing with kindness" that she was barred from night work at the State Department because a "woman should not work eighteen hours a day" although foreign service officers often did (Dulles, 1980, p. 237). She was excluded from participation at international conferences even though she had years of foreign service experience (p. 237). Dulles reports providing substantial contributions to the State Department even with the discriminatory barriers. Her position in 1952 was to run the "Berlin Desk" where she "was charged with the reconstruction of Berlin and concerned with policy toward the city" (p. 241). Her official title was "Special Assistant to the Director, Office of German Affairs, responsible for Berlin matters" (p. 277). As in Austria, she was to funnel resources into the Cold War-torn city and to rehabilitate it. In West Berlin this work included constructing a conference hall and a hospital. Though she made contributions, she continued to face barriers to full participation in Berlin policy. In 1959 she was barred from participating both in preparatory meetings in Washington D.C. and the main conference on Berlin in Geneva. She knew she would not be able to participate as "[n]o woman had participated in any international Berlin conference" (p. 276).

There is one documented experience of a woman's unanticipated inclusion in men's space. Katharine Bement Davis earned her political economy Ph.D. in 1900 at the University of Chicago. En route to that accomplishment, she writes of unjustified ambivalence about using a seminar room that the male students used:

> The men fellows used for working purposes a seminar room opening off the small library of the department. I had rather understood that they had not favored the innovation of a woman in the department, so I naturally hesitated about joining them there. But one day one of the young men, I think it was Herbert Davenport, now professor of economics at Cornell University came out to me and suggested that I bring my work in and join the other Fellows. I did. And from then on I had a beautiful time.
>
> *Fitzpatrick, 1990, p. 75*

In the example of Davis it seems her acquiescence to perceived exclusion based on sex was the driving factor in her initial isolation from inter-collegial interactions.

Women's contributions to experiences of discrimination

As the Davis seminar room example suggests, women economists sometimes subconsciously colluded in their own oppression. Repeated recipients of messages of inferiority, it is not unusual that some of these messages become internalized. Once oppressive beliefs become internalized, women economists might have contributed to the discriminatory forces that undermined their full participation. There are many ways that the discriminated can participate in their own oppression. In the examples below, this participation manifested in expectations of relatively poor performance, behaving tentatively in interactions with colleagues, submitting to prejudicial views, and perpetuating discriminatory beliefs.

Caroline Ware reminisces in a letter to a friend about Ware's year at Oxford circa 1921: "The thing that used to dishearten me was the women's own expectation of inferiority which made them surprised when they achieved better academic records than the men (which they usually did, being a more rigorously selected group etc.)" (Scott, 2006, p. 70). Eleanor Lansing Dulles explicitly identifies that if women were uncertain or hesitant in workplace activities, they could reinforce sex discrimination (Dulles, 1980, p. 240). Katharine Bement Davis specifically wrote that it was her hesitancy that undermined her ability to profit from collegial interactions with men students in a seminar room.

John Maynard Keynes identifies that Mary Paley Marshall respected and accepted men's "strict principles": although she was one of the first women to receive college level training in economics in Great Britain, there is no public record of her admonishing husband Alfred's belief in the intellectual inferiority of women. Keynes also describes that Mary never asked for or expected "anything for herself. It was always in the forefront of her thought that she must not be a trouble to anyone" (Keynes, 1944, p. 276). Though Mary Paley Marshall was co-author of a book in economics with her husband, Alfred Marshall, and an economics lecturer:

> she never, to the best of my [Keynes's] recollection, discoursed on an economic topic with a visitor, or even took part in the everlasting economic talks of Balliol Croft. For the serious discussion she would leave the dining-room to the men . . . and the most ignorant Miss could not have pretended less than she to academic attainment.
>
> *Keynes, 1944, p. 277*

In two documented cases, women on the receiving end of logic used to justify sex discrimination propagated that logic. Both Sophonisba Breckinridge of the University of Chicago (in her younger years) and Theresa McMahon of the University of Washington colluded in the predominant opinion that withholding funding for women graduate students was justified because of the belief that any woman receiving funding would ultimately withdraw from studies to marry. In contrast, the African American woman economist Phyllis Ann Wallace met discriminatory obstacles with an attitude of: "You do your work and that's it" (Malveaux, 1997, p. 133).

Conclusion

People involved in the construction of economic thought absorbed and reinforced societal norms of sex discrimination in the nineteenth and twentieth centuries. Women economists were indoctrinated into beliefs about their alleged inferiority, had less access to resources and fewer opportunities than their male counterparts. This chapter highlights the documentation of discriminatory treatment toward women contributing to economic thought. The evidence on these pages is mostly uncluttered with analysis, intentionally so—to allow the accumulation of anecdotes to speak directly to the reader. Given that cultural norms reinforced non-communication of such experiences, the information available for any given case is anecdotal and incomplete; and documented sources likely exclude offenses that society shuttered, those glares too harsh to bear.

To date, there is only one formal case of academic discrimination in early twentieth-century economics—that of Edith Abbott and Sophonisba Breckinridge at the University of Chicago. Incomplete information of the other specific claims about discrimination leave each case open to questions of validity, thus these are "anecdotes." Did the discrimination exist and impede a woman's abilities? Or was the woman alleging discrimination hiding inadequate ability? No single example suggesting sex discrimination is itself immune from such questions as the latter. But by drawing upon so many distinct examples of discrimination from a variety of sources, it is obvious that in the aggregate, women attempting to do economics faced exclusion and ostracism because of their sex.

Beyond questioning factuality, the term "anecdote" evokes humorous intent in conveying an incident. How often do we people—women and men—wink or nod, shrug shoulders, raise hands palm-side up, feigning sarcastic resignation to yet another case in the historically persistent deluge of belittling treatment afforded womanhood? The reality is that discrimination and ostracism wound. Sarcastic receipt is social wrapping over each welt that emerges in heart-consciousness. And the examples presented here are the easier ones, the ones that were more socially acceptable to document.

It is doubtful that there is much more detail on the cases of sex discrimination present in this chapter. Preserved papers collections of women economists in many academic archives and other institutional records likely hold additional fragmentary accounts. Whether women contributing to economic thought through the twentieth century faced even more severe forms of sexual harassment or outright abuse than what is in these anecdotes is a relevant question worthy of deeper inquiry. Surveys and interviews of middle- and end-career women economists might yield insight into the mid- and late twentieth century.

Women economists' responses range over a wide spectrum: succumbing to discrimination, drawing upon resources to manage in spite of it, excelling because of it. The ability to carry on and contribute to the production of economic knowledge seems stronger for some than others while discrimination and harassment take a toll. Better understanding of the mechanisms that both undermine and support women economists' abilities to transcend discrimination is warranted in future research.[4]

Discrimination is typically considered problematic because it reduces human capability. But discrimination in academia has another important negative implication: it affects the growth of knowledge. Effective discrimination suppresses voice, narrowing academic scope, perspective, insight. But academic discrimination of women was only partially effective. Some women did carry on and contribute to economic thought. How do exclusionary and harassing experiences shape world views, assumptions, methodological preferences, mental compartmentalization of evidence, theoretical ideation, etc.? The effect of sexual harassment on the construction of economic knowledge by the harassed is an important area for future exploration.

Notes

1 Thanks to Zach Cober for research support on women in the sciences.
2 Personal communication with Joseph Persky, April 2016.
3 This anecdote was initially identified in Bumb (n.d.).
4 Women also received support from men in the pursuit of economic knowledge. Research documenting support and inclusion would provide a fuller picture of the experiences of early women economists because of their sex.

References

Becchio, Giandomenica. 2018. "Austrian School Women Economists." In Kirsten Madden and Robert W. Dimand, eds., *The Routledge Handbook of the History of Women's Economic Thought*. London: Routledge, 309–24.

Beller, Andrea H. and D. Elizabeth Kiss. June 2008 Working Paper Revision of 1999 draft. "On the Contribution of Hazel Kyrk to Family Economics."

Bernasek, Alexandra and Douglas Kinnear. 2000. "Ruth Alice Allen (1889–1979)." In Robert W. Dimand, Mary Ann Dimand and Evelyn L. Forget, eds., *A Biographical Dictionary of Women Economists*. Cheltenham, UK: Edward Elgar, pp. 8–11.

Breckinridge, Sophonisba. 1933. "University Women in the New Order." *Journal of the American Association of University Women*, XXVI (4): 195–9.

Broder, Ivy. 2010. "Women's Leadership in Economics." In Karen O'Connor, ed., *Gender and Women's Leadership: A Reference Handbook*. Thousand Oaks, CA; London; New Delhi; Singapore: Sage Publications, Chapter 69.

Bumb, Jenn. n.d. "Annie Marion MacLean." Available at: http://faculty.webster.edu/woolflm/anniemaclean.html (accessed 9/15/2015).

Clifford, Geraldine Jonçich. 1983. "Shaking Dangerous Questions from the Crease: Gender and American Higher Education." *Feminist Issues*, 3 (Fall): 3–62.

Dimand, Robert W. 2000a. "Emily Greene Balch (1867–1961)." In Robert W. Dimand, Mary Ann Dimand and Evelyn L. Forget, eds., *A Biographical Dictionary of Women Economists*. Cheltenham, UK: Edward Elgar, pp. 21–5.

Dimand, Robert W. 2000b. "Theresa Schmid McMahon (1878–1961)." in Robert W. Dimand, Mary Ann Dimand and Evelyn L. Forget, eds., *A Biographical Dictionary of Women Economists*. Cheltenham, UK: Edward Elgar, pp. 304–6.

Douglas, Dorothy W. 1919. "American Minimum Wage Laws at Work." *American Economic Review* 9 (4): 701–38.
Douglas, Dorothy W. 1920. "The Cost of Living for Working Women: A Criticism of Current Theories." *The Quarterly Journal of Economics* 34 (2): 225–59.
Dulles, Eleanor Lansing. 1980. *Chances of a Lifetime*. Toronto, Canada: Prentice Hall.
Dzuback, Mary Ann. 2003. "Gender and the Politics of Knowledge." *History of Education Quarterly* 43 (Summer): 171–95.
Dzuback, Mary Ann. 2006. "Berkeley Women Economists, Public Policy, and Civic Sensibility." In Donald Warren and John J. Patrick, eds., *Civic and Moral Learning in America*. New York: Palgrave Macmillan, pp. 153–72.
Fitzpatrick, Ellen. 1990. *Endless Crusade: Women Social Scientists and Progressive Reform*. New York: Oxford University Press.
Folbre, Nancy. 1998. "The 'Sphere of Women' in Early Twentieth-Century Economics." In Helene Silverberg, ed., *Gender and American Social Science: The Formative Years*. Princeton, NJ: Princeton University Press, pp. 35–60.
Gilson, Mary Barnett. 1940. *What's Past is Prologue*. New York: Harper & Brothers.
Guide to the Mary Jean Bowman Papers 1916–1998. Available at: www.lib.uchicago.edu/e/scrc/finding aids/view.php?eadid=ICU.SPCL.BOWMANMJ (accessed 7/14/2015).
Hammond, Claire Holton. 1993. "American Women and the Professionalization of Economics." *Review of Social Economy*, 51 (3): 347–70.
Hammond, Claire Holton. 2000. "Sophonisba Breckinridge (1866–1948)." In Robert W. Dimand, Mary Ann Dimand and Evelyn L. Forget, eds., *A Biographical Dictionary of Women Economists*. Cheltenham, UK: Edward Elgar, pp. 81–9.
Harvard University Catalogue 1915–1916. 1916. Cambridge, MA: Harvard University. Available at: https://babel.hathitrust.org/cgi/pt?id=mdp.39015065458658;view=1up;seq=936 (accessed 4/21/2016).
Harvard University Catalogue 1920–21. 1920. Cambridge, MA: Harvard University. Available at: https://babel.hathitrust.org/cgi/pt?id=mdp.39015065447776;view=1up;seq=3 (accessed 4/21/2016).
Howe, Florence. 1989. "Practical in her Theories: Theresa McMahon, 1878–1961." In Geraldine Jonçich Clifford, ed., *Lone Voyagers: Academic Women in Coeducational Universities 1870–1937*. New York: The Feminist Press at the City University of New York, pp. 223–38.
Hutchinson, Emilie J. 1928. "Women and the Ph.D." *Bulletin of the American Association of University Professors*, 14 (8) (December): 587–92.
Hutchinson, Emilie Josephine. 1930. *Women and the Ph.D.: Facts from the Experiences of 1,025 Women Who Have Taken the Degree of Doctor of Philosophy since 1877*. Institute of Women's Professional Relations Bulletin, no. 2. Greensboro, NC: North Carolina College for Women.
Ivory, Christine. 2000. "Julie-Victoire Daubié (1824–74)." In Robert W. Dimand, Mary Ann Dimand and Evelyn L. Forget, eds., *A Biographical Dictionary of Women Economists*. Cheltenham, UK: Edward Elgar, pp. 125–9.
Jacobsen, Joyce P. 2000. "Margaret Gordon (1910–94)." In Robert W. Dimand, Mary Ann Dimand and Evelyn L. Forget, eds., *A Biographical Dictionary of Women Economists*. Cheltenham, UK: Edward Elgar, pp. 196–200.
Kasper, Sherry Davis. 2012. "Eveline Mabel Burns: The Neglected Contributions of a Social Security Pioneer." *Journal of the History of Economic Thought*, 34 (3): 321–37.
Keohane, John. "Biography of Paul H. Douglas." Available at: www.bowdoin.edu/economics/curriculum-requirements/douglas-biography.shtml (accessed 7/21/2015).
Keynes, John Maynard. 1944. "Obituary, Mary Paley Marshall (1850–1944)." *The Economic Journal*, 54 (214): 268–84.
Kohlstedt, Sally Gregory. 2004. "Sustaining Gains: Reflections on Women in Science and Technology in 20th-Century United States." *NWSA Journal*, 16 (1): 1–26. Accessed February 2017 from www.jstor.org/stable/4317032.
Libby, Barbara S. 1990. "Women in the Economics Profession, 1900–1940: Factors in their Declining Visibility." *Essays in Economic and Business History*, Volume VIII. Ed Perkins, ed. South Carolina: University of South Carolina History Department.
Lobdell, Richard A. 2000. "Jessica Blanche Peixotto (1864–1941)." In Robert W. Dimand, Mary Ann Dimand and Evelyn L. Forget, eds., *A Biographical Dictionary of Women Economists*. Cheltenham, UK: Edward Elgar, pp. 328–30.
Lonn, Ella. 1924. "Academic Status of Women on University Faculties." *Journal of the American Association of University Women*, 17 (January): 5–11.

MacKenzie, Norman and Jeanne MacKenzie. 1977. *The Fabians*. New York: Simon and Schuster.
MacLean, Annie Marion. 1932. "Twenty Years of Sociology by Correspondence." *American Journal of Sociology*, 28 (4): 461–72.
Madden, Kirsten K., Janet A. Seiz and Michele Pujol. 2004. *A Bibliography of Female Economic Thought to 1940*. London: Routledge.
Malveaux, Julianne. 1991. "Missed Opportunity: Sadie Tanner Mossell Alexander and the Economics Profession." *American Economic Review Papers and Proceedings*, 81 (2): 307–10.
Malveaux, Julianne. 1997. "Tilting Against the Wind: Reflections on the Life and Work of Dr. Phyllis Ann Wallace." In D. Boston, ed., *A Different Vision: African American Economic Thought*, Volume 1. London and New York: Routledge.
Marshall, Alfred and Mary Paley Marshall. 1879. *The Economics of Industry*. London: Macmillan.
Marshall, Mary Paley. 1934. *What I Remember*. Cambridge: Cambridge University Press.
McMahon, Theresa Schmid, 1989. "My Story." In Geraldine Jonçich Clifford, ed., *Lone Voyagers: Academic Women in Coeducational Universities 1870–1937*. New York: The Feminist Press at the City University of New York, pp. 238–80.
McWilliams Tullberg, Rita. 1995. "Mary Paley Marshall, 1850–1944." In Mary Ann Dimand, Robert W. Dimand and Evelyn L. Forget, eds., *Women of Value: Feminist Essays on the History of Women in Economics*. Aldershot, UK: Edward Elgar, pp. 150–93.
McWilliams Tullberg, Rita. 2004. "Hollond [*née* Tappan], Marjorie (1895–1977), Economist and Academic Administrator." Available at: www.oxforddnb.com/ (accessed 9/22/2015).
Newcomer, Mabel. 1959. *A Century of Higher Education for American Women*. New York: Harper and Company.
Rostek, Joanna. 2014. "Female Authority and Political Economy: Jane Marcet's and Harriet Martineau's Contradictory Strategy in Disseminating Economic Knowledge." In Silvia Mergenthal and Reingard M. Nischik, eds., *Proceedings of the Conference of the German Association of University Teachers of English*, Volume XXXV. Trier: WVT Wissenschaftlicher Verlag Trier, pp. 21–34.
Rutherford, Malcolm. 2004. "Institutional Economics at Columbia University." *History of Political Economy*, 36 (Spring): 31–78.
Ryan, Christopher K. and Ramakrishna Vaitheswaran. 2000. "Barbara Ward (1914–81)." In Robert W. Dimand, Mary Ann Dimand and Evelyn L. Forget, eds., *A Biographical Dictionary of Women Economists*. Cheltenham, UK: Edward Elgar, pp. 445–59.
Scott, Anne Firor, ed. 2006. *Pauli Murray and Caroline Ware: Forty Years of Letters in Black and White*. Chapel Hill, NC: The University of North Carolina Press.
Shackleford, Jean. 1995. "Mabel Newcomer and the Economics Profession: 1917–1957." Unpublished working paper.
Simon, Rita James, Shirley Merritt Clark and Larry L. Tifft. 1966. "Of Nepotism, Marriage, and the Pursuit of an Academic Career." *Sociology of Education*, 39 (4): 344–58.
Strober, Myra H. 1975. "Women Economists: Career Aspirations, Education, and Training." *American Economic Review* 65 (2): 92–9.
Thorne, Alison Comish. 1995. "Women Mentoring Women in Economics in the 1930s." In Mary Ann Dimand, Robert W. Dimand, and Evelyn L. Forget, eds., *Women of Value: Feminist Essays on the History of Women in Economics*. Aldershot, UK: Edward Elgar, pp. 60–70.
Thorne, Barrie. 1997. *Feminist Sociology: Life Histories of a Movement*. Barbara Laslett and Barrie Thorne, eds. Rutgers, NJ: Rutgers University Press.
Wobbe, Theresa. 2000. "Käthe Leichter. 1895–1942." In Robert W. Dimand, Mary Ann Dimand and Evelyn L. Forget, eds., *A Biographical Dictionary of Women Economists*. Cheltenham, UK: Edward Elgar, pp. 254–6.

10

THE POINT IS TO *CHANGE* IT

Three lives of applied Marxism

Zoe Sherman

> The philosophers have only *interpreted* the world, in various ways; the point is to *change* it.
>
> *Karl Marx,* Theses on Feuerbach

Introduction

Eleanor Marx, Rosa Luxemburg, and Raya Dunayevskaya all spent their lives immersed in Marxist theory and political action. They all found the worlds they were born into worthy of their efforts but wanting. Marxism was for all of them a theory of the process of change and therefore a practical tool for participating in the practice of making change. This chapter highlights areas of their practice that clearly expressed the theoretical understanding they derived from Marx—and their practice and experience, in turn, shaped their choice and interpretation of theory.

Eleanor Marx, youngest daughter of the famous Karl and his wife Jenny, was born in England in 1855. She was most politically active in England from the 1880s until her death in 1898 (Kapp 1976; Holmes 2014). Rosa Luxemburg was born into a Jewish family in Russian-occupied Poland in 1871 and was most active in Germany and Poland from the mid-1890s until she was assassinated in 1919 (Nettl 1969; Ettinger 1986). Raya Dunayevskaya was born in Ukraine in 1910—she then immigrated to the U.S. with her family as a child. Her long career, mostly centered in the U.S., spanned the middle of the twentieth century, from the mid-1930s to her death in 1987 (Howard and King 2000). Despite important differences in these contexts, the three all lived in times and places where capitalist development was yielding remarkable technological advances and increases in the production of goods. But they could not see this development as a pure triumph of human progress. They were keenly aware of the unequal distribution of productive work and the unequal distribution of economic rewards. They viewed the dire poverty that persisted in their home countries and the subjugation of far-off populations by their home countries' colonial occupations as core features of capitalism. They agreed with K. Marx's assessment that capitalism is inherently exploitative and alienating: workers' labor produces value that is appropriated by capitalists. With this exploitative relationship at the core of economic production, all human relations are damaged.

They devoted themselves, therefore, to the struggle to remake the economy, and the whole social world, in line with participatory democracy and non-exploitative values. To those fearful that the socialist criticism of private property meant socialists wanted to strip everyone of their personal belongings, Eleanor Marx explained that the goal was quite the contrary: those who now have nothing would, far from being denied belongings, for the first time be able to say "my coat," "my watch." But, she continued, no one would be able to say "*my* factory" or "*my* land" and certainly no one would be able to say about another person's body "*my* hands" (Kapp 1976, p. 138). The vision of how to practice democratic, non-exploitative values evolved. The public ownership of factories and land that E. Marx favored in the 1880s, for example, was not convincing to Dunayevskaya in 1940. Rather than abolishing the capitalist–worker divide, Dunayevskaya argued, the state takeover of factories in Soviet Russia incorporated the role of a capitalist into the activities of the state (Howard and King 2000, p. 150). However, the most important principle in E. Marx's late-nineteenth-century critique, that no one should be able to say "my hands" when referring to another person, remained intact in Dunayevskaya's mid-twentieth-century critique. Indeed, several common threads bind together the work of all three.

An important theme that weaves through the work of all three is the complex entanglement of revolutionary consciousness, human agency, and institutional structures. Early in their own intellectual development K. Marx and his collaborator Friedrich Engels traced out the strands of this entanglement. Humans, K. Marx and Engels noted, are a social species—we can only be fully human in community with others. But while we cannot be fully human in isolation, the social structures of the communities in which we are human together may also damage and diminish us (Marx and Engels 1970, p. 83). K. Marx and Engels charged that this was so of the structure of society in their time and place; E. Marx, Luxemburg, and Dunayevskaya all considered it still true in their times and places. A person struggling to endure this unsatisfactory state of society may develop a revolutionary consciousness, a vision that things could be different. The vision alone cannot change the world if the material basis of society remains unchanged. That is, if the existing institutional structures, within which workers' labor produces value and owners of capital appropriate it, remain in place, we cannot philosophize our way to a more just world. However, revolutionary consciousness can inspire and inform the exercise of agency; thought, therefore, is part of the revolutionary process that can change a society's institutions (Marx and Engels 1970, pp. 93–94). E. Marx, Luxemburg, and Dunayevskaya all embraced this conclusion. They worked ceaselessly to communicate their critique of existing institutions. They worked, too, to reach and apply an understanding of how individual agency could gather into collective action by building smaller-scale institutions (e.g. unions, political parties, activist organizations) within the overarching large-scale institutions of society. And they worked to steer the collective action of the smaller-scale institutions they joined or founded toward the goal of changing the large-scale institutions of society for the better.

Another theme these three share is what we would now call intersectionality; E. Marx, Luxemburg, and Dunayevskaya all were deeply enmeshed in navigating and reshaping the interrelations of class identity, gender identity, and national, ethnic, or racial identities. Marxism's emphasis on class was, for them, no hindrance to their use of Marx's theory of revolution for working simultaneously toward a revolution of gender relations and international cooperation.

Revolutionary consciousness, human agency, and institutional structure

In *The German Ideology*, Marx and Engels assert that the lived experiences of the proletariat under capitalism can foster the emergence of a new consciousness. Spending the workday under the autocratic rule of an employer and producing the wealth enjoyed by others while living in poverty cannot be endured forever. Workers sharing this experience with their peers may form "a consciousness of the necessity of a fundamental revolution." This consciousness is made concrete in acts of revolution. Participating in revolutionary acts, in turn, further develops consciousness (Marx and Engels 1970, pp. 93–94). Marx and Engels' story is braided together from three major strands: institutional structure of the economy (the capitalists have power over the lives of workers), the workers' potential to develop a revolutionary consciousness (they can come to recognize that capitalists wield power over them and object), and their agency (they resist the capitalists' exercises of power and try to increase their own power). Someone intent on influencing the course of history must work with the strands of this braid.

Consciousness

One way to enter the tangle—and one that E. Marx, Luxemburg, and Dunayevskaya all worked at—is by grabbing hold of the strand of consciousness. If the institutional structure of class oppression fosters discontent, and discontent fosters a search for answers, there is an opening for critique. All three believed that if they could find people in a persuadable moment and be persuasive in their analysis of what is wrong and what could be different, they had the potential to transform inchoate discontent into a revolutionary consciousness.

Although she had been outspoken about politics since childhood, Eleanor Marx began her teaching and public speaking career with literary topics. She had a lifelong passion for literature and theater, which she saw as venues in which social conflicts could be illuminated and examined under the spotlights and in which other lives could be imagined. Her topics and venues shifted more and more to the overtly political from the mid-1880s through the 1890s. She made most effective use of her theatrical training not playing a fictional character on stage, though she tried that, but performing a public version of herself on the dais at public rallies. Even those with whom she was frequently in conflict considered her to be an electrifying public speaker. One listener described the effect of her speech as to make ideas that were radical challenges to the existing English power structure sound utterly reasonable and very attractive—but she did not shy away from taking a combative stance. She was so much in demand in 1897 that her voice gave out and she ran a notice in the socialist paper *Justice* expressing her regret that she could accept no more outdoor speaking invitations until her voice recovered (Kapp 1976; Holmes 2014, pp. 292, 299, 410).

Luxemburg, too, was known as a riveting public speaker. She progressed much farther in her formal education than had Eleanor Marx; her in-class debates with Professor Julius Wolf while enrolled in the University of Zurich in Switzerland might have been her first experience of holding the center of attention in a room and feeling an audience respond. She had an ambition to be influential and she judged that the best position from which to wield influence would be within the German Social Democratic Party (SPD). So after completing her graduate studies in 1898 she went to Germany—she finessed immigration restrictions with a sham marriage—and offered her services. The SPD leadership promptly dispatched her to Silesia, a Polish-speaking region of Germany or a German-occupied region of Poland, depending on one's perspective. She was elated at discovering and developing her confidence as a speaker and loved the feeling of connecting with an audience. Once recalled from Silesia to Berlin, which was the center of gravity for most of her activities for the remainder of her life, Luxemburg exercised her rhetorical skills in German as well. She did so as a speaker at SPD Congresses, international meetings, and as a revered and renowned teacher at the SPD school (Nettl 1969; Ettinger 1986).

Luxemburg also left a larger (attributed) print trail than did Eleanor Marx. She contributed extensively to theoretical debates within the SPD, which were carried out in large part in the pages of a variety of party papers. She believed it mattered what those in the SPD thought and it mattered what the SPD communicated to the outside world, so Luxemburg spoke and wrote constantly in an attempt to sway the party to her way of thinking and draw the wider public to the party (Nettl 1969; Ettinger 1986).

Dunayevskaya, like Luxemburg, made her mark on debates within organized Marxism. The Russian Revolution and the formation of the U.S.S.R. were, according to their leaders' claims, putting Marxist principles into practice. Unsurprisingly, those revolutionaries never reached a full consensus on what those Marxist principles were and how best to realize them in practice. Russian debates and power struggles, therefore, mattered to Marxists around the world. Leon Trotsky had played a major role in the revolution but, when Stalin rose to power in the 1920s, Trotsky's criticism of top-down autocratic political control earned him a trip into exile in Mexico and later death by assassination. During Trotsky's exile, Dunayevskaya served for a time (1937–1939) as his personal secretary. Then, in the 1940s she became a prominent voice of dissent among Trotsky's allies. In the 1950s she broke entirely with Trotskyism and began writing extensively on the newly emerging Marxist-Humanist strand within the evolution of Marxist thought (Howard and King 2000; Fromm 1966, p. 74).

But Dunayevskaya was not only interested in debates with others who already described themselves as Marxists. She also listened to, spoke to, and wrote for activists organizing around issues of labor, racial justice, and women's liberation. She was central in the 1955 founding of the News and Letters Committees, an activist organization, and the affiliated *News and Letters*, a biweekly newspaper. *News and Letters* published articles and letters, often by manufacturing workers, intended primarily for an industrial working-class readership. She collaborated in this project with Detroit autoworker Charles Denby; both Dunayevskaya and Denby remained in leadership positions in the organization for the remaining thirty(ish) years of their lives. *News and Letters* was meant as a venue for communication among writers and readers who shared many of the concerns that motivated Dunayevskaya, even if they did not enter the conversation already sharing the theoretical language of Marxist Humanism (News and Letters Committees; Raya Dunayevskaya Collection).

E. Marx, Luxemburg, and Dunayevskaya were convinced that the world could be better than it was, but to make it better would require understanding it, and understanding is not easy. As Dunayevskaya put it, theory "is not something one 'picks up' en route to somewhere else. It requires labor, hard labor, to work out" (Dunayevskaya 2002, p. 282). They each worked to share their understanding with others through public speaking and writing for a wide public readership because the construction of a revolutionary consciousness is an experience worth sharing. When shared widely enough, this consciousness becomes not just a private experience, but a social force.

Agency

When the daily experience of class oppression that is institutionalized in the fabric of society combines with exposure to revolutionary ideas, and when that combination results in a widely shared revolutionary consciousness, that consciousness can manifest in concrete actions. The oppressed can exercise agency to resist their oppression.

The fall and winter of 1887–1888 had been especially hard times in England. A sharp economic downturn and bitter weather combined to leave a wide swath of the working class hungry and cold. Gaunt, malnourished people haunted the streets of London's working-class East

End. E. Marx wrote to a friend, "in the streets here one sees so many starving people—people with hunger in every line of their faces that one cannot but be wretched" (Kapp 1976, pp. 220–222). The plight of the dockworkers pained E. Marx as much as anything she saw. There could hardly be a more vivid illustration of Karl Marx's theory of the reserve army of labor: more men than employers would hire crowded the docks each morning and fought one other to be among the few who secured the miserably underpaid day work on offer. Wooden railings were replaced with iron to better withstand the stampede; some, especially smaller men, were injured when crushed against the fence. E. Marx marveled that they fought each other rather than uniting to fight the exploiting class and surmised that the exploiting class feared such a shift could be imminent (Kapp 1976, pp. 262–263). Indeed, the shift came.

From 1888 to 1890, in one workplace after another, conditions that workers had endured without serious protest for years came to seem unendurable, and in one workplace after another, workers took on considerable risk and hardship to fight for change. Each action produced a shift in consciousness among those who had not taken action yet—and then, in one surge after another, more did take action. In those tumultuous years, E. Marx observed how discontented resignation tipped into discontented protest and she engaged with the back-and-forth between consciousness and action. She took part in marches and demonstrations—for free speech, for eight-hour workday legislation, for striking workers—as an organizer and speaker. Although there was no fundamental revolution in the institutions that structure a capitalist economy, many of the labor actions that bubbled up from below achieved some surface-level but real material changes such as increased pay and shorter work hours (Kapp 1976; Holmes 2014).

A decade and a half later, Luxemburg watched the events unfolding in Russia. As E. Marx had seen in England in 1888–1890, but on an even larger scale, a wave of labor actions and political demonstrations built up over the better part of a decade without much central organization and crested in 1905. Russia's government at the turn of the twentieth century was more absolutist and repressive than England's (where E. Marx was most active) or Germany's (where Luxemburg was based). Russian workers did not have political rights to freedom of assembly and freedom of speech, but they assembled and spoke nonetheless. In 1905 they did not (yet) entirely overthrow the institutions of governance by monarchy and capitalist control of economic production. Nevertheless, workplace actions won reduced working hours and raised wages, and political demonstrations won increased civic freedoms (Luxemburg 2004, pp. 181–187).

Luxemburg disseminated her analysis of this eruption of action in the pamphlet *The Mass Strike, the Political Party, and the Trade Unions*, published in 1906. The pamphlet's core argument can be summarized this way: Each action alters the consciousness of revolutionary class. The altered consciousness of the revolutionary class then changes the chances of a next action taking place and shapes the form the next action will take. (So far this echoes K. Marx and Engels' essays of the 1840s.) For these reasons, Luxemburg concluded that the urgent political lesson for her time was that revolutionary change cannot be plotted in advance and does not proceed through a predictable series of phases that follow in linear order. Instead, an unpredictable, experimental series of actions, temporary partial advances, and temporary partial setbacks unfold outside of the control of any central command structure. A mass strike cannot be marked on your calendar in advance (Luxemburg 2004).

Many of Luxemburg's colleagues in the SPD believed they held the option of a mass strike in reserve, though they had never attempted to call one. This, she argued, was a grave mistake. The leadership of the party could not call a shared revolutionary consciousness into being at will and ensure that the masses were ready for an action that they had so far refrained from taking. Indeed, the facts of the case in Russia were the reverse. Russians engaged in "a multiplicity of the most varied forms of action," and these were not orchestrated in advance (Luxemburg 2004, pp. 172–173). The centrally organized demonstration strike might appear, because of the extensive coordination required, to be "the most mature form of the mass strike" but a mass strike is more likely, in fact, to be most important "in the *beginnings* of the movement." Mass strikes raise consciousness; heightened consciousness then leads to fighting strikes—Luxemburg's term for a workplace-based action with employment, wage, working conditions, or work time demands. With the slight loosening of political repression achieved in the strikes, the room to maneuver politically grew and more coordinated collective action could emerge. Political demonstration strikes and economic fighting strikes interact in "complete reciprocal action" (ibid., pp. 185–187, 193–195).

Luxemburg believed that whatever the concessions that might be won from employers, those are not the enduring achievement of an economic fighting strike. Increasing the standard of living, she wrote, is not an end goal and is not, on its own, lasting—capital will claw back what it ceded under duress. What lasts, in Luxemburg's view, is the "mental sediment." The first outbreak of action in Russia, she wrote,

> *reacted inwardly all the more powerfully as it for the first time awoke class feeling and class consciousness in millions upon millions as if by an electric shock. And this awakening of class feeling expressed itself forthwith in the circumstances that the proletarian mass, counted by millions, quite suddenly and sharply came to realize how intolerable was that social and economic existence which they had patiently endured for decades in the chains of capitalism. Thereupon there began a spontaneous general shaking of and tugging at these chains.*

Political education, she wrote, is achieved "by the fight and in the fight" (Luxemburg 2004, pp. 181–185).

Dunayevskaya not only recognized a reciprocal relationship between consciousness and agency, but she collapsed the distinction between the two. She pointed to the U.S. coal miners' general strike of 1949–1950 as a turning point in her intellectual development. She saw the coal miners' strike action as itself a form of theory; the strikers' demands—which transcended simple wage bargaining to emphasize the quality of life below and above ground—were working out a humanist philosophy. She concluded that action, what she often called "masses in motion," is a force of history, as Luxemburg had so clearly seen, *and also* a force of reason. She credited Marx with the recognition that practice was a source of philosophy and developed her analysis by tracing Marx's intellectual roots in Hegel. She put particular emphasis on Hegel's concept of negation as a positive, multi-step movement forward: first a negation of (reaction against) the conditions of the world as it is, then reaction against the first negation (Dunayevskaya 2002, pp. 275, 295–297).

Just as she had found philosophy in the coal miners' strike in 1950, over the following decades she found philosophy in the movements fighting racial exclusion and sex-based hierarchies. Race and sex, like class, are built into the structure of social institutions. She saw the movements that aimed to dismantle and replace the existing institutions of inequality as living, breathing embodiments of the second negation at the core of her philosophy. She pointed out, for example, that the Women's Movement was a reaction against the Left not from outside but from *within* the Left, pushing it farther. Leftists asked why workers produced value appropriated by capitalists (first negation). Feminists asked why male Leftists still expected women to be sexually subservient and to do all the cooking and cleaning and childcare (negation of the first negation). Dunayevskaya's developing Marxist-Humanist philosophy was rooted in the lived struggles for dignity. She wrote, "Absolute humanism is surely the articulation needed to sum up a class*less, non*-racist, *non*-sexist society, where truly new human relations self-develop" (Dunayevskaya 2002, pp. 282–283).

But even though action is a source of theory it must also, if it is to have any hope of more than momentary success, come from theory. Philosophy and social change come "not by practice alone" (Dunayevskaya 2002, p. 275). Philosophy was, for her, more than a tool for interpreting revolutionary change. Instead, philosophy was a tool for making revolutionary change—and the philosophical tools needed to make change emerged from the practice of making change. Neither is fully determined by or entirely prior to the other. She insisted that in Marx's own writing, in his adaptation of Hegel's principle of second negativity, there was a philosophy of revolution that was an indispensable tool for sought-after revolutions, not only in economic class relations but also in the racial and sexual order. Thinking out a philosophy of revolution, she wrote, is not something to be studied "in the manner in which one gets a degree"; it is "an urgent task *to do*" (Dunayevskaya 2002, p. 287).

Institutions

One way to describe the braiding together of consciousness, agency, and institutions is to begin the story with institutions—this is what K. Marx and Engels did when they wrote that the miseries and contradictions of the existing structures of society spark "a consciousness of the necessity of a fundamental revolution." If those of revolutionary consciousness exercise their agency and succeed, the story can circle back to institutions, but to institutions that have been transformed. A different type and scale of institution is also important in the middle of the story: along the way to fundamental transformation of the large-scale structures of society that we inherit from our ancestors and deed to our descendants, revolutionaries will need smaller-scale institutions of voluntary affiliation such as unions, political parties, and activist organizations to coordinate their collective actions. E. Marx, Luxemburg, and Dunayevskaya were all intellectually interested and actively involved in the question of how to build effective institutions of this second type, social change organizations. Some action for social change can bubble up, seemingly spontaneously, and an effective organization must harness the impetus for positive change through organizing, but without stifling the impulses that emerge unplanned.

During the 1880s and 1890s, Eleanor Marx took part in English socialist organizations that aimed for a class transformation at the national, perhaps international level. These social change organizations were not rooted in any particular workplace or category of worker, and even included members from relatively privileged backgrounds whose interest in socialism was more ethical than material (Kapp 1976; Holmes 2014). E. Marx, along with everyone else in these groups, continuously struggled with organizational strategy, especially the tension between the potential benefits of a big tent and the contrasting potential benefits of a tight consensus. She was a consistent free speech advocate, and if promoting openness to debate and dissent within the nation is good, surely there is some good to be derived from accommodating debate and dissent within an organization smaller than the nation, too. However, a voluntary membership organization and a nation are not the same, and the attempt to accommodate too wide a variety of opinion within an organization risks leaving the organization unable to take collective action. E. Marx did not follow a rigid, consistently applied principle regarding the right level of openness for organizations in general, but instead made a judgment specific to each organizational struggle she confronted (Kapp 1976; Holmes 2014).

She participated in splits; she was a founding member of the Socialist League, which split off from the Social Democratic Federation in 1884, arguing that the disagreements within the Social Democratic Federation were too significant and their educational mission needed a more unified body. In 1888 the Socialist League itself split apart. E. Marx was among those dissatisfied with the organization's self-imposed restriction to education and its abstinence from participation in Parliamentary government, with all the messiness and compromises that political action entails (Kapp 1976, pp. 44–72, 197–199, 248). Yet at the same time that she felt it necessary to break away from larger organizations whose positions she could not countenance, she lamented the fracturing of the movement and took part in a failed attempt to call a meeting exploring the possibility of reuniting the various socialist organizations. To no avail. English socialism remained profoundly schismatic (Kapp 1976, pp. 52–53, 248, 264–265).

England was not uniquely fractious. During his lifetime, Karl Marx and his collaborators formed the First International Workingmen's Association to promote working-class solidarity, disseminate Marxist theory, and foment social change across Europe. Contentious disputes within and among a number of countries led to the dissolution of the organization. Similar disputes nearly derailed the formation of a Second International Workingmen's Association, whose organizers intended to pick up the work begun by the first. But somehow or another, with the contribution made during the planning stages by E. Marx's cajoling and corresponding, an inaugural Congress of the Second International was organized to take place in Paris in the summer of 1889. With the continual contribution made by her translation throughout the proceedings, the Congress was held and some business successfully accomplished. The parties present agreed to return to their respective countries and organize May Day demonstrations in favor of the eight-hour workday (Kapp 1976, pp. 291–315).

Upon her return to England, E. Marx found that a wave of more spontaneous actions was already under way, having bubbled up from outside the ranks of self-identified socialists. Several groups of workers in England were a step ahead of the Second International's call for the eight-hour workday and had begun to agitate for reduced work hours without having any institutional affiliation with the Second International (Kapp 1976, pp. 291–321; Holmes 2014, pp. 317–333). However, even though the socialist organizations she already belonged to did little to start the labor revolt, E. Marx never believed that heightened class-consciousness and spontaneous action would be enough to sustain the changes the revolt achieved. Even if the revolt did not result in fundamental transformation of capitalist class relations, the concessions won from employers could be institutionalized by means of union representation and legislation establishing labor standards.

When 100,000 dockworkers went on strike and all but shut down commerce in the city of London, E. Marx helped out with behind-the-scenes clerical tasks and correspondence, in addition to taking the stage to speak at the massive public demonstrations. The dockworkers' action achieved some, though not all, the workers' demands and also resulted in the formation of a union. In her speeches to striking Telegraph and Cable Workers, E. Marx asserted that the most important achievement of the recently concluded dockworkers' strike was the union. She emphasized that an increase in wages, should workers win one, could not be a lasting victory unless the strike also resulted in organization. Strikes could disrupt the existing disproportionate power held by capitalists, but a union could provide an institutional structure for the workers' continuing exercise of power. So some of her organizational efforts shifted toward the new organizations that were arising from spontaneous revolts. When the newly formed Gasworkers Union held their first election, she became an important mentor for Will Thorne, the General Secretary, tutoring him in the literacy and record-keeping skills needed in his new position. She was also nominated for the Executive Council of the Gasworkers Union herself and was the only nominee to be unanimously elected (Kapp 1976, pp. 328–347).

At the May Day demonstration organized in fulfillment of the plans formed at the inaugural Congress of the Second International, E. Marx urged the use of state power, as well as union organization. She said to the crowd assembled in Hyde Park,

> *Those of us who have gone through all the worry of the Dock Strike, and especially the Gasworkers' Strike, and have seen the men, women and children stand round us, have had enough of strikes, and we are determined to secure an eight hours' day by legal enactment; unless we do so, it will be taken from us at the first opportunity.*
>
> *E. Marx 1890*

Small-scale victories won through action can only be maintained if they reform existing institutions of society, and victories can only be expanded upon—reform can only blossom into revolution—if there are effective social change organizations continuing the struggle.

Luxemburg confronted as E. Marx did, the challenges of building social change organizations that could take aim at society's large-scale institutions. She, too, engaged with the dynamic interplay between top-down organization and bottom-up emergent action. While E. Marx's thoughts on these matters must mostly be reconstructed from her activism, Luxemburg wrote more sustained analyses. It is Luxemburg's vocabulary of spontaneity vs. organization (or so it is rendered in English translation) that has provided an enduring mental toolkit for thinking about this question.

Early in her career Luxemburg was involved in an organizational schism. There was already an established Polish Socialist Party (PPS), but the PPS advocated Polish independence and Luxemburg was resolutely opposed to all nationalist movements. She felt unable to work for or with the PPS but for practical, tactical reasons, she needed a national party affiliation: she wanted to have standing for representation at the upcoming Congress of the Second International. Her solution was to lead the formation of a new socialist party, named Social Democracy of the Kingdom of Poland (SDKP), in 1893 (Nettl 1969, pp. 45–58).

However, despite starting (and later ending) her career with an organizational split, she spent most of her working life committed to dissent within a big tent. Her drive to be at the center of things took her to Germany and she joined the German Social Democratic Party (SPD)—Germany's SPD had a stable institutional structure and operated publicly after the 1890 repeal of Germany's anti-socialist laws. Once a member, she maintained loyalty to the party through a great many disputes and debates. She was sometimes a representative of the party, and often a voice of dissent within the party, but consistently worked within the existing party structure. During her years of active membership in the SPD, 1898–1914, the party was sufficiently democratic and well supplied with outlets for dissenting voices to accommodate—but not contain—her (Nettl 1969).

Luxemburg's appreciation for internal dissent and debate informed her critique of Lenin's push for centralization of authority over the Russian socialist movement. Luxemburg's article entitled "Organizational Questions of Russian Social Democracy," written in response to Lenin's book *One Step Forward, Two Steps Back*, was published in *Neue Zeit* in 1904. Lenin argued that in order to change the centralized institutions of economic and political power in Russia, the socialist movement must be similarly centralized. In her article, Luxemburg agreed that organization at a national scale was essential and she admitted that the extremes of authoritarianism in czarist Russia posed problems for the Russian socialist movement that differed somewhat from the problems faced by socialist movements in places with more developed bourgeois republican governments.[1] She insisted passionately, however, that Lenin's call for a Central Committee with ultimate authority, including the authority to organize fully subordinate local committees and select local leaders, was the wrong approach. Certainly, she agreed, Russian social democracy must have a nationally united organizational structure. But local party affiliates need enough autonomy from the central leadership to seize opportunities that present themselves at the smaller scale, to experiment, to cultivate creativity and self-discipline, not obedience. Building a central authority "that alone thinks, acts and decides for everyone," would mean only substituting blind obedience to a new authority for blind obedience to the old authority. It would blunt rather than develop revolutionary consciousness and the capacity for agency (Luxemburg 2004, pp. 250–254).

The doctrinal flexibility and organizational openness Luxemburg urged for Russian social democracy in the 1900s did not come to pass. At the outbreak of World War I, the SPD, too, failed her in this. The SPD had won representation in the German government and from their seats of newfound power capitulated completely to nationalism and militarism. Luxemburg felt betrayed; she broke with the party and joined with like-minded colleagues to form the German Communist Party. Once Germany conceded defeat and World War I ended, the social divisions that had been suppressed in the name of nationalism resurfaced. Luxemburg, as ever, stood on the side of the revolutionary overthrow of capitalism. The SPD, once a social change organization but now a defender of the institutional status quo, no longer stood for any such thing. They ordered her assassination. She was murdered in 1919 (Nettl 1969; Ettinger 1986).

Raya Dunayevskaya was deeply appreciative of Luxemburg's prescience (Dunayevskaya 1991[1981]). Luxemburg's warning to Lenin went unheeded and the U.S.S.R. did substitute one form of authoritarianism for another. Dunayevskaya picked up the argument two decades after Luxemburg's death: Without democratic institutions, she insisted, the U.S.S.R. could not be truly socialist, either. During the 1940s she reached the conclusion that the U.S.S.R. was best understood as State Capitalist, not Communist. State ownership might have substituted for private ownership, but exploitative relations of production remained. In her first treatment of this idea, written under her oft-used pseudonym Freddie James, she wrote, "The Soviet Government occupies in relation to the whole economic system the position which a capitalist occupies in relation to a single enterprise." The relation of government to citizen is "the real economic relation of state-capitalist-exploiter to the propertyless exploited" (quoted in Howard and King 2000, p. 150). The identity of the exploiter did not excuse the exploitative content of the relation.[2] She expanded this analysis in two articles in the *American Economic Review* in 1944 and 1945; her articles were part of a larger debate in the pages of *AER* over the relation between Soviet practice and Marxist theory. (Dunayevskaya also translated the full text of a Soviet article on the teaching of Marxist theory into English for the *AER*—the Soviet article prompted the particular round of the debate that she entered (Raya Dunayevskaya Collection; Dunayevskaya 1944, 1945).)

As she developed her analytical critique of society-wide institutional structures—of the U.S.S.R., the U.S., and elsewhere—Dunayevskaya, like E. Marx and Luxemburg, struggled with the challenges of social change organizations. Initially, her concerns about the development of the U.S.S.R. led her to her work as Trotsky's personal secretary during his exile. But in 1939, when she reached the judgment that the rot went deeper than Trotsky could admit, she left that post. (Trotsky was assassinated the next year.) In the 1950s, Dunayevskaya broke off her remaining affiliation with groups loyal to Trotsky and followed her concern with human relations into new theoretical work and new organizational affiliations (Raya Dunayevskaya Collection; Howard and King 2000, p. 150).

Dunayevskaya's admiration for Luxemburg did not lead to emulation of Luxemburg's practice of dissent from within an organization. Instead, Dunayevskaya aimed to displace philosophical disagreements onto the external relations of one social change organization with another rather than sustaining internal disagreements. She wrote, "[W]hen a principle of philosophy *and* revolution is not in the 'program,' one should never join that organization, though one could participate in individual joint action against capitalism" (Dunayevskaya 2002, p. 298). Using her organizational practice to guide the interpretation of her difficult writing suggests her meaning was this: When distinct organizations agree on a particular goal for changing some aspect of the larger institutions of society, they can coordinate on a particular action, but should not merge permanently. By spearheading the formation of the News and Letters Committee (see above) and maintaining leadership over the following decades, she was able to keep the organization's philosophical position well aligned with her own as she engaged in Civil Rights, Women's Movement, and labor activism, sometimes in conjunction with people and groups who approached the issues from a different angle (Raya Dunayevskaya Collection).

None of the three, E. Marx, Luxemburg, or Dunayevskaya, resolved the tension between spontaneity and organization. Revolution needs room for dissent and experimentation, so the larger the organization, the greater the need to allow for spontaneity within the organization and oppose excessive centralization. But when spontaneity succeeds, the gains have to be institutionalized if they are not to be lost. The organizations E. Marx helped establish to institutionalize the gains won in the hard-fought labor actions of 1888–1890 soon became a constraint on further change. Unions maintained modest concessions from employers but blocked more radically revolutionary demands, a pattern not at all unique to the London Gasworkers (Friedman 2008). Luxemburg hoped to preserve the space for spontaneity by allowing dissent within the same organizations that work to coordinate revolutionary action and institutionalize revolutionary change. She demonstrated her principled commitment to allowing dissent at a Congress of the Second International: She listened to an address in which Jean Jaurès, speaking in French, denounced her views and then, when no other translator was available, she translated his speech into equally pointed German herself (Nettl 1969, p. 125; Dunayevskaya 1991[1981]). While the German Social Democratic Party had little real power outside the administration of its own organization, it approximated Luxemburg's ideal of internal dissent. With state power to wield, however, the SPD became murderously repressive. Dunayevskaya saw that the puzzle of spontaneity vs. organization has no solution. Even the second negativity, although it moves us forward, is not the end of history. Challenging inequalities within groups dedicated to revolutionary change, as in the example of the Women's Movement challenging male Leftists, raises the question of what happens *after* the envisioned revolution. Dunayevskaya's conclusion (and her reading of Marx's phrase "revolution in permanence") was that there is no utopian end state. When past changes are institutionalized, they become new constraints. "[R]evolution must be continuous *after* the overthrow of capitalism" (Dunayevskaya 1991, pp. xxix–xxxi; 2002, p. 297).

Class and its intersections with race and gender

Dunayevskaya concluded that the overthrow of capitalism is not sufficient because, as she, Luxemburg, and E. Marx all understood, capitalist class exploitation is not the only source of human suffering, the only obstacle to human flourishing. Multiple dimensions of unequal power are interrelated. Gender, race, nationality, and class all interact in complex ways.

Eleanor Marx was particularly attuned to the injuries of sex. She saw the burdens borne by her mother Jenny Marx and by the family's lifelong servant Helen Demuth. They tied their fates to a man who was impeccably revolutionary, but that was no protection against the particular degradations endured by women *as* women in their time and place.[3] As the youngest in the family, E. Marx saw her two elder sisters fall to a similar fate: They both married French revolutionaries and then followed wherever their husbands' political activities took them, keeping house in unpredictable circumstances, bearing and too often losing children. She wanted more autonomy and more direct engagement with the public sphere than the older women in her family had (Kapp 1976; Homes 2014).

In 1886 she and her long-time *de facto* (though never *de jure*) husband Edward Aveling co-authored an essay published in the *Westminster Review* entitled "The Woman Question, From a Socialist Perspective." They later revised the essay and published it with some commercial success as a freestanding pamphlet. In this work they explore the interrelation of class and sex. They diagnose the ills of a capitalist class society that is also structured by unequal gender relations; the two are, they argue inseparable. "The woman question," they write, "is one of the organization of society as a whole." Women's exclusion from well-paid employment makes them economically dependent on men and therefore subject to any arbitrary abuses of power men may subject them to. "Women are the creatures of an organized tyranny of men, as the workers are the creatures of an organized tyranny of idlers." But men, too, stand to gain from women's emancipation. Because women and men are rigidly forced into separate economic roles, they are alienated from one another, prevented from enjoying the richer social and sexual relationships that more shared experiences would foster. "But when each sex is incomplete . . . and when, as a rule, neither of them comes into real, thorough, habitual free contact, mind to mind, with the other, the being is neither whole nor entire." Men and women both could be liberated by a feminist approach to socialism (or a socialist approach to feminism). Indeed, E. Marx and Aveling conclude that women's emancipation cannot occur without socialism, nor can socialism achieve its aims without a revolution in sex roles (Aveling and Marx 1886).

By contrast, few would be emancipated in any substantive way by the women's rights demands then being put forth by some upper-class women. The many women who were wageworkers or dependent on their working-class husbands' wages would not be relieved of their exploitation by expanding women's property rights and access to higher education; extending the privileges already enjoyed by elite men to elite women would do nothing for the non-elite majority. E. Marx was certainly not interested in supporting a cross-gender alliance of the elites to protect their class privileges, but she saw an urgent need for a cross-gender alliance of the working class to challenge the privileges of the elites. Viewing women as full and equal human beings, therefore, has profound consequences for the socialist imagination and the project of class mobilization. (Plenty of male trade unionists, alas, were not persuaded.) She must have gotten tired of having to remind socialism's moralizing critics, over and over, that socialism's call for property in common does *not* mean wives in common; women are human beings, not property (Aveling and Marx 1886; Holmes 2014, pp. 259–267; Kapp 1976, pp. 85–86, 164).

Although published as a single-authored work under Friedrich Engels' name, *The Origins of the Family, Private Property, and the State* can also be taken as an indicator of E. Marx's views. She and Engels were frequent companions during the development of Engels' essay, as was true for the many years they both lived in London, and her perspectives likely informed his writing. She, in turn, found his rendering of the ideas useful. In a letter to the editor of a periodical titled *Justice*, she drew particular attention to a quotation that she felt an earlier article had not fully appreciated: "[I]n the family the man is the bourgeois, the woman represents the proletarian" (Engels 1884; Holmes 2014, p. 258; E. Marx 1896).

Eleanor Marx was also a vocal advocate for national self-determination. As a teen she identified passionately with the cause of Irish independence and continued throughout her life to oppose English imperialism everywhere it manifested. In 1885 she participated in the Socialist League's protests against imperialist war in Sudan. The League's pamphlet countered the nationalist rhetoric designed to drum up support for the war by pointing to the class division of interests within England. The primary beneficiaries of colonialism, they charged, are the capitalists who gain access to new markets, new materials, new sources of labor. But who risks their lives?

> *Is it the market-hunting classes themselves? . . . No! But the sons and brothers of the working classes at home. . . . They it is who conquer, for the wealthy middle and upper classes, new lands for exploitation, fresh populations for pillage.*
>
> *Socialist League pamphlet, as quoted in Kapp 1976, pp. 66–67*

This position is consistent with the views E. Marx shared in letters with friends and with her consistent support for similar protests. She saw national self-determination for colonized regions of the world as a way to constrain the reach of the capitalists based in the imperialist center. As strongly as E. Marx opposed the international expansion of the reach of the ruling class, she advocated the international cooperation of the working class. She was bitterly disappointed whenever English workers opted to protect their relative privilege over workers in colonized or less developed nations rather than to challenge the ruling elites in solidarity with those other workers (Kapp 1976, pp. 291–317).

Luxemburg, more than either E. Marx or Dunayevskaya, seemed to wish that divisions along lines of gender or national identity would go away and stop bothering her. She rejected the SPD leadership's initial attempts to assign her to "the woman question," seeing that for someone like herself, with ambitions to be influential, the woman question was a dead end. Urging her to take it up was a move to marginalize her in the party (Dunayevskaya 1991, pp. 1–3). She succeeded in remaining outside the woman question pigeonhole—photographs of party conferences and Congresses of the Second International often show her as the one woman among a sea of black-suited men.

Yet despite her reluctance to speak or write at length on the woman question, Luxemburg, like E. Marx, saw socialism and women's emancipation as inseparable. She avoided being too closely identified with women's issues in order to retain influence on other questions, but was a long-time close friend and collaborator of Clara Zetkin, who was for many years at the helm of the socialist Women's Movement in Germany and beyond. Luxemburg urged the women assembled in 1907 for the first International Socialist Women's Conference to maintain an independent organizational identity, rather than to merge with and risk being silenced by male-dominated socialist organizations (Dunayevskaya 1991, p. 13). She expressed admiration for Zetkin's work organizing women as women—not just as workers—to be leaders, thinkers, revolutionaries. Luxemburg saw capitalism's disregard for the caregiving and housekeeping work most often done by women as a clear illustration of the inhumanity of capitalism as an economic system.

> From [a capitalist] point of view, the music-hall dancer whose legs sweep profit into her employer's pocket is a productive worker, whereas all the toil of the proletarian women and mothers in the four walls of their homes is considered unproductive. This sounds brutal and insane, but corresponds exactly to the brutality and insanity of our present capitalist economy.
>
> *Luxemburg 2004, p. 241*

She was uncompromisingly committed to full universal suffrage—she reacted with disgust and disdain to those who called male-only suffrage "universal." As strong as her disgust for so-called socialists who would sell out women's rights was, her disgust for the upper-class women's rights movement might have been even stronger. She called bourgeois women "parasites of the parasites of the social body" whose only function is the biological reproduction of the ruling class. Elite women could be fierce in their objections to male prerogatives, she observed, but "would trot like docile lambs in the cap of conservative and clerical reaction if they had suffrage" (Luxemburg 2004, pp. 240–241).

Luxemburg's commitment to international cooperation led her, quite out of step with most of the Left at the time, to oppose all nationalist movements. Her dissertation research on the economic development of Poland convinced her that, as onerous as the political subjugation of Poland by the Russians and Germans was, the country's economic development depended on its economic integration with these larger units. She believed that economic development would lay the groundwork for the maturation of the proletariat and thereby for future revolution. Nationalist movements would simply empower local elites and distract workers from class-consciousness with nationalist jingoism. Patriotism did not resonate with her—and because of her Jewish background other people's patriotism often did not include her in their definition of the nation—so she could not appreciate the strength of anyone else's identification with their nation rather than their class. Luxemburg's biographer Nettl observed, "[T]he only real fatherland she knew or wanted [was] the proletariat in general and German Social Democracy in particular" (Nettl 1969, p. 20).

Nationalist movements among the colonized were the dominant form of resistance to colonialism. Luxemburg simultaneously opposed these nationalist movements and articulated a bitter, thorough critique of colonialism. During a period when European powers were busily vying with each other for control of other continents, she was the first and most prominent figure to push the socialist movement to position colonialism as a core issue in the critique of capitalism. Her largest scale theoretical work, *The Accumulation of Capital (A Contribution to an Explanation of Imperialism)*, first published in 1913, argued that colonial expansion is a necessary feature of capitalism. Capital's drive to expand can never be contained within the already-capitalist regions of the world but must continuously reach into new, not-yet-capitalist regions and metabolize them.

Luxemburg did not just argue the point in the abstract. *The Accumulation of Capital* also details what colonization looks like in the colonies. She described English rule of India—"Not until 1867 was England able to appreciate the results of her noble efforts in this respect. In the terrible famine of that year a million people were killed in the Orissa district alone"—and French rule of Algeria—by the late 1860s "more than forty years of French rule culminated in wide-spread famine and a disastrous mortality rate among the Arabs" (Chapter 27). She explained the means by which China was opened up as a market for European capitalists, with the English leading the way: brutal military slaughters (Chapter 28). She illuminated the commonalities between the extension of capitalist power in North America and in South Africa: first violent depopulation and displacement of native people to make way for settlers' petty production, then the destruction of petty production to make way for large-scale capital. In the U.S., American Indians who survived the violence were "driven like cattle to the West to be folded in reservations like so many sheep," and then the European settlers, in turn, were "driven beyond the Mississippi to make way for capital." In South Africa the Boers, Dutch settlers, had by the 1860s gained control of the land and "built their peasant economy like parasites on the backs of the Negroes, compelling them to do slave-labor for them." Then English capital sought to displace Boer peasant economy. "Both competitors had precisely the same aim: to subject, expel or destroy the colored peoples, to appropriate their land and press them into service by the abolition of their social organizations" (Chapter 29). The racial difference of colonized people in Africa and Asia made the harms of imperialism too often invisible to Europeans, and Luxemburg herself sometimes wrote in the language of racial labels and stereotypes that was current in Europe, but still she insisted that her readers see that colonized people had prior complex societies and that European domination, achieved through the violent destruction of their existing social institutions, caused tremendous human suffering (Luxemburg 1951[1913]; Dunayevskaya 1991[1981]).

Dunayevskaya admired Luxemburg, but objected to the theoretical basis of *The Accumulation of Capital*. She found enduring value in Luxemburg's empirical account of imperialism as experienced by the conquered, but in her 1981 book *Rosa Luxemburg, Women's Liberation, and Marx's Philosophy of Revolution*, she charged that Luxemburg painted the colonized as passive victims. Luxemburg's theory assumed that only the capitalist proletariat could be a revolutionary class and so did not identify the colonized as a potentially resistant, revolutionary force with agency of their own (Dunayevskaya 1991[1981], pp. 36–42). Dunayevskaya's reading of K. Marx's philosophy of revolution differed from Luxemburg's. In Dunayevskaya's interpretation, the proletariat is *a* revolutionary class, but not *the only* revolutionary class. K. Marx's account of the process of change can apply to other collective oppressions, the emergence of other collective subjectivities, other impulses to set the masses into motion. There are multiple dimensions of inequality and no one dimension is prior to the rest.

Instead, resistance in multiple dimensions is necessary. We cannot solve capitalist exploitation first, and then racism next, and then sexism. (Any other ordering would be equally impossible.) Negation, in the sense Dunayevskaya adapted from Marx's Hegelianism, is most powerfully positive when it is multifaceted. Her work with the News and Letters Committee, for example, integrated concerns with racial justice and labor organizing. White-only and white-majority unions often sought to preserve their relative status at the expense of nonwhite workers, but Dunayevskaya rejected this practice. In the early 1960s as national liberation movements strengthened African resistance to the direct European colonial rule Luxemburg had critiqued, she traveled extensively in West Africa to learn about the struggles and organizing strategies of workers who could rely neither on U.S.-and-Europe-dominated international labor organizations nor on African elites to prioritize their interests (Dunayevskaya 1962). Dunayevskaya found the theoretical principle of second negativity in Marx's philosophy of revolution and she found it in the practice of the Women's Movement (see above). The theory fit the experience, so she believed the Women's Movement could learn from Marxism—indeed she was sure all liberation movements could learn from Marxist Humanism. But Marxism also had to listen to feminism. She insisted that interpreting all social life as dependent first of all on economic class was an error, despite the fact that many Marxists did so. Furthermore it was an error she did not believe K. Marx himself made (Lovato 2015).

E. Marx, Luxemburg, and Dunayevskaya all saw the need to pursue both-and, not either-or battles for emancipation. They did not, however, agree in every particular. They differed in the dimensions they chose to emphasize. Dunayevskaya criticized *The Origins of the Family* for misinterpreting K. Marx's notes on which it was based and reducing the complexity of gender to class; she criticized *The Accumulation of Capital* for its assumption that the proletariat was the only revolutionary class (Dunayevskaya 1991[1981], pp. xxi–xxii, 36–42). So she was at odds with E. Marx and Luxemburg on certain points. Nevertheless, all saw that economic exploitation is not the entirety of an exploited worker's experience, and class is not the only facet of anybody's identity.

Conclusion

Eleanor Marx, Rosa Luxemburg, and Raya Dunayevskaya were simultaneously theorists and activists, meaning they lived the entanglement of thought and action. All three were very much of their times and all three sought to be a bridge to a different time: a better future in which human flourishing takes a decisive lead over human suffering.

The emergence of a new revolutionary consciousness among all people, enabling us all to be aware of and effectively exercise our own agency, is both the means and the ends of the social change E. Marx, Luxemburg, and Dunayevskaya envisioned. All three were communicators and educators, with ambitions to directly influence thought. Luxemburg expressed her desire "to act on people like a thunderclap, to grip them by the head" (Nettl 1969, p. 109). The transformed consciousness, if their ambitions were to be realized, would not be objects of private contemplation among so many isolated individuals, but rather would be the raw material of mass social movement. The mass social movement would, in turn, reflect back on the consciousness of those touched by the upheaval and carry the potential to remake the large-scale institutions of society. Those mass movements encompass a tension between spontaneous action and coordinated organization. E. Marx, Luxemburg, and Dunayevskaya were organizers as well as being thinkers, and were continually confronted with questions of when and how and to what extent to institutionalize the social movements in which they took part. All three saw inequalities of class, race, and gender as inextricably linked and wrestled with the challenge of how to act on this knowledge when no action can tackle everything at once.

Revolution for human liberation is not a discrete task any of them ever expected to complete in their own time. It is a task that will never be completed for all time. But all three were sure that it was a task worth doing, in whatever flawed and partial way they could manage in their circumstances.

Notes

1 Despite Luxemburg's famous opposition to "opportunism"—maintaining a hold on a modicum of political power by settling for modest reforms, a practice she denounced most pointedly in her critique of her SPD colleague Eduard Bernstein—she supported republican government as an expansion of space for action. Rights of assembly, speech, and suffrage make the next stage more feasible. Indeed, she argued that the newly arising capitalist elites will only support civil liberties as long as they are useful in capitalists' struggle against the aristocracy. The true long-term defenders of republican liberties are socialists.
2 Dunayevskaya represented this position in debate with prominent Marxist theorist Ernest Mandel at the 1947 Conference of the Fourth International. The Second International that E. Marx helped to launch 1889 and Luxemburg took part in during the 1890s and 1900s had, phoenix-like, gone through two more dissolutions and rebirths by then.
3 Some of Jenny Marx's surviving letters, begging friends for money when K. Marx did not generate enough for household expenses and she had little access to other resources, are excruciating to read. Helen Demuth, in the midst of navigating her complicated status in the Marx household, bore a child she could not keep and raise herself; E. Marx only discovered later in her life that the child's father, never acknowledged, was almost certainly K. Marx.

References

Aveling, Edward and Eleanor Marx. 1886. *The Woman Question*. Available at: www.marxists.org/archive/eleanor-marx/works/womanq.htm (accessed June 6, 2016).

Dunayevskaya, Raya. 1944. "A New Revision of Marxian Economics." *American Economic Review* 34: 531–537.

Dunayevskaya, Raya. 1945. "Revision of Reaffirmation of Marxism? A Rejoinder." *American Economic Review* 35: 660–664.

Dunayevskaya, Raya. 1962. "Out of Colonization into the Fire." *Africa Today* 9(10): 10–11+15.

Dunayevskaya, Raya. 1991 [1981]. *Rosa Luxemburg, Women's Liberation, and Marx's Philosophy of Revolution*. Urbana and Chicago: University of Illinois Press.

Dunayevskaya, Raya. 2002. *The Power of Negativity: Selected Writings on the Dialectic in Hegel and Marx*. Edited by Peter Hudis and Kevin B. Anderson. Lanham, MD: Lexington Books.

Engels, Friedrich. 1884. *The Origins of the Family, Private Property, and the State*. Available at: www.marxists.org/archive/marx/works/1884/origin-family/ (accessed June 6, 2016).

Ettinger, Elzbieta. 1986. *Rosa Luxumburg: A Life*. Boston, MA: Beacon Press.

Friedman, Gerald. 2008. *Reigniting the Labor Movement*. New York: Routledge.

Fromm, Erich. 1966. *Marx's Concept of Man*. New York: Frederick Ungar Publishing Co.
Holmes, Rachel. 2014. *Eleanor Marx: A Life*. New York: Bloomsbury Press.
Howard, M.C. and J.E. King. 2000. "Raya Dunayevskaya," in Robert W. Dimand, Mary Ann Dimand, and Evelyn Forget, eds., *A Biographical Dictionary of Women Economists*, pp. 149–151. Northampton, MA: Edward Elgar.
Kapp, Yvonne. 1976. *Eleanor Marx, Volume II*. New York: Pantheon Books.
Lovato, Brian. 2015. "New Forces of Resistance." *Rethinking Marxism* 27: 464–478.
Luxemburg, Rosa. 1951[1913]. *The Accumulation of Capital (A Contribution to an Explanation of Imperialism)*. London: Routledge.
Luxemburg, Rosa. 2004. *The Rosa Luxemburg Reader*. Edited by Peter Hudis and Kevin B. Anderson. New York: Monthly Review Press.
Marx, Eleanor. 1890. *Speech on the First May Day*. Available at: www.marxists.org/archive/eleanor-marx/works/mayday.htm (accessed June 1, 2016).
Marx, Eleanor. 1896. *The Proletarian in the Home*. Available at: www.marxists.org/archive/eleanor-marx/1896/11/proletarian-home.htm (accessed June 1, 2016).
Marx, Karl and Friedrich Engels. 1970. *The German Ideology*. Edited by C.J. Arthur. New York: International Publishers.
Nettl, J.P. 1969. *Rosa Luxemburg*, abridged edition. New York: Schocken Books.
The News and Letters Committees. www.newsandletters.org (accessed February 12, 2016).
The Raya Dunayevskaya Collection. www.rayadunayevskaya.org (accessed February 12, 2016).

PART III

Beginning in the early 20th century

11

WOMEN ECONOMISTS IN THE ACADEMY

Struggles and strategies, 1900–1940

Mary Ann Dzuback[1]

The Social Science Research Council (SSRC) held a meeting in New York in December of 1931, the first to focus on social science research in the colleges. The participants included representatives from twelve liberal arts colleges, most in the northeastern United States. The meeting was the result of a number of factors: the expansion of social sciences into the colleges, the growth in social science Ph.D. production, and the increasing commitment of some colleges to supporting and encouraging faculty research over the previous forty years. The meeting came at the urging of Marion Edwards Park, President of Bryn Mawr College, an institution that had long supported faculty research and developed Ph.D. programs for young women when American universities denied them entry. Park, like other college presidents, was wrestling with the tension between research and teaching resources for college faculties. Research had long been considered the province of research universities and the production of new knowledge the province of their male faculty. But women had been completing Ph.D.s in the social sciences for nearly forty years prior to this meeting, most at the very same research universities as their male research counterparts: Columbia, the University of Chicago, Harvard (Radcliffe), the University of Pennsylvania, Yale, and the universities of Michigan, Wisconsin, and California. In economics alone, women Ph.D.s reached just over 20 percent of the total in the early 1920s, before declining to a low of 10 percent in the middle 1950s.[2] Yet most of these same women were not perceived as productive researchers worthy of university positions and, instead, were recommended for and pushed to take teaching positions largely in the women's colleges. The women economists who filled these positions are the focus of this chapter.

The tension on college campuses, which was evident in the SSRC meeting report, had grown over forty years, as more faculty saw themselves as knowledge producers as well as teachers and as college budgets grew only slowly in the first three decades of the twentieth century. Universities had far more resources to support research and had begun accommodating faculty research by adjusting teaching loads, developing funding sources, expanding their libraries, and providing equipment for faculty and graduate students to use in their scholarly projects.

This chapter examines women economists in the colleges and the strategies they developed to ensure strong economics programs in their institutions, to train young women in economics, to push their institutions to accommodate their research commitments, and to use their research to influence policy at the local, national, and international levels. Given women academic economists' relative marginality in this period, in the sense that they were not typically faculty in the research institutions where the leading economists were located from the 1910s to the 1940s in the U.S., it is useful to consider their work in relation to power and knowledge production. Foucault argued that power is not a commodity, something to be possessed. Rather it is diffuse, relational, and located not only in structures and laws, but also in practices, techniques, and processes of everyday interactions. These interactions, in particular institutional contexts and moments, can enable those seen as marginalized to call into existence bodies of knowledge that provide effective means of social participation, resistance, and critique. His theory of power is useful for exploring how women navigated their teaching institutions, establishing practices and processes new to these institutions, to make them receptive to both the production of knowledge in addition to teaching, and to women as producers of knowledge, not only transmitters of knowledge, within them.[3]

The colleges that had the strongest economics departments and the most consistent support for women economists by the 1920s included Barnard under Emilie Hutchinson, Bryn Mawr under Susan Kingsbury, Mount Holyoke under Amy Hewes, Goucher under Elinor Pancoast, Smith under Esther Lowenthal, and Vassar under Mabel Newcomer. A very small number of women economists did find places in research universities, mostly as "lone voyagers," but there were two exceptions: the University of California at Berkeley, to which I allude here, and the Industrial Research Department at the Wharton School at the University of Pennsylvania, which I will address briefly in relation to the colleges. For the purposes of this chapter, I focus on Smith, Mount Holyoke, and Goucher, with a brief mention of Bryn Mawr because they offer different kinds of strategies shaped by both the women themselves and by the institutional cultures in each. Smith developed a special research unit for historians and economists, and economists played a major role in this unit. Mount Holyoke and Goucher very slowly increased economics faculty. But the women economists in each of those places made significant research contributions to local and state agencies and typically worked with their sociology colleagues to do so. This contribution to local communities was key to their strategies as scholars—they focused on what was at hand. They used the knowledge their research generated to influence change and reform. Mount Holyoke developed an externally financed statistics lab to support student and faculty research. Taken together, these colleges educated at least two generations of young women in economics in this period, including those who pursued economics graduate degrees and then educated the next two generations until women economists were able to breach the departments in the research universities in the 1980s and 1990s. Moreover, a number of these economists were so respected in the field that they were elected to officer positions in the major professional organizations. Such efforts were means of exercising power to challenge gendered assumptions about the production of knowledge.[4]

According to the SSRC report, colleges were at a distinct disadvantage as environments for social science research because their libraries, though quite adequate for students, lacked the depth and range faculty needed for their own research and for staying current with developments in their fields. Universities had local research councils financed by philanthropic foundations providing support for faculty research; colleges did not have access to these. Few colleges provided research funds and the men's and coeducational colleges tended to provide more funding for faculty travel for research and conference presentations. Moreover, at all the colleges, male faculty tended to receive higher salaries, which enabled them to better support their own research. By the early 1930s, seven of the twelve colleges represented in the report expected faculty to do research; four of these were women's colleges and two of the remaining three were coeducational.[5]

The SSRC report recommended the following measures to support faculty social science research: colleges should develop sources of research funding among alumnae, much like

Wellesley's alumnae fund; colleges should provide funds from administrative budgets for faculty research; the SSRC should consider rotating matching grants among the colleges to encourage this development. Another factor was time for research. Most colleges did not have a paid sabbatical leave policy throughout most of the early twentieth century; faculty research occurred over the summer. Teaching loads were heavy and few adjustments were made, even for those who supervised undergraduate honors students and programs, which made research and writing more difficult during the academic year. The SSRC report recommended that shorter and more frequent sabbatical leaves be granted, that teaching loads be redistributed, and that students be supported in, and encouraged to pursue, research.

The SSRC report made clear the challenges college faculty faced in sustaining research programs. But women faculty had already developed research programs in economics in the colleges by 1931. They had also increased the presence of economists on their campuses and established connections with state and federal agencies through the scholarship they produced. Moreover they had already brought students into their research programs and located funds to help support their work. These efforts represent the strategies—which were particularly critical for women scholars who were denied positions at research universities—that women economists used to transform their institutions from being largely focused on teaching to expecting faculty to sustain a commitment to research. And all of these strategies enabled women economists to challenge the gendered practices and definitions that shaped academia in the early twentieth century.

These women's critical and heterodox approaches to research in economics merit recognition. The field itself allowed for far more diverse approaches in the early part of the twentieth century than prevailed in the discipline beginning in the late 1930s. But the women economists' marginality from the research university enabled them to explore areas of economics outside the mainstream—or what was becoming mainstream during their academic careers. A number traveled to Soviet Russia in the 1930s to examine changes in the Soviet economy and their impact on families, women, children, and industrial labor. They explored transitional economies in the context of the failure of the "free" market economy and capitalist industrial contraction in the 1930s. They presented their work in traditional conference formats and disciplinary journals and at international gatherings. And in some cases they risked their own faculty positions in the process.[6]

Mount Holyoke

Mount Holyoke College, and the women economists there, offer a telling example of how they accomplished this transformation. Appointed in 1901, President Mary Emma Woolley was committed to increasing the academic credentials of the faculty. She fostered an institutional culture in which women faculty exercised considerable power in shaping the social science programs in their departments, as well as the professional criteria for their colleagues' advancement. She sought faculty with demonstrated interest in research, and appointed a number of strong women scholars to the history department, from which economics, sociology, and political science grew. At Mount Holyoke, women faculty received sabbatical leaves, supervised Master's students who were financed by graduate fellowships from their own colleges and from Mount Holyoke alumnae, and contributed their research expertise to local, state, national, and international agencies. Amy Hewes (1905–1943) provides a case in point for demonstrating how these strategies unfolded at Mount Holyoke.[7]

Hewes arrived at Mount Holyoke in 1905, after Woolley had begun encouraging faculty to complete doctorates and increase the academic quality of the college's programs. Hewes, a

University of Chicago sociology Ph.D. (1903) appointed to teach economics and sociology, used two approaches to justify her own research and to encourage a research culture in the college. First, she taught seminar-style courses related to her own research interests, which had a field component in factories and other work places in the Connecticut River Valley. Second, she obtained funding to support the development of a statistical laboratory on campus for both undergraduate and Master's-level research. Disputes with a colleague in the history department over Hewes' focus on contemporary economics rather than economic history and theory led Woolley to create a department of economics and sociology in 1908 for Hewes' work. Hewes' shift from sociology to economics suggests the fluidity of disciplinary boundaries in this early period of academic social science in the U.S.[8]

University researchers routinely drew graduate students into their research programs and used university funds and infrastructure to support them. In a college, Hewes did not have access to that kind or level of resources. As Foucault suggested about those on the margins, she employed the tools and resources she found at Mount Holyoke: students on one hand and alumnae donors on the other. She also strategically used her socioeconomic and geographic context to make a case for the value of her research. In addition, she closely examined labor and economic conditions in Britain and the Soviet Union, in the 1920s and early 1930s. These studies followed a fairly coherent path, shaped first by Hewes' concerns about the dehumanization and exploitation of labor under capitalism, and second by her interest in alternative ways of organizing industry: guild socialism in Britain and socialism and communism in the Soviet Union. She particularly focused on workers' power in negotiating both wages and conditions of labor and published in the leading economics journals of the period.[9]

Hewes included both undergraduate and Masters' students in her local projects. She conducted studies on such topics as women in arms industries, industrial home work, minimum wage law, working conditions in textile mills, trade unions in Russia and elsewhere, and regulation of the coal industry in Britain. She frequently was asked by state and federal agencies to explore problems for them. She served on the Massachusetts Minimum Wage Commission in an investigation of seven industries, which resulted in passage of the first minimum wage law in the U.S. in 1912. In order to better prepare students for economic research, she began offering a course in statistics in 1912; enrollment grew steadily. Students subsequently conducted research into "Occupations of Mount Holyoke Undergraduates during the Summer of 1918." At the Holyoke Chamber of Commerce's request, they studied non-English-speaking workers in factories in the industrial town of Holyoke. Hewes and students also completed a report on children leaving school for work in Holyoke, requested and partially financed by the Massachusetts Child Labor Committee. Because, like most colleges, Mount Holyoke did not have the capacity to carry out sophisticated data collection and analysis, Hewes sought support for a statistics laboratory on campus. When the student work was published and widely praised by a member of the United States Employment Service, and graduates working at the U.S. Department of Labor were noted as exceptionally skilled, trustee Joseph Skinner contributed financing for a statistics lab in the basement of one of the classroom buildings. The fact that sixty-eight students enrolled in the course by the late 1910s suggested high and increasing demand.[10]

Within a year, an additional donor appeared: Dorothy Whitney Straight, a wealthy New York philanthropist and social reformer, who, with her husband Willard Straight, published the *New Republic*. She provided funding to expand the work of the lab and enable the college to offer graduate fellowships in statistical work. That Straight saw the work as important is significant; she was deeply interested in industrial problems and local economies. Students not only were invited into industrial work places in the Connecticut River Valley to collect data, but also were given access to data at social service agencies including the New York Charity

Organization Society and research institutions including the Judge Baker Foundation. Such access for the purposes of research and publication was critical for these students and the faculty. In addition, faculty were able to supervise graduate students, brought to Mount Holyoke to study statistics and conduct statistical research in state and private social welfare agencies, through the research program financed by Skinner and then Straight.[11]

Straight's funding was not the only source of support for the economists at Mount Holyoke. Alzada Comstock (1913–1954) and Ethel Dietrich (1917–1941) were appointed under Hewes' leadership. Comstock, whose research focused on taxation and finance in modern states, received a Guggenheim Fellowship in 1926 to study post-war financial reform in Hungary. Hewes, in contrast, financed her research in part by using the opportunities her public service commitments presented: for example, labor and industrial economics through her work with the Industrial Service Sector of the U.S. Army during World War I. Dietrich studied international trade through her work as special investigator in the women's branch of the industrial service department of the Ordnance Department during World War I, for the International Labor Office and for the Committee on International Peace, and, in the 1940s and 1950s, in the Office of Exports on the Board of Economic Welfare. She also served as an economic advisor for the Military Government of Germany in the post-war period and in other capacities as a member of international delegations on trade.[12]

Hewes' efforts to engage students in statistical and field research in economics and sociology had a strong impact on them, increasing their interest in research and expanding their understanding of social and economic issues. Her teaching put them in close contact with those who were dealing with these issues on the ground: in the declining industries of the Connecticut River Valley, in social service agencies working with the poor, young people, and others, and in municipal offices developing research-based public policy. Hewes' own experiences conducting research and shaping policy had an impact on her teaching and increased the visibility of the college's economics research. Emma Woolley noted that:

> The theory that a college is sufficient unto itself, is a relic of a by-gone day. At a time when educational institutions must appeal to the public for support, it is only just for them to give freely in return.[13]

Hewes demonstrated that attitude through the research she pursued in the 1930s and she exercised a particular form of intellectual power by publishing her investigations of alternative means of organizing economic systems.

Smith

Smith College developed an early commitment to the social sciences in departments headed by male faculty. By the early 1900s, the senior (male) faculty began to accept women faculty with Ph.D.s. The economics department added sociology in the 1910s, which was dominated by men. But the faculty of economics after 1910 was almost entirely composed of women. Although men created and developed social science programs at Smith, and used the college to launch their own scholarly careers, as women with doctorates were added and slowly promoted, they gained increasing power in shaping those programs from the 1910s through the 1960s. Esther Lowenthal (1911–1952) was key to the department's development.[14]

Lowenthal had studied economics at Oxford and completed her Ph.D. at Columbia before joining the Smith faculty in 1911. Her dissertation on the Ricardian socialists was published in the same year. She moved up through the ranks from assistant to full professor by 1921, and eventually served as chair of the economics department and dean of the faculty before retiring forty-one years after arriving at Smith. She published one article and supervised the work of students and colleagues in *Smith College Studies in History*. She also participated in bringing two women faculty into the department: Dorothy Wolff Douglas (1924–1951) and Dorothy Bacon (1927–1954). A student remembered that Lowenthal was a scholar of "towering capability," who was "a superb teacher" and "somewhat aloof," but had "a logical mind which is sharp as a knife." This same student, Elizabeth Stoffregan (May), who later completed the Ph.D. in economics at the London School of Economics and taught at Goucher College, was an economic analyst at the U.S. Treasury, a fiscal analyst at the U.S. Bureau of the Budget, and eventually returned to academe at Wheaton College, serving on the board of the Export/Import Bank of the U.S. in the 1960s.[15]

Bacon came to Smith a year before finishing her Ph.D. at Radcliffe in 1928. She took research and service sabbatical leaves to work for the Works Progress Administration and the Federal Deposit Insurance Corporation in the 1930s. She focused her research on money flows during the 1930s, cost price problems, and the development of federal level credit institutions. By the 1940s, she was working with the federal Office of Price Administration. By the 1950s, she was consulting with the Brookings Institution, had been a research associate of the National Bureau of Economic Research, and received grants from the SSRC. She published a monograph on the recent economic history of five towns around Northampton, Massachusetts, in the late 1930s, and was completing a book on the development of Philippine credit institutions by 1970.[16]

Dorothy Wolff Douglas was appointed instructor in the economics department in 1924, the year before she finished her Ph.D. at Columbia in French economic history. At that point she was married to Paul H. Douglas, who moved from a position at the University of Chicago to one at Amherst to keep their family together. Dorothy Douglas was divorced and caring for four children by 1930, when she was promoted to assistant professor. Raised in a wealthy New York family, she had already been contributing from her independent income to social and political causes. Like Hewes at Mount Holyoke, her own research and politics focused on labor issues and labor legislation. With Katherine Lumpkin, for example, she published *Child Workers in America* (1937). She believed that it was critical to have a solid understanding of economic history to inform contemporary policy making with regard to labor issues, and decided to support such work at Smith in the 1930s. The focus was on the Connecticut River Valley. With a $3,500 donation from Douglas for the first two years, the promise of the same amount for the second two years, and the stipulation that the Smith committee guiding the work be composed of five faculty members from economics and history, the college established the Council on Industrial Studies. Douglas suggested that the college contribute up to $1,500 beginning in the second two years. After those four years her support would end and the college could decide whether to continue to support the Council, which it did until 1948.[17]

Katherine D. Lumpkin served as the Council's first director (1932–1939) before moving to a position at the Institute of Labor Studies in Northampton (1939–1953), and eventually to a professorship in sociology at Wells College in New York (1957–1967). Lumpkin had finished a sociology Ph.D. at the University of Wisconsin in 1928, with a dissertation on delinquent girls, taught at Mount Holyoke, and conducted research with the SSRC and at Bryn Mawr College. By 1932, Douglas and Lumpkin were partners and lived together in Northampton with Douglas's four children.[18]

The Council offered the opportunity to examine the Depression's impact on the region and to assist women graduate students toward completion of their theses at a time when such financial support for women was scarce. The Council chose doctoral students from other institutions to receive Council fellowships, and provided mentors. The studies produced under Council auspices examined the industrial history of the valley. One goal was to collect and preserve the papers and other materials that were being lost as various textile, metals, and paper making industries folded or moved out of the region in the 1920s and 1930s. Another was to encourage regional studies in the United States and provide an institutional umbrella for coordinated and cooperative research. As Lumpkin framed it:

> We want to study transportation, agriculture, business organization, the rise and in some cases the decline of particular industries, the movement of factories within the region and to the outside, and the shifting of industrial and farm labor, the sources and movement of local capital.[19]

The studies uncovered more than Lumpkin, Douglas, and Lowenthal expected: diaries, collections of correspondence going back to the colonial period, oral recollections of older residents, publications by mill girls in Chicopee, as well as the expected business papers and town records. To locate these sources and carry on the fieldwork, industrial sites were crucial to the Council's work. But Lumpkin and the first fellows encountered some reluctance from industries to open their books and records. Lumpkin placed advertisements in local papers and surveyed Mount Holyoke alumnae in the region for papers and other materials in private hands. In the end, researchers produced a mix of historical and contemporary studies. They examined a variety of topics, including the extent of manufacturing shut downs and worker displacement by the 1930s, the economic history of Chicopee, a history of industry on the Mill River, a history of early nineteenth-century metals industries and one of agricultural transformations in the nineteenth century. By 1938, five of approximately seven projects were being used for dissertation work. In addition, in Douglas and the other five members of the Council's executive committee, these students had regular contacts with economics scholars who could help guide and critique their work. Many of the studies of the 1930s and 1940s were published in the *Smith College Studies in History* series.[20]

Douglas and Lumpkin explored questions outside the boundaries of mainstream economics and published in venues sponsored by or addressing Communist Party concerns in the U.S. Although their work in these areas disturbed some on the faculty at Smith, they were able to conduct it under the auspices of their faculty positions. For example, Douglas and Lumpkin examined the place of child labor in American economic life—where it had been restricted and where it continued to flourish, in order to illuminate the issues related to the ratification of the 1924 child labor amendment to the Constitution. Douglas explored transitional economic systems in Poland and Czechoslovakia, the influence of the Soviet Union on labor practices, and the historical transformations since World War I in these countries. She also studied the shift to stronger labor union activity in Mexico in the middle 1930s, to include more democratic means of organizing labor, for the Marxist scholarly journal *Science and Society*. Lumpkin published a piece on the expanding access Black and working class citizens had to public spaces in the 1930s in the USSR.[21]

Lowenthal, Bacon, and Douglas provided leadership, substantial support, and scholarly recognition for research at Smith. They employed different strategies and practices to enhance their institutional power to transform the college and ensure that the knowledge they produced left an invaluable legacy of research on the Connecticut River Valley. In Bacon's case, her impact helped shape federal monetary policy. Douglas's financial support for developing scholars and scholarship in the Connecticut River Valley and her own ongoing research created opportunities for economics training for graduate students at Smith. Douglas, too, used her power to challenge assumptions about the impact of communism and political change on labor and economic organization. Lowenthal provided the leadership that enabled faculty and students to continue their work. Together, they ensured more than four decades of continuous commitment to economics research and teaching for women at Smith.

Goucher

Goucher College was one of the few southern women's institutions that offered a full four years of college-level work at the turn of the century. Goucher had historically modeled its curriculum on the undergraduate work at Johns Hopkins, though with fewer faculty and financial resources. Most southern women's colleges held conservative views of women's proper roles and place; they all developed social science departments more slowly than the northern colleges. Although many of these institutions expanded economics courses in the 1930s, those courses typically emphasized women's roles as consumers. Goucher's economics and sociology department rarely had more than two faculty members throughout the 1920s and most of the 1930s. At the same time, the paternalistic administration of the college through the 1920s slowed growth of faculty scholarship. When economist Elinor Pancoast (1924–1960) arrived, Goucher's President William W. Guth tightly controlled both faculty and curricular development, which left her little room to maneuver to expand teaching in economics. His successor William Allan Robertson encouraged faculty involvement in reorganizing the curriculum and relied on Pancoast's leadership to develop what became Goucher's "New Plan." The New Plan introduced a separation between the first and last two years of the undergraduate program, individual student course selection in accordance with the goals of the program, and general examinations at the end of the sophomore year. The faculty were divided into three divisions, one of which was the social science division. Within this climate of reform, broadened goals for education, and openness to ideas, Pancoast pushed for innovations in economics and sociology instruction and in the college's relations with the community.[22]

Pancoast completed her Ph.D. in economics at the University of Chicago in 1927, three years after taking her position at Goucher. Her research largely concerned labor conditions and industrial issues, as well as the impact of the economy on low-wage workers, the poor, the aged, and adult education. She moved from an instructor to full professor at Goucher and continued to publish until she retired in 1960. In a highly unusual move at a southern women's college, she introduced three kinds of activities related to her research and teaching interests: establishing an educational program in economics for women workers in industry, taking students on field trips to local government agencies, and establishing and maintaining a cooperative dormitory in which students reduced costs by performing much of the daily labor themselves. Pancoast's innovations provided Goucher's largely middle-class white students with opportunities to understand economic issues across class and on a practical level.[23]

The goal of the worker's education program was to help both "industrial women" and college women "develop new powers of appreciation and understanding" that worked across class and experience. To that end, in 1932 Pancoast persuaded the Baltimore chapter of Goucher alumnae to work with Baltimore's Worker's Education Committee to establish night classes for women workers. The classes were held on the Goucher campus, and students were invited to make use of the library. The first classes focused on history, economics, and English. Goucher faculty and alumnae volunteered to teach, and the Goucher alumnae club raised funds for student scholarships, textbooks, and other needs. Undergraduate students became interested in the program and invited the women workers to meet with them to read poetry and discuss books. Although this gesture could be read as maternalist from the middle class to the working class (and it might well have been that for many participants), Pancoast saw it as a potentially "enlightening experience to those college women who care to participate. It is the sincere testimony of one faculty member who has been meeting with these workers in industry this past year that they have much to teach." She suggested that it would not only be industrial women, "but college women," who "develop new powers of appreciation and understanding."[24]

Pancoast's approach to teaching economics and interacting with students suggests a broad understanding of the impact of a changing economy on both the working poor and the middle class. The cooperative dormitory enabled many Goucher students to remain in college in the 1930s and provided them with help "in other than financial ways," presumably by exposing them to the rigors of building maintenance and appreciation of domestic laborers and to having to work with peers and the college administration to maintain the building. The outside field trips demonstrated to students the ways that economics research could have an impact on the operation of government and the opportunities open to women researchers. One trip, to the Federal Bureau of Standards, introduced students to the application of statistical work and to a number of Goucher alumnae working at the Bureau.[25]

Pancoast was widely admired by students for her rigorous teaching and prodigious research and publication as well as her innovations. One remembered that

> Instead of a dead weight of knowledge which we undergraduates half expected to crush a young woman who knew all about trade unions, marginal costs, and the comparative theory of international trade, we discovered a sprightliness of spirit and an objectivity of thought that were challenging and disturbing. We were disturbed because Dr. Pancoast persuaded us to see that there were more things in the world of economic problems than we had dreamed of . . . Dr. Pancoast led us to perceive that it was not what we wanted to believe about economics that mattered; it was what was true.[26]

Pancoast's research at Goucher was closely tied to the needs of Baltimore and Maryland. Similarly to Hewes at Mount Holyoke, as well as Douglas at Smith, Pancoast used her position at Goucher and the research-based knowledge she produced to open the college, its students, faculty, administration, and alumnae, to the kinds of contributions, through research, that faculty could make locally, and to state and local agencies. Her research focused on what was needed within particular historical moments. In the 1920s, she studied labor unions and employers' lockouts, as well as protective labor legislation for women. In "The Prohibition of Night Work for Women" (Pancoast 1927b), for example, she argued that night work was not healthy for women or men, but was particularly detrimental to women during childbearing years, largely because of the combined stresses on health of lower wages (than men) and reduced bargaining power, as well as social expectations for work in the home, rather than "greater innate physical weakness." In the 1930s and 1940s her work focused on the problems of economic stability and security for the elderly and low- and middle-income families and their health, and on the impact on labor of industrial relocation. In the middle 1950s, working with five other colleges, she organized a three-weeklong workshop on economic education for sixty teachers from Maryland, Pennsylvania, Washington, D.C., and Minnesota. The conference was exemplary of her teaching and research commitments—to broaden understanding of economics and to produce knowledge that could be used in making economic and other policy decisions affecting people's daily lives and life chances. This commitment continued into the 1960s, with work for the state on aging and social insurance.[27]

Pancoast was the only professor of economics at Goucher, but she did have other women faculty colleagues working in areas of interest to economists, including chair of the economics and sociology department sociologist Mollie Ray Carroll, who studied social insurance programs and was considered an expert on unemployment insurance. Without institutional support for expanding economics (and other social sciences) and providing steady financing for research, though, Pancoast was limited in her ability to develop the kinds of strategies to promote research that women economists used at Mount Holyoke and Smith. At the same time, she used her limited institutional power to contribute to a larger understanding of the impact of the fluctuations of the economy and the labor market on some of society's most vulnerable citizens.

Bryn Mawr

Bryn Mawr College, in contrast, devoted more resources to the development of social science research. The only institution among the women's colleges with a longstanding Ph.D. program, the college added a graduate Department of Social Economy and Social Research, headed by Susan Kingsbury (1915–1936), and financed with a bequest from an alumna. By 1940, fifteen women had finished social economy Ph.D.s and assumed academic posts as well as research and administrative positions in a variety of public and social service agencies. Forty had completed Master's degrees, become social workers, and/or pursued further degrees, or worked in industry. The program manifested a commitment to social economic scholarship and, similarly to the other colleges explored here, encouraged students to conduct research on local industries (as well as social service agency populations) in the Philadelphia area.[28]

Kingsbury had already established a reputation as a scholar of economic history. Her Ph.D. from Columbia (1905) and her subsequent work as a professor of history and economics at Simmons College and as research director of the Women's Educational and Industrial Union in Boston gave her significant power in her three-year negotiation with M. Carey Thomas over the terms of her appointment at Bryn Mawr. She made clear that those making economic and social policies affecting workers and the poor needed a deeper understanding of the conditions of poverty and circumstances of workers and that she would only direct a unit that was committed to graduate research and training, and that provided funds for faculty and student research. The alumna bequest assisted with the funding, as did solicitations from other sources, including John D. Rockefeller, whose $100,000 established the Grace Dodge Professorship of Social Economy. Kingsbury also brought in women economists as faculty, including Anne Bezanson, who subsequently headed the industrial relations department at the University of Pennsylvania, and Eleanor Lansing Dulles, who was on the faculty between 1928 and 1935, before becoming Chief in the Division of Old-Age Benefits Research at the Social Security Board in Washington, D.C. Mildred Fairchild (Woodbury) (1929–1947) was another Kingsbury appointment. Fairchild Woodbury chaired the department after Kingsbury retired in 1936.[29]

Kingsbury and Fairchild Woodbury published key studies of the Soviet economy in the 1930s, when social scientists and others were exploring alternatives to capitalism in the context of the failures of free market theory evidenced by the Depression. They examined the impact of the planned economy on Russia in the 1920s and early 1930s and found large decreases in unemployment and increases in food production and manufacturing in this period. In a major study financed by the America Russia Institute, Society for Cultural Relations with Soviet Russia, and the SSRC, they studied the effects of Soviet communism on the reorganization and productivity of labor and the social impacts of this reorganization on women and the family into the 1930s.[30]

The Bryn Mawr case suggests what a women's college, with a historic commitment to providing for research as well as teaching, and access to philanthropic funding to support the research, could accomplish in the first four decades of the twentieth century. At the same time, it was not a research university. It was a college, which meant that it did not work under the same set of research-driven expectations as universities. By the late 1920s, when Rockefeller funding for social science research was centered in the Laura Spelman Rockefeller Memorial (LSRM) and later the Rockefeller Foundation (RF), rather than the Rockefeller family, those funds were directed to the research universities and only rarely to the colleges. The Social Economy and Social Research Department continued its work, but finding support for that work became more difficult in succeeding decades. Kingsbury and Fairchild's work on the Soviet Union was an exception in the 1930s, as interest in new ways of organizing economies generated interest among funding agencies and economists. They were able to take advantage of the diversity of research in the field to pursue these studies before the discipline increasingly narrowed after the 1930s.

Women economists at universities: Penn and Berkeley

The University of Pennsylvania

The University of Pennsylvania, whose industrial research department (IRD) was well supported, presents a contrast to the college cases. Research in industrial relations was the focus. Penn's IRD was initially financed by the Carnegie Corporation, the Philadelphia Association for the Discussion of Employment Problems, and the university, under the direction of Joseph Willits in 1921, who co-founded the department with Anne Bezanson and appointed her as his assistant director. In 1928–1929, after the Carnegie Corporation ended its support, the department received a five-year grant from the LSRM, effectively tripling the budget for that period. The grant was given on condition that the university increase its support over the same period.[31]

The department was established to offer courses in industrial relations and to pursue "co-operative industrial research in the Philadelphia community" and into "the economic and social problems of business." As funding grew throughout the 1920s, the purposes expanded to include conducting "fundamental studies of the economic and human problems and phenomena of industry." This expansion gave the faculty and research associates considerable latitude in designing projects, a latitude always tempered by the idea that the research itself would be done in a coordinated fashion rather than by lone scholars in isolation.[32]

Rockefeller support for Penn's IRD continued into the middle 1940s, although at a reduced level. As a result of this financing, approximately one-third of its total budget over two decades, the department created an enormous body of research. This work encompassed personnel and labor relations; the hosiery, upholstery, textile, and bituminous coal industries; and community labor studies that included examinations of labor market trends, personnel relations, wages, and transportation. Anne Bezanson was the driving force in the department and she effectively ran it after Willits became Dean of the Wharton School in 1933. She had finished her Ph.D. at Radcliffe in 1929, and was appointed professor of industrial research, the first woman tenured at the University of Pennsylvania. She became associate director of the department until 1939, when Willits left for the Rockefeller Foundation and she became director (and consultant to the RF). Willits called her the "real architect of the Industrial Research Department." Bezanson herself focused on "a massive, two-decade undertaking that in the end produced one of the foundation-pieces of modern scholarship in economic history: her five-volume history of prices in Philadelphia between 1720 and 1896."[33]

Under her and Willits' leadership, the department hired several women to conduct research, including Eleanor Lansing Dulles, who contributed a number of studies, and Gladys

Palmer, who directed the research after Bezanson's retirement. These appointments occurred at a time when the University of Pennsylvania appointed no other women to its social science faculty. Converted to a unit in the Wharton School in the 1960s, the IRD's work continued into the 1980s.

Berkeley

Women economists at the University of California at Berkeley between 1904 and 1960 offer another example to suggest how university support contrasted with the experiences of women economists in the colleges. The Berkeley women conducted social economy research and sustained a policy reform commitment in the economics department, even as that department increasingly went the way of academic social science—less and less reform-oriented over these decades, and more and more focused on developing theory and quantitatively based methodologies. These latter emphases distanced faculty research from both the social context of economic activity and from state policymaking. The women principally responsible for sustaining the policy orientation in the department were Jessica Peixotto, Barbara Nachtrieb Armstrong, and Emily Huntington. Peixotto, who had obtained the Ph.D. in political economy at Berkeley in 1900, remained in the department from 1904 to 1935, until she retired. Armstrong worked in the department from 1914 to 1919 as an assistant (during which time she also completed law school and practiced law), completing the Ph.D. in economics in 1928, when she moved full-time to the law school, but continued her economic research and participated in committee and other work related to the economics department's activities. She was one of the significant designers of the old age pension portion of the Social Security Act in the 1930s. Huntington remained an active researcher in the economics department from 1928 until her retirement in 1961.

Peixotto, Armstrong, and Huntington developed three strategies to continue their policy commitment and train students in research. First, they claimed an area of economic research that was not well developed in the department and developed it. Peixotto focused largely on consumer economics, Armstrong on social insurance programs and the intersection between law and economics, and Huntington on labor and industrial economics. Second, they conducted their research in a department that also maintained a commitment to a clinical program in social work, which Peixotto had developed with another colleague Lucy Stebbin, enabling them to offer course work based on their policy research, to hire other women to work in clinical as well as research capacities, and to establish an institutional justification for their own teaching and scholarship. Third, they received and sustained external as well as internal funding for their research, which they disseminated to the relevant local, state, and federal government departments and offices.[34]

Peixotto's work attracted financing from a local wealthy woman donor, Clara Hellman Heller. The Heller Committee on Research in Social Economy was a crucial source of support for both Peixotto's and Huntington's work. The Heller Committee provided the funds and internal legitimacy that enabled Peixotto to expand studies in social economics, to contribute to the graduate curricular program in social service, and to employ research and teaching assistants for both programs. The committee allowed them to define projects and carry them forward through the worst years of the Depression. It also helped them acquire an external reputation. As a result of the research she conducted under the committee's auspices, Peixotto was known as one of the pioneers of consumer economics and was elected vice-president of the American Economics Association in 1928.[35] Huntington assumed leadership of the Heller Committee when Peixotto retired in 1935 and headed the committee's work throughout most of the next 16 years, until its funding ended in 1951. Her research included economics and policy, social insurance, consumer economics, and labor market and employment problems. Her work was in part shaped by her commitment to "the problems and deprivations of the low income population," an area of study that held "little interest" for economic analysts "until well into the 1930's."[36]

Peixotto, Armstrong, and Huntington used the kind of institutional legitimacy Berkeley provided in academic economics to support their research. They created a significant place for women economists at the University of California, which expanded women social scientists' capacity to pursue research that influenced public policy and reform into the 1960s, when Huntington retired. The university appointed no women to economics between Huntington's retirement and the 1980s. Yet the presence of these women in economics at Berkeley for nearly sixty years is significant in itself. Their accomplishments in the institution, in the field of economics, and in the public policy and reform arenas are noteworthy. Geraldine Clifford has argued that one important reason for examining the history of women in higher education institutions is to analyze how they changed those institutions. Peixotto and her female colleagues transformed the economics department and the university in a number of ways that increased the contributions of the university to social and economic research and policy in both prosperous and troubled times. Their presence in economics meant that male and female students had female academic professional role models, which proved to be a decisive influence on men students, including Paul Taylor, Charles Gulick, and Clark Kerr. Kerr took four seminars with Peixotto and recalled that her subject matter was not in the mainstream of classical economics, and that she spent a great deal of time with her students. In the bullpen of faculty desks in economics—open to students and faculty—she was "respected and accepted." Moreover, the economics department was more diverse than most in the 1930s, he noted, in viewpoints and in gender. Their female mentors also profoundly affected women who studied at Berkeley, many of whom went on to graduate degrees or social service work.[37]

Alice O'Connor suggests that such efforts to develop "poverty knowledge" challenged a fundamental assumption in classical economics: that poverty was a natural outcome of economic processes. The researchers at Berkeley refused to succumb to the theories developing in the 1920s that offered cultural rationales for group and individual poverty. Instead, as they contributed to research on California and elsewhere, they continued to see poverty and unemployment as systemic, structural phenomena that occurred as a result of larger economic and labor market forces, as well as the distribution of wealth—a "problem of political and social economy."[38]

Conclusion

As this analysis of women economists at Mount Holyoke, Smith, Goucher, and Bryn Mawr and the comparison to women economists at Berkeley and Penn, suggest, women economists in the colleges encountered a number of obstacles in their efforts to sustain their identities as productive scholars. Yet they used the knowledge they produced in powerful ways to shape institutional and disciplinary change and raise challenges to disciplinary assumptions. They faced a constrained employment market for women academic economists in this period when almost no tenure-line positions were open to women scholars in the research universities. Unlike their counterparts at Berkeley and the IRD at Penn, they did not have the benefits of research university status and recognition of scholarship as a primary faculty commitment. Nor did they have access to the resources increasingly available at the research universities. Except for Bryn Mawr, they had little expectation of training doctoral students or access to the kinds of research assistance doctoral students routinely provided their mentors in the research universities. They did not have the kinds of access to research funding that, for example, the University of Chicago had from the LSRM and the Rockefeller Foundation in the 1920s and 1930s. They could not take the kinds of research sabbaticals increasingly available at the universities. Finally, they lacked the prestige conferred on scholars in the research universities in this period, as social sciences were gaining ground in the academy and losing their connections to the social service and social policy commitments, as well as contributions to local economic community research, that were at their roots in the United States.

Although college women economists found significantly fewer resources than their colleagues in the research universities, they continued to be productive scholars. They developed localized institutional power and used that power to transform the colleges to accommodate them as researchers. From the margins of the field, when compared with their male counterparts at Columbia, Chicago, Penn, Harvard, Wisconsin, and Michigan, they developed strategies to support their research. Their research practices—including students, and targeting their research questions on local economic and historical transformations—enabled them to develop both institutional and professional power. Notably, Penn and Berkeley efforts headed by women economists also maintained strong local and state-level research programs. They raised funds from alumnae and other donors and used the funding to spur institutional financial contributions. They trained students, some of whom later joined college and university faculties and government and nonprofit agencies as economic and social researchers. Except in the most financially constrained context, such as Goucher's, they increased the presence of women economists in their institutions. They ensured the continuation of women's leadership within their departments and institutions. Finally, in the case of Hewes, Douglas and Lumpkin, and Fairchild Woodbury and Kingsbury, they investigated alternative economic systems in the face of exploitative labor practices and the failures of Western capitalism in the 1930s.

Certain key factors enabled these women to transform the colleges to accommodate their work as scholars and, more important, develop institutional resources to sustain their work. All of these economists created new areas of study in their colleges. They introduced economics into the college curriculum and engaged students in examining local economic institutions and problems as part of their undergraduate or graduate training. They helped students understand the benefits in interdisciplinary work; social economics as a research area is a prime example of this phenomenon. Extending faculty activity into the rich variety of research venues of the 1910s through 1930s was a means of demonstrating to college administrators the importance of economic research to their identities and of illustrating for local leaders the value of research to their planning and policy making. As Woolley of Mount Holyoke argued, women economists in the colleges created productive, often research-based town–gown relationships where they had not existed before. They used their knowledge to address pressing local, state, and federal problems, as well as major transformations in other countries. Their students joined them in the research or benefited from it in their classrooms. Administrative and trustee support, developing in response to the reputations of particular faculty also were significant in furthering women economists' scholarship in the colleges and increasing their institutional power.

Locating sources of funding, working with local, state and federal agencies, increasing the presence of economists, and drawing students into research programs were successful strategies that generated support for their own work and for developing the next generation of women economists. These activities would not have been possible had college women economists not engaged in practices, techniques, and interactions, with the knowledge they produced, to challenge gender norms in academia, transform their institutions, and address larger social and economic issues with their work, stretching the boundaries of the discipline and challenging some of its then current assumptions. Taken together, these kinds of strategies enabled women economics scholars in the women's colleges to extend their power into the male world of academic scholarship and to contribute to shaping knowledge in the discipline and the social sciences.

Notes

1 The author thanks the Spencer Foundation and the Rockefeller Archive Center for their generous support for some of the research that informs this chapter.

2 The Carnegie Commission, 1975, Chart 10, 90. See also similar figures for the other social sciences: Harmon, 1978, Table 4, 17, in which the percentage of women obtaining Ph.D.s in all fields increased from 8.8 in 1900–04 to 15.4 in 1925–29, before declining to a low of 9.4 in 1950–54.

3 I am grateful to Margaret Nash for pointing to the usefulness of Foucault's power/knowledge argument in the examination of gender and power in educational spaces: Margaret Nash, Comments made at "Historiographical Trends in U.S. Women's and Gender History: Revisiting Eisenmann's 'Creating a Framework for Interpreting U.S. Women's Educational History'," at the History of Education Society annual meeting, November 7, 2015. See also Foucault, 1980, 89, 99–101, for example.

4 Clifford, 1989. Susan Kingsbury was elected Vice-President of the American Economic Association (1919); Jessica Peixotto of the University of California, Berkeley was Vice-President of the American Economic Association (1928); Anne Bezanson of the University of Pennsylvania was President of the Economic History Association (1946–48).

5 "Summary of the Conference on Research in the Social Sciences in Colleges Held at the Social Science Research Council, December 12 and 13, 1931," Ethel B. Dietrich papers, File 1, Faculty Files, Mount Holyoke College Archives (FF, MHCA).

6 Thanks to Robert Dimand for urging me to discuss these scholars' politically diverse, critical, and heterodox contributions to the history of economics when I presented an earlier version of this chapter at the History of Economics Society meeting in 2016.

7 Dzuback, summer 2003: 185–86.

8 *Annual Report of the President, Bulletin of Mount Holyoke College, 1908–1909* (Series 3, January, 1910), 10, Mount Holyoke College Archives (MHCA). Useful histories of the college under Woolley: Cole, 1940, ch.11; Marks, 1955.

9 Hewes, 1920, 1922a, 1922b, 1925, 1926, 1932. On her books, see Hewes, 1915, 1917, 1930.

10 Emma Woolley, "President's Report, 1918–1919," 2–3; Amy Hewes, "Report of the Department of Economics and Sociology, 1919–1920," and "Report of the Department of Economics and Sociology, 1921–1922," Economics and Sociology Department Records (ESDR), MHCA. See also Amy Hewes, Faculty Files, MHCA.

11 *Report of the President, 1920–1923, Mount Holyoke College Bulletin* (Series 17, November, 1923); *Report of the President and Treasurer, 1923–1924, Mount Holyoke College Bulletin* (Series 18, November 1924); "Report of the Department of Economics and Sociology, 1923–1924," ESDR, MHCA.

12 See Faculty Biographical Files, Mount Holyoke College Archives (FBF, MHCA), for vitas and other college material on Comstock and Hewes. Amy Hewes, "Report of the Department of Economics and Sociology, 1923–1924," Economics and Sociology Department Records, MHCA. Straight was a wealthy reformer who, with her husband Willard, published the *New Republic.* See also Groenewegen, 2000, on Hewes' career and contributions. As Groenwegen notes, Hewes' (1925), was one of the few articles by a women published in that journal.

13 Woolley, *Report of the President, 1923*, 13. On Straight, see Rauchway, 2001, chapters 1 and 4; Swanberg, 1980. On Hewes' policy work and public service: Amy Hewes Papers, Faculty Files (AH, FF), MHCA. On her influence on students, see Demond, 1943; Madeleine P. Grant, "In Memorian—Amy Hewes," *Mount Holyoke Alumnae Quarterly*, copy in AH, FF, MHCA. And see Deegan, 1991.

14 See Fuller, 1920; and see Page, 1982, ch. 4; Faculty Files, Smith College Archives (FF, SCA).

15 Elizabeth Stoffregan May, in Jacqueline Van Voris, *College: A Smith Mosaic* (Smith College, 1975), 77. See also FF, SCA; Hyman and Moore, 1997; Lowenthal, 1927.

16 On Bacon, see FF, SCA. She published articles in the *Review of Economic Statistics*, the *Journal of the American Statistical Association* and the *National Encyclopedia* in her areas of expertise. Her study *Recent Economic History of the Five Towns* was published by both *Smith College Studies in History* in 1937 and, I believe, by the Works Progress Administration in April 1938.

17 "Suggested plan," ca. 1932 (n.d.), Box 38, W.A. Neilson Papers, Smith College Archive (WAN, SCA); and other materials in Box 398, Presidential Papers (William A. Neilson) (PP, WAN), SCA.
18 See FF, SCA; Jacquelyn Dowd Hall, 1998, 2000; and Lumpkin, 1947. While at Amherst, Paul Douglas collaborated with mathematician Charles Cobb, with whom he developed the Cobb-Douglas formula, a model of an economic system's total production as a function of the amounts of labor used and of capital investment over a period of time. Again, thanks to Robert Dimand for this information.
19 Lumpkin, 1937, SCA.
20 See, for example, Lumpkin, "Brief Resume of the Work of the Council of Industrial Studies, 1932–1938," Box 398, PP (WAN), and "Report of the Director of Research of the Council of Industrial Studies" in Report(s) of the President, 1933–1938, SCA. See also *Smith College Studies in History*, vols 19, 21, 23, 24, 26, 28, 33, 37. The students who completed the projects as part of their dissertation included Vera Shlakman, *Economic History of a Factory Town* (1934); Thelma Kistler, *The Rise of Railroads in the Connecticut River Valley* (1938); Margaret E. Martin, *Merchants and Trade of the Connecticut River Valley* (1939); Margaret Richards Pabst, *Agricultural Trends in the Connecticut River Valley Region of Massachusetts, 1800–1900* (1941). Agnes Hannay, *A Chronicle of Industry on the Mill River* (1936) did not use her research for the dissertation. Mabel Van Abel started work on *Shutdowns in the Connecticut Valley* (1934), but left to marry; the work was completed by Katherine Lumpkin. Margaret Brainerd (Rolph) began a study of the metals industry, but left after a year to marry.
21 Douglas and Lumpkin, 1937; Douglas, 1972 (1953), 1940, and 1930; and Lumpkin, 1937.
22 McCandless, 1999, on southern colleges; 79 on social sciences; Knipp and Thomas, 1938; and Musser, 1990.
23 On Pancoast, see files at Goucher College Archives and Reynolds, 1959. Her nine publications are listed in the bibliography. Pancoast, "Effects of Changes in Location of Industries on Labor," Report for the National Resources Planning Board, 1941. See the following for descriptions of the industrial education program: Pancoast, 1933; Reynolds, 1933; Knipp and Thomas, 1938; Musser, 1990, 20–22. The field trip and dormitory innovations are described in Musser, 1990, and Knipp and Thomas, 1938.
24 Elinor Pancoast, 1933, 30.
25 Knipp and Thomas, 1938, 548.
26 Reynolds, 1959, 11.
27 Pancoast, 1927b, 3; 1930; 1938; 1940; 1945; 1954; 1962.
28 Bryn Mawr College, *Carola Woerishoffer Graduate Department of Social Economy and Social Research: Degrees and Certificates Conferred, 1915–1930*, Graduate School of Social Work and Social Research Records, Bryn Mawr College Archives (BMCA); 11 of the 15 theses were published in some form by 1939. See Dzuback, 1993, for a full account of the department.
29 Toba Kerson, "Susan Myra Kingsbury", Florence Peterson and Frederica de Laguna, "Susan Myra Kingsbury," both in Susan M. Kingsbury Papers (SMK)-BMCA; Watson, 1950 and Woodbury, 1971. The Thomas–Kingsbury correspondence is located in the M. Carey Thomas Papers, BMCA. See Dzuback, 1993, for full documentation.
30 Kingsbury and Fairchild, 1931, and Kingsbury and Fairchild, 1935.
31 The Carnegie Corporation shifted support from research institutes to popular education in the mid-to-late 1920s (Josiah H. Penniman to Beardsley Ruml, 13 June 1927, and other materials in box 75, file 792, Laura Spelman Rockefeller Memorial File, series 3, RAC). The university's obligation increased from $10,000 (1928–1929) to $40,000 (1931–1932); the LSRM's decreased from $50,000 (1927–1928) to $10,000 (1931–1932). See also Dzuback, 2004.
32 *University of Pennsylvania: The Wharton School of Finance and Commerce, Announcement, 1922–1923* (Philadelphia: University Press of Pennsylvania, 1921), 66; Announcement, *1934–1935*, 26; *Moving into the Eighties: The Wharton School's Industrial Research Unit and Labor Relations Council* (University of Pennsylvania Archives), 7. According to Steven A. Sass (1982, 208), LSRM funding increased the budget to over $110,000. Eventually Bezanson and Palmer received faculty appointments.
33 Dzuback, 1993; *Moving into the Eighties*, 7; Sass, 1982, 210, for quote. The Rockefeller Foundation appropriated $50,000 over two years in 1932 and $75,000 over five years in 1935; see "Minutes," 9 May 1932 and 17 April 1935, box 5, file 78; in 1939, the Foundation gave $11,000 for two specific projects and in 1940, $105,000 for three years (Thompson to Williams, 25 October 1939, box 8, file 112, and "Minutes" 17 May 1940, box 5, file 78); all in RFA, RG 1.1, series 241, RAC. See also, Dzuback, 2008, 55–62.
34 Dzuback, 2006. See also, Dzuback, 2008, 62–64.
35 Joseph Dorfman, 1959, 570–578; Cookingham, 1987.
36 Huntington, "A Career in Economics and Social Insurance," University of California Oral History Collection, Bancroft Library, 40; 1942, v.

37 Author interview with Clark Kerr, 14 May 1996. Clifford, 1983.

38 Dorfman, 1959, 570–578; Cookingham, 1987. Clifford, 1983, 15. Huntington, "A Career in Economics and Social Insurance," v. See essays in Hatfield, ed., 1935 by former students on topics such as the American Federation of Labor, care of the indigent ill, British health and unemployment insurance, self-help cooperatives, unemployment relief, changing functions of the American family, infant mortality, and historical analyses of various economic reformers. O'Connor, 2001, 25, 27.

Bibliography

Carnegie Commission on Higher Education. (1975). *Opportunities for Women in Higher Education: Their Current Participation, Prospects for the Future, and Recommendations for Action.* New York: McGraw Hill.

Clifford, G. (1983). "Shaking Dangerous Questions from the Crease: Gender and American Higher Education." *Feminist Issues* 3. 3–62.

Clifford, G. (1989). *Lone Voyagers: Academic Women in Coeducational Universities, 1870–1937.* New York: Feminist Press at the City University of New York.

Cole, A. (1940). *A Hundred Years of Mount Holyoke College: The Evolution of an Educational Ideal.* New Haven, CT: Yale University.

Cookingham, M. (1987). "Social Economists and Reform: Berkeley, 1906–1961." *History of Political Economy* 19. 47–65.

Deegan, M.J. (1991). "Amy Hewes (1877–1970)." In *Women in Sociology: A Bio-bibliographical Sourcebook.* Ed. Mary Jo Deegan. New York: Greenwood. 164–71.

Demond, H. (1943). "Amy Hewes: Professor Emeritus of Economics and Sociology." *Mount Holyoke Alumnae Quarterly* 27. 45–46.

Dorfman, J. (1959). *The Economic Mind in American Civilization*, Volume Five. New York: Viking.

Douglas, D. (1930). *Mexican Labor: A Bulwark of Democracy.* New York: American League for Peace and Democracy.

Douglas, D. (1940). "Land and Labor in Mexico." *Science and Society*. 127–52.

Douglas, D. (1972/1953). *Transitional Economic Systems: The Polish-Czech Example.* New York: Monthly Review Press.

Douglas, D. and Lumpkin, K. (1937). *Child Workers in America.* New York: McBride & Company.

Dzuback, M.A. (1993). "Women and Social Research at Bryn Mawr College, 1915–1940." *History of Education Quarterly* 33. 579–608.

Dzuback, M.A. (2003). "Gender and the Politics of Knowledge." *History of Education Quarterly* 43. 171–95.

Dzuback, M.A. (2004). "Creative Financing in Social Science: Women Scholars and Early Research." In *Women and Philanthropy in Education.* Ed. A. Walton. Bloomington: Indiana University Press. 105–26.

Dzuback, M.A. (2006). "Berkeley Women Economists, Public Policy, and Civic Sensibility." In *Civic and Moral Learning in America.* Ed. D. Warren and J. Patrick. New York: Palgrave Macmillan. 153–71.

Dzuback, M.A. (2008). "Gender, Professional Knowledge, and Institutional Power: Women Social Scientists and the Research University." In *The "Woman Question" and Higher Education: Perspectives on Gender and Knowledge Production in America.* Ed. A.M. May. Cheltenham: Edward Elgar. 52–76.

Foucault, M. (1980). *Power/Knowledge: Selected Interviews and Other Writings, 1972–1977.* New York: Pantheon.

Fuller, M. (1920). "Development of History and Government in Smith College, 1875 1920." *Smith College Studies in History* 5. 139–73.

Groenewegen, P. (2000). "Amy Hewes." In *A Biographical Dictionary of Women Economists* Ed. R. Dimand, M.A. Dimand and E. Forget. Cheltenham, UK: Edward Elgar. 209–11.

Hall, J. (1998). "Open Secrets: Memory, Imagination, and the Refashioning of Southern Identity." *American Quarterly* 50. 110–24.

Hall, J. (2000). "'To Widen the Reach of Our Love': Autobiography, History, and Desire." *Feminist Studies* 26. 231–47.

Harmon, L. (1978). *A Century of Doctorates: Data Analyses of Growth and Change.* Washington, DC: National Academy of Sciences.

Hatfield, H. Ed. (1935). *Essays in Honor of Jessica Blanche Peixotto.* Berkeley: University of California.

Hewes, A. (1915). *Industrial Home Work.* Boston, MA: Women's Educational and Industrial Union.

Hewes, A. (1917). *Women as Munitions Makers.* New York: The Russell Sage Foundation.

Hewes, A. (1920). "Labor Conditions in Soviet Russia." *Journal of Political Economy* 28. 774–83.

Hewes, A. (1922a). "Guild Socialism: A Two Years' Test." *The American Economic Review* 12. 209–37.

Hewes, A. (1922b). "Russian Wage Systems under Communism." *Journal of Political Economy* 30. 274–78.
Hewes, A. (1925). "The Changing Structure of the Bargaining Unit of Labor." *Quarterly Journal of Economics* 39. 612–34.
Hewes, A. (1926). "The Task of the English Coal Commission." *The Journal of Political Economy* 34. 1–12.
Hewes, A. (1930). *The Contribution of Economics to Social Work*. New York: Columbia University.
Hewes, A. (1932). "The Transformation of Soviet Trade Unions." *The American Economic Review* 22. 605–19.
Huntington, E. (1942). *Doors to Jobs: A Study of the Organization of the Labor Market in California*. Berkeley: University of California.
Hyman, P. and Moore, D. Eds. (1997). *Jewish Women in America: An Historical Encyclopedia*. Volume I. New York: Routledge. 879.
Kingsbury, S. and Fairchild, M. (1931). *Employment and Unemployment in Pre-War and Soviet Russia Report*. Amsterdam: World Economic Congress, 1929–1930.
Kingsbury, S. and Fairchild, M. (1935). *Factory, Family, and Woman in the Soviet Union*. New York: G.P. Putnam's Sons.
Knipp, A. and Thomas, T. (1938). *The History of Goucher College*. Baltimore, MD: Goucher College.
Lowenthal, E. (1927). "Labor Policy of Oneida Community, Ltd." *Journal of Political Economy* 35. 114–26.
Lumpkin, K. (1937). "Democratic Ways in the USSR." *Soviet Russia Today*. 10–11, 29–30.
Lumpkin, K. (1947). *The Making of a Southerner*. New York: Alfred A. Knopf.
Marks, J. (1955). *Life and Letters of Mary Emma Woolley*. Washington, DC: Public Affairs.
McCandless, A. (1999). *The Past in the Present: Women's Higher Education in the Twentieth-Century American South*. Tuscaloosa: University of Alabama Press.
Musser, F. (1990). *The History of Goucher College, 1930–1985*. Baltimore, MD: Johns Hopkins University.
O'Connor, A. (2001). *Poverty Knowledge: Social Science, Social Policy, and the Poor in Twentieth-Century U.S. History*. Princeton, NJ: Princeton University.
Page, C. (1982). *Fifty Years in the Sociological Enterprise: A Lucky Journey*. Amherst: University of Massachusetts Press.
Pancoast, E. (1927a). "The International Photo-Engravers' Union." Ph.D. dissertation, University of Chicago.
Pancoast, E. (1927b). *The Prohibition of Night Work for Women*. Committee on Women in Industry, National League of Women Voters.
Pancoast, E. (1930). *A Study of Old-Age Dependency in the City of Baltimore, 1930*. Baltimore, MD: n.p.
Pancoast, E. (1933). "Goucher 'Pioneers' Again." *Goucher Alumnae Quarterly* 11. 29–30.
Pancoast, E. (1938). "Social Education in Our Adult Summer School." *Social Education* 11. 536–40.
Pancoast, E. (1940). *Budgets for Low Income Families*. Baltimore, MD: Baltimore Council of Social Agencies.
Pancoast, E. (1945). "Federal Programs for Family Security." *The Councillor* 10. 1–7.
Pancoast, E. (1954). "The Goucher Workshop on Economic Education." Goucher Alumnae Quarterly 3. 10–12.
Pancoast, E. (1962). *Income of Older Persons in Maryland: Report Prepared for the Commission's Committee on Income and Social Services*. Baltimore, MD: State Coordinating Commission on the Problems of Aging.
Rauchway, E. (2001). *The Refuge of Affections: Family and American Reform Politics, 1900–1920*. New York: Columbia University Press.
Reynolds, A. (1933). "Workers' Education at Goucher." *Goucher Alumnae Quarterly* 11. 29–30.
Reynolds, A. (1959). "Elinor Pancoast." *Goucher Alumnae Quarterly* 27. 11–12.
Sass, S. (1982). *The Pragmatic Imagination: A History of the Wharton School, 1881–1981*. Philadelphia: University of Pennsylvania.
Swanberg, W. (1980). *Whitney Father, Whitney Heiress: Two Generations of One of America's Richest Families*. New York: Charles Scribner's Sons.
Watson, A. (1950). "A Tribute to Susan M. Kingsbury." *Bryn Mawr Alumnae Bulletin* 20. 12–13, 13–14.
Woodbury, M. (1971). "Susan Myra Kingsbury." In *Notable American Women, 1607–1950*. Vol. III. Ed. Edward T. James, *et al.* 3 vols. Cambridge, MA: Harvard University. 335–36.

12

DAUGHTERS OF COMMONS

Wisconsin women and Institutionalism

Marianne Johnson

Introduction

One of the top four programs in the United States throughout the first third of the 20th century (Froman 1942), Wisconsin was known for an Institutional approach that was "empirical, focused on institutions, and social control" (Rutherford 2006, 168). What distinguished Wisconsin Institutionalism was a commitment to Progressive reform, an emphasis on field research, historical case studies, and a focus on the larger cultural and legal environment. While having many contributors, the defining individual of Wisconsin Institutionalism was John R. Commons. Commons arrived at Wisconsin in 1904 and quickly became the epicenter of the department, overseeing an expansive research agenda and orchestrating nation-wide political advocacy for labor reforms including unemployment insurance, social security, and the minimum wage (Kato 2009; Kaufman 1993; Rutherford 2011; Tilman 2008). Commons "contributed in one way or another to practically every piece of social and labor legislation that has been enacted in the twentieth century" (Barbash 1993, 69). He was "the intellectual origin of the New Deal, of labor legislation, of social security, of the whole movement in the country toward a welfare state" (Boulding 1957, 7). His policy work was underpinned by a complicated and unwieldy theoretical structure, which he laid out in the *Legal Foundations of Capitalism* (1924) and *Institutional Economics* (1934).

Though an "illiberal reformer" who rationalized labor laws on eugenic grounds and embraced lower minimum wages for women and minorities (Leonard 2016), Commons was unusually supportive of female students at Wisconsin. During Commons' tenure, Wisconsin ranked fourth in the production of women doctoral candidates, following only Columbia, Chicago and Harvard.[1] Compared to institutions where women were often "lone voyagers" (Jonçich Clifford 1989), women at Wisconsin participated widely in department activities, including Commons' famous "Friday Nighters", a dinner and discussion group for students.[2] Women wrote papers and books; they contributed to collaborative research projects, including Commons' vast labor histories. Women co-authored Institutional textbooks and engaged in field studies. They authored legislation and ran government agencies.

Women have received little attention by those writing the history of Wisconsin Institutionalism (Johnson 2011 and 2015; Kaufman 1993; Lampman 1993; Rutherford 2006 and 2011; Tilman 2008). Yet, the daughters of Commons made important contributions both to the body of work considered Wisconsin Institutionalist as well as to its diffusion. Rather than drawing conclusions from individual cases and generalizing, I adopt a prosopographic approach, investigating the common characteristics of this historical group, whose individual biographies are often obscured. By examining typical Wisconsin women economists, we can develop a picture of their contributions to Institutionalism. This is done by collecting data on more than 40 women who matriculated at Wisconsin – PhDs, Master's students, and undergraduates – and looking for phenomena that transcend individual experiences.[3] In doing so, two important themes emerge. By actively including women in his research program, Commons vastly expanded the army of people well-equipped to contribute to his social-political agenda. This allowed Wisconsin Institutionalism to achieve a much larger footprint than would have otherwise been possible, as women made significant contributions to the spread of Wisconsin Institutionalism though publications, teaching, and applications.

However, this is not just a story about the contributions of women to the Institutionalist tradition, but also about using their experiences to elucidate unresolved questions in the history of economic thought. Those that study Institutionalism have long sought to understand its rapid marginalization and decline in the post-war period (Backhouse 1998; Biddle 1998; Johnson 2015; Lampman 1993; Rutherford 2011 and 2015). The story of Wisconsin's women economists illustrates how Wisconsin Institutionalism's broadly defined approach to economics and economic research contributed to its decline. By embracing government work, statistical data collection without underlying theory, and multi-disciplinary studies, Wisconsin diluted its brand of economics until it was no longer clearly recognized as economic theory proper. This was particularly evident in the careers of Wisconsin-trained women economists who became practicing sociologists, social workers, government researchers and administrators of nonprofit organizations, lobbying groups, and government programs.

Wisconsin women economists as a historical group

To understand the historical significance of Wisconsin's women economists, it is important to first form a picture of their place in the department and to consider how Wisconsin compared to other leading institutions. The University of Wisconsin produced its first PhD in economics in 1893. Entering with the second class was Helen Page Bates who became the first woman to earn a PhD in economics in the United States (1896). She arrived with funding as a University Scholar; subsequent years were funded by fellowships and teaching (Hammond 1993). Bates was also the first woman to serve as a lecturer in economics at Wisconsin, hired by Richard T. Ely to satisfy the rapidly increasing demand for undergraduate economics courses.[4]

While the absolute number of women pursuing graduate education at Wisconsin was large, Wisconsin was typical in the percentage of women in economics graduate programs at the time (Libby 1990). Women represented 9.6 percent of PhDs and 21.4 percent of Master's degrees granted at Wisconsin before 1940 (Table 12.1).[5] What was unusual is the extent to which these women were associated with Commons. Though a prolific advisor generally, Commons played an out-sized role in the education of women. During Commons' tenure, Margaret Pryor Glicksman was the only woman to complete a dissertation in economics under another professor at Wisconsin.

Women were more likely than men to work on labor and social reform issues at Wisconsin. They were also more likely to undertake projects that involved empirical case studies and fieldwork.[6] For example, Helen Sumner Woodbury's dissertation cum book of "two years' study of suffrage in Colorado . . . gathered together a valuable collection of data from which important conclusions can be drawn as to the actual effects of equal suffrage upon politics, upon legislation" and which was based on statistical analysis of 1,200 questionnaires she developed (Nearing 1910, 259–260).

Table 12.1 Wisconsin women economists*

	*PhDs granted to women (out of total)***	*Master's degrees granted to women (out of total)***
Before 1900	1 (12)	3 (10)
1900–1910	5 (27)	4 (40)
1911–1920	0 (25)	13 (78)
1921–1930	7 (52)	24 (86)
1931–1940	5 (70)	20 (89)
Total	18 (186)	64 (303)

Notes

*During some of this period, the Economics Department was also responsible for courses in Sociology, Social Work, Accounting, and Finance, complicating counting PhDs. For example, William Kiekhofer wrote to Teresa Schmid McMahon asking if she wanted to be listed as a sociologist or economist for the departmental records. "Although I am an economist now, I really was a sociologist in 1911" she responded (Schmid McMahon to Kiekhofer, 18 November 1930, Schmid McMahon Papers, University of Washington, Box 1, Folder 5).

**University of Wisconsin Graduation Bulletins, 1892–1940.

In addition to the 18 women that completed PhDs at Wisconsin, eight more can be found in the *American Economic Review* list of doctoral candidates. While some pursued traditional topics in labor economics such as unpaid services or the labor conditions of a particular industry, half were at the intersection of eugenics and social policy.[7] Their titles reflect a national interest by Progressives during this period in eugenics as the basis of social reform (Leonard 2016).

Many of Commons' Master's students also made significant contributions to the dissemination of Wisconsin Institutionalism including Florence Peterson, Alice Shoemaker, Maud Swett, and Helen Witmer. Much like the PhD dissertations, the Masters theses completed by Wisconsin women emphasized field research and social reform. Swett wrote a *Summary of Labor Laws in Effect* (1909) for Commons; her thesis was funded by the American Association for Labor Legislation (A.A.L.L.). Ely's daughter, Anna Ely Morehouse, based her 1919 thesis on undercover work in machine-works and canning factories in Milwaukee.[8] Peterson's thesis relied on extensive data collection on the number of shoeworkers, unionization rates, and shoes produced in her *History of Shoe Works' Organizations* in the Midwest (1930).

As apparent in Table 12.1, the number of graduate students increased dramatically throughout the first third of the 20th century, and Wisconsin, like many other schools, commonly accepted large numbers of students without providing funding. However, unlike at other institutions where women rarely received stipends or fellowships (Dzuback 2006), at Wisconsin, Commons actively worked to find paid employment opportunities for at least some of his female students. For example, Genevieve Townsend received a legislative scholarship in economics for graduate work. When that was exhausted, Commons secured a position for her as a research assistant to the Department of Economics paid by a grant from the Consumer Credit Institute of America. Helen Sumner Woodbury initially funded her graduate education by working as Ely's secretary. After her first year, Commons had Sumner Woodbury appointed as an honorary fellow in political economy and then employed as a correspondence instructor. Margaret Pryor Glicksman and Elizabeth Brandeis Raushenbush eventually achieved professorships in economics at Wisconsin. Many other women were hired at the behest of Commons to university administrative work and as instructors in various extension programs.[9]

It would be misleading to focus exclusively on graduate students, as many of the women undergraduates who studied with Commons contributed to the spread of Wisconsin Institutionalism in significant ways, particularly Irene Osgood Andrews with the A.A.L.L. and Katherine Lenroot at the Children's Bureau in Washington, D.C. There was a notable presence of women undergraduates from the earliest years, with a reasonable estimate that women made up approximately 16 percent of undergraduate degree earners in economics before 1940.[10] Several were supported by on-going scholarships, including Orphia Leavitt who received the Women's Club Scholarship for study in economics (1893). Helen Page Bates received the same scholarship the following year. Throughout this period, women earned honors for theses on economics subjects. Their theses reflected much the same interests of Wisconsin women graduate students, nearly all focusing on labor economics, economic issues of mothers and children, pensioning, women's paid work (e.g. laundries, canning factories), and women's unions. Some Wisconsin undergraduates chose to pursue graduate work at other centers of Institutionalism.[11]

The contributions of these women to Institutionalism through their publications, their teaching, and their policy work are considered in the next sections. Their stories indicate the extent to which women added to the body of Institutionalist thought and to its diffusion in the academy, in government, and to the broader public.

Publishing Institutionalism

One way to consider the contribution of women to Wisconsin Institutionalism is by examining their publications. Publications have long conferred status, for authors and for their universities. Including the contributions by both faculty and PhDs of an institution, Roger Backhouse (1998) sampled publications in the *American Economic Review* (every volume), the *Journal of Political Economy* (every fifth volume), and the *Quarterly Journal of Economics* (every fifth volume). Based on his sample estimates, he calculated that Wisconsin ranked seventh nationally for publications in top economics journals before 1940. Several women contributed to this ranking, including Ethel Dietrich, Constance Kiehl, Elizabeth Brandeis Raushenbush, and Helen Witmer. Their well-cited publications appeared in the *American Economic Review*, the *Journal of Political Economy* and the *Quarterly Journal of Economics* (Table 12.2).

The publications listed in Table 12.2 reflect a marked interest in policy analysis and social issues, consistent with Commons' labor reform agenda. Unlike women at other institutions, Wisconsin women did not contribute much to research on household management or consumer economics, instead focusing on issues that would now be classified as labor economics, industrial relations, and social work. Their work represented original contributions to economic thought. Wisconsin women employed the empirical Institutionalist methods of case study and legal-historical analysis supplemented by data collection and basic statistical analysis. None adopted the mathematical formulism popular at schools such as Chicago or Harvard. A review of Ethel Dietrich's *World Trade* (1939) emphasized her Institutionalist approach, noting she abandoned classical trade theory and instead "proceed[ed] immediately to a discussion of the role which governments play" and that "the factual material here presented needed to be accumulated, for there has not been a book of like subject matter during the past decade" (Phelps 1940, 460). Frequently canvassed topics included regulations on child labor, minimum wages, and unemployment insurance programs. Google Scholar provides a convenient method to benchmark the impact of a particular scholarly work. The numbers of identified citations are provided for books, journal articles, pamphlets, and studies, searchable either by title or by author name. In total, there are more than 2,000 Google Scholar citations to works listed in Table 12.2, of which sole-authored articles, books, and studies by Wisconsin women earned more than 700 Google Scholar citations.

Table 12.2 Publications of Wisconsin women (all degree levels)[12]

Name (degree)	*Notable books or reports*	*Publication impact**
Irene Osgood Andrews (AB)	*Women Workers in Milwaukee Tanneries* (1909); *Minimum Wage Legislation* (1914); *The Relation of Irregular Employment to the Living Wage for Women* (1915); *Economic Effects of the War upon Women and Children in Great Britain* (1918)	JSTOR hits: 11 Book reviews of Andrews' work: 4 Additionally dozens of articles in *American Labor Legislative Review* Google Scholar citations: 57
Ethel Dietrich (PhD)	*World Trade* (1939); *Far Eastern Trade of the United States* (1940)	JSTOR hits: 8 Articles: 4 (1 *JPE*, and 3 *AER*) Book reviews written by Dietrich: 1 Book reviews of Dietrich's work: 3 Google Scholar citations: 46
Elsie Glück (PhD)	*John Mitchell, Miner, Labor's Bargain with the Gilded Age* (1929); *Labor Movement in the United States 1860–1895* (1929)	JSTOR hits: 7 Book reviews written by Glück: 1 Book reviews of Glück's work: 2 AEA conference program: 1 Google Scholar citations: 60
Constance Kiehel (PhD)	*Unemployment Insurance in Belgium* (1931)	JSTOR hits: 2 Articles: 1 (*AER*) Book reviews of Kiehel's work: 1 Google Scholar citations: 11
Katherine Lumpkin (PhD)	*The South in Progress* (1942); *Child Workers in America* (1936); *The Making of a Southerner* (1947)	JSTOR hits: 9 Articles: 1 (*Phylon*) Book reviews of Lumpkin's work: 5 Google Scholar citations: 2
Emma Lundberg (MA)	*Unto the Least of These: Social Services for Children* (1947)	JSTOR hits: 6 Articles: 1 (*AAAPSS*) Book reviews of Lundberg's work: 5 Google Scholar citations: 20
Theresa Schmid McMahon (PhD)	*Women and Economic Evolution* (1912); *Social and Economic Standards of Living* (1925)	JSTOR hits: 3 Book reviews of McMahon's work: 1 AEA conference program: 1 Google Scholar citations: 36
Elizabeth Paschal (PhD)	Education pedagogy publications, e.g., *Encouraging the Excellent* (1960) Paschal's thesis, *Worker's Equity in His Job*, was not published as a book.	JSTOR hits: 8 AEA conference program: 1 Google Scholar citations: 26
Florence Peterson (MA)	*Alleviation of Unemployment in Wisconsin* (1931) with Don Lescohier; *American Labor Unions* (1945); *Survey of Labor Economics* (1947)	JSTOR hits: 25 Book reviews by Peterson: 3 Book reviews of Peterson's work: 6 Google Scholar citations: 265
Elizabeth Brandeis Raushenbush (PhD)	Co-author of *History of Labor in the United States* (1935) with Don Lescohier; *Organized Labor and Protective Labor Legislation* (1957) Reports: The Migrant Labor Problem in Wisconsin (1962)	JSTOR hits: 6 Articles: 2 (1 *AER*) Book reviews by Brandeis Raushenbush: 4 Book reviews of Brandeis Raushenbush: 2

(continued)

Table 12.2 (continued)

Name (degree)	*Notable books or reports*	*Publication impact**
Raushenbush (cont.)		AEA Conference program: 1 Google Scholar citations: 29 Google Scholar citations to volumes of *History of Labor in the United States* co-authored by Brandeis Raushenbush: 137
Helen Leland Witmer (MA)	*The Field of Parent Education* (1936); *Social Work: An Analysis of a Social Institution* (1942); *Independent Adoptions* (1963)	JSTOR hits: 26 Articles: 6 (1 *QJE*) Google Scholar citations > 400
Helen Sumner Woodbury (PhD)	*Equal Suffrage* (1909); "History of Women in Industry in the United States" (1910); co-author of *Documentary History of American Industrial Society* with Commons (1910); co-author of *History of Labor in the United States* (1918), *Working Children of Boston* (1922)	JSTOR hits: 22 Book reviews written by Sumner Woodbury: 2 Book reviews of Sumner Woodbury's work: 10 Google Scholar citations to works sole-authored by Sumner Woodbury: 1 Google Scholar citations to volumes of *History of Labor in the United States* co-authored by Sumner Woodbury: 769 Google Scholar citations to volumes of *A Documentary History of American Industrial Society* co-authored by Sumner Woodbury: 233

Notes

*JSTOR hits refer to the records returned by the searchable academic database JSTOR when an author's name is entered as the search criterion. JSTOR hits include journal publications, book reviews by, book reviews of, references to, and AEA annual conference participation (paper, discussant, or round table) in economics, political science, and sociology journals. *AER* indicates the *American Economic Review*. *JPE* indicates *Journal of Political Economy*. *QJE* indicates *Quarterly Journal of Economics*. *AAAPSS* is the *Annals of the American Academy of Political and Social Science*.

Wisconsin women authored 11 book reviews, and their books, exclusive of the large joint projects discussed below, received 28 reviews in journals indexed by JSTOR (Table 12.2). That these women had more reviews of than reviews by indicates that they were considered authors in their own right, receiving disciplinary scrutiny. Nearly every review emphasized the strongly Institutional approach taken by Wisconsin women. For example, Amy Hughes wrote of Irene Osgood Andrews' *Economic Effects of the War upon Women and Children in Great Britain* (1918) that "it takes the form of a documentary study of official and other sources of material . . . very naturally it is written from the author's point of view as a person primarily interested in labor legislation" (Hughes 1919, 722). Theresa Schmid McMahon's *Women and Economic Evolution* (1912) was "superficial" and full of typographical errors (*JPE* 1913, 876), Aaron Director found that "Elsie Glück is a very excellent example" of "the recent vogue in biographical literature" (1932, 424). Otherwise, the reviews were not particularly notable for being either unusually positive or negative.

Women were collaborators on significant departmental projects. Irene Osgood Andrews, Elizabeth Brandeis Raushenbush, and Helen Sumner Woodbury contributed to the multi-volume *History of Labor in the United States*, a project supervised by Commons and funded by the American Bureau of Industrial Research. Sumner Woodbury co-authored with Commons *Trade Unionism and Labor Problems* (1905) and parts of the ten-volume *Documentary History of American Industrial Society* (1910–1911). These projects garner more than 1,000 Google Scholar citations and were highly praised in contemporary reviews (Bogart 1910; Cross 1918; Johnson 1910). Though chiding Commons for "his usual modesty" and giving "his assistants . . . full and complete credit for those parts of which they had the writing," Ira Cross appreciated that in "Dr. Helen Sumner's" contribution, the data are more readily available and the story more focused (1918, 668–669). George Barnett (1919, 341) wrote that "Miss Sumner's history of the period from 1827 to 1837 contains a definitive study of the rise and development of workingman's parties – a chapter in the history of American labor hitherto only half written."

Sumner Woodbury also co-authored the Institutionalist textbook *Labor Problems* (1905) with T.S. Adams. The book went through nine editions by 1920 and was the most popular labor economics textbook in the country. Determined an "excellent textbook" that covered women and child labor, immigration, poverty, unemployment, strikes, cooperatives, and labor laws, among its many topics (Cummings 1906, 396). *Labor Problems* did much to advance the Wisconsin Institutionalist position on labor reform by advocating for workday limits, minimum wages, and unemployment insurance. Florence Peterson provided an updated view of the Institutional approach in her *Survey of Labor Economics* (1947). By "historically and descriptively" treating the institutions of labor, the book was an "outstanding success" (Kirkaldy 1948, 200). Peterson's book paved the way for the development of Industrial Relations as an independent field of study (Kaufman 1993).

The varied contributions by women to economic thought and Wisconsin Institutionalism were recognized and appreciated by their peers. Four Wisconsin women presented at the American Economic Association's annual conference (Table 12.2). Another was chosen to serve on the committee to award the first E.A. Karlesen prize given by the American Economic Association for the best paper on a theme. The selection provides evidence of the esteem in which Irene Osgood Andrews was held by the profession, despite only holding a bachelor's degree.[13]

Teaching Institutionalism

Women made significant contributions to training the next generation of Wisconsin Institutionalists and to spreading Wisconsin Institutionalism beyond the boundaries of the state and the confines of the university. Of the 18 women who earned PhDs in economics at Wisconsin before 1940, ten held full-time faculty positions for at least part of their career (Appendix 12.1). Five women were associated with women's colleges, including the prestigious institutions of Mount Holyoke and Bryn Mawr. Others found places in the large state universities of the Midwest and West, including at the University of Washington, Ohio State University, University of Iowa, University of Minnesota, UCLA, and the University of Wisconsin.

A leading figure of Wisconsin Institutionalism by any measure, Elizabeth Brandeis Raushenbush taught at Wisconsin for 42 years. As such, she was important in determining the direction of the department. She aligned herself firmly with the Institutionalist faction of Martin Glaeser, Harold Groves, Selig Perlman, and Edwin Witte. This group guaranteed that Wisconsin remained a center of Institutionalism long after Institutionalism had been marginalized in the profession more generally (Johnson 2015; Rutherford 2011).

As an instructor, Brandeis Raushenbush adopted Commons' teaching strategy, requiring students to "attend hearings and legislative sessions and follow the progress of bills dealing with labor issues" (Raushenbush and Brandeis Raushenbush 1979, 15).[14] She regularly offered courses in economic history, labor economics, and labor legislation, all from a distinctly Institutionalist perspective. The courses "focused on 'government action in relation to labor,' protective legislation and its constitutionality, collective bargaining and its legal status, and the work of the Wisconsin Industrial Commission" (Rutherford 2006, 167).

Teresa Schmid McMahon joined the faculty at the University of Washington after earning her PhD in 1909 for a dissertation completed under Commons and E.A. Ross. In Washington, she was a "thorn of Liberalism in the sides of a conservative U.W. administration" (Theresa Schmid McMahon Papers, Box 1, Folder 1). Schmid McMahon was deeply involved with the Progressive labor movement, including the Socialists Society and the Central Labor Council. In her teaching, she followed the Wisconsin model of having students engage directly in local labor and political activities (Theresa Schmid McMahon Papers, Box 1, Folder 1). Though offered a job at the University of Chicago by Paul Douglas, her lifelong interest in teaching labor activism led her to decline, since she "was never interested in being a theorist" (Howe 1989, 230 and 237). Schmid McMahon recommended several students to graduate work at Wisconsin, including Ewan Clague, who became the Commissioner of Labor Statistics for the U.S. Department of Labor (1946–1965).

Beyond traditional collegiate education, Wisconsin women played a significant role in educating the public on labor issues through worker and summer schools and community outreach programs. The University of Wisconsin Extension School for Workers was established by Commons as a collaboration between the YWCA and the University of Wisconsin to provide summer programs for women factory workers. The schools were designed both to educate workers in fundamentals such as reading and arithmetic and to foster a thorough knowledge of labor laws, unionization, and the rights of workers to agitate for reform. The school was run almost entirely by his female students. Both Genevieve Townsend and Alice Shoemaker administered the program and taught courses. They also worked as field agents, recruiting students and collecting data and information on various industries. The historical importance of the school and its close association with Institutionalism has long been recognized (Schwarztrauber 1950; Hoeveler 2016).

Conflating research, teaching and activism, many Wisconsin-trained women worked in community outreach including settlement houses where the data collected were used to argue for social reform and the inhabitants trained to advocate for change (Appendix 12.1). Wisconsin women were also active in the cooperative movement. Popular among Midwest farmers from the 1870s, the cooperative movement grew to include retail stores, dairies, and banks in the early part of the 20th century. The University of Wisconsin Credit Union emerged out of a line of investigative research conducted by Margaret Pryor Glicksman, particularly her work on the 1927 Uniform Small Loan Law and related legislation. Anna Campbell Davis, "one of the ablest students that have ever been in my [Commons'] classes" was also involved, as were Genevieve Townsend and Alice Shoemaker (University of Wisconsin Credit Union 2011). Women comprised four of nine board members and two of three members of the credit committee; all were Commons' students. Beyond banking services, the credit union provided financial education to the community.

Applying Institutionalism

Institutionalism is defined more by its body of varied types of work – reports, legislation, legal-historical studies, advocacy, speeches – than by a handful of foundational documents.

As a school of thought, Institutionalism went beyond academics to deliberately engage politicians and the public to influence economic policy. Therefore, what constitutes contributions to Wisconsin Institutionalism must be broadly defined to include these applications (Rutherford 2006 and 2011). In doing so, the importance of Wisconsin women in building this body of work becomes apparent. The strong connection between research and political activism can be seen in the careers of many of Commons' female students. Their work for government agencies and for political organizations was thus an important way in which Institutionalism was diffused.

One implication of Commons' emphasis on practical experience and policy reform was "to the young Wisconsin Institutionalist . . . a position in government likely seemed more exciting and important than it would have seemed to a graduate student trained in a more orthodox program" (Biddle 1998, 113–114). Wisconsin graduates of all sexes were more likely than those from comparable schools to spend a portion of their early career years working for government (Biddle 1998). In Commons' obituary, it was reported that more than 30 former students became economists for the federal government (*Milwaukee Journal*, 13 May, 1945, 12). At the annual Commons birthday dinner in 1950, Witte listed some, including several prominent women:

> Commons' students went everywhere and many of them made great contributions . . . [they] have made real contributions of a practical nature to human betterment . . . [including those] whose careers were mainly in the public service . . . Arthur Altmeyer, William Leiserson, Katherine Lenroot, Ewan Clague – and on a state level, Paul Rauschenbush, Maud Swett, and Meredith Givens.
>
> *Genovese 1998, 116*

Their inclusion in the list is indicative of the depth to which women were integrated into the policymaking agenda of the Wisconsin Institutionalists.

Government was the primary employer of more than half of Wisconsin's female economists (Appendix 12.1), more than double the rate at which men from Wisconsin took jobs in government (Biddle 1998).[15] Many worked for the Women's and the Children's Bureaus in Washington, D.C., including Elizabeth Brandeis Raushenbush, Elizabeth Paschal, Helen Witmer, and Marie Correll. Katherine Lenroot became the third Chief of the Children's Bureau and Witmer the Director of the Division of Research. Helen Sumner Woodbury conducted research for various federal government agencies as an independent contractor before joining the Children's Bureau as an industrial expert. She later became the assistant chief and chief investigator (Lobdell 2000). Paschal became the first female division chief at the Social Security Administration, overseeing the Program Planning Branch of the Bureau of Old Age and Survivors Insurance. Florence Peterson spent many years as the director of industrial relations at the Bureau of Labor Statistics. Gertrude Schmidt Weiss was at the Department of Labor along with Ruth Scandrett, who was their senior industrial economist. Margaret Smith worked at the Bureau of Human Nutrition and Home Economics and for the Department of Agriculture; Margaret Purcell also worked for the Department of Agriculture. Wisconsin economists also had a high profile at the U.S. Department of Labor, the Bureau of Labor Statistics, and the Social Security Administration as well as at the Industrial Commission of Wisconsin.[16]

In these positions, Wisconsin women used Institutional methods and insights to foster reform. The influence of Wisconsin Institutionalism can be seen in the studies conducted and the collection of expansive data sets. Many Wisconsin women, such as Elizabeth Paschal and Helen Witmer, started their government careers as researchers, hired based on their field work experience at Wisconsin. Katherine Lenroot and Emma Lundberg oversaw extensive surveys on the juvenile court system for the Children's Bureau. Lundberg's *Public Aid to Mothers with Dependent Children* (1928) reported on data collected about the women and children in various government programs, identifying ages, locations, and programs used. She also looked at aid in relation to standards of living. She did a similar analysis for the state of New York. She also wrote a number of government handbooks (1927). Florence Peterson wrote a definitive history of strikes in the United States, chronicling more than 80 separate incidences for the Bureau of Labor Statistics (1938). These projects were leveraged to influence policy makers and to underpin legislation (Rutherford 2011). Wisconsin women were almost exclusively responsible for the development and implementation of New Deal programs for women and children.[17]

Besides those working in government, many other Wisconsin women applied Institutionalist theory and methods by writing legislation. Elizabeth Brandeis Raushenbush was a co-author of the nation's first unemployment insurance program, the Wisconsin Unemployment Reserves Act (1934), and she assisted in drafting significant portions of the Social Security Act. Emma Lundberg later added the child welfare provisions to the Act. Katherine Lenroot made substantial contributions to the minimum wage law in Wisconsin and to Aid to Dependent Children (Title V and VI of the Social Security Act). Both Irene Osgood Andrews and Teresa Schmid McMahon contributed to state-level minimum wage legislation, limits to the working day, maternity policies, and labor law enforcement. As part of this, each served on state-level minimum wage boards.

Applications of Institutionalism came not only from within government but also from organizations attempting to change government. The academic research conducted by Wisconsin economists was meant to support labor reform, and the two often went hand-in-hand. Many women worked as contract researchers for the A.A.L.L., whose organizational brief was to craft progressive labor legislation on worker rights, worker safety, and unemployment and social insurance programs (Kaufman 2003; Leonard 2016). A major contributor, the A.A.L.L. relied on Irene Osgood Andrews as the long-time assistant secretary. Osgood Andrews wrote extensively on labor issues for *American Legislative Labor Review* as part of her job, directly influencing labor laws on maternity leave, minimum wages, factory inspections, and child labor.

Though only obliquely glimpsed, it is evident that while women lacked opportunities generally, Wisconsin was one place where there were a large number of women studying economics and where women were given real opportunities to practice economics. Commons' particular teaching and working methods meant that undergraduate and graduate students got experience in field research, writing legislation, and policy making. This created skills as well as opportunities, though primarily in government agencies. Whether government and organizations such as the A.A.L.L. were the preferred choices for employment by Wisconsin women, or became the choice because the opportunities in academics were few, is unknown.

Women and the decline of Wisconsin Institutionalism

By the end of the Second World War, Wisconsin Institutionalism was in decline. Wisconsin had lost its position in the national departmental rankings (Lampman 1993). Wisconsin faculty dropped from seventh to eleventh in terms of the share of publications in the *American Economic*

Review; publications by Wisconsin PhDs in top journals fell precipitously (Backhouse 1998). Increasingly, Wisconsin was finding it difficult to place graduates in good positions (Johnson 2015; Lampman 1993; Rutherford 2011).[18] Rutherford (2011 and 2016) suggests that several factors were at play in Wisconsin's decline: the rise of Keynesianism and mathematical economics, Wisconsin Institutionalism's lack of a theoretical core, Wisconsin's tendency to hire their own students, and the central importance of Commons' personality. Others attribute competition from Sociology, Industrial Relations, and Social Work to siphoning off talent from the economics program (Kaufman 1993). That so many Wisconsin-trained economists chose government over academia has been cited as another reason for the decline of Wisconsin Institutionalism, as fewer academics were available to train subsequent generations (Backhouse 1998; Biddle 1998). The history of Wisconsin's women economists offers useful insights for understanding the relative importance of these various factors in explaining the decline of Wisconsin Institutionalism.

As a preliminary step, it is necessary to consider why women came to study at Wisconsin in the first place. The women who enrolled at Wisconsin were much less likely to be local than their male counterparts, and hence chose to go to Wisconsin, not out of convenience, but for other reasons. Looming large was Commons' national reputation. Elizabeth Paschal stated that "that's really why I went to the University of Wisconsin, to do graduate study with John R. Commons" (1996, 103). Teresa Schmid McMahon, Elizabeth Brandeis Raushenbush, and Jean Scobie Davis make the same claim (Lampman 1993; Davis 2014). New York socialite Evelyn Preston chose to pursue a Masters' degree at Wisconsin because of her interest in labor reform and the institution's association with Commons (Tamboukou 2017).

Commons provided the energy and central focus for the department for nearly 20 years, which was much missed following his retirement in 1933. Wisconsin Institutionalism correspondingly lost much of its identity and impetus for innovation. Reflective of these changes, the number of women doctoral students at Wisconsin dwindled to nearly zero, though the numbers at Columbia, Chicago, Harvard and other institutions grew. Between 1935 and 1940, the immediate period following Commons' retirement, Wisconsin reported three women doctoral candidates to the *AER* list. Columbia reported 79, Chicago reported 34, Harvard reported 35, and all other institutions combined reported 85 women doctoral candidates. That Wisconsin was no longer able to attract some of the great woman scholars of the era meant fewer publications and fewer qualified candidates for academic and high-level government positions over the next decade.

A second factor at the intersection of the story of Wisconsin women and the decline of Wisconsin Institutionalism was competition from newly established fields in Industrial Relations and Social Work (Kaufman 1993). While there was overlap between economics generally and these fields, the extent of the overlap of interest was much more strongly evident at Wisconsin than at other top programs. Formidable scholars and activists who had trained under Commons, including Helen Clarke, Helen Witmer, and Katherine Lumpkin became increasingly associated with Social Work, and Florence Peterson with Industrial Relations. In the process, their publications moved out of economic journals and into journals related to these new fields. Their books were reviewed in *Social Forces*, the *American Journal of Sociology*, the *British Journal of Sociology*, *American Sociological Review*, *Journal of Educational Sociology*, and the *Journal of Health and Human Behavior*.

Compounding the problem, the University of Wisconsin established its School for Social Work in 1946, which was spun off from the Economics Department, taking faculty, students, and resources (Lampman 1993). Social Work doctoral degree candidates were entirely women for the school's first decade. Whether this was by choice or by encouragement is unknown; but it is apparent from the Graduation Bulletins that women interested in topics at the intersection of economics, sociology, and social reform were matriculating in the School for Social Work rather than the Economics Department.

A third and more controversial explanation centers on the employment options for Wisconsin-trained women economists. Commons invested time and resources in the intellectual development of his women students. This paid off in their contributions to his research agenda and in terms of effecting labor and social reform in government. However, to carry on as a strong academic program, sufficient students must be placed in academia in economics departments. During this period, there were few opportunities for women to achieve good placements at ranking institutions that trained graduate students. Elizabeth Paschal, for example, was frustrated by the lack of opportunities for women in academia and thus went to work in government (Paschal 1996, 37–38). Even the women surveyed here who had opportunities at top-ranking institutions were often not teaching graduate students (Grace Zorbaugh, Katherine Lumpkin), did not supervise PhD students (Elizabeth Brandeis Raushenbush, Theresa Schmid McMahon), or worked in departments other than economics (Katherine Lumpkin, Margaret Schaffner, Helen Witmer).

While evidence supporting the "failure to replicate" hypothesis is highly mixed for men (Biddle 1998), it is apparent that many talented women graduates went to work in government where they were less likely to publish in economics journals or to train new Institutionalists. As Elizabeth Paschal (1996, 126) noted: "I had a doctorate in labor economics and had worked for the American Federation of Labor. But I was not working as an economist particularly" at the U.S. Department of Labor.

Conclusions

This chapter examines the contributions made by women economists to Wisconsin Institutionalism. They did so through their publications, their teaching, and their applications in government, legislative work, and social reform efforts. They also did so by disproportionately exhibiting many of the features used to distinguish Wisconsin Institutionalists – a focus on labor economics, empiricism, policy and legislative activism, as well as a tendency to be employed in government (Leonard 2016; Johnson 2015; Rutherford 2011). Thus, Wisconsin-trained women both reinforced perceptions of what Wisconsin Institutionalism was and played a pivotal role in diffusing the Institutional viewpoint.

Their story also uniquely contributes to our understanding of the reasons for the decline of Wisconsin Institutionalism in the post-war period. Lacking a theoretical core or a clearly defined methodology, Wisconsin Institutionalism's success was in the volume of work created under Commons and the ability of Commons and his students to motivate labor and social reforms. Once Commons retired, the central core of what could be defined as Wisconsin Institutionalism lacked his stabilizing influence and fragmented. Wisconsin's brand of economics became diluted until it was no longer clearly recognized as economic theory proper. While many factors played a role, the stories of Wisconsin's women economists illustrate the importance of Commons for recruiting students, the role competition from new fields of study played, and the impact of placing few students in academic jobs in economics on publications for the field of economics. The loss of these women thus both contributed to Wisconsin's decline and was reflective of it.

Appendix 12.1 Summary of contributions by women to Wisconsin Institutionalism

Name *Degree and date*	*Dissertation title* *Number of publications listed in Google Scholar*	*Government and legislative work*	*Applications and activism*	*Academic or related positions*
Irene Osgood Andrews (1879–1963) AB 1905	— 11 She wrote extensively for the *American Labor Legislative Review*	National Industrial Commission With the A.A.L.L.: minimum wages, working conditions, factory inspections, maternity policies	Associated Charities in Minneapolis, Red Cross, Northwestern Settlement, University Settlement House in Milwaukee	—
Helen Page Bates (1870–1933) PhD 1896	State Irrigation in the Australian Colonies 1	—	Hull House, Goodrich House	Lecturer at Wisconsin, Professor of Economics at Rockford College, Librarian for Dept. of Economics, UC Berkeley
Anna Campbell Davis (1896–1991) PhD 1927	Law and Economics in the Commodity Transaction —	District Supervisor Family Relief Agency in Illinois, Women's Division of Wisconsin Civil Works, Wisconsin Committee on Women's Employment	Women's suffrage movement, YWCA, ACLU, and Women's International League for Peace and Freedom, Madison Consumer's Cooperative, University of Wisconsin Credit Union	—
Jean Scobie Davis (1892–1985) PhD 1929	Labor Management in Southern Cotton Mills —	New York State Correctional Facility, Board of Visitors to the New York State Reformatory for Women	Settlement houses in NYC, summer camp for low-wage workers, field work on the development of professional social work in the south and investigator of prison conditions in the U.K., Russia and Finland	Professor of Economics at Wells College; also instructor/assistant professor at Agnes Scott College, Bryn Mawr Summer School for Women Workers, Vassar College, Piece College and the American Women's College in Beirut
Ethel Dietrich (1891– unknown) PhD 1921	Collective Bargaining in the Book and Job Printing Industry 13	Unknown	Unknown	Professor of Economics at Mount Holyoke

(continued)

Appendix 12.1 (continued)

Name *Degree and date*	*Dissertation title* *Number of publications listed in Google Scholar*	*Government and legislative work*	*Applications and activism*	*Academic or related positions*
Margaret Pryor Glicksman (1894–1972) PhD 1927	Place of Consumption in Economic Theory 1	War Industry Commission Research and report to support the 1927 Uniform Small Loan Law, resulted in state bills in 1931	First board member and director for University of Wisconsin Credit Union, Madison League of Women Voters	Instructor of Economics at Wisconsin (until 1936 when forced to retire due to anti-nepotism laws)
Elsie Glück (1908–1997) PhD 1929	John Mitchell, Miner: Labor's Bargain with the Gilded Age 8	Works Progress Administration	International Ladies' Garment Workers' Union, other women's trade unions	Part-time instructor at the New School for Social Research
Constance Kiehel (unknown) PhD 1935	Unemployment Insurance in Belgium 11	Division of Research and Statistics, Social Security Board	Unknown	—
Katherine Lenroot (1896–1984) BA 1912	— 30 Primarily Children's Bureau Reports and articles on Children's health, education, and safety	WI State Industrial Commission, Children's Bureau (including Chief), Advisory Committee of Social Questions, League of Nations, consultant to the United Nations WI Minimum Wage, Reform of Juvenile Care, Children's Welfare, developed Aid to Dependent Children (Title V and VI of Social Security)	President of the National Conference of Social Work, various positions with the League of Nations on children's welfare, created the United Nations International Children's Emergency Fund, Secretary to the UN on issues of child welfare	—
Katherine Lumpkin (1897–1988) PhD in Sociology in 1928 (Commons on Committee)	Social Situations and Girl Delinquency: A Study of the Commitments to the Wisconsin Industrial School 2	State Board of Directors for Citizen's Association for Justice	YWCA National Student Secretary, activist against racial oppression, League of Women Voters	Instructor Mount Holyoke, post-doctoral research fellow at Social Science Research Council, Research Director of the Council of Industrial Studies of Smith College, Professor of Sociology at Wells College, extension instructor University of Virginia

Emma Octavia Lundberg (1881–1954) MA 1914	— 20	Industrial Commission of Wisconsin, Director of the Social Services Division of the Children's Bureau, Director of Research and Statistics at the New York Temporary Emergency Relief Administration Social Security Act (children welfare provisions)	Children's Welfare League of America	—
Theresa Schmid McMahon (1878–1963) PhD 1909	Evolution of Home Industry and its Effects upon Women 4	WA Minimum Wage Board, National Advisory Board on Social Security WA state minimum wage, 8-hour work day, women's labor rights	Hull House	Professor of Economics, University of Washington
Jane Newell (unknown) PhD 1908	The Women's Christian Temperance Union 2	—	—	Professor of Economics at Wellesley College
Elizabeth Paschal (1903–1997?) PhD 1933	Worker's Equity in His Job 3	Economist at the Bureau of Home Economics, U.S. Department of Labor Statistics, U.S. Department of Agriculture, Social Security Administration	Ford Foundation	Occasional Professor, Marietta College, Eureka College, New Jersey College for Women
Florence Peterson (1881–1968) MA 1930	— 3	Wisconsin State Industrial Commission, Bureau of Labor Statistics	—	—

(continued)

Appendix 12.1 (continued)

Name *Degree and date*	*Dissertation title* *Number of publications listed in Google Scholar*	*Government and legislative work*	*Applications and activism*	*Academic or related positions*
Elizabeth Brandeis Raushenbush (1896–1984) PhD 1928	Wage Earner and the Common Rule 11	Minimum Wage Board, Wisconsin State Industrial Commission, Social Security Board, Migratory Labor in WI, Labor Department's Advisory Committee on Young Workers WI state unemployment insurance law; national unemployment insurance, Social Security law	—	Lecturer then Professor of Economics at Wisconsin
Margaret Schaffner (unknown) PhD 1902	Labor Contract with Collective Bargaining 2	—	—	Instructor of Economics and Sociology at the University of Iowa
Alice Shoemaker (1892–1973) MA 1927	— —	US Department of Labor Women's labor rights, women's education	First volunteer member of the University of Wisconsin Union's Credit Committee, YWCA	Wisconsin Extension School for Workers, Summer Schools for Working Women/ Industrial Workers, Director of Program
Maude Swett (1895–1964) MA 1912	— 1	Director of the Women and Child Division of the Wisconsin State Industrial Commission Children's welfare laws, family welfare laws	—	—

Genevieve Townsend (1901–1966) MA 1933 (?)	— 1	Supervisor of the Public Welfare Departments	Study of small money loans in Wisconsin, including investigative field work on banks, employer's plans, pawnbrokers, etc. Industrial Secretary YWCA, Secretary-Treasurer of Local Union 223 of the American Federation of Teachers	Research Assistant for Wisconsin Department of Economics, Summer School for Industrial Workers
Jennie Turner (unknown) PhD 1922	The Right to Organize 4	Supervisor of Teacher Training for the State Board of Education in Wisconsin	Women's rights, apprentice education	Courses for the State Board of Vocational and Adult Education
Gertrude Schmidt Weiss (unknown) PhD 1933	History of Labor Legislation in Wisconsin —	U.S. Department of Labor & Bureau of Home Economics Extensive government reports on family income and expenditures	—	—
Helen Witmer (1898–1979) MA 1925	— 78	Massachusetts Division of Corrections, Director of Research for the United State Children's Bureau	Director of fact-finding for the White House Conference on Children and Youth	Assistant Professor of Sociology at the University of Minnesota, Director of Research at the Smith College School for Social Work, UCLA
Helen Sumner Woodbury (1876–1933) PhD 1908	The Labor Movement in America, 1827–1837 28	Contract Government Work, Children's Bureau	—	—
Grace M. Zorbaugh (dates unknown) PhD 1926	Commuted Awards in Wisconsin Workmen's Compensation 5	—	Industrial investigations, credit unions, employment cooperatives	Associate Professor of Economics and Dean of Women, The Ohio State University

Notes

1 An estimate of the absolute numbers of women pursuing doctoral degrees in economics across institutions can be made from the *American Economic Review*'s (*AER*) "Lists of Doctoral Dissertations in Political Economy in Progress in American Universities and Colleges." Between 1910 and 1932, Wisconsin had 25 women doctoral candidates in economics. Columbia had 72, Chicago had 57 and Harvard/Radcliffe had 42. Only 71 women pursued PhDs at all other institutions combined.

2 Elizabeth Paschal remembered "Commons was, of course, a very unusual man. He had his graduate students come to his house about once a week for dinner, all the graduate students . . . [it was] a very inspiring and interesting situation" (1996, 30).

3 Twenty-five of these women are detailed in Appendix 12.1.

4 Helen Stuart Campbell's experience at Wisconsin is illustrative of the difficulties faced by women in this early period. A social reformer, popular lecturer, and activist in the settlement house movement, evidences many of the interests of the Wisconsin Institutionalists.

Stuart Campbell came to study at Wisconsin with Ely in 1893. During this time, Ely wrote the introduction to her book, *Women Wage-Earners* (1893), which had previously won the AEA essay competition in 1891. Ely persuaded the university regents to invite Campbell to give a series of lectures, which she did in the spring of 1895. These were published as *Household Economics* (1897). However, despite Ely's efforts, the university did not offer Stuart Campbell a permanent position. See Davis (2000) for details.

5 In addition to the 17 PhDs listed by Lampman (1993), I identify Jane Newell from the University of Wisconsin Graduation Bulletin for 1908. Kirsten Madden (2002) reports Wisconsin granted 26 PhDs to women with dissertation titles associated with economic concepts between 1900 and 1940. Some of the difference is likely attributable to degrees issued by related departments such as Sociology, Social Work, Business or Home Economics.

6 Out of the 48 dissertations overseen by Commons (42 percent of the total at Wisconsin during this period), 30 dealt directly with labor issues. Ten of these were produced by women (out of 12 by women in total).

7 These include Caroline MacGill on unpaid services (1910), Roberta Pritchard on heredity in relation to the control of defectives (1910), Rhonda White (Wisconsin AB) on the morality of the city population (1910), Emma Lundberg (Wisconsin BA, MA) on personal inefficiency as related to family and social conditions (1911), Roberta Hodgson (Wisconsin BA) on types and traits of Negros of Athens, Georgia (1911), Katherine Lumpkin on social situations and girl delinquency (1928), Marie Correll on the paper industry in its technological business and labor aspects (1930), and Ruth Dunham (Wisconsin BA, MA) on the relation between tobacco cultivation and western land speculation (1940). The last three were listed as completed by *AER* but were not listed in the University of Wisconsin Graduation Bulletin.

8 Ely reported that his daughter was studying for a PhD in economics (Ely 1938, 205), but it was apparently not completed. Ely Morehouse became a notable proponent of racial justice and, as part of her activities, published a revised version of *Social Problems, A Study of Present Day Conditions* (1931) with Ezra Thayer Towne.

9 Additional women trained by Commons and holding Master's or undergraduate degrees who taught economics courses at Wisconsin include Alma Bridgeman, Mary Shine Peterson, Miriam Frye, Irene Hensey, and Helen Clarke (Lampman 1993, 292). It should be noted that women were much more likely to be placed in secretarial and administrative-assistant jobs and less likely to be recommended to the NBER or to receive grant funding.

10 It is difficult to achieve good estimates of the number of women earning undergraduate degrees in economics at Wisconsin because the university did not list students by major in the graduation bulletins until 1921 and then only sporadically thereafter.

11 Rosalind Tough (BA and MA from Wisconsin 1924, 1925) earned her PhD at Northwestern. Frieda Figelman and Nina Miller earned their undergraduate degrees from Wisconsin (1909, 1915) and their PhDs from Columbia (1915, 1921).

12 Grace Zorbaugh and Gertrude Schmidt Weiss each had two hits, one reference for their dissertation and one for AEA membership. Jean Scobie Davis had her dissertation listed. Margaret Schaffner had one publication in the *AAAPSS*.

13 The prize was established to offer $1,500 for the best essay on the subject of "What can a man afford?" Somewhat ironically, the first award was shared by Paul and Dorothy Douglas (Fetter 1921, v–vi). Osgood Andrews served on the committee with James Tufts, Professor of Philosophy at the University of Chicago, and Frank Fetter, Professor of Political Economy at Princeton.

14 Commons required undergraduates in his labor economics course to conduct research in support of new legislation and to testify in local or state hearings as part of the course requirements. Katherine Lenroot believed that her experience preparing a minimum wage brief and testifying before the state legislature led to her first job with the Wisconsin State Industrial Commission (Biographical Note, Katherine Lenroot Papers).

15 One difficulty with chronicling the careers of women economists is that they were more likely to be part-time or engaged in contract work than men during this period. Many of the women trained at Wisconsin held multiple and sometimes overlapping jobs. For example, Elsie Glück not only worked for the Works Progress Administration (WPA), she also taught courses in Labor and Contemporary American Economics for the New School for Social Research.

16 Elizabeth Paschal credited her first position to the Wisconsin network in D.C. "I suppose someone from the University of Wisconsin recommended me for it. There were a number of people in the Bureau of Labor Statistics who had graduated from Wisconsin" (1996, 45).

17 Details on the development and adoption of such programs can be found in Leonard (2016).

18 Martin Bronfenbrenner placed some of the blame on Alma Bridgeman, a Wisconsin MA and the department secretary, for recommending "inferior graduate students to good places" (in Lampman 1993, 136). Another loyal Commons supporter, Bridgeman played a significant role in assigning teaching assistantships, allocating fellowships, and recommending graduate students for employment outside the university. Bronfenbrenner's claim is representative of his personal antipathy to Bridgman and his general dislike of Institutionalism (Johnson 2015).

References

Adams, T.S. and Helen Sumner. 1905 (and later editions). *Labor Problems: A Textbook*. New York: MacMillan & Co. Ltd.

American Association for Labor Legislation Records. 1905–1943. Kheel Center for Labor-Management Documentation and Archives, Cornell University Library.

Andrews, Irene Osgood. 1918. *Economic Effects of the War upon Women and Children in Great Britain*. New York: Oxford University Press.

Backhouse, Roger. 1998. "The Transformation of U.S. Economics, 1920–1960, Viewed through a Survey of Journal Articles," *History of Political Economy* 30 (Supplement): 85–107.

Barbash, Jack. 1993. "Commons as a Labor Economist," in *Economists at Wisconsin: 1892–1992*, ed. R. Lampmann, 69–71. Madison, WI: The Board of Regents of the University of Wisconsin System.

Barnett, George. 1919. "Review: *History of Labor in the United States*," *American Economic Review* 9 (2): 340–342.

Biddle, Jeff. 1998. "Institutional Economics: A Case of Reproductive Failure?" *History of Political Economy* 30 (Supplement): 108–133.

Bogart, Ernest. 1910. "Review: *A Documentary History of American Industrial Society* by John R. Commons, Helen L. Sumner," *The Economic Bulletin* 3 (4): 414–416.

Boulding, Kenneth. 1957. "A New Look at Institutionalism," *American Economic Review* 47 (2): 1–12.

Campbell, Helen Stuart. 1893. *Women Wage Earners: Their Past, Their Present, and Their Future*. Boston, MA: Roberts Brothers.

Campbell, Helen Stuart. 1897. *Household Economics*. New York: G.P. Putnam's Sons.

Commons, John R. 1924. *Legal Foundations of Capitalism*. New York: Macmillan.

Commons, John R. 1934. *Institutional Economics*. New York: Macmillan.

Commons, John R. and Helen Sumner [Woodbury]. 1905. *Trade Unionism and Labour Problems*. New York: Ginn & Co.

Commons, John R., Ulrich Philips, Eugene Gilmore, Helen Sumner, and John Andrews. 1910–1911. *A Documentary History of American Industrial Society*, 10 Volumes. Cleveland, OH: Arthur H. Clark, Co.

Commons, John R., David Saposs, Helen Sumner, Edward Mittleman, Henry Hoagland, John Andrews, and Selig Perlman. 1918. *History of Labor in the United States*, 2 Volumes. New York: Macmillan.

Cross, Ira. 1918. "Review: *History of Labor in the United States*," *Quarterly Journal of Economics* 32 (4): 667–673.

Cummings, John. 1906. "Review: *Labor Problems*: A Textbook by Thomas Sewall Adams; Helen Sumner," *Journal of Political Economy* 14 (6): 396–399.

Davis, Jean Scobie. 2014. Jean Scobie Davis Papers, 1892–1985. Bryn Mawr College. Available at: http://dla.library.upenn.edu/dla/pacscl/ead.pdf?id=PACSCL_BMC_USPBmBMCM85

Davis, John. 2000. "Helen Stuart Campbell," in *Biographical Dictionary of Women Economists*, eds. R. Dimand, M. Dimand, and E. Forget, 101–103. Cheltenham, UK: Edward Elgar.

Dietrich, Ethel. 1939. *World Trade*. New York: Henry Holt.

Director, Aaron. 1932. "Review: *John Mitchell, Miner: Labor's Bargain with the Gilded Age* by Elise Glück," *Journal of Political Economy* 40 (3): 424–427.

Dzuback, Mary Ann. 2006. "Berkeley Women Economists, Public Policy, and Civic Sensibility," in *Civic and Moral Learning in America*, eds. D. Warren and J. Patrick, 153–171. New York: Palgrave Macmillan.

Ely, Richard T. 1938. *Ground under Our Feet: An Autobiography*. New York: Macmillan.

Fetter, Frank A. 1921. "Two Essays Awarded the Karelsen Prizes by the American Economic Association," *American Economic Review* 11 (4): v–vii.

Froman, Lewis A. 1942. "Graduate Students in Economics, 1904–1940," *American Economic Review* 32 (4): 817–826.

Genovese, Frank. 1998. "In Memoriam: Robert J. Lampman, 1920–1997," *American Journal of Economics and Sociology* 57 (1): 115–120.

Glück, Elsie. 1929. *John Mitchell, Miner: Labor's Bargain with the Gilded Age*. New York: John Day Co.

Hammond, Claire. 1993. "American Women and the Professionalization of Economics," *Review of Social Economy* 51 (4): 347–370.

Hoeveler, J. David. 2016. *John Bascom and the Origins of the Wisconsin Idea*. Madison, WI: University of Wisconsin Press.

Howe, Florence. 1989. "Practical in Her Theories: Theresa Schmid McMahon," in *Lone Voyagers: Academic Women in Coeducational Universities 1870–1937*, ed. G.J. Clifford, 223–280. New York: The Feminist Press at the City University of New York.

Hughes, Amy. 1919. "Review: *Economic Effects of the War upon Women and Children in Great Britain* by Irene Osgood Andrews," *Journal of Political Economy* 27 (8): 722–724.

Johnson, Emory. 1910. "Review: *A Documentary History of American Industrial Society* by John R. Commons, Ulrich B. Phillips, Eugene A. Gilmore, Helen L. Sumner, John B. Andrews," *Annals of the American Academy of Political and Social Science* 36 (2): 211–216.

Johnson, Marianne. 2011. "Public Finance and Wisconsin Institutionalism, 1892–1929," *Journal of Economic Issues* 45 (4): 967–985.

Johnson, Marianne. 2015. "Harold Groves, Wisconsin Institutionalism, and Postwar Public Finance," *Journal of Economic Issues* 49 (6): 691–710.

Jonçich Clifford, Geraldine. 1989. *Lone Voyagers: Academic Women in Coeducational Institutions, 1870–1937*. New York, NY: The Feminist Press.

Journal of Political Economy. 1913. "Review: *Women and Economic Evolution* by Theresa Schmid McMahon," *Journal of Political Economy* 21 (9): 876.

Kato, Ken. 2009. "American Unemployment Insurance Schemes of the 1910s: J.R. Commons, J.B. Andrews, and I.M. Rubinow," *History of Economic Thought* 50 (2): 38–55.

Kaufman, Bruce. 1993. *The Origins and Evolution of the Field of Industrial Relations in the United States*. Ithaca, NY: Cornell University Press.

Kaufman, Bruce. 2003. "John R. Commons and the Wisconsin School on industrial Relations Strategy and Policy," *Industrial and Labor Relations Review* 56: 324–348.

Kirkaldy, H.S. 1948. "Review: *Survey of Labor Economics* by Florence Peterson," *Economic Journal* 58 (230): 260–262.

Lampman, Robert. 1993. *Economists at Wisconsin: 1892–1992*. Madison, WI: The Board of Regents of the University of Wisconsin System.

Lenroot, Katherine. 1909–1974. "Katherine F. Lenroot Papers," Archival Collections, Rare Book and Manuscript Library, Columbia University Libraries. Available at: www.columbia.edu/cu/lweb/archival/collections/ldpd_4079022/

Leonard, Thomas C. 2016. *Illiberal Reformers: Race, Eugenics, and American Economics in the Progressive Era*. New Haven, CT: Princeton University Press.

Libby, Barbara. 1990. "Women in the Economics Profession, 1900–1940: Factors in their Declining Visibility," *Essays in Economic and Business History*, Volume VIII. E. Perkins, ed. South Carolina: University of South Carolina History Department.

Lobdell, Richard. 2000. "Helen Laura Sumner Woodbury (1876–1933)," in *A Biographical Dictionary of Women Economists*, eds. M. Dimand, R. Dimand, and E. Forget, 470–471. Northampton, MA: Edward Elgar.

Lundberg, Emma. 1927. *Handbook for the Use of Boards of Directors, Superintendents, and Staffs of Institutions for Dependent Children*. Washington, DC: U.S. Government Printing Office.
Lundberg, Emma. 1928. *Public Aid to Mothers with Dependent Children, Extent and Fundamental Principles*. Washington, DC: U.S. Government Printing Office.
Madden, Kirsten. 2002. "Female Contributions to Economic Thought, 1900–1940," *History of Political Economy* 34 (1): 1–30.
McMahon, Theresa Schmid. 1889–1960. *Theresa Schmid McMahon Papers*. Special Collections, University of Washington.
McMahon, Theresa Schmid. 1912. *Women and Economic Evolution*. Madison, WI: Bulletin of the University of Wisconsin.
Morehouse, Anna Ely and Ezra Towne Taylor. 1931. *Social Problems: A Study of Present-Day Social Conditions*. New York, NY: Macmillan Company.
Nearing, Nellie Marguerite Seeds. 1910. "Review: *Equal Suffrage* by Helen Sumner," *Annals of the American Academy of Political and Social Science* 35 (2): 259–260.
Paschal, Elizabeth. 1996. "Pioneering Career Woman: New Deal Labor Economist, Social Security Administration Program Chief, Ford Foundation Executive," an Oral History Conducted in 1955 by the West Bay Wellesley Club, Inc. and the Regional Oral History Office, The Bancroft Library, University of California, Berkeley. Available at: http://digitalassets.lib.berkeley.edu/roho/ucb/text/paschal_elizabeth.pdf
Peterson, Florence. 1930. *A History of Shoe Workers' Organizations with Especial Reference to Ohio, Missouri, Illinois, and Wisconsin*. MA Thesis. University of Wisconsin, Madison.
Peterson, Florence. 1938. *Strikes in the United States, 1880–1936*. Washington, DC: U.S. Government Printing Office.
Peterson, Florence. 1947. *Survey of Labor Economics*. New York, NY: Harper and Brothers.
Phelps, D.M. 1940. "Review: *World Trade* by Ethel Dietrich," *Journal of Political Economy* 48 (3): 460–461.
Raushenbush, Paul and Elizabeth Brandeis Papers. 1918–1980. Wisconsin Historical Society Archives.
Rutherford, Malcolm. 2006. "Wisconsin Institutionalism: John R. Commons and His Students," *Labor History* 47 (2): 161–188.
Rutherford, Malcolm. 2011. *The Institutional Movement in American Economics, 1918–1947*. New York: Cambridge University Press.
Rutherford, Malcolm. 2015. "American Institutionalism After 1945," *Research in the History of Economic Thought and Methodology* 33: 95–123.
Schwarztrauber, Ernest. 1950. "University of Wisconsin School for Workers," *ILR Review* 3 (4): 542–547.
Sumner, Helen [later Woodbury]. 1909. *Equal Suffrage*. New York: Harper Brothers.
Tamboukou, Maria. 2017. *Women Workers' Education, Life Narratives and Politics*. London: Palgrave Macmillan.
Tilman, Rick. 2008. "John R. Commons, the New Deal and the American Tradition of Empirical Collectivism," *Journal of Economic Issues* 42 (3): 823–851.
University of Wisconsin Credit Union. 2011. "Celebrating Our Founders and the Wisconsin Idea." Available at: www.uwcu.org/media/1502/our-founders.pdf
University of Wisconsin Graduation Bulletins. 1892–1940. Madison, WI: University of Wisconsin.
Wisconsin Catalogue and Bulletin. 1890–1930. Madison, WI: University of Wisconsin.

13

WOMEN ECONOMISTS OF PROMISE?

Six Hart, Schaffner and Marx Prize winners in the early twentieth century[1]

Kirsten Madden

Fifty-three monographs with publication dates between 1907 and 1932 received the Hart, Schaffner, and Marx Prize in the U.S.A. In the opinion of a 1929 book reviewer:

> The cult of competitions is widespread today, but few of the winning plays, poems, and plans for peace, prosperity or prohibition have won much approval. In one field, however, a competition has thoroughly justified its existence, for the Hart, Schaffner and Marx Prize Essays have consistently, during the last twenty years, been valuable contributions to economic literature, and many of their authors have subsequently stepped to the very front of the academic field.[2]

The Hart, Schaffner, and Marx Prize provided financial incentives to encourage study of economics. First prize included a $1,000 award, second prize a $500 award. The annual award committee consisted of three to five members, typically filled by the following men: J. Laurence Laughlin of the University of Chicago, J.B. Clark and Wesley C. Mitchell, both of Columbia University, Edwin F. Gay, in association with Harvard University and the *New York Evening Post*, Theodore E. Burton of Washington D.C., Henry C. Adams of the University of Michigan, and Horace White of New York City.

Frank Knight, Edwin Nourse, Harold Moulton, and Edgar Furniss are a few of the men who won either first or second prize, and Simon Kuznets received honorable mention. Major journals such as the *American Economic Review* announced the prize winners each year. An award-winning series with the Hart, Schaffner, and Marx label provided publication exposure for the award recipients. The award-winning books often received academic journal reviews.

Eleven percent of the 53 Hart, Marx, and Schaffner award winners were women.[3] The first woman to receive the award was Yetta Scheftel in 1915; the final woman to receive the award was Alma Herbst in 1930. Table 13.1 lists the six women prize winners by name and university affiliation for each prize winner's doctoral studies, thesis title, year receiving the award, and prize recognition level.

All but one woman earned her Ph.D. from the University of Chicago, the institutional home of prize committee chairman, J.L. Laughlin. A prize committee member was the thesis director

Table 13.1 Women winning the Hart, Schaffner and Marx Prize[i] in the U.S.A.[ii]

Name & university affiliation (doctorate)	*Thesis title*	*Award year*	*Recognition level*
Yetta Scheftel (Univ. of Chicago)	The taxation of land value; a study of certain discriminatory taxes on land	1915	1st prize
Hazel Kyrk (Univ. of Chicago)	A theory of consumption	1921	1st prize
Mollie Ray Carroll (Univ. of Chicago)	Labor and politics; the attitude of the American Federation of Labor toward legislation and politics	1922	Honorable mention
Helen Fisher Hohman (Univ. of Chicago)	The development of social insurance and minimum wage legislation in Great Britain; a study of British social legislation in relation to a minimum standard of living	1928	1st prize
Caroline Ware (Radcliffe College)	The early New England cotton manufacture; a study in industrial beginnings	1929	1st prize
Alma Herbst (Univ. of Chicago)	The Negro in the slaughtering and meat-packing industry in Chicago	1930	2nd prize

[i] All six of these women received a Hart, Schaffner and Marx Class A award, which "included any American without restriction." Class B awards targeted undergraduate research.

[ii] Women received awards for their economic thought in Great Britain as well. At the London School of Economics (LSE), four women received the LSE Hutchinson Silver Medal before 1940: Eileen Power (1923); Dorothy Swaine Thomas (1924); Eveline Mabel Burns (1926); and Margaret James (1926–27).

for the other woman, Caroline Ware. Initial investigation into the men prize winners shows more variation in PhD-granting affiliation than that for the women, though other personal connections between the men winners and the prize awarding committee members certainly might have existed. Nonetheless, receiving merit-based awards may have implications for productivity and for career path trajectory.

The literature analyzing economics awards hypothesizes numerous potential career effects. Awards may change pre-award issuance behavior of the pool of people who believe they are potential award recipients. For instance, an award might induce potential recipients to undertake actions desired by the award giver or an award might more broadly stimulate productivity in pursuit of the reward. Receipt of awards may change the post-award issuance behaviors of award recipients, particularly productivity. Some recipients might increase productivity, perhaps in connection to a rise in self-esteem; other recipients' efforts may stagnate (a resting on laurels phenomenon), reflected in lower post-award productivity. There are also social ramifications of publicized awards. Assuming the award is perceived as merit-based, when publicized, the award might serve as a signaling device across a community for desirable researcher characteristics such as intellectual innovation or discipline. The award winner could be the recipient of disciplinary status effects.[4] It seems reasonable to posit that the Hart, Schaffner, and Marx award winners' productivity and disciplinary status might have been affected.

Though six women did earn the Hart, Schaffner, and Marx award for their economic thought in the early twentieth century, substantial gender discrimination substantially impeded women's career progress in economics specifically and in academia generally.[5] Women adapted to the discriminatory barriers in constructing and disseminating economics knowledge, seeking "reasonable lives despite the obstacles their own socialization and the larger society placed in their paths."[6] Three recognized adaptation strategies include "superperformance," "subordination," and "separatism." Superperforming women were "pathbreaking pioneers, outperforming their male colleagues on most measures of professional success and commitment," their stellar career outcomes likely the combined result of "individual drive and genius and circumstance."[7] Women who maintained careers in economics also adapted via subordination, settling into low- or no-status positions as teachers or administrators for high schools, normal schools, and teaching colleges, or relegated to lower-status, low-pay, and unstable positions in colleges and universities. Separatists (some of whom also warrant recognition as innovators) moved to women's colleges, focused on niche publications in areas ignored by mainstream economists, moved into economics-related academic departments (such as home economics and social work), took careers in government, or focused on social service.[8] An extreme separatist response might include dropping out of economics altogether. For the women who pursued careers associated with academic economics, it was likely that those women economists who were heterosexual opted for career over marriage and childbearing.

Given the discriminatory barriers, it is remarkable that over 250 women earning Ph.D.s in the U.S.A., the U.K., and Germany wrote theses on economics topics before 1941.[9] The women receiving the Hart, Schaffner and Marx Prize had remarkable intellectual ability and/or a networking connection with the established men economists issuing the award. How did their careers fare? How did economists specifically, and academia generally, receive their work?

Yetta Scheftel (circa 1893–?)

There is minimal biographical record about Dr. Yetta Scheftel.[10] She completed her undergraduate A.B. at Northwestern University in 1906. Her 1907 thesis, "Persistence of Poverty," earned for Scheftel an M.A. degree in sociology from the University of Chicago. There is a record that she attended the University of Berlin from 1908–09. Scheftel enrolled again in graduate school with the University of Chicago in 1912 and 1913.[11] Scheftel appears on the "Fellows" and the "Graduate Students" list for 1913–14 with the Department of Political Economy at the University of Chicago.

Scheftel was a paid staff member of the Illinois Survey from roughly 1913 to 1916, charged with "making an exhaustive study of the settlement of the Military Tract in Illinois"[12] for use in The Centennial History of Illinois.[13] She completed her portion of this study by 1915–16 under the direction of Clarence W. Alvord. Scheftel's historical products include a published book review in *The Mississippi Valley Historical Review* in 1915.

While Scheftel undertook her historical academic ventures, she worked on a research monograph which she acknowledges was inspired by Professor Robert F. Hoxie of the University of Chicago. Hoxie died in 1916.[14] Scheftel did not complete her Ph.D.[15] Her monograph, *The Taxation of Land Value: A Study of Certain Discriminatory Taxes on Land*, received first prize in the Hart, Schaffner, and Marx Company of Chicago's Political Economy essay contest for 1915.

A range of periodicals publicized Scheftel's awards, including newspapers such as *The Evening Missourian* of Columbia (p. 3, Wed. Dec. 1, 1915) and *The New York Times*, academic journals such as *The American Economic Review* and *The American Political Science Review*, and the Bureau of Labor Statistics publication, *The Monthly Labor Review*.

The *New York Times* "Notable Book in Brief Review" headline mis-states Scheftel's gender: "**Mr**. Yetta Scheftel's Prize Essay on the Taxation of Land Value . . . ." The *Times* article of March 25, 1917 might have reported Scheftel's thesis due to its political relevance in the state:

> New York is to be the next battle ground of the single tax crusade. It is right to call it a crusade, for its motive is as much social reform as fiscal fitness. The battle will be fought in New York because the strategists of the campaign have selected it to break the force of defeats elsewhere.

A number of journals published reviews of *The Taxation of Land Value*. The *Annals of the American Academy of Political and Social Science* review judges that:

> Miss Scheftel has prepared a judicious, well-balanced treatment of land-value taxation in those countries where the scheme has been chiefly tried. The history of Australasian land taxes, German taxes on value increment, English land-value duties, and municipal land taxes in Canada is carefully outlined. Study is also given to the fiscal, economic and social effects of such taxes.[16]

The rest of the book review is descriptive except for a comment that the bibliography is "valuable." *The American Political Science Review* describes Scheftel's book as "the newest and in many respects the best study of what is commonly known as the single tax" with "careful discussions of the tax upon land values as a source of revenue and as an instrument of social reform respectively . . . excellent bibliography."[17]

A June 1917 book review provides a deeper analytical review of Scheftel (1916), identifying weaknesses as well as strengths. In his *American Economic Review* assessment, Arthur N. Young of Princeton University wrote that this thesis "well may be said to be the first attempt 'to present fully the experience with the system of the countries which have introduced'" a land tax. Young highlights Scheftel's "careful and complete account of the complicated land taxes of Australasia, Germany and Great Britain" but Young states that another researcher provides more exhaustive coverage of taxes in Western Canada than Scheftel. Though "[h]er work shows careful and painstaking research," Scheftel's critical analysis perhaps "attempted too much." Young identifies a few areas of "loose" treatment of economic theory. Though Young agrees with other reviewers concerning the excellence of Scheftel's bibliography, he describes as "inadequate" the four-page index.

Scheftel enrolled in Rush Medical College of the University of Chicago from 1916 to 1920, earning a medical degree in 1921.[18] According to a 1940 U.S. Census record, a Yetta Scheftel of Chicago was a physician in private practice.

Scheftel (1916) is the last academic reference in the social sciences that Yetta published. She had a promising academic career. The promise Scheftel showed in academic capability is apparent in the fact that her dissertation is cited and briefly discussed in four journals published 40 to 60 years *after* her work, in 1957, 1959, 1961, and 1977. In the journal article, "How College Textbooks Treat Land Value Taxation," footnote 11 documents that:

> Recognition of the stimulating effect of a land value tax policy can be found in the literature of nearly half a century ago. See, for example, Yetta Scheftel . . . Her investigation showed that "the land tax" had been found to increase the amount of building, decrease the amount of vacant land and stimulate business.

Hazel Kyrk (1886–1957)[19]

Self-supporting by age 17, Hazel Kyrk worked for the household of economist Leon Carroll Marshall while working toward an undergraduate degree at Ohio Wesleyan University. The personal connection with Marshall might have influenced Kyrk's choice to study economics. Though Kyrk's intellectual capacity and tenacity were likely the driving forces shaping her biography, Marshall's patronage probably helped her obtain an academic position in the 1920s at the University of Chicago with such appointments sparse for academic women.

Kyrk earned her bachelor's degree in 1910. Intermingling academic employment, wartime work in Britain with James Alfred Field, and pursuing higher education, Kyrk completed her Ph.D. from the economics department in 1920. She worked for short spurts in a variety of institutions of higher education, including a stint at Oberlin College. Evidence from the Oberlin College archives suggests that negative reception by male students toward a woman professor drove her decision to depart from Oberlin.[20]

Hired in 1925 by the University of Chicago, by 1930 Kyrk obtained a joint appointment in the Economics and Home Economics departments. Kyrk became full professor in 1941 and retired from her joint appointment in 1952. This mature phase of her professional career was stable and conducive to Kyrk making major academic contributions. She mentored over 30 graduate students, including Margaret Reid who herself became an academic leader. In service, Kyrk worked for a variety of federal agencies such as the Bureau of Labor Statistics, the Office of Price Stabilization, and the Bureau of Home Economics. Her intellectual contributions through government include partial responsibility for a statistical forerunner to base year pricing for the U.S. consumer price index. Kyrk's major intellectual contributions rest in her interdisciplinary, institutionalist treatment of the consumer as well as being a pioneer in home economics where she retired as a recognized "leader in the field" (Beller and Kiss 2008, p. 16). Summarizing Kyrk's work life, Beller and Kiss write "by the standards of today, Kyrk had a solid career; in the context of her times, it was a remarkable career" (p. 16).

The literature on Hazel Kyrk documents little with regard to her personal life. There is no evidence of non-work-related personal relationships, except that Kyrk raised a foster daughter (Lobdell 2000, p. 253).

Kyrk's thesis received two distinct assessments in two economics journals. The *Quarterly Journal of Economics* review classifies Kyrk's thesis as institutional economics—falling within the scope of "social psychology" where factors such as "instincts, folkways, and social classes" drive consumer behavior (p. 344). The reviewer, Z. Clark Dickinson, did not favor the institutionalist school. According to Dickinson, Kyrk undertook a detailed pursuit of only one path of inquiry in consumption economics (want creation), but for Dickinson there are five paths of useful inquiry. Though Kyrk "touched on all" five topics, she did so "quite inadequately" because of her antagonism toward the approach to consumption based on marginal utility. Dickinson suggests that reliance upon an instinct-driven theory generates circular reasoning. Though Dickinson is highly critical of Kyrk's approach to consumption economics, he describes her work as "clearly and pleasingly written" with plenty of evidence, "a sound groundwork of economic principles and of level-headed, original thinking."

In 1926, the second review appeared in *The Economic Journal.* This review opens by stating that Kyrk's work "is both a plea for a complete study of the economics of consumption, and an important contribution to it" (p. 241). MacGregor, the reviewer, clearly sympathizes with Kyrk's analytical framework, describing it as "[t]rue to the best modern psychology." With Kyrk charting "some new paths" in her exploration of the consumption "hinterland," MacGregor excuses the book's "diffuseness" because "so much is brought under review." The review closes that the prize-winning publication has "well-deserved approval of such examiners as J. B. Clark, J. L. Laughlin, and Wesley Mitchell," the Hart, Marx and Schaffner award committee.

After her thesis, Kyrk published six books as sole author. Two of these books are narrow in their subject appeal, one covering the baking industry from 1849 through 1923 and the second analyzing household expenditures and cost of living for Iowa farms. The single-authored books which received academic attention via journal review are *Economic Problems of the Family* (1929) and its major revision, *The Family in the American Economy* (1953). Kyrk also participated in the creation of three co-authored books in consumption and in family economics.

There are at least 16 reviews of Kyrk's books across academic disciplines. Four of Kyrk's books received journal review, though only two reviews after her thesis appeared in economics journals (*Industrial and Labor Relations Review* and the Italian journal, *Giornale degli Economisti e Annali di Economia*). Kyrk's book, *Economic Problems of the Family* received three interdisciplinary reviews. Nine reviewers assessed *The Family in the American Economy* in interdisciplinary journals across economics, sociology, social work, and demography. The final book reviewed was a co-authored publication with Day Monroe and Ursula B. Stone.

Kyrk published 12 single-authored journal articles from 1929 through 1950 and one co-authored article; these were published across eight distinct interdisciplinary journals. The journal subject matters range from farm economics to educational sociology to marketing to home economics. The majority of these articles are in two general areas: consumption and family economics. In 1950, Kyrk also published one article in the *American Economic Review Papers and Proceedings* about income distribution as a potential economic welfare measure. There is a record that Kyrk participated in the conference of the American Economic Association in 1939.

Hazel Kyrk published over 60 book reviews in academic journals between 1925 and 1957. The *Journal of Political Economy* published at least 15 of these, most of which concerned consumption. Kyrk was also a frequent reviewer for the *Social Service Review* and for the *American Journal of Sociology*. The book reviews tended to address consumption, household economics, the cost of living or the standard of living.

Kyrk's institutionalist economics insights make a splash in economics circles with the publication of her thesis. Kyrk benefited early in her career from recognized intellectual capability and from a personal connection with an established male economist. Throughout her career, she was a prolific publisher in interdisciplinary venues. Kyrk's intellectual paradigm (institutionalism) was in a field that fell out of fashion in economics, though she was a leader in the trend of consumption economics in the first half of the twentieth century. Her interdisciplinary approach also fell out of fashion in economics over the twentieth century. She had noteworthy influence on a fleet of graduate students coming out of the University of Chicago. She made important contributions to U.S. federal government tracking of economic statistics. Given the constraints on women's advances in academia, Kyrk's career trajectory was of the superperforming category; in comparison to men with Ph.D.s in the twentieth century, Kyrk's career might be described as solid and relatively unremarkable.

Mollie Ray Carroll (1890–1994[21])

Mollie Ray Carroll earned three degrees at the University of Chicago. With 363 other undergraduate degree recipients, Carroll completed her first Chicago degree, a Ph.B, in 1911. Her undergraduate extra-curricular activities included serving as vice president of the Young Women's Christian League (YWCL) of the University of Chicago. In 1913 she was secretary of the Lawrence, Kansas YWCA, after which she must have returned to Chicago, completing her master's degree in 1915.

Carroll held two positions of employment after earning her master's degree. From 1917–18 she was a special agent and assistant inspector under Grace Abbott for the Child Labor Division of the U.S. Children's Bureau. Carroll described her professional responsibilities as a Greenwood, South Carolina child labor inspector:

> My job has been very interesting too. Sent down here to aid in the enforcement of the Federal Child Labor Law, now some eight months old, I find the district which I cover every month to be comprised, industrially, chiefly of cotton mills. My task is mainly the ascertaining of the ages of the children, seeing them and their parents, and looking up records of age. I have handled more family Bibles than I knew could exist in one section of the country.[22]

From 1918–20 Carroll was a staff lecturer at the Chicago School of Civics and Philanthropy. This School was associated with the settlement house movement of the early twentieth century, combining social work education and job experience. Social workers resided in settlement houses and the houses provided food, shelter, and education for the income-poor.

Carroll earned her Ph.D. from the University of Chicago Sociology Department in 1920. Her Ph.D. thesis, *Labor and Politics: The Attitude of the American Federation of Labor Toward Legislation and Politics*, received a Hart, Schaffner and Marx "honorable mention" in 1922.

Carroll's thesis received no reviews from economics journals. The two interdisciplinary reviews that do exist are lackluster. Primarily descriptive in nature, *The Journal of Negro History* review identifies that the thesis mostly omits coverage of race in its discussion of the American Federation of Labor. Addressing topics emphasized by the book, this review questions the adequacy of Carroll's coverage. Whereas adequacy of coverage is questioned in the first review, "concise" is the descriptive term used in the second review. *The Annals of the American Academy of Political and Social Science* review identifies historical and contemporary political events left out of Carroll's thesis. This second review describes the "concise" thesis as "well-planned." An allusion to partiality in coverage is suggested via the descriptive phrase, "sympathetic survey" of American Federation of Labor political policy. Nonetheless, the second review concludes that the book is "a helpful handbook" for the specialist and an easy, illuminating read for the generalist.

A *New York Times* book review[23] also conveys a lackluster reception for Carroll's thesis beyond the Hart, Schaffner and Marx award committee members. Though she "packed a good deal of information in her book gleaned from the official organs of the American Federation of Labor," the *Times* reviewer writes of Carroll's thesis that "its title is too big for its contents. Labor and politics are both vast subjects; to tie them up makes them almost fearsome. Yet Miss Carroll's book is not fearsome in any respect."

In 1920 Carroll became associate professor at a women's school, Goucher College in Maryland. In 1922 she was professor and chair of the Goucher College Department of Economics and Sociology. Carroll was a Guggenheim Memorial Foundation fellow in 1927–28 and spent a couple years in Germany researching the German unemployment insurance system. The 1931 *American Economic Review* book review of Carroll's German unemployment insurance monograph identifies the timeliness of the book and that it is a "careful" study presenting "invaluable, disinterested testimony."

By 1932, Carroll had left her Goucher College position and worked at the University of Chicago Settlement. A few career-oriented factoids are available. While working for Goucher College, she gave professional talks in both South Carolina and Georgia in Spring 1925. Carroll was actively involved with the League of Women Voters for decades. She served as a national vice president of the League, participated in at least one League convention leading a discussion about problems associated with women in industry (1926), and wrote about economics for the League. Carroll may have returned to the University of Chicago and its Graduate School of Social Service Administration (an administrative outgrowth of the earlier Chicago School of Civics and Philanthropy) in 1926 to teach two summer courses titled, "The Field of Social Work" and "Child Welfare Problems." In Spring 1930, she was one of more than 1,250 economists who signed "The Economists' Tariff Protest of 1930" opposing the Hawley-Smoot tariff bill.

By 1935–36, Carroll was the Executive Head Resident of the University of Chicago Settlement and an associate professor of social economy with her alma mater. During this year, she also was secretary for the board of directors of the Chicago Douglas Smith Fund and was director of research for the New York City Workers' Education Bureau. Carroll published twice with the Workers' Education Bureau Press on the topics of trade unions and worker education.

By 1941, Carroll was a research adviser[24] with the Labor Standards Division in the United States Department of Labor. In 1946, she was Senior Technical Adviser of the Training Division for the Social Security Board. In 1950, she served as a labor economist with the Social Security Administration.

In 1965 a "Dr. Mollie Ray Carroll of Fairfax, Va" provided critical testimony for a U.S. Senate Immigration and Naturalization Subcommittee to the Judiciary Committee. Carroll testified with the opinion that:

> while America has been built by the vision and energy of immigrants, including your ancestors and mine, the so-called melting pot has often not melted. Masses of poorly screened immigrants have too often become undigested lumps of frustrated, undiluted foreign ideology and habits, pawns of some of the world's worst elements.[25]

It is unclear when or why this xenophobia developed.

From 1923 to 1939, Carroll published four books (including her thesis), one of which came in two editions. All four books received published academic review across interdisciplinary journals. Her thesis and the book on German unemployment insurance that she published as a result of her Guggenheim fellowship are the more substantial academic contributions. The 1930 text of *Our Wants and How They Are Satisfied* is under 70 pages long, providing a common sense explanation of economic principles for the National League of Women Voters. Hazel Kyrk's two-paragraph review describes the contents and purpose. The *Southern Economic Journal* review of *What is Collective Bargaining?* identifies Carroll's unique position on collective bargaining. The reviewer concludes that though "[m]any readers will accuse Miss Carroll of being too idealistic and too far from the day-to-day struggle for existence," her book does rise to its purpose to encourage reasoned communication. Beyond the four books that received journal review, Carroll published a few more tracts printed by the National League of Women Voters in the mid-1920s.

Carroll published 21 times in interdisciplinary periodicals through the 1920s and the 1930s. Her major publication outlet links to her Ph.D. thesis topic: Carroll published nine articles between 1925 and 1938 in the *American Federationist*, the "official magazine of the American Federation of Labor." She published three times each in *American Labor Legislation Review*, in *Social Forces*, and in the *Journal of Adult Education*, twice in *Social Service Review*, and one article about German social statistics appears in the *Journal of the American Statistical Association*.

Carroll was one of five in an American Economic Association round table panel covering unemployment and public works. Her contribution on German public works appears after J.B. Clark's comments in the 1930 papers and proceedings issue of the *American Economic Review*.

Carroll published over 35 book reviews in academic journals between 1919 and 1936, with roughly half published in *Social Service Review*. A few of the remaining reviews appear in established economics journals such as the *Journal of Political Economy* and the *American Economic Review*. The rest are interdisciplinary publications with broad range, extending across sociology, religion, ethics, history, and statistics. Eight of the books reviewed from 1929 forward have German titles, suggesting Carroll continued using the German- language skills acquired during her time in that country to facilitate international exchange of knowledge. Only five book reviews appear before 1930. Most of her 1930s' book review titles revolve around employment and unemployment relief.

Carroll's professional life iterated between U.S. federal government and academic spheres. She clearly maintained networking ties to the University of Chicago at least 15 years after earning her terminal degree. Though her 1920 Ph.D. thesis was worthy of honorable mention, it took a full decade for Carroll to receive passing attention for her research on a second subject, German insurance, from the American Economic Association, and even then this was only in the form of conference participation and book reviews.

The electronic records about Mollie Ray Carroll suggest that she was an active academic contributor until the mid-1930s. Her academic contributions were numerous and diverse in scope, though perhaps not the quality or type of work to receive disciplinary recognition. After the mid-1930s, her academic contributions cease. She worked briefly for the federal government before earning her Ph.D.—her initial federal employment possibly the result of social networking through Edith Abbott of the University of Chicago and her sister Grace Abbott. Carroll returned to federal employment in later life. It is unclear whether Carroll's return to federal bureaucracy was due to personal desire or whether she was pushed away from academia. Throughout her career, Carroll made contributions in the field of labor. Beyond dedication of her thesis to her parents, no records of substance turn up about her personal life.

Helen Fisher Hohman (1894–1972)[26]

Helen Fisher Hohman completed an undergraduate degree at the University of Illinois in 1916. Married in 1919, her spouse, economist Elmo P. Hohman, was also an Illinois alum. By 1919, Helen graduated from a two-year program at the New York School of Social Work and worked as an economics department assistant with teaching responsibilities for a year at Vassar College, an appointment which lasted until 1920. While Elmo worked on a second degree at Harvard University, Helen and Elmo had teaching appointments at Simmons College for the 1921–22 school year.

Hohman's split attention across the fields of social work and economics led her to write a piece about the importance of both professions. In a 1922 alumni magazine publication, Hohman describes her diaspora: "economists dub me a sentimental reformer, and the social workers pity me as a useless juggler of the metaphysics of supply and demand. Therefore I welcome this opportunity to recommend myself to both parties." Perceiving herself with two professional homelands and foretelling her migration to economics, Hohman concludes to her social work audience:

> As social workers we can never save the world by case work alone, as economists we cannot fully comprehend our problem; but as cooperators and coordinators, to use familiar terms, we can enrich our contribution to the great tasks to which we are committed. So I believe that they also serve, who only teach and study economics.[27]

In the mid-1920s, Hohman pursued graduate study in economics. During her graduate work, she published an article with the *Journal of Political Economy* on cost of living adjustments to wages. By 1928, she earned a Ph.D. from the University of Chicago with the completion of her thesis, "The Trade Board Acts and the Social Insurance Acts in Relation to a Minimum Standard of Living in Great Britain: A Study in Attitudes toward Poverty and Methods of Dealing with It, 1880–1926."

The *American Economic Review* announced that Hohman's dissertation received first prize in the 1928 Hart, Schaffner and Marx competition and acknowledged that an honorable mention went to Simon S. Kuznets for his "Secular Movements in Production and Prices." The 1928 version of Hohman's dissertation research received no reviews in journals. Hohman's 1933 publication of this doctoral study, titled *The Development of Social Insurance and Minimum Wage Legislation in Great Britain: A Study of British Social Legislation in Relation to a Minimum Standard of Living*, did receive attention from five interdisciplinary journals (including sociology, history and political science), though it was only reviewed by one major economics journal, the *Journal of Political Economy*. In contrast, Kuznets' "honorable mention" received eight journal reviews in 1930 and in 1931, including the *American Economic Review, The Economic Journal*, and *Journal of Political Economy*.

Given that the Hart, Schaffner & Marx Prize committee rated Hohman's research monograph as the worthier research product, it is unclear why Kuznets received multiple reviews in major economics journals and Hohman's work was not received until 1933 and then only by one major economics journal. Like Kuznets' book, Hohman's 1926 journal publication is technical. In contrast, the *Journal of Political Economy* review of Hohman (1933) identifies that her award-winning thesis "method of treatment is historical rather than analytical" and criticizes the work for undertaking no international comparison of social insurance. Perhaps thesis methodology had some effect on disciplinary reception of the two scholars' works. Some of the journal attention Kuznets receives is critical. An open question is whether receiving critical disciplinary attention has more positive career impact than receiving no professional attention.

After earning her doctorate, Hohman compiled and edited "Essays on Population and other papers by James Alfred Field" at the University of Chicago, which was published in 1931. This publication received four reviews in interdisciplinary journals.

In 1932 Helen gave birth to a daughter, Elinor. Her husband, Elmo, served as an economics professor with Northwestern University from the early 1930s through the 1950s. Evidence from Northwestern University archives suggests that, although Helen signed book reviews in economics journals in association with Northwestern, her official teaching duties in economics were limited to lecturing, to summer courses, and to teach for her husband in his absence; she held no permanent academic rank with Northwestern. For example, in two archived *Daily Northwestern* newspaper articles about Helen, she is identified as the wife of Elmo—she is not identified individually with university rank. It is only after publishing her book on Swedish social insurance that she is identified as "Dr. Helen Hohman."

Social insurance was the central topic of Hohman's post-graduate publications. Her research in social insurance spanned countries in North America and Europe. She served as a consultant for the U.S. federal government's Bureau of Research and Statistics of the Social Security Board, when she studied the Swedish social insurance program. *Old Age in Sweden* identifies that Helen Hohman traveled in Europe during the summer of 1937. Her summer activities included direct observation of the Swedish social insurance program and review of Swedish documents. She also consulted with Social Insurance Section staff in the International Labor Office in Geneva. Hohman thanks both Gunnar Myrdal and Bertil Ohlin in the acknowledgments, two male economists with noteworthy contributions that continue to receive attention in the early twenty-first century.

Three reviewers assessed *Old Age in Sweden*. The *Journal of Political Economy* review provides both a descriptive account and a positive assessment, concluding that Hohman's work is "a comprehensive and accurate source of information on the Swedish experience." In 1940, the *American Economic Review* published a Hohman article about American public assistance.

Hohman's publishing career after 1940 appears to rest on the intellectual capital she developed in her formative research years. These later social insurance publications emphasize Great Britain, Sweden, and cost of living adjustments. Only one publication branches out from her earlier emphases, though as a handbook for professional social service provisioners, it is not an academic heavyweight. Hohman published over 40 book reviews, of which 26 appear in major economics journals.

At the age of 53 in a February 2, 1947 radio broadcast titled "Is America Going Feminine?" Helen Hohman was one of four speakers. The concept "feminine" was presented derisively in the broadcast. The broadcast included two conservative male speakers who tied women's social role to effective child rearing. Helen's minimal commentary was moderate and reactive to the extremely vocal, conservative views expressed by the men. Perhaps she was reflecting on her own life circumstances in the following commentary:

> Most women in the United States are married. Most women have children. And it is the woman with a family and the unbroken family that we are concerned about today. I think that the very fact that so much of her life, of her former activities, have been taken out of the home means that now she has leisure that she never had before. She has smaller families. A woman who has six children doesn't have any problem of leisure. Good or bad, that is the fact. Therefore, the modern woman cannot find within the home, after the children have passed infancy, things to do that take all of her interest and all of her capacities.

She continues:

> I think that there are some women who find their total expression within the home. Others, probably most, need some contacts outside of the home, some kind of sociability, some common purpose, working for things that are not just their own families, their own husbands, their own children.

Her daughter and two grandchildren survived Helen Hohman. It seems reasonable to conjecture that when her daughter grew out of infancy, Hohman chose to interlace academic pursuits around her familial role. Hohman seems to have chosen part-time research economist with lifetime academic service at Northwestern University. Her research caught passing attention from two major economics journals. That Hohman coupled serious pursuit of academics on an erratic basis while married to an economist and raising a child is noteworthy given the time period and gender-centric social constraints.

Caroline Ware (1899–1990)[28]

Caroline Ware's intellectual accomplishments span academic disciplines, institutions, and countries. Her contributions in history overshadow her work in economics, and she had substantial research programs in community development, women's issues, race relations, and worker's education. Running parallel with this active research agenda, Ware held appointments at four institutions of higher learning between 1925 and 1961, where teaching was also an important responsibility. Her academic appointments were at Vassar College, Sarah Lawrence College, the American University Graduate School, and the School of Social Work at Howard University.

Lee and Warren (2000) identify many public agencies for which Ware labored. These include the National Recovery Administration's Consumer Advisory Board and consumer groups associated with the National Emergency Council, the National Defense Advisory Board, President Truman's Council of Economic Advisors, and President Kennedy's Consumer Advisory Council.

According to the American Association of University Women, Ware "led AAUW in the fight to establish a consumer agency in the federal government and testified on behalf of AAUW on consumer interests and fair-housing issues."[29] Ware also published in 1962 for the United States President's Commission on the Status of Women, and the YWCA republished this work in 1963.

Experience in Puerto Rico in the late 1940s spurred Ware's contributions in community development. According to Lee and Samuels, from 1962–1976 Ware "was a technical advisor in community development and cultural affairs for the United Nations" and traveled in Latin America. She published a number of tracts in Spanish on this subject matter from 1953 to 1963.

Ware's Radcliffe Ph.D. in 1925 kickstarted her energized career. She received the $1,000 Hart, Schaffner, and Marx first prize in 1929 for *The Early New England Cotton Manufacture: A Study in Industrial Beginnings*. Interestingly, Professor Edwin F. Gay of Harvard University both directed her thesis and was one of four members on the award committee. Ware credits both Gay and the "critical cooperation" of her husband, Gardiner C. Means in the preface to her thesis.

Book reviews credit Ware's efforts to unearth historical documents for her thesis. Visiting historical societies in New England, she "found boxes and boxes filled with a jumble of half-rotted letters, accounts, letter-books and production-sheets." After "[t]hree days of sorting and arranging" Ware constructed an "amazingly full" record of the first cotton-spinning firm in the Northeastern United States. In her quest for randomly preserved records in "family attics or deserted barns" she consulted a town clerk, a banker, and then a judge who led her to a cotton-spinning entrepreneur's descendant. This descendant "remembered having some old books in the attic belonging to some ancestor" which included a variety of business records such as sales accounts and expense receipts (Ware, 1926, p. 5). Ware also compiled records from personal mill visits, accompanied by "letters of introduction to persons in authority" (p. 6). Ware's quest for original source material turned up piecemeal documents, each of which Ware fitted "into the fragmentary picture to change the shading or to strengthen a line" (p. 6). The meticulous thesis research uncovering historical documents and piecing them together is one basis for Ware's influence with the history discipline.

Ware's award-winning thesis received three journal reviews, including one by Delmar Leighton in the *American Economic Review*. Leighton identifies that Ware worked a large amount of historical material to construct a 70-year history of cotton manufacturing in New England. Ware provides "value . . . for historical students" in her source data and a 16-page bibliography (p. 316). Ware's thesis illuminates understanding of finance, marketing, and labor force management in a capital-intense industry start-up and makes an "able attempt" to assess community development effects of the industry. Using one-half of the review, Leighton takes Ware to task for emphasizing "exploitation" in her thesis.

The New England Quarterly review also uses most of its space to clarify Ware's exposition in her chapter about "exploitation and reform." This second review explains why Ware's chapter on exploitation is a "one-sided" treatment: she over-emphasized a boarding-house method of labor hiring and under-emphasized a family-hiring method (pp. 561–62). This second reviewer is gracious about her error, concluding: "The student of economic history will be grateful to Miss Ware for this study in industrial beginnings; if he regrets that she had slighted certain aspects of the story . . . his regret is merely that these topics did not fall entirely within the scope of her volume" (p. 562).

The Mississippi Valley Historical Review coverage of Ware's thesis begins quite positively. Ware's thesis "measures up well with the best [Hart, Schaffner and Marx awarded] monographs" and "is a substantial and worth while contribution to the history" of the U.S. industrial revolution. Two criticisms concern the "dry detailed treatment" typical of academic work and a wish that there were more breadth in coverage to related economic issues such as international trade (p. 572).

Over her career, Ware published at least 12 journal articles. Two of these articles appear in economics journals. Her 1926 *Quarterly Journal of Economics* publication related to her thesis topic. In 1949, Ware published an article in *Industrial and Labor Relations Review* about her work on university programs for workers' education.

Ware participated in research resulting in at least 20 monographs. These monographs mostly span her interdisciplinary career from 1931 until 1966, with one co-authored work in 1981. Roughly two-thirds of these publications were authored by Ware alone, the remainder with co-authors. The subject matter of Ware's monographs exhibit breadth of knowledge. The topics of her single-authored monographs in economics ranged from the consumer to worker education to women's issues to community development. Her work about community development in Latin America was published in English, Spanish, and Portuguese.

Records suggest Ware published nine reviews of others' publications, none of which appeared in economics journals. In contrast, Ware received at least 24 academic reviews of books that she penned alone or with co-authors. The reviews appear across disciplines and journal topics. The work that received the most immediate attention of reviewers is Ware's *The Cultural Approach to History* (1940). This book received at least 12 interdisciplinary reviews, though none in economics. Economists' reviews of Ware's broad-reaching intellectual contributions were limited to her thesis (reviewed in *American Economic Review*), to *Labor Education in Universities* (reviewed in *Journal of Political Economy* and in *Industrial and Labor Relations Review*), and to *The Modern Economy in Action*, co-authored with her husband (reviewed in the *American Economic Review*).

Ware married economist Gardiner C. Means in 1927, separated by his death in 1988. According to Lee and Samuels (2000, p. 462), Caroline Ware

> married Means . . . with the very clear intention of combining a career with marriage and children (although for physical reasons the marriage remained childless). She long believed that women did not have to choose between children and career. Indicative of her desire to combine marriage and a career, Ware retained her maiden name, a very unusual, but not unheard of, practice then. Apropros of this, she later reported that she then had more status than her husband and did not want to set aside her own name; and that when her husband achieved more status than she, she did not want to ride on his coat-tails. Their relationship was complex, although she reported that they lived in mutually supportive harmony for 60 years.

Preserving the marriage did involve at least one major career-impacting decision by Caroline. She resigned from her Vassar teaching position when Means moved to Washington in 1933 to work for the federal government, and afterwards found "university history departments reluctant to hire women."[30]

Alma Herbst (1892–1968)

A Delta Delta Delta sorority member and president of a Columbus, Ohio branch of the YWCA in her undergraduate years, Alma Herbst earned an A.B. degree from the Ohio State University in 1914. From 1914 to 1916, she was industrial secretary for the YWCA in Pittsburgh, Pennsylvania. From 1918–1923 she was with the New York National Board of the YWCA. Herbst also worked with the Bryn Mawr summer school for women from 1922 to 1923. She must have shifted into academic studies thereafter; from 1926 to 1928 she was a research assistant at the University of Chicago.

Herbst earned a Ph.D. from the University of Chicago in 1930. Her dissertation, *The Negro in the Slaughtering and Meat-Packing Industry in Chicago*, won second prize in the 1930 Hart, Schaffner and Marx competition, and like the other women award winners, was in Class A, including any American without restriction. The preface to her award-winning dissertation credits Professor Harry A. Millis of the University of Chicago "for his generous criticisms and helpful suggestions during every stage of the work."

Herbst's thesis received at least three book reviews shortly after publication. As a University of Chicago Press publication, the *Social Service Review*'s interest in reviewing Herbst's thesis was perhaps due to institutional, geographic, and topical overlap between the thesis and the journal. *The Mississippi Valley Historical Review* likely reviewed the thesis due to its subject matter. Both reviews are positive about the thesis. For example, reviewer "M.R.C."[31] of the *Social Service Review* describes the thesis as objective, based on "much valuable factual material," and states that Herbst handles "vexing questions . . . with courage and scientific caution." The *Mississippi* reviewer describes Herbst's approach as "clean-cut" and "interesting" with "[a]bundant statistical tables and charts." Both reviews relay that Herbst collected her own observations for this study. The *Mississippi* review suggests that "a bit more in the way of case studies and negro folk-opinion might have added somewhat to the interest and value of the treatment."

A third book review by Alain Locke (1932) provides a perspective shift about the validity of the book in a broader socio-historic context. A leading figure in the Harlem Renaissance, Locke's review of Herbst provides insight into the book's reception by a contemporary African American intellect. Locke commends the book for its objectivity and its accuracy. He empathizes with "the average reader, pardonably weary with graphs and statistics." Most importantly, Locke's review contextualizes Herbst's thesis in the socio-political context of race, labor, and industry, and socioeconomic discord in early 1900s' Chicago. Locke encourages Herbst's audience to "[r]ead this book not merely as a study of the Negro in the 'Meat-Packing Industry,' but as the story of America's black pawns of labor."

At least 13 publications reference Herbst's thesis, 12 of which date between 1972 and 2015. These references elicit material from Herbst's thesis to address a variety of labor- and race-related topics including promotion, labor termination, labor productivity, and employee loyalty toward a firm during labor strife.

Her Ohio State University appointment began as assistant from 1929 to 1930. In December 1930, the *American Economic Review* announced that Herbst "advanced from assistant to instructor of economics at Ohio State University."[32] She was promoted to assistant professor in 1933, associate professor in 1938, and was full professor in 1943 until her retirement in 1962. Herbst's Ohio State University career centered on teaching in labor and industrial relations and service to her university and her local community.

Though her award-winning dissertation continues to receive attention in the early twenty-first century, Herbst has no discernible track record of research productivity beyond her 1930 thesis and one book review in 1942. The only publication she listed in official

Ohio State University employment records is her Ph.D. thesis.[33] Though her thesis received accolades, her academic publishing career appears effectively to have both begun and ended with the dissertation.

Herbst overlapped her academic focus in labor with many of her local service activities. In 1932 she instructed adult education classes in economics principles at the Columbus Central YWCA. She was acting director of the Bryn Mawr summer school for workers in industry for the summer of 1934. Herbst ran the first survey of Ohio State University student working conditions in 1939. In 1946, she was a faculty adviser to the University Industrial Relations Club. Herbst was a member of a Committee on Teaching in Industrial Relations in 1949. She was partially responsible for "the first Midwestern Conference" held in Columbus, Ohio bringing together 27 people from ten midwestern colleges and universities in the U.S. This conference focus was on teaching and curriculum planning in labor-related and industrial relations subjects.[34] In 1947, Herbst was one of a nine-member board reviewing minimum wage scales of local hotels and restaurants.[35]

In Ohio State University online thesis records, Herbst appears as the thesis adviser to one master's level student and to another doctoral level student. Both thesis dates are 1961 and both have labor-related titles. Curiously, no other thesis adviser records turn up in searches of Herbst's name, though this could be due to spotty library online recordkeeping in naming thesis advisers. She clearly had more than two graduate students as reported by the Board of Trustees announcing her death:

> [T]estimony to Professor Herbst's constructive professionalism was the caliber of graduate students who took graduate degrees under her guidance and embarked on eminent professional careers. A number of the outstanding specialists in labor and industrial relations in the nation today were students of Professor Herbst and profited from her stimulating mind and critical and constructive evaluation of their work.[36]

Parnes (2001) recounts a story of initial favoritism and a later falling out in his work relationship with Herbst at the Ohio State University. According to Parnes, the interpersonal conflict between the two was initiated by Herbst in the 1940s. The story revolves around the establishment of a "school for trade unionists at Ohio State," something desired by Herbst. Though Parnes and Herbst shared similar broad views on this program, they differed in their preferences over its details. The result was a severing of their personal interaction, a break which, according to Parnes, was triggered by Herbst making a negative comment toward Parnes. The account suggests that there were at least three male faculty members in the Commerce program at Ohio State who had negative interactions with or held negative opinions about Herbst (Parnes 2001, pp. 47–48).

Herbst realized her mature research promise by overlapping scholarship with teaching and with community and university service. Along with Ohio State colleague Ruth Spitz, Herbst is noted as having made "progress" with "an analytical study of the Ohio Federation of Labor and the Ohio CIO Council in an effort to examine the changing role of the Ohio labor federations in the fields of citizenship and community participation."[37] Reflecting on research productivity in her 1943–44 annual report to the university, she wrote:

> My research has centered about present critical and rapidly changing labor problems both in the U.S. and foreign countries. Time has been taken to put materials in form for *possible* publication—*but studies thus have been made indispensable for teaching.*

In her 1946–47 annual report, she writes that her "own research projects cover those most needed to produce new teaching materials—Collective bargaining; Conciliation and Mediation . . . ; Labor and Internationalism." Herbst also "wrote a monograph published and copyrighted by the Ohio Chamber of Commerce, [titled] 'Governmental Agencies for Settlement of Industrial Disputes'." In community relations she reported maintaining "constant contacts with both trade union and employer groups." She wrote of serving employers and employees by "drawing up and negotiating their trade agreements" as well as having "been called in as a mediator."

Alma Herbst retired from the Ohio State University in 1962 with 33 years of service and was professor emerita by 1968. In 1961 and 1965 and again in Winter 1967–68, the name "Alma Herbst" appears in the journal *Educational Horizons*. In her retirement year, Herbst received a $1,000 prize for distinguished teaching at the university. Herbst commented on her award:

> My most rewarding teaching experience has been the unique privilege of association and comradeship with students in the quest for truth . . . there comes a realization of the sacred worth of personality and the uniqueness of irreplaceable talent. All are fellow members of the human race. As the core of life emerges so also are relationships in the home, on the job, and in the larger community established. To the teacher it is rewarding to recognize the dedication of former students to responsible areas of the government, in international affairs, in academic life, in labor-management relations, in business, in politics, in the home, and in service activities. The bond of a continuing free way of life is sealed in mutual gratitude and love long after the formal 'Commencement' date.

Herbst died in her home of a heart attack in 1968. Re-enforcing one of her annual report notes that she was not married, her listed survivors included only a brother, nieces and nephews. The Board of Trustees' announcement of Herbst's death included this statement about her undergraduate teaching: "her classes were distinguished by a realistic, knowledgeable, and eminently practical exploration of complex facets of labor problems and industrial relations. She attracted and interested many students to her field of specialization at the undergraduate level."

In 1994, the Ohio State University economics department established an Alma Herbst Memorial Lecture Fund in labor economics with support from Dr. Virgil C. Crisafulli and Martha Bair Crisafulli. Crisafulli earned an M.A. in 1940 and a Ph.D. in 1954, both degrees from the Ohio State University. Both theses focused on labor economics. It seems reasonable to conjecture that Crisafulli was a student of Herbst.

Perhaps Herbst's Ph.D. thesis award facilitated an appointment from the institution which granted her undergraduate degree. A 40-year relationship between a mid-twentieth-century woman economist and a major university's economics department is a substantial accomplishment. If Herbst's goal was a teaching position at her alma mater, then it seems that her personal aspirations were realized. The academic research promise embodied in Herbst's thesis, which continues to be recognized 85 years since publication, was not realized in any other attention-grabbing venues. It seems Herbst prioritized teaching and local community service. Not much should be made of a documented interpersonal conflict that might have existed with certain colleagues, as another doctorate and his wife valued Herbst's academic career enough to endow a lecture fund in her honor. An emerging picture of Herbst's professional accomplishments is that of a solidly institutionalized academic who emphasized teaching, personal and localized arenas as the receiving grounds for her professional efforts.

Assessing the career outcomes of six women economist-award winners (based on available information)

Six women received accolades for their Ph.D. theses from the Hart, Schaffner and Marx committee in the first few decades of the twentieth century. There is limited theoretical and empirical support that awards might increase recipient productivity and disciplinary reception in economics. Nonetheless, an early career award is certainly not a strong predictor of lifetime outcomes, particularly for academicians experiencing discriminatory barriers. Given the limited opportunities available to women in economics throughout the twentieth century, analyzing how a group of early twentieth-century women award winners fared in career and life is instructive.

Available information suggests that Caroline Ware and Hazel Kyrk had strong academic career outcomes. Caroline Ware made substantial lasting methodological academic contributions, though in the discipline of history, not economics. Kyrk pioneered the initiation of a new academic discipline. The careers of Alma Herbst and Mollie Ray Carroll played out admirably given gender discrimination, but otherwise do not stand out. Helen Hohman intermingled child rearing with part-time academic pursuits. Yetta Scheftel is an example of an early twentieth-century woman who dropped out of economics to pursue a different profession.

Commonly accepted twentieth-century indicators of "superperformance" in academic economics include publications and book reviews of one's own monographs in major economics journals[38] and appointments with major universities and prestigious private colleges. Considering only these indicators as reflected in Table 13.2, the economics outcomes of the careers of Kyrk, Hohman, and Ware stand out among the women award winners. The award-winning theses of all three were each reviewed in at least one major economics journal. Hohman had two publications and Ware had one publication in major economics journals. The post-graduate research monographs of Hohman and Ware each received book reviews in major economics journals. Kyrk had a career-long appointment with the economics departments of a major U.S. university. In contrast, Carroll had only one book review of her research by a major economics journal and one conference participation. Herbst had a lifelong appointment with the economics department of a major public university but is otherwise invisible.

However, as Table 13.2 suggests, based on exposure through major economics journals, none of the award winners' careers stand out. The highest frequency of exposure is three, not particularly noteworthy for a lifelong career. Though the women have negligible exposure as authors in major economics journals, a few were prolific book reviewers of other economists' works. For example, Hohman reviewed 29 books by other economists in major economics journals and Kyrk reviewed 15.

Table 13.2 Some career productivity criteria

Name	*Major economics journal thesis review*	*Permanent academic appointment*	*Major economics journal review, non-thesis*	*Major economics journal publication*	*Book reviews by her in a major economics journal*
Scheftel	1	No			
Kyrk	2	Yes (Chicago)			15
Carroll	0	Yes (Goucher)	1		5
Hohman	1	No (Northwestern lecturer)	2	2	29
Ware	1	Yes (4 schools)	3	1	
Herbst	0	Yes (Ohio State)			

Of the five women who persevered in academia, none contributed substantially to the major twentieth-century trends in economic thought: neoclassical economics or macroeconomics theory or econometric methodology. The research of all five women does include applications of empirical economics. Kyrk was involved in the construction of a statistical forerunner to the consumer price index, and Hohman contributed on cost of living adjustments to wages. Ware's and Herbst's theses stand out in their collection of unique primary source data. Carroll provided insights on German social statistics to an American academic audience. Generally speaking though, the five women were socio-political economists who did not fit the narrowing disciplinary norms that developed.

A definition of "superperformer" women economists is "pathbreaking pioneers, outperforming their male colleagues on most measures of professional success and commitment."[39] If their male colleagues' average performance is the comparative yardstick, it does not seem that even Kyrk, Hohman, and Ware had stellar economics careers. From this comparative yardstick, it might be more reasonable to classify the three women as "status quo" academic economists who made contributions to the discipline that received passing recognition.

It is reasonable, though, to question the appropriateness of the typical male economist as the comparative standard: in his correspondence with Hazel Kyrk, Marshall identified a gender-segregated academic labor market that was more difficult for women economists; it seems reasonable to conjecture that unequal treatment based on gender existed in publication venues. Furthermore, academic disciplines were not distinct in the first half of the twentieth century. The remainder of this assessment considers the women economists more broadly.

Two clearly created high-quality, innovative interdisciplinary contributions during their careers: Caroline Ware in historical method, workers' education, and community development in Latin America; and Hazel Kyrk in her institutionalist approach to consumption and by leading in the creation of a new discipline concerning family economics. Helen Hohman's contribution in social insurance, Alma Herbst's thesis on race in the Chicago meat-packing industry, and Mollie Ray Carroll's mid-career research on German unemployment insurance were each insightful contributions but do not reflect a career of realized intellectual promise.

The five women pursued interdisciplinary interests, though at different levels. Carroll, Hohman, and Herbst show a taste for interdisciplinary inquiry: Carroll's breadth of interest in her book review subject matter; Hohman in early attempts to cross social work and economics; and Herbst in taking on the issue of race in labor economics during the early twentieth century. Far more interdisciplinary are the lifelong contributions of Ware (in history, economics and development, and worker's education) and Kyrk (economics, consumption, and family). Ware and Kyrk are appropriately classified as "superperfomer separatists": both were "pathbreaking pioneers," individually driven and energized with sparks of genius. Both were also separatist-innovators, responsible for breaking new ground in academic thought. The separatist nature of their groundbreaking contributions did not leave career trails that attracted the attention or the respect of the typical twentieth-century male economist.

Networking is apparent in some of the careers of these five women economists. Institutional networking beyond their degree-granting and career-long university connections appear more limited for Hohman and Herbst relative to the other three. Ware stands out for her institutional web of interconnections: four relatively long-term academic appointments, federal government service including contributions to two US presidential councils, and extended work with the United Nations. Kyrk and Carroll also had career-long institutional connections with federal government agencies. Four of the five women traveled abroad: Kyrk to England during World War I, Carroll and Hohman to Europe during the interwar period, and extensive travel by Ware with the United Nations, particularly in Latin America. The international travel must have expanded the minds and influenced the intellectual creativity of each.

Supportive people-networking links are obvious in the careers of Kyrk, Ware, and Hohman, suggestive in Carroll's case, and mostly non-apparent for Herbst. Kyrk received early career support from Leon Carroll Marshall and traveled with James Alfred Field, as well as benefitting from federal agency networking links with women such as Ursula Batchelder Stone and Day Monroe (a graduate student of Kyrk's). Kyrk's deep mentoring of many graduate students was also likely important in her network expansion over time. Hohman had four noteworthy connections with leading male economists: husband Elmo Hohman, James Alfred Field, and two Swedish economists. There is no evidence of networking between Hohman and other women economists. Ware likely benefited early on from her thesis adviser, Edwin Gay's connection to the Hart, Schaffner and Marx committee, as well as lifelong interactive influence with her economist-spouse, Gardiner Means. Ware also had a host of co-authored publications, indicating strong networking capacity in research. The only obvious network for Carroll is in her early connections to the women of the Chicago program, including Grace Abbott who headed the first federal agency employing Carroll. Kyrk had substantial influence on graduate students, and it seems likely that Herbst and Ware had some mentees who diffused variations of their mentors' thinking and methods.

Available information on the personal lives of all six women is limited. Two (Hohman and Ware) were married to male economists. Because both couples maintained academic pursuits for both partners and lifelong marriages, it seems reasonable to posit that the women, particularly Ware, received more benefit than difficulty from their marriages. Two (Kyrk and Hohman) carried responsibility for a dependent child. Responsibility for a dependant may divert attention away from career, though there might have been unintended positive effects if human capital developed through parenting transferred into interpersonal skills in their careers. There is no information on important social circles, friendships, and intimate relationships for Kyrk, Carroll, Herbst or Scheftel.

There is variation in the career outcomes of the six women award winners listed in Table 13.3. Because Scheftel dropped out of economics altogether, her career might tentatively constitute an extreme case of "separatism." Carroll's career manifested separatist classification by teaching in a women's college and when she shifted permanently into federal bureaucratic employment. Hohman made two noteworthy research contributions in economics beyond her thesis but because her career seems to have taken secondary status to family, can be considered "subordinate" from an academic career perspective. With an active localized, decades-long academic appointment at a major state university but no discernible non-localized research productivity, Herbst is "status quo." Kyrk and Ware stand out as superperforming-separatists—both made contributions within economics, but are known for their contributions outside the discipline. In all but one case, these six *her*stories suggest that, with early disciplinary recognition, the award-winning women economists navigated gender discrimination in academia, leaving a paper trail of careers that created knowledge in specific spheres of inquiry.

Table 13.3 Career outcomes assessment for six women economics award winners

Name	*Overall career assessment (based on available information)*
Yetta Scheftel	Extreme "separatist" (economics drop-out)
Hazel Kyrk	Superperformer and separatist
Mollie Ray Carroll	Separatist
Helen Hohman	Subordinate
Caroline Ware	Superperformer and separatist
Alma Herbst	Status quo

Notes

1 Thanks for editorial support from Millersville University undergraduate research assistant, Sammie Bigham.
2 *Minnesota History*, June 1929, volume 10, number 2, p. 178.
3 Though assessing the first decade of economists' careers rather than one monograph, compare the John Bates Clark Medal winners: from 1947–1999, 0 women received this award out of 26 award recipients (0%); from 1947–2015, 3 women received this award out of 37 award recipients (8.11%).
4 See Frey and Neckermann (2010) and Chan et al. (2013).
5 See Madden, Kirsten, "Anecdotes of Discrimination: Barriers to Women's Participation in Economic Thought During the Late Nineteenth and Early Twentieth Centuries," Chapter 9 this volume.
6 Forget, 1995, p. 26 who cites Glazer, Penina Migdal, and Miriam Slater (1987) *Unequal Colleagues: The Entrance of Women into the Professions, 1890–1940*. New Brunswick, NJ: Rutgers University Press.
7 Ibid., p. 34.
8 Ibid., pp. 34–36.
9 These theses are scattered throughout the references in Madden, Seiz, and Pujol (2004).
10 Except where otherwise noted, biographical details for all six women in this chapter are from documents turned up through Google searches. Full sets of references for biographical details are available upon request.
11 Correspondence with University of Chicago Special Collections, ask@lib.uchicago.edu, 2/5/2016.
12 Described as such by Solon J. Buck in "Historical Activities in the Old Northwest and Eastern Canada, 1913–1914," *The Mississippi Valley Historical Review*, 1 (1) (June 1914): 57–94.
13 The University of Illinois at Urbana-Champaign, Illinois History and Lincoln Manuscript Collections houses the completed eight-chapter manuscript.
14 Preface by Lucie B. Hoxie and Nathan Fine in *Trade Unionism in the United States*, Robert Franklin Hoxie, New York: D. Appleton & Co., 1921.
15 Correspondence with University of Chicago Special Collections, ask@lib.uchicago.edu, 2/5/2016.
16 See the review by "F.T.S." in *Annals of the American Academy of Political and Social Science*, 72 (July 1917): 240.
17 No author attributed, in "Minor Notices" section of *The American Political Science Review*, 11 (3) (August 1917): 597.
18 Correspondence with University of Chicago Special Collections, ask@lib.uchicago.edu, 2/5/2016.
19 The biographical account of Kyrk draws from three secondary sources. Beller and Kiss (2008) presents detailed biographical information; Lobdell (2000) provides a few additional biographical details; and van Velsen (2003) primarily provides analysis of Kyrk's intellectual contributions.
20 Beller and Kiss 2008, p. 5.
21 Year of death from *Goucher Library News*, Vol. 38, No. 3, June 1994, p. 7.
22 "The Letter Box," in *The University of Chicago Magazine*, Vol X, No. 1, November, 1917 (Chicago: The Alumni Council), p. 309.
23 Rose C. Feld 1923. "Two Centuries of the Labor Feud . . ." *The New York Times*, Feb. 4, p. BR8.
24 "Says War Nations Cut Hours of Work," *The New York Times*, Feb. 19, 1941, p. 26.
25 "National Quotas for Immigration to End," *CQ Almanac*, 1965, https://library.cqpress.com/cqalmanac/document.php?id=cqal65-1259481 (10/15/2015 access date).
26 Northwestern University emailed a digital copy of one folder of information preserved from Elmo Hohman and of three items preserved in Helen Fisher Hohman's archive. The biographical facts in this account draw from the Northwestern University archives and from Google searches.
27 "She Also Serves Who Teaches Economics," *Alumni Magazine*, which is the Bulletin of New York School of Social Work, July 1922, pp. 26–27.
28 Lee and Samuel's entry to Dimand et al. (2000) *A Biographical Dictionary of Women Economists*, pp. 460–64, is the source for Ware's biographical profile. Anne Firor Scott (2006) also provides biographical information in *Pauli Murray and Caroline Ware: Forty Years of Letters in Black and White*, as summarized in "Caroline Farrar Ware. Brief life of a multifaceted public citizen: 1899–1990," *Harvard Magazine* online, 2009, http://harvardmagazine.com/2009/05/caroline-farrar-ware (10/19/2015 access date).
29 American Association of University Women website, www.aauw.org/2012/08/14/from-the-archives-caroline-ware/ (10/19/2015 access date).
30 Anne Firor Scott, "Caroline Farrar Ware. Brief life of a multifaceted public citizen: 1899–1990," *Harvard Magazine* online, 2009 http://harvardmagazine.com/2009/05/caroline-farrar-ware (11/5/2015 access date).

31 Mollie Ray Carroll?
32 In the "Notes" of *American Economic Review*, 20 (4) (Dec., 1930): 798–811.
33 The Ohio State University Archival Office (archives@osu.edu) responded to a December 22, 2016 email inquiry and provided the few documents they have in association with the employment of Alma Herbst.
34 Industrial and Labor Relations Review, 3 (2) (Jan., 1950): 309.
35 *Lantern* (of The Ohio State University), June 26, 1947, p. 8.
36 From OSU official archived records obtained via email correspondence with librarian Halle R. Mare, 12/22/2015.
37 In the "News and Notes" section of the January 1955 issue of *Industrial and Labor Relations Review*.
38 "Major" economics journals in the twentieth century include the *American Economic Review, Journal of Political Economy, Quarterly Journal of Economics*, and *The Economic Journal*.
39 Forget, 1995, p. 34

References

References for specific undocumented biographical details are available upon request.

Beller, Andrea H. and D. Elizabeth Kiss. June 2008 Working Paper Revision of 1999 draft. "On the Contribution of Hazel Kyrk to Family Economics."

Carroll, Mollie Ray. 1923. "Labor and Politics: The Attitude of the American Federation of Labor toward Legislation and Politics." Cambridge, MA: The Riverside Press. Hart, Schaffner & Marx Prize Essay, no. 33.

Chan, Ho Fai, Bruno S. Frey, Jana Gallus and Benno Torgler. February 2013. "Does the John Bates Clark Medal Boost Subsequent Productivity and Citation Success?" University of Zurich Department of Economics Working Paper Series ISSN 1664-705X (online), Working Paper No. 111. (https://ideas.repec.org/p/cra/wpaper/2013-02.html, August 2015 access date.)

Forget, Evelyn L. 1995. "American Women Economists, 1900–1940: Doctoral Dissertations and Research Specialization," in Mary Ann Dimand, Robert W. Dimand and Evelyn L. Forget, eds., *Women of Value: Feminist Essays on the History of Women in Economics*. Aldershot, UK and Brookfield, VT: Elgar, pp. 25–38.

Frey, Bruno S. and Susanne Neckermann. October 2010. "Awards as Signals." Institute for Empirical Research in Economics University of Zurich Working Paper Series ISSN 1424-0459, Working Paper No. 513. (https://ideas.repec.org/p/zur/iewwpx/513.html, August 2015 access date).

Herbst, Alma. 1932. "The Negro in the Slaughtering and Meat-Packing Industry in Chicago." Hart, Schaffner & Marx prize essays, 52. Boston: Houghton Mifflin/Herbst, Alma. (1930) 'The Negro in the Slaughtering and Meat Packing Industry in Chicago', Ph.D. Thesis, University of Chicago (economics).

Hohman, Elmo P. Faculty Biographical Files, Northwestern University Archives, Evanston IL. Materials emailed in a .pdf file, 12/21/2015.

Hohman, Helen Fisher. 1922. "She Also Serves Who Teaches Economics." *The Alumni Magazine* for the New York School of Social Work (July): 26–27.

——. 1928. "The Trade Board Acts and the Social Insurance Acts in Relation to a Minimum Standard of Living in Great Britain – A Study of Attitudes toward Poverty and Methods of Dealing with It – 1880–1926." Ph.D. thesis, University of Chicago (economics).

Hohman, Helen Fisher. Faculty Biographical Files, Northwestern University Archives, Evanston IL. Materials emailed in a .pdf file, 12/21/2015.

Kyrk, Hazel. 1923. "A Theory of Consumption." Boston and New York: Houghton Mifflin; London: Pitman.

Lee, Frederic S. and Warren J. Samuels. 2000. "Caroline Farrar Ware (1899–1990)," in Robert W. Dimand, Mary Ann Dimand and Evelyn Forget, eds., *A Biographical Dictionary of Women Economists*. Cheltenham, UK: Edward Elgar Publishing, Inc., pp. 460–64.

Lobdell, Richard A. 2000. Hazel Kyrk (1886–1957). In Robert W. Dimand, Mary Ann Dimand and Evelyn Forget, eds., *A Biographical Dictionary of Women Economists*, Cheltenham, United Kingdom: Edward Elgar Publishing, Inc., pp. 251–53.

Locke, Alain. 1932. "Black Pawns of Labor: Reviews of *The Negro in The Slaughtering and Meat-Packing Industry in Chicago*, by Alma Herbst; and the *Free Negro Family*, by E. Franklin Frazier." *Survey*, 68: 699–700.

Madden, Kirsten K., Janet A. Seiz and Michele Pujol. 2004. *A Bibliography of Female Economic Thought to 1940*. London: Routledge.
Parnes, Herbert S. (2001). *A Prof's Life: It's More than Teaching*. Lincoln, NE: Writer's Showcase.
Scheftel, Yetta. 1907. "Persistence of Poverty." M.A. thesis, University of Chicago (sociology).
——. 1915. Review of "Ross's 'Old World in the New'." *The Mississippi Valley Historical Review*, 1 (4) (March): 617–30.
——. 1915–16. "The Settlement of the Military Tract in the State of Illinois: A Study of the Western Movement." Prepared for The Centennial History of Illinois. Manuscript available at The University of Illinois at Urbana-Champaign, Illinois History and Lincoln Manuscript Collections (www.library.illinois.edu/ihx/archon/?p=collections/controlcard&id=254 10/1/2015 access).
——. 1916. "The Taxation of Land Value: A Study of Certain Discriminatory Taxes on Land." Boston, MA: Houghton Mifflin Company. Hart, Schaffner & Marx prize essays 22.
Van Velsen, Susan. 2003. "Hazel Kyrk and the Ethics of Consumption," in Drucilla K. Barker and Edith Kuiper, eds., *Toward a Feminist Philosophy of Economics*. London: Routledge, Chapter 3.
Ware, Caroline Farrar. 1925. "The Industrial Revolution in the New England Cotton Industry." Ph.D. thesis, Radcliffe College (history). Published as: 1931. "The Early New England Cotton Manufacture: A Study in Industrial Beginnings." Boston: Houghton Mifflin. Reprinted New York: Russell and Russell, 1966.
——. 1926. "New England's Cotton Mills: How the Records for Their Story Were Discovered." *Bulletin of the Business Historical Society*, 1 (4): 4–7.
Young, Arthur N. 1917. "Review of *The Taxation of Land Value* by Yetta Scheftel." *The American Economic Review*, 7 (2) (June): 415–16.

14

EARLY WOMEN ECONOMISTS AT COLUMBIA UNIVERSITY

Contributions in the struggle for labor protection in the Lochner era

Clara Elisabetta Mattei[1]

The 1910s and 1920s were critical for the development of labor legislation in the United States. A shift in the role of the state was being negotiated in the regulation of the economy, especially of the labor market. A heterogeneous network of progressive activists, of which academics were a constituent (Hart 1994, 67), fought for enactment of protective labor legislation, while conservative efforts, primarily embodied by Lochner era[2] Federal Courts, upheld freedom of contract and laissez-faire.

A peculiar feature of early American progressive labor legislation was that, until the New Deal, it aimed at protecting women, not men workers. The constitutionality of the law was based upon a recognition of the "difference between the sexes." Women were accorded special status due to their economic weakness and their reproductive role. The words of Justice David Josiah Brewer are noteworthy:

> That woman's physical structure and the performance of maternal functions place her at a disadvantage in the struggle for subsistence is obvious . . . as healthy mothers are essential to vigorous offspring, the physical well-being of woman becomes an object of public interest and care in order to preserve the strength and vigor of the race.
>
> *208 U.S. 412 at 412 [1908]*

The common interest for a vigorous race overruled the classical principle of "liberty of contract" and legitimized government exercise of police power[3] to protect the health, morals and safety of the community.

Of all labor legislation, minimum wage laws were the most controversial, since, in the words of its opponents, wage fixing represented the emblem of the "expression of the paternalistic and socialistic tendencies of the day" (Woloch 2015, 106). In 1912 Massachusetts enacted the first minimum wage law only for women workers, a year later seven more states and the District of Columbia followed. Up until 1923 its constitutionality was upheld on the basis of the above-mentioned sex-dividing philosophy.

Scientific expertise was broadly deployed by courts. The canonical narrative views the progressive advocacy of sex-specific wage legislation as a strategy to exploit the police power loophole of the constitution and thus escape the vetoes of the conservative courts who were unwilling to allow for regulation of male labor contracts. Leonard (2005 and 2016) shows that such a view is at best incomplete if not misleading. The stance of reform economists Henry Seager, Richard Ely, and John Commons "was also the product of reformers' ambivalence, sometimes even hostility, toward women's labor-force participation" (Leonard 2005, 772).

This chapter considers the progressive Columbia School of women economists as an important exception to the sexist progressive trend. Emilie Josephine Hutchinson and Elizabeth Faulkner Baker viewed labor legislation, in particular minimum wage legislation, as a full-blown "labor problem" rather than a "sex problem" (Hutchinson 1919, 80). They proposed universal extension of labor legislation as a fundamental pillar for socio-economic improvement of American capitalist society. Such a far-reaching outlook posed a convincing challenge to feminist opponents of protective labor legislation, who, starting from the beginning of the 1920s, fought against minimum wages in the name of equal opportunities. The feminist opposition argument to labor legislation was based on the idea that protective legislation for women diminished competitiveness of women workers, causing unemployment and discrimination of jobs: "freedom of contract" had to be extended to all. Hutchinson and Baker's analysis dispelled the feminist opposition argument, advocating for universal labor protection.

In the first section I introduce the two women economists, embedding their scholarship within the main sequence of judicial events on minimum wage laws. The latter exemplify the historical turnover of the three major ideological blocks: the conservative courts, the reform progressives, and the equal rights feminists. The following two sections discuss Baker and Hutchinson's method of analysis, together with their reform proposals, which disclose their distance with respect to Leonard's (2005) mainstream progressives. The fourth section discusses the two economists' response to criticisms against wage legislation, in particular the problem of legally induced disemployment,[4] highlighting a further element of divergence from mainstream progressives. In the fifth section, I discuss two indispensable components for Baker's and Hutchinson's reform agenda: unionization and socio-economic education. I study original archival material that discloses Hutchinson's primary involvement in The Barnard Summer School for Women Workers in Industry, a ground-breaking practical experiment for disseminating socio-economic consciousness among women workers.

Hutchinson, Baker, and their time

Hutchinson and Baker were pioneer women professors of economics at Barnard College, the women's college affiliated with Columbia University. The major historical works on labor laws cite them as contemporary experts on the topic (Hart 1994; Woloch 2015). Yet, until now, their life and works have not been unearthed. I use the material of the Columbia and Barnard Archives, together with their publications, to give these women their due significance.

Emilie Hutchinson (1877, Yarmouth USA–1938, New York City) graduated with honors from the Barnard class of 1905. After five years of instructorship in economics at Mount Holyoke and Wellesley colleges, in 1913 "her alma mater invited her to fill the first position ever offered to a woman in an Economics department" (Baker 1938, Hutchinson's Obituary, Barnard Archives). While teaching at Barnard, Hutchinson received her MA from Columbia University (1908) and took her doctorate in economics at the same institution. In 1919 she defended her thesis called *Women's Wages: A Study of the Wages of Industrial Women and Measures*

Suggested to Increase Them, soon published by Columbia University Press. She was then promoted to Associate Professor in Economics at Barnard and held the post of Head of the Department of Economics until her death. Hutchinson taught an eclectic variety of courses: from economic history to economic theories and consumer behavior. Beginning in 1919, Baker assisted Hutchinson with the core course entitled "Outlines in Economics." The two women taught the course together for almost twenty years. In the Barnard Bulletin of 1938, Baker wrote an affectionate obituary of her senior colleague and former PhD supervisor. In 1940 Baker replaced Hutchinson as head of the department, a post she held until her retirement in 1952.

Contrarily to Hutchinson, Baker (1885, Kansas–1973, Washington) was not a Barnard alumna. She received her Bachelor's degree from the University of California, Berkeley in 1914. However, just like Hutchinson, she gained her MA and PhD in economics at Columbia University. Her interest in the topic of labor relations, and especially in the status of women in industry, is evident from her 1919 MA dissertation entitled "Some of the Economic and Social Causes and Effects, Especially upon the Family, of the Employment of Married Women in Industry." In that same year Baker was appointed at Barnard to teach the course "Women and Labor." In 1925, she defended her PhD dissertation *Protective Labor Legislation, with Special Reference to Women in the State of New York*, published by Columbia University Press (1925). Baker served as a faculty member of the Barnard College economics department for thirty-three years (1919–1952), first as Assistant Professor and, from 1938 onward, as Associate Professor.[5] In 1933 her famous book, *Displacement of Men by Machines*, was published, and in 1964, twelve years after retirement, she published *Technology and Woman's Work.*

Both women economists combined their academic career with "practical and humane interests" (Saulnier 1973, *Baker's Obituary*, Barnard Archives). While teaching at Wellesley College, Hutchinson was a volunteer worker for the Women's Trade Union League of Boston. For two years (1905–07) she was secretary of the Women's Auxiliary to the Civil Service Reform Association of New York. In 1917 Hutchinson took a year's leave of absence from Barnard to act as manager of the Intercollegiate Bureau of Occupations.[6] As for Baker, her obituary reads: "Her career was particularly notable . . . as an outstanding example of service and accomplishment in education, research and public service" (Saulnier, 1973). During WWII she served as Panel Chairman in Region II, New York, for the War Relations Board. Baker was also a member of the National Planning Association and, from 1946 to 1948, distinguished member of the New York sector of the Society for Advancement of Management. Apart from scholarly journals, such as the *American Economic Review*, both Baker and Hutchinson intervened in the national press, in particular the *New York Times*.[7] The Columbia women produced a scholarship that was constantly concerned with the real world of policymaking. This is clear, in the first place, from their dissertations.

Emilie Hutchinson and Elizabeth Baker wrote their PhD theses on the subject of minimum wage legislation during a critical historical moment: an age of transition. In 1919, when Hutchinson defended *Women's Wages*, American Progressives had much to celebrate. In 1912 the State of Massachusetts passed the first act providing for a minimum wage for women while establishing a commission to study industrial conditions and to set wage rates. By 1919 minimum wage laws were applied in fourteen states, the District of Columbia, and Puerto Rico. Yet, at the eve of the new decade, circumstances changed dramatically. *Adkins v. Children's Hospital* of (1923), declared the unconstitutionality of the District of Columbia minimum wage law. The United States Supreme Court confirmed the decision of the District. The event sanctioned the death knell of protective wage legislation up until the New Deal.

Baker and Hutchinson were well aware of complex political contrasts at play. Both women dedicated a chapter of their theses to "The Controversy." A schematic reconstruction of the ideological collision pictures three major forces at play.[8] The Courts' rulings expressed the passage of historical force from one ideological block to another: from laissez-faire to progressive creed, then once more, from progressive creed to laissez-faire, though, this time, imbued with legal feminist ideology. Political pressures apart, the judiciary was informed by expert reports and opinions.

In a first moment, the contrast was mainly between the conservative block fighting for the respect of laissez-faire principles as constitutive elements in the American Constitution and the progressive social reformers that obtained single-sex laws through the principle of woman's peculiar biological and social role. Until 1919 the constitutionality of wage legislation for women was affirmed on the basis of the legitimate use of police power to promote public welfare. The progressive case for women's labor legislation was not posed as a matter of exploitation of the lowest skilled and ill-remunerated workers, but rather as a national obligation, pertaining exclusively to women, to produce "vigorous offspring" (Baker 1925, 83–85).

The landmark case *Muller v. Oregon* (1908) that inaugurated the success of progressive women's labor legislation was won on the grounds of the necessary protection of the integrity of the home and the race by limiting female wage labor. Baker denounces the conservative *animus* of progressive wage legislation:

> From this it seems there are mixed motives underlying the advocacy of special laws for women. One of the fundamental motives is not the protection of women's health but the retention either of a tradition or of a job [men's jobs]. This motive appears in the form of a health and a morals disguise.
>
> *Baker 1925, 444*

Beginning in 1920, a second ideological contrast emerged. The Women's National Party (WNP) split from the reformers of the National Consumers League (NCL), declaring the elimination of women's labor protection as its main goal. The conflict between the principles of protection and equality fully ensued. Led by Alice Paul, the WNP campaigned for equal opportunities, selecting legal equality as their exclusive socio-political concern. Protective labor legislation ought to be abolished: it made labor competition more difficult for women, creating unemployment, especially among skilled women workers. In this view, "freedom of contract" had to be extended to all.[9] The *Columbia v. Adkins* case of 1923 confirmed the victory for the so-called legal feminists, marking also a conservative counterattack against progressives. Indeed, as Baker well explains,

> A two-fold attack was made upon the law, – first upon the very principle of legal minimum wage which is a "price-fixing law" and an infringement of the right of free contract, and then upon its special application to women "who are legally as capable of contracting for themselves as men," and therefore a denial of the equal protection of the laws.
>
> *Baker 1925, 88–89*

The recognition of women's equality came with the rejection of "the tendency of the hour to socialize property rights" (Baker 1925, 86), "paternalism," price fixing, and even "Sovietism"; all dangerous phenomena that, according to the conservative forces, had characterized the past decade (Baker 1925, 86). The 1923 case sanctioned the comeback of the principles of the famous *Lochner v. New York* case (1905) that had inaugurated courts' rulings against labor legislation.[10] By 1930 only six minimum wage laws remained in place: all were either unenforced or otherwise ineffective (Woloch 2015, 127–128).

Baker and Hutchinson observed the complex overturn of events. The two academics were also attentive to the intellectual debate that informed the judiciary. They shared a stance that represented an exception with respect to the mainstream progressive field. They were surely not the only exception, yet one that deserves attention for its scope and modernity. Their position dialogued and challenged the stance of equal rights feminists who had revolted against labor legislation.

As any authentic progressive, Hutchinson and Baker supported state intervention and deeply believed in the power of economic expertise. As progressives, Hutchinson and Baker were supporters of female minimum wage legislation. Yet, in contrast with mainstream progressives, minimum wage legislation was not a means to preserve women in their traditional role of homemakers. On the contrary, it was the first fundamental instrument for society to adjust to the structural economic and social changes of capitalism that presented women as crucial components of the labor force.

In order to support their claim, Hutchinson and Baker undertook an economic analysis of the effects of minimum wage legislation. They considered the main concern of the equal rights feminists: disemployment caused by these laws. Baker and Hutchinson were conscious of the limits of single-sex wage legislation. However, their critical analysis brought them to support universal wage laws.

Advocacy of wage laws for all workers distinguished the position of the two Columbia economists from both mainstream feminists and mainstream progressives. The two economists saw minimum wage legislation as a basic component of a broader set of tools for the welfare of workers. Political organization through unionization and economic instruction were crucial in their eyes. These ideas stemmed from their approach to economics, receptive to the interlock between economic, cultural, and political factors.

The historical approach

Baker and Hutchinson held a common view regarding minimum wage legislation. It is plausible to think that this shared vision derived from a more fundamental commonality: the scope and method of economic analysis. This aspect explains their distance from the "sexist mainstream" discussed by Leonard (2005 and 2016).

Hutchinson and Baker approached the topic of labor legislation from a broad economic and historical perspective. The Columbia scholars were not interested in the women's question per se; they were concerned with women's socio-economic position as a crucial element to analyze the evolution of the capitalist economy.[11] They stressed that as the economic system changes, so does its socio-economic organization. The opening of Hutchinson's 1929 article, "The Economic Problem of Women," is very telling of this approach:

> The advent of the machine age roughly dated the passing of one social and economic order and the beginning of another that is still in the process of unfolding its peculiar and distinctive characteristics. Economic, political, and social problems have presented themselves with bewildering rapidity, and have created an atmosphere of stress and strain throughout our social life. One of the problems of major importance in this rapidly changing order centers in the economic position and function of women.
>
> *Hutchinson 1929, 132*

In Hutchinson's historical analysis, the transition from the domestic system of industry to machine production was the principal reason for the emergence of the strict division of labor between men and women. When the home was the chief setting of economic activity, men and women were jointly producers and consumers. Once profit became the leading aim of production and traditional family activities were taken out of the home "the function of women in the home steadily lost its importance in production until it fell to a minimum, and emerged associated primarily with consumption" (Hutchinson 1929, 132). In their role as consumers, women lost all of their financial independence. As Baker also put it, their legal and social position adjusted to the new economic setting: "under the common law, the economic status of a married woman was practically that of a slave" (Baker 1927, 273).

Yet, as capitalism matured and unskilled labor increased its ranks, many women joined the labor force, primarily to compensate for the fact that, in the lowest income group, "the earnings of men have been insufficient to support their wives and daughters" (Hutchinson 1929, 132). For Baker and Hutchinson, it was an undeniable historical fact that the evolution of the capitalist economy meant a continuing increase of women in the labor market, in particular in industrial occupations. Since 1880, when the national census began to record separately the number of men and women gainfully employed, "the steadily increasing number of women working for money has been a matter of general interest and concern." World War I, Hutchinson remarked, merely ignited a structural change that had been going on for the last decades (see Hutchinson 1919, 12).

The history of capitalism revealed how the traditional division of labor between men and women was deeply economically and socially constructed, thus historically contingent: "The trend of women's gainful employment has been running counter to the general assumption that men are the 'natural' breadwinners in the present economic order" (Hutchinson 1929, 133).

In sum, Baker and Hutchinson's broad method of historical analysis pushed them to analyze the topic of women's labor in a dynamic fashion. This marked the first fundamental difference with respect to Leonard's (2005) progressives: women's labor is not an unnatural and exceptional phenomenon; rather, it is one of the crucial aspects that define the evolution of capitalism. Women's roles as caregivers hold nothing biologically innate. In this perspective, women's labor and wage conditions did not represent "a sex problem" but rather the topical problem for the analysis of the evolving economic system.

In her thesis, Hutchinson sets the common agenda: "we must look forward to the continued importance of the unskilled woman worker and her labor problem" (Hutchinson 1919, 13). Indeed, the same dynamic approach is visible in Baker, who writes:

> The apparent facts force recognition by the impartial observer "that women are in industry to stay" . . . Social change is inevitable . . . without being dogmatic it is as logical to declare that our economic order must return to that of the 1750s as to say that women must take themselves out of industry.
>
> *Baker 1925, 443–444*

Hutchinson and Baker's method displays a flavor of historical materialism. As the production structure and the labor market evolve, women recover an economic position as producers that they had lost with the passage from the traditional economy to the machine age. Thus, Hutchinson and Baker predicted that social relations would modify accordingly with the economic structure. The household and family relations would eventually advance into forms of joint economic and child-bearing responsibilities between men and women. As Baker also insists, motherhood would eventually be transformed into parenthood.

However, the two economists were well aware of the complexity of processes of socio-economic transformations. In fact, Baker and Hutchinson did not endorse a deterministic version of historical materialism: a crucial element of their analysis rested in the appreciation of the strong power of tradition and culture as conservative forces, contrasting the evolution of women's role.[12] This insight gives a strong reason for Hutchinson and Baker's support of wage legislation as an institutional measure to counteract the forceful reaction to economic change. Let us first discuss the influence of non-economic forces on women's wages.

Beyond economic forces: the significance of wage legislation

Baker and Hutchinson focused on wages as they represented "a specific test of woman's economic status" (Hutchinson 1919, 179). In her first chapters of *Women's Wages*, Hutchinson studies available data on wages and their relations with the costs of living: census and federal investigations, labor bureaus statistics, and investigating commissions. The findings revealed that wages of industrial women "are compressed within a narrow range from four to eight dollars a week" (p. 25). Furthermore, wages of the majority of industrial women "fall short of the amount required to maintain a normal standard of life . . . to this extent industrial women at present fail self-support" (p. 50).

From this data, the two economists conclude, women are "a distinct class of wage earners" (Hutchinson 1919, 66). They embody the weakest and worst remunerated component of the labor force: a class of the most exploited workers. Baker and Hutchinson affirm that a satisfying explanation of women's particular economic condition must account for extra-economic forces, in particular, custom and tradition. The working of the law of supply and demand fails to account for this extreme level of exploitation. Hutchinson's phrasing is clear:

> The outcome of the whole situation is that the industrial employment of girls becomes subject to peculiar and distinctive influences that operate to hold their wages at a low level—lower than would result from the working of purely economic forces. Custom and tradition in themselves dictate the offer of lower wages to women than to men and put definite limit to their occupational opportunities.
>
> *1919, 66*

Hutchinson devotes an entire chapter of her thesis to the "Factors Affecting Wages." It is clear that economic rationales are impossible to disentangle from socio-cultural factors. A summary of the chapter conveys the idea:

> Women are usually young and inexperienced, hence predominating in the lower grades of jobs; they stay in industry a comparatively brief time, too brief to reach the maximum earnings possible in even their own types of work; they cannot rely to any extent upon a strong organization to defend and promote their interests; and finally, their economic status in the family, closely connected as it is to their child-bearing function, contributes a further restriction upon their vocational opportunity.
>
> *1919, 66*

Baker's thesis echoes these ideas, stressing the conservative force of tradition as a determining factor on woman's labor condition (Baker 1925, 445). Thus, at present, the challenge for women is "to wrestle with the problem of adjusting their necessities and obligations as producers to the claims of an environment still largely dominated by the tradition of economic dependence and restricted economic opportunity" (Hutchinson 1919, 179).

Baker and Hutchinson conceived wage legislation for women as a primary element in opposing conservative social forces. This point brings about a contrasting interpretation of the meaning of women's wage legislation with respect to Leonard's progressives. Wage legislation is not demanded as an instrument to keep women outside the labor market. Rather, it is a means for social practices to adjust to the structural economic changes of women as gainfully employed actors of the economy.

Writing after 1921, when the feminist criticism of single-sex labor legislation exploded, Baker was perceptive of the controversial interpretation of labor legislation: its emancipatory role for women was challenged. To tackle this topic, we must first discuss the criticism of wage legislation, particularly regarding unemployment.

Criticism of wage legislation

Disemployment effect?

The main criticism against wage legislation considered it as an interference with the natural law of supply and demand, producing "greater evils than it is aimed to cure" (Hutchinson 1919, 90), as it fundamentally caused unemployment, especially of the most unskilled. Minimum wage laws "seem likely to lead either to lessened profits or higher prices of goods. Either process leads again to some curtailment of the operations or some employment of others to take the place of women" (Taussig 1916, 428).[13] This position, based on neoclassical price theory, was well known to our authors. Hutchinson located it theoretically: it was the result of a particular "social philosophy" (Hutchinson 1919, 96) that deeply clashed with progressive ideas of state interventionism: "The argument savors of laissez-faire and an optimistic reliance upon natural law which can be trusted to bring all things right in the long run" (p. 91).

Six years later, in her thesis, Baker revealed the connection of neoclassical attacks with the feminist equal opportunities movement: the feminist opposition argument against wage legislation deployed neoclassical theory to strengthen its stance. For both critics the main effects of minimum wage legislation were unemployment for women and discrimination of jobs. Baker wrote, "The principle of special protection is being challenged as unattainable and irrational – as prejudicial to women rather than advantageous" (Baker 1925, 342).

Leonard shows that the majority of leading progressives were in favor of labor reform exactly *because* they thought binding minimum wages would disemploy workers. What distinguished them from their neoclassical counterparts was their value judgment: legally induced disemployment was not a social cost but a putative social benefit, "as it performed the eugenic service of rising wages by ridding the labor force of the 'unemployables'" (Leonard 2005, 766). Among the "unemployables," Sidney Webb famously classified "child-bearing women" and those "deficient in strength" (Webb 1920, 785).

In opposition to these views, Baker and Hutchinson held a position that was in line with today's minimum wage advocates: minimum wages did not disemploy women workers. Hutchinson contested the assumption of a zero sum game between lower profits and higher prices that would occur with labor legislation, thus causing unemployment. Rather, there subsisted a positive correlation between wage laws and economic progress, and the latter phenomenon would increase the number of employed workers. Wage legislation acted as a catalyst for investment in improved machinery. Since employers could "no longer nibble at wages" (Hutchinson 1919, 88) legislation prompted "a challenge of established business methods. It will forcibly urge employers to conserve their profits by compensating advantages in some form of greater efficiency of production" (Hutchinson 1919, 88).

In this framework, a virtuous process of selective evolution among firms took place: "The practice of establishing minimum rates in putting a premium upon efficient management tends to drive out of business the inferior establishments that exist in every trade" (Hutchinson 1919, 88). Labor laws benefit society as a whole. Wage laws protect society against the pernicious socio-economic effects of parasitic industries that had subsisted at "the expense of the vigor, health and morality of its employees." "If an industry can maintain itself only by paying its workers less than a living wage, it is socially an unprofitable enterprise. Rightly it should be forced out of existence" (p. 83). "Mr. Webb" is cited in Hutchinson's thesis to support this view. Yet, she differs from the Webbian progressive thesis in two major respects.

In the first place, Hutchinson accepted that during the selective process a degree of displacement of adult workers occurred: some businesses failed and, contemporaneously, employers would "weed out" their less efficient workers. However, she firmly claimed that the disemployment effect would be only temporary. Technological innovation fostered economic growth, hence the less efficient worker would be absorbed into other businesses, while new workers would be taken on board to replace them. Hutchinson's conclusion is firm: "The result has been that the increased cost of labor has been offset by superior methods of management, thus constituting a gain for the employee and no loss for the employer" (p. 119).

The author noted that the Massachusetts minimum wage commission corroborated her views:

> The increases in wages have been large throughout the industry, and at the same time the capital investment in the industry and the value of the product have materially increased. The employment of women and minors have not given way to the employment of men, nor has the minimum become the maximum.
>
> *Massachusetts Minimum Wage commission (1915, 1), in Hutchinson 1919, 126*

Second, while the author endorsed Webb's evolutionary approach concerning the progress by selection of institutional capacity, she completely disregarded any eugenic notion of innate capabilities of workers, especially women. Biological determinism was demystified and no mention of the concept of "unemployables" was made. The material conditions, in particular the investment and management capacities of the firm, retained absolute priority to explain labor productivity. An integral part of these material conditions was workers' nutrition and health: as their wage increased so did their physical strength and thus their productivity. Empirical evidence supported this point as well; for example, the 1915 reports by R.H. Tawney on minimum wages in tailoring.

Together with Baker, Hutchinson considered empirical studies as a fundamental component of their scholarship on minimum wages. "Nothing short of actual experience of the social and economic effects of minimum-wage legislation can settle the controversy between its advocates and opponents" (Hutchinson 1919, 97). Hutchinson looked at the foreign precedents of Victoria (New Zealand) and Great Britain, while both women carefully analyzed the data deriving from various US industrial commissions or State Labor Bureaus commissions.[14] The two authors discussed the epistemological limits[15] of these enquiries at length, invoking greater effort in deploying economic expertise to collect larger and unbiased material (Baker 1925, 424: Hutchinson 1929, 129).

Nevertheless, the available evidence confirmed that "no substantial fact refutes the results of those who defend the general benefits of wage legislation" (Hutchinson 1919, 123). In summary, in the states where the minimum wage law was actually applied, the social problem of sweating had been eliminated (Hutchinson 1919, 98). Also, the fear of a leveling down of all wages to the minimum wage had been discarded. The Wisconsin Commission of 1920 testified that the general level of wages had advanced since minimum laws passed; it was specifically the youngest and most inexperienced women that had benefited (Baker 1925, 406; Hutchinson 1919, 105).

Baker agreed with these findings: minimum wages, far from being detrimental to women's employment, ameliorated their labor conditions, and thus society's welfare as a whole. Baker fully approved the Hutchinsonian analysis to refute the criticism of the positive correlation between labor legislation and unemployment. To the contrary, minimum wages enhanced industrial efficiency, economic progress, and wider employment of unskilled women workers (Baker 1925, 404–428). However, writing in 1925, Baker was receptive to feminist protests for equal rights, taking their motivations with serious scholarly concern.

Baker and the feminist critique

Baker asked: "Why then the growing opposition for protective labor legislation for women?" (Baker 1926, 531). She answered:

> [T]he protestants explain that these laws do not always protect, that they often shackle instead. They urge that women have small chance before their profit seeking employers to secure desirable occupations when there are restrictions placed on what they can offer while men can give their services on their own terms.
>
> *1929, 266*

For Baker, recent empirical studies[16] revealed that, in industries where women predominated, such as mercantile establishments and many factories, Hutchinson's findings held true: wage laws, and labor laws in general, did not cause women's unemployment and benefited men workers by raising the general labor conditions. But, the feminist's worries had relevance in *particular* sectors where men predominated, such as in the printing and transportation services. In these cases, which concerned a minority of privileged women, who "through superior skill and opportunities have built the strength to dignify their relations with their employers" (Baker 1926, 532), labor legislation based only upon sex was of "doubtful value" as it caused women's loss of jobs in those sectors. It is important to note that Baker's concern applied especially to other forms of labor legislation that concerned limitation of working hours and night work, rather than minimum wage laws, which were relevant to unskilled workers.

Baker attributed great symbolic value to the minority of skilled women workers as they represented the vanguard of women's economic enfranchisement. They were "the economic standard bearers in the progress of women" (Baker 1925, 428), or better, the women at the "industrial frontiers" (Baker 1929, 276). They embodied the first who struggled against the conservative forces of tradition and prejudice in coherence with the economic changes of the time. Hence, their economic conditions were relevant to all women workers since "they are building the ladder upon which greater numbers of women may climb to a place in the sun" (Baker 1926, 532).

Even if partially agreeing with the feminist diagnosis, in harmony with Hutchinson, Baker did not agree with its solution, that is, the abolition of protective labor legislation so as to grant "freedom of contract" to all employers. The *Columbia v. Adkins* case (1923) exemplified such a view, liberalizing the labor market and slashing previous labor reforms.

By contrast, Hutchinson and Baker proposed a solution that was coherent with their historical materialism: freedom of form did not mean freedom of substance. Workers who did not receive a living wage lacked *any* bargaining power. With little unionization and ruthless competition among them, their freedom of contract was pure illusion. The majority of women formed the ranks of the unskilled workers who lingered in a structurally subordinated condition:

> Under the present system of wage payment the weakness of women's bargaining power may be inferred from the very nature of the work they do . . . Boys and girls just out of the elementary schools, immigrants with no industrial training, young women and older ones too, forced to earn a living and with no preparation for it—all these fill the ranks of the unskilled worker . . . To the employer the most important question is "which will do it the more cheaply".
>
> *Hutchinson 1919, 82*

State intervention had to establish a basic wage in order to "rise the plane of competition and restrict its working in the interest of the common good" (Hutchinson 1919, 96). Any higher wage than this basic one may be a matter of bargaining, "but at least a living wage becomes a charge upon industry" (p. 83).

In this framework, there is no logical reason for fixing wage legislation only for women. There is no dividing line between women wage earners and men wage earners as regards "their helplessness in the face of diverse industrial conditions" (Baker 1925, 440). Hence, emphasis should be put upon "the need of a plan for progressive legislation beginning with the most helpless of our workers whether they be male or female" (p. 441).

An important paragraph comes from Baker's 1929 article, "At the Crossroads in the Legal Protection of Women in Industry." Its words deserve full mention as they eloquently express Baker's ambitious reform agenda in favor of universal labor laws:

> We appear, then, to have arrived at the crossroads in the legal protection of women in industry. Which way shall be our next turn? One road is toward more and more laws for women; another leads to none—to the abrogation of laws which do not apply alike to men and women. Should the opposing forces prove equally potent we seem doomed to stand still. But there is still another way . . . Let the present statutes for women remain for the present at least, with some necessary exceptions for the victimized minorities. Drive hard for the extension of these laws to include men as well. Aim as rapidly as possible to wipe out sex discrimination in the labor law by raising the status of all sub-level workers to the level of those better off. Present a program of legislation for men and women workers with solid economic foundation, one which is abreast of the time. Let this program be developed by an informed and industrious commission with the progress of women at heart . . . If we sincerely desire to advance the position of women in industry, is not this the road to take?
>
> *Baker 1929, 279*

In sum, Baker and Hutchinson supported universal minimum wage legislation as a fundamental measure for society to embrace the changed economic conditions of women in the workforce and promote socio-economic progress.[17] However, their common analytical framework that emphasized the intertwine between economic-political forces and power relations, together with tradition and culture in determining the economic outcome, shaped their reform proposals to more extreme consequences. Baker and Hutchinson envisaged the minimum wage law only as one component of a larger set of emancipatory tools explored in the next and final section.

Unionization and education

A universal minimum wage provides the basic "civilization standard for wage payment" (Hutchinson 1919, 175) in a historical moment in which labor organization is weak. This is particularly true for women, the great majority of whom are unorganized. Baker wrote: "If all workmen were successfully organized, it is conceivable that there would be little need for their protection by law. But the facts are far from this—perhaps one-fourth of the organizeable workers in the country are members of unions" (Baker 1925, 454).

Both authors were aware that wage legislation by itself fell short of a complete solution for low wages. For example, it could not tackle the structural problem of the irregularity of employment in industries for low-skilled workers. Hence, wage legislation marked just the first step in establishing the economic claims of women as a class of workers that could be fulfilled through political organization (Hutchinson 1919, 179).

Baker and Hutchinson contradicted the concern of labor unions about legal regulation of wages as causing diminished voluntary action. Empirical evidence underlined the positive relation between wage laws and worker's organizing power. Hutchinson cited Tawney's enquiry[18] showing how minimum wage laws encouraged trade unionism. They helped create class-consciousness and overcome the main material obstacle of trade unionism in the past: the low earnings of certain groups of workers who could not afford union participation.

The main obstacle to unionization of women rested in the powerful counteracting force of the tradition of economic dependence that permeated American society. Baker and Hutchinson were convinced that only an educative effort upon all members of society could secure women's economic emancipation. Baker's thesis demonstrated how the enforcement of labor legislation could not merely rely upon formal laws. Compliance was truly effective only once employers internalized progressive values (see Baker 1925, Ch. V).

Most important of all was the educational process of the industrial woman worker. The perseverance of prejudice and exploitation rested primarily in the resigned attitude of women, who had internalized their subordinated role in the labor force and their traditional identity as housewives (Hutchinson 1919, 13). To raise workers' prospective and consciousness, Baker and Hutchinson envisioned two types of interrelated pedagogic processes: vocational training together with general economic/political instruction. While they only wrote about the former, they put the latter into practice.

Vocational training endowed workers with practical skills in order to best fit their callings. It raised the opportunities of the unskilled women workers, increasing the value of their labor, and especially combated the stereotypical ideas of only certain types of jobs being fit for women (Hutchinson 1919, 172). Baker and Hutchinson intervened in the press to invoke the promotion of vocational training on a nationwide scale.[19]

The two economists engaged directly to provide economic and political instruction. Both professors taught classes for women undergraduates at Barnard College. The topics of the courses disclose an agenda of raising understanding about the competing forces of economic transformation and tradition. In the year of her appointment (1914–1915), Hutchinson inaugurated the first course in the economics department explicitly devoted to "the study of the economic relations of women" (Barnard Archives, Barnard College Announcement 1914–1915). It was called "Women in Industry." The following year she taught "Women in Gainful Occupations," described as "a study of economic and social occupations of women" (Barnard Archives, Yearbook). She repeated this course for the following ten years. In alignment with her methodological framework, she juxtaposed these courses with broader investigations in the history and theories of capitalism.[20]

Baker's syllabi reveal a similar teaching method to her senior colleague. Baker taught central issues for the analysis and development of the capitalist economy, considering the evolution of women's role in the labor market as its integral component.[21]

Students at Barnard learned economic theory and the relation between such theory and the real world, with special emphasis on the socio-economic condition of the worker. Yet, Hutchinson's and Baker's educational efforts did not merely concern the elites who could afford college education: Barnard College took part in one of the most innovative educational projects for workers in the country.[22] *The Barnard Summer School for Woman Workers in Industry* took place from 1927 to 1932. It offered "seven weeks of study with proper degree of recreation and opportunity for health building to 50 workers from 9 am to 9 pm" together with "a scholarship and a subsidy for living expenses in order to compensate for the work lost" (Report 1932, "The first five years," Barnard Archives).

The summer school provided classes all "closely linked with the world of the twentieth century." In addition, 200 workers, men and women, attended an evening class once a week to discuss "current social and labor problems." The importance of knowledge to raise the socio-economic alertness of workers, is clear from the 1932 "plan of teaching":

> For such students it is of first importance to understand the current economic problems which concern them as workers in industry, they also wish to learn something of the world they live in, and to develop talents and resources for leisure time. The courses therefore focus attention on the workers' experience, drawing from literature, sociology, history, government, economics, psychology and the natural sciences, to give a broad basis of fact and develop perspective and understanding.
>
> *Report 1932, "The first five years," Barnard Archives*

The school's spirit was to create a locus of exchange between women of different classes in order to discuss contemporary socio-economic issues.

> The summer school . . . with daily discussion by industrial workers on their own financial problems, is of vital interest to Columbia students attending classes in economics and in education. Each summer graduates, undergraduates, and members of the Barnard College Faculty have taken an active part in the summer school as instructors, educators and committee members.
>
> *Report 1932, "The first five years," Barnard Archives*

In the *Columbia Alumnae Bulletin* of 1929, Emilie Hutchinson wrote an enthusiastic report about the summer school. It provides a vivid image not only of the multiclass but also of the multi-ethnic environment:

> An interesting group they were, they came from various great city industries . . . every branch of the labor movement and at least 12 locales were represented. On the other hand, 1/3 of the students did not belong to any labor organization. Only four girls were American born: they had come from Russia, Poland, Rumania, Czecho-Slovakia, and Germany, just before the war or soon after . . . I was very much impressed with their high degree of intelligence and with the concrete and realistic way in which they carried out their work.
>
> *p. 7*

Emilie Hutchinson held a primary role in the organization of the summer school. She was both permanent instructor and chair of the curriculum committee. Her syllabus in economic history was detailed in the analysis of the evolution of the economic structure since the Middle Ages, giving special attention to the changing condition of workers and current economic problems, including modern imperialism, the labor movement in Europe and in the United States and the origin and growth of socialism.

Numerous depositions of the students attest the success of this pedagogic experiment. A worker writes: "I'm beginning to understand, my mind is becoming clear and concentrated on the problems workers face." And: "I am finding a school at last that helps me by showing me how to find an answer to perplexing problems which concern our social welfare" (Report 1930). Especially interesting for testing the perceptiveness of the student-workers are the *Barnard Reports*: the school's magazine had a section devoted to a "series of papers typical of those written by students in connection to their classroom studies." Students' knowledge was extensive. For example, they learned the difference between Fabian socialism and syndicalism or that between anti-labor law and anti-labor injunction. Specifically, these records reveal a diffused conviction about the value of instruction and political organization to raise the socio-economic condition of workers. One example out of many:

> Even under the present system, a great deal could be done through trade unions . . . The unions tend to raise wages and shorten hours . . . On the whole workers who belong to unions play an important part in deciding wages, hours, working conditions and many other things.
>
> *"Prosperity for American Workers" by an anonymous student, Barnard Report 1931, Barnard Archives*

Conclusion

Hutchinson and Baker were the first women economists to gain academic positions at Barnard College. Since their PhD years, during the so-called Lochner era, they directly engaged with the heated socio-economic debate on women's economic condition and protective labor legislation. Certainly, Baker and Hutchinson shared the progressive traditions of statism and expertise. Nonetheless, this essay shows that the two Columbia economists put forth a common contribution to the topic of minimum wage legislation that deeply distinguished them from the position of the "mainstream progressive view" as described by Leonard (2016).

The Columbia economists focused on women's labor condition as the most topical subject in order to analyze the evolution of the capitalist economy. Their historical approach marked the first fundamental difference with respect to Leonard's progressives: women's participation in the labor market was not an unnatural and exceptional phenomenon; rather, it was one of the crucial aspects of the development of capitalism.

Baker and Hutchinson's perspective was that "women are in industry to stay" and that "social change is inevitable," as it followed the change in the productive structure of society. Hence, women's social role as caregivers was not biologically innate and would eventually be transformed into joint responsibilities of parenthood.

It follows that wage legislation for women was not invoked as an instrument to keep women outside the labor market through legally induced disemployment. On the contrary, it was a means for social practices to adjust to the structural economic changes of women as gainfully employed actors in the economy. Contrary to Leonard's mainstream progressives, neoclassical economists, and equal rights feminists, Hutchinson denied that minimum wage legislation induced permanent disemployment for women. In fact, minimum wages provoked firms to invest in productivity and boost efficiency, thus propelling economic growth and greater overall employment. These ideas found positive corroborations in the enquiries of the time.

The Columbia economists' analysis was receptive of the interlock between economic, cultural, and political factors, thus stressing the limits of labor legislation. In order for the conservative forces to be fully defeated, Baker and Hutchinson envisioned the indispensability of other social tools. First, political organization was the sole means to gain enduring economic achievements above the basic threshold of minimum wages. Legislation could only provide the first boost for voluntary action. In Baker's words, "If all workmen were successfully organized, it is conceivable that there would be little need for their protection by law" (Baker 1925, 454).

For both economists it was really through political-economic instruction of workers, especially women, that both minimum wage laws and labor organization could be secured. Hutchinson and Baker envisaged their teaching activity was an integral part of their progressive reform agenda. The Barnard Summer School for Women Workers was a vanguard experience of socio-economic education. Women workers were taught about current economic problems, labor unions, and alternative theories of political economy. The school aroused the awareness of their identity as productive agents of society with economic and political rights.

The vanguard significance of Hutchinson and Baker's reform agenda is fully assessable in light of the political and legal context of the 1920s. The two Columbia economists proposed an ambitious doctrine of universal labor legislation in a moment in which USA protective labor laws were overturned. The two women were attentive observers of the contemporary legal events and of their ideological underpinnings. They firmly rejected the sexist progressive ideas that had shaped protective reforms until 1920. Simultaneously they contrasted the legal feminist efforts to abolish labor legislation, efforts that won their battle in 1923 and ruled for more than a decade. Notwithstanding the setback of wage laws, Baker and Hutchinson strove for their reform principles, teaching their ideas to many college and working women. This study discloses how Baker and Hutchinson were among the ideological precursors of the New Deal labor reform. The Fair Labor Standards Act of 1938 (FLSA), represented a landmark law in the nation's social and economic development. Reflecting the beliefs of our Columbia economists, it extended labor legislation, including minimum wages, universally to all American workers, independent of sex.

Notes

1 A special thanks to Sarah Witte, reference librarian of the Women Studies Sector at Columbia University, who has guided me through the immense archival material, a crucial aid to undertake this research.

2 Named after the famous *Lochner v. New York* (198 US 45, 1905) case, the Lochner era comprises the four decades (1897–1937) during which the Supreme Court substantively applied the due process clauses of the Fifth and Fourteenth Amendments of the American Constitution in order to strike down state and federal regulation, in particular labor legislation, that infringed constitutional rights to property and freedom of contract. See Giocoli (2016).

3 In United States constitutional law, police power grants states the authority to regulate private behavior for the betterment of the health, safety, morals, and general welfare of their inhabitants. A classic definition of police power is "the power of promoting the public welfare by restraining and regulating the use of liberty and property" (Freund 1904, iii). On the origins of this doctrine, see Siegel 1991; Novak 1996, Ch. 1; Giocoli (2016).

4 I use the term "disemployment" rather than "unemployment" in order to stress the *causal connection* that is at the basis of the criticism to minimum wages. Minimum wages for women *cause* women to lose employment they would otherwise have in a free labor market setting. The idea is that, if minimum wages are set above the market clearing price, women are expelled from the employability category.

5 Prior to graduate studies, she taught Economics while serving as Dean of Women at Lewiston State Normal School in Idaho (1915–1917) and at Washington State Normal School (1917–1918).

6 From 1929 to 1935 Hutchinson also served as chair of the Committee on Fellowships of the American Association of University Women (Barnard College Alumnae Monthly, 1938, Barnard Archives).

7 See: Hutchinson, *New York Times*, March 2, 1933, and *New York Times*, July 6, 1913. In both cases Hutchinson defends the cause of women as an integral part of the labor force.
8 See Woloch 2015; Hart 1994; Lehrer 1987; Baker 1925.
9 For details about the clashes between Alice Paul and Florence Kelly, respectively the leaders of WNP and CNL, see Chapter 5 of Woloch (2015) and Chapter 6 of Hart (1994).
10 The Lochner case was often cited by the courts as the virtuous precedent that, in the words of Chief Justice Taft, in those years had wrongly "been overruled sub silentio" (Baker 1925, 90).
11 This emerges also from their teaching interests. Hutchinson taught economic history and Baker focused on mechanization and technological change as critical elements of socio-economic evolution.
12 Lack of citations on the part of Baker and Hutchinson does not permit us to find out to what degree institutionalism had direct influence on their thought.
13 Other authors in the Marginalist school expressed the same concern, for example, Alfred Marshall (1897) and A. C. Pigou (1913). For an overview of the progressive position on minimum wage see Prasch (1999).
14 Among others, Hutchinson cited the Massachusetts minimum wage commission (1916) and The Oregon Bureau of Labour commission (1914); Baker considered the Industrial commission of Wisconsin (1920), Minimum wage board of the District of Columbia (1923), and California Bureau of Labor Statistics (1923).
15 Hutchinson remarked that "in all probability difficulties encountered by employers in making the adjustment and failure itself will be ascribed to the restricted legislation rather than to personal incompetency" (1919, 110). Furthermore, there was the inherent difficulty of disentangling the influence of one specific factor (wage laws) in a highly complex set of circumstances. Business cycles were among the factors complicating the statistical results.
16 Baker (1929) principally discusses the findings of the Report of the Women's Bureau of the United States Department of Labor: "The Effects of Labor Legislation on the Employment Opportunities of Women" (1928), Bulletin No. 64, 1928.
17 For evidence of Hutchinson's support to universal minimum wages see Chapters V and VI and the Conclusion of her dissertation (Hutchinson 1919).
18 Tawney, Minimum Rates in the Tailoring Industry (London 1915).
19 See Baker 1925, 1929; Hutchinson 1928, 1929. See also *New York Herald Tribune*, "Higher Incomes Reward Women Who Specialize," Sept. 9, 1928, page A14.
20 Her course "Economic Theories," inaugurated in 1923–1924, studied "the leading types of economic theories since the industrial revolution, with special attention to the background in economic history." Hutchinson was also responsible for the course in economic history.
21 The first courses Baker taught autonomously in 1924–1925 were called "Financial and Business Organization" and "Labor in Industry and Society."
22 This pioneering project was part of a larger movement for workers' summer school:

> Working together as an affiliated group the Summer Schools of Barnard, Bryn Mawr college, [that launched the project in 1921] and the University of Wisconsin are studying questions of curriculum and teaching method for the adult industrial worker and helping the former students to continue the Study program.
>
> *Report 1932 "The first five years", Barnard Archives*

Bibliography

Archival sources

Barnard Archives and Special Collections, Barnard Library, Barnard College

Barnard College Summer School for Women Workers in Industry, 1927–1933; Series I and II; Barnard Archives and Special Collections, Barnard Library, Barnard College.
Biographical Files
Barnard Announcements and Year Books (1910–1952)

Columbia Archives, Rare Books and Manuscripts, Columbia University

Baker, Elizabeth, *Some of the Economic and Social Causes and Effects, Especially upon the Family, of the Employment of Married Women in Industry*, Master's Thesis, May 1919.

Newspapers

The New York Times, "Women Fire Inspectors: Commissioner Johnson Accused of Discriminating Against Them." Agatha Schurzemilie and E.J. Hutchinson, July 6, 1913, page 10.

The New York Times, "Women and Machines: We Might Abolish Men Also and End Unemployment." Hutchinson, March 2, 1933.

The New York Times, "Emilie Hutchinson of Barnard Dead: Associate Professor Head of Department of Economics and Author of Books." Jan. 13, 1938.

The New York Times, "Prof. Elizabeth F. Baker Dies; Taught Economics at Barnard: Studied Printing Plants New York Times." Feb. 1, 1973.

New York Herald Tribune, "Higher Incomes Reward Women Who Specialize." Sept. 9, 1928, page A14.

Primary sources

Baker, Elizabeth F. 1925. *Protective Labor Legislation: With Special Reference to the Women in the State of New York*. New York: Columbia University Press.

——. 1926. "Do Women in Industry need Special Protection?" *The Survey*, 55 (10): 529–532, 582–585.

——. 1927. "The Economics of Marriage." *The World Tomorrow*, June, 271–274.

——. 1929. "At the Crossroads in the Legal Protection of Women in Industry." *The Annals of the American Academy of Political and Social Science*, Vol. 143, "Women in the Modern World," 265–279.

——. 1933. *Displacement of Men by Machines*. New York: Columbia University Press.

——. 1957. *Printers and Technology: A History of the International Printing Pressmen and Assistants' Union*. New York: Columbia University Press.

——. 1964. *Technology and Woman's Work*. New York: Columbia University Press.

Hutchinson, Emilie J. 1914. "The Socializing Influence of the Ballot upon Women." *The Annals of the American Academy of Political and Social Science*, Vol. 56, "Women in Public Life," 105–110.

——. 1915. "Vocational Interests of College Women." *Columbia University Quarterly*, June, 227–229.

——. 1915. "Book Review: The Public Schools and Women in Office Service." *Political Science Quarterly*, 30 (3): 517–518.

——. 1918. "Reviews." *Political Science Quarterly*, 33 (1): 113–114.

——. 1919. *Women's Wages: A Study of Wages of Industrial Women and Measures Suggested to Increase Them*. New York: Columbia University Press.

——. 1928. "Women and the Ph.D." *Bulletin of the American Association of University Professors*, 14 (8): 587–592.

——. 1929. "The Economic Problems of Women." *The Annals of the American Academy of Political and Social Science*, Vol. 143, "Women in the Modern World," 132–136.

Secondary sources

Freund, Ernest. 1904. *Police Power*. Chicago, IL: Callaghan and Co.

Giocoli, Nicola. 2016. "The Classical Limits to Police Power: Adam Smith and the Economic Foundations of the Slaughterhouse Dissents". Working Paper for HES conference.

Hart, Vivien.1994. *Bound By Our Constitution: Women, Workers, and the Minimum Wage*. Princeton, NJ: Princeton University Press.

Lehrer, Susan. 1987. *Protective Labor Legislation for Women 1905–1925*. Albany: State University of New York Press.

Leonard, Thomas. 2000. "The Very Idea of Applying Economics: The Modern Minimum-Wage Controversy and its Antecedents." In Roger E. Backhouse and Jeff Biddle (eds) *Toward a History of Applied Economics*, 117–144. Durham, NC: Duke University Press.

——. 2005. "Protecting Family and Race: The Progressive Case for Regulating Women's Work." *American Journal of Economics and Sociology*, 64 (3): 757–791.

——. 2016. *Illiberal Reformers*. Princeton, NJ: Princeton University Press.
Marshall, Alfred. 1897. "The Old Generation of Economists and the New." *Quarterly Journal of Economics*, 11 (2): 115–135.
Novak, William J. 1996. *The People's Welfare: Law and Regulation in Nineteenth-century America*. Chapel Hill: University of North Carolina Press.
Pigou, Arthur Cecil. 1913. *Unemployment*. London: William and Norgate.
Prasch, Robert. 1999. "Retrospectives: American Economists in the Progressive Era on the Minimum Wage." *The Journal of Economic Perspectives*, 13 (2): 221–230.
Siegel, S. A. 1991. "Lochner Era Jurisprudence and the American Constitutional Tradition." *North Carolina Law Review*, 70 (1): 111.
Taussig, F. W. 1916. "Minimum Wages for Women." *Quarterly Journal of Economics*, 30 (3): 411–442.
Woloch, Nancy. 2015. *A Class by Herself: Protective Laws for Women Workers, 1890s–1990s*. Princeton, NJ: Princeton University Press.

15

CHINESE ECONOMIC DEVELOPMENT AND CHINESE WOMEN ECONOMISTS

A study of overseas doctoral dissertations

Yue Xiao[1]

Introduction

Modern China refers to the time period from the beginning of the First Opium War in 1840 to the establishment of the People's Republic of China in 1949. During this turbulent one hundred years, the Chinese economy experienced sharp reform with the collapse of feudalism and the introduction of western capitalism. Centered on the opening of foreign trade in China, Chinese economists searched for policies around which to build economic reforms. Among them, three women economists played a significant part. They offered novel insights on the most pressing changes that China should make in order to survive the impact of western economics on the traditional Chinese structure. And these three inserted women's voices in an area formerly dominated by men. However, they have received almost no attention from the history of economic thought.

This chapter explores these three women's doctoral dissertations chronologically. Mabel Ping-hua Lee's[2] doctoral dissertation "The Economic History of China: With Special Reference to Agriculture," was the first modern survey of Chinese agricultural economic history. Facing the unprecedented political and economic changes caused by the expansion of foreign trade, Lee emphasized the importance of learning from agricultural adjustments and policy reforms in the past. Chung-ying Kuo's[3] "British Trade in China, 1894–1914" focused on China's imports from Britain in Sino-British[4] trade. Britain was one of the pioneer western countries to build a trade relationship with China, and had a primary influence on the development of modern China's economy. By carefully reviewing the history of British trade in China, Kuo's study served as an excellent example of foreign trade analysis. Yu-pu Pan's[5] doctoral research, "International Capital Movements and Capital Formation," studied the theory of international capital flows, a major topic of international economics, and its relation to China's economic development. These three pioneering women offered important economic proposals aimed at coping with Chinese new reality.[6]

Under reform, many changes were involved in the process of economic development. It is understandable that these three women did not focus on the same topic. However, all their works discussed economic changes associated with modernization and industrialization.

Furthermore, their economic thought was a reflection of different levels of their Chinese heritage and experience of study abroad. Mabel Lee incorporated a balance of Chinese and western economic thought, while Chung-ying Kuo and Yu-pu Pan were much more influenced by western thought.

The structure of this paper is as follows. The next section introduces the historical background of this study. The following sections, present Mabel Lee, Chung-ying Kuo and Yu-pu Pan and their respective dissertations. The chapter ends with a conclusion.

Historical background

Women's education in modern China

The origin of modern women's education in China was closely related to foreign missionaries and missionary schools. When Robert Morrison[7] founded the Anglo-Chinese College in Malacca in 1818, he brought church schools into China (Morrison 1839, 355). After the First Opium War[8] (1840–1842), the scale of missionary schools expanded due to the treaties signed by the Qing government as the defeated nation. In addition to creating unequal trading rights for foreign powers, these treaties granted those countries with privileges to Christian missionaries and to open schools in China. In just 13 years from 1847 to 1860, foreign missionaries established 12 women church schools in the five treaty ports with foreign trade (He 1996, 235). From the mid-nineteenth century to the early twentieth century, most of the missionary schools founded in China were owned by American churches. By the year 1914, American Christian churches opened nearly 2,000 primary missionary schools: 45,000 students were enrolled, and 208 schools opened for higher learning with 25,000 students (Wang 1998, 190). These missionary schools not only promoted the development of women's education in modern China, but also made possible women's overseas education.

In fact, before missionary schools there were no other educational institutions that offered women the opportunity to pursue higher education in China. The reason why China did not have higher education for women was mainly a result of the long dominant feudal ethical code. In imperial China, the traditional thought of "male superiority" remained unshakable for more than 2,000 years. Women were confined to the domestic sphere and socially disadvantaged. Their thought and morality were restrained by the "three obediences and the four virtues"[9] of the feudal Confucian ideas. The Chinese proverb "a woman without talent is virtuous" suggested the standard of value and the principal life creed designed for women. For thousands of years, women were purposely refused education and deliberately kept in the dark, so that they would be contented with their domestic lives and not question patriarchy. The right of receiving education from schools was exclusively for men in ancient China. Only a few women from scholarly families or official families had the opportunity to receive education from home tutors, for the purpose of better serving their future husbands in the household and serving their children in education. Most Chinese women were illiterate and unschooled. Therefore, modern women's higher education was not a product of China's own traditional development, but the outcome of the introduction of western culture. The church schools played the significant "maternal role" in the growing process of the first generation of Chinese intellectual women (Wang 1996, 65).

The Qing government issued a constitution for women's schools in 1907 and eventually recognized women's education as part of the official education system. The primary education of women has been promoted nationwide ever since. However, it was not until the establishment of the Republic of China that the Chinese set up their own school for women's higher education. The first women's university of China was the Beijing Female Higher Normal College, officially named in 1919.

Karl Marx once said, "Social progress can be measured exactly by the social position of the fair sex." With the collapsing feudal system and the introduction of the capitalist system in China, social reforms improved the development of women's liberation and women enjoyed more opportunities to receive education.

The trend of studying abroad

The First Opium War fundamentally changed the social nature of China. The Qing Dynasty was rocked by the outside world and a tide of revolution started in all areas of ideology in China. The self-sufficient natural economy that had dominated China for so long was violently impacted by western capitalism as China became involved in the world market. This revolution forced the Chinese to learn from the strengths of the western world, thus stimulating a great interest in western higher learning. In Yuan Wei's "Illustrated Treatise on the Maritime Kingdoms," he put forward the famous proposition: "Learn from the advanced technologies of the foreigners in order to compete with them" (1999 [1847], 67). Most of the patriots of the period drew useful lessons from the painful failure of the war, and accepted Wei's idea of striving for self-improvement. The nationwide tide of the study abroad movement is one of the main results of this thought: "To learn from the foreigners."

The first Chinese student who studied abroad in America was Yung Wing.[10] He was brought to America by Reverend Samuel Robbins Brown in 1847. When Yung Wing returned to China after graduation, he tried with endless effort to encourage authorities to send more students abroad for study. Eventually persuaded by Yung Wing and starting in 1872, the Qing government launched the Chinese Educational Mission, sending young Chinese students to study in America.[11] Many students of this program later made significant contributions to the reform of China in engineering and the social sciences. The success of these early students laid a strong foundation for future study abroad programs. The number of students studying abroad grew each year under the government's support.

Gender differences

As missionaries laid the foundation of women's education, the study abroad trend pushed forward the progress of women's higher education in foreign countries. In 1885 China's first woman student, Yamei Kin[12] (1864–1934), earned a doctorate of medicine from the Women's Medical College of the New York Infirmary. The first female student came nearly four decades later than the earliest male student. Besides Kin, three other women students obtained medical degrees in American universities. These three women were King-eng Hn[13] (1865–1929), Mary Stone[14] (1873–1954), and Ida Kahn[15] (1873–1931). The four women students' chances to study abroad were all somehow related to the missionary influence, and their choice of medicine was strongly influenced by the missionary schools. Caring, self-sacrifice and empathy traits required by medical service were believed to match feminine qualities, impacted by religious doctrine. After these four women students returned to China, they made a great contribution in the medical service industry.[16] When Qichao Liang, an influential reformist in the late Qing Dynasty, saw the momentous accomplishments by these women students, he praised their achievements and set them as role models. In the Hundred Days' Reform launched by Qichao Liang, he vigorously promoted the idea of women's education. Liang believed that Chinese women should be educated so that they could support the country in time of need (Ye 1994, 318–321). Early women's education was not promoted for the purpose of individual development, but for the well-being of the nation.

After the feudal autocratic rule of the Qing Dynasty was overthrown by the bourgeois democratic revolution in 1911, the number of women students increased. The social climate for women to be educated was more open than ever before. From the beginning of this trend for studying abroad to the end of the later period of Nanjing Nationalist Government, the number of women students rose continuously; the imbalanced ratio between men and women improved; though there were always more men students, the growth rate of female students was higher than for male students.[17] Nonetheless, a gender difference continued in overseas students from modern China.

It is clear that in modern China, missionaries started the trend of opening formal educational opportunities to women and created opportunities for Chinese students to study abroad. In the early stages, the American schools that Chinese students went to were recommended by missionaries. Later, impressed by early Chinese students' performances, more schools opened to Chinese students.

Gradually, western economic thought was introduced into China by overseas students. Nationalism, pragmatism and effectiveness are three prominent traits of Chinese economists in modern China. They fought to save their deeply troubled country from economic break down and played an essential part in the development of modern China's economy. Women economists shared the same traits as their male colleagues. They sought solutions to their country's most urgent economic problems. However, their efforts did not receive the same level of serious attention.

Mabel Lee

Introduction to Mabel Lee

Mabel Ping-hua Lee (1897–1966) was the first Chinese woman student graduating from Columbia University with a doctoral degree. Being an overseas student in America was rare among the large population of modern China; being a doctoral student in economics was even rarer; and being a woman economics student was a singularity. Her work on the economic history of China's agriculture was unprecedented in China's economic studies.

Mabel Lee was born in Guangzhou in 1897. Like most of the early female overseas students, Mabel Lee's chance to go to America was connected with missionaries. As the only child of a Baptist minister, Towe Lee, who worked in the American Baptist Home Mission Society, Mabel Lee went to America with her mother, reuniting with her father in the summer of 1900 at the age of four. Lee showed her interest in politics at an early age by joining in social reform. She participated in the demonstration of the "Feminist Movement" in New York on horseback when she was 16 years old. Influenced by the liberal democratic environment, Lee gained feminist consciousness at a young age. After earning her master's degree, Lee received a scholarship from the "Boxer Indemnity Scholarship Program" to go on with her studies at Columbia University. The Chinese government stated that Lee excelled in research on the agricultural economy, and hence was willing to grant her the scholarship. She was the first woman student to win this scholarship (Cai 2008, 35).

Mabel Lee's student life

Before entering Columbia University, Lee studied history and philosophy at Barnard College. Then she transferred to education administration and earned her master's degree of education at Barnard College. Lee was active among the Chinese overseas students. She published several articles in *The Chinese Students' Monthly*,[18] including "The Meaning of Women's Suffrage." In 1914, she gave an English speech at the Eastern Conference on the topic of "Chinese Patriotism." Her speech was so successful that it won her a wide reputation among Chinese overseas students. In 1915, she became the English secretary of the Chinese Students' Alliance in America. In a photo[19] of the members of the Alliance, Mabel Lee was the only woman student, sitting middle-front among the other 36 male students. "A single red flower in the midst of thick foliage" describes the photo well. In autumn of 1916, Lee campaigned for president of the Chinese Students' Alliance with Tse-ven Soong,[20] who came from one of the four most wealthy and powerful families[21] in China and later became the finance minister of the national government. Lee narrowly lost to Soong after three rounds of competitions. She was fearless in the face of a strong rival. Lee made a potent statement to the Chinese on both sides of the Pacific Ocean that women's intelligence and social competence were equal to men's. In an age when most Chinese women were housewives, it was astonishing to picture Lee's vigorous and social life.

In 1917, Lee became a Ph.D. student in economics at Columbia University. Then she shouldered the responsibility of vice president of the Columbia Chinese Club and the associate editor of *The Chinese Students' Monthly*. Lee graduated from Columbia University in 1921 with high academic credentials. She was selected by the Board of Council of Columbia University as the University Scholar in Economics for her excellent research work in agricultural economy. Lee was the first Chinese student to receive this honor (Bieler 2004, 185–186).

In 1923 Lee went to Europe to investigate postwar economics. She was offered a job at Xiamen University as the department head that year (Zou 2016, 542). Everything seemed promising until she received the news of her father's sudden death in 1924. She threw everything aside, returned for her father's funeral and decided to stay in New York. She declined the other employment offers, inherited her father's career in the Baptist church, and became the chairman of the Morning Star Mission. In memory of her father, Lee built a memorial hall in 1936.

Remaining single her whole life, Lee passed away in 1966. She did not pursue her career in economics after she devoted herself to Christ. Lee's thesis, "The Economic History of China: With Special Reference to Agriculture" (1921) was her first and last economics book.

Mabel Lee's economic thought

Mabel Lee's doctoral dissertation was the first modern survey of Chinese agricultural economic history. It was included in the series of "Studies in History, Economics, and Public Law" (Volume 99) published by Columbia University in 1921. Her thesis consisted of three main parts: History; selection from sources; and special topics. It covered the history of Chinese agriculture from Huangdi[22] in 2697 BC to the Qing Dynasty (1644–1911), divided into 16 time periods. Lee's motivation for carrying out this survey was inspired by her supervisor Professor Vladimir G. Simkhovitch. In Professor Simkhovitch's "Rome's Fall Reconsidered,"[23] he analyzed the close relationship between land deterioration and the progressive disintegration of the ancient Roman Empire. That history prompted Lee to consider the mysterious situation in China: How did China survive soil exhaustion, while the other ancient civilizations of Egypt,

Babylonia and Rome all declined because of soil depletion? The people in ancient China must have expended a great deal of effort to avoid land deterioration. The emperors must have formulated policies and laws, and the farmers must have conducted aggressive management measures. Lee searched the classical Chinese canon to find data related to this subject. In her dissertation, Lee made a clear division of the source materials, placing quotations under each dynasty, emperor and specific event. She made abundant references to 117 ancient books[24] concerning agriculture and economic governance, skillfully translated by her from Chinese to English. Most of these books had never been translated before. In this way, Lee introduced ancient Chinese economic thought to the west.

Lee noted that ancient Chinese history was closely related to emperors and dynasties, while modern Chinese history was mainly shaped by foreign relations, revolutions, and civil strife. After studying the classical books, she found that Chinese economists generally fell into two schools of thought: the traditional school and the practical school. Lee explained the traditional school are the ones "who looked back upon the time of Yao and Shun and the sages for precepts to remedy every situation," and the practical school are those "who disregarded all authority of classical times and set out to solve each new individual problem as they themselves understood it."[25] Under the influence of western economic thought, the practical school was in fierce combat with the classical school. In the face of the sudden prodigious change, Lee argued that it was crucial to take ideas from both these schools into consideration. As she wrote in her thesis:

> As the classical school erred when it did not fully appreciate the new situations, so too the practical school could only succeed insofar as it was correct in its comprehension of the conditions presented, and the extent of its success was in accordance with the degree to which it took into consideration all the elements in the case. The writings of both schools, however, are valuable in helping us to a better understanding of the historical conditions. In every case they have been found to concur in the description of facts and the recording of events, thereby giving us more definite knowledge of the general conditions of the times.
>
> *Lee 1921, 15–16*

Lee's middle-ground opinion on these two schools' thought was a reflection of the "doctrine of the mean."[26] This attitude turned out to be more helpful in times of reform, when no one knew what method would suit China's actual conditions the best. Lee's thesis clearly brought together both the influences of being raised in China and nurturing China-specific thought along with the influences of the experience of study in the west.

In the semi-colonial and semi-feudal society (1840–1919), uncritical acceptance of western economic thought was unpractical and irresponsible. By taking both advantages and disadvantages of the two schools into consideration, Lee cherished the wisdom of the ancient sages and embraced the new ideas of the west. Lee (1921, 17) stated that: "We must search the old records for data, but the facts thus ascertained can be valuable only as we interpret them in the light of modern science."

Even though the disturbances of the Xinhai Revolution[27] (1911) ended, economic reform remained ahead. With the introduction of technology and machinery, China would need to adapt to survive. Adjustments in agriculture had to be made, but how would this impact the farmers? Since the majority of China's people were farmers, the implications of agricultural readjustment would affect the lives of millions. Lee's work on historical Chinese agricultural policy had implications for Chinese transition to a capitalist world order.

Changes of policy and land protection

Lee elaborated the changes of agricultural policy from the Tsing Tien system[28] (started in Shang Dynasty, 1600BC–1046BC) to the early years of the Republic of China. The Tsing Tien system of slave agriculture marked the beginning of land tenure, land distribution and land taxation. In the Spring and Autumn Period (770BC–221BC), the creation of the iron plough and the oxe-nyoke increased productivity. After the Reforms of Shong Yang,[29] the Tsing Tien system was abolished, and individual private ownership of land was now protected by law. However, the private ownership of land aggravated the situation of large-scale land holdings. It further caused a decrease in national tax revenue and an increase in the gap between rich and poor, intensifying social conflicts. From the Northern Wei Dynasty (368–534) to the Tang Dynasty (618–907), the modified Tsing Tien system[30] was carried out to prevent the big landlords, bureaucrats and nobles devouring the lands. Both small-scale peasant agriculture and tenantry were very common in the Song Dynasty (960–1279), and became the main mode of rural land management in the Qing Dynasty (1636–1912).[31]

The course of change and development of land taxation interacted with land policy. The heavy tax on land per "mu"[32] in the Spring and Autumn Period accelerated the collapse of the Tsing Tien system. A legal subject system was created in the Qin Dynasty (221 BC–207 BC) to levy the land tax, adult poll tax, juvenile poll tax, corvée and military service on farmers. The heavy tax soon roused a people's rebellion. After the Qin Dynasty, the idea of reducing the burden of taxation and cost was adopted by the emperors in the Han Dynasty (202–220). In coordination with the modified Tsing Tien system, a corvée and household tax was levied to reduce the heavy tax burdens of the farmers. Government collected grain, piece goods, instead of currency. In the later Tang Dynasty, the Bi-Annual Tax (780) was enacted. It unified taxes of various kinds, and was mainly based on a land tax and household tax. It was called the Bi-Annual Tax because the government collected taxes twice a year in summer and autumn. The single tax in silver issued in the Ming Dynasty greatly simplified the tax system by combining the land tax, corvée and sundry taxes together. The System of Assessment According to Farmland launched in the Qing Dynasty was the last significant tax reform in Chinese feudal society. It abolished the poll tax which had lasted for 2,000 years. It is clear that the reforms in the land system and tax policy, which protected the interests of the broad masses of farmers and reduced their burden, improved productivity and developed the economy.

Beyond providing a detailed explanation of land taxation history, the stories Lee told demonstrated that throughout Chinese history, land protection was deeply rooted in Chinese people's minds. The idea to "adjust measures to local conditions"[33] that came from an ancient sage had a profound influence. Farming should be based on geographical environment, climate and natural resources. The Twenty-Four Solar Terms invented by farmers manifested the wisdom of ancient Chinese people on how and when to cultivate land. Chinese farmers regarded land as a living organism and believed that land had its "rhythm." The doctrine of Taoism[34] told people to follow the rules of nature. Every living thing depends on each other for existence in a cycle. What mankind obtained from the earth must be returned. The use of organic fertilizer benefited the ecological system. From generation to generation, China's agriculture was based on sustainable farming. The ancient wisdom on land protection greatly slowed down the natural speed of soil degradation. In modern times, population control and improvement of mechanization are vital to sustainable agriculture.

Lee's coverage of Chinese thought here is obviously reflecting China-specific elements, fused with the western-driven question of sustainability arising from her supervisor Professor Simkhovitch.

Summary

As the first woman Ph.D. economist in China, Lee engaged in religious service after her graduation. Choosing not to marry, and supporting herself on her own salary were privileges for women in that time period. Only a few women receiving higher education and achieving economic independence were able to enjoy the liberty of staying single. In the mission founded by her, Lee helped thousands of new immigrants to learn English and supported many people spiritually.

Lee's doctoral dissertation was the first book on agricultural economics written by overseas students from modern China. It illustrated the changes of policies in agriculture and explained sustainable land use in ancient Chinese agriculture. To address agricultural reform in modern times, Lee emphasized a balanced view between Chinese traditional economic thought and contemporary western economic thought. Of the three women economists discussed in this chapter, Lee was the one who went beyond studying the Chinese economy from a western perspective to being reflective of a China-historic approach. Particularly she found a middle ground between the classics and the practical school. Her economic thought reflected Chinese classic philosophy.

Chung-ying Kuo

Chung-ying Kuo[35] was born in 1912 and died in 1965.[36] Kuo's biography is nearly a blank page. The only evidence of her existence in the history of overseas women students is her doctoral dissertation. Kuo studied with Professor Paul Knaplund in the history and political science department of the University of Wisconsin. After Kuo finished her dissertation, titled "British Trade in China, 1894–1914," she received her doctoral degree in 1947.

Chung-ying Kuo's economic thought

As a beneficiary of the trend for studying abroad initiated by missionaries, Kuo recognized the revitalizing effects of cultural contact between the east and the west, and realized the importance of carrying out reforms in social and economic development. In her dissertation preface, Kuo stated: "Free thinking, adequate environment and convenient working conditions in a secure society are prerequisite for the development of a person's knowledge and, eventually, for his or her accomplishment."[37] This idea of free thinking illustrates the influence western thought had on Kuo. As an overseas student in the US, she embraced the idea of liberal thought. Kuo's dissertation focused on the first western country forcing China to open markets. Her detailed study on British trade in China served as a historical review and provided a reference point for future foreign trade relations.

When Kuo collected materials for her thesis, both Britain and China were at war against common enemies. In this time of great difficulty, the British government supported China by abolishing the privileges that Britain had enjoyed. Kuo thought this abolition of British extraterritoriality in China reflected continuously changing British policy. Her study dealt with the changes of policies and Sino-British relations, from the First Sino-Japanese War (1894) to the eve of the First World War (1914).

The earliest attempt made by Britain to establish a trade relationship with China was in the 1600s. When Captain John Weddell landed on Macao in 1637, he intended to develop trade with the Chinese government. He failed because the Portuguese were standing in the way. In 1670, the British East India Company opened trade in Xiamen and Taiwan. In order to cope with the expanding trade business of the British East India Company, a private organization, Gong-Hang,[38] was formed by the merchants group in Guangdong in 1720. This monopolistic organization ruled foreign trade on the Chinese side for more than a century, even after Britain stopped hiring the East India Company to trade with China in 1834. Little by little, conflicts accumulated between Britain and China. In addition, Britain had trade deficits since the beginning of Sino-British trade. As a result, the First Opium War broke out in 1840. The treaties signed after the war fundamentally changed China's social nature. China turned from a feudal society to a semi-colonial and semi-feudal society. The Treaty of Nanjing laid the foundation of British trade in China by instituting the treaty port system.

Kuo analyzed the development of the trade policies, dividing them into five periods. In the first period, 1894 to 1898, British trade flourished in both value and quantity. In 1894, China was defeated by Japanese invaders. The Treaty of Shimonoseki extended the scope of foreign investment of capital to railways and mining enterprises. The incompetent Qing government lost the integrity of its territory. Britain determined to protect its commercial supremacy in China, and constantly tried to block other countries such as Russia, France and Germany. Britain kept its dominant right in the Yangtze valley, railway construction, and mining. In the second period, 1899 to 1901, British trade fluctuated extensively because China was suffering from the wars initiated by the Boxer Rebellion and the invasion of the Siege of the International Legations. In 1899, an English man A. E. Hippisley suggested the American government maintain the "Open Door Policy" in China, along with other countries. In the third period, British trade boomed from 1902 to 1905. After the Boxer Rebellion, there was a new feature of British policy in China called the "Balance of Power." At this time, Russia occupied a large territory in the north of China. Britain was eager to gain an ally against Russia. The Anglo-Japanese alliance was formed in 1902. In the fourth period, from 1906 to 1911, Sino-British trade was strained. After the defeat of Russia, Japan became the new threat to the British "Balance of Power." Britain renewed the alliance with Japan to restrain Japan's power in China. In the fifth period, from 1912 to 1914, British trade recovered again. After the Chinese revolution, the Chinese Republic was founded in 1911. Britain supported the new government by offering a reorganization loan, in order to create a stable economic environment for trade. When the First World War broke out in 1914, all policies that Britain had made in the past were subordinated to the purpose of winning the war.

According to Kuo, the fluctuations that Britain experienced through the years in trade with China were mainly caused by:

> [D]islocation of domestic affairs and international complications in China; the competition of other traders with Britain, like Japan, Russia, Germany, France, U.S. and even the growth of domestic Chinese industries; and the change of the monetary unit from silver to sterling.
>
> *Kuo 1947, 198*

Kuo regarded the influence of British trade in China as a remarkably beneficial event in a historical perspective. Before 1800, western products were insignificant to the Chinese people, and the Chinese market was unimportant to westerners. After 1800, British manufacturing goods such as cottons, woolens and metals swarmed onto the Chinese market. These three kinds of products were the leading exports of British trade in China. Machinery, another article imported from Britain, was significant in the process of China's modernization. By opening trade ports, cities such as Shanghai, Tianjin, Guangdong, Wuhan, Beijing and Shenzhen prospered. Open trade brought huge changes in communication technology, railways, customs administration, education, medical science and factory-based manufacturing. China was both used as an extractive country, with

Britain benefiting, but also obtained British technology for mass production and increased material standard of living for those in China. As Kuo summarized, "China was on the way of being modernized and having better relations with other members of the family of nations."[39]

Unlike Mabel Lee, Kuo's thesis had a more explicitly western character. Kuo advocated "free" trade following norms of western economics that she likely would have learned through graduate training in the US. Kuo's thesis ignored the historical problems that British trade imposed on China, such as the lost tariff autonomy, serious outflow of silver and unfavorable balance of trade. Because there is a limited biographical record, we do not know whether western thought shaped her in China. Her free trade stance makes it reasonable to conjecture that western influences (such as missionaries) might have had an effect on Kuo during her youth in China. We assume that her thesis was certainly informed by the influence of her study abroad.

Summary

Kuo's dissertation, divides Sino-British trade from 1894 to 1914 into five time periods. Kuo generalized the features of British trade in each period and assessed the impact of British trade policy changes on China's economy. She was a firm advocate of free markets and the open trade and she highlighted the benefits of this trade for China.

Kuo had a promising start in this field. Her work was certainly comparable to her male colleagues.[40] As one of a small number of doctorates with cross-cultural experiences, Kuo could have made substantial contributions to the study of foreign trade if she had carried on with her research. We have no records of her subsequent work. Perhaps this is because she was a woman.

Yu-pu Pan

Introduction to Yu-pu Pan

Yu-pu Pan (1914–1997) was the first woman Ph.D. of Shenyang.[41] From 1925 to 1928, Pan received her high school education in Fengtian Provincial Women's Normal School. She entered the National Northeastern University in 1934 and gained her Bachelor of Science degree in 1938. After two years teaching at the university, she became a graduate student in statistics at Nankai Institute of Economics. In 1943, Pan translated an article "Revenue Policy of Britain in War Times" written by Walter Hill, which was published in *Time and Tide*.[42] In China, Pan married Gengnian Hu, a famous politician, but after he fell in love with another woman, Pan divorced him.

In her early 30s, Pan went abroad to study at the University of Illinois in 1945. One year later, she earned her master's degree with a thesis entitled, "A Comparative Study of the Theory of Interest." Pan received her doctoral degree under the guidance of Professor Ralph H. Blodgett at the University of Illinois in 1948 (Zou 2016, 212).

Sometime after graduating, Pan became the supervisor of the statistical department in the United Nations, specializing in statistics of life indices. Pan was granted U.S. permanent residence in 1957. After 27 years of service, she retired from the United Nations and returned to China. In May 1978, Pan was hired by the world economy department of the Chinese academy of social sciences as a special researcher. The next year, she was selected as the director of the first council of the Statistical Society of China.

Pan's ex-husband, Gengnian Hu, had a daughter named Yinmeng Hu from his second marriage. Yinmeng Hu was a popular actress in Taiwan in the 1970s. When Yinmeng Hu went to study in America, she was treated as family by Pan. Hu wrote of Pan in her autobiography *The Journal of the Soul*:

> This woman used to bind her feet is now standing on her own full feet in America. Her independence and generosity impressed me deeply. I think a woman's feet are not so much fettered by tradition, but wrapped by her own fear living inside her heart. As one of the women from the last generation, she did not give up on herself and deny her potential ability after her husband's abandonment. Instead, she became a strong independent woman and made the most of her life.
>
> *Hu 2006, 101*

The *New York Times* printed an obituary of Yu-pu Pan on September 24, 1997. It stated: "She will be greatly missed by her family and friends for her warmth, strength and loving spirit."[43]

Yu-pu Pan's economic thought

Pan started her studies at the University of Illinois in 1945, the same year China won the second Sino-Japanese War (1931–1945). At that time, industrialization was a major concern of Chinese economists. Available capital was needed desperately in the postwar period. Pan's doctoral dissertation was timely, dealing with international capital movements. Particularly relevant are the last two chapters which discuss the relation between capital and economic development.

In the theory of marginal productivity, factors of production are valued by their marginal products. In the theoretical context of long-term equilibrium, factors of production used in different firms, industries and regions should eventually be equal. Pan stated in the preface to her dissertation that "[a]s the world is bound together more and more by the facilities of communication and transportation, international equilibrium becomes as important as interregional equilibrium from the long-run point of view."

Among the factors of production, capital is the most mobile. Pan regarded the study of international capital movements as part of international trade theory, and thought that the relationship between international capital movements and the formation of domestic capital required systematic study within a general equilibrium framework.

The causes of international capital movements

Different interest rates in two countries were the main cause of international capital movements. Knut Wicksell (1954) stated that the rise of interest rates in one country could attract large capital inflows from foreign countries and prevent the outflow of domestic capital. However, in the classical theory of interest, economists mainly focused on equilibrium between international capital movements and short-term interest rates. Pan's idea on capital movements belonged to new classical theory. She believed that the differences in countries' interest rates were caused by differences in their productivity of capital. She also indicated, "International lending does not necessarily mean a reduction of productive power in the remitting country; nor does borrowing mean definitely an increase of it in the receiving country" (1948, 218). Although the costs involved in international capital movements were higher than domestic capital movements, both lending and borrowing countries would benefit from the capital movements in the long run.

Early economists tended to think that international capital movements were caused by a single reason. By the late nineteenth century, however, economists believed that international capital movements were not simply caused by interest rate differentials; they also took personal investment preferences and investors' risk aversion into consideration.

After the Second World War, the world's political and economic situation was significantly changed. Economic imbalances between less-developed and developed countries were large. Usually, capital would flow from the less-developed countries with high interest rates to developed countries with low interest rates in order to avoid risk. However, Pan found that in the postwar years, the situation was different. Capital tended to flow from areas of higher marginal productivity to lower ones—that is, from developed to developing countries—instead of the expected flow from low to high. After the war, the imbalance of economic development and the frequent fluctuations of monetary exchange rates of countries in the world accelerated the flow of international capital. The opening up of China facilitated the capital flow from developed countries to developing China.

Pan also addressed the issue of capital flight from developing economies (1948, 82–85). Pan explained that capital flight brought a decline in wealth and exchange rates. Since capital flight normally occurs unexpectedly and suddenly, the country losing capital (developing country) will suffer the consequences of production shrinking and a sharp rise in the interest rate. Therefore, it will further cause imbalance in economics, trade, revenue and expenditure.

Economic development and the utilization of capital

Economic development and accumulation of capital are inseparable with mutual effects on each other. The level of technology and utilization of capital affect economic development, and in turn affect capital formation. A country's progress in industrialization is closely pegged to the accumulation of capital.

As a less-developed country, Pan thought China had two ways to obtain necessary capital for its industrialization and economic development: either raising its domestic capital or borrowing from foreign countries. Pan studied the dissertation of another overseas student, Peigang Zhang.[44] She agreed with Zhang's argument that the postwar years should become the prime time for China's industrialization. The increased demands of expanding manufacturing required large capital infusions. The introduction of foreign machinery in agriculture was also necessary to feed the growing industrial population. However, the aftermath of eight years of war made it difficult for China to gather capital from domestic savings, and consequently, foreign capital was indispensable. As for the speed of capital inflow, Pan argued that it should match the expansion of the borrowing country's productive power.

A general study would shed some light on this complicated problem, with specific cases requiring more detailed analyses. In general, Pan held that foreign capital should be distributed equally to support domestic industries, export industries and public service. But Pan deemed that China was an "immature borrower" at the time. The efficiency of capital was crucial because borrowing involved problems of repayment. Under these circumstances, and to avoid debt accumulation from loans, she advocated that foreign capital be used in building public utilities to increase the productive power of the nation.

Pan's conclusions on international capital mobility resonated with the ideas in the western development literature of the second half of the twentieth century. Her dissertation builds on important contributors to the understanding of capital flows and its influence on development, including the classical theory and contemporary contributions by economists such as Ragnar Nurkse (1953). Her studies demonstrated a clear influence of the predominant views in US economics programs and of western economic thought of the neoclassical variety.

In terms of the existence of western influence in her childhood, it is clear that her early childhood was one of a traditional upbringing for many girls in China in the early twentieth century: her feet were bound. Whether she was affected by liberal thought through education or missionary contact in her later education is unclear. It seems reasonable to infer that missionary activity had more influence on the early stage of women's higher education abroad. Later on, as the educational system developed in China, this influence faded.

Summary

Pan's dissertation dealt with the urgent problems of capital in the best time for Chinese industrialization. She analyzed the causes of international capital movements and formation, the relationship between capital and development, and the utilization of capital in the context of China's actual conditions after the war. Pan's cutting-edge studies, as well as her keen sense of economics made her stand out in the field. Pan put forward novel ideas, such as counter-intuitive capital flows and capital accumulation for public investment expenditure to support China's industrial development. Her western-based economic thought was new in the study of the Chinese economy.

Among these three women economists from modern China, Pan was the only one who actually persisted in economic research and made a career of it. The high-quality doctoral dissertation she accomplished was a solid stepping stone to her later contributions in economics.

Conclusion

Three women economists in modern China have been studied in this chapter. First, Mabel Lee thoroughly investigated the history of Chinese agricultural economy. Lee listed the changes in land policy, land tax policy, and land conservation policy of each dynasty. In the China of Lee's time period, the distribution of land was greatly imbalanced. The rent and tax on land were heavy, thus intensifying the poverty of farmers. In order to develop agricultural and industrial production, the outdated land system had to be changed. Lee's suggestions to learn from the thought of ancient sages and to adopt agricultural reform policies for sustainable development continue to be valuable today. Second, Chung-ying Kuo addressed the policy changes in British trade in China. Kuo saw the irresistible historical trend of international trade and embraced the positive side of British trade. Kuo emphasized the advantages of foreign trade brought to social and economic development, such as the improvement of living standards, communication technology, transportation, etc. Third, Yu-pu Pan analyzed international capital movements. Pan pointed out that, for a developing country, it was important to draw foreign capital to construct the nation. A wise utilization of international capital could benefit domestic capital formation and avoid the accumulation of loans. Although Pan's study of capital movements belonged to the early stage of this theory, her insights on the relations between capital movements and formation are still worthy of reference and consideration.

In the study of the Chinese economy, these women merged their knowledge of Chinese society with the economics that they learned in the US. However, deeper reflection finds that only Lee actively considered elements of Chinese thought and Chinese classical philosophy in her analysis of the Chinese economy. By contrast, the economic thought of Kuo and Pan primarily reflected standard economic views of the west. Kuo attached importance to the benefits of trade with Great Britain, and to a certain extent ignored the negative realities of this trade experience during the nineteenth century. Pan's analysis of capital flows in the postwar years of China also shows the influence of western economic thought.

Overseas students played a significant role in the process of China's social change and modernization. A few women were a part of this movement to study abroad in China. Certainly, the chaos of the times did not make for an easy transition to professional life. Even for these accomplished women, academic economics remained elusive: The first woman left academia for her own reasons; the second disappeared from the academic field for unknown reasons. Only the third built a solid meaningful career in economic research. However, they all demonstrated the strong side of femininity. As intellectual women, they led by example in breaking the conventional role imposed on women. Their research, which contributed to the study of economic development in modern China, demonstrates the potential of Chinese women in economics.

Of course, the individual initiative of these three women played out against institutional constraints. Their access to early education was influenced by the western missionary movement of the day. Importantly, support for graduate studies also came from the Chinese government, which was willing to support women in higher education. This demonstrated the liberal influence in early twentieth-century China. However, only a few women actually had the opportunities to study abroad, so this also indicated the limitation of the liberal trend in that period.

Notes

1 I would like to give special thanks to Professor Joseph Persky, Professor Kirsten Madden, Professor Jinwen Zou and Chuanyi Guo, for their kindly encouragement and endless support to help me finish this chapter. I am also very thankful to the Departments of Economics in both Zhongnan University of Economics and Law and University of Illinois at Chicago. The Ph.D. student exchange program I attended from 2016 to 2017 was very beneficial to my research.

2 Mabel Lee's Chinese name is written as 李美步.

3 Chung-ying Kuo is written as 郭冲颖 in Chinese.

4 Sino refers to China. It means the ancient-to-modern history of China, the culture of China, or the Chinese people.

5 Yu-pu Pan is written as 潘玉璞 in Chinese.

6 Besides these three women economists, two other women earned their Ph.D.s in economics in the first half of the twentieth century. Meng-ban Wu 吴孟班 graduated from University of Paris in 1931, her dissertation, "The Development of Modern China's Business," was written in French. Shu-chuang Ting Kuan 丁关淑庄 graduated from Radcliffe College in 1948. Her dissertation was titled "Simple Dynamics of Income, Investment and Consumption." Because of the lack of materials, these two dissertations are not discussed in this chapter. Any further study of these women is welcomed within the field.

7 Robert Morrison was the first missionary of the Protestant Church in China. He started his mission in 1807. One of his contributions was that he pioneered translating the Bible into Chinese.

8 The First Opium War, or the First Anglo-Chinese War, was launched by Britain to reverse its trade deficit with China. It marked the beginning of China's modern history.

9 "Three obediences and four virtues" is written as 三从四德 in Chinese. "Three obediences" means a woman should obey her father before marriage, obey her husband during married life, and obey her son in widowhood; "four virtues" were fidelity, physical charm, propriety in speech and efficiency in needlework. It is a saying that comes from one of the Confucian classic books, *Etiquette, Mourning, and the Story of Zixia*.

10 Yung Wing's Chinese name is written as 容闳. After three years of studying at Wilbraham & Monson Academy, he was enrolled in Yale University as the first Chinese student. In 1854, Yung Wing earned his bachelor's degree in literature, and graduated from Yale University with honors.

11 According to Yung Wing's book *My Life in China and America*, in total 120 students aged 10 to 16 were sent to study in New England.

12 Yamei Kin's Chinese name is written as 金雅梅.

13 King-eng Hn's Chinese name is written as 柯金英.

14 Mary Stone's Chinese name is written as 石美玉.

15 Ida Kahn's Chinese name is written as 康爱德.

16 For example: Yamei Kin was the founder of the first nursing school, Beiyang Women's Medical School, and the first Women's Hospital, Beiyang Women's Hospital; King-eng Hn was the director of Woolston Memorial Hospital in Fujian; Mary Stone opened Danforth Hospital at Jiujiang.

17 This summary is drawn from the book *A Survey of Chinese Students in American Universities and Colleges in the Past One Hundred Years*, published in 1954 by China Institute in America in New York. Yichi Mei was the chairman of the institute.

18 *The Chinese Students' Monthly* (1906–1931) was the first and most influential magazine published by the Chinese students in America. It discussed the important topics in China, included education, society, industry, agriculture, politics and economics.

19 This photo was published in *The Chinese Students' Monthly* in 1919, Vol. 3, No. 2, page 1.

20 Tse-ven Soong's Chinese name is written as 宋子文.

21 Four families controlled China's politics and economy in the first half of the twentieth century. They were Jiang, Song, Kong and Chen families. Tse-ven Soong belonged to the Song family.

22 Huangdi was the first leader of the ancient Huaxia tribal league.

23 *Political Science Quarterly* 31, no. 2 (1916): 201–243.

24 These books include *Shu King* (尚书), *Chow Li* (周礼), *Han Book* (汉书), *Qimin Yaoshu* (齐民要术), *Mengxi Bitan* (梦溪笔谈), *Nongzheng Quanshu* (农政全书), *Shennong Bencaojing* (神农本草经), etc.

25 Lee 1921, 15.

26 Doctrine of the mean, 中庸, is one the main doctrines of Confucianism. In James Legge's translation of the text, the goal of the mean is to maintain balance and harmony, directing the mind to a state of constant equilibrium. The person who follows the mean is on a path of duty and must never leave it. A superior person is cautious, a gentle teacher and shows no contempt for his or her inferiors. She or he always does what is natural according to her or his status in the world. Even common men and women can carry the mean into their practices, as long as they do not exceed their natural order.

27 Xinhai Revolution, or the Chinese Revolution in 1911, was a revolution that overthrew China's last imperial dynasty (the Qing dynasty), and established the Republic of China.

28 The Tsing Tien system, 井田制, was a slaveholder-owning land system. This system distributed land. "A square area of land was divided into nine identically-sized sections; the eight outer sections were privately cultivated by serfs and the center section was communally cultivated on behalf of the landowning aristocrat" (Zhufu 1981, 7). The advantages of this system were: It saved expenses; unified customs; improved production; made the exchange of commodities easier; had mutual protection among farmers; closed social relations, and generated cooperation.

29 Shong Yang (395BC–338BC) is written as 商鞅 in Chinese. He was a politician, reformist, and thinker during the Spring and Autumn Period. Shang was the most important representative of the legalist school.

30 What Lee called modified Tsing Tien system is now known as 均田制. It was a system that declared all land was owned by the nation or the emperor. The free land was assigned by the government to individual farmers according to the population of the area. After farming on the land for a certain number of years, the famers could own the land.

31 Lee (1921) made a timetable of the changes in land systems. See chronological table 1, page 11.

32 Mu, 亩, is a unit of measurement. One "mu" is approximately 666.667 square meters.

33 The saying came from the book "Wu Yue Chun Qiu" (吴越春秋) by Hua Zhao (赵晔) in the Han Dynasty.

34 Taoism is a religious or philosophical tradition in China. The central thought of Taoism is to live in harmony with the Tao (道). Tao is the nature of everything, and the orbit of all things. In Taoism, it is "the One, which is natural, spontaneous, eternal, nameless, and indescribable. It is at once the beginning of all things and the way in which all things pursue their course" (Chan 1963, 136).

35 Kuo's English name was Margret. Her husband was Justin Yun-Kung Shen (1909–1982). She added her husband's last name "Shen (沈)" in her family name after marriage. In modern China, as a tradition, some women would drop their surname and take that of their husband, or add their husband's name in front of their own surname after the marriage.

36 Information about her death remained unknown until now. Ying and Trautwein (2013) stated that Kuo's birth year was 1912. Kuo's death date is on a gravestone in Rock Creek Cemetery (Washington DC (www.findagrave.com/memorial/44383292)). The inscription matches her name and birth year. This is assuming that after Kuo's graduation she moved to Washington DC.

37 Kuo 1947, iii.

38 Chinese: 公行. Like the British East India Company, Gong-Hang was also a monopoly organization controlling all the foreign trade in China. It worked as the middleman in imports and exports; it set prices of the export goods; and collected customs duties.

39 Kuo 1947, 247.

40 Other works on foreign trade by male overseas students are the following dissertations: Chong-Su See's *Chinese Foreign Trade* (1919), Shu-Lun Pan's *The Trade of the United States with China* (1924) and Chee-Hsien Wu's *Two Decades of Soviet Foreign Trade* (1947).
41 Fan, Hua. "People of Shenyang." *Shenyang Evening News*, May 23, 2008.
42 *Time and Tide* was a semimonthly journal that started publication in Wuhan in 1938 and ended in 1949. It was a comprehensive political publication during the Second Sino-Japanese War. The aim of publication was to unite Chinese people to build the confidence to win the war.
43 Paid Notice: Deaths PAN, YUPU, DR., *The New York Times*, September 28, 1997.
44 Peigang Zhang, 张培刚, was the father of development economics in China. Zhang graduated from Harvard University in 1945. His influential doctoral dissertation was "Agriculture and Industrialization."

References

Bieler, Stacey. *"Patriots" or "Traitors"? A History of American-Educated Chinese Students.* New York: M.E. Sharpe, Inc., 2004.
Cai, Dengshan. "The Saint Lady in Hu Shi's Heart." *Book Town* 1 (2008): 35–37.
Chan, Wing-tsit. *A Source Book in Chinese Philosophy.* Princeton University Press, 1963.
Fan, Hua. "People of Shenyang." *Shenyang Evening News*, May 23, 2008.
He, Xiaoxia. *Church Schools and the Modernization of Education in China.* Guangzhuo: Guangdong Education Publishing House, 1996.
Hu, Yinmeng. *The Journal of the Soul.* Shanghai: Orient Publishing Center, 2006.
Kuo, Chung-ying. "British Trade in China, 1894–1914." Madison: University of Wisconsin, 1947.
Lee, Mabel Ping-hua. *The Economic History of China: With Special Reference to Agriculture.* New York: Columbia University Press, 1921.
Legge, James. *The Chinese Classics: The Life and Works of Mencius.* Vol. 2. London: Trübner & Company, 1875.
Mei, Yichi. *A Survey of Chinese Students in American Universities and Colleges in the Past One Hundred Years.* New York: China Institute in America, 1954.
Morrison, Elisa A. *Memoirs of the Life and Labours of Robert Morrison.* London: Longman, Orme, Brown, and Longmans, 1839.
Nurkse, Ragnar. *Problems of Capital Formation in Underdeveloped Countries.* London: Oxford University Press, 1953.
Pan, Shu-Lun. "The Trade of the United States with China, 1784–1923." New York: Columbia University, 1924.
Pan, Yu-pu. *International Capital Movements and Capital Formation.* University of Illinois, 1948.
See, Chong-Su. *The Foreign Trade of China.* New York: Columbia University Press, 1919.
Wang, Daozhi. *The History of Chinese and Foreign Educational Exchanges.* Hunan: Hunan Education Press, 1998.
Wang, Qisheng. "The Historical Evolution of Women's Higher Education in Church School." *Journal of Central China Normal University* 2 (1996): 65.
Wei, Yuan. *Illustrated Treatise on the Maritime Kingdoms.* Zhengzhou: Zhongzhou Guji, 1999. No publisher available for 1847 edition.
Wicksell, Knut. *Value, Capital, and Rent.* Translated by S. H. Frowein. London: George Allen and Unwin Ltd., 1954.
Wing, Yung. *My Life in China and America.* Shanghai: The Commercial Press, 1915.
Wu, Chee Hsien. "Two Decades of Soviet Foreign Trade." Cambridge, MA: Harvard University, 1947.
Ye, Weili. "'Nü Liuxuesheng': The Story of American-Educated Chinese Women, 1880s–1920s." *Modern China* 20 (1994): 321.
Ying, Ma, and Hans-Michael Trautwein, eds. *Thoughts on Economic Development in China.* London: Routledge, 2013.
Zhufu, Fu. "The Economic History of China: Some Special Problems." *Modern China* 7 (1981): 7.
Zou, Jinwen. *The Development of Economics in Modern China: Centered on Overseas Students'* Doctoral Dissertations. Beijing: China Renmin University Press, 2016.

PART IV

Spanning the mid-20th century

16
AUSTRIAN SCHOOL WOMEN ECONOMISTS

Giandomenica Becchio

Three generations of Viennese male economists worked in Vienna, either at the university or in private economic institutions, between the 1870s and early 1930s (Mises 1984). They are responsible for constructing the foundations of the Austrian School of economics. These men were a cohesive group of economists who developed an economic theory combining human and social dynamics with classical liberalism. To the first generation belonged founding father Carl Menger (1840–1921), who in 1871 published his *Principles* (Menger 1871), Eugene Böhm-Bawerk (1851–1914), and Friedrich Wieser (1851–1926). Their immediate followers (the second generation) were: Joseph Schumpeter (1883–1950), Gottfried Haberler (1900–1995), Hans Mayer (1879–1975), and Ludwig Mises (1881–1973). In the third generation are Friedrich Hayek (1899–1992), Paul Rosenstein-Rodan (1902–1985), Ludwig Lachman (1906–1990),[1] and Fritz Machlup (1902–1983), (Holcombe 2014; Boettke and Coyne 2015).

The Austrian School of economics focused on building an economic theory describing the spontaneous dynamics of individual economic action and innovation in a framework of free institutions guaranteeing economic growth and social development. From a methodological perspective, the common feature of Austrian scholars was their peculiar way of reasoning, known as methodological individualism. An implication of methodological individualism is the necessity to understand individual decision-making processes in order to explain macroeconomic phenomena. In the Austrian School of economics, methodological individualism is rooted in the application of dispersed knowledge to decision-making processes (as in Menger's passage from individual needs to economic laws), and in the importance of introducing time to understand economic phenomena (as in Böhm-Bawerk's description of production processes, and in Wieser's notion of marginal utility). Schumpeter, Mises, and Hayek made methodological individualism even stronger. From a theoretical perspective, they fought against any form of planned economy, even during Europe's interwar years, and later against Keynesianism as well. They considered any form of economic policy as a rupture of the spontaneous, although imperfect, economic order. Furthermore, they stressed the importance of creativity in economic activity, especially in Schumpeter's notions of entrepreneurship. This notion of creativity specifically contrasts with the static mechanism of expected utility/profit function maximization as depicted in neoclassical economics.

Economists of the Austrian School, from Menger to Hayek, had a great influence on Viennese students of political economy in the early twentieth century. Among them, many women economists had a significant role. The aim of this chapter is to identify four generations of the Austrian School of women economists from the first decade of twentieth century to 1970s, and to determine their role in the history of the Austrian School. There is a particular focus on their novel theoretical contribution as well as on their ability to extend and disseminate the Austrian paradigm.

A time-period taxonomy of the four generations of Austrian School women economists

The Austrian School women economists shared with their mentors and colleagues the main features of Austrian economics: economic theory focused on an individual's plan for coordination and decentralized knowledge; the disutility of any monetary policy as well as of any governmental intervention to minimize distortions; the fundamental role of innovation to explain the link between growth and development; and a specific interest in the history of political economy.

Starting in the early twentieth century, four generations of Austrian School women economists arose (see Table 16.1). The first two generations were Viennese economists active between the early twentieth century and 1938 before the massive emigration due to the *Anschluss*. The first generation (up to 1919) was formed by students of Böhm-Bawerk and Mises, although they received their academic training and degrees outside Austria due to the persistent ban against female students in Austrian universities. The second generation (active during the interwar period) finally had the opportunity to enroll in and graduate from the University of Vienna: formally students of Mayer, they were massively influenced by Mises. The first and second generations of Austrian School economists share some peculiar features: besides all being Viennese, they belonged to the Jewish middle class and were subjected to stringent anti-Semitic attitudes in academia (and society in general); they strongly supported classical liberalism as the non-negotiable vision for their economic analysis; and they were very active in fighting for women's emancipation, especially for their participation in the public sphere (Klausinger 2014; Timms 2009). The third generation of Austrian School women economists were no longer

Table 16.1 Austrian School women economists in chronological order

First generation: Students of Böhm-Bawerk's and Wieser's at the University of Vienna 1900–1919	Else Cronbach (1879–1913) Louise Sommer (1889–1964) Toni (Kassowitz) Stolper (1890–1988)
Second generation: Students of Mises' extramural seminars 1920s-1930s	Marianne Herzfeld (1893–1976) Martha Braun (1898–1990) Helene Lieser (1898–1962) Gertrude Lovasy (1902–1974) Elly Spiro (1903–2001) Ilse (Schüller) Mintz (1904–1978)
Third generation: Students of Hayek's at the LSE (1930s–1940s) and of Mises' at NYU (1950s–1960s)	Marjorie Grice-Hutchinson (1909–2003) Vera Smith Lutz (1912–1976) Mary Sennholz (1913-2017) Bettina Bien Greaves (1917-)
Fourth generation: The Austrian revival associated with Hayek winning the Nobel Prize: (1974 onwards)	Sudha Shenoy (1943–2008) and many more active since the 1990s

from Austria: it was formed by Hayek's students at LSE (1930s–1970s) and by Mises' students at NYU (1938–1960s). A fourth, more recent generation began after the so-called Austrian revival in the 1970s with the work of Sudha Shenoy.[2] The number of Austrian School women economists significantly increased in the first two decades of the twenty-first century.

The first generation

It was not easy for female students to study economics in Vienna before World War I. Although in 1897 they had been admitted to the school of philosophy, they could not be officially enrolled in economic programs offered at the school of law. This was the main reason that the first generation of Austrian School women economists received their degrees either in Germany or in Switzerland, in spite of the fact that they were students of Böhm-Bawerk and Wieser. Members of this first generation were educated in the so-called fin-de-siècle Vienna, a period of seeming prosperity, which dramatically changed after the World War I.

Else Cronbach (1879–1913) was a student of Böhm-Bawerk and Wieser, and received her Ph.D. in political science in Berlin. She became involved in the foundation of the future *Nationalökonomische Gesellschaft* along with her friends and colleagues Ludwig von Mises, Emil Perels, and Karl Pribram (Pribram 1913). As Mises recalled, the *Nationalökonomische Gesellschaft* was founded in 1918 and represented, besides Mises' *Privatseminar*, an occasion to regularly discuss economic problems. The society was dismissed in 1938 by Hans Mayer (Wieser's successor at the University of Vienna) due to the anti-Semitic ban against Jews. Cronbach authored several publications on international trade, until her career was abruptly interrupted by her death at the age of 34 (Nautz 1997).

Louise Sommer (1889–1964), a student of Wieser and deeply influenced by Menger's work, received her Ph.D. in 1919 at the University of Genève, where she lived during the interwar period, earning her livelihood teaching as an adjunct and working as a freelance journalist. Her research mainly focused on economic history (Sommer 1920, 1925), history of economic thought (Sommer 1927a, 1960), methodology (Sommer 1932), and international economics (Sommer 1935, 1950). A close friend of Mises, whom she met after World War I, she shared with him the conception of socialism as a liberticidal principle (Hülsmann 2007).

Antonia (Kassowitz) Stolper (1890–1988), enrolled in 1911 at the school of law as the only female student, however, she was forced to move to Berlin to get her Ph.D. (1917). A student of Böhm-Bawerk and Wieser, she mainly worked on macroeconomics (national policy). In 1921, she married Gustav Stolper, the editor of both *Der Österreichische Volkswirt* and *Der Deutsche Volkswirt*, the most respected liberal economic journals in German-speaking countries of that time.

The second generation

In 1919, Viennese female students were finally allowed to register in the school of law in the University of Vienna, where they might also be enrolled in political economy programs. Hence, starting from the interwar period, Austrian female students were either granted access or allowed to get a Ph.D. in *Nationaloekonomie* in Vienna. Unfortunately, it was Mayer, not Mises, who got Wieser's chair. Hence, from 1920 to 1934, both male and female students of economics were officially Mayer's students, but mainly trained by Mises in his extramural meetings.[3] Among Mises's circle of attendees, there were many female students: Marianne Herzfeld, Martha Braun, Helene Lieser, Gertrude Lovasy, Elly Spiro and Ilse Mintz attended his weekly seminar. Lovasy and Mintz were also involved in the Austrian Institute for Business Cycle

Research, founded by Mises and Hayek in 1927 (Feichtinger 2001; Nautz 2000b; Hülsmann 2007; Klausinger 2016a).

Marianne Herzfeld (1893–1976) received her Ph.D. in history in Vienna and worked as a secretary in the Austrian Banker's Association until 1938, when she escaped from Vienna to Scotland.

Martha (Hermann) Braun (1898–1990) studied under the supervision of Wieser, Weber, and Mises. In 1921, her Ph.D. in political economy was one of the first for women graduates in Vienna, with a dissertation on monetary economics. In the 1920s, she worked in the Viennese Chamber of Commerce. She was forced to emigrate to the United States in 1939 (after a year spent in London), where she was employed as an economic analyst on behalf of the State Department (1944–1947). From 1947 to 1969, she taught at Brooklyn College in New York. After her retirement, she lectured at New York University.

Helene Lieser (1898–1962) obtained a Ph.D. in economic policy in 1920 in Vienna, where she was a regular member of the *Nationalökonomische Gesellschaft*, until her expulsion in 1938, and worked in the Austrian Banker's Association up to 1939 when she left Austria.

Gertrud Lovasy (1902–1974) earned her Ph.D. in Vienna in 1928, with a thesis on cartels in the Austrian iron industry. In 1938 she left Vienna. In 1939, she reached the United States where she worked on international cartels at the International Monetary Fund (Lovasy 1947).

Elly (Offenheimer) Spiro (1903–2001) obtained her Ph.D. in economics in Vienna in 1922. She reviewed several books for the *Zeitschrift für Nationalökonomie* and attended Mises' seminar until 1929, when she moved to Frankfurt. Escaping from Germany in November 1938, she settled in San Francisco in 1941 and stayed in touch with Mises, Machlup, and Hayek (Nautz 2002).

Ilse (Schüller) Mintz (1904–1978) was the daughter of Richard Schüller, one of Carl Menger's top students. After gaining a Ph.D. in 1927, she worked at the Institute under Hayek's supervision before escaping to the USA in the 1930s. She studied statistics at Columbia, earning another Ph.D. in 1951. Member staff of the National Bureau of Economic Research from 1951 to 1973, she focused her work on business cycle theory and foreign trade policy (Nautz 2000c).

The third generation

The *Anschluss* (1938) was the traumatic event that ended the Austrian School of economics in Austria and affected the destiny of its women economists. In fact, the third generation of Austrian women economists was formed by Hayek's students at the LSE (1931–1945) and Mises' students at NYU seminars (1951–1969). Although none were from Vienna, women economists of the third generation were considered 'Austrian' in the sense that they were educated on the basic principles of Austrian economics.

Two women economists emerged at the LSE: Marjorie Grice-Hutchinson, whose works dealt especially with history of economic thought, and Vera Smith Lutz, who mainly studied monetary economics and economic development. Grice-Hutchinson (1909–2003) was enrolled at the LSE as a Ph.D. student in economics and completed her degree under Hayek's supervision. He suggested she work on the historical manuscripts from the School of Salamanca. Smith Lutz (1912–1976) was a British student of both Robbins and Hayek at the LSE, receiving her Ph.D. in 1935 as Hayek's protégé: her thesis criticized the central banking system (Smith Lutz [1936] 1990).

At NYU, Mary Sennholz (1913–2017) and Bettina Bien Greaves (1917–) were regulars at Mises' seminars, and both spent many years at the Foundation of Economic Education (FEE) working to enhance the Austrian School of economics tradition. Sennholz edited a volume about Mises on the occasion of his 60th birthday (Sennholz 1956), and authored a biography of Leonard Read (Sennholz 1993); her last book was a collection of articles she edited for *The Freeman* (Sennholz 1997). During Bien Greaves's tenure as editor of *The Freeman* (1955 to 1999), Bien Greaves focused her interests on the effects of taxation on growth and unemployment during 1955–1970. From the 1970s to her retirement, she continued to edit many publications on the free market economy, and she compiled a monumental bibliography on Mises (Bien Greaves and McGee 1993). Also, Bien Greaves wrote a syllabus on a basic course in economics for high school students. The syllabus was basically a handbook on the Austrian School principles of economics: it begins from the analysis of individual needs to clarify the nature of economic principles (prices, savings, entrepreneurship, labor, money, credit, competition, etc.), enriched by examples from the history of economic thought and economic history (Bien Greaves 1975).

The fourth generation

The last generation of Austrian women economists started in the 1970s during the so-called Austrian revival, which took place in the United States (Vaughn 1994) and more recently developed outside the United States. The Austrian revival began after Hayek won the Nobel Prize in Economics (1974), and continued, especially through the initiative of Lachman, Kirzner, and Rothbard, who had been Mises' students. Under their supervision, a conference in South Royalton (Vermont) was organized by the Institute of Human Studies in 1974; one year later, Lachman and Kirzner started the 'Austrian Economics Seminar' at NYU to pave the way for an easier circulation of ideas among Austrian scholars.[4]

During the meeting of the South Royalton conference (1974), particular attention was given to Austrian methodological issues, such as the definition of human action and the role of markets in an anti-neoclassical perspective. Monetary issues, such as free banking and the role of monetary institutions to challenge Keynesian neoclassical theory were also priorities in the agenda (Dolan 1976). Among attendees, there was only one woman economist: Indian scholar Sudha Shenoy (1943–2008). According to an interview Shenoy gave a few years before her death, she had always been a Hayekian scholar (Shenoy 2003). Perhaps she was influenced by her father who was a student of Hayek at the LSE. She applied Hayek's economics not only to monetary themes against Keynes' legacy (Shenoy 1972), but also to the analysis of the economies of Eastern Europe (Shenoy 1989) and developing countries (Shenoy 1963, 1971, 1991).

The fourth (and current) generation is an entirely new generation of women academics associated with Austrian economics that might shed new light and perspective on their economic proposals. Most of them earned their Ph.D.s at George Mason University, and are especially working around the commonalities between Austrian economics, the Virginia School and institutionalism of the Bloomington School. Among them is Karen Vaughn, who, in 1996, was elected as the first President of the Society for the Development of Austrian Economics, and whose current research interests include a pro-market view of feminism. Other fourth-generation Austrian women economists include Bobbi Herzberg, Emily Chamlee Wright, Jayme Lemke, Diana Thomas, Shruti Rajagopalan, Abby Hall, Liya Palagashvili, Meghan Teague, Arielle John, Neera Badhwar, and Audrey Redford. Deirdre McCloskey might be included in the fourth generation of Austrian women economists. In the mid-1990s during an AEA meeting, McCloskey proudly announced: "I am an economist in transition . . . I am transitioning from a Chicago [neoclassical] economist to an Austrian economist."[5] Although very serious, she joked about her personal experience as a transgender person; in fact McCloskey referred to herself crossing from the world of a male economist embedded into the traditional neoclassical Chicago School to an Austrian woman economist; this crossing she described as emblematic of the necessity to re-think economics by introducing a 'feminine eye' against the discipline's male orientation, as well as recognizing a feminine style of reasoning in economics (McCloskey, 1993).

Main theoretical contributions by Austrian School women economists

Austrian School women economists focused their research on topics specific to Austrian economics, and extended Austrian concepts to their specific research fields (see Table 16.2). The Austrian women made contributions of substance to the development of the Austrian School paradigm. Although it is not possible to cover the entirety of the Austrian contributions from these women economists, a broad picture of their work drawn from a meaningful sample of their research is feasible, with special, but not exclusive, focus on their original contributions. Table 16.2 provides a schematic overview of the research topics undertaken by the Austrian School's women economists which are emphasized here.

Stolper was a fierce adversary of any form of government intervention. But the other first-generation women economists were somewhat open to some measure of government intervention in the economy when contingent social problems were particularly urgent (Cronbach 1907, 1910; Sommer 1935; Braun 1929). Cronbach and Braun were inclined toward minimal intervention of the state to guarantee decent conditions for life of agricultural and industrial workers in Austria and in Germany. Sommer advocated government to give some order to international trade. Braun advocated government to partially moderate the effects of business cycles, although she was against any form of taxation on industries.

Second-generation economists were particularly interested in understanding the hyperinflation that ensued after World War I and studied the general rise of unemployment that followed in Central Europe. They gave special attention to monetary issues: advocating against any monetary policy that favors inflation in order to reduce unemployment.

Second-, third-, and fourth-generation economists, who were students of Mises and Hayek during the interwar period and immediately thereafter, fought against regulation in international trade. They also explained the damage caused to development and growth by interventionism. These contributions include some originality concerning the business cycle and development in emerging countries. The battle against interventionism, especially after World War II, was in particular directed against any Keynesian policy.

Table 16.2 Some research topics of Austrian School women economists

On monetary theory and policy	First generation: Cronbach, Stolper, Sommer Second generation: Herzfeld, Braun, Lieser, Lovasy Third generation: Smith Lutz, Bien Greaves
On international trade	First generation: Sommer Second generation: Lovasy
Against Keynesianism	Second generation: Smith Lutz Fourth generation: Shenoy
On development and the business cycle	Second generation: Mintz Fourth generation: Shenoy
History of political economy	First generation: Sommer Second generation: Spiro, Lieser, Third generation: Grice-Hutchinson, Bien Greaves, Sennholz Fourth generation: Shenoy

Last, but not least, these women gave particular consideration to the history of political economy, seen as a necessary complement to theoretical analysis.

On monetary theory and policy

Research on monetary issues was central for Austrian School women economists since Stolper's Ph.D. (1917) (Table 16.2). They converged on the idea explained by Mises and Hayek that any attempt to cure depression by monetary policy would worsen circumstances from the initial situation. This is particularly valid in frantic periods during and after war. In fact, the nature of money, which obeys the laws of supply and demand, would simply make any monetary policy useless and often dangerous.

During the interwar period in Germany and Austria, hyperinflation became a dangerous economic and social problem. Stolper wrote several articles in the *Deutsche Volkswirt* against the Weimar government program, which was prone to an active monetary policy in order to reduce unemployment. She insisted that the prosperity brought about by inflation was an illusion because the value of real wages would decrease and, consequently, the middle-lower classes would suffer economically. Furthermore, businessmen would shift from their productive activities to speculation, and this would increase unemployment.

Like Stolper, both Lieser and Herzfeld demonstrated the social damages of inflation in Vienna: they insisted on the disutility of inflation in reducing national debt and unemployment. Lieser's thesis (1920), supervised by Mises and Spann, adopted an historical example, showing that monetary policy adopted during the Napoleonic wars in Austria (1811–1816) worsened the initial situation of hyperinflation and led to two periods of bankruptcy within a few years (Nautz 2000a). Herzfeld further attacked the general idea that inflation creates prosperity and wealth (the 'inflationist view of history' as defined by Mises): a reduced purchasing power is the main consequence of inflation, incorrectly considered a necessary condition of economic progress. Economic theory shows that any monetary policy (inflationary or deflationary) merely promotes financial growth for a segment of the population to the detriment of others. Furthermore, inflation leads to ill-conceived investment of capital and overconsumption, and ends with an inevitable breakdown of the currency system (Herzfeld 1926).

A turning point in research concerning the impact of inflation was Braun's first book (1929), an attempt to apply a micro-foundation analysis for economic policy (Leischko 2002; Backhaus 2005). Her approach was no longer historical, but essentially theoretical: she developed a microeconomic analysis to show inopportunity arising from state interference in market forces. For example, she criticized the practicability of Pigou's theory of taxation on industry due to the increase of manufacturing and production overhead. In her book, Braun distinguished economics as a theoretical discipline derived from economic policy, which rests outside economics: monetary policy, which is part of the theoretical component of economics, must remain free from any political interference, although a moderate state interventionist policy could be pursued for some contingencies.

The same theoretical approach was pursued by Smith Lutz in her doctoral thesis, which was enriched by historical examples concerning the central banking system in England, Scotland, France, USA, Germany, and Belgium. She worked under the supervision of Hayek at the LSE (Smith Lutz [1936] 1990). In her thesis, mainly based on Mises (1928), she proposed a system of free banking. The privately circulated currency of commercial banks was supposed to compete with the nationally issued currency, given the fact, at that time, that national monetary systems usually performed poorly. Smith Lutz's thesis is an historical reconstruction on the genesis of the central bank in Europe and in the United States. In this reconstruction, she showed that the system of central banking—in contrast to free banking—had prevailed because of a "combination of political motives and historical accident which played a much more important part than any well-considered economic principle" (Smith Lutz [1936] 1990, 5). According to Smith Lutz, central banking had been established as a monopoly for political reasons connected with the exigencies of state finance. Once established, "the superiority of central banking over the alternative system became a dogma" (Yeager 1990, 19), reinforced by the expectation that under a multiple banking system, there will be regular failures of individual banks, as well as monetary instability (inflation). Smith Lutz pointed out that crises often originate from the central banking system. She supported the idea that private banks keep stable reserve proportions:

> [T]he major fluctuations come from changes in the amount of cash provided by the central banks. We find that the commercial banks keep relatively stable reserve proportions and that their lending activities follow fairly closely (except in the pit of the depression) movements in central bank money.
>
> *Smith Lutz 1990, 52*[6]

The battle against the use of monetary policy to moderately increase inflation continued after World War II. Bettina Bien Greaves shared with Mises the idea that government regulation and control of economic life is opposite to freedom. This antipathy toward government intervention covered many policies, including manipulating prices, fixing wages, hampering imports or exports, and, above all, managing the money supply. For Bien Greaves, freedom flourishes within capitalism; state control makes people unable to cooperate on their own.

On international trade

International free circulation of money and commodities was another common feature for Austrian School women economists. Again, like the argument on monetary policy, first-generation economists were more open to possible intervention in regulating international trade. For example, Louise Sommer dealt especially with the European situation. Deeply influenced by political realism, Sommer claimed that inequality is inevitable in political and economic relations, and international commercial policy is not an exception. She claimed that international stability cannot be grounded in a hypothetical desire for equality. Instead, she introduced a 'scheme of preferential tariffs' and generated calculations of total export trade for each European country in order to find a proper balance (Bidwell 1937). Later, after World War II, Sommer considered the Monnet-Schumann plan. This plan was the French-German agreement on steel and coal trade introduced in 1947 for the partial restoration of national economies and the reconstruction after World War II. For Sommer, the Monnet-Schumann plan was "an important approach to the final aim of the unification of Western Europe" (Sommer 1950, 80).

Economists of the second generation were definitely against any form of government intervention in regulating the economy. Mises-trained Gertrude Lovasy (1941, 1962; Lovasy and Zassenhaus 1953) is the most emblematic example. In her first publication on international trade with imperfect competition, Lovasy (1941) analyzed Chamberlin's book and Robinson's work on monopolistic/imperfect competition. According to Lovasy, monopolistic/imperfect competition is characterized by decreasing costs of production as well as downward sloping demand curves, which can be influenced by producers. She explained that international trade can exploit decreasing costs by increasing trade volume, but the existence of imperfect substitution across international products reduces international trade volume (Lovasy 1941). For Lovasy, international trade expansions result from taking advantage of decreasing costs and international trade contractions result from imperfect substitution. In the 1950s and 1960s, Lovasy worked on the possible consequences of fluctuations in international trade as well as on the relation between inflation and export in a worldwide context. She was intolerant toward the intergovernmental cartels that were accepted by American policy of that time (Pauly 2003).

In a later publication, Lovasy combined her critique of monetary policy as inflation-inducing with an effective policy of regulation in international trade. In several papers on the relation between inflation and export in Western countries, she focused her attention on the unexpected consequences of inflation hampering the increase of exports and delaying their diversification. According to Lovasy, inflationary prices can spread to the export sector, but mainly through adjustment of wages to cope with a higher cost of living: the immediate consequence is thus an increase of costs that discourage exports. Lovasy insisted that inflation has a dangerous long-term effect: it makes investment more expensive, which reduces exports, and can lead to price control policies on basic living commodities. Although the effect of inflation on exports may be adjusted by a gradual devaluation of the exchange rate, continuous devaluation causes a lack of confidence in the currency (Lovasy 1962).

Anti-Keynesianism

The attack against Keynesian economics especially involved Hayek-trained Smith Lutz (Graziani 1983) and Shenoy. Smith Lutz's book, *Theory of Investment of the Firm* (Smith Lutz and Lutz 1951), tried to merge neoclassical economics and Austrian theories. The book introduced time, as an extension of Böhm-Bawerk's emphasis, into a standard model of investments in an anti-Keynesian perspective by "integrating the theory of production with the theory of capital as the latter applies to the individual firm" (Smith Lutz and Lutz 1951, 4). As Smith Lutz wrote later, their purpose was to "develop a unified theory of production and investment under a cost minimization (and profit maximization) behavior criterion" (Smith 1959, 61).[7]

In her works on the relation between monetary factors and the rate of employment (Smith Lutz 1952), she defended the classical dichotomy between real and monetary factors. Her defense used Modigliani's model against the Keynesian view that the amount of money and liquidity preferences are determinants of the real levels of macroeconomic variables. She analyzed the role of monetary factors in wage policy under perfect competition and imperfect competition, as well as the dependence of monetary factors on saving schedule and on real demand for cash balances, and found that they are not related with a reduction of unemployment. Against unemployment, Smith Lutz advocated free market dynamics. According to her there were two ways of fighting against unemployment:

> One is to attack the elements of monopoly power in both the labor and the product markets directly. The other is to introduce government control over the real rate of earnings by physical means (rationing), which is in effect another indirect method of restricting the power of organized labor to bargain for a given level of real wages.
>
> *Ibid., 272*

Lutz Smith came out against this second way of fighting unemployment.

Smith Lutz's interest in macro dynamics was developed in the analysis of workers' well-being. In the 1960s, she compared some European nations, in particular Italy (Smith Lutz 1962) and France (Smith Lutz 1969), to understand the effects of unions in determining wage policy. In her book on French economic planning (1969) Smith Lutz claimed unions were still convinced that capitalism is based on class struggle and they never realized that there are other social constraints in the improvement of the conditions for the working class. Therefore, she presented her theory on wage dualism. Wage dualism arose from increased wages concentrated in the large-firm sector; consequently labor demand in this sector fell through substitutes of capital. This process led the unemployed toward the small-firm sector, driving wages lower than wages in a hypothetical unified labor market. This misallocation of resources will generate, as an inevitable consequence, a decrease of GDP. Contrary to a Keynesian approach, which would have explained this problem as resulting from lack of aggregate demand, Smith Lutz insisted on the necessity to transform the local economic system, based on agriculture, into a modern industrialized system. Her advocacy for transformation was not with a specific public economic plan, but emphasized private sector development. Following a peculiarly Austrian argument, Smith Lutz strongly defended the free market against any form of planned economy because of the role of uncertainty in determining any decision based on policy. Smith Lutz considered "economic development as a spontaneous product of the market, provided that the market is left to act according to its natural rules without hindrance or interference" (Graziani 1983, 23).

Another fierce adversary of Keynesianism among Austrian School women economists was Shenoy, who at the Royalton conference (1974) presented a paper on inflation, recession, and stagflation that was later co-authored with O'Driscoll (1976). They attacked both Keynesianism and monetarism for relying on the general assumption that, over the long term, the real side of the economy is in equilibrium, and that monetary factors influence "only the price level or money income and not the structure of relative prices or the composition of real output" (O'Driscoll and Shenoy 1976, 185). The authors suggested, as the only possible alternative to Keynesianism and monetarism, a development of Hayekian analysis based on the fact that any monetary changes in real terms will break the spontaneous economic order.

More important in her battle against Keynesianism is Shenoy's contribution to *A Tiger by the Tail* (Shenoy 1972). This paper is a historical reconstruction of the debate between Hayek and Keynes after the publication of Hayek's *Prices and Production* (1931). Shenoy recognized that the main fault of Keynes' macroeconomics was his neglect of the real structure of production and his insistence on aggregative macro concepts. According to Shenoy, Hayek's approach to macroeconomics, based on an analysis of the structure of relative prices and their interrelations as an allocative tool, is much more able to explain macro dynamics than Keynes' macroeconomics.

On development and business cycles

This research field, which is peculiar to Austrian economics, was central especially in Mintz (1959, 1970) and Shenoy (1963, 1971).

Mintz presented development as a consequence of Schumpeter's notion of innovation, which is inevitably linked with the business cycle. For Schumpeter, innovation leads to high profits; profits push imitators to enter the market; imitators increase supply and profits decrease; later imitators are unable to pay their debt, and crisis begins; at some point new innovation will stop the crisis. As a result, business cycles do not need any intervention.

In her book on the relation between trade balances and business fluctuations, Mintz considered the business cycle as the unavoidable consequence of economic development dynamics. She coined the term 'growth cycles', calculated as deviations from long-run trends, in order to explain that there are two different types of business cycles: business cycles that are essential in economic development (in Schumpeter's terms), and sectoral business cycles which affect only certain economic indicators. According to Mintz, and this is her original contribution to that debate, both cycles give shape to what she called the inevitable 'growth cycle.' Hence any government's attempt to reduce instability, even in smaller sectors, might alter the structure of the economy as a whole by reducing the phase of expansion: depression phases in naturally induced cycles have a short-term negative impact while the unattended consequence of a government policy to reduce depression might have much worse consequences in the long run (Mintz 1970).

Shenoy addressed development using the Hayekian notion of spontaneous order. Shenoy (1963) applied Austrian ideas to the economy of India. She employed Hayek's argument against socialist control of an economy in order to criticize the Indian government's economic plan. The Indian government's intention was oriented to strengthen heavy industries, but, according to Shenoy, this plan was bound to fail for three reasons: (1) it would weaken exports; (2) it would create inflation to cover a budget deficit; and (3) it would increase corruption, because the system of issuing import licenses would have been distributed by unfair means; i.e., through collusion between potential licensees and government. In Shenoy (1971) on the Indian economy, she suggested the abolition of industrial licensing and capital issues controls, as well as the refusal to introduce any form of exchange and price regulation or trade and distribution control, especially those applied to road transport and textiles.[8]

According to Shenoy, development works only in a spontaneous way through innovations, not in a designed way planned by a political agenda. Spontaneous innovations generate a better capital structure, "which gradually emerges over time in the context of privately evolved legal rules" (Shenoy 1991, 20). This is what happened in the modern age for Western countries: industrial revolutions happened as consequences of a combination of the accumulation of capital, entrepreneurial spirit, and the rule of law. Thus the only duty government has is to guarantee private property and individual freedoms. Any other governmental intervention is regarded by Shenoy as a possible cause of perverse capital structure, which leads to structural underdevelopment. The high level of corruption among politicians, and their lack of any specific competence or knowledge, might stop or delay development, and structural underdevelopment was bound to arise.

History of political economy

Austrian women's contributions to the history of political economy span all four generations. Sommer, Spiro, Grice-Hutchinson, Bien Greaves, Sennholz, and Shenoy specifically devoted a consistent part of their research to the history of political economy. Sommer wrote on mercantilism, cameralism, and Galiani (Sommer 1927b, 1935), and on methodology (1928, 1932). Spiro's dissertation was on the nature of the credit as discussed by Owen, Proudhon, and Solvay (Nautz 1997). Bien Greaves and Sennholz worked on liberalism with Mises and Leonard Read.[9] The most original contributions (both related to the typical Austrian approach to economics) were Grice-Hutchinson's research on the School of Salamanca (1952) and Shenoy's book on early modern England ([2001] 2010) which attempts to analyze consumption, distribution, and production in terms of Austrian economic theory.

Under Hayek's supervision, Grice-Hutchinson wrote her thesis on the nature of markets and monetary theory in the School of Salamanca founded by Francisco de Vitoria in the early XVI century (1952). Scholars of the School of Salamanca were well known in Spain, but almost forgotten abroad. Hayek was interested in introducing them to an English-speaking audience because he considered them as forerunners of the Austrian School. Grice-Hutchinson presented the Salamanca scholars as the founders of the subjective theory of value, later developed by Jevons, Walras, and Menger; she also considered the significant influence they had on Adam Smith via Pufendorf and Grotius. According to Rothbard, her book was fundamental to understanding the historical tradition of the "subjective-value analysis based on consumer wants alongside the competing objective conception of the just price based on labor and costs" (Rothbard 1976, 52).

Besides their subjective-utility approach, Grice-Hutchinson highlighted that Salamanca supported free markets over protectionism and a minimal role of the state in economic policy and fiscal matters. She explained that the School of Salamanca arose in a very peculiar period of Spanish modern history: a period when a massive quantity of gold and silver had been transferred from the New World colonies to Europe. This phenomenon increased inflation and made usury more evident. As Grice-Hutchinson wrote:

> The School's original contribution to monetary theory consists, in its formulation of a psychological theory of value applied to both goods and money, of the quantity theory, and of a theory of foreign exchange that closely resembles the modern purchasing power parity theory.
>
> *Grice-Hutchinson 1952, 47–48*

Hence, Salamanca illustrated a subjective theory of value, which attempted to analyze the psychological motives of economic activity. Furthermore, they regarded money as a useless measure of value, since its own value is subject to fluctuations. In fact, they refused the classical distinction between intrinsic and extrinsic value of money.

Grice-Hutchinson was the first to identify that the School of Salamanca provided a quantity theory of money: Martín de Azpilcueta Navarro, in 1556 and a dozen years before Jean Bodin, explained that the inflation in the sixteenth century occurred as a consequence of the gold and silver arriving from the New World. More surprisingly, scholars of the School of Salamanca initially formulated a basic purchasing power parity on the theory of exchange. When they were asked to solve the monetary phenomenon according to which "when money was sent from foreign countries to Spain a considerably larger sum was usually repaid in Spain than had been delivered abroad" (Grice-Hutchinson 1952, 54) but not vice versa, they suggested a subjective theory of value: "since the agio could not be explained by objective factors, it must be derived from a variation in the subjective value of money in the different countries" (Grice-Hutchinson 1952, 55).

In her Ph.D. thesis, Shenoy ([2001] 2010) applied some specific features of the Austrian School of economics to a particular case study; namely, the history of early modern England. She adopted Menger's organicism, Mises' market process, and Hayek's catallaxy in order to explain the rise of complex phenomena. Complex phenomena such as language, customs, or money, arise spontaneously in an "un-designed [and] historical-developed social order" (Shenoy [2001] 2010, 11). Specific manifestations of complex phenomena such as French, the custom of marriage, or the American dollar, inevitably need to be coordinated by a legal set of rules. In fact, following Hayek's line of thinking, Shenoy considered catallaxy and common law (as a system of private case-law) as two sides of the same coin, and she considered the interdependence between theoretical analysis and historical studies as fundamental in order to understand human action. In her analysis, Shenoy explicitly adopted Austrian categories to criticize neoclassical economics.[10]

Concluding remarks

The story of the four generations of the Austrian School women economists has been neglected for decades, with the exception of some references in Mises' memoir and a few other very recent publications on the Viennese milieu around the Austrian School of economics. Although they failed to accede to academic positions in Vienna, mainly due to a combination of adverse conditions (initially, a ban against women in academia, later the racial ostracism against Jews, and a persistent and generalized suspicion against classical liberals), their contributions were often original, and their work played an important part in the history of the Austrian School as a whole.

Embedded in the complex Austrian society between the end of the nineteenth century and the interwar years, the first two generations of Austrian School women economists frequently handled the economic problems of their time from a theoretical perspective. Their research revealed that they shared the typical features of the Austrian School of economics, especially the disutility of any economic policy (with some exceptions), in keeping with their more influential and well-known male counterparts. Furthermore, in some cases, they were able to make original contributions to some typical Austrian themes: e.g., the case of Braun's pioneering study on the micro-foundation of monetary economics; that of Sommer's study on international economic relations; Mintz's analysis of business cycles; and Lovasy's investigations into the effects of inflation on international trade.

The third and fourth generation of Austrian School women economists developed their economic analysis mainly under the influence of Mises and Hayek in London and in the United States. Like their Viennese predecessors, they were authentically 'Austrians' because of their adherence to Austrian ideals. The third and fourth generations also enriched the Austrian tradition with some original ideas, such as Smith Lutz's theory of wage dualism, and Shenoy's application of Austrian economic categories to the analysis of growth and development in developing countries.

Their contributions extended the Austrian ideas by applying the commonly accepted Austrian paradigm into new contexts (new historical studies, specific histories of economic thought, as in Cronbach, Sommer, Spiro, Grice-Hutchinson, Bien Greaves), into new fields (development economics and economies of developing countries—such as India—as in Mintz, Lovasy, Shenoy). They also disseminated Austrian economics, especially in their battle against Keynesian economics and in their works on monetary policy (as in Stolper, Braun, Herzfeld, Lieser, Lovasy, Smith Lutz, Shenoy).

For the reasons mentioned above, Austrian School women economists have a special place in the history of women's economic thought as well as in the broader field of the history of economics. They made noteworthy contributions as scholars, as members of a cohesive school of economics, whose role in the history of the discipline has been and still is enormous. As classical liberals, Austrian School women economists of the first and the second generations were also impressive examples of the broader story of women's cultural emancipation, which took place in Europe from the end of the nineteenth century. These women defied the limitations that culture imposed on their gender, participating and contributing to deep academic inquiry from a classical liberal perspective; and, as classical liberals, Austrian School women economists of the following generations never stopped fighting for freedom and liberty through their contributions to economic theory.

Notes

1 Although German, Lachman is embedded into the Austrian School of economics' tradition for his theoretical and methodological works. Furthermore, he was first student, then colleague, of Hayek in the 1930s at the LSE.

2 Shenoy has been chosen as emblematic of the latest generation of Austrian School women economists mainly because she has had a significant role in the so-called Austrian revival and because she applied, for the first time, the Austrian economics perspectives to underdeveloped economies.

3 During the interwar period in Vienna, economists of the historical Austrian School (1871–1938), like many other Viennese scholars, were very active mainly outside academia: they attended informal seminars, opened to scholars with different backgrounds who often were regular attendees of several circles. This kind of audience created a network of peers whose cultural exchange made Vienna a unique place for the development of a pluralistic approach within social disciplines (Craver 1986; Hülsmann 2007; Mises [1978] 2013; Dekker 2014, 2016; Klausinger 2016; Wright 2016).

4 Kirzner realized his Ph.D. in 1957 under the supervision of Mises, and he spent his entire career at NYU, where he became full professor in 1968, until his retirement in 2001 (Ebeling 2001). That seminar, renamed Colloquium on Market Institutions & Economic Processes, is still scheduled at NYU, under the supervision of Mario Rizzo.

5 As reported by Boettke in www.coordinationproblem.org/2011/12/mccloskeys-transition-to-austrian-economics.html (retrieved on June 2, 2018).

6 As retrieved from http://oll.libertyfund.org/titles/smith-the-rationale-of-central-banking-and-the-free-banking-alternative.

7 According to Vernon Smith's review, Smith Lutz failed to solve the problem "that no production function analysis is possible when processes employing durable goods are analyzed ... [because] the cost minimization problem, properly formulated, does apply" (Smith 1959, 62).

8 Shenoy's fight against protectionism and planning in the Indian economy is better understood in the context of the cultural and historical frameworks. Since the 1930s, a planning apparatus for Indian economic development had been set up in India, and it was renewed after Independence in 1947 especially involving the industrial sector. There were very few opponents to this economic policy; among them, the liberal economist Bellikoth Ragunath *Shenoy*, Sudha's father, later joined by his daughter and others (Bauer 1998; Shenoy 2003; Manish et al. 2015).

9 Read was the founder of the Foundation for Economic Education, one of the first Libertarian institutions in the United States.

10 In contrast to neoclassical economics, Shenoy explicitly followed McCloskey's argument that economists are not scientists, but story-telling historians: "neoclassical economists are even further removed from even the remotest possibility of learning about the issues involved in studying human action" (Shenoy [2001] 2010, 60).

References

Backhaus, J. (2005) 'Taxation: An Austrian Approach', in Backhaus, J. (Ed.) *Modern Application of Austrian Thought*. London: Routledge, pp. 115–138.

Bauer, P. (1998) 'B. R. Shenoy: Stature and Impact'. *Cato Journal*, Vol. 18:1, pp. 1–10.

Bidwell, P. (1937) 'Review of *Neugestaltung der Handelspolitik* by L. Sommer'. *Journal of Political Economy*, Vol. 45:2, pp. 253–255.

Bien Greaves, B. (1975) *Free Market Economics: A Syllabus*. Irvington-on-Hudson, NY: Foundation for Economic Education.

Bien Greaves, B. and McGee, R. (1993) *Mises: An Annotated Bibliography*. Irvington-on-Hudson, NY: Foundation for Economic Education.

Boettke, P. and Coyne, C. (Eds.) (2015) *The Oxford Handbook of Austrian Economics*. New York: Oxford University Press.

Braun, M. S. (1929) *Theorie der staatlichen Wirtschaftspolitik*. Wien, Leipzig: Franz Deuticke.

Craver, E. (1986) 'The Emigration of the Austrian Economists'. *History of Political Economy*, Vol. 18:1, pp. 1–32.

Cronbach E. (1907) *Die österreichische Spitzenhausindustrie: Ein Beitrag zur Frage der Hausindustriepolitik*. Wien, Leipzig: Deuticke.

Cronbach (1910) *Österreichische Gesellschaft für Arbeiterschutz. Die Bedeutung von Organisationen und Tarifverträgen in der österreichischen Hausindustrie mit specieller Berücksichtigung der Konfektionsindustrie und der Gablonzer Glaskurzwarenindustrie*. Wien: Karl Brakl.

Dekker, E. (2014) 'The Vienna Circles: Cultivating Economic Knowledge outside Academia'. *Erasmus Journal for Philosophy and Economics*, Vol. 7:2, pp. 30–53.

Dekker, E. (2016) *The Viennese Students of Civilization*. Cambridge: Cambridge University Press.

Dolan, E. (Ed.) (1976) *The Foundations of Modern Austrian Economics*. Kansas City: Sheed and Ward Inc.

Feichtinger, J. (2001) *Wissenschaft zwischen den Kulturen. Österreichische Hochschullehrer in der Emigration 1933–1945*. Frankfurt am Main and New York: Campus Verlag.

Freidenreich, H. (2009) 'Käthe Leichter', in Hyman, P. and Ofer, D. (Eds.) *Jewish Women: A Comprehensive Historical Encyclopedia*. Jewish Women's Archive. As retrieved on 3/8/2017 from https://jwa.org/encyclopedia/toc/L.

Graziani, A. (1983) 'The Macroeconomic Theory of Vera C. Lutz'. *Banca Nazionale del Lavoro Quarterly Review*, Vol. 36:146, pp. 3–27.

Grice-Hutchinson, M. (1952) *The School of Salamanca: Readings in Spanish Monetary Theory, 1544–1605*. Oxford: Clarendon Press.

Hagemann, H. (forthcoming) 'Louise Sommer (1889–1964)', in Dimand, R. and Forget, E. (Eds.) *A Biographical Dictionary of Woman Economists*, 2nd enlarged edition. Aldershot: Edward Elgar. pp. 1–6.
Hayek, F. (1931) *Prices and Production*. London: Routledge.
Herzfeld, M. (1926) 'Die Geschichte als Funktion der Geldbewegung'. *Archiv fur Sozialwissenschaft und Sozialpolitik*, Vol. 56, pp. 654–686.
Holcombe, R. (2014) *The Austrian School of Economics*. Cheltenham: Edward Elgar.
Hülsmann, J. (2007) *Mises: The Last Knight of Liberalism*. Auburn, AL: Ludwig von Mises Institute.
Klausinger, H. (2014) 'Academic Anti-Semitism and the Austrian School: Vienna, 1918–1945'. *Atlantic Economic Journal*, Vol. 42:2, pp. 1–14.
Klausinger, H. (2016) 'The Nationalökonomische Gesellschaft (Austrian Economic Association) in the Interwar Period and Beyond'. *History of Economic Thought and Methodology*, 34A, pp. 9–43.
Klausinger, H. (2016a) 'The Austrian Economists, Hayek, and the Anschluss'. Paper presented for the ESHET 20th Annual Conference. Paris: Sorbonne.
Leischko, H. (2002) 'Braun, Martha Stephanie', in Keintzel, B. and Korotin, I. (Eds.) *Wissenschafterinnen in und aus Österreich. Leben – Werk – Wirken*. Vienna: Böhlau Verlag, pp. 92–95.
Lovasy, G. (1941) 'International Trade under Imperfect Competition'. *The Quarterly Journal of Economics*, Vol. 55:4, pp. 567–583.
Lovasy, G. (1947) *International Cartels: A League of Nations Memorandum*. New York: Lake Success.
Lovasy, G. (1962) 'Inflation and Exports in Primary Producing Countries'. *Staff Papers (International Monetary Fund)*, Vol. 9:1, pp. 37–69.
Lovasy, G. and Zassenhaus, H. (1953) 'Short-Run Fluctuations in U.S. Imports of Raw Materials, 1928–39 and 1947–52'. *Staff Papers (International Monetary Fund)*, Vol 3:2, pp. 270–289.
Manish, G., Rajagopalan, S., Sutter, D., and White, L. (2015) 'Liberalism in India'. *Econ Journal Watch*, Vol. 12:3, pp. 432–459.
McCloskey, D. (1993) 'Some Consequences of a Conjunctive Economics', in Ferber, M. A. and Nelson, J. A. (Eds.) *Beyond Economic Man: Feminist Theory and Economics*. Chicago, IL: University of Chicago Press, pp. 69–93.
Menger, C. (1871) *Grundsätze der Volkswirtschaftslehre*. Vienna: Braumüller.
Mintz, I. (1959) *Trade Balances During Business Cycles: U.S. and Britain Since 1880*. New York: National Bureau of Economic Research.
Mintz, I. (1970) *Dating Postwar Business Cycles: Methods and Their Application to Western Germany, 1950–67*. New York: National Bureau of Economic Research.
Mises, L. (1928) *Geldwertstabilisierung und Konjunkturpolitik*. Jena: Verlag von Gustav Fischer.
Mises, L. ([1978] 2013) *Notes and Recollection*. Indianapolis: Liberty Fund.
Mises, L. (1984) *The Historical Setting of the Austrian School of Economics*. New York: Arlington House.
Nautz, J. (1997) 'Zwischen Emanzitation und Integration. Die Frauen der Wiener Schule für Nationalökonomie'. In Fisher L. and Brix E. (Eds.) *Die Frauen der Wiener Moderne*. Wien, Munich: Verlag für Geschichte und Politik, pp. 64–82.
Nautz, J. (2000a) 'Helene Lieser', in Dimand, R., Dimand M., and Forget, E. (Eds.) *A Biographical Dictionary of Women Economists*. Cheltenham: Edward Elgar, pp. 259–260.
Nautz, J. (2000b) 'Gertrud von Lovasy', in Dimand, R., Dimand, M., and Forget, E. (Eds.) *A Biographical Dictionary of Women Economists*. Cheltenham: Edward Elgar, pp. 260–261.
Nautz, J. (2000c) 'Ilse Schüller Mintz', in Dimand, R., Dimand, M., and Forget, E. (Eds.) *A Biographical Dictionary of Women Economists*. Cheltenham: Edward Elgar, pp. 311–312.
Nautz, J. (2002) 'Offen(heimer) Elly', in Keintzel, B. and Korotin, I. (Eds.) *Wissenschafterinnen in und aus Österreich. Leben – Werk – Wirken*. Wien: Böhlau Verlag, pp. 540–541.
O'Driscoll, G. and Shenoy, S. (1976) 'Inflation, Stagflation, and Recession', in Dolan, E. (Ed.) *The Foundations of Modern Austrian Economics*. Kansas City: Sheed and Ward Inc., pp. 185–211.
Pauly, L. (2003) 'International Financial Institutions and National Economic Governance: Aspects of the New Adjustment Agenda in Historical Perspective', in Flandreau, M., Holtfrerich, C., and James, H. (Eds.) *International Financial History in the Twentieth Century*. Cambridge: Cambridge University Press, pp. 239–264.
Pribram, K. (1913) 'Dr. Else Cronbach'. *Neues Frauenleben*, Vol. 15:5, pp. 3–4.
Rothbard, M. (1976) 'New Light on the Prehistory of the Austrian School', in Dolan, E. (Ed.) *The Foundations of Modern Austrian Economics*. Kansas City: Sheed and Ward Inc, pp. 52–77.
Sennholz, M. (Ed.) (1956) *On Freedom and Free Enterprise: Essays in Honor of Ludwig von Mises*. Princeton, NJ: Van Nostrand.

Sennholz, M. (1993) *Leonard E. Read: Philosopher of Freedom*. Irvington-on-Hudson, NY: Foundation for Economic Education.
Sennholz, M. (Ed.) (1997) *Faith of Our Fathers*. Irvington-on-Hudson, NY: Foundation for Economic Education.
Shenoy, S. (1963) *Indian Planning and Economic Development*. New York: Asia Publishing House.
Shenoy, S. (1971) *India: Progress or Poverty*. London: IEA.
Shenoy, S. (1972) 'The Debate: 1931–1971', in Shenoy, S. (Ed.) *Tiger by the Tail: The Keynesian Legacy of Inflation by F.A. Hayek*. London: Institute of Economic Affairs, pp. 1–14.
Shenoy, S. (1989) 'Comment on Some Implications of the Hayekian (Austrian) Analysis for Eastern Europe', in Hayek, F. *Order – With or Without Design?* London: Centre for Research into Communist Economies, pp. 189–198.
Shenoy, S. (1991) 'Austrian Capital Theory and the Underdeveloped Areas: An Overview?', in Ebeling, R. (Ed.) *Austrian Economics: Perspectives on the Past and Prospects for the Future*. Hillsdale, MI: Hillsdale College Press, pp. 379–423.
Shenoy, S. ([2001] 2010) *Towards a Theoretical Framework for British and International Economic History*. Auburn, AL: Ludwig von Mises Institute.
Shenoy, S. (2003) 'The Global Perspective: An Interview with Sudha Shenoy'. *Austrian Economics Newsletter*, Vol. 23:4, pp. 1–8.
Smith, V. (1959) 'The Theory of Investments and Production'. *The Quarterly Journal of Economics*, Vol. 73:1, pp. 61–87.
Smith Lutz, V. ([1936] 1990) *The Rationale of Central Banking and the Free Banking Alternative*. Indianapolis: Liberty Fund.
Smith Lutz, V. and Lutz, F. (1951) *Theory of Investment of the Firm*. Princeton, NJ: Princeton University Press.
Smith Lutz, V. (1952) 'Real and Monetary Factors in the Determination of Employment Levels'. *The Quarterly Journal of Economics*. Vol. 66:2, pp. 251–272.
Smith Lutz, V. (1962) *Italy, a Study in Economic Development*. London, New York: Oxford University Press.
Smith Lutz, V. (1969) *Central Planning for the Market Economy: An Analysis of the French Theory and Experience*. Harlow: Longmans for the Institute of Economic Affairs.
Sommer, L. (1920) *Die Österreichischen Kameralisten in dogmengeschichtlicher Darstellung* (Vol. 1). Vienna: Scientiaverlag Aalen.
Sommer, L. (1925) *Die Österreichischen Kameralisten in dogmengeschichtlicher Darstellung* (Vol. 2). Vienna: Scientiaverlag Aalen.
Sommer, L. (1927a) 'Mercantilisme et la Théorie de la Valeur'. *Revue d'histoire économique et sociale*. Vol. 15:1, pp. 5–24.
Sommer, L. (1927b) 'Abbé Galiani und das physiokratische System'. *Zeitschrift für Volkswirtschaft und Sozialpolitik*, New Series, Vol. 5:4–6, pp. 318–341.
Sommer, L. (1928) 'Zur Methode der exakten und historischen Nationalökonomie'. *Schmollers Jahrbuch*, Vol. 52, pp. 611–653.
Sommer, L. (1932) 'Das geisteswissenschaftliche Phänomen des "Methodenstreits": Analogien ud Präzedentien', in *Festschrift für Carl Grünenberg zum 70 Geburstag*. Leipzig.
Sommer, L. (1935) *Neugestaltung der Handelspolitik*. Vienna: Österreichischer Wirtschaftsverlag.
Sommer, L. (1950) 'The Franco-German Steel and Coal Pact: THE MONNET-SCHUMANN PLAN'. *World Affairs*, Vol. 113:3, pp. 80–82.
Sommer, L. (1960) *Essays in European Economic Thought*. Princeton, NJ: Van Nostrand Company.
Timms, E. (2009) 'Cultural Parameters between the Wars: A Reassessment of the Vienna Circles', in Holmes, D. and Silverman, L. (Eds.) *Interwar Vienna: Culture between Tradition and Modernity*. Rochester, NY: Camden House, pp. 21–31.
Vaughn, K. (1994) *Austrian Economics in America: The Migration of a Tradition*. New York and Melbourne: Cambridge University Press.
Wright, C. (2016) 'The 1920s Viennese Intellectual Community as a Center for Ideas Exchange: A Network Analysis'. *History of Political Economy*, Vol. 48:4, pp. 593–634.
Yeager, L. (1990) 'Preface', in Smith Lutz, V. *The Rationale of Central Banking and the Free Banking Alternative*. Indianapolis: Liberty Fund, pp. 1–38.

17
PLACING WOMEN'S ECONOMICS WITHIN SOVIET ECONOMIC DISCOURSE
1920s–1991

Anna Klimina

Introduction

After the Bolshevik 1917 Revolution, the challenge for the newly formed socialist government was to envision and then build a workable society, without having any detailed plans. What were available for this massive social engineering experiment were Marxist concepts and insights, which were adopted and adapted to guide a transition to socialism in a predominantly backward country. Through that process, Soviet[1] economic science was born. To understand the logic and ideological underpinning of the construction and development of Soviet economics, some historical context needs to be provided. An assessment of women's contributions within Soviet economic thought cannot be meaningfully done without taking account of dramatic shifts in the social and political reality of Soviet socialism.

My discussion of Soviet women's economics begins with an overview of the period from the 1920s to the mid-1960s. During that period, foundational ideas were developed that continued to dominate Soviet economic discourse until the 1991 collapse of the Soviet Union. In fact, those ideas actively blocked reforms that could have prevented that collapse. In these crucial decades, the New Economic Policy (NEP) experiment was replaced with a command economy, and the Soviet Political Economy, its apologetic, was constructed and reached its zenith, a work in which women, along with men, had a long-lasting impact.

In the era of Soviet reforms, from the early 1960s to the early 1990s, Soviet economists, faced with the increasingly undeniable problem of economic inefficiency, reoriented their focus from how a planned economy was supposed to function to how it actually operated. Efficiency and optimality were finally recognized, if not by an overwhelming majority, as key economic problems. Applied mathematical methods in support of economic planning, once practically forbidden, gained wider acceptance. Ways of decentralizing and democratizing the Soviet command economy, such as establishing participatory economics, reducing price controls, and emphasizing economic motivation, could at last be discussed. And, beginning with Gorbachev's 1985–1991 *Perestroika*[2] movement, state-guided market socialism seemed feasible in certain academic and political circles.

However, Party officials did not consistently support suggested reforms. Since what could be researched, publicly discussed, and published was determined by the over-shadowing power of the Communist Party, the treatment of the above-mentioned initiatives is fragmented and incomplete in official economic literature. In this essay only what has been officially published is used to assess Soviet economic thought and its women's voices. The unique contribution of this chapter is to highlight women's contributions to this important period of history, with its consequences.

Soviet women's economics in a command economy and its ideologically defensive economic science

Formation of Soviet economics in 1920s and early 1930s

By the end of 1920, Lenin's government had won the civil war, and Bolshevik plans for comprehensive centralized governance were being implemented. The important step in this construction of an authoritarian economic order was to crush syndicalist workers' opposition in 1919 to early 1920, which had advocated ownership of productive property and decentralized control over the economy by worker collectives and their independent trade unions. Thereafter Bolsheviks were free to nationalize all industrial property and place it under centralized control of a single state-appointed enterprise director. From that point on, the advancement of socialism came to be exclusively associated with expansion of state ownership of property, and, consequently, state power over the economy (Lewin 1974: 83). However, the Bolshevik policies of 1918–1921—total nationalization, centralization of production and distribution, abolition of the monetary system, and, most importantly, compulsory requisitions of food surplus from the peasantry—ruined Russia's economy and provoked powerful mass protests.

Thus, in March 1921, Lenin introduced the NEP to restore Russia's economy and then accelerate its industrialization. NEP aimed at using peasants' private initiative as well as private enterprise in industry and trade (Lenin [1921] 1973: 60–78).

This period, when market relations were adopted into the reality of socialist construction, is the most interesting and intellectually exciting time in the history of Soviet economics. Its consequences were long-lasting. In the midst of NEP, Bolshevik leaders and those intellectuals still alive and remaining in the country[3] engaged in what became known as the Industrialization Debates concerning possible methods of building socialism[4] and the nature of Soviet central planning. Because the establishment of Soviet planning practices is important for our analysis of women's involvement in the formation of Soviet orthodoxy, a brief summary of its history follows.

In economic literature, the discussion of the nature of Soviet planning is known as the "genetic-teleological dispute." Supporters of the "genetic school," non-Bolshevik economists Vladimir Bazarov (1874–1937), Vladimir Groman (1874–1940), Abram Ginzburg (1878–1937) and Nikolai Kondratiev (1892–1938), argued that economic planning should be based on extrapolating existing trends of economic development; planners should study these trends and adjust economic policy accordingly, to determine efficient use of economic resources and "employ scarce capital to the best advantage" (Bazarov 1927: 45; see also Kondratiev 1927). In contrast, the teleological school contended that the Soviet economy should be determined by the "freely chosen political goals" of Soviet leaders; planners should subordinate economic decisions to these goals without considering economic reality (Strumilin 1927: 20–21). The "teleological school" became the official doctrine of Soviet planners after the debates among economists were ended by Joseph Stalin[5] (1879–1953), who directly supported teleologists (Lange 1945: 130–131).

It is at this point in the history of Russia's transition into the Soviet Union that minimal education for women had the clearest consequences. In the early stages of the Russian Revolution, women who were educated enough to become passionate about a possible new democratic order could participate actively. In the 1920s, however, the intense intellectual debates required a more thorough education than women had until then received. What narrowed the possibility even further for women to contribute was the important question of loyalty to the dictatorial Bolshevik rule. It so happened that most of the women who supported the Russian Revolution were not Bolshevik supporters. Therefore, by 1925, those women who openly challenged authority were already outside Russia, either because they escaped after being pronounced "enemies of the state," like Ariadna Tyrkova, or because they were expelled from Soviet territory, like Ekaterina Kuskova and Lydia Dan.[6] Alexandra Kollontai, a special case, was sent to Sweden as Head of the USSR diplomatic mission after her open disagreement with Lenin over industrial democracy in the USSR.[7] Thus the debates of 1925–1928 on the architecture of the Soviet planning system included no women's voices that opposed the Stalinist vision for socialism.

Those few educated women who remained in the country accepted, as their own, the official Party line and its dogmatic Marxist-Leninist teaching. In fact, in the mid-1920s, the most interesting contribution to the future development of the ideologically defensive Soviet economics was made by a woman, Sofia Shachnovskaya (1898–19?),[8] who pioneered the framework within which a special field known as "a critique of bourgeoisistic [Western] economic theories" was developed.

Her story, although mostly conjectural, reveals much about the political dynamics within Soviet-style economics. Little is known of her beyond those publications that are available. They demonstrate her evident training in economic theory,[9] which, with the addition of her unquestioning loyalty to Bolshevik rule,[10] enabled Shachnovskaya in 1923 to become one of the founders of the State Planning (Gosplan) Research Institute, and in the late 1920s, its deputy director. In the first part of the 1930s, Stalin organized purges of many pre-1917 trained professionals, for fear that the "planned economy would be built by alien hands" (Strumilin 1932: 37):

> [T]rumped-up charges of "willful wrecking and sabotage" were brought against thousands of industrial managers, engineers, academicians, economists, and planners who were arrested and either executed or sentenced to harsh prison terms.
>
> *Treml 1969: 196*

Later, Stalin widened his definition of "enemy of the people" to include all political opposition—the Left Deviationists led by Leon Trotsky (1879–1940) and the Right Deviationists led by Nikolai Bukharin (1888–1938). In this Great Purge at the end of the 1930s, even Party loyalists were swept up with supporters of Trotsky and Bukharin. So despite her published pro-Bolshevik rhetoric, Shachnovskaya was arrested, imprisoned in Siberia, and disappeared from scholarly discourse (Alekseeva et al. 2017: 84; *Stalin's Lists*: 466). Her contributions were thus made during two major historical developments of great importance for the fate of Soviet economics.

The first major development followed Lenin's recognition that Marx's economic teaching was "the most profound, comprehensive and detailed confirmation and application of his theory" (Lenin [1914] 1974: 59). The Soviet Party officials made this assertion a non-negotiable central core of their ideological dogma. Marxist economic theory was thus the only allowable truth, and any deviation constituted an attack on the entire Marxist edifice. Party loyalists in academe thus conducted all of their economic research to develop and substantiate this official paradigm. This is the context in which Shachnovskaya did her innovative work.

Her crucial contribution appears in her large two-part 1926 journal article entitled "Dynamics of discount and problems of its regulation" (Shachnovskaya 1926). In it, Shachnovskaya, rather superciliously, superficially, and selectively described Western economic approaches to the analysis of capital and interest rate, and to the subsequent role of monetary movements in explanation of cyclical phenomena. She focused on Gustav Cassel's views on credit expansion and contraction, specifically on his identification of the essential cause of the business cycle: the insufficiency of savings. After her intentionally brief description of Cassel's position, Shachnovskaya argued that his "shallow" theory of undersaving/overinvestment, which explained how the business cycle is self-regulated through fluctuations in discount rates, "reveals" Cassel's "bourgeoisistic inability" to "understand objective laws of capitalism." According to her, Cassel could not see that imbalances between savings and investment, the cause of economic crises, cannot be successfully resolved through adjustment in the discount rate; economic crises, the inevitable by-product of exploitative capitalist relations of production, can be eradicated only through the abolition of capitalism (1926, 11: 82–83, 88). Then, to substantiate the validity of her arguments, Shachnovskaya juxtaposed Cassel's theory with the official Party understanding of Marx's explanation of business cycles, which, in her opinion, "convincingly demonstrated" that as long as "private ownership of property and power of bourgeoisie" exist, the exploitation of workers by the owners of capital will remain "the main cause of economic crises" (Shachnovskaya 1926, 11: 87–88).

Shachnovskaya was among the first Soviet scholars to present Marx as the ultimate authority in any theoretical discussion, and his theory as the highest point of the development of economic knowledge, against which all other views had to be measured. Basically, she was the originator of Leninist/Stalinist dogmatism in the Soviet historico-economic science; her style and tone were very unlike those of Isaak Rubin,[11] for example, whose open-minded 1927 research on contemporary Western economists (Rubin 1927) was written courteously and impartially. In contrast, Shachnovskaya's approach initiated the pugnacious propagandist framework within which the Soviet analysis of Western economic thought was subsequently conducted. In the understated words of Ronald Meek, that framework was not "sufficiently polite" (Meek 1955: 244). From the 1930s to the 1950s such analysis was especially noticeable for its consistently hostile criticisms of Western economics, both orthodox and heterodox (Balabkins 1958). As Meek, who visited the USSR in the early 1950s, succinctly put it, in the USSR, students study Western economists "in order to find out for themselves why [these economists] should be dismissed" (1955: 243).

Overall, succeeding generations of Soviet economists[12] were trained in this dismissive approach to Western economic thought and were expected, for the most part (see "Khrushchev's thaw" below), to follow it right into the 1980s.[13] Ironically, in Soviet economic literature, Shachnovskaya—due to her alleged status as the "enemy of the people"—was never given credit for her innovative application of the Party's ideological dogmatism.

The other major historical development that impacted Soviet economic science was the elimination of NEP by the end of the 1920s. The NEP years, 1921–1928, were viewed by Stalin and his supporters only as a temporary retreat from their envisioned model of socialism based on the supremacy of state ownership of productive property and dictatorial teleological planning. The end of NEP, with its relative freedom of speech, changed the political atmosphere dramatically; coupled with political repression of the purges, it led to a command totalitarian society, in which political pluralism was eradicated.

By the 1930s, however, and despite the more repressive environment generally, women had been granted full access to the same education offered to men and were equal participants in all aspects of society.

The years of Soviet economic orthodoxy and their long-lasting consequences

In the early 1930s, the science of theoretical economics in the USSR was totally replaced with what was called Political Economy, a "historically oriented and descriptive field, with strong Marxist-Leninist ideological underpinning" (Alexeev et al. 1992: 139). The two chief branches of Soviet Political Economy, the "principal economic discipline" in the USSR (Ostrovitjanov 1968: 21), became (1) Political Economy of Capitalism, intended to examine market economies through the lens of Marxism-Leninism, and (2) Political Economy of Socialism, meant to justify socialism and communicate the Party's policies. If one chose to study capitalism, the only acceptable approach was the "assessment of the process of 'disintegration of capitalism'" and its "intensifying contradictions" (Treml 1969: 198); any focus on Western economic thought had to be done for the purpose of critiquing.

There were also applied branches of economic studies, which included economic statistics, demography, accounting, and economics of industry, transport, and agriculture; but, again, in that period, even statistics research was conducted primarily through "Marxist-Leninist perspectives," which meant "offering quantitative support" for Party decisions ("Planned Sabotage" 1930: 140). Most notable for her unusual zeal in carrying out this approach in statistics is the well-educated and highly placed Maria Smith-Falkner (1878–1968).[14] In 1930, during a discussion among Marxist economists suggestively entitled "Planned Sabotage and Statistical Theory," she declared that since "mathematical statistics, based on probability theory," examines disorderly mass data and random phenomena, it is suitable only for "chaotic capitalism," and is not appropriate for a "planned economy" and "organized data collection" ("Planned Sabotage" 1930: 143; see also Smith-Falkner 1934: 227–228). Smith-Falkner actually argued that pre-1917-trained statistics specialists who used "vulgar marginal analysis" and "mathematical formalism" were "saboteurs" harmful to the Marxist cause, and called for all genuine Marxists in the field to become the "GPU [predecessor of KGB] of scientific thought in the field of statistics and its application to Soviet planning" ("Planned Sabotage": 141, 143, 168).

Smith-Falkner was thus instrumental in making certain that these views were shared by all scholars. Those who did not support the now-official Party view of statistics, including many scholars from Kondratiev's Institute of Conjuncture and Chayanov's Institute for Agricultural Economics, lost their positions, were imprisoned, and disappeared. Among those scholars were several women-statisticians. Olga Pryakhina (?–193?) was a member of Kondratiev's Conjuncture Institute, whom Kondratiev specifically thanked for "her work of a directly statistical nature" in his *Problems of Economic Fluctuations* (1925) (Kondratiev [1925] 1984: 34–35). S. (?) Platova (?–193?) was a member of Chayanov's Institute for Agricultural Economics and one of the authors of *Methods of Quantitative Calculation of the Effectiveness of Land* (1925), a study edited by Chayanov (Jasny 1972: 201). Anna Khriashcheva (?–193?) began her professional career doing statistical work for rural self-government (*zemstvo*); during the 1920s, she was the Head of the Department of Agricultural Censuses of the Central Statistical Administration (Campbell 2012: 178–179). Khriashcheva was known for her innovative methodology to analyze stratification of peasants' households (1925). After Chayanov and Kondratiev were arrested in 1930, and their respective institutes destroyed, these women, along with many other "bourgeois specialists" trained before 1917, disappeared from Soviet statistical discourse. As a result of the ideologically motivated activities of Smith-Falkner and of others, the use of mathematical statistics and overall mathematics in economics was not resumed until the early 1960s.

That is why it is safe to conclude that between the late 1930s and late 1950s, "all Soviet economics was political economy," while the academic training of economists was "reduced to an inane study of the writings of the 'founding fathers' and to purely technical subjects such as accounting, technology of production, cost analysis, and the like" (Treml 1969: 198). As Pekka Sutela (1991: 12) deftly summarizes,

> [T]he Stalinist revolution in economics meant the total suppression of all previous scholarship, the killing of some of the best brains in the field, and the occupation of research institutes, journals and universities by young Stalinists. They were to spend the decades to come in propagating Marxism and commenting upon the decisions of the party-state.

This is the political context that must be kept in mind as we discuss women's voices in the 1930s–1950s. Although in the 1920s, during the Industrialization Debates, only a few women could have participated because of the lack of education, in subsequent years, the Soviet Union eliminated that difference[15] with pioneering laws that gave women equal opportunities and pay, substantial protection of gender equality in many occupations, and considerable assistance in bringing up children. These changes led to an increase in educational attainment and, in turn, an increase in the number of women economists. However, under Stalin's regime the newly trained economists, both men and women, for the reasons explained above, did not actually contribute to economic science as it is understood in the West. They simply contributed to the validation of the ideologically proper doctrine of Marxist-Leninist Political Economy.

The prevailing dogmatism in official economic theory manifested itself most particularly in early Soviet attempts to reconsider the theory of the general crisis of capitalism, in light of events that seemed to contradict it. According to the official Marxist-Leninist view, in advanced capitalist countries, which were already at the monopolistic stage of capitalist development and, thus, on "the eve of the socialist revolution of the proletariat," the general crisis of capitalism must necessarily be "aggravated" and the working class reduced to "absolute and permanent impoverishment." The misery under capitalism can only grow and real wages fall for all but the "working class aristocracy," that is, trade union leaders.[16]

Eugene Varga's[17] book *Changes in the Capitalist Economy as a Result of the Second World War* (1946), however, pointed out the inaccuracy of the prevailing dogmatism. Based on his research of main trends in Western capitalism from the end of the 1920s to the mid-1940s, including the emergence of Keynes' "anti-Depression" economics, Varga concluded that in advanced capitalist countries the greatly increased role of the state in regulating the business cycle assured some degree of stability and reduced the danger of chronic mass unemployment (1946: 9–12). In contrast to the official doctrine of the "inevitable decay of Western capitalism," Varga predicted, with absolute accuracy, the "upward swing" of the economies of "United States, Canada and other countries" due to an "increase in [American] productive capacities during the war" and further development of state interventionism (1946: 67). He also argued that the "strengthening of the political role of the working class in all the countries that had fought in the war" might lessen contradictions between capital and labor (1946: 38). Shortly after its publication, in 1947,[18] Varga's book was subjected to a public discussion, the majority of the participants denouncing it as anti-Marxist (*Soviet views* . . . 1948). Varga was particularly accused of making too much of the progressive possibilities of state regulation under capitalism.

To defend Soviet beliefs in the inevitability of the deepening of the general crisis of capitalism, an army of Soviet academic propagandists went to work to discredit Varga's findings. The announcement in June 1947 of the "Marshall Plan for Europe" added urgency to their task of discovering and substantiating a positive link between growth in state interventionism in capitalist countries and the intensification of the decay of capitalism.

During these agonized discussions, Maria Smith-Falkner, the trusted Party loyalist discussed earlier, proposed an original direction for the now ideologically necessary research: expanding Lenin's 1917 theory of state monopoly capitalism to vindicate propagandist Soviet dogmas. Her innovation was to argue that the modern rise of state intervention in a capitalist economy is the next, more sophisticated phase of the general crisis of capitalism. The initial phase of the crisis had begun in 1914–1917 with what Lenin described as "an emergence of state-monopoly capitalism"[19] (*Soviet views* [1947] 1948: 10). Smith-Falkner explained that in this new "state interventionist" phase of the crisis, the state still remains a servant of large-scale capital; its "bourgeois state institutions" cannot help oppressed workers to lessen their misery (ibid.: 13–14).[20] Party ideologists welcomed this reading of Lenin. In 1949, presumably to preserve his life, Varga admitted that his views about state interventionism were "premature and incorrect" because they deviated from "the evaluation of contemporary imperialism [as predatory, bestial, and dying] by Lenin and Stalin" (1949: 4).

To this "government-sponsored and Kremlin-blessed" (Balabkins 1958: 459) scholarship on capitalism a notable contributor is Elizaveta Khmelnitskaya (1902–1969), a long-time colleague of Varga, and a member of the Communist Party since 1918. From the end of the 1940s, she began to argue extensively that, since Lenin's time, the ways through which capitalist states defend "the interests of bourgeoisie" have become more sophisticated (1959: 82–84). Khmelnitskaya explained that when Lenin first coined the term "state monopoly capitalism," that capitalism had only started to emerge, and its main form was large-scale state ownership of capitalist productive property, created to "increase and guarantee the income of millionaires in some branch of industry who are on the verge of bankruptcy" (Lenin [1916] 1974: 218). With the development of "wide-scale state interventionism," first and foremost the macroeconomic management after World War II, the state primarily serves capitalists, not through the creation of state monopolies, "but through the redistribution of state funds" and "increased military spending," aimed at controlling the business cycle and thus creating stable and most favorable conditions for profit generation at the expense of the working class. It is for this reason, according to Khmelnitskaya, that even if the working class was not becoming more impoverished in absolute terms, its standards of living must tend to deteriorate "in relative terms" (1967: 63–65). In her research, Khmelnitskaya focused primarily on analyzing state-monopoly capitalism in post-WWII West Germany. What she perceived, for her specific purpose of propaganda, was a growing militarization of the German economy and an "increase in exploitation of labor in the country" (1959: 15).

For her work, specifically this contribution to Soviet ideology, Khmelnitskaya is honored by inclusion in a seminal Soviet monograph of 1989, *A History of Political Economy of Capitalism* (*HPEC*),[21] which assesses the achievement of Soviet scholars of capitalism over 50 years. She was one of fourteen most prominent names in the field, and the only woman. Her work is prized for her "skillful development" of Leninist analysis of "state monopoly capitalism" to expose the "exploitative nature of state regulation in post-WWII West Germany" (*HPEC*: 370–371). Whether or not she acquired any information about West Germany that would have called into question her evaluation of capitalism is not known. What is clear is that without great personal risk, she would not have been able to present views that were not officially endorsed.

Starting with the Khrushchev thaw,[22] when more congenial relations between the USSR and the West were established, some Soviet scholars began to admit that the state in a capitalist society is indeed able to intervene effectively to improve the operation of the economy, and that workers do have some pro-labor influence on state policies (Menshikov 1964; cf. Nordahl 1974: 259). A few Soviet historians of Western economic thought actually published articles and monographs with a less negative perception of Keynesianism and heterodox institutionalism, and regarded writers such as John Galbraith and Joan Robinson with greater warmth than might otherwise be expected (Osadchaya [1971] 1974; cf. Zweynert 2018: 35–45). Textbooks, however, were not changed; their dismissive tone toward Western theories was not softened.

Among a privileged echelon of Soviet academics, trusted researchers with strong ties to the Soviet political establishment were permitted, briefly, to sidestep the usual automatic denigration of Western views. Hence, they were able to discuss, more positively, Galbraith's ideas about a potential increase in similarities of organizational forms of economic management between capitalism and socialism due to the development of technology and people's needs (Galbraith 1967: 483–485). In this regard, Kama Kozlova (1931–), a scholar of international economics, published a noteworthy article, in which she acknowledged, positively, the interesting character of Galbraith's ideas (1968: 142–144). After the 1968 uprising in Prague, however, anti-Western rhetoric regained its dominance in Soviet Political Economy, and until the end of the 1980s, Galbraith's ideas about increasing convergence of industrial societies were viewed only as a sophisticated "attempt of right socialist theoreticians to misrepresent the collectivist nature of Soviet economic order" (*History of Economic Thought*,[23] 1983: 482; cf. Zweynert 2018: 36–40).

To return to the political economy of socialism, much of what has been produced by Soviet political economists, especially by those of the older generation who learned to adapt to Stalinist politics and ideological necessities, had little enduring significance. Such a typical scholar is Olimpiada Kozlova (1906–1986), for example, whose specialty was economics and organization of socialist production. In *A Biobibliographical Dictionary of Russian and Soviet Economists*, Robert Campbell characterizes Kozlova as "one of the thoroughly conventional economists, party loyalists (she joined the party in 1932), and activists," whose works epitomized "a strongly formulaic treatment of an unimaginative agenda" (2012: 205). Consequently, when restrictions on independent thought were gradually lifted, beginning with Gorbachev's 1985–1991 *Perestroika*, it became apparent that the scholarship of many orthodox political economists was "a matter of history, but [history] of ideology rather than of economic science" (Lavigne 1997: 480). Most of these scholars were not useful in the *Perestroika* debates.

However, those scholars who were formed during "the Khrushchev era of de-Stalinization" strove in their work "to offer theories on how the Soviet system should function, which they equalled with how it could be reformed" (Sutela 2008: 160). Quite often, these reform-minded economists tried to achieve their goals by bringing together economically relevant knowledge from different fields. To such, often incomplete, economic ideas during the era of Soviet reforms we will now turn.

Women's voices in the era of reform: from the 1960s through the 1980s

Overall, reform economics emerged out of the necessity to restore Soviet economic growth which, since the end of 1950s, had begun to decelerate. The urgent need to reorient the economy from extensive growth based on expansion of inputs, to "its intensive pattern, driven by increases in factor productivity and efficiency in production" (Aganbegyan 1984: 3–5) had become apparent. It had also become clear that to achieve an increase in efficiency, deep changes were required in the way in which the economy was managed, enterprises operated, enterprise and industry performance assessed, prices formed, and workplace incentives structured.

Since the major theme of reform economics was increased efficiency and optimization of production structure, reformers began seeing mathematical methods as an indispensable tool (Fedorenko and Shkliarevsky 1981–1982: 123). The starting point of such recognition was Leonid Kantorovich's (1912–1986) pioneering application to economics of the techniques of mathematical programming (Kantorovich [1959] 1965), a process that led to the development of the mathematics-based Theory of the Optimal Functioning of the Socialist Economy (SOFE), which outlined the necessary reforms. To advance research in mathematical economics and, thus, in SOFE, the Central Economic-Mathematical Institute (CEMI) was established in 1963. Many scholars with a background in mathematics, both women and men, were employed by the institute. A celebratory 50th anniversary booklet published in 2013, mentioned for special recognition the following women: Ella Borisova for her research in the field of cybernetics and linear programming (1964), Natalia Rimashevskaya and Ninel Rabkina for work on mathematical modelling for assessing standards of living (1972), Victoria Kiseleva for quantitative policy modelling (1973), Yelena Riumina for ecological modelling (1980), Irina Shubkina for mathematical modelling of enterprise management (1983), and Lyudmila Zelikina for research in stochastic economics (Zelikin 1999: 849). The problem was that any increase in mathematical rationalization inevitably led many reformist economists to advocate pro-market reforms: use of shadow prices in optimal planning and "cost-accounting" (*khozraschet*) system in assessment of enterprise results; a shift to multi-level models in iterative plans; establishment of inter-enterprise contracting for materials and product flows; introduction of "dual price systems" to optimally reflect "socialist market" conditions; and use of enterprise profitability as a decision-making criterion. All of which contradicted Marxist-Leninist ideology of Soviet planning. Ideological restrictions prevented serious attention being given to many ideas offered by the Institute researchers;[24] much of their work failed to influence actual planning decisions, and remained under-used. Such constraints basically stopped the comprehensive reform process by the mid-1970s. It was resumed, in its fullness, only near the end of Gorbachev's *Perestroika*, with SOFE researchers working as government advisers.

Far more successful during the reform years were the mathematicians whose work was not ideologically restricted because economic implications were not immediately evident. The most outstanding example is Olga Bondareva (1937–1991), who was internationally recognized as a leading game theorist in the Soviet Union. Following the seminal ideas of John von Neumann and Oskar Morgenstern (1944), Bondareva made substantial contributions to methods of optimization in, and solutions of, cooperative games. Bondareva is best known as one of two discoverers of the Bondareva–Shapley theorem, derived independently by Shapley in 1967 and Bondareva in 1963. In her pathbreaking 1963 article, based on her Ph.D. dissertation, Bondareva, like Shapley, introduced the notion of a core as a general solution concept for cooperative games, and provided a necessary and sufficient condition for the core of a cooperative game with side payments to be declared non-empty (see Bondareva 1963, 1983). Bondareva published over 70 works on game theory and probability theory; she was a member of the American Mathematical Society as well as a member of the editorial board of *Games and Economic Behavior* (Rosenmueller 1992: 310). However, given that at that time most Soviet economists were not familiar with game theory and operations research (Alexeev et al. 1992: 139, 141), explorations in these fields remained the domain of theoretical mathematics, and not of Soviet economics. Bondareva's work, as well as that of her colleague, another well-known mathematician Yelena Yanovskaya ([1972] 1974), never actually dealt with the range of economic problems to which various mathematical techniques were applied in Soviet economics,[25] and, thus, they remained virtually unknown to the majority of Soviet economists.

Once we move into the period of Gorbachev's 1985–1991 *Perestroika*, reformist voices gain full hearing. *Perestroika*'s foundational principles of transparency and utmost publicity (*glasnost*) allowed reform-economists greater freedom and encouraged, finally, a thorough consideration of several pressing issues: the inefficient Soviet system of ownership, unsatisfactory work attitudes, and the existence in socialism of conflicting economic interests and a shadow economy. After 1989, there was even freedom to analyze the introduction of market "elements" within the Soviet system and negative social consequences of economic decentralization and intended price liberalization.

It is in that changed context that Tatiana Zaslavskaia (1927–2013), the author of the highly popularized term "*Perestroika*," and Rosalina Ryvkina (1926–) rose to prominence as leading women's voices of reform. Zaslavskaia initially researched work incentives under socialism but, in the 1980s, she began exploring potential improvements in economic efficiency through decentralization of Soviet economic decision processes. In particular, she argued against the assumption that, as socialism moved closer to communism, relations of ownership would be simplified—everything would be owned by the state (*Political Economy of Socialism* 1982: 78). She saw the necessity of potential complexity and multi-dimensionality of ownership relations (Zaslavskaia 1986a: 61–73; 1986b: 5–8). Such a revision, in her opinion, was necessary in order to alleviate the growing disparity between "the greater educational level of the modern workers" that leads to their desire for "greater independence [and 'more control'] in their work," and perpetual worker separation from property (power) and resources (1986a: 66–68; 1986b: 15–17). Ryvkina furthered that argument, clarifying that "worker alienation from property" is reflected in "their indifference toward work, the low level of involvement, the low quality of work and of produced output" (1987: 35). At the same time both Zaslavskaia and Ryvkina emphasized that the delineation of state property, which existed mostly in a form of large-scale state enterprises, should be "socialist" and conducted along fairly inclusive and collective lines, and without decreeing large-scale private property rights.

They, together with their colleagues Natalia Figurnova (1940–) and Irina Starodubrovskaya (1961–), proposed, as the principal approach to democratization of the relations of state ownership of large-scale productive property, a reintroduction of "shared" ownership[26] according to which there are three co-dependent, co-existing levels of ownership: the state level, the enterprise (firm) level, and the worker (employee) level (Zaslavskaia 1987: 35–37; Figurnova 1989: 68–69; Starodubrovskaya 1990: 31–37). Without being entirely transformed into the property of worker collectives or turned over into private hands, such a tripartite version of large-scale ownership, in the view of Zaslavskaia, offered possibilities for worker co-ownership and co-decision making regarding enterprise plans, allocation of resources, election of managers, and profit (revenue) sharing, all of which would increase economic motivation of workers and promote workplace democracy (Zaslavskaia, 1986b: 5–9). In a similar vein, Ninel Rabkina (1924–) and Natalia Vladova (1927–) explained that multi-leveled co-ownership of the means of production within enterprise that provides workers with significant control and decision-making rights will better address the diverse economic interests in a workplace, moderate their potential conflicts, and reduce worker alienation (Vladova and Rabkina 1988: 80–84; see also Ryvkina and Yadov 1989: 247–248). Tatiana Kuznetsova (1987) and Zemfira Kalugina (1938–) (1987), on the other hand, pointed out that for small- and medium-sized enterprises, both in industry and agriculture, the development of worker cooperatives would result in increased worker commitment and involvement.

The Soviet reform dialogue about the nature of state ownership under socialism signified the beginning of recognition of a profound contrast between the normative vision for socialism and the actual (and often negative) economic reality of a command economic system. Soviet scholars finally acknowledged what they had previously denied: the existence of a second economy in the country.[27] Among the first economists who not only addressed this issue but also publicly provided actual estimates of its scope was Tatiana Koriagina (1943–). She defined the shadow (second) economy as the "scope of services rendered outside a legal framework and not reflected in the official statistics" (1989: 62). According to her estimations, illicitly obtained personal wealth in the USSR at the end of the 1980s amounted to 200–240 billion Soviet rubles, or about 25 percent of all personal wealth (ibid.: 60–61). Basically, Koriagina's analysis pioneered Soviet/Russian studies into corruption and non-transparency as major legacies of the Soviet system. Once liberal market reforms were implemented, these conditions created abundant opportunities for the blatant theft of state assets by commercialized enterprise directors and entrepreneurially minded government officials, and led to the emergence of oligarchy in Russia. By the summer of 1989, the time when the core reform laws (Law on the State Enterprise, Law on Cooperatives, Law on Self-Employment, Law on Land Reform, and Law on Peasant Farm) were adopted, the *Perestroika* approach had become more radical. In July 1990, the need for using market mechanisms to coordinate most of the economy had been publicly acknowledged by Gorbachev (1990: 1). In 1990–1991, small- and medium-size privatization was openly advocated by many leading Soviet economists; the need to create labor and capital markets "as soon as practically possible" was acknowledged; the necessity of "meaningful," deregulated prices was recognized (Ryvkina et al. 1990: 267–271). In April 1991, a law was adopted "On the General Principles of Entrepreneurship by Citizens," which allowed individuals to trade and employ others. In the words of Alec Nove, this public permission for entrepreneurship signified that, "for the first time since 1930 private trade ceased to be punishable 'speculation,' and private employment no longer noxious 'exploitation'" (1992: 417).

Among women economists who spoke out about the negative consequences of the intended liberalization of economy—decline in living standards, the emergence of unemployment, and increased inequality—Natalia Rimashevskaya (1932–2017), a notable SOFE economist, argued that the negative results of market reforms could be lessened, if the state would support access to jobs, guarantee income programs, and provide a state-funded, wide-ranging system of social benefits, especially subsidized health care and education (Rimashevskaya and Gritsenko 1990: 60–64). Meanwhile Nellie Pavlova (1945–), and Ninel Rabkina explained that "new ownership," in terms of state-funded social benefits, created by the state outside the workplace, would have ensured adequate living standards and have offset reform costs (Pavlova and Rimashevskaya 1987: 21–25; see also Ryvkina et al. 1990). Unfortunately, their advice was ignored.

Under the conditions of an accelerated disintegration of the country and worsening economic situation, a group of economists (S. Shatalin, G. Yavlinsky, E. Yasin, N. Petrakov, and others), in summer of 1990, drafted a so-called *500 day Program* for a decidedly radical transition to an alternative, market-based system, a program that envisaged large-scale privatization, radical price liberalization, and total deregulation of the economy (*500 Days Transition to the Market* 1991: 27–47). At that time Larisa Piyasheva (1947–2003) rose to prominence as the first woman-advocate of such radical marketization (Piyasheva 1991). The *500 day Program* approved in Russia in September 1990, signified the end of *Perestroika* reform strategy. After the collapse of the USSR, this program was implemented, with minor changes, and led to a total replacement of the economic system, bringing the era of Soviet economic thought to an end.

Conclusion

This chapter, based on historical and bibliographic research, provides a concise history of women's economic thought in the Soviet Union. It argues that the involvement of Soviet women in economic science cannot be readily compared to the experience of women economists in

Western cultures; very different socio-political forces were at work in the authoritarian Soviet Union. My main point is that in the Soviet system women economists either functioned within the prevailing ideological currents of thought, or were completely marginalized, mostly through exile or imprisonment.

During the 1920s, when a multiplicity of voices were briefly heard, women were not yet sufficiently educated to become noticeably involved, not as they had been during the actual revolution. Thereafter, as Soviets extended equal education to all citizens, women and men, the ability of women to contribute to economic thought was solely determined by their willingness to parrot the Party line. Interestingly, from the 1920s to the1960s, women were quite influential in shaping Soviet Marxist-Leninist orthodoxy, within which the analysis of Western economic thought, assessment of modern capitalism, and justification of Soviet-style socialism were conducted. Sofia Shachnovskaya, Maria Smith-Falkner, and Elizaveta Khmelnitskaya are discussed as cases in point.

The more interesting period in the development of Soviet economics is the era of Soviet reforms, from the early 1960s to the early 1990s, during which the mathematical methods of planning were introduced, and the need to democratize the Soviet economic system was openly recognized. In mathematical economics, especially in game theory which had no ideological restrictions, the greater freedom of thought resulted in economic research that was on a par with Western economic scholarship. Olga Bondareva, a leading game theorist in the Soviet Union, is a prime example here. The nascent reform economics was not thoroughly developed until Gorbachev's 1985–1991 *Perestroika*, when many ideological constraints were removed. That opened the door for the daring policy proposals of Tatiana Zaslavskaia, Rosalina Ryvkina, Nina Rimashevskaya, and the other reformers—establishing the tripartite model of large-scale ownership of productive property, and instituting and nurturing democratic and participatory processes throughout the Soviet economy. These proposals constitute an original contribution of Soviet reform scholars to the political economy of modern social democracy.

Notes

1 The Soviet Union was officially established in December 1922 with the union of the Russian, Ukrainian, Byelorussian, and Transcaucasian Soviet republics, each ruled by local Bolshevik parties.

2 The literal meaning of *Perestroika* is comprehensive restructuring.

3 Most dissenting intellectuals had already been exiled or killed or imprisoned. According to the study of Vladimir Telytsyn, 108 academic economists left Russia between 1917 and 1923 (cited in Kojima 2008: 123).

4 Soviet industrialization debates have been thoroughly addressed in economic literature concerning Soviet economic thought of the 1920s (Erlich 1960; Nove 1992: 78–158).

5 Stalin succeeded Lenin in 1924 as the leader of the Soviet Union.

6 Their fate was not specific to women. Many other philosophers, historians, and writers who did not want to "work [in Soviet Russia] only as directed by the dictatorship of the proletariat" (Finkel 2003: 590) were likewise banished or had chosen to flee.

7 Kollontai returned to the USSR only in 1947.

8 Because records of those who were targeted during Stalin's purges were routinely destroyed, it is now almost impossible to acquire full information about her. Even if political victims of Stalinism survived the years of imprisonment, as Shachnovskaya did (she returned to Moscow in 1955 (Alekseeva et al. 2017: 89)), they remained obscured, out of the public eye and out of official documents. Their books were often destroyed, although their journal articles can still be accessed.

9 Presumably, judging by her command of other languages and familiarity with the most recent Western scholarship, Shachnovskaya was educated in Europe, like Maria Smith-Falkner (1878–1968), another Bolshevik Party loyalist and statistics professor, beginning in the early days of the Soviet rule, who in 1901–1905 studied economics at the University of London. She will be discussed more fully later.

10 Shachnovskaya joined the Communist Party in 1919.
11 Isaak Rubin (1886–1937) was a well-known theoretician of Marxism, which he interpreted in a non-orthodox Party manner. Rubin was a professor of Marxist economics and, from 1926 on, a research associate at the Marx-Engels Research Institute, until he was arrested in 1930. He was executed in 1937 (Boldyrev and Kragh 2015).
12 In the mid-1980s, the author of this chapter was also trained in this primary method of analysis.
13 See treatment of Western economic thought in the standard 2-volume Soviet undergraduate textbook in Political Economy – *Political Economy, Vol. 1: Capitalism* and *Political Economy, Vol. 2: Socialism* – required texts for those specializing in political economy until the end of the 1980s. In these textbooks, each topic ended with an entire paragraph on erroneous Western views related to that topic, with appropriate "correction" from Marx, Lenin, and Party documents.
14 In 1939 she became a corresponding member of the Academy of Sciences of the USSR.
15 In the album *"USSR: Country of Women's Equality"* (1938), one could read: "There is no single area of scientific exploration in which a woman couldn't take part like a leader and organizer, like a teacher, researcher, and scientific worker" (cited in Valkova 2008: 160).
16 In 1954 all these points, which had been repeatedly made over at least ten years' worth of academic discussions, were succinctly summarized in the first edition of an official Soviet textbook in Political Economy, prepared by the Institute of Economics of the Academy of Sciences of the USSR under the general editorship of hard-core Marxist Konstantin Ostrovitjanov (*Political Economy*, 1954).
17 From 1927 to 1947, Eugene Varga (1879–1964) was the Head of the Institute of World Economy and World Politics, and the chief editor of its journal *World Economics and World Politics*.
18 The discussion took place in Moscow in 1947; an English-language translation of the discussion, entitled "Soviet views . . ." was published in Washington in 1948.
19 To Lenin, in state monopoly capitalism, "the colossal power of the state" is combined with "the colossal power of capitalism into a single mechanism," which seeks to ensure "ten-fold increases in capitalist profits" through the exploitation, ruination and impoverishment of the working class (Lenin [1917] 1974: 403).
20 At the time of this discussion, Varga did not support Smith-Falkner's views (*Soviet views* . . . [1947] 1948: 62).
21 In the history of Soviet economics this monograph is unique, and is commonly referred to by its title, namely *History of Political Economy of Capitalism* (or *HPEC* here) rather than the authors' last names.
22 The "Khrushchev thaw" was a distinct period of relative freedom and cultural liberalization from the time of Stalin's death in 1953 to the 1965 reversal of Khrushchev's policies of "de-Stalinization" by Leonid Brezhnev, Nikita Khrushchev's successor as the new leader of the Soviet Union.
23 This textbook is the one and only approved undergraduate textbook in the history of economic thought that was used in the USSR in the 1980s; it is commonly referred to by its title, and not under the editors' names.
24 As Pekka Sutela observes, in the USSR "mathematical economists have been a small minority whose theories have often met with incomprehension or outright hostility" (1991: 52).
25 However, their work in game theory and conflict resolution had much wider use in Soviet defence studies (Hagemann et al. 2016).
26 Originally this idea had been introduced in the late 1960s by Vladimir Korniernko (1966).
27 Yet among many Sovietologists, it had been common knowledge since the late 1950s that the economic system of the Soviet Union was characterized by falsified economic statistics, illegal networking, a booming parallel production, and informal bargaining between the state bureaucracy and economic management (Grossman 1982).

References

Aganbegyan, A. 1984. "Important Positive Changes in the Economic Life of the Country" (in Russian), *EKO: Economics and Organization of Industrial Production*, 6: 3–16

Alekseeva, E., Onopenko, Ya. & Fillipov, A. 2017. "The History of Institute of Economics (according to the archival documents)" (in Russian), *Herald of the Russian Academy of Sciences*, 87 (2): 82–94

Alexeev, M., Gaddy, C. & Leitzel, J. 1992, "Economics in the Former Soviet Union", *The Journal of Economic Perspectives*, 6 (2): 137–148

Balabkins, N. 1958. "Soviet View of Contemporary Western Economic Thought", *Il Politico*, 23: 446–467

Bazarov, V. 1927. "On Our Economic Perspectives and Perspective Plans" (in Russian), *Economic Review*, 5: 31–53

Boldyrev, I. & Kragh, M. 2015. "Isaak Rubin: Historian of Economic Thought during the Stalinization of Social Science in Soviet Russia", *Journal of the History of Economic Thought*, 37(3): 363–386

Bondareva, O. 1963. "Some Applications of Linear Programming Methods to the Theory of Cooperative Games" (in Russian), *Problems of Cybernetics*, 10: 119–139

——. 1983. "Extensive Coverings and Some Necessary Conditions of Existence of Solutions in Cooperative Games", *Herald of Leningrad University (Mathematics)*, 19 (1): 12–27

Borisova, E. 1964. *Iterative Method in Solving Linear Programming Problems*, Moscow: Central Economic-Mathematical Institute

Campbell, R. 2012. *A Biobibliographical Dictionary of Russian and Soviet Economists*, London: Routledge

Erlich, A. 1960. *The Soviet Industrialization Debate, 1924–1928*, Cambridge, MA: Harvard University Press

Fedorenko, N. & Shkliarevsky, G. 1981–1982. "The Application of Mathematical Methods to the Study of Economic Processes", *International Studies of Management & Organization*, 11 (3/4): 123–141

Figurnova, N. 1989. "Monopolistic Tendencies in the Economy of Socialism and Distortions in Economic Growth" (in Russian), *Problems of Economy*, 8: 96–106

Finkel, S. 2003. "Purging the Public Intellectual: The 1922 Expulsions from Soviet Russia", *Russian Review*, 62 (4): 589–613

Galbraith, J. K. 1967. *The New Industrial State*, London: Penguin Books

Gorbachev, M. 1990. "Closing Speech as the Congress of People's Deputies of the Soviet Union" (in Russian), *Pravda*, January 27

Grossman, G. 1982. "The Second Economy in the USSR". In Tanzi, Vito, Ed., *The Underground Economy in the United States and Abroad*. Lexington, MA: D.C. Heath: 245–270

Hagemann, H., Kufenko, V. & Raskov, D. 2016. "Game Theory Modeling for the Cold War on Both Sides of the Iron Curtain", *History of the Human Sciences*, 29 (4–5): 99–124

History of Economic Thought: a Textbook, 1983 (in Russian), edited by Ryndina, M., Vasilevskiy, E. & Golosov, V., Moscow: Vishaya shkola

History of Political Economy of Capitalism (*HPEC*), 1989 (in Russian), edited by Demin, A., Raskov, N. & Shirokorad, L., Leningrad: Leningrad University Press

Jasny, N. 1972. *Soviet Economists of the Twentieth Century: Names to Be Remembered*, Cambridge: Cambridge University Press

Kalugina, Z. 1987. "Social Qualities of Workers and Ways of Their Improvement", *EKO: Economics and Organization of Industrial Production*, 7: 27–40

Kantorovich, L. 1965. *The Best Use of Economic Resources*, Cambridge, MA: Harvard University Press

Khmelnitskaya, E. 1959. *Monopolistic Capitalism of Western Germany* (in Russian), Moscow: Institute of International Relations Press

——. 1967. "Historical Place of State Monopoly Capitalism" (in Russian), *World Economy and International Relations*, 9: 62–77

Kiseleva, V. 1973. *Modelling of Economic Processes* (in Russian), Moscow: Nauka

Kojima, Sh. 2008. "Exiled Russian Economists and the USSR: Brutzkus and Prokopovich". In Barnett, V. & Zweynert, J., Eds., *Economics in Russia: Studies in Intellectual History*. Burlington: Ashgate: 123–140

Kondratiev, N. [1925] 1984. *The Long Wave Cycle*, translated by Guy, D., New York: Richardson & Snyder

——. 1927. "Plan and Foresight" (in Russian), *Directions of Agricultural Development*, 2: 3–36

Koriagina, T. 1989. "Shadow Services and Legal Services" (in Russian), *EKO: Economics and Organization of Industrial Production*, 2: 60–65

Korniernko, V. 1966. "The Main Features of Ownership under Socialism" (in Russian), *Economy of Soviet Ukraine*, 3: 13–20

Kozlova, K. 1968. "New Industrial State of John Galbraith" (in Russian), *World Economy and International Relations*, 1: 142–150

Kuznetsova, T. 1987. "Cooperative Relations in Socialist Economy" (in Russian), *Problems of Economy*, 4: 25–34

Lange, O. 1945. "Marxian Economics in the Soviet Union", *The American Economic Review*, 35 (1): 127–133

Lavigne, M. 1997. "The Political Economy of Socialism: What Is Left?" *Europe-Asia Studies*, 49 (3): 479–486

Lenin, V. [1914] 1974. "Karl Marx". In *Lenin's Collected Works*, Volume 21, Moscow: Progress Publishers: 43–91

——. [1916] 1974. "Imperialism, the Highest Stage of Capitalism". In *Lenin's Collected Works*, Volume 22, Moscow: Progress Publishers: 185–304
——. [1917] 1974. "War and Revolution". In *Lenin's Collected Works*, Volume 24, Moscow: Progress Publishers: 398–421
——. [1921] 1973. "The New Economic Policy and the Tasks of the Political Education Departments: Report to the Second All-Russia Congress of Political Education Departments, October 17, 1921". In *Lenin's Collected Works*, Volume 33, Moscow: Progress Publishers: 60–80
Lewin, M. 1974. *Political Undercurrents in Soviet Economic Debates: From Bukharin to the Modern Reformers*, Princeton, NJ: Princeton University Press
Meek, R. 1955. "Some Conversations with Soviet Economists", *Soviet Studies*, 6 (3): 238–246
Menshikov, S. 1964. *The Economic Policy of the Kennedy Administration, 1961–1963* (in Russian), Moscow: Mysl
Neumann J. & Morgenstern O. 1944. *Theory of Games and Economic Behavior*, Princeton, NJ: Princeton University Press
Nordahl, R. 1974. "Stalinist Ideology: The Case of the Stalinist Interpretation of Monopoly Capitalist Politics", *Soviet Studies*, 26 (2): 239–259
Nove, A. 1992. *An Economic History of the USSR: 1917–1991*, London: Penguin Books
Osadchaya, I. [1971] 1974. *From Keynes to Neoclassical Synthesis: A Critical Analysis*, Moscow: Progress Publishers
Ostrovitjanov, K. 1968. *System of Economic Science* (in Russian), Moscow: Nauka
Pavlova, N. & Rimashevskaya, N. 1987. "The System of Pension Security" (in Russian), *Problems of Economy*, 6: 21–31
Piyasheva, L. 1991. "Economic Freedom: A Great Bubble or a Faint Chance to Survive?", *Cato Journal*, 11 (2): 293–298
"Planned Sabotage and Statistical Theory, 1930" (in Russian), *Planned Economy* 8, (10–11): 139–168
Political Economy: A Textbook, 1954. (in Russian), edited by Ostrovitjanov, K. et al., Moscow: Politizdat
Political Economy: A Textbook. Vol. 1: Capitalism, 1976 (in Russian), edited by Rumiantsev, A. et al., Moscow: Politizdat
Political Economy: A Textbook. Vol. 2: Socialism, 1982 (in Russian), edited by Rumiantsev, A. et al., Moscow: Politizdat
Rimashevskaya, N. & Gritsenko, N. 1990. "Everything for People?" (in Russian), *Communist*, 3: 59–68
Rimashevskaya, N. & Rabkina, N. 1972. *Foundations of Differentiation in Wages and Incomes: Methods of Economic-mathematical Modelling* (in Russian), Moscow: Economika
Riumina, Y. 1980. *Ecological Factor in Economic-mathematical Models* (in Russian), Moscow: Nauka
Rosenmueller, J. 1992. "Olga Nikolajevna Bondareva: 1937–1991", *International Journal of Game Theory*, 20: 309–312
Rubin, I. (1927). *Modern Western Economists* (in Russian), Moscow: Gosizdat
Ryvkina, R. 1987. "Overcoming the Breaking Mechanism" (in Russian), *Soviet Estonia*, 11: 28–37
Ryvkina, R. & Yadov, V. 1989. *Social Mechanism of Organization and Development of Production* (in Russian), Moscow: Nauka
Ryvkina, R., Kosals, L. & Sharnina, O. 1990. *Social Mechanism of Economic Reform* (in Russian), Novosibirsk: Siberian Department of the Academy of Sciences Press
Shachnovskaya, S. 1926. "Dynamics of Discount and the Problems of Its Regulation" (in Russian), *Planned Economy*, 4 (11): 81–104, (12): 74–98
Shubkina, I. 1983. *Economic-mathematical Models of Enterprise Management* (in Russian), Moscow: Nauka
Smith-Falkner, M. 1934. "Against Idealistic and Mechanistic Concepts in the Theory of Soviet Statistics" (in Russian), *Planned Economy*, 12 (7): 217–231
Stalin's Lists of Political Victims, Memorial Scientific Information and Enlightenment Center, MSIEC, f. 3, op. 24, d. 421, l. 446 (in Russian). Available at: http://stalin.memo.ru/spravki/13-446.HTM
Starodubrovskaya, I. 1990. "Foundations of Antimonopoly Policy" (in Russian), *Problems of Economy*, 6: 31–37
Strumilin, S. 1927. "On the Future Five-year Plan of 1926/1927–1930/1931" (in Russian), *Planned Economy*, 5 (3): 17–54
——. 1932. *Problems of Planning in the USSR* (in Russian), Leningrad: USSR Academy of Sciences Press
Soviet views on the post-war world economy: an official critique of Eugene Varga's "Changes in the economy of capitalism resulting from the Second World War", translated by L Gruliow, 1948, Washington: Public Affairs Press

Sutela, P. 1991. *Economic Thought and Economic Reform in the Soviet Union*, New York: Cambridge University Press
——. 2008. "Soviet Economics after Stalin: between Orthodoxy and Reform". In Barnett, V. & Zweynert, J., Eds., *Economics in Russia: Studies in Intellectual History*, Burlington: Ashgate: 157–172
Treml, V. 1969. "Interaction of Economic Thought and Economic Policy in the Soviet Union", *History of Political Economy*, 1 (1): 187–216.
Valkova, O. 2008. "The Conquest of Science: Women and Science in Russia, 1860–1940", Osiris, Second Series, Vol. 23, *Intelligentsia Science: The Russian Century, 1860–1960*: 136–165
Varga, E. 1946. *Changes in the Capitalist Economy as a Result of the Second World War* (in Russian), Moscow: USSR Academy of Sciences Press
——. 1949. "Against Reformist Tendencies in Works on Imperialism" (in Russian), *Voprosy Economiki*, 11 (3): 4–16
Vladova, N. & Rabkina, N. 1988. "Property and the Market" (in Russian), *Problems of Economy*, 10: 76–86
Yanovskaya, Y. [1972] 1974. "Infinite Zero-sum Two-person Games", *Journal of Soviet Mathematics*, 2 (5): 520–541
Zaslavskaia, T. 1986a. "Social Justice and the Human Factor in Economic Development" (in Russian), *Communist*, 13: 61–73
——. 1986b. "Creative Activity of the Masses: Social Reserves of Growth" (in Russian), *EKO: Economics and Organization of Industrial Production*, 1: 3–25
——. 1987. "The Need for Restructuring is Dictated, of Course, Not Only by the Economy" (in Russian), *Science and Life*, 11: 35–37
Zelikin, M. 1999. "Lyudmila Zelikina (1942–1996)" (in Russian), *Differential Equations*, 35 (6): 848–849
Zweynert, J. 2018, *When Ideas Fail: Economic Thought, the Failure of Transition and the Rise of Institutional Instability in Post-Soviet Russia.* New York: Routledge
500 Days Transition to the Market: The Concept and Program. New York: St. Martin's Press, 1991

18

URSULA HICKS' AND VERA LUTZ'S CONTRIBUTIONS TO DEVELOPMENT FINANCE[1]

Lucy Brillant

Introduction

The London School of Economics (LSE) seems to have occupied a special place in the emergence of development economics as a field of research. Indeed, by its openness, the LSE welcomed some overseas students from India and other countries within the British Empire. The term "economic development" appeared for the first time in the work of LSE historians in the 1920s such as Vera Anstey and Lillian Knowles (Arndt, 1981, p. 458).[2] A fair number of economists and practitioners, who would later specialize in the field of development economics, were trained at the LSE: Colin Clark, researcher at the LSE from 1928 to 1929; Arthur Lewis in 1932; Nicholas Kaldor, assistant professor from 1932 to 1947; Albert Hirschman, student from 1935 to 1936; Ursula Webb Hicks and Vera Smith Lutz, doctoral students in the 1930s and Alice Amsden in the late 1960s. Contributions focused mainly on two broad kinds of factors enhancing economic growth: the real factors (productivity, capital and land endowments and the growth of the population) and monetary factors (access to liquidity, aid or external loans, and the existence of a sound financial infrastructure). It seems that a small number of scholars in the 1950s analyzed the importance of banking institutions to enhance economic growth in developing countries.

Two influential researches underlined that economic growth goes hand in hand with the development of finance (Goldsmith, 1969 and Gurley and Shaw, 1955), but their analysis was oriented to countries already developed. Ursula Hicks and Vera Lutz were two of the few scholars giving importance to money and banking issues for economic development. Hicks and Lutz can be included in a list of fifteen outstanding female researchers and practitioners in the discipline of development economics. Of note in this list are Alice Amsden, France Stewart, Nancy Birdsall, Irma Adelman and Anne Krueger (Cooley and Van Der Meulen Rodgers, 1999).

Philippe Hugon distinguished four broad periods in the evolution of development economics (2007, pp. 719–720). In the first period from 1960 to 1968, studies in economic development focused mainly on the implementation of development plans in the context of decolonization. The second period from 1968 to 1980 was marked by fights for freedom and the recognition of the Third World. The period from 1980 to 1995 was characterized by the openness of developing to international markets. In the last period from 1995 to 2007 there was a shift in emphasis with an intensification to the fight against poverty in the context of the deconstruction of liberal beliefs. Hicks' work makes an obvious contribution to the first period in the 1960s. Lutz's works both predate and extend into the first period, but are distinct: Lutz studied development characteristics of non-colonized countries (France and Italy), emphasizing the concept of economic dualism.

Some common features can be observed between Hicks' and Lutz's experiences in academics. They both earned doctorates at the LSE, and their first researches dealt with developed countries. Lutz's first academic work was about the evolution of banking practices and the birth of central banks in Western Europe and Northern America. Hicks began working on the evolution of public finance in England. These two women's interest in developing countries rose almost at the same time, in the 1950s. During her career Hicks studied a long list of countries from different regions of the world such as India, Pakistan and Afghanistan, South East Asian countries (Malaya), the East, West and Central African states such as Nigeria, and also countries such as Jamaica in Latin America. Lutz focused only on southern Italy whose development lagged markedly behind that of the north (1950, 1951, 1956, 1958, 1962a, 1962b). Hicks and Lutz show an evident interest for finance and banking issues. Hicks published *Development Finance* in 1965, and Lutz, in addition to her doctoral work on free-banking practices in 1936, discussed the role of banking institutions in the debate about dualism between the north and the south of Italy.

Hicks' definition of economic development appears on the first page of *Development Finance*:

> By "economic development" I simply mean growth in real income per head, while not losing sight of the fact that an increase in the gross national product is unacceptable unless it also implies some betterment of the lot of the mass of the people. Economic development has a social and redistributional as well as an economic aspect.
>
> *Hicks, 1965, p. 1*

Lutz's *A Study in Economic Development* (1962a) is limited to the case of underdeveloped regions in southern Italy. Lutz, like many observers of the time, thought that the economic performance of Italy could be improved if the gap in development between the northern and the southern regions was reduced. Emphasizing dualism as a central feature of Italian underdevelopment, Lutz indicates "the direction which the growth process would have to follow to achieve economic unification" (1962a, p. 12). Economic unification via the reduction of economic dualism and large differences in standard of living can be considered as Lutz's definition of economic development. Influenced by Hayek, she was generally skeptical of government intervention. But in the Italian case she encouraged limited policy intervention to assist the south. Her enthusiasm for policy intervention was tempered though, as previous interventions "have, however, not sufficed to remove the large disparity in levels of economic and social progress between the two geographical areas" (1962a, p. 3).

This chapter does not cover all Hicks' and Lutz's contributions to development economics. Hicks' many experiences in developing countries make this task quite difficult.[3] This chapter primarily narrows the focus to the role of the banking system in the process of economic development. Those economists both recognized that the main goal of a central bank, notably in Great Britain after the First World War, was to stabilize and manage money in order to limit instabilities of prices and deficits of the balance of payments. In developing countries, the stakes were different. Hicks encouraged the establishment of central banks to guide the policies of private banks participating in the public securities market. Lutz lacked Hicks' academic knowledge and consulting experience, but offers some interesting insights into the role of banking to enhance economic development. Beginning as early as her doctoral dissertation, Lutz is a partisan of free-banking practices, which discredits the utility of central banks. However, her view evolved starting in the late 1940s, and by 1962 she supports conservative monetary policy of the Central Bank of Italy in *A Study in Economic Development* (1962a).

The plan is the following. The next section offers a bibliographical profile of Hicks and Lutz and presents their intellectual backgrounds. The third section analyzes a convergence of thought between Hicks and Lutz on the nature of credit and its importance for the economic development. The fourth section presents Hicks' thought about the role of a central bank in developing countries. The fifth section is about Lutz's theory of economic dualism and the sixth develops her evolution of thought about central banking from 1936 to 1962. The seventh section is the conclusion of this chapter.

Bibliographical profile[4]

Hicks did her PhD dissertation at the LSE under the supervision of Lionel Robbins (1938, p. xxxvii). Even if Robbins had affinities with conservative thinkers such as Ludwig von Mises and Friedrich Hayek, it did not much influence Hicks. She was mostly influenced by John Maynard Keynes[5] and John Richard Hicks. Hicks' research specialized in the history of British public finance. She taught this course at Nuffield College (Oxford) for many years. There, Wilfred David, who did his PhD thesis under her supervision, wrote that "one of Lady Hicks's major contributions lies in the application of the theories of fiscal policy and the financial approach to the problems of the less developed countries" (1973, p. xiii). On Hicks' book *Development Finance: Planning and Control*, David wrote that it is "one of the best available studies of the development process from the fiscal and financial angles" (1973, p. xiv).

In a book written in Hicks' honor, David (1973) distinguished two phases in which her contributions to economics unfold. A first phase from 1938 to 1954 concerns her interest in the history of British public finance. Her PhD dissertation *The Finance of British Government 1920–1936* (1938) is reckoned as "the first attempt by a scholar to quantify the major aspects of British public finance" (David, 1973, p. xi). Hicks is also identified as a pioneer with her method of cost/benefit analysis enabling a country to choose the plan that offers the greatest present value of benefits over costs. She wrote two other books on this topic (1947 and 1954). Martin Feldstein also identifies that Hicks contributed to a framework for evaluating public investment projects in developing countries using cost/benefit analysis (Feldstein, 1973, p. 4).

A second phase begins in the 1960s with Hicks' new interest in the development of developing countries. She wrote three books about economic development (1961, 1965, and 1978 with John R. Hicks), and she participated in a collective book edited by J.R. Hicks about the economic development of Ceylon (1959) where she advised the young central bank.[6] During this phase, she directed the thesis of some bright young economists at Oxford who later occupied key positions in institutions and universities: Gamani Corea, Martin Feldstein and Nicholas Kaldor.

Hicks' interests passed on through the work trajectories of her thesis advisees. Corea joined the central bank of Ceylon at its creation in 1950 as one of a group of "young recruits" (Kelegama, 2004, p. 15). He became the director of economic research from 1960 to 1965, and deputy governor from 1970 to 1973. Feldstein specialized in public finance in developed countries (1985) and Nicholas Kaldor focused on the case of developing countries (1963), in addition to his numerous contributions on economic growth.

Hicks was also a civil servant. She served as an economic adviser for the governments in the Caribbean, India, Jamaica, Malaysia, Nigeria (as part of its "advisory Commission") and Uganda. In 1965, with Margaret Hall, Hicks was one of the first women allowed to join the Oxford University Political Economy Club (FitzGerald and Heyer, 2011, p. 40). She was also one of the founders of the *Review of Economic Studies*, and managing editor from 1933 to 1961.

Lutz did her PhD dissertation at the LSE under the supervision of Friedrich Von Hayek. She did not follow an academic career like Hicks – she never occupied a position at a university. Lutz's first research, published in 1936, was on free-banking practices and questions the existence of central banks at the top of the banking system. Some write that Lutz continued Hayek's work on the evolution of money and banking; Hayek might have delegated this project when he was appointed Professor at the LSE (Huerta de Soto, 2012, p. 631). Lutz's contribution to the free-banking debate is acknowledged by several economists. Capie et al. (1995) wrote notably that "Vera Smith's (1936) book [. . .] is simultaneously one of the major studies of central banking and a sustained plea for the resumption of Free Banking" (p. 86). This issue was not extensively studied in the twentieth century as White noted (2014, p. 8), with the exception of Ludwig von Mises (1928). A renewed interest in this topic arose in the late 1970s (with Hayek's book, 1976, p. 19) and in the 1980s with the works of White (1984) and Selgin (1988). Both recognize the quality of the empirical work of Lutz's book.[7] Lutz, with her husband Friedrich Lutz, was a member of the Mont Pelerin Society.[8]

Lutz's interest in development economics arose in the 1950s as European countries adopted public investment plans in the aftermath of war. Lutz limited her research to the case of southern Italy and France, where she disputed the strongly held belief of others that public plans would enhance economic growth.[9] Lutz's objective was to reveal the inconsistency of public plans (Guirao and Lynch, 2015, p. 47). Lutz's views on markets and social justice appear in *Central Planning for the Market Economy* (1969). In this book she challenged the plan adopted by the French Government from 1947 to the mid-1960s to fix commodity prices (a policy of "indicative" planning). This kind of policy runs counter to her liberal philosophy, killing the spirit of entrepreneurship. To fix prices would deprive private firms from setting their own prices. Lutz supports the "Austrian view" according to which economic efficiency is improved if the decisions of private agents determine prices in a market economy:

> The collection of information and prediction are themselves competitive activities; and the right of individual operators to exploit their particular advantages or talents in this domain cannot be suppressed without striking at the roots of free enterprise and risk-taking.
>
> *Lutz, 1969, p. 117*[10]

The most famous part of Lutz's work is probably that dealing with her researches on the economic development of Italy. With Friedrich Lutz, Vera Lutz was part of a team of liberal thinkers appointed as economic experts by the Bank of Italy in the late 1940s (Baffi, 1985, as noted by de Cecco, 2011, p. 17).[11] On this topic she published one book (1962a) and several articles (1950, 1956, 1958). Those researches, notably "The Growth Process in a 'Dual' Economic System" (*Banca Nazionale del Lavoro Quarterly Review*, 1958) had a strong impact in Italy, with a direct reaction: economist Luigi Spaventa rejected Lutz's thesis (1959). Italian economist Mazzochi considered that Lutz opened the debate about the origins of dualism in Italy (1965, p. 716). De Cecco wrote that Lutz's "line of argumentation was the one which had the strongest influence on Italian public debate for years to come" (2011, p. 19; see also Toniolo, 2013, p. 147 on Lutz's influence).

The nature of money and the development of private commercial banks

A convergence of some of the thought of Hicks and Lutz can be observed in their approach to money and credit. Both recognize that credit plays an important role in economic development. In Hicks' words, "The provision of credit for private enterprise is vital to development" (1965, p. 58). On her side, considering the effect of credit on the quantity of bank notes in circulation, Lutz wrote that "a paper currency is a desirable adjunct to a country's commercial development" (1936, p. 10).

The word "credit", both in Hicks' and Lutz's writings, has double meaning. First, it can be considered as the funds that credit institutions are willing to lend to businesses. Here, lending capacity of banks depends on the amount of savings collected from depositors. Credit also has a second meaning. It corresponds to the situation where banks respond to the demand for liquidity from businesses (Hicks, 1965, p. 58 and Lutz, 1936, p. 172). A bill of exchange – characterizing indebtedness – can also be considered as a credit. The bill of exchange represents a promise to deliver money at a future date. For instance, if a wholesaler A delivers goods to a retailer B and B promises to pay A in money at a later date, then B has a debt with A. The process of production can start once A accepts the bill of exchange (i.e. the indebtedness) of B. If A cannot wait to receive money at the agreed date, A can discount its bill with a bank, the bank exchanging the bill for money. Banks provide liquidity to traders who need money before the maturity date (for instance to pay their workforce).

One major problem that developing countries face is the lack of credit as defined above (Hicks, 1965, pp. 52, 57). The market for bills of exchange is weak, and the amount of savings is low. The weak development of the market for bills of exchange can be due to "lending risk", that is, the lack of confidence across merchants in their capacity to reimburse debt by maturity (Hicks, 1965, p. 58). This risk dissuades traders from issuing bills of exchange and reduces confidence in the bills market. As a result, trade decreases between merchants.

On her side, Lutz illustrated the importance of confidence in the means of exchange against which bills are convertible. She took the case of the Goldsmiths in seventeenth-century England. Goldsmith notes were certificates of indebtedness issued by banks when merchants deposited gold. Merchants could recover their gold with a simple presentation of Goldsmiths to the bank. With the spread in their use, traders became confident in the value of Goldsmiths. Those notes started to be used as money – not merely as gold certificates – with merchants accepting them as means of payment for goods (p. 11).

Another point of convergence of thought can be observed between Hicks and Lutz. They seem to agree on the fact that in occidental countries the formation of the banking and financial system is the result of a long historical process. Banking developed spontaneously without intervention of the State:

> We can roughly summarise the course of events and swings of policy in the evolution of banks of issue before 1875 under four phases. The first was a preliminary period when banks were only just beginning to emerge, and they were theoretically at liberty to form freely even if it was only because they were not yet obtrusive enough to catch the eye of the legislative authority.
>
> *Lutz, 1936, pp. 10–11*

> In an advanced country the commercial banks are far from being the only sources of credit or depositories for savings. Over the years many other institutions, such as insurance companies and building societies, have developed spontaneously.
>
> *Hicks, 1965, p. 58*

Lutz only studied the case of already developed countries, and did not express views on the development of banks in developing countries. Hicks provides interesting insights into developing economy banking in *Public Finance* (1965), where she affirms that development banks should be deliberately created. Hicks encourages the adoption of public plans in order to help countries to develop their economies. It is clear for Hicks that the quality of a plan depends on access to resources such as raw materials and an efficient workforce. Equally clear for Hicks is the need to include the impact of financing the plan in overall cost calculations (1965, p. 35). Hicks encourages countries to be financially independent, for instance by developing their own commercial credit market and by increasing private savings, in order to avoid dependence on foreign aid and loans (1965, p. 38).[12] The formation of domestic saving is necessary for independence from foreign funds. Unfortunately, this is rarely the case in most developing countries, but not because households do not save. The sense of saving is quite present in the minds of peasants in developing countries, as Hicks identifies in the case of Nigerian cocoa farmers (1965, pp. 47–48). The problem is the absence of a sound banking system which centralizes secured savings and provides these pooled funds to private merchants and to public infrastructure investment in water, roads, schools and hospitals.

To sum up, parallels can be drawn on the meaning of credit in Hicks' and Lutz's thoughts. They consider that banks have the double function to provide liquidity on the market for bills of exchange, and also to collect savings. The rate of interest is the rate at which bills are exchangeable against money. Their thoughts also converge on the fact that banking systems emerged without the intervention of public authorities in most developed countries. However, their views diverge about the role of central banks.

Ursula Hicks on central banking practices

One original aspect of Ursula Hicks in the field of development finance deals with the task of a central bank. In the 1950s, it was unusual to think that central banking practices were a way of promoting economic development. Most economists sought solutions from central banks for the high inflation observed in Western countries, not for reducing poverty in low-income regions of the world. Hicks, however, belongs to the few researchers who thought that developing countries require a sound banking system for sustained growth (David, 1973, p. xiii). For her, the knowledge and long experience of developed countries should serve to establish sound financial infrastructure elsewhere (1965, p. 52). She considered that in a developing country, "such institutions [central banks] are needed here and now, and so must be deliberately created" (p. 58). The central bank can be financed almost wholly out of government funds when no other source is available (p. 55). Those institutions should not be in competition with private banks, and must be capable of giving independent advice "on the basis of its own economic and statistical research" (p. 55).

Hicks presents four main roles of a central bank in developing economies, closely linked to each other. The first role of a central bank is "to build up an internal banking structure almost from the bottom. One way of doing this is to establish a commercial bank with public funds, which will follow an aggressive policy of "selling" banking even in remote rural areas" (Hicks, 1965, p. 57). Recall that Hicks perceived high "lending risk" in developing economies, which discourages lenders to invest in projects (p. 58). The higher the lending risk, the higher is the interest rate charged on loans. The existence of a strong banking system, supervised by a central bank, would lead to reductions in interest rates on the money market and on the market for commercial loans. It would also lead to reductions in cash hoarding, and the facilitation of funding for productive investments. Credit should develop for small and/or large businesses with the establishment of Industrial Development Corporation and an Agricultural Credit Corporation (p. 58) deliberately created by the State. Under the guidance of the central bank, these development banks implement a policy of selective credit. For instance, the central bank can encourage the banking sector to ensure low credit rates to the companies of a chosen sector: "[I]t [the central bank] should be given powers to encourage investment in particular lines by selective credit controls through the banks and through such financial institutions as insurance companies and building societies" (Hicks, 1965, p. 56).

Second, once the banking system is established, the central bank should facilitate public borrowing: "[I]t [the central bank] will have to conform to the government's general economic policy" (Hicks, 1965, p. 55). One way to reach this objective is to seek low interest rates charged on Treasury bonds, either by direct purchases of the public bonds by the central bank, or by keeping low the main lending rate from the central bank. Here Hicks had in mind an original mechanism: by announcing its policy, the central bank could promote the belief among private investors that lending rates will remain low. If investors believe this, they would be encouraged to purchase and hold long-term assets such as the Treasury bonds. The additional purchases lead to a rise in the price, and therefore decrease the interest rates of Treasury bonds.[13] This would be favorable to public finance.

A third role of the central bank in a developing economy is to encourage the formation of a private capital market. Hicks thought that the purchase of Treasury bonds could support the development of a capital market. The goal is to encourage private agents to keep their savings in the form of those bonds (which are less risky than private stock) instead of investing in a bank deposit or hoarding wealth in the form of precious metal. Agents might then become more willing to finance private stocks. Hicks had in mind the British experience, where the development of the market for Treasury bonds came before the emergence of the market for stocks:

> Experience shows that government debt is a perfectly good foundation for security trading.
>
> *Hicks, 1965, p. 59*

> For those [developing countries] who have not the nucleus of a market in long-term loans will be, to start with (and perhaps for a considerable time), trading in government debt.
>
> *Hicks, 1965, p. 59 fn*

Another advantage of Treasury debt dealing is more original. Hicks thought that new issue of Treasury bonds was a good thing for borrowers in capital markets, because "additional long-term debt provides extended collateral for loans" (Hicks, 1947, p. 363). If the quality of the public debt is better than the quality of the private stock, private investors have an interest in holding Treasury bonds in their portfolio. This difference in the quality of the debt is due to the powers of raising taxes by the State.[14]

A fourth role is to ensure stability in the value of money, the volatility of which is impacted by foreign and domestic factors (Hicks, 1965, p. 53). The domestic factor is the quantity of credit contracted by private businesses; if too much credit is created, money can depreciate because of the rise in prices. In order to avoid a depreciation of money, the central bank should control the money supply and impose reserve requirements on commercial banks. External factors that influence the money supply center around foreign trade. Also note that Hicks believed the central bank should form a pool of foreign currencies in order to avoid violent exchange rate fluctuations (pp. 52–53).

Vera Lutz about economic "dualism" in Italy and the failure of Keynesian budgetary and monetary policies

Lutz extended Arthur Lewis's theory of dualism (1954) to the Italian case[15] and questioned the effectiveness of public plans (such as the "Vanoni plan" launched in 1954) which were supposed to narrow dualism between the north and the south of Italy.[16] She wrote that all the efforts made by the Italian government to promote industrialization in the south – either by increasing the money supply or by investing in public funds – had been unsuccessful:

> The results achieved by more than ten years of Southern policy have, by fairly general admission, fallen short of expectations. The "infrastructure" of industry that was built failed – in spite of additional incentives of a more directly cost-reducing kind – to attract an industrial "superstructure" on the scale that had been anticipated. And little or no progress was made towards closing the income-gap between the two regions.
>
> *1962a, p. 130*

In 1947, the Italian Government created an association in order to develop the south of Italy, called the SMIREV (Associazione per lo Sviluppo dell'Industria nel Mezzogiorno). From 1947 to 1957, the SMIREV voted in 340 laws aimed at raising the industrialization and living standards of the south (Lutz, 1962a, pp. 101, 122). The main purposes of policy were to allow tax relief, credit facilities[17] and grants to southern private enterprises (as presented in Chapter 6 of *Italy, a Study in Economic Development*, 1962a). In addition, the Bank of Italy and the finance of the government were closely linked: the Treasury had privileged access to the funds of commercial banks, and also it had priority over the use of the funds that were deposited by the public with the Postal Administration (Lutz, 1962a, p. 169).

The failure of public plans conducted in southern Italy is due, according to Lutz, to problems specific to Italy (1962a, p. 298). First, it is due to the high income elasticity of demand for agricultural products and the rigidity of the supply of agricultural products (1962a, p. 138); second, the level of wages was rigid because of powerful trade unions in the north (Lutz, 1950, pp. 83–84). Third, there was a difference of skills between northern and southern workers; and finally, the geographic location of southern Italy limited the competitiveness of its products (1962a, p. 135). The first and second points are considered in the next two paragraphs.

A main concern in southern Italy was the lack of spirit of entrepreneurship and the related unwillingness of farmers to modernize their production equipment.[18] Because of that, the supply of food products was inelastic to price in southern Italy (Lutz, 1962a, p. 138), and this was a major issue considering population pressure. In addition, at a national scale, the income elasticity of demand for food products was higher than the income elasticity of industrial products.[19] This created imbalanced growth between the (northern) industrial and (southern) agricultural sectors (1962a, pp. 133–137). On the basis of these observations, Lutz presented a case where the government creates additional revenue in the south, in order to reduce the gap of development between northern and southern regions (the industrial plan conducted by the Italian government from 1947). Rising income in the south would engender a rise in consumption of food and industrial products. Because the income elasticity of the demand for food produce was higher than the income elasticity for industrial produce, and also because the food supply was inelastic in the south, the price of food products would increase more than the price of industrial products. The declining relative prices of industrial goods in comparison with the prices of food products would reduce the profit rate in the industrial sector.

A solution to restore the margin of producers would be to reduce wages in the industrial sector, Lutz explained, but the workers' unions were making it impossible. Powerful workers' unions engendered higher wages in the north than in the south. Companies were therefore encouraged to invest in capital-using techniques instead of recruiting labor force. In the south, however, companies were not constrained by workers unions so wages were lower than in the north. Lutz's remedy for the economic dualism in Italy was to reduce the power of unions in the north, which would increase the demand for labor, and then to encourage (with financial assistance) the departure of southern Italian workers to the north in order to work in the industrial sector (Lutz, 1962, pp. 314–315).[20]

In an article published in the *Quarterly Journal of Economics*, Lutz expressed her view on Keynesian monetary policies. She was skeptical that these policies would encourage new investments. The stimulus can only be found in the reduction of the power of the workers' unions:

> [W]hen the real wage rate is fixed, a policy of monetary expansion is not much more likely to be an answer to the unemployment problem when imperfect competition prevails in the product market than when perfect competition prevails. . . . Public works likewise . . . would be of no avail unless they succeeded either in bringing about a redistribution of income of the kind described, or else in decreasing the degree of monopoly in some other manner. It appears that the only remedy adequate to the present case is a direct attack on the elements of monopoly power in both the labor and the product markets.
>
> *1952, p. 262*

The two kinds of rigidities presented above – the inelasticity of the supply of food product and the rigidity to the decrease of wages – were, according to Lutz, the main factors of economic dualism in Italy. Public interventions such as expansive monetary policies or public plans aiming at industrializing the south would not enable full utilization of resources in Italy. One reason is that

> there never had existed in Italy any pre-constituted balance of capital equipment commensurate in size and composition with a situation of full or near-full employment of labour, just as there never had existed that proportion of skilled to unskilled labour which corresponds to such a situation [of a previous state of full utilization of resources].
>
> *Lutz, 1962a, p. 298*

An expansionary monetary policy would therefore not solve the problem of the rigidity of the supply of food products in southern Italy:

> As was observed in earlier chapters, the process of providing, within a near future, the necessary increase in the supplies of the higher-quality foodstuffs and of other goods must be a highly complex one, depending on many more things than monetary policy.
>
> *Lutz, 1962a, p. 301*

According to Lutz, the State should help southern families to emigrate to the north – the only public intervention that Lutz advised. Internal migration would reduce the population pressure and the excess demand for food products in the south. It would bring additional workers to the north who could specialize into the industrial sector, knowing that "the North . . . is better situated than is the South for expanding industrial exports" (Lutz, 1962a, p. 144). Lutz saw internal migration as the best way to fight economic dualism in Italy.

Central banking in Vera Lutz's thought: from a rejection (1936) to an adoption for economic development (1962a)

In her doctoral work *The Rationale of Central Banking and the Free Banking Alternative* (1936), Lutz was very critical toward creation of central banks in most European countries (England, France, Germany and Scotland), and Northern America (Canada and the United States). Her advocacy of free banking was audacious in the late 1930s, where a majority of economists supported Keynesian-style monetary and budgetary policies. Lutz applauded free-banking practices, and was critical toward the creation of central banks, who, in her view, harmed the functioning of the banking system and the economy in general. The "scientific management" of money by the central bank in order to stabilize prices (Lutz, 1936, p. 190) led to "catastrophic disturbance" (p. 194). Lutz wrote:

> Out of the realization of the central bank's power to determine the volume of credit there arose the notion that it should consciously direct monetary policy along "scientific lines". The question then arises: What is to be the criterion of this "scientific management"? The criterion which has so far usually been adopted, namely, that of the stability of the general price level, has been suspect in theory and just as unfortunate in practice.
>
> *1936, pp. 189–190*

Lutz's use of "instabilities" is close to Wicksell's definition: they are generated by discrepancies between the monetary rate (which is the interest rates charged on loans by the banking system) and the natural rate (being the profit rate of firms). Lutz thought that centralizing liquidity within a central bank, and giving central bank control over the price of liquidity on the money market would not reduce monetary-induced price instability. Lutz wrote:

> The most satisfactory theory yet offered in explanation of booms and depressions, however, is one which at that time was undeveloped and which finds the perpetually disequilibrating force in monetary disturbances expressing themselves in a divergence between the "natural" and market rates of interest and between voluntary savings and real investments.
>
> *1936, p. 7*

Disappointed about the direction of banking practices coupled with frequent interventions of central banks in the early years of the interwar period (1919–1939), Lutz undertook the ambitious task of deconstructing the dominant belief that capitalism could not work without a central bank. To do so, Lutz studied the origins of central banking in capitalist economies by surveying the history of the financial structure of Canada, England, France, Germany, Scotland and the United States. According to Lutz, the establishment of central banks (except in the United States) is the result of "a combination of political motives and historical accident which played a much more important part than any well-considered economic principle" (Lutz, 1936, pp. 4–5). In England, for instance, pressure from politicians gave birth to the Bank of England: it "was the result of a long series of Government manipulations" (Lutz, 1936, pp. 22–23). Central banks, she continues, were created to be subordinated to the State and to ease public spending.

This idea was already apparent in Bagehot (1877), quoted several times by Lutz (1936, pp. 22, 23, 123, 133). Bagehot was a British banker who became famous for his book *Lombard Street* (1877) dealing with the relationship between the Bank of England and

London's financial and money market. Lutz wrote that Bagehot supported the fact that the Bank of England's first objective in 1694 was to facilitate the borrowing of the government (1877, p. 92), and also, that "[he] continued to make frequent reference to the superior qualities of a plural banking system" (Lutz, 1936, p. 133).

Disagreeing with influential economists and partisans of central banking interventions of her time, such as Ralph George Hawtrey and John Maynard Keynes, Lutz did not think that the central bank exerts a stabilizing role in economy by controlling interest rates. History shows that attributing such power to the central bank gave rise to great monetary disturbances that harmed the economy. Lutz had in mind the special facilities granted to the State to finance public spending which had been a major cause of inflation:

> While recognizing that the maladjustments may be due, not to the specific form of the banking system, but rather to at present unresolved technical difficulties, common to any system, in maintaining equilibrium between savings and investments, or in stabilizing the effective quantity of circulating media, it seems not improbable that the tendencies to misdirection are magnified by the form of the system, in particular that part of it which entrusts the determination of the volume of credit to a single authority, between which and the Government there exist reciprocal incentives to paternalism. It is not unlikely that the bolstering up of banking systems by their Governments is a factor which makes for instability.
>
> *1936, p. 7*

Further, to oblige banks to centralize a part of their reserve in a single supra bank renders banks less prudent. It should be the responsibility of each private bank to ensure its own solvency. Even if a big financial crisis occurs that forces banks into bankruptcy, Lutz thought that at least one prudent bank would survive the crisis – and savers could transfer any remaining solvent savings (Lutz, 1936, p. 185). The best way to encourage banking prudence is to allow the "law of bankruptcy":

> To the vast majority of people government interference in matters of banking has become so much an integral part of the accepted institutions that to suggest its abandonment is to invite ridicule. One result of this attitude is that insolvency in the sphere of banking has won exception from the rule applied in other lines of business that it must be paid for by liquidation, and it is important also to point out that since the laws of bankruptcy have almost never been strictly applied to banking we should be diffident of drawing the conclusion that actual experiences prove the unworkability of free competition in banking.
>
> *Lutz, 1936, p. 185*

Passages discussing the role of central banking in the development of a country are not easy to find in Lutz's later works. She was clearly against the privilege of Italian Government benefiting from loans from the Bank of Italy. Those loans served to create State-owned industries and to give subsidies to private industries. This was part of the development plan aimed at reducing the development gap between the north and the south of Italy. Lutz thought that those plans were ineffective at solving economic dualism.

Lutz put an emphasis on the fight against inflation. In her eyes, stable prices were an essential ingredient in development "for a recovery of personal savings, for a revival of bond markets, for a reduction in the amount of capital tied up in business hedging against rising commodity prices" (Lutz, 1962a, p. 325). In the aftermath of the Second World War, the level of commodity prices was rising in Italy. As Lutz wrote, before the stabilization of September 1947, the wholesale price level was fifty-five times higher than its level in 1938 (Lutz, 1962a, p. 297). One major cause of that rise was the note issue associated with "wheat bills" due to the Italian Government's support of high prices of wheat (Lutz and Lutz, 1950, p. 5). The Bank of Italy had to, without limit, discount bills issued by the organization pooling wheat, who purchased wheat at a price that was over twenty times the pre-war price (as explained by Masera, 1983, p. 32; see also Lutz 1962b, p. 164 and also Lutz and Lutz, 1950, pp. 5–6). In September 1947, the Government and the Bank of Italy had to find ways to stop the rise of commodity prices. Luigi Einaudi, appointed Minister of the Budget and also Governor of the Bank of Italy in September 1947, implemented a successful monetary policy of restrictive credit,[21] without reducing public spending (Lutz, 1962a, pp. 215, 297): "Professor Einaudi . . . was instrumental in carrying out these restrictive policies" (Lutz and Lutz, 1950, p. 12). Thanks to this policy, the value of the lira was rapidly stabilized, and the level of inflation was reduced in Italy.

Lutz's support for restrictive monetary policy seems to contradict her doctoral thesis in 1936, where she wrote against Hawtrey's monetary rule.[22] This rule aimed at stabilizing prices by controlling the quantity of money (Lutz, 1936, pp. 190–191). Such monetary policy, called "scientific management" of money by Lutz (1936, p. 190), was according to her a strong factor of "disturbance" in the economy:

> There is not much doubt that the present banking system is actively responsible for disturbances . . . it seems to be an indisputable fact that the major fluctuations come from changes in the amount of cash provided by the central banks . . . fluctuations, while not being entirely eliminated, would be much reduced under free banking. And it is undoubtedly true that such a system is much less capable of monetary manipulation than a system of central control.
>
> *Lutz, 1936, pp. 194–195*

However, this apparent contradiction in Lutz's thought might not reflect a radical change in her view. One can suppose that Lutz adapted herself to a world with growing support for central banking practices, and that she found some benefits that she did not grasp while she was a doctoral student. Indeed, her view about central banking practices changed around the same time that she became interested in issues in development economics. In her writings about Italy, she clearly thought that monetary policy could favor the development of some less-advanced regions, by ensuring stability in the value of money (Lutz, 1962a, p. 325) and therefore limiting inflation which discourages agents from saving. Instead of public plans, Lutz is in favor of policies encouraging voluntary private savings, which can be used to finance projects in developing regions, such as the south of Italy:

> [T]he encouragement of voluntary private savings as a means of financing the increase in real capital resources which are necessary in order to allow the number of workers who can be employed at a given level of real wages to expand, an aim which can be reached by continuing the policy of maintaining stability of the lira.
>
> *Lutz, 1962a, pp. 83–84*

Concluding remarks

Hicks and Lutz provide contributions to the first generation of scholars who became interested in the field of development economics (Knight, 1991, p. 10). Though belonging to two different schools, both women promoted the transfer of knowledge and experience from developed to developing economies. Observing the development of banking in England (in Hicks' works), and more generally in occidental countries (in Lutz's PhD Thesis), Lutz and Hicks shared the idea that a sound banking system was necessary to ensure the proper functioning of the economy, despite an apparent opposition about the organization of such a system. Indeed, Lutz was for free banking, and Hicks for central banking. They nevertheless both considered that savings should be secured, liquidity should be provided to businesses when needed and the value of money should be kept stable by adopting relevant monetary policies.

In Hugon's fourth period of the evolution of development economics (1995–2007) there was a change in the dominant mentality supporting liberalization policies as well as knowledge transfer intended to support development. For example, Escobar (2012) denounces the practice of replicating the institutions and policies of "advanced" economies within countries where growth of domestic produce, industrialization, and mechanized, capital-intensive production in agriculture are low (p. 4). In this view, pursuing the goal of economic progress through the model of industrialized countries has caused more damage than benefit to the situation.

Lutz is less susceptible to Escobar's criticism, because, for the case of southern Italy, she did not think that public plans ("several hundreds of industrial plants," 1962a, p. 122) would help the economy to develop. She was also very critical toward plans conducted in France in the post-war period, as explained in one article and two books especially written for this issue (1964, 1965, 1969). Public plans, adopted by a majority of occidental countries after the Second World War, harmed more than helped countries by killing the spirit of entrepreneurship, and depriving economic agents from perceiving "real" signals of markets (Lutz, 1969, p. 117).

In some ways, Hicks contributed partly to the policy transfer process criticized by Escobar, although it is difficult to know how "lucrative" her civil servant functions were in the developing world.[23] However, she does not completely succumb to the Escobar critic because she never imposed a liberal model to follow. As a specialist of the evolution of British Finance from the nineteenth century until the 1930s (Hicks, 1938, 1947, 1954), her goal was to help former British colonies adapt economically with their newly gained independence. Hicks' introduction to *Development from Below* (1961) is insightful about this issue. After the war, Hicks observed an evolution of mentalities about the way to enhance economic development. It became more and more accepted that local governments had a role to play, and Hicks worked for their establishment:

> As soon as British people began to settle overseas, they set to work creating local institutions on the model of those to which they were accustomed; from these origins the democracy of the United States and of the older Dominions has grown up. That part of the expansion, and transplantation, of British local government will, however, lie, for the most part, outside our subject. Local democracy of that sort was a natural growth; no deliberate policy lay behind it . . . There is nevertheless something that is quite novel about the recent experience: what is it? . . . Since the last war local government has been regarded as a means, not only to political, but also to economic development.
>
> *Hicks, 1961, pp. 3–4*

The basis of national economic progress in Hicks' eyes, should come first by the existence of strong institutions –a local government and a central bank – which would collect public revenue, then secure and employ funds in the most efficient way. Before opening their economy to international trade, countries should be aware of the risks. Far from encouraging liberal policies, Hicks insisted on the need to be prepared to face risks of a shortage of foreign exchange or the risk of price volatility before opening the economy to international markets (Hicks, 1965).

Notes

1 This paper was presented in May 2017 at the European Society for the History of Economic Thought (ESHET) organized at the University of Antwerp. I would like to warmly thank Kirsten Madden (editor) without whom this chapter would not have this present form. I also thank very much Robert Dimand (co-editor with Kirsten Madden), and Farida Kahn (discussant) for their insightful help. I am also grateful to Nicolas Barbaroux, Harro Maas and Nathalie Sigot for their discussion during the session. This paper was also presented to the seminar of the LEDi in April 2017, I which to thank all the participants (Ludovic Desmedt, Jean-Luc Bailly, Xavier Bradley, Jimmy Lopez) and the PhD students present there (Emmanuelle Leturque).

2 Dr. Sheetal Bharat identified that Vera Anstey and Lillian Knowles were instrumental in coining the phrase "economic development". This term appears in the title of their respective books entitled *The Economic Development of the British Overseas Empire* (London: George Routledge and Sons, 1924) and *The Economic Development of India* (London: Longmans, Green, 1929).

3 In the Preface of *Development from Below* (1961) Hicks gives a description of her functions as a civil servant in several developing countries. She stresses the various development plans conducted in different parts of Africa (Ghana, Kenya, Nigeria, Sierra Leone, Tanganyika, Uganda) and in India and Sri Lanka (called Ceylon in the 1960s). Later in the 1960s she also advised some Asian countries such as Malaya.

4 The bibliographical profile for Ursula Hicks draws on material out of Jacobsen (2000).

5 Hicks wrote that Keynes's *General Theory* was a major source of inspiration for her work. About John Richard Hicks, she was very supportive of the *Social Framework* (1946).

6 As explained by Sue Van Atta and Edita A. Tan (July 21, 1970, University of Philippines).

7 "The Rationale of Central Banking is a rare classic in monetary economics. It provides still the best account available of how and why the United-States and several European countries acquired the central banks that dominate their monetary system today" (Lawrence White, writing on the back cover of Lutz (1936) [1990]).

8 The Mont Pelerin Society is a think tank founded by Hayek in 1947. It gathers politicians, economists and thinkers who advocate freedom for individuals, enterprises and markets. Milton Friedman, Maurice Allais and James Buchanan were members of the Mont Pelerin Society.

9 In 1961 Chancellor of the Exchequer Selwyn Lloyd, and two years later Christopher Saunders, suggested implementing planning policies in England. Lutz worried about those political directions (1969, p. 62).

10 Despite authoring two books (1965, 1969) and one chapter written in 1964, Lutz's works about the French economy did not receive much attention from economists (except Kindleberger, 1967).

11 See also Maes, 2008, p. 2

12 Irma Adelman assessed the effectiveness of foreign aid in Greece in a paper written with Chenery in 1966. Like Hicks, Adelman encourages limiting the reliance on foreign aid.

13 This method of influencing rates by playing on the expectations of private agents was discovered in the 1930s, and presented by Keynes (1930, I and II, and 1936) and also by John R. Hicks (1939).

14 However, if the State has a high credit risk, private investors lose confidence and the public debt ceases to be liquid. Hicks assumes the State is credible: its debt is more trustworthy than the debt of private companies thanks to the power of raising taxes.

15 Arthur Lewis is credited with contributing the idea of economic dualism in the context of economic development, without explicitly coining this term. Italian economist Spaventa gives the following definition of dualism:

> Dualism is a paradox, in that a sector remains backward even though the economy as a whole is growing and the overall rates of capital accumulation and of income growth continue at a high level: growth taking place in a part of the economic system does not benefit the remainder: and the excess labour force in one sector is not absorbed by capital accumulation in the other.
>
> *1959, pp. 201–202*

Lutz did not claim explicitly that her researches were influenced by Lewis's theory. There is only one reference to Lewis in footnote 13, p. 137 in Lutz (1962a). Spaventa however wrote that she extended Lewis's theory to the Italian case in earlier works (1959, p. 203).

16 Lutz wrote

> It had been a popular exercise at one time to make calculations of the total volume of public works and other investment expenditures that would be required, especially in the South, to get rid of unemployment there within a shorter or longer period.
>
> *1962a, p. 299*

17 The credit facilities were mostly given to agricultural companies. During the years 1946–1947, the price of wheat was twenty times higher than its pre-war price. The organizations pooling wheat were purchasing wheat at a higher price than the price at which they could resell wheat to mills. To cover the difference, they were allowed to issue bills and banks accepted them. The Bank of Italy had to accept the rediscounting of those bills when banks asked for it (Lutz, 1962a, pp. 163–164).

18 Lutz raises these issues, quoting Professor Rossi Doria:

> Professor Rossi Doria has devoted many of his writings of recent years to the task of presenting – in the new light of modern techniques – the hard realities of the situation in the Mezzogiorno as, in his present view and that of many others, they still remain. His general conclusion is that, even allowing for the improvements that modern science and engineering have made possible, the pessimism of Fortunato was substantially justified. . . . Often lack of capital or lack of knowledge may stand in the way of this and other types of progress. Over a great part of Southern agriculture, however, other limitations exist. These are connected partly with irremediable physical conditions, and partly with the present excessive population pressure.
>
> *Rossi Doria,* 10 anni di policia agrarian nel Mezzogiorno, 1958, *p. xviii, in Lutz, 1962, p. 169*

19 "It seems probable, then, that the condition of zero elasticity of supply of food, in the face of a rise in industrial productivity due to investment, will have one of the following consequences" (Lutz, 1962a, p. 138).

20 Lutz wrote:

> If the demand for labour in the North of the country continues at the same high level, the most efficacious form of government aid to the South . . . may be financial and other assistance to workers and their families for migrating. The consequent relief of population pressure on the South may well be the factor which finally tips the balance in favour of that process of "autonomous" economic development and industrialization within the area which will gradually bring the average income per head there closer to parity with that in the North.
>
> *Lutz, 1962a, pp. 314–315*

21 Lutz wrote that "credit controls – meaning the amount that the central bank allows the banks and saving banks to borrowing the form of 'ordinary' discounts and advances – has been the strictest" (Lutz, 1962b, pp. 171–172).

22 This rule was presented during the Genoa Conference in 1922 (Hawtrey, 1923, p. 61).

23 Quoting Rahnema (1991), Escobar underlined that working as planners, civil servants or experts for the government of developing countries was a "lucrative industry" (2012, p. 46).

References

Adelman, Irma and Chenery, Hollis B. (1966). "The Foreign Aid and Economic Development: The Case of Greece". *The Review of Economics and Statistics*, vol. 48, no. 1, pp. 1–19

Arndt, Heinz Wolfgang (1981). "Economic Development: A Semantic History". *Economic Development and Cultural Change*. The University of Chicago Press, vol. 29, no. 3, pp. 457–466

Bagehot, Walter (1877). *Lombard Street, a Description of the Money Market*. Third edition. Henry S. King and Co.

Capie, Forrest, Goodhart, Charles, Fischer, Stanley and Schnadt, Norbert (1995). *The Future of Central Banking: The Tercentenary Symposium of the Bank of England*. Cambridge University Press

Cooley, Jane C. and Van Der Meulen Rodgers, Yana (1999). "Outstanding Female Economists in the Analysis and Practice of Development Economics". *World Development*, vol. 27, no. 8, August 1999, pp. 1397–1411

De Cecco, Marcello (2011). "The Italian Economy Seen from Abroad over 150 years". *Quaderni di Storia Economica, Economic History Working Paper*, October 2011, Banca d'Italia Eurosystema

David, Wilfred L. (1973). *Public Finance, Planning and Economic Development: Essays in Honor of Ursula Hicks*. St. Martins Press

Escobar, Arturo (2012). *Encountering Development: The Making and Unmaking of the Third World*. Second edition. Princeton University Press

Feldstein, Martin (1973). "Cost Benefit Analysis in Developing Countries: The Evaluation of Projects Financed by Aid and External Loans". In David, Wilfred L. (ed.) *Public Finance, Planning and Economic Development*, pp. 3–19. St. Martin's Press

Feldstein, Martin (1985). "Debt and Taxes in the Theory of Public Finance". Working Paper no. 1433

FitzGerald, Valpy and Heyer, Judith (2011). *Overcoming the Persistence of Inequality and Poverty*. Palgrave MacMillan

Goldsmith, Raymond (1969). *Financial Structure and Development*. Yale University Press

Guirao, Fernando and Lynch, Frances M. B. (2015). *Alan S. Milward and Contemporary European History: Collected Academic Reviews*. Routledge

Gurley, J. and Shaw, E. (1955). "Financial Aspect of Economic Development". *The American Economic Review*, vol. 45, no. 4, pp. 515–538

Hawtrey, Ralph George (1923). *Monetary Reconstruction*. Longsman, Green and Co.

Hayek, F. (1976) [2009]. *Choice in Currency: a Way to Stop Inflation*. First published by The Institute of Economic Affairs in 1976, and republished in cooperation with The Ludwig von Mises Institute in 2009

Hicks, John Richard (1939). *Value and Capital*. Clarendon Press

Hicks, John Richard (1959). *Papers by Visiting Economists*. Planning Secretariat, National Planning Council, Ceylon

Hicks, Ursula Kathleen (1938) [1970]. *The Finance of British Government 1920–1936*. Second edition with a new introduction. The Clarendon Press

Hicks, Ursula Kathleen (1946). "The Terminology of Tax Analysis". *The Economic Journal*, vol. 56, no. 221, pp. 38–50

Hicks, Ursula Kathleen (1947). *Public Finance*. Pitman Publishing Corporation

Hicks, Ursula Kathleen (1954). *British Public Finances: Their Structure and Development, 1880–1952*. Oxford University Press

Hicks, Ursula Kathleen (1961). *Development from Below: Local Government Finance in Developing Countries of the Commonwealth*. Oxford University Press

Hicks, Ursula Kathleen (1965). *Development Finance: Planning and Control*. Oxford University Press

Hicks, Ursula Kathleen and Hicks, John Richard (1978). *Federalism, Failure and Success: A Comparative Study*. Oxford University Press

Huerta de Soto, Jesus (2012). *Money, Bank, Credit and Economic Cycle*. Third edition. Ludwig von Mises Institute

Hugon, Philippe (2007). "Retour sur une cinquantaine d'années d'économie du développement dans la revue tiers monde". *Revue Tiers Monde*, vol. 3, no. 191, pp. 717–741

Jacobsen, Joyce P. (2000). "Ursula Hicks". In Dimand, Robert W., Dimand, Mary Ann and Forget, Evelyn L. (eds) *A Biographical Dictionary of Women Economists*, pp. 211–215. Edward Elgar Publisher Ltd

Kaldor, Nicolas (1963). "Taxation for Economic Development". *The Journal of Modern African Studies*, vol. 1, no. 1, pp. 7–23

Kelegama, Salman (2004). *Economic Policy in Sri Lanka: Issues and Debates. A Festschrift in Honour of Gamani Corea*. Sage Publications, India

Keynes, John Maynard (1930). *A Treatise on Money*. Volumes I and II. First edition. Palgrave Macmillan

Keynes, John Maynard (1936). "The General Theory of Employment, Interest and Money". In Moggridge, D. (ed.) *The Collected Writing of John Maynard Keynes*, volume 7. Palgrave Macmillan, for the Royal Economic Society

Kindleberger, Charles P. (1967). *Europe's Post War Growth: The Role of the Labor Supply*. Harvard University Press

Knight, J. B. (1991). "The Evolution of Development Economics". In Balasubramanyam, V. N. and Lall, S. (eds) *Current Issues in Development Economics*, pp. 10–22. Palgrave

Lewis, Arthur (1954). "Economic Development with Unlimited Supplies of Labor". *The Manchester School*, vol. 22, no. 2, pp. 139–191

Lutz, Vera (signed Vera C. Smith) (1936) [1990]. *The Rationale of Central Banking and the Free Banking Alternative*. Preface by Leland B. Yeager. King and Sons Ltd

Lutz, Vera (1950). "Italy: Economic Recovery and Development". In Howard Sylvester Ellis, *The Economics of Freedom: The Progress and Future of Aid to Europe*, pp. 299–350. Published for the Council on Foreign Relations by Harper; Royal Institute of International Affairs

Lutz, Vera (1951). "Old and New Instruments of Credit Control". Proceedings of the First International Conference, Volume II, pp. 165–182

Lutz, Vera (1952). "Real and Monetary Factors in the Determination of Employment Levels". *Quarterly Journal of Economics*, vol. 66, no. 2, pp. 251–272

Lutz, Vera (1956). "Some Characteristics of Italian Economic Development, 1950–1955". *Banca Nazionale del Lavoro Quarterly Review*, no. 39, pp. 153–185

Lutz, Vera (1958). "The Growth Process in a 'Dual' Economic System". *Banca Nazionale del Lavoro Quarterly Review*, pp. 179–324

Lutz, Vera (1962a). *Italy: A Study in Economic Development*. Royal Institute of International Affairs. Oxford University Press

Lutz, Vera (1962b). "The Central Bank and the System of Credit Control". In Sayers, Richard Sidney (ed.) *Banking in Western Europe*, pp. 154–173. Clarendon Press

Lutz, Vera (1964). "The French 'Miracle'". In Hennessy, Jossleyn, Lutz, Vera, Scimone, Giuseppe and Powell, J. Enoch, *Economic Miracles: Studies in the Resurgence of the French, German and Italian Economies Since the Second World War*, pp. 75–167. Andre Deutsch

Lutz, Vera (1965). *French Planning*. American Institute for Public Policy Research, Washington

Lutz, Vera (1969). *Central Planning for the Market Economy: An Analysis of the French Theory and Experience*. Longmans for the Institute of Economic Affairs

Lutz, Vera and Lutz, Friedrich (1950). "Monetary and Foreign Exchange Policy in Italy". *Princeton Studies in International Finance*, vol. 27, no. 1, pp. 1–45

Maes, Ivo (2008). "The Spread of Keynesian Economics: A Comparison of the Belgian and Italian Experiences (1945–1970)". *Journal of the History of Economic Thought*, vol. 30, no. 4, pp. 491–509

Masera, Rainer (1983). "Inflation, Stabilisation and Economic Recovery in Italy after the War: Vera Lutz's Assessment". *Banca Nationale del Lavoro, PSL Quarterly Review*, vol, 36, no. 144, pp. 29–50

Mazzochi, Giancarlo (1965). "Dualisme et disparités regionals". *Revue Économique*, vol. 16, no. 5, pp. 708–730

Mises, Ludwig von (1928). *Geldwertstabilisierung und Konjunkturpolitik*. G. Fischer, Jena

Rahnema, Majid (1991). *Global Poverty: A Pauperizing Myth*. Intercultural Institute of Montreal

Spaventa, Luigi (1959). "Dualism in Economic Growth". *Banca Nazionale del Lavoro Quarterly Review*, vol. 12, no. 51, pp. 386–434

Toniolo, Gianni (2013). *The Oxford Handbook of the Italian Economy Since Unification*. Oxford University Press

White, Lawrence H. (2014). "Free Banking in History and Theory". *GMU Working Paper in Economics* no. 14-07. George Mason University, Department of Economics, pp. 1–31

19

THE TWO FACES OF ECONOMIC FORECASTING IN ITALY

Vera Cao Pinna and Almerina Ipsevich

Marcella Corsi and Giulia Zacchia

Introduction

This chapter aims to analyse the contributions made by two Italian women economists, now almost completely forgotten, but who were at the forefront of political and economic debate in the 1960s and 1970s, Vera Cao Pinna and Almerina Ipsevich. Both women gave an impulse to applied economic research as support to political economics during the post-war economic reconstruction in Italy, although their ideologies and theories were very different.

Vera Cao Pinna is described as a "kind and powerful woman, courageous and unconventional, who made a firm contribution to the economic debate in Italy and Europe during the last fifty years".[1] It is thanks to her that inter-industry relationships between different industrial sectors were introduced in Italy, using the so-called input-output tables designed by Wassily Leontief in the US during the 1940s. And Almerina Ipsevich is remembered as the "real mother of business cycle analysis in this country (Italy)".[2]

Both of them, however dialectically, have been cornerstones in the development of applied economics in Italy when applied economics research was concentrated in public- and private-sector research centres, and less so at university level because of its interdisciplinary nature (at the crossroads of political economics, economic politics, economic statistics, etc.). Indeed, these two women were at the top of the two main research centres of applied economics, ISCO and the Economic Planning Study Centre, where they carried their innovative ideas forward.

Their divergent methodological approaches contributed to the birth and evolution of two main Italian schools of economic forecasting:

- one more based in structure and planning, represented by the Economic Planning Study Centre (Centro di Studi e Piani Economici) directed by Vera Cao Pinna;
- one more de-structural, linked to the business cycle analysis carried out at ISCO (Italian Institute for Business Cycle Analysis) under the supervision of Almerina Ipsevich.

Thanks to the memories of their respective families, colleagues and students and some archival research, we are able to shed some light on their private and professional lives. It was important to collect all available recollections, anecdotes and archival materials in order to portray these two women's contributions to economics, which otherwise, would have been forgotten.

The social context: Italy in the late 1950s to the 1970s

Women economists' (in)visibility

Vera Cao Pinna and Almerina Ipsevich were undoubtedly pioneers. They were women economists in influential positions in the 1960s and 1970s in Italy. To provide historical context on the (in)visibility of women economists in the years of the activity of the two women, we analysed the articles published by women authors in economic journals in Italy (see Figure 19.1).

From 1956 to 1969, on average only 1.4% of the authors published in twelve main Italian economics journals[3] were women. During this period, the highest share is recorded in 1956 when women wrote 3.8% of the articles. During the 1960s the share of articles written by women fell, not because fewer women were writing but because the overall number of articles rose. Though women's visibility increased in the second half of the 1970s, women still contributed less than 10% of the journal articles published in Italy by the end of the 1970s.

In the journals analysed women contributed to various fields, such as applied economics,[4] political economy,[5] taxation,[6] demography,[7] and history of economic thought.[8] During the 1970s, interest shifted toward finance and its impact upon day-to-day life[9] and toward wages and the redistribution of earnings.[10] Italian economic dualism and the "Southern Question" remained a constant interest over the decades for women economists in Italian economic journals. The British economist Vera Lutz addressed this topic in 1953, 1954, and 1958, as did Wilma Rotondo decades later (1978a, 1978b).

Women editors-in-chief existed during this time period, such as Enrichetta Spina and Valeria Luzzato. Both served as editors of the journal *Ricerche Economiche*, and also wrote many articles on different economic issues, especially during the 1950s. At that time, the role of editors-in-chief was administrative; these two women carried out mainly secretarial and editing activities. This editing process was no small feat, usually culminating in the re-writing of whole articles for publication. The women did not receive any publication credit for their contributions.

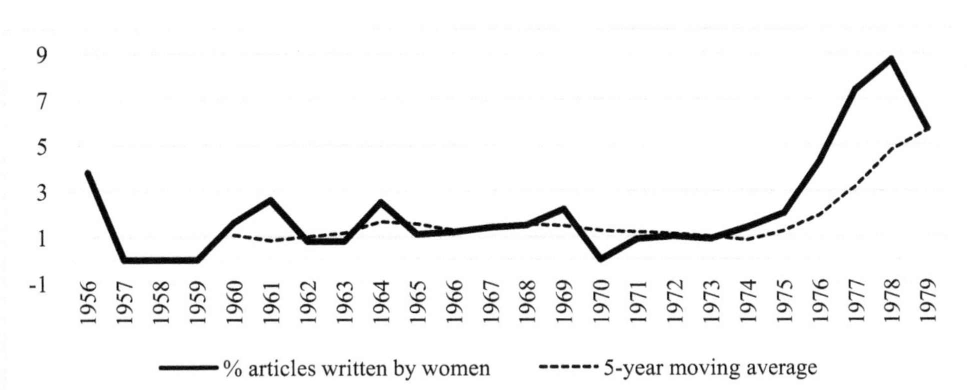

Figure 19.1 Visibility of women in Italian economic journals 1956–79

Just a few of the female authors of journal articles worked in academia, but none held an economics chair. None of the academic women was younger than 50 years old, since women usually were appointed only after their mentor's retirement. Examples include:

- Nora Federici who in 1962, at the age of 51, was the first woman to be appointed Professor of Statistics at Sapienza University of Rome;
- Costanza Costantino who in 1967, at the age of 54, was the first woman Professor of Finance at the University of Turin;
- Francesca Duchini who in 1973, at the age of 54, became Professor in the History of Economics at the Catholic University of Milan.

We found an almost complete absence of women professors in Italy, except those in faculties of Humanities and the Arts. This was a male-dominated academic network that implies the very few successful women had to rely on support from their male mentors. Two examples are Nora Federici, with the support of Corrado Gini[11] and Costanza Costantino with the support of Attilio Garino Canina and Alfredo Scotto.[12]

As a consequence of this male-dominated academic context, even in the largest Italian University (Sapienza University of Rome), where both Cao Pinna and Ipsevich studied, no chairs were awarded to women at the Faculty of Economics before 1972. When Cao Pinna was a student of economics (1931–34), the entire faculty had only male professors. The only woman working there was the librarian. Even among students the number of women was very low. For example, during her first year of university training in 1931, Vera Cao Pinna had twenty-three female colleagues, a mere 5% of the total number of students. Moreover, in the same year there had only been one female graduate in economics. Twenty-four years later in 1955 when Cao Pinna began to work as adjunct professor there, the situation had changed very little: there was just one female professor, Maria Castellani, who taught Financial Mathematics, and for the next ten years Professors Castellani and Cao Pinna were the only women in the Department of Economics at Sapienza University of Rome. As reported in Figure 19.2, the number of undergraduate students tripled from 1956 (2,539 students) to 1969 (8,549) and the share of female students increased from 7% in 1956 to 25% in 1969. But in economics departments, the share

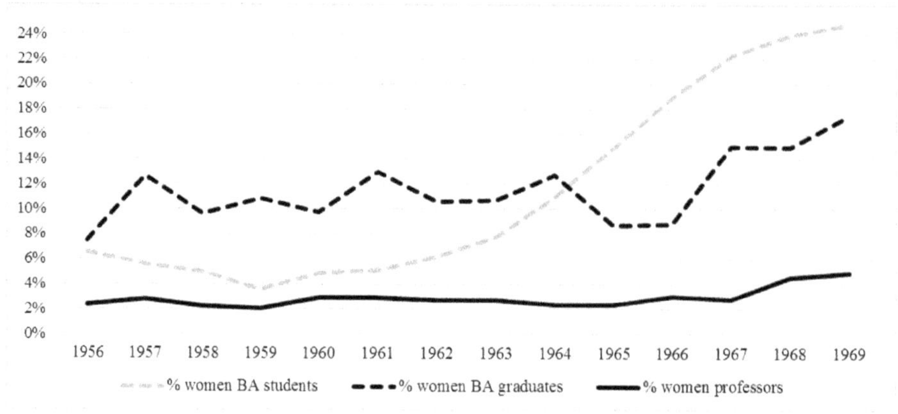

Figure 19.2 Women among registered BA students, BA graduates and professors in Economics at Sapienza University of Rome from 1956 to 1969

of women professors always remained below 5% of the total: considering together tenured and non-tenured professors in 1959, there were only two women among eighty-six professors; in 1969, there were only eight women out of a total of 162 professors.

The economic debate: economic planning in Italy and its historical context

After the Second World War, the Italian economy had to be reconstructed from scratch. Cao Pinna and Ipsevich both contributed to the post-war economic debates in Italy and Europe. Along with Ferdinando di Finizio, Libero Lenti and Gastone Miconi, the two women economists were an integral part of that group of economists and statisticians who described the analytical instruments needed to begin the first experiments in economic policy.

Following international trends that included the Marshall Plan and the OECD, in Italy in the late 1940s the debate focused mainly on three areas:

- economic planning versus *laissez-faire*;
- long-term versus short-term forecasting;
- formal input-output modelling versus informal short-term forecasting.

The term economic planning indicates the adoption, by the state, of coordinated programs in various fields of the economy. These coordinated programs extend across fiscal and monetary policies to housing and public investment in public companies, in order to meet specific economic objectives, such as GDP growth, reduction of inequality or economic dualism. Economic planning involves the pursuit of set goals, taking into account practical, real world constraints.

Economic planning is different from the central planning that is characteristic of socialist countries. In centralised planning, a central authority within the government makes the main investment decisions on production levels and prices of various products. In contrast, economic planning is based on predictions of the behaviour of economic subjects who are separate from the public operators, such as economic trends in major overseas countries and the investment decisions of private companies.

Beginning in the early 1960s in Italy, some attempts were made to adopt economic planning policies, but they failed mainly because of the inefficiency of the public administration. The history of the first implementation in Italy of economic planning and its evolution is useful to understand the social and political context in which Cao Pinna and Ipsevich worked.

The first years after the end of the Second World War (1945–47) were the years of reconstruction. The United States, through the Marshall Plan, provided the aid necessary to rebuild production capacity (machinery and equipment) destroyed during the war, and to buy raw materials and energy to allow the resumption of production. In 1947 Luigi Einaudi, Governor of the Bank of Italy, implemented a severely restrictive monetary policy, which blocked the inflation that had been high during the war and in the immediately following years. However, the restrictive policies of Einaudi also caused a fall in investment and a slowdown in growth in a period when unemployment was still high. It was not until 1949 that Italy's production returned to pre-war levels. In 1950, an agricultural reform was carried out allowing many landless farmers to become owners of small pieces of arable land. In the same year, the *Cassa del Mezzogiorno* (Fund for the South) was established. This was a public effort by the government to build infrastructure (such as roads, bridges, hydroelectric power stations, irrigation, etc.) in the southern regions (also called *Mezzogiorno*). The *Cassa del Mezzogiorno* had the aim of stimulating economic growth and development in less-developed southern Italy in order to fight economic dualism,[13] that is, to narrow the economic gap between the richer northern and much poorer southern regions of Italy.

The decade 1953–63 is usually labelled as the "economic miracle" phase in Italy. There was a rapid growth in investment and then a rapid growth in exports, both favourable to development. Throughout this period, real wages grew less than productivity, favouring firms' profits – and thus their investments – and favouring Italian industries' competitiveness in international markets. In 1954 the Vanoni Plan[14] became the first exercise of economic planning in Italy for the decade 1955–64; this plan focused on employment and income. The Vanoni Plan aimed to reach four main targets under the condition of an annual 5% increase in GNP, better international cooperation and a greater propensity toward savings:

- greater stability in labour employment,
- a better balance of payments,
- a reduction of the gap between northern and southern Italy,
- a reduction of employment in agriculture.

The fragility of the Vanoni Plan led Prime Minister Amintore Fanfani to set up a committee of economists in 1961 (chaired by Giuseppe Ugo Papi) to improve the plan; their improvements were never implemented. Meanwhile in 1963, for the first time in over fifty years, real wages rose more than productivity; this meant a redistribution of income in favour of workers. The reduction in unemployment, especially in the northern regions in the years of the "economic miracle" provided greater bargaining power for trade unions. But the wage increase caused an upward pressure on prices, and the increased consumption of imports worsened the trade balance. Therefore, the Bank of Italy adopted a restrictive monetary policy, which resulted in a sharp slowdown in growth in 1964, marking the end of the growth process of the "economic miracle". The inflationary pressures of 1963 and the slowdown of growth in 1964 revived concern about the underlying Italian economic problem: the economic dualism between the southern and the northern regions.

The decade 1963–73 can be considered the real programming phase, because the state tried to address the underlying problems of the Italian economy with programming tools. The first attempt (the Vanoni Plan of 1954) was never implemented, but after a long period of fierce debate that began in 1963, the first "Five Year Plan" – proposed by La Malfa – was approved by parliament in July 1967. In a period of slower growth (after the "monetary tightening" of 1963, investment was especially slow to recover), economic planning aimed to promote a more rational use of available resources. In 1969, after the "hot autumn" (*autunno caldo* in Italian) characterised by mass strikes and student protest, there was a new wage explosion. Moreover, in 1969, the approval of the Workers' Statute by the parliament marked a clear improvement in the bargaining position of workers and trade unions in Italy. In 1970–71 economic growth slowed further. The expansion of public spending caused, in the second half of 1972, a recovery which, however, was accompanied by inflation and deterioration in the balance of payments.

Finally, the oil crisis of 1973–74 and the consequent dramatic increase in the price of oil drastically worsened the problem of inflation and the balance of payments; mainly because Italy was dependent on foreign countries for its energy supply.

Following the major industrialised countries, Italy was forced to adopt restrictive policies.

In 1975, for the first time in the post-war period, national income decreased, unemployment grew and inflation rose. A second wave of oil price increases occurred in 1979–80, followed by a new recession in Italy and much of the rest of the world. This marked the end of this particular economic planning project in Italy.

Vera Cao Pinna and Almerina Ipsevich had an active role, even though antithetical, during these years of debate and preparation of the first Italian attempts at economic planning.

Vera Cao Pinna and Almerina Ipsevich: two parallel lives

Reconstructing the biographies of these two economists is particularly difficult because only limited documentation remains (for Cao Pinna see Fornengo 1997 and 2000). Thus, personal interviews with their relatives, former colleagues and friends have been essential to writing this chapter.[15]

In both families a father figure is almost completely absent, whereas bonds with the mother are very strong. Both women moved to Rome and studied at the same university, albeit in different fields (Cao Pinna graduated in Economics and Ipsevich in Political Science). Neither Almerina Ipsevich nor Vera Cao Pinna settled down to raise a family. They never married, never had children, and lived with their mothers for most of their lives. Their mothers grew old and became increasingly ill, and this conditioned the work they were able to do: they made fewer and fewer visits overseas, and worked increasingly from home.

The strong bonds between Cao Pinna and her mother and sister (Maria) were stressed in private correspondence dating back to 1986 between Renato Guarini (her fellow) and her friend Estelle Leontief[16] found from archival research among the few documents now available.[17] These three women (Maria, Vera and their mother) lived for one another, shut off in their own personal world right through to the last days of their lives. They all died within twenty days of each other.

Another common element is that both Cao Pinna and Ipsevich were very reserved people. Both preferred to have no one, even their closest colleagues or friends, know their personal lives. They also rarely spoke about their professional achievements with family or close friends.

Although they were heavily burdened with family duties, Vera Cao Pinna and Almerina Ipsevich were invested with great responsibilities in economics and for many years represented Italy on international economics committees, where they interacted with some of the world's most important scholars and politicians. We cannot provide a detailed list of the conferences and meetings that they attended, but from the collected documents it emerges clearly that Vera Cao Pinna was frequently called to give lectures overseas. In 1956 she spoke at the Faculty of Statistics and Economics at the University of Madrid; in 1960, she went to Cairo for the Institute for National Planning of the United Arab Republic; and in 1964 she delivered lectures in Paris at CESD-Paris (Centre européen de formation des statisticiens économistes des pays en voie de développement) on planning methods as part of balanced regional economic development. For her part, Almerina Ipsevich was a member of international committees in the European Community and participated as an expert in the OECD group on short-term forecasting. It seems apparent that both women loved their jobs. All those who dealt with them for whatever reason say that their whole lives revolved around research work and mentoring/teaching.

Cao Pinna dedicated her whole life to studying comparative economics, to applying Leontief's input-output model (activities that started in ISCO and then developed in the Economic Planning Study Centre or *Centro di Studi e Piani Economici*), and to teaching econometrics at university. The importance of her work was never formally recognised by the university system in Italy but has been recognised by her students. Students embraced her teachings and the salient characteristics of her scientific method: "methodological insights, critical rigour, and attention to empirical testing".[18] However, Italian academia never recognised her scientific value – Vera Cao Pinna was never appointed professor, always teaching with temporary contracts. In her curriculum vitae, Pinna identifies her "innovative" field of research as the main reason for her academic failures. While she was interested and deeply involved in describing and analysing the new structure of the Italian post-war economy using applied economics and statistical models, the contextual Italian academics were mostly concentrated on developing theoretical models, seemingly without concern for how those models fit into reality.

Things were different in other countries where Vera Cao Pinna and her applied economics research were really appreciated. Before her lectureship in Economic Statistics at Sapienza University of Rome was renewed in 1961, Cao Pinna had been a member of the scientific committee of the Department of Applied Economics at the Université libre de Bruxelles (1959), where she actively followed the research programme. She was the founder and Deputy President of the *Association Scientifique Européenne pour la Prévision Économique à Long Terme* (ASEPELT), founded in 1961 to bring together the best econometricians from

Table 19.1 Two biographies compared

Vera Cao Pinna	*Almerina Ipsevich*

Photograph: Unione Sarda	**Photograph:** Cristina and Giovanna Ipsevich
Date of birth: 23 December 1909	**Date of birth:** 18 November 1920
Studies: graduated in Economics (BA level) at the Royal Higher Institute for Economics and Business Studies in Rome (later to become the Faculty of Economics at Sapienza University of Rome) in 1934.	**Studies:** graduated in Political Science (BA level) at University of Rome (later to become the Faculty of Political Science at Sapienza University of Rome) in 1944.
Work: [1947–1951] US Embassy in Italy: Economic Analyst. [1952–1953] Italian Division of the Mutual Security Agency [1954–1955] National Committee for Business Cycle Analysis. [1955–1957] ISCO (Italian Institute for Business Cycle Analysis) [1958–1964] Banco di Sicilia: Economic Analyst. [1965–1975] Economic Planning Study Centre – *Centro di Studi e Piani Economici*: Chief Research officer. [1976–1986] Information Technology and Systems Study Institute (ISIS): Director of Research	**Work:** [1948–1954] National Committee for Business Cycle Analysis [1955–1995] ISCO (Italian Institute for Business Cycle Analysis): Research officer, then Director (1973) and Vice President (1993).
Date of death: 11 June 1986	**Date of death:** 18 March 2003

all over Europe. She contributed actively to the scientific dissemination of works by the ASEPELT by making detailed critical analyses of the main sources of statistics and the methods conventionally used to measure consumption.[19] Wassily Leontief, Nobel prize-winner, mentor and friend of Vera Cao Pinna remembers her, in an Italian local newspaper article, as the woman who "understood the importance of statistics and mathematics to understand economics in depth", and stressed that she was the first Italian economist to "deal with measuring production, with creating a link – a real liaison – between theory and the empirical observation of economic facts".[20]

Almerina Ipsevich, on the other hand, dedicated her professional life[21] to ISCO (Italian Institute for Business Cycle Analysis).[22] She started working there in 1955 as assistant of the first President, Gustavo Miconi, and then became director in 1973, and vice president in 1992. She concentrated her efforts, as reported in one of her notes,

> to define constantly new fields of research to maintain a frontier role between statistical and economic analyses, that, starting from the intuition of a phenomenon, allows to construct and to provide new data, intelligently prepared and checked to formulate the first hypothesis of individual behaviours.

A whole group of economists, statisticians, economics journalists, civil servants and industrialists grew up with her, and they respected her curiosity and her approach to the day-to-day observation of events, which would then be summarised using an economic and social approach, never taking anything for granted.

Vera Cao Pinna and Almerina Ipsevich: a methodological contrast

Although the lives of these two women were similar, when we look at the contents of what they said and wrote it is easy to see their ideological distance.

The two women fell on opposing sides of the economic debate surrounding applied economics: short-term economic analysis (business cycle analysis) and the analysis of relationships between sectors. At the time, many people believed there was rivalry between Vera Cao Pinna and Almerina Ipsevich, but those who actually knew them said that these two women were parts of related, though completely separate, networks.

Ipsevich was reticent and rarely moved outside Rome. She was a moderate right-winger, mainly linked in her work to the banker and politician Guido Carli and industrialist Franco Mattei. Cao Pinna on the other hand worked mainly for the Ministry for Economic Planning, for the Italian delegation of the US Mutual Security Agency, and at university.

From the analysis of their curriculum vitae (see Table 19.1) we find that the two women worked from 1954 to 1957 in the same institution (the National Committee for Business Cycle Analysis, later ISCO, Italian Institute for Business Cycle Analysis) on applied economics but on different perspectives:

- Cao Pinna was research director of the Input-Output Unit, working on the update of the first input-output table for Italy;
- Ipsevich was also a research director, working instead on short-term forecasting.

While Cao Pinna was adapting the Italian input-output tables to evaluate the impact of the US-financed Marshall Plan for reconstruction of a country ravaged by war,[23] Ipsevich was working on a series of data collection techniques and the data processing that would characterise the research activities of the Institute in the next decades.

In 1957, Cao Pinna decided to leave ISCO because, as she explains in her curriculum vitae, "the Institute (ISCO) had begun to concentrate more on short-term economic analysis" (Cao Pinna's own note).

Although we cannot say that there was rivalry between Vera Cao Pinna and Almerina Ipsevich, we can argue that they had different ideological and methodological approaches to economic forecasting.

Economic forecasting, *stricto sensu*, is the identification and quantification of certain developments related to both real and monetary economic aspects of society (economic growth, inflation, employment, etc.). When preparing an economic forecast, due account must be taken of many different elements. One of the most important of these is the period of time to which the forecast has been applied.

A difference is usually made between short- and medium-/long-term forecasting. There is an economic explanation for this. The idea behind medium-term forecasting is that specification must be made of the time needed for families, companies and central or local government to reach certain targets, and this is the time we need to see if certain variables have settled down. In contrast, short-term forecasts can be made by observing the immediate effects upon a pre-existing situation and by studying what changes arise.

For economic forecasting in Italy during that time, in addition to the various national ministries, there were two main Institutes: the ISCO which, as we described above, concentrated mainly on short-term forecasts; and the Economic Planning Study Centre (*Centro di Studi e Piani Economici)*, for long-term forecasts, where Vera Cao Pinna worked from 1965 to 1975 in order to "specialize further in economic forecasting and analysis" (Cao Pinna's curriculum vitae).

Ipsevich preferred short-term forecasts of 12–18 months, where structures were considered unchangeable; Cao Pinna emphasised the medium and long term, and analysed structural changes to economic systems. This difference between the two, as well as the timescale of their forecasts, can be seen in their different methodological approaches. Ipsevich was willing to use any element, including economic sentiment indicators, which would help in analysing upward or downward trends in possible economic scenarios. In contrast, Cao Pinna relied more upon formalised structure and based all her models on the Leontief matrix.

They can, therefore, be described as two sides of the economic forecasting coin: on the one hand, Cao Pinna used quantitative methods that, considering only the quantities in a series of data, were supposed to show future trends in economic variables. In contrast, Ipsevich advocated the development of qualitative methods, useful for eluding the more determinist quantitative methods. She mainly wanted to understand changes in phenomena as a way of understanding the direction in which such changes were leading.

Cao Pinna used formal statistical methods in forecasting to represent those factors that influence economic variables. She refined and adapted to the Italian and European situation those models, which were based on the dealings between economic sectors that could be obtained using double-entry input-output tables. These were the methods devised by her friend and master Wassily Leontief in the 1940s, although historical precedent can be seen in Quesnay's *Tableau économique* (1758). Cao Pinna herself speaks of the

> statistical and mathematical analysis of interdependence between the various forms of economic activity (manufacturing, consuming, investing) [. . . that] allows one to describe the structure of an economic system in numerical terms and to explain how it develops. . . . Statistical analysis uses a large, double-entry table called the *matrix* of

> economic interdependence. . . . In practical application of the model for forecasting purposes, it is (therefore) necessary and sufficient to estimate the probable fluctuations in final demand {Y}, to determine the orders of magnitude of changes which (in conditions of relative price stability in a system) such fluctuations will give rise to at a general level of activity and to the structure of a national production system.
>
> *Cao Pinna, 1961a*

In 1952 Cao Pinna had already become a pioneer in drawing up, with Hollis B. Chenery and Paul G. Clark,[24] and a small number of young researchers, the first ever table of structural interdependences for Italy related to the year 1950. This 1950 table was the first application of input-output analysis to Italian economic problems.

The input-output table was used to illustrate some of the features of the Italian economy described in the book, co-authored by Cao Pinna, *The Structure and Growth of the Italian Economy* prepared by the Mutual Security Agency. As reported in the introduction, the book is innovative in the sense that:

> Up to now, most attention has been given to the development of the theoretical scheme and the compilation of the basic tables. The application of input-output analysis to practical problems of economic policy is only just beginning. It is as an illustration of such practical applications that our work in Italy may be of some general significance.
>
> *Chenery et al., 1953, p. 5*

The general significance of this applied work on Italy was identified by established economists such as David Henderson, chief economist at the Economics and Statistics Department at the OECD,

> [T]his is a most impressive piece of applied economic research, which deserves a wider circulation than it seems likely to get in its present form. It should be of interest to all economists who are concerned with the quantitative aspects of national economic problems.
>
> *Henderson, 1955, p. 151*

One main innovation of Cao Pinna was outlining a regional input-output model in which the north and south of Italy are distinguished. A second innovation was her use of the input-output model to estimate the effects of economic policies toward achieving the aim, as agreed upon by the OECD countries,[25] of a 5% yearly increase in total output between 1951 and 1956.

When she was working at ISCO, Cao Pinna directed the updating of the national input-output tables to 1953. She also acted as lead consultant for the Italian Statistical Institute (ISTAT) in creating tables for the years 1959 and 1965. After that, ISTAT began drawing up the series of tables. The introduction of intersectoral tables became an integral part of the national accounts in Italy and in European countries from 1970, with the introduction of the European System of Integrated Economic Accounts (ESA). Currently all industrialised countries frequently publish input-output tables, as do many countries in the developing world.

Almerina Ipsevich, who had a great sensitivity for economics and who was amazingly skilled in observing numbers, instead introduced quarterly reports on economic trends in Italy. In particular, she pushed to have quarterly income surveys in Italy (rather than yearly) mainly because of increased reliability of the use of quarterly statistics in estimates and forecasting performance.

As reported in one of her few notes that we found, Ipsevich firmly believed in the importance of data and data collecting, "because any researcher that wants to investigate new phenomena must also build the data in the sense of putting in place methods and research for gathering the needed data" (Ipsevich's own note).

She worked toward data-based analysis by introducing at ISCO the Short-term Economic Business Tendency Surveys for qualitative data collecting about the economic short-term forecast. The surveys consisted of questionnaires distributed to entrepreneurs and managers about their perceptions of the current situation and their expectations for the near future, regarding both their own business and the general situation of the national economy. Answers obtained from the survey were aggregated in the form of *balances* (differences between positive and negative answers). Balances were then used to build indicators about production expectations.

Ipsevich also worked at ISCO on an *informal*[26] forecasting process based on the interplay between experts who forecast how certain variables were likely to change. It is a complicated process that requires careful selection of information, a firm understanding of economic theory and statistical and mathematical tools and, especially, great experience in sifting through all the various signals. This can only be achieved by continuously observing the economy, especially its short-term fluctuations, where details from the past are mixed up with predictions of the future. The ISCO forecasting model was short-term (eighteen months), starting from the assumption that most of the relevant trends are predetermined by observable events. Consequently, such trends were extrapolated by using a series of indicators, and then brought into line with national official statistical figures.

Vera Cao Pinna and Almerina Ipsevich are therefore two kindred spirits of applied economics through their use of statistics. On the one hand, both contributed to "technical" statistics concerning the definition of formalised statistical models to be used to understand the current situation and make forecasts. On the other, both contributed to "data" statistics, the use of which involves great care in selecting their source and in defining what information can be used to observe an economy.

In light of the first attempts at economic planning in Italy, the distance between Vera Cao Pinna and Almerina Ipsevich widens enormously.

On one side, Vera Cao Pinna was a key person advocating models for economic planning based on input-output tables. The objective was to turn the Italian economy back toward collective consumption with planners selecting specific sectors to emphasise in the economy, using input-output estimates of final demand. Cao Pinna believed "that even a country like Italy could promptly build its own future by means of economic planning or, at least, by a more coordinated positioning of politics, general and sectorial, based on serious in-depth studies" (Cao Pinna, 1971, p. 20). On the other side, Almerina Ipsevich, along with Guido Carli (Bank of Italy) and Emilio Colombo (Treasury Minister), were magnets for those who felt that the economy should follow market trends, without being forced in any direction but to avoid inflation which would inevitably result from wage increases and limits placed upon supply.

Ipsevich was firmly against medium-term planning because she saw this as running an economy by law. She critically saw this as the first step toward centralised planning and socialism.

Cao Pinna tried, using econometric models and "her" tables, to contribute to economic policy changes.[27] Indeed, she took an active part in the economic planning, during the preparatory stages of the Vanoni Plan of 1954 by forecasting private consumption levels for 1964. In 1961 she also designed an econometric model (based on the input-output analysis) for the Economic Planning Minister to ensure compatibility and consistency in statistics for the first part of the 1965–69 planning measures. She then presented a critical analysis of the structure and limits of this model to the World Conference of Econometricians.

Ipsevich, instead, was an active member of a committee of experts created in 1968 by the Italian Statistical Institute (ISTAT) for designing new statistical analyses and methods for estimating national accounts.

As we explained previously in this chapter, the "hot autumn" of 1969 saw a series of long strikes; new collective bargaining agreements and wage increases exacerbated contrasts between the supporters and non-supporters of public intervention in economics. The oil crises, the lowering of supply and then the onset of stagflation all contributed to the death of economic planning. Cao Pinna regretted having to see "a trend towards documenting and overlooking the rhythm of development . . . rather than looking towards a brighter future" (Cao Pinna, 1971, p. 25).

Final thoughts

We have shown the contribution made by two women economists in Italy during the 1960s and 1970s who had been more or less forgotten. A final consideration concerns the "silent" contribution made by so many women in the past, whose contributions are in danger of being lost forever because women did not sign their works with their full names.

It is so in the case of Almerina Ipsevich whose full name never appeared in publications although she directed and supervised the research publications edited by ISCO. She signed just one publication with her initials (A.I.) and it is only thanks to her colleague Giovanni De Cindio that we were able to find it and to piece together her contribution to the economic profession in Italy.

Vera Cao Pinna, instead, was an innovator, choosing a field of research completely new at the time: input-output analysis. This innovation unfortunately turned out to be a failure for her recognition in Italy. Although she was well known by many of her colleagues in other countries, Cao Pinna was pushed aside by Italian universities, which refused to award her a professorship in economic statistics. Furthermore, Cao Pinna was not credited as the mother of input-output analysis in Italy by the Italian Statistical Institute (ISTAT). ISTAT does not even mention her name on their webpage dedicated to intersectional analyses.

Let us wind up by reprinting a brief summary of the lives of these women given by Innocenzo Cipolletta, who knew and worked with both of them:

> Vera Cao Pinna challenged a men's world, that of post-war Italy, and stood out as a leading scholar in her analysis of the relationships between sectors. In doing so, she advanced our understanding of the structure of the Italian economy and its economic policy after reconstruction. . . . Almerina Ipsevich pragmatically introduced interdisciplinary analysis because she really understood statistics without allowing herself to be overwhelmed by formulas like many of her contemporaries. Her greatest contribution has been how to understand reality by looking at the exceptions rather than at the rules.
>
> *Interview conducted with the present authors on 27/01/2014*

Notes

1 Claudio Mazziotta (1986).

2 *Il Sole 24 Ore*, 21/03/2003, p. 11.

3 We analysed a wide range of journals in terms of editorial boards and research fields: journals published by banks' research centres such as *BNL Quarterly Review, Moneta e Credito, Rassegna Economica, Bancaria* and *Review of Economic Conditions in Italy*; journals close to the Confederation of Italian Industry

including *Rivista di Politica Economica, L'industria* and *Mondo Aperto*; and finally journals more linked to academia such as *Il Giornale degli Economisti* and *Annali di Economia, Rivista Internazionale di Scienze Sociali, Ricerche Economiche* and *Economia Internazionale*.

4 The studies on applied economics include Vera Cao Pinna 1952, 1954, 1955, 1956a, 1956b, 1958 and Enrichetta Spina, 1955, 1959, 1960, 1961, 1963, 1965.

5 The political economy studies include Danila Cremona Della Casa, 1953, 1961.

6 The taxation studies include Costanza Costantino, 1951, 1955, 1956, 1958.

7 The demography studies include Nora Federici, 1953a, 1953b, 1954a, 1954b.

8 The history of economic thought studies include Francesca Duchini, 1957a, 1957b.

9 Gianna Maria Sanacuore has two pieces on finance in 1972 and 1973.

10 Renata Targetti Lenti has three pieces on wages and earnings redistribution in 1974, 1975, 1977.

11 Nora Federici's academic mentor was Corrado Gini, Professor of Statistics at Sapienza University of Rome, a prominent statistician, demographer and sociologist who developed the Gini coefficient, a measure of the income inequality in a society still commonly used in the literature.

12 Costanza Costantino's academic mentors were both Attilio Garino Canina (whose biography she would later write), Director of the Institute of Finance at the Department of Economics at Trieste University, and Alfredo Scotto from the Department of Economics at Genoa University.

13 Dualism between northern and southern Italy has deep historical roots, consolidated (and even extended) after the country's political unification in 1861. See Galasso (2014) for an excellent analysis of Italian dualism.

14 The Vanoni Plan was the ten-year plan for developing employment and wages for 1955–64. It took the name of the economist and Minister for Economic Planning who drew it up.

15 We wish to thank the following for sharing their memories with us: Innocenzo Cipolletta and Giovanni De Cindio who worked with Almerina Ipsevich at ISCO; Cristina and Giovanna Ipsevich, nieces of Almerina Ipsevich who gave us biographical details, photos and a curriculum vitae written by their aunt; Dolly Tommasi, a close friend of Almerina Ipsevich when she was in Agesci; Francesca Pizzetti from the Centro Documentale Agesci, who showed us the Officer Reports and other materials by Almerina Ipsevich. Thanks are also due to Alessandro Roncaglia, who worked both with Almerina Ipsevich and Vera Cao Pinna and to Renato Guarini, who worked with Vera Cao Pinna from 1959 to 1960 on the input-output tables for Italy. Cao Pinna left him all her work and books.

16 Wife of Wassily Leontief. They usually met during their respective visits to America and Italy.

17 Unfortunately, most of the books, notes and letters belonging to Vera Cao Pinna inherited by Renato Guarini have been lost in the intervening years.

18 From the memorial lecture given by Renato Guarini in Cagliari, organised in memory of Vera Cao Pinna on 18/11/1988.

19 See Cao Pinna 1962 and 1963.

20 Leontief's interview, *L'Unione Sarda*, 19 November 1988, p. 6.

21 In parallel with her work at ISCO, in her spare time she was part of AGI (Association of Female Italian Catholic Guides and Scouts). At AGI she was a real leader and landmark figure for many generations of Catholic girls.

22 ISCO (*Istituto Nazionale per lo Studio della Congiuntura*), incorporating the former National Committee for Business Cycle Analysis, was formally founded in 1955 with the support of Ezio Vanoni, Finance Minister and later Minister for Economic Planning. The aim of the institute was to monitor and examine economic trends in Italy, with an eye also on the world economy. Gastone Miconi, a lawyer at the National Court of Audit who believed in the relevance of statistics, and the economist Ferdinando Di Fenizio, were its founding members. For a complete analysis, see De Cindio (1993).

23 There was a specific target set for all OECD countries.

24 Hollis B. Chenery and Paul G. Clark worked with Wassily Leontief at the Harvard Economic Research Project. Chenery, director of the Italian Division of the Mutual Security Agency (the MSA was responsible for the development and administration of US military and economic post-war assistance programs in Europe), called Vera Cao Pinna to Rome – she was in Paris – from 1951 to 1953 to work on the construction of the first input-output table, drawn up for Italy for the year 1950.

25 The Organisation for European Economic Cooperation (OEEC) was established in 1948 to run the US-financed Marshall Plan. By making individual governments recognise the interdependence of their economies, it paved the way for a new era of cooperation that was to change the face of Europe. Encouraged by its success and the prospect of carrying its work forward on a global stage, Canada and the US joined OEEC members in signing the new Organisation for Economic Co-operation and

Development (OECD) Convention on 14 December 1960. The OECD was then officially born on 30 September 1961, when the Convention entered into force.

26 The *informal* method or *ingenuous* forecast can be extremely subjective, but it allows a greater amount of information to be considered. As Löwenthal (1988) stresses, forecasting thus becomes the product of the "accumulated wisdom" of the analyst, or the result of his/her experience and ability in detecting new trends. See Cipolletta (1992) for details of the method used.

27 Several works in this context are highly revelatory: Cao Pinna 1956a, 1961b and 1969.

References

Cao Pinna, V. (1952), "Nuovi metodi di programmazione economica: la input output analysis", *Rivista di Politica Economica*, XLII (1): 34–53.

Cao Pinna, V. (1954), "Le discussioni di Varenna sulla teoria della input output analysis", *Economia Internazionale*, VII (3): 573–605.

Cao Pinna, V. (1955), "Applicazioni ed esperienze del metodo input output in vari paesi", *Economia Internazionale*, VIII (2): 97–143.

Cao Pinna, V. (1956a), "Alcuni suggerimenti dottrinari e pratici sulla metodologia della programmazione economica", *Rassegna Economica*, XX (4): 681–700.

Cao Pinna, V. (1956b), "Stabilità e progresso dell'economia mondiale nelle discussioni del I congresso dell'Associazione Internazionale delle Scienze Economiche", *Rivista di Politica Economica*, XLVI (7–8): 605–645.

Cao Pinna, V. (1958), "Principali caratteristiche strutturali di due economie mediterranee, Spagna e Italia", *Economia Internazionale*, XI (2): 259–311.

Cao Pinna, V. (1961a), "Interdipendenze strutturali", *Enciclopedia Italiana*, Treccani.

Cao Pinna, V. (1961b), *Schema metodologico per una programmazione 'indicativa' dello sviluppo economico sul piano regionale*, Centro Nazionale di Prevenzione e di Difesa Sociale.

Cao Pinna, V. (1962), "Validité théorique et empirique d'une prévision globale de la croissance de l'économie italienne", in R.C. Geary (ed.), *Europe's Future Consumption*, Amsterdam, North-Holland, 111–161.

Cao Pinna, V. (1963), "Critique des méthodes de prévision de la consommation et suggestions pratiques", in J. Sandee (ed.), *Europe's Future Consumption*, Amsterdam, North-Holland, 245–261.

Cao Pinna, V. (1969) *Tentativo di compilazione di un sistema multi-regionale di contabilità intersettoriale*, Centro di Studi e Piani Economici.

Cao Pinna, V. (1971), *Econometria e pianificazione: raccolta di saggi in memoria di Camillo Righi*, Milano, Etas Kompass.

Chenery, H.B., Clark, P. and V. Cao Pinna (1953), *The Structure and Growth of the Italian Economy*, Rome, U.S. Mutual Security Agency.

Cipolletta, I. (1992), "Il percorso di uno statistico: dall'Italia del miracolo economico ai timori del declino industriale", *Statistica & Società*, III (2): 3–7.

Costantino, C. (1951), "La sensibilità alla congiuntura delle imposte italiane sui consumi", *Rivista Internazionale di Scienze Sociali*, LIX (4): 313–333.

Costantino, C. (1955), "Ancora sulla divergenza di opinioni intorno alla traslocazione dell'imposta generale del reddito", *Giornale Degli Economisti e Annali di Economia*, XIV (5–6): 254–280.

Costantino, C. (1956), "Finanza pubblica in Danimarca", *Rivista di Politica Economica*, XLVI (12): 1123–1140.

Costantino, C. (1958), "Sulle moderne dottrine relative all'incidenza delle imposte sul reddito", *Giornale Degli Economisti e Annali di Economia*, XVII (5–6): 265–292.

Cremona Della Casa, D. (1953), "Il *pigouvian effect*", *Rivista di Politica Economica*, XLIII (9): 914–923.

Cremona Della Casa, D. (1961), "Note sulle curve d'indifferenza", *Giornale degli Economisti e Annali di Economia*, XX (7–8): 482–502.

De Cindio, G. (1993), "L'attività di ricerca dell'ISCO", *Rassegna di Lavori dell'ISCO*, X (1): 1–14.

Dimand, R.W. (1995), "The Neglect of Women's Contribution to Economics", in Dimand, M.A., Dimand, R.W. and E.L. Forget (eds.), *Women of Value*, Cheltenham, Edward Elgar, 39–59.

Duchini, F. (1957a), "La pianificazione nei paesi dell'Europa orientale", *Rivista Internazionale di Scienze Sociali*, LXV (1): 25–44.

Duchini, F. (1957b), "Teorie contemporanee del profitto", *Rivista Internazionale di Scienze Sociali*, LXV (6): 541–545.

Federici, N. (1953a), "Aspetti della situazione demografica italiana in base ai primi risultati del censimento del 1951", *Moneta e Credito*, VI (23): 373–410.

Federici, N. (1953b), "Some Aspect of the Italian Demografic Situation: the First Results of 1951 Census", *BNL Quarterly Review*, VI (25): 107–118.

Federici, N. (1954a), "Recent Forecasts of the Future Growth of Population in Italy", *BNL Quarterly Review*, VII (28): 58–69.

Federici, N. (1954b), "Recenti previsioni sul futuro sviluppo demografico dell'Italia", *Moneta e Credito*, VII (25): 32–47.

Fornengo, G. (1997), "Vera Cao Pinna (1909–1986): un'antesignana dell'econometria in Italia", *Storia del Pensiero Economico*, 33–34: 159–182.

Fornengo, G. (2000), "Vera Cao Pinna", in Dimand, R.W., Dimand, M.A. and E.L. Forget (eds.), *A Biographical Dictionary of Women Economists*, Cheltenham, Edward Elgar, 343–346.

Galasso, G. (2014), *Alle origini del dualismo italiano: Regno di Sicilia e Italia Centro-Settentrionale dagli Altavilla agli Angiò (1100–1350)*, Soveria Mannelli, Rubbettino Editore.

Henderson, P.D. (1955), "Review: The Structure and Growth of the Italian Economy", *The Economic Journal*, 65 (257): 149–151.

Ipsevich, A. (1959), "Appunto sulla rilevazione del reddito trimestrale", in AA.VV. (1963), *Rassegna dei lavori interni dell'ISCO*, pp. 133–141.

Löwenthal, P. (1988), *Analyse conjoncturelle: vigie de l'économie*, Editions Universitaires De Boek.

L'unione Sarda (1988), *Intervista: il Nobel Wassily Leontief, professore di Modigliani e Samuelson*, L'Unione Sarda, 14 November, p. 6.

Lutz, V.C. (1953), "Italian Economic Developments in 1952 as Reported by the Bank of Italy", *BNL Quarterly Review*, VI (25): 92–106.

Lutz, V.C. (1954), "Development Problems in Southern Italy: The Second Conference of the Cassa per il Mezzogiorno", *BNL Quarterly Review*, VII (28–29): 46–51.

Lutz, V.C. (1958), "The Growth Process in a 'Dual' Economic System", *BNL Quarterly Review*, XI (46): 279–324.

Mazziotta, C. (1986), "Ricordando Vera Cao Pinna", *Politica ed Economia*, XVII (9): 15–17.

Rotondo, W. (1978a), "Destinazione settoriale delle risorse finanziarie affluite alla Cassa per il Mezzogiorno e investimenti realizzati o indotti", *Rassegna Economica*, XLII (6): 1465–1482.

Rotondo, W. (1978b), "Impegni e flussi di spesa dello Stato per la Cassa per il Mezzogiorno", *Rassegna Economica*, XLII (3): 709–721.

Sanacuore, G.M. (1972), "Analisi di alcuni modelli di coordinamento tra politica monetaria e politica finanziaria in una economia aperta", *Rivista di Politica Economica*, LXII (3): 316–348.

Sanacuore, G.M. (1973), "Friedman e i neokeynesiani, una controversia ancora aperta", *Rivista di Politica Economica*, LXIII (8–9): 961–978.

Spina, E. (1955), "L'industria elettrica britannica in regime statale", *Ricerche Economiche*, IX (6):1–24.

Spina, E. (1959), "Lo sviluppo economico dei paesi comunisti dell'Europa orientale", *Ricerche Economiche*, XIII(1): 41–68.

Spina, E. (1960), "La determinazione dell'efficienza economica degli investimenti nell'URSS", *Ricerche Economiche*, XIV (4): 473–504.

Spina, E. (1961), "Il Commonwealth e l'integrazione europea", *Ricerche Economiche*, XV (1): 26–60.

Spina, E. (1963), "Sulla funzione dei prezzi nell'economia dei paesi socialisti", *Ricerche Economiche*, XVII (3): 284–300.

Spina, E. (1965), "La bilancia dei pagamenti degli Stati Uniti e la liquidità internazionale", *Ricerche Economiche*, XIX (1): 94–106.

Targetti Lenti, R. (1974), "Un'analisi disaggregata delle variazioni salariali", *Giornale degli Economisti e Ennali di Economia*, XXXIII (1, 2): 103–134.

Targetti Lenti, R. (1975), "Prezzi, costo del lavoro e margini di profitto in un'economia aperta", *Rivista di Politica Economica*, LXV (3): 327–364.

Targetti Lenti, R. (1977), "Risorse naturali, rendite e distribuzione dei redditi", *Giornale degli Economisti e Annali di Economia*, XXXVI (7–8): 419–457.

PART V

Beginning mid-20th, extending into the 21st century

20
THE FIRST 100 YEARS OF FEMALE ECONOMISTS IN SUB-SAHARAN AFRICA

Lola Fowler and Robert W. Dimand

Introduction

The earliest literature on economic thought on Africa was not by Africans. The economic experience of West Africa was surveyed and analyzed first by writers from colonizing countries (e.g. Lady Flora Lugard 1905; Allan McPhee 1926; Margery Perham, ed. 1946–48a, b), often associated with colonial administration (see Barbara Ingham 1992). Africans had no chance to tell their own story until centuries after the onset of European economic contact with sub-Saharan Africa, toward the demise of colonialism. Two such scholars in the African diaspora are Howard University's George W. Brown, a pioneer with *Economic History of Liberia* penned as his 1938 LSE PhD dissertation and published in 1941, and *Politics in West Africa* as the most eminent example by Nobel laureate W. Arthur Lewis in 1965. Even later are contributions by African men working at African universities (e.g. R. Olufemi Ekundare 1973, at the University of Ife).[1]

The African Economic Research Consortium (AERC 1994, 2010) has given recent attention and encouragement to increasing participation of women in economics in Africa, as graduate students, university teachers, and in government. The 2016/17 AERC Annual Report states that 32% of participants in AERC research activities that year were women. Notably, approximately half of the 43 participants across two AERC econometrics workshops in 2016 and 2017 were women of Africa, and 13 out of 25 new fellowships for AERC's Collaborative PhD Programme went to women. Of 1,140 members in the Association for the Advancement of African Women Economists (AAAWE),[2] 898 were African women economists, of whom 695 lived in Africa (410 professionals, 285 students) and 203 outside Africa (92 professionals, 111 students).[3] The AAAWE has active branches in Ghana, Nigeria, South Africa and Uganda (see Asiedu 2015). Despite its substantial membership, the AAAWE reports:

> Data suggests that the lack of female representation is even more pervasive in African countries, especially in academia. The Economics Department at the University of Burundi has 15 male faculty members and NO female faculty members; the Economics Department at the University of Cape Coast in Ghana also has 18 male faculty members and NO female members. Women constitute only 10% (3 women and 27 men) of the Economics Department faculty at the University of Dar es Salaam
>
> *AAAWE website; emphasis in the original*

Yet several African women economists have attained prominence, primarily in the public sector rather than academia.[4]

This chapter examines the first generation of female economists in Africa. After an introductory overview, the next three sections deal with Southern Africa, East Africa and West Africa, highlighting female economists from each region. There is a short biography of each female economist from the respective sub-region in Africa, followed by their contributions to the economic history of their country. Notice is taken of their writings (articles and books) as well as of books and articles about them. This chapter considers the contributions only of female economists originally from Africa, whether white or black, excluding for example Polly Hill, who spent a decade at the University of Ghana before returning to Cambridge (see Dimand and Saffu 2017).

Economic history of Africa in relation to African women economists, introductory overview

Patrick Manning (1987) aptly identified that there are three separate literatures on economic history in Africa, the pre-colonial, colonial and post-colonial literature. Pre-colonial West Africa economic literature focused mainly on trade, especially along the trans-Saharan trade routes. Gold, ivory and slaves including skilled troops were traded for salts, beads and metal goods. Koumbi Saleh was a major trade center in the Ghana Empire (*c.*300–*c.*1235) and trade flourished under it through to the Kanem Bornu Empire. The accounts of such economic activities were recorded by Islamic scholars, notable among whom was the celebrated traveler Ibn Battuta of Tangier. The pre-colonial period also saw the rise of female political and economic leaders such as Amina of Zaria (Nigeria), Queen Nzhingha (Angola) and Yaa Asantewa. These women promoted trade, resisted European takeover and the slave trade, but were more noted for their role in national defense.

The colonial literature focused on international trade and government. There exist divergent views on data and perspective for this period. There is a colonial view and a national view which included those opposed to forms of colonialism but who accepted colonial data and worked within a colonial framework.

Foray Bay College, the first college in Africa founded during the colonial period in 1827, began issuing degrees in 1856 when it became affiliated with Durham College, England, but its focus was on the liberal arts of the time which did not include political economy. Foray Bay College is notable for preparing the first set of formally educated Africans who would later advocate for self-rule. The University of Cape Town was established in 1829 and later taught economics as a discipline and thus the first generation of indigenous African economists emerged during the early 20th century. For example, Sheila van der Horst graduated from the University of Cape Town in 1930 and, after earning a PhD at the London School of Economics, returned to teach from 1933 until she retired in 1974 (Archer and Heywood 2003). Several female economists wrote book reviews published in economic journals at the time. A few women published their own papers, notably in the *South African Journal of Economics* from its foundation in 1933 (Pollak 1933a, 1933b, 1936, 1940; Van der Horst 1934, 1935, 1939, 1941). It was common to find these economists employing their pens as weapons to caution against the evils of their day. This chapter studies examples of such women: Hansi Pauline Pollak, Helen Suzman and Sheila van der Horst from South Africa. These were the first generation of university-educated women, members of the white liberal opposition to apartheid and outspoken opponents of the white supremacist National Party. Their contribution in addressing economic and political issues remained relevant long after their time.

Post-colonial literature indicates the growing female literacy levels in Africa as more and more women attained post-secondary education. This study showcases Gloria Nikoi of Ghana, Dambisa Moyo of Zambia, Ngozi Okonjo-Iweala of Nigeria and Ellen Johnson Sirleaf of Liberia to mention a few. Though African women economists are substantially under-represented in African universities, several African female economists have taken up high-ranking political positions as well as positions in international economics agencies, such as the World Bank, and have significantly affected the economic wellbeing of their respective countries. Curiously, there is no prominent African woman economist in Francophone Africa. In contrast, in Tanzania, Ghana, Namibia, Liberia and Nigeria, female economists have emerged as finance ministers, a foreign affairs minister, central bankers, and even a prime minister! These women are perceived as technocrats (hence, not perceived by politicians as rivals) with internationally recognized skills and credentials from reputable institutions such as Harvard, Oxford, and Massachusetts Institute of Technology (MIT), with World Bank experience and the like. These credentials matter to aid donors such as the International Monetary Fund and Paris Club. From Hansi Pollak to Ngozi Okonjo-Iweala, the voices of African female economists are now heard around the world.

Southern Africa

Hansi Pollak – South Africa[5]

Hansi Pauline Pollak, economist, sociologist, welfare worker and activist, was born in Johannesburg in 1905. Pollak published actively in economics in the 1930s. She published several articles in the early volumes of the *South African Journal of Economics* (Pollak 1933a, 1933b, 1936, 1940, and two book reviews in 1934), on such topics as women workers in Witwatersrand industries and the growth of the European-descended population in South Africa.

She served as an officer in South Africa's Women's Army Auxiliary Services during World War II. In 1944 she was seconded to undertake welfare among refugees and displaced persons, as deputy director of welfare, for five United Nations Refugee Relief Association (UNRRA) camps in the Middle East. She was also director of field services among displaced persons in the British, French and American occupied zones in Germany.

Pollak served as director of welfare services for the World Council of Churches from 1953 to 1954. She was involved in working for the South African Institute of Race Relations (SAIRR) and served on the executive from 1954. SAIRR, established in 1929, is among the most liberal research and policy organizations in South Africa. It is concerned with promoting ideas and policies to free South Africa from unemployment, poverty and dependency. However, by 1948 it had lost one of its most powerful political allies – Jan Hofmeyr – and the pro-apartheid National Party had gained a stranglehold on the political scene in South Africa. Pollak was elected vice president of the SAIRR on three separate occasions and also became an honorary member of the organization.

From 1962 she became a professor and head of the Department of Sociology and Social Work at the University of Natal. She later started an Educational Bursary Fund, aimed at offering education bursaries to less privileged children. In 1980 she was awarded an honorary doctorate in social science by the University of Natal in recognition of her community welfare work. Notable later publications include *Housing and Human Needs in South Africa* (1972) and *Pensions and Welfare: A Review of Differentiation and Discrimination* (1977). Pollak died in Cape Town in 1982 (South African History Online, Web, March 22, 2015).

Activist

Dr. Pollak was the first woman to publish in the *South African Journal of Economics* in the 1933 inaugural issue, followed by Sheila van der Horst who published there from the second volume onwards. Few other women joined them in that journal until 1960, when Mary V. Piercy of the University of the Witwatersrand became a very active contributor, with seven articles from June 1960 to December 1963. The *South African Journal of Economics* was conspicuously open compared to the dominant forces in South African society, for instance publishing in 1960 an article (on banking and finance in the Sudan) by Andrew F. Brimmer, later the first African-American member of the Federal Reserve Board. Pollak wrote articles regarding labor laws, welfare issues and demography, and compared the economic conditions of blacks in the United States with those in South Africa. She was a community activist who tried to advance peaceful racial relations in her homeland while condemning racist policies through education. In a letter she wrote to Z.K. Mathews, a political activist and fellow academician, she expressed her admiration and support on behalf of the Natal Regional Committee of SAIRR in her capacity as chairperson of the committee. Mr. Mathews had resigned his position when his school (now the University of Fort Hare) was relegated from being a university to a mere ethnic college for the Xhosa community alone. An education fellowship has been instituted in her name in recognition of her support of education, particularly for the under-privileged.[6]

Helen Suzman – South Africa[7]

Helen Suzman was born Helen Gavronski to Lithuanian Jewish parents on November 7, 1917, in Germiston, Transvaal, South Africa (see Suzman 1994; Godsell 2011; Renwick 2013). She graduated from the University of the Witwatersrand in 1940 with a degree in Economics and Economic History. She worked with the South African War Supplies Board as a statistician then went on to lecture in her alma mater until 1952. While at the university, she became a member of the SAIRR (of which, like Pollak and Van der Horst, she was a leader) as well as forming a chapter for the United Party (UP) in the school. She became a member of parliament in 1953 under the umbrella of the UP representing the Houghton Constituency, thus beginning a remarkable career in politics. Dissension within the UP caused Mrs. Suzman to resign and form the new Progressive Party with a few others that same year.

She was often a lone voice for change and stood staunchly against the pro-Apartheid National Party policies. She spent 36 years in parliament and did not waver in her resolve for change in South Africa long after retirement. She was a Dame Commander of the British Empire (DBE) and the holder of several honorary degrees from universities across the world. She was nominated for the Nobel Peace Prize twice. She died on New Year's Day in 2009 at the age of 91.

Politician and anti-apartheid fighter

Helen Suzman struck some as a deceptive figure. Elegant, poised and immaculately coiffured, she held her own for 13 years as the lone liberal member in parliament. In parliament she was often heckled for her ancestry. She attacked her opponents fearlessly and unrelentingly with her sharp tongue and quick wit. P.W. Botha, a South African former prime minister, is quoted as referring to her as a "vicious little cat" while an earlier prime minister once told her, "I've written you off" to which she retorted, "The whole world has written you off." She was notorious for asking endless embarrassing questions about the repressive apartheid regime. When reprimanded by government minister that her questions embarrassed her country, she responded that it was their answers that caused the country embarrassment (*The Economist*, January 10, 2009, p. 77).

Unlike other members of parliament, she used her positions to give voice to the marginalized in society, some of whom she came to know by visiting prison and slums. Late President Nelson Mandela recounted her visits during his imprisonment with affection. Among her friends and admirers is 1994 Nobel Peace Prize winner Archbishop Desmond Tutu. Though praiseworthy, Suzman is not free from criticism. Among other anti-apartheid groups, she has been criticized along with her liberal colleagues for supporting a qualified franchise under which only educated blacks with at least a college degree could vote.

She stood true to liberal beliefs in "free markets, capitalism, the paramountcy of democracy and civil institutions and equal opportunity" (*Economist*, January 10, 2009, p. 77). It is in this respect that she opposed economic sanctions against South Africa. She believed, instead, that non-violence and boycott by South African blacks could lead to change. While her tenure in parliament did not hinder the National Party apartheid regime or stop any law, she made a stand for freedom and justice. In the words of Mandela, "No-one can do more than her duty on earth" (*Economist*, January 18, 2014, p. 70).

Sheila Van der Horst – South Africa

Sheila van der Horst was born on October 27, 1909 to an English mother of feminist conviction and Dr. J.G. van der Horst who was among the foremost Afrikaner financiers. She graduated from the University of Cape Town in 1930 and earned a PhD from the London School of Economics. She lectured at the University of Cape Town from 1933, retiring in 1974, and then served four terms as an elected member of the University Council after her retirement. In 1993, Van der Horst was awarded an Honorary Doctorate of Economic Science honoris causa from the University of Cape Town.[8]

She wrote *Native Labour in South Africa* (1942), a revision of her doctoral thesis, and this has become a landmark study in labor economics, reissued by another publisher in 1971. She also is author of the book *African Workers in Town: A Study of Labour in Cape Town* (1964). Her concern and views on the economic effects of apartheid and on racial and gender inequality are encapsulated in many of her writings, among which are "Equal Pay for Equal Work" (1954), "The Effects of Industrialization on Race Relations in South Africa" (1965a), *Lessons from the South African Labour Market* (1965b), *Women as an Economic Force in South Africa* (1976), *Discrimination in Employment and Wages* (1977), and *Race Discrimination in South Africa* (1981). She also wrote on macroeconomic policy issues: how to finance South Africa's participation in World War II (Van der Horst 1941); inflation (1944); and full employment (1946).

She served on the Council of the Economic Society of South Africa and was a member of the Executive Committee and Chairman of the Cape Western Regional Committee of the SAIRR. In her obituary (Archer and Heywood 2003), she is remembered as a gifted person with clear understanding of many intellectual and moral dilemmas of her time. She remained liberal and an avowed critic of sectionalism and concentration of power. Throughout her career she published and taught under her maiden name rather than taking the name of her husband, the Cape Town lawyer Stanley Field.

The academic labor economist

By the 1950s, the South African population could be grouped into four categories. The natives Africans (or Bantu) were the majority, numbering about 8.5 million. The 2.5 million

Whites were mainly descendants of servants to the original Dutch East India Company as well as European immigrants. The Coloured population were mixed bloods, products of intermarriage and concubinage, and numbered about 1 million, and the 366,000 Indians or Asians were descendants of indentured labor from India brought to work in the sugar plantations on the Natal coast (Van der Horst 1955, pp. 72–73). Dr. Van der Horst traces a comprehensive historical picture of the evolution of native labor.

The first stage shows the unsuccessful attempts by the Cape government to control natives seeking work from adjoining territories. The next stage saw the spread of agricultural farming and discovery of gold and diamonds. These factors increased the demand for labor. Government intervened by imposing heavy taxes on natives thereby enforcing labor. As wages rose due to supply shortages, the Transvaal Chamber of Mines set itself up as a monopoly to control employment and recruitment to mines. Blacks continued to perform the majority of manual labor while Whites possessed the management skill, capital and initiative. The third stage witnessed economic forces leading to a common system of production with the majority in some form of paid employment. Native labor became increasingly feared as competition. The Whites saw them as a hostile proletariat. This led to the institution of different forms of job preservation, ownership restrictions on the occupation of land and freedom of movement.

Dr. Van der Horst highlighted the wage disparity among the different racial groups with Africans earning on average 10–12.5% of White earnings for similar work. Besides outright discrimination, she attributed the perpetuation of such inequality to "innate differences in upbringing, environment, employment opportunities, education and property acquisition" (Van der Horst 1955, p. 74). It is no wonder that stagnation and poverty prevailed.

Dr. Van der Horst's economic analysis was delivered for a general audience to stress the need for adjustment and mutual accommodation. She stressed the cost of discrimination particularly the difficulty of enforcement, as well as social and cultural erosion. Apartheid, she argued, is "manifest instability, injustice and wastefulness. It is economically impracticable and is used by its proponents to make racial discrimination morally acceptable" (1955, p. 82).

She pleaded for an end to those restrictive practices and the overcoming of disparities in social services and education which impeded "progress in the community as a whole, and the Native population in particular" (Van der Horst, 1942, p. 324). Such labor policies, she argued were based "on a short view of European advantage, preferring the convenience of the present generation of the European population to the prospects of prosperity and peace of their descendants" (Van der Horst 1942, p. 325). She noted that as economies become global, the economic outlook could not be divorced from the political. South Africa implemented these necessary changes, albeit 50 years later with the end of apartheid.

Saara Kuugongelwa-Amadhila – Namibia[9]

Saara Kuugongelwa-Amadhila is the current, and Namibia's first female, prime minister. She was born at Otamanzi in Omusati region of Namibia on October 12, 1967. She went into exile in 1980 and continued her elementary and secondary school education in Sierra Leone. She went to the United States where she obtained a Bachelor's degree in Economics in 1994 from Lincoln University, Pennsylvania, a renowned historically black college, and then returned home. She began her political career as a desk officer in the Office of the President during the administration of President Sam Nujuoma and gained prominence shortly thereafter when appointed director general at the National Planning Commission at the age of 27.

She is a member of the South West African Peoples Organization (SWAPO) and has been a member of the National Assembly since 1995. Within SWAPO, she is credited with turning the party's financial fortunes around in her position as Secretary for Economic Affairs. She served as Namibian Minister of Finance from 2003 to 2015 becoming not only the first female to hold that position but also the longest serving finance minister in the country's history.

A shrewd politician, Kuugongelwa-Amadhila is known to avoid partisan in-fighting while learning fast and on the job how to navigate the often-tricky political minefield. Her tenure as finance minister is reputed for its fiscal discipline and ambitious targets. In her first staff meeting address to her ministry in 2012, arresting the misuse of public funds was given top priority. Her first budget as minister is remembered for limiting government spending. She presented Namibia's first budget surplus in the 2006–07 financial year. With her as prime minister, Namibia can confidently look forward to achieving further successes.

Dambisa Felicia Moyo – Zambia[10]

Dr. Dambisa Moyo was born in Lusaka on February 2, 1969 without an official birth certificate. She obtained her Bachelor's degree in Chemistry and a Master of Business Administration, both degrees from the American University, Washington D.C. She earned another Master's but this time in Public Administration from the John F. Kennedy School of Government, Harvard University in 1997. She obtained her doctorate in Economics from St. Antony's College, Oxford in 2002. Her dissertation topic was titled, "Essays on the determinants of the components of savings in developing countries".

She is renowned, and controversial, as a global economist and author who has made the *Time Magazine* best seller list with each of her books. Her notable books include, *Dead Aid: Why Aid Is Not Working and How There Is a Better Way for Africa* (2009), *How the West Was Lost* (2011) and *Winner Takes All: China's Race for Resources and What it Means for the Rest of the World* (2012). She is a recipient of the Presidential Medal of Freedom and of the Friedrich Hayek Lifetime Achievement Award (2013) as well as earning a place on *Time Magazine*'s 100 most influential people (2009) and Oprah's 20 remarkable visionaries (2009). Dr. Moyo is a regular contributor to several financial journals and networks such as the *Financial Times, Wall Street Journal*, CNN and Bloomberg.

She worked as an economist at Goldman Sachs and as a consultant to the World Bank. She serves on the board of such global organizations as Barclay's Bank, SABMiller and Barrick Gold. In addition, she serves on the World Economic Forum's Network of Global Agenda Councils on Global Imbalances, and is a patron of Absolute Return for Kids (known as ARK) which is an international children's charity.

International economist and author

Dr. Moyo is a macroeconomic analyst, and her book *Dead Aid*, in particular, has received more attention than any other book to come out of Africa in recent times. One indisputable fact among both admirers and critics of Dr. Moyo is her impressive resumé. However, the manner in which that translates into opinion about her books is another matter. *Dead Aid* declares that financial aid to Africa has not improved but worsened the lot of its people, as the majority of the continent continues to wallow in poverty. This is compounded by the fact that African leaders see such aid as easy free money and are not accountable, thus perpetuating the vicious cycle of over dependency, market distortion, corruption and need for more aid. She offers an alternative in private capital raised either domestically or from international investors so that the leaders are accountable either to these lenders or to taxpayers. She uses examples of other successful countries which have employed micro-finance such as Bangladesh through its

Grameen banks. Prior policies in most African countries, she alleges, have hindered the growth of home-grown capitalists.

Most of her critics argue that Dr. Moyo tends to gloss over valid historical details. An example is the case she makes of government aid policies hampering the growth of an entrepreneurial elite who will invest in their own countries. Critics show aid hampering entrepreneurship not to be the case in at least one example. A government aid project instituted during the colonial era in the southern province of Zambia was to build up capitalist farmers among Tonga people. This class "went into dramatic decline with tragic consequences" as aid was reduced or cut from them (Moorsom 2010, p. 365).

She is also accused of being another neoliberal stooge who has provided ammunition for anti-aid groups instead of pushing for effective aid. It is agreed that international financial aid to Africa is not without its flaws, such as being self-serving and promoting protectionism, but no aid is equally damning (Moorsom 2010).

Moyo seems to suggest cures, but critics understand that is no uniform cure for Africa's economic woes, at least not one that has worked in Asia or the West. The reason is that they do not share similar history or trajectory. Colonialism has robbed nations of whatever identity they had prior and superimposed its own ideology. These nations now must sew up a patchwork of who they think they are with who they have been taught to be. For example, Nigeria is approximately 923,768 square kilometers in area (574,003 square miles) with over 520 languages: the implication is that Nigeria has a new language approximately every 1,000 square miles. The different sub-groups within each nation must jointly build a nation under their current dispensation as equals, which is no small feat as they are usually historically unequal. This inequality and failure to achieve consensus is at the root of most civil strife and political instability, and forms a backdrop for post-independent policies of these countries.

The existence of effective and functioning infrastructure and market framework amid a stable political climate is crucial for economic growth and development, aid or no aid. As for the idea in Moyo (2012) that the investment from China is the elixir for Africa's economic progress, that remains to be seen as it is early days yet. A word of caution about private capital and free trade. Both concepts are business centered and not motivated by patriotism. While the parties are bargaining as equals and there are returns on investment it might work. However, when the governments change or business cycle dips, the investor pulls back. What happens to the poor farmer whose crop has been wiped out and who has a family to feed without the intervention of the state?[11]

East Africa

Hamdani Zakia Meghji – Tanzania[12]

Zakia Hamdani Meghji was born on December 31, 1946, in Zanzibar where she had her early education. She obtained her Bachelor's in Education (1971) and Master's in Economic History (1979), both from the University of Dar es Salaam. Her Master's thesis was on women workers. She worked as a lecturer at the Moshi University College of Cooperative and Business Studies, then as programme officer at the International Cooperative Alliance (AIC). Meghji entered politics in 1985 as a member of parliament where she serves to date. In her political career, she has served as minister of health from 1992 to 1995, minister of natural resources and tourism from 1995–2005 and minister of finance from 2006 to 2008. She also served as president of the Africa Travel Association for two terms, where she is reputed to have introduced many important and timely initiatives in terms of developing the tourism sector, sponsoring promotional tours in the USA, and introducing a Tourism Awards Programme. She remains the longest serving tourism minister in the country, and has brought many positive changes in the ministry. She has co-authored a book on women and cooperatives with late husband Ramadhan Meghji and Clement Kwayu (Meghi et al. 1985). The book focuses on women and cooperatives as agents of economic change, particularly rural development in Tanzania.

Saada Mkuya Salum – Tanzania[13]

Saada Mkuya Salum was born in 1975. There is no official record of when and where. She is the second female to hold the office of finance minister in Tanzania since its independence. She holds a Master's of Business Administration from Herriot-Watt University in Edinburgh, Scotland, and is currently studying for a business PhD from the Open University of Tanzania (OUT). She served as commissioner of external finance in the Zanzibar government. She was subsequently appointed deputy finance minister in 2012 and became minister for finance and planning upon the death of her predecessor William Mgimwa. Salum also serves as a governor at the International Monetary Fund and of the Eastern and Southern African Trade and Development Bank.

West Africa

Olubanke King Akerele – Liberia[14]

Olubanke King Akerele was born May 11, 1946. Her grandfather was Charles B. King, the 16th President of Liberia. She studied at the University of Ibadan, Nigeria, and Brandeis University in Massachusetts where she obtained a B.A. in Economics. She earned an M.A. in Manpower Economics from Northeastern University in Boston and another M.A. in Economics of Education from Columbia University. She worked for the United Nations for 20 years in various capacities which included deputy director of the United Nations Development Program for Women. The United Nations Economic Commission for Africa published her studies on *Women and the Fishing Industry in Liberia: Measures of Women's Participation* (Akerele 1979a), *Women Workers in Ghana, Kenya, Zambia: A Comparative Analysis of Women's Employment in the Modern Wage Sector* (1979b), and *Traditional Palm Oil Processing: Women's Role and the Application of Appropriate Technology* (1983). Akerele served as minister of commerce and industry under President Johnson Sirleaf in 2005. She was later made minister of foreign affairs in a cabinet shake-up in 2007. As foreign minister it was her challenge to attract international investment toward rebuilding a country recently devastated by civil war. She resigned the position in 2010 when there was another cabinet reshuffle.

Akerele is a champion of women in leadership and believes that women leaders have a unique perspective toward real positive change. She is the author of several books including *The "How" of Integration of Women in Development Planning* (1981), *Women's Leadership in Post-Conflict Liberia: My Journey* (2012) and *The "Growing" of Africa's Emergent Leadership* (2014).

Tinuke Johnson – Nigeria[15]

Dr. Tinuke Lola Johnson was born 1942 at Onse Agbedi, Ogun State, Nigeria. She attended the University of West London and London School of Economics where she earned her Bachelor's and an M.Sc. (Statistics) in 1966. Her PhD was obtained from the University of Ilorin, Nigeria, in 2009 at the age of 67 with a doctoral thesis on the "Effects of Correlation and Identification Status on Methods of Estimating Parameters of System of Simultaneous Equations Models."

Dr. Johnson began her career as an assistant statistician in the British Ministry of Health between 1966 and 1970 where she was the first black professional. She lectured part-time at both the University of West London and the North Western Polytechnic, London. Upon her return to Nigeria in 1970, she took up a lecturer position at the University of Ibadan, Nigeria's premier university, where she rose to become a reader. In conjunction with the then acting head of department, they developed the Bachelor's, Master's, Postgraduate Diploma and Doctorate programs. Along with a few other pioneering colleagues, she succeeded in separating the Mathematics and Statistics Department from the Computer Science Department. She worked briefly at Bowen University, Iwo, Osun State in Nigeria between January 2003 and February 2005.

Dr. Johnson is no stranger to pioneering in her professional life. She holds the distinction of being the first female professionally accredited statistician in Africa (*a fortiori* Nigeria), the only non-British professional statistician in the British Civil Service before 1970, co-author of the first statistics textbook in Africa and the first female head of department of statistics in Africa as well.

She is widely published and is among the first indigenous Nigerian females to publish in the *Nigerian Journal of Economic and Social Studies* (Johnson 1973). Her publication credits include *Cost Benefit Analysis of Education in Nigeria* (1981; with Prof. Segun Adesina) and *Statistics for Beginners* and its workbook (1975; jointly with late Prof. S. Adamu). She is the holder of several awards and scholarships. Dr. Johnson is an elected Fellow of the Nigerian Statistical Association (NSA), and is the managing director and chief consultant of DENT Projects Limited.

Mother of statistics

In her book *Statistics and its Development in Nigeria* (2013) Dr. Johnson reflects on personal gains and pains of over 40 years of teaching statistics in universities across Nigeria while tracing the inception of a statistics department in the Faculty of Social Sciences at the University of Ibadan. She mentions the hostilities involved in obtaining recognition as a professional within the Faculty of Social Sciences as well as a deployment from the economics department. Her career path within the university was often thwarted by internal politics among her superiors. She was not only denied promotion at times but nearly obliterated from the department's history! Perhaps the most painful example of such victimization was the abrupt withdrawal of her PhD supervisor due to "personal reasons" at the point of submitting a title. The incident caused her much mental anguish. With encouragement from family and colleagues she summoned courage to obtain her doctorate from the University of Ilorin 33 years later at the age of 67 years.

Dr. Johnson believes that statistics, like geography, should be located in both Social Science and Science Faculties. She remains a strong advocate for mentoring of junior colleagues in the academy as well as promoting statistics outside academia through her consultancy work.

Gloria Nikoi - Ghana[16]

Gloria Amon Nikoi (née Addae) was born in Ghana in 1930. She was one of the few females to attend the prestigious Achimota College, Accra. Most of the early students of this school went on to play important roles in the development of Ghana. She obtained her degree in Economics and Modern History from St Andrew's University in Scotland (Nikoi 1998, p. 128). She is a career public servant who has held several public and international positions. From 1969 to 1974, she was Deputy Chief of Mission to the United Nations, then she worked as a senior official in the Ministry of Foreign Affairs. She later was the foreign affairs minister under the Armed Forces Revolutionary Council (AFRC) government of Flight Lieutenant Jerry Rawlings in 1979 and has remained the only woman to hold such a position. In 1981 she became chairperson of the Bank of Housing and Construction.

She has served as director of the African Development Bank (ADB) where she advised also on gender issues. She was part of the Ghanaian delegation to the Lagos Plan for Action for Economic Development of Africa (1980–2000). This was a draft of an action plan by African leaders blaming the International Monetary Fund and World Bank for the stringent conditions placed on African nations that aggravated their economic woes, particularly the Structural Adjustment Program. She was the first chairperson of the Council of the Ghana Stock Exchange when it was inaugurated on November 12, 1990.

Career diplomat and champion of gender issues

Gender issues are particularly dear to Mrs. Nikoi, particularly development from the grassroots level up. She sees women as necessary agents of economic change and development. As such her view on development is aimed at empowering women and building on the traditional structures toward achieving progress.

She illustrated the prominence of women in commerce, particularly in urban distribution of cloth from wholesale purchase to the petty trader retail efforts. She used the number of passbook holders, deposit and credits pattern to show that the majority, by far, were women ([Nikoi] Addae 1956).

Her paper "Change Agents in the Development of Financial Services for Small Scale Enterprises in Ghana" (1995) furthered this view and advocated that financial services providers bridge the gap between the formal and informal financial economy. To achieve self-reliance and sustainable growth, she opined that production, productivity and incomes of private entrepreneurs in the informal and small-scale enterprise (SSE) sectors must grow. Such growth must be accomplished through innovative and bold policies that target rural and inner-city areas. This is no surprise since such sectors have traditionally been, and continue to be, dominated by women. These SSE are grassroots enterprises and already have the capabilities and human capital to perform credit and financial services which formal financial institutions could promote by divesting of such functions. By extension, rural banks are more decentralized and accessible and thus are better able to serve informal and SSE sectors and make the needed critical improvement to the local economy (Nikoi 1995, p. 155).

Olufunmilayo Oloruntimehin – Nigeria[17]

Professor Olufunmilayo Oloruntimehin was born on June 17, 1942. She was a Professor of Criminology at the Obafemi Awolowo University for 30 years in the sociology department. Her research area covered sociology, criminology and sociology of law, but she was also among the first women published in the *Nigerian Journal of Economic and Social Studies*. In her writings as well as through her outreach programs, she continues to advocate for societal change toward those incarcerated and their rehabilitation back into civil society. She is particularly focused on helping to alleviate the plight of women in prison with their innocent children. She strives to bring attention to the inhumane conditions in Nigerian prisons and those unjustly imprisoned. Professor Oloruntimehin is another example of many unsung female heroes in Africa.

Ngozi Okonjo-Iweala – Nigeria[18]

Dr. Okonjo-Iweala was born in Ogwashi-Uku, Delta State, Nigeria. She was educated at Harvard University where she earned an A.B. in Economics, graduating magna cum laude. She obtained a PhD in regional economics and development from the MIT in 1981. Her dissertation topic was on credit policy, rural financial markets and Nigeria's agricultural development.

She received an international fellowship from the American Association of University Women (AAUW) which supported her doctoral studies.

She started her career at the World Bank in 1982 as a development economist, rising to the position of vice president and corporate secretary in 2002. She served two terms as minister of finance in Nigeria first under the Obasanjo administration (2003 to 2006) and later under the administration of President Goodluck Jonathan (2011 to 2015) with the additional office of coordinating minister for the economy.[19] She briefly served as minister of foreign affairs. She was appointed a managing director of the World Bank from 2007 to 2011, and was one of three nominees for World Bank president in 2012. Had she been elected, women would have led four of the world's major public financial institutions, with Christine Lagarde at the International Monetary Fund (IMF), Janet Yellen at the Federal Reserve and, from 2013, Elvira Nabiullina as governor of the Russian Central Bank. Okonjo-Iweala lost to Dartmouth College president Jim Yong Kim, the U.S. nominee, despite her stellar qualifications and emphatic endorsement by *The Economist*. As a member of the Governing Council of Nigeria Sovereign Investment Authority, she provided advice and counsel to the Board of Directors. She was also an adviser to the World Bank on the Stolen Assets Recovery initiative. Other World Bank positions include director of operations in the Middle East and North Africa region, and country director for the South-East Asia and Mongolia Country unit. She was a member of the Boards of Governors of the ADB, the IMF, and the Islamic Development Bank. She is a member or chair of numerous boards and advisory groups in the public, private and non-governmental sectors, including DATA, the Clinton Global Initiative, the Nelson Mandela Institution and the African Institutes of Science and Technology, and Friends of the Global Fund Africa.

She is also a recipient of numerous awards and honors including *Time Magazine* European Hero 2004, *Euromoney Magazine* Global Finance Minister of the Year 2005, *Financial Times-The Banker* African Finance Minister of the Year 2005. She has Honorary Doctorates of Law from Colby College in 2007 and Brown University in 2006 and an Honorary Doctorate of Humane Letters from Northern Caribbean University, Jamaica.

Reformer or politician?

Nigeria discovered oil in commercial quantities in the 1960s and steadily shifted focus from an agricultural-based economy with an emerging mineral extraction sector to an economy that is oil based. Nigeria was never able to translate the significant oil wealth into a better standard of living for its people. Rather, it exhibited all the classic economic woes of Dutch disease – a sudden influx of foreign exchange income that causes inflation and appreciation of the real exchange rate, resulting in contraction of other parts of the economy (Okonjo-Iweala 2012, p. 3). While other resource-rich countries such as Norway and Canada have turned their Dutch disease symptoms around, Nigeria continues to grapple with a struggling economy and the majority of its populace living in poverty.

This was the scene for Dr. Okonjo-Iweala's debut as minister of finance in 2003. She stated that her initial task was to establish credibility, fairness and social trust. She formed an economic team that shared this vision and who identified four major challenges responsible for the poor state of the economy. These were: weak economic management, volatile public spending, and monoculture production; weak and institutionalized corruption in governance; bureaucratic inefficiencies that are hostile to the private sector (Okonjo-Iweala 2012, p. 14).

Dr. Okonjo-Iweala, with members of her economic team, outlined their tasks as follows:

1 address macroeconomic volatility and fight corruption;
2 address structural features that hinder private-sector enterprise by promoting privatization, deregulation and liberalization;
3 reform the civil service, trade and tariffs, customs and the banking sector;
4 restore social trust and growth; and
5 obtain debt relief.

They were successful in implementing several of the reforms outlined above. They improved Nigeria's financial stability and fostered greater fiscal transparency by de-linking oil prices used to formulate the budget from the more volatile world price. This led to US$17 billion in savings through the Excess Crude Account which was deployed to shore up the economy when oil prices fell (Okonjo-Iweala 2012, p. 120). The launch of structural reforms to many loss-making enterprises led to improved outlook and performance of the financial sector. Setting up the Economic and Financial Crimes Commission (EFCC) led to the investigation, arrest, conviction and jail time for members of the rulers who had stolen public funds with impunity. Her efforts through her team led to the recovery of stolen assets from Switzerland alone worth US$505 million. This is considerable for a country unable to pay its medical doctors and teachers for months on end.

The successful negotiation with the Paris Club to eliminate US$30 billion of Nigeria's external debt is, arguably, one of Dr. Okonjo-Iweala's major accomplishments as finance minister. To a large extent it "acted as a signal that policies had improved and this further improved investor confidence" and "as a consequence there was an increase in foreign direct investment and portfolio flows" (Okonjo-Iweala 2012, p. 121). She noted, however, that she and her team could have done better by focusing on the politics and political economy of the reforms. Regardless, her reforms gave hope to Nigerians about their prospects and the future of their country. It revealed that there are selfless Nigerians willing to heed the national call to service. Dr. Okonjo-Iweala is among them.

Ellen Johnson Sirleaf – Liberia[20]

Mrs. Ellen Johnson Sirleaf was born in Monrovia on October 29, 1938. She earned an Associate degree in Accounting and a Bachelor's in Economics, both from Madison Business College, Madison. She received a Master of Public Administration degree from Harvard's John F. Kennedy School of Government, a degree that included economics (see Johnson Sirleaf 2009; Scully 2016; Cooper 2018). She began her political career as assistant minister of finance under the administration of President William Tolbert. Army Sergeant Samuel Doe overthrew Tolbert's government and offered Johnson Sirleaf the position of president of the Liberian Bank of Development and Investment, which she initially accepted. She later fled to exile in Nairobi.

She subsequently worked in the international banking community in such institutions as the World Bank, Citibank and Equator Bank (a subsidiary of HSBC). During this time, she also ran for Senate representing the Monteserrado County in 1985. She was sentenced to 10 years in prison for speaking out against Doe's regime. She won the Senate seat but refused to accept as a protest against election fraud. This time she went into exile in the United States.

Johnson Sirleaf supported Charles Taylor in his bloody rebellion against President Samuel Doe though she later disagreed with him. In 1997, she ran unsuccessfully against Charles Taylor who later charged her with treason. However, after Taylor was removed, and in 2005 as leader of the United Party, she was elected President of Liberia, becoming the first African woman to be elected head of state and the first black elected female president. She completed her second term as president in 2018 in a tenure that is marked by growth and political stability. She shared the Nobel Peace Prize with two other women, Tawakkul Karman and Leymah Gbowee, for non-violent struggle for the safety of women and women's right to full participation in peace-building work.

Madam President

In 2002, Johnson Sirleaf co-wrote *Women, War and Peace* with Elisabeth Rehn saying, "As former Defence and Finance Ministers, and as Presidential candidates, we understand the world of politics, and we have a keen sense for ripe political moments." This quote profoundly expresses the timing of her political strategies which has led to numerous successes. She is a relentless champion of women's rights and empowerment, particularly toward equipping women with proper support and training, recommendations that she and Rehn included in their study. She also supports the mobilization of women leaders as a member of the Council of Women World leaders. As president, Johnson Sirleaf issued an executive order mandating elementary education that is free and compulsory for school-aged children. Her administration has achieved debt relief from the country's creditors, including the IMF, Paris Club and other bilateral creditors. She maintained an open foreign policy with the international community and mended previously strained relations with Liberia's neighbors. Her limited tolerance for corruption among public officials and decisiveness earned her the moniker "Iron Lady": she dismissed her whole cabinet in November 2010 replacing them roughly a month later without seven of the original members. However, *The Economist*, September 7, 2013, p. 50, subtitled an article about her, "The president keeps the peace but fails to reduce graft."

Another major criticism of President Johnson Sirleaf concerned her decision to go against the recommendation of the Truth and Reconciliation Commission (TRC) which she established. The TRC included her in a list of people who should be banned from holding public office. Her response to the crisis posed by the Ebola virus was also controversial, as would have been any policies by any government facing that crisis. However, it is undisputed that she has done much good in Liberia: according to *The Economist*, she is "arguably the best President the country has ever had."

Conclusion

The women of Africa in this chapter are but a few that have risen to prominence internationally and locally. There remain many more whose efforts are undocumented but whose legacy carries on in their students, their children and others affected by their works. Whether by adopting a liberal approach to economic development or by advocating state support of cooperatives and impoverished farmers, African female economists offered substantial solutions and implemented needed changes. They contributed to economics and to economic policy-making, both as academics and as central bankers, government ministers and public officials. Female economists have sometimes been aided in attaining influential positions closed to other African women through the prestige of gaining such credentials as Harvard or MIT degrees or experience at the World Bank or United Nations, and by being viewed by politicians as technocrats rather than as rival politicians. Whether staring down political opponents alone or fighting corruption to redeem a national image, these women are strategists as well as the muscle that brings those policies to life. This is the power of education, and particularly formal education, playing an indispensable role for African female economists to emerge, find their voices, share their ideas and aspire to public offices. These ideas, dreams and aspirations are the ones that will ultimately shape Africa into the global giant she is meant to be.

Notes

1 Gerardo Serra provides an overview of the development of writing on economics in Africa (in Barnett 2015).
2 AAAWE was founded in March 2012 at the initiative of Elizabeth Asiedu, an economics professor at the University of Kansas.
3 Data taken from AAAWE website, March 2017.
4 Two such women not documented in detail in this chapter are Sarah Alade, deputy governor of the Bank of Nigeria, and Frannie A. Léautier, treasurer of the African Economics Research Consortium and former chief operating officer and senior vice-president of the African Development in Abidjan, Côte d'Ivoire.
5 Some information on Hansi Pollak is from www.sahistory.org.za/dated-event/hansi-pauline-pollak-welfare-worker-and-social-activist-born (accessed May 2015).
6 www.sahistory.org.za/dated-event/hansi-pauline-pollak-welfare-worker-and-social-activist-born (accessed May 2015).
7 Some biographical information is available from the following sources. Obituaries: "Helen Suzman, Relentless Challenger of Apartheid System, is dead at 91," *Globe and Mail* (Toronto), December 31, 2008; "Helen Suzman" *The Economist*, January 10, 2009. Also see "Helen Suzman" (2015). The Biography.com website. Retrieved 02:19, May 17, 2015 from www.biography.com/people/helen-suzman-9499766
8 Information from Archer and Heywood 2003 obituary.
9 For biographical information, see "Namibia: Profile – Saara Kuugongelwa-Amadhila, all Africa Vol. 0826 (2015, March). Retrieved from http:allafrica.com/stories/201503120826.html
10 Biographical information on Moyo drawn from blurbs in her books, and from Simon Houpt, "The Private Life of a Public Intellectual," *The Globe and Mail* (Toronto), April 23, 2011, p. B5.
11 The ideas in this paragraph and the one before it are Fowler's, based on reading several of Moyo's critics; particularly Moorsom (2010), Madelene Bunting (*The Guardian*, retrieved May 2015 from www.theguardian.com/books/2009/feb/14/aid-africa-dambisa-moyo) and Kevin Watkins (retrieved May 2015 from www.huffingtonpost.com/kevin-watkins/why-idead-aidi-is-dead-wr_b_191193.html).
12 Biographical information retrieved May 2015 from https://prabook.com/web/zakia_hamdani.meghji/429033.
13 Biographical information drawn from sources linked to Wikipedia: two 2014 Reuters articles on appointment of Saada Mukya Salum as Tanzania's minister of finance, retrieved May 2015 from https://af.reuters.com/article/commoditiesNews/idAFL6N0RU14N20141001 and https://live.worldbank.org/experts/saada-mkuya-salum
14 Akerele (2012), her autobiography, is the source for biography facts.
15 Biographical information is from Johnson (2013).
16 For Gloria Nikoi's career time line see www.guide2womenleaders.com/Ghana.htm.
17 Biographical information retrieved May 2015 from www.wisewomenawardsng.org/prof-mrs-olufunmilayo-oloruntimehin/ and https://blerf.org/index.php/biography/oloruntimehin-professor-olufunmilayo-yetunde/. Note: her birth year is different across these two sources.
18 Biographical information drawn from Okonjo-Iweala (2012).
19 The government of President Buhari, which took office in 2015, also had a woman as finance minister, an accountant rather than an economist.
20 See Scully (2016). Biographical information is also from Sirleaf (2009).

References

Primary sources

Adamu, S. O., and Tinuke L. Johnson (1975) *Statistics for Beginners*. Ibadan, Nigeria: Onibonoje Press.
Adesina, Segun, and Tinuke L. Johnson (1981) *Cost-Benefit Analysis of Education in Nigeria*. Lagos, Nigeria: Lagos University Press.
Akerele, Olubanke King (1979a) *Women and the Fishing Industry in Liberia: Measures of Women's Participation*. Addis Ababa: United Nations Economic Commission for Africa.
—— (1979b) *Women Workers in Ghana, Kenya, Zambia: A Comparative Analysis of Women's Employment in the Modern Wage Sector*. Addis Ababa: United Nations Economic Commission for Africa.

—— (1981) "Discussion paper." Seminar on development planning and women. Esami, Arusha, Tanzania, June 17.
—— (1983) *Traditional Palm Oil Processing: Women's Role and the Application of Appropriate Technology*. Addis Ababa: United Nations Economic Commission for Africa.
—— (2012) *Women's Leadership in Post-Conflict Liberia: My Journey*. Tema, Ghana: Digibooks.
—— (2014) *The "Growing" of Africa's Emergent Leadership*. Paris: Club Millennium.
Johnson, Tinuke Lola (1973) "Efficiency of Government Health Services in Lagos," *Nigerian Journal of Economic and Social Studies* 15: 391–404.
Johnson, T. L. (2013) *Statistics and its Development in Nigeria: 40 Years of Statistics Department Ibadan (Gains and Pains) My Personal Recollection*. Ibadan, Nigeria: Department of Statistics, University of Ibadan.
Johnson Sirleaf, Ellen (2009) *The Child Will Be Great: Memoir of a Remarkable Life by Africa's First Woman President*. New York: HarperCollins.
Meghi, Hamdani Zakia, Ramadhan Meghi, and Clement Kwayu (1985) *The Woman Co-operator and Development*. Kijabe, Tanzania: Maarifa Publishers.
Moyo, Dambisa F. (2009) *Dead Aid: Why Aid is Not Working and How There is a Better Way for Africa*, with a foreword by Niall Ferguson. New York: Farrar, Strauss and Giroux, London: Allen Lane, and Vancouver: Douglas & McIntyre.
—— (2011) *How the West Was Lost: Fifty Years of Economic Folly and the Stark Choices that Lie Ahead*. London: Penguin.
—— (2012) *Winner Takes All: China's Race for Resources and What it Means for the Rest of the World*. New York: HarperCollins.
[Nikoi] Addae, Gloria (1956) "The Retailing of Imported Textiles in Accra Market," in *Proceedings, 3rd Annual Conference, West African Institute of Social and Economic Research*.
Nikoi, Gloria (1995) "Change Agents in the Development of Financial Services for Small-Scale Enterprises in Ghana," in Philip English and Georges-Maurice Hénault, eds., *Agents of Change: Studies on the Policy Environment for Small Enterprise in Africa*. Ottawa: International Development Research Centre, pp. 144–160.
—— (1998) *Gender and Development*. Accra, Ghana: Ghana Universities Press and University of Cape Coast Publications Unit.
Okonjo-Iweala, Ngozi (2012) *Reforming the Unreformable: Lessons from Nigeria*. Cambridge, MA: MIT Press.
Okonjo-Iweala, Ngozi, Charles Chukwuma Soludo, and Mansur Muhtar (2003) *The Debt Trap: Towards a Sustainable Debt Strategy*. Africa World Press
Pollak, Hansi P. (1933a) "Women Workers in Witswatersrand Industries," *South African Journal of Economics* 1: 58–68.
—— (1933b) "The Economic Position Attained by the Negro in America by 1930 and the Influence of the Depression on Him," *South African Journal of Economics* 1: 433–50.
—— (1936) "European Population Growth since Union: An Analysis of the Birth, Fertility and Death Rates with Reference to the Future Increase of Population," *South African Journal of Economics* 4: 1–42.
—— (1940) "State and Private Provisions for Soldiers' Dependents," *South African Journal of Economics* 8: 446–74.
—— (1972) *Housing and Human Needs in South Africa: A Summary and Evaluation*. Johannesburg: South African Institute of Race Relations.
—— (1977) *Pensions and Welfare: A Review of Differentiation and Discrimination and Current Trends in State Social Pensions and Welfare*. Cape Town: University of Cape Town Centre for Intergroup Studies.
Rehn, Elizabeth, and Ellen Johnson Sirleaf (2002) *Women, War and Peace: The Independent Expert's Assessment of the Impact of Armed Conflict on Women and Women's Role in Peace-Building*. New York: Kumarian Press for the United Nations Development Fund for Women.
Suzman, Helen (1994) *In No Uncertain Terms: Memoirs*. London: Mandarin.
Van der Horst, Sheila T. (1934) "Poor Law Legislation," *South African Journal of Economics* 2: 298–305.
—— (1935) "Some Effects of Industrial Legislation on the Market for Native Labour in South Africa," *South African Journal of Economics* 3: 481–501.
—— (1939) "Report of the Native Farm Labour Committee, 1937–39," *South African Journal of Economics* 7: 462–71.
—— (1941) "Financing the South African War Effort," *South African Journal of Economics* 9: 66–84, 184–89.
—— (1942) *Native Labour in South Africa*. Oxford, UK: Oxford University Press; reprinted London: Frank Cass, 1971.
—— (1944) "Inflation in South Africa: Some Comments on the Annual Address of the Governor of the Reserve Bank," *South African Journal of Economics* 12: 238–40.

—— (1946) "Some Reflections on Full Employment," *South African Journal of Economics* 14: 1–16.
—— (1954) "Equal Pay for Equal Work," *South African Journal of Economics* 22: 187–209.
—— (1955) "The Union of South Africa: Economic Problems in a Multiracial Situation," *Annals of the American Academy of Political and Social Science*, Volume 298: *Contemporary Africa Trends and Issues*, pp. 71–83.
—— (1964) *African Workers in Town: A Study of Labour in Cape Town*. Oxford, UK: Oxford University Press.
—— (1965a) "The Effects of Industrialization on Race Relations in South Africa," in Guy Hunter, ed., *Industrialization and Race Relations*. Oxford, UK: Oxford University Press.
—— (1965b) *Lessons from the South African Labour Market*. London: Pergamon Press.
—— (1976) *Women as an Economic Force in South Africa*. Rondebosch: Abe Bailey Institute of Interracial Studies, and Cape Town: University of Cape Town Centre for Intergroup Studies.
—— (1977) *Discrimination in Employment and Wages*. Cape Town: University of Cape Town Centre for Intergroup Studies.
—— (1981) *Race Discrimination in South Africa: A Review*. Cape Town: D. Phillip.

Secondary sources

African Economics Research Consortium (1994) *Addressing Gender Bias: Graduate Training in Economics*. Nairobi: AERC.
—— (2010) *Women in Economic Research and Graduate Training in Southern Africa*. Nairobi: AERC.
—— (2017) *Annual Report 2016/17*. Nairobi: AERC.
Archer, Sean, and Jeanne Heywood (2003) "Obituary: Sheila van der Horst (1909–2001)," *South African Journal of Economics* 71: 211–14.
Asiedu, Elizabeth (2015) "The Association for the Advancement of African Women Economists," *CSWEP Newsletter* (Committee for the Status of Women in the Economics Profession, American Economic Association).
Association for the Advancement of African Women Economists (AAAWE), website: aaawe.org.
Barnett, Vincent, ed. (2015) *Routledge Handbook of the History of Global Economic Thought*. London and New York: Routledge.
Brown, George W. (1941) *Economic History of Liberia*. Washington, DC: Associated Publishers.
Cooper, Helen (2018) *Madame President: The Extraordinary Journey of Ellen Sirleaf Johnson*. New York: Simon and Schuster.
Dimand, Robert W., and Kojo Saffu (2017) "Polly Hill (1914–2005)," in Robert Cord, ed., *The Palgrave Companion to Cambridge Economics*. London: Palgrave Macmillan, Vol. 2, pp. 857–70.
Ekundare, Richard Olufemi (1973) *An Economic History of Nigeria 1860–1960*. New York: Africana Publishing.
Godsell, Gillian (2011) *Helen Suzman*. Cape Town: Maskew Miller Longman.
Ingham, Barbara (1992) "Shaping Opinion on Development Policy: Economists at the Colonial Office during World War II," *History of Political Economy* 24: 689–710.
Lewis, W. Arthur (1965) *Politics in West Africa*. Toronto: Oxford University Press (the Whidden Lectures at McMaster University).
Lugard, Lady Flora (1905) *A Tropical Dependency*. London: James Nisbet.
Manning, Patrick (1987) "The Prospect of African Economic History: Is Today Included in the Long Run?" *African Studies Review* 30(2): 49–62.
McPhee, Allan (1926) *The Economic Revolution in British West Africa*. London: Routledge.
Moorsom, Toby Leon (2010) "The Zombies of Development Economics: Dambisa Moyo's *Dead Aid* and the Fictional African Entrepreneurs," *Review of African Political Economy*, 37(125): 361–71.
Perham, Margery, ed. (1946–48a) *Mining, Commerce and Finance in Nigeria*. London: Faber & Faber.
—— (1946–48b) *The Native Economics of Nigeria*. London: Faber & Faber.
Renwick, Robin (2013) *Helen Suzman: Bright Star in a Dark Chamber*. London: Biteback Publishing.
Scully, Pamela (2016) *Ellen Johnson Sirleaf*. Athens: Ohio University Press.

21

WOMEN ECONOMISTS OF THE ARAB HOMELAND[1]

Talia Yousef and Robert W. Dimand

Researcher's approach, limitations and position

This research aims to identify the role of Arab women in the field of economics within the Arab nations of the Middle East and North Africa (MENA). In doing so, the research goal is to highlight the extent of female participation in modern economics within the Arab Homeland, in comparison to the rest of the world. For consistency and to allow for a relevant comparison between female participation in economics within this region versus female participation in economics elsewhere, the field of Islamic economics will be excluded from this study. Even though Islamic economics has a profound history existing long before Adam Smith (see e.g. Hosseini 2003; Islahi 2015), this study focuses on female participation in the field of modern liberal economics.

It is essential to highlight the positionality of one of the authors as an Arab-Canadian female scholar. This author's position has both benefits and limitations. The benefits of the author's position are an expanded scope of study, because many research results were retrieved in both English and Arabic. The author's expanded access to material in the Arabic language sets a limitation on the countries and women included in this survey. Because of the limitation to data and content in the Arabic, English and French languages, only the Arab nations within MENA can be included in this research. Thus, this research excludes female participation in the field of economics in non-Arab nations that might be included in the Western definition of the Middle East, such as Turkey, Iran and Israel.

The lead author mitigates the prospect of orientalist or subjective Western bias, as the researcher is linked to the research subject as a female Arab economist herself, though in North America rather than in an Arab nation. As an Arab researcher, it is necessary to identify the nations included in the research by the local definition rather than the orientalist Western definition. The modern term "Middle East" was coined as a British colonial military term referring to all Islamic "othered" nations in the "middle", between Britain and Colonial India. Although the term fell into common use, "Middle East" was neither accepted nor used by the inhabitants of the region until very recently. A commonly used local term for the region is الوطن العربي – in Arabic (or "Al-Watan Al-Arabi"), directly translated as "The Arab Nation." In research studying numerous maps of the "Middle East" published from within the region, Karen Culcasi (2012) translates the commonly used term as the "Arab Homeland":

> One can easily deduce that the Arab Homeland includes the states of Morocco, Tunisia, Algeria, Libya, Egypt, Sudan, Palestine (Israel is not included), Lebanon, Syria, Jordan, Iraq, Kuwait, Saudi Arabia, Oman, the UAE and Yemen. On nearly all Arab Homeland maps that have been published since the 1960s, these states have consistently comprised the Arab Homeland.[2]

Many Arabs, including the lead author, do not identify with or recognize the term "Middle East" in reference to Arab nations, because that term was imposed by Western colonizers. This research focuses on the Arab nations within the region that have linguistic and cultural commonalities.

Socio-economic context: Arab women in education and the labor force

Table 21.1 shows that labor force participation rates have been low for women in many of the countries of the Arab Homeland in recent decades. Average female labor force participation rates are 21% in 1990 and only 23% in 2016. There are noteworthy exceptions: Qatar, Kuwait, and the United Arab Emirates, which clearly indicate that a low women's labor force participation rate is not a necessary outcome in this region of the world. Though beyond the scope of

Table 21.1 Female labor force participation rates and national GDP, 1990 versus 2016

	1990 female labor force participation rate (ages 15+)	*1990 GDP ($ billions)*	*2016 female labor force participation rate (ages 15+)*	*2016 GDP ($ billions)*
Algeria	10	62.045	17	156.08
Bahrain	28	4.23	39	31.859
Egypt	26	43.13	23	336.297
Iraq	11	179.886	15	171.48
Jordan	9	4.16	14	38.655
Kuwait	35	18.428	48	114.041
Lebanon	18	2.838	24	47.537
Libya	18	28.902	28	*
Mauritania	25	1.02	29	4.635
Morocco	27	30.18	25	101.445
Oman	17	11.685	30	66.293
Qatar	41	7.36	53	152.469
Saudi Arabia	14	117.63	20	646.438
Sudan	27	12.409	24	95.584
Syria	18	12.309	12	2007: 40.405*
Tunisia	20	12.291	25	42.063
UAE	25	50.701	42	348.743
West Bank and Gaza	9	1994: 2.843*	18	13.397
Yemen	16	5.647	26	27.318
Arab World	21		23	
World	52		49	

Source: World Bank, 2016. https://data.worldbank.org/indicator/SL.TLF.CACT.FE.ZS

*For the purpose of consistency, all data presented have been retrieved from the World Bank. Thus, any data which the World Bank does not have nor provide for public record, is omitted. This does not mean that the labor force in these regions did not exist at that time. Rather, for a variety of possible reasons, that information was not accessible to, or was omitted by, the World Bank.

Table 21.2 Female labor force participation, female population and total population

Country	*2016 female labor force participation rate (ages 15+)*	*Female population (% of total)*	*Total population*
Algeria	17	49.5	40 606 052
Bahrain	39	37.9	1 425 171
Egypt	23	49.4	95 688 681
Iraq	15	49.4	37 202 572
Jordan	14	49.4	9 455 802
Kuwait	48	42.6	4 052 584
Lebanon	24	49.8	6 006 668
Libya	28	49.6	6 293 253
Mauritania	29	49.6	4 301 018
Morocco	25	50.5	35 276 786
Oman	30	34.6	4 424 762
Qatar	53	24.8	2 569 804
Saudi Arabia	20	43.1	32 375 687
Sudan	24	50.0	39 578 828
Syria	12	49.4	18 430 453
Tunisia	25	50.6	11 403 248
UAE	42	27.2	9 269 612
West Bank and Gaza	18	49.3	4 551 566
Yemen	26	49.5	27 584 213
Arab World	23	48.2	
World	49		

Source: World Bank, 2016. https://data.worldbank.org/indicator/SL.TLF.CACT.FE.ZS

this chapter, it is relevant to note that the low female labor force participation rates are due to a vast array of reasons, including political and economic disruptions imposed by nations outside the Arab Homeland.

Where there are high female labor force participation rates in the Arab Homeland, this is correlated with high per capita GDP. Thus, oil-rich and foreign investment-attracting countries such as the nations of the Arabian Gulf provide women the greatest means to enter the workforce simply based on higher availability of jobs. This is the case for all Arabian Gulf nations, except for Saudi Arabia.

In assessing the role of women in the labor force, Saudi Arabia is an outlier: it exhibits the absolute highest GDP among other Arab nations, yet has one of the lower female labor force participation rates. Unlike other Arab nations, Saudi Arabia has imposed strict patriarchal laws on its female citizens, falsely using Islam as a justification for its policies. Such limitations imposed on women include the fact that, unlike other Arab-speaking nations and until quite recently, women in Saudi Arabia have not been permitted to drive, run for political positions past the municipal level, or work without a male guardian's permission. These patriarchal policies are not at all correlated with Islamic law, which traditionally prioritizes and promotes women's right to work, own land and contribute to their communities.[3] This disconnect with Saudi Arabia's policies on women and Islam is further strengthened by the fact that all other Arabian Gulf nations are also ruled by conservative Muslim monarchs, and yet the other wealthy Gulf nations exhibit higher female labor force participation rates. Thus, Saudi Arabia is a unique case with its own socio-economic context. In the sense of female contributions to the field of economics, Saudi Arabia's unique differences set a limitation on women to participate in economics in the political realm, but might not have as much of a negative impact on their contributions within the academic realm.

In contrast to the wealthy economies of the Arabian Gulf, the nations of the Levant which include Lebanon, Syria, Jordan and the West Bank and Gaza, exhibit weaker economies and worse female labor participation rates. In addition to the economic limitations which differentiate the Levant from the Arabian Gulf, the Levantine nations are all less than a century out of British and French colonization, in which the displacement of people from their traditional lands and socio-economic roles was a key contributor to the rise of poverty. The high poverty rates of Jordan and Lebanon are associated with millions of displaced refugees from former Palestine and now from Syria as well. The nations with lowest GDP as of 2016, and the lowest female labor force participation rates have much in common. On one hand, there is the effect of political instability and war which impacted the economies of Iraq and Syria. On the other hand, there is the very recent settler-colonialism which impacted the economies of Algeria and the West Bank and Gaza. The context of colonialism in the Levant and North Africa is essential to providing socio-economic context. This is especially relevant as women in the Levant and North Africa traditionally held key economic roles in their previous communal structures, most of which were destroyed with colonialism and the imposition of new economic structures.

> Private property and capitalist relations of production in the context of an expanding market economy transformed class structure. In the rural areas a complex process of social differentiation and stratification occurred, characterized by inequalities in landholding and new social relationships of production and distribution.[4]

Colonial impact not only affects the key economic roles of women by imposing capitalism and land privatization, but in the case of the West Bank and Gaza caused the displacement of, and was the root cause of poverty for, millions of Palestinian refugees. Such context is important to factor in, to address the Western-centered biases that falsely lay the blame on Islam: historical studies highlight the fact that within the traditional cultures of the Levant especially, women held very key economic roles within their communities. Therefore, it is essential to understand the political relations and their economic impacts which have had long-term impact on the economic status of women in the Arab Homeland.

One other major impact of colonialism in the modern economies of the Arab Homeland is the main language use in post-colonial Arab nations. In the Levant and Egypt, both Arabic and English are the professional languages, while in North Africa, French and Arabic are the professional languages. These sub-regional differences have effects on women's advanced education. More women from the Levant and Egypt earn their Ph.D.s from English-language universities in the UK and North America. Many women in North Africa seek completion of their Ph.D.s in modern economics in France due to their French proficiency. Lebanon is an outlier, as it recognizes all three languages, French, English and Arabic as common. The vast majority of Lebanese academics being trilingual, they have the option of completing dissertations and teaching or practicing economics in any of the three languages.

In Lebanon especially, but also in parts of Jordan, and most of North Africa it is becoming increasingly uncommon to complete one's post-secondary education in the Arabic language. Lebanon and Egypt were the first to adopt American universities and implement Western systems of higher education, which initially created the advantage of feminist advocacy in the early 20th century and early female enrollment in education. Yet their initial advancements did not allow them to exceed other Arab nations in the labor force participation of women due to different experiences of political instability from the civil war in Lebanon, to the Egyptian revolution in 2011.

A history of women in education in the Arab Homeland

Although the observed emergence of Arab women graduating with Ph.D. degrees in modern economics began in the mid-1960s, the accomplishments are not limited to such recent involvement. The world's first university, the University of Al-Karaouine in Fez, Morocco, was actually founded by an Arab woman, Fatima Al-Fihri, in 859 AD.[5]

The legacy of educated Arab women was strengthened in 1885 when Tabat M. Islambouly graduated from the Women's Medical College of Pennsylvania, which is now Drexel University in Pennsylvania. Tabat Islambouly was the first Arab medical student to graduate from an American university. She became a successful medical physician in the Arab Homeland.

> Tabat Islambouly is also believed to have gone back to Damascus, and then was in Cairo, Egypt in 1919 according to the alumnae list of that year. After that, the college lost touch with her and it's not known what happened to her ultimately.[6]

As one of the first Arab nations to adopt Western economic structures, Lebanon holds the record for the earliest admittance of females into modern universities within the Arab Homeland. The first three females to graduate within Arab nations were Adele Kassab, Rosa Kulunjian, and Ossanna Maksoudian, who enrolled at the American University of Beirut (AUB) in 1905.[7] The three graduated in 1908 with Nursing Certificates. The AUB implemented coeducation in 1921 with little feminist advocacy or pressure to do so, but as a natural progression to reinstate the traditional economic roles of Arab women within the rising Western economic structures. The coeducation expansion of 1921 was a decision that resulted from an executive observation within the university that other departments required female influence. This expansion encouraged the enrollment of female students in faculties other than Nursing, including the School of Medicine, Pharmacy, Dentistry, and the pre-medical program in the School of Arts and Sciences. As the enrollment of female students increased, Lebanese women began to graduate in a variety of fields, enhancing the contributions of Arab women to the economy. The first Arab woman to be granted a degree from a university in the region was Miss Sara Levy from Palestine, who gained a Ph.C. in Pharmacy from the AUB in 1925.[8] According to the AUB Archives,[9] the next women to be the first to graduate in their field were as follows:

- Munirah F. Jaffri, who graduated with a B.A. in Arts and Sciences in 1926
- Gladys F. Shanklin, who graduated with a B.A. in Arts and Sciences in 1926
- Fortune Azriel who graduated with a D.D.S Dentistry in 1926
- Edma Abou Shadid who gained her B.A. in Arts and Sciences in 1926, and then an M.D. in Medicine in 1931 from AUB. She also continued post-graduate studies from 1932–1933 in Paris and London. Dr. Shadid practiced as a clinical assistant in gynecology and obstetrics at AUB from 1933–1935. She then worked as a government physician at the Royal Hospital of Baghdad from 1935–1942. She became the first woman to open a private practice in Baghdad from 1942 to 1945, then moved to work in the U.S.A.

By 1947, which commemorated the silver jubilee of coeducation at the AUB, there were 113 female students enrolled across every single department within the university except for the engineering school. These accomplishments for women were published in "the *kulliyah* magazine" (college magazine) in 1950,[10] which, after presenting the absence of females in the engineering department, wrote "any feminine team of three to force open its gates", empowering and encouraging women to challenge that male-dominated field. The AUB was the first university in the region to enroll female students, and actively advocated for further academic achievements and economic contributions of women.

Egypt paved the path of progress in women's rights and participation in a variety of ways. As the oldest economy within the Arab Homeland, it could be expected that a nation with such a powerful history of politics, trade, and innovation would be one of the first to exhibit female participation in the field of modern economics. As the Egyptian economy grew, the demand for women in the labor force increased and an Arab feminist movement gained mainstream attention. The Egyptian Feminist Union (EFU) was the first women's rights advocacy group in the Middle East, emerging in Egypt in 1923.[11] Led by Huda Sharawi, the EFU successfully advocated for many women's issues including female enrollment in universities. The EFU's advocacy was successful, resulting in female admission to the Egyptian National University in 1928, now internationally recognized as the University of Cairo.[12]

Since the number of modern universities in the Arab Homeland before the 1950s was limited, all universities that were founded later in the 20th century enrolled both female and male students upon opening. For example, the University of Jordan has practiced coeducation since its founding day in 1962.[13] All Arabic universities accept female students equally based on academic ability, and provide equal means of academic and economic achievement for both men and women. Extreme cases that will be evaluated later are nations such as Saudi Arabia, in which gender segregation exists in higher education but, nonetheless, women are not excluded from studying any academic fields.

Female economists in Lebanon

As the first nation to include female students in higher education, along with a historical context of social progressiveness, Lebanon holds the record for the earliest observed involvement of Arab female economists.

The first observed record of an Arab female economics instructor was Ms. Mona Baroody at the American Junior College for Women within the AUB, in 1944.[14] Ms. Mona Baroody first held the position of secretary at the American Office of War Information in Beirut from 1943 to 1944, then later became an instructor of economics from 1944–1946. In 1947, she married an economics instructor, Faisal Farouk Damlouji, who taught economics at the School of Commerce in Baghdad from 1943. The family became better known for Damlouji's diplomatic work in the Iraqi Embassy in London, and later as the Assistant Director General of the economics department in the Foreign Ministry of Baghdad, a position he took over in 1951.

The next Arab woman to make a professional contribution within the field of economics was Ms. Salwa Mansur Jurdak, born in 1927 in Beirut, Lebanon. Ms. Jurdak received her Bachelor of Arts degree in 1947, her M.A. degree in 1948 and became an instructor at the Beirut College for Women within the AUB in 1949. She was the second female economics professor in the Arab Homeland, also teaching subjects such as history and political science since November 1949. The inclusion of female faculty was not limited at the AUB, as the economic positions of women were traditionally valued in the Levant. In 1951, another female faculty member began teaching economics at the AUB. Mrs. James Baster had an M.A. from Columbia University and lectured economics at AUB from 1951 to 1953.

The AUB was the first university among Arab nations to hire a female economist, and continues to have strong female presence within their Economics Faculty. In fact, the chair of the department of economics from 2011 to 2015 is Dr. Nisreen Salti. Dr. Salti received her Ph.D. in Economics from Princeton University in 2006, and in that year joined the AUB. When surveyed as a primary source, Dr. Salti clarifies that she never faced any barriers in pursuing an education or gaining a career within economics. She also states: "In the Middle East, as it is elsewhere, the field of economics tends to be male-dominated, but this has been changing in the Middle East as it has been in the rest of the world."[15] This quote by the chair of the economics department at AUB in 2015 indicates that the involvement of Middle Eastern female economists continues to evolve alongside that of female economists across the world, and also along with the constant growth of the field of economics. Retrieved from her professional website, two topics of recent interest include health economics (for example, see Salti and Raad 2010; Salti and Ghatta 2016) and public finance (for example, see Salti 2015 and Salti et al. 2015).

The references cited here, along with her many other publications and ongoing research show that this Arab economist is not only contributing to the field of economics, but she is using her platform as an economist to contribute positively by addressing social and economic issues within the Arab Homeland. Her work is often published and recognized on an international level, as she continually succeeds to release economic research that brings forth relevant and influential data. The Faculty of Economics at the AUB includes many other successful female economists.

Female economists in Egypt

Among the many Egyptian universities that benefit from the contributions of female economics professors, the University of Cairo holds the largest number within a department of economics with 88 female economics professionals.[16] Not only did the University of Cairo enact the first enrollment of female students within Egypt, but it also hired numerous female economists in the 1960s who were among the first Arab women to gain Ph.D. degrees in economics. An emeritus faculty member, Dr. Salwa Ali Soliman Farghali (recognized as Dr. Soliman) obtained a Ph.D. in Economics in 1966 from the University of Southern California.[17] Her Ph.D. dissertation appears to also be the first publication within economics by an Arab woman. Her thesis was published as a book titled "Planning under Socialism—and Risk" in 1966. In this publication, Dr. Soliman examines the role of "risk" with emphasis in the economic system of the United Arab Emirates. Her main hypothesis is that all economic systems face risk, centrally planned as well as market-based. Her second hypothesis is that

> under socialist centrally-planned systems, the situations which originally represent cases of "risk" are affected by new conditions that turn them into situations of "uncertainty," and that this fact gives a strong justification to the arbitrariness in decision-making under these systems.
>
> *p. 2*

As she taught at the University of Cairo, she was responsible for many publications in Arabic, one of which was a first edition political economy textbook which introduces the applied economics aspects within mixed economic systems, discussing the rules and foundations upon which economic policies should be built and clarifying the fundamental objectives such economic policies should seek to achieve.

Another significant University of Cairo emeritus faculty member and alumna is Dr. Hanaa A. Kheir-El-Din who gained her Bachelor's degree in Economics with highest honors from the University of Cairo in 1961. She acquired her Ph.D. in Economics in 1967 at Massachusetts Institute of Technology in the U.S.A., where she conducted a successful dissertation titled "A Quadratic Programming Approach to the Problem of Optimal Pricing and Use of Cotton in

Egypt." Dr. Kheir-El-Din's success within economics includes public service as an economic advisor for ministries in the Arab Homeland since 1968. Her economic contributions were prominent in the following list of highly influential advisory roles:[18] Economic advisor at the Ministry of Treasury (1968–1969); economic advisor at the Arab Corporation for Investment Guarantee in Kuwait (1974–1975); economic consultant evaluating all investment in construction within the Ministry of Planning of Kuwait (1977–1978); economic advisor within the Ministry of Economy in Cairo, Egypt (1978–1980); economic advisor to the Minister of Economy and Foreign Trade in Egypt (1981–1985); economic advisor to the Minister of Economic Cooperation in Egypt (1986–1993); economic advisor to the Minister of Economy and Foreign Trade (1994–1996); and member of the Ministry of Foreign Affairs, Sweden (2005–2008).

Dr. Kheir-El-Din's vast success is not limited to her many influential advisory roles within economics ministries, as she has succeeded in roles such as the director of research within the Economic Policy Initiative Consortium from 1997–1998. Her expertise was utilized often in her participation as a board member at the United Nations University (Kokusai rengō daigaku), located in Shibuya, Tokyo, Japan, and also in the Egyptian Competition Authority, the Economics Committee of the Supreme Council of Culture in Egypt, the Egyptian Capital Market Authority, and the Executive Committee of the Social Fund for Development in Egypt. Dr. Kheir-El-Din received an Award of Honour by the Economics Research Forum (ERF) alongside other successful researchers. The ERF acts as a professional local network within Egypt, which recognizes the successes of high-quality economic research, promoting sustainable economic development in the Middle East and North Africa region.[19]

In consecutive order, the next Egyptian emeritus faculty member from the University of Cairo who was one of the first Arab females to contribute to the field of economics is Dr. Nadia Hassan Soliman. She completed her M.Sc. in 1969 at the University of Cairo with a dissertation on "Agricultural Land Taxation in the U.A.R." Her thesis was conducted and reported in English and it aimed to find a taxation system that maximized the tax revenue from land without neglecting the equity of tax and its income distributional effects and balancing the issue of land taxes as dis-incentives for agricultural development.

The successful female economists from the University of Cairo have held a variety of influential roles and have made an impact in the field of economics within the Arab Homeland.

Within the field of economics, there are many groups and councils that utilize economics expertise to advocate policy and legislation. The Egyptian Center of Economics Studies (ECES) funds and publishes a wide variety of economic research, as an independent and non-profit organization. With the contributions of international experience and the thorough evaluation of many stakeholders, the organization aims to continually increase economic efficiency and social justice within Egypt. The ECES provides research to propose effective economic policies and introduce institutional and legislative reforms within Egypt. The ECES is divided into three categories of involvement; the board of directors, the ECES members, and the ECES research team. Four of the 41 ECES members are women who work in influential roles within the Egyptian economy. The research team of 21 includes 10 female economists. All the managing roles within the team are held by female economists while many of the male economists on the team contribute as supporting staff.

Dr. Abla Abdel-Latif is the executive director and director of research within the Egyptian Center of Economic Studies. With over 20 years of teaching experience as a Professor of Economics at the American University in Cairo, she has also participated in research within the ERF and is the author of many publications within international refereed journals. She is currently the chairwoman of the Presidential Advisory Council for Economic Development, a member of the Central Bank of Egypt's Coordinating Council, and is the first female board member at the National Bank of Egypt. She currently holds the role of the main economic advisor to the president of the republic of Egypt. Her economics contributions have been recognized by Western academics: she received a special award for outstanding achievement and excellence in research from Sussex University in the UK.[20]

The other female economists on the ECES research team include Magda Awadallah the deputy director of finance and administration. She has over 30 years' experience. Her previous international contributions include the finance accounts manager at the USAID-funded National Council of Negro Women, Inc., and work with the International Development and Energy Associates, Louis Berger International, Inc., and the UNDP/FAO Regional Fisheries Project. Rama Said is the senior economist at the Egyptian Center for Economics Studies and is also the senior economist at the Ministry of Trade and Industry, where she is responsible for creating strategic documents and policy-oriented research papers on behalf of the ministry. Maya Ehab is an economist at ECES who has previously worked as the team leader at the Egyptian Competition Authority and has served as a visiting fellow at the United Nations Conference on Trade and Development in Geneva. Other roles successfully achieved by women on the ECES research team include three economics research analysts, the executive assistant to the executive director, the editor and translator, and the events, operations and membership officer.

Female economists: Saudi Arabia

Saudi Arabian laws and policies pertaining to women's rights exhibit uncommon limitations and restrictions, with very little, if any, room for political advocacy and resistance. Social and socio-economic barriers imposed on Saudi Arabian women by the state, until quite recently, included the inability to drive, inability to study abroad without a male guardian and inability to work without the permission of a male guardian. These restrictions limit the means and accessibility of labor force participation for Saudi Arabian women in the overall workforce, let alone the field of economics.

Yet despite the unparalleled restrictions Saudi Arabian women face, some do have the means to contribute to academic economics. The controversial policies which enforce gender-based segregation create a demand for all-female faculty. It is common for Islamic universities, which include all universities in Saudi Arabia, to provide separate faculties for males and females. The idea is to provide both genders with access to the same education and awards, but all lectures and academic sessions are segregated. Despite this gender-based segregation being problematic from a Western feminist perspective, it can be argued that there arises an economic benefit from these structures. First, the availability of two faculties for each field of study provides opportunities for female student enrollment and a guaranteed higher rate of female students to be accepted into universities. A second beneficial aspect of the segregation of faculties is that it encourages women to succeed in higher levels of education and to pursue well-paid and economically stable work as professors.

In one university alone, there exists a faculty of 20 Saudi Arabian women working within the field of economics.[21] One of these women economists of Saudi Arabia is Dr. Lubna Mohamed Abu Alaa Abdullah. She is an economics professor at King Abd Al Aziz University in Jedda, and her first research publication was in 1989 on "The Factors Affecting Household Saving, an Attempt to Measure the Qualitative Impact."[22] She specializes in teaching macroeconomics. Some of the other research topics she explores in her publications include oil revenues in Saudi Arabia and the role of barter deals in Egyptian exports.

Islamic universities, Al-Azhar University

Islamic universities offer a variety of world-renowned fields of study, with the university operations maintaining Islamic religious ethics and standards. All levels of education are equally available for males and females. Although Islamic universities are the norm within Saudi Arabia, they are quite rare among the rest of the Arab nations. Most universities in the Arab Homeland operate in correlation with Western education systems. There are many American universities throughout Arab countries such as Lebanon, UAE and Egypt. Many other universities offer all disciplines in the English language and operate in correlation to the UK education system. In the North Africa region, most universities operate in closer correlation to the French education system, and offer all disciplines in French rather than English. Therefore, it can be observed that Islamic universities are not very common outside of Saudi Arabia, and segregation of genders in higher education is also not common in Arab countries.

There is a noteworthy exception. Al-Azhar University in Egypt is a well-renowned Islamic university which practices gender segregation, and, like Saudi Arabia, provides the specialized labor demand for female faculty in Egypt. Apart from the discipline of Islamic economics, the business school at Al-Azhar University includes a gender-segregated economics department.

Other examples of female economists in the Arab Homeland

In Iraq, the historically dominant University of Baghdad first founded its College of Administration and Economics in 1947, then known as the Economics Business College. Almost half of the staff at the University of Baghdad are females, with 3125 female staff in comparison to 3517 male staff.[23] The university's small faculty of economics professors includes two female faculty members with Ph.D.s in Economics (Dr. Hala Khalid Hameed, assistant professor; Dr. Raphe Qasim, lecturer) and one female faculty (Basma Khalil Namik) lecturing with an M.Sc. in Economics.

The Iraq Economists Network has qualified Iraqi economists connecting to discuss and debate current issues including but not limited to monetary policy, inflation, fiscal policy, oil policy, trade policy and tariffs. One of the nine experts overviewing the network is Dr. Salam Smesim.[24] Prior to receiving her Ph.D. in Economics in 1999, she contributed to the field of economics as an economics teacher within commercial secondary schools in 1982. She was the founding dean of the College of Administration and Economics at the University of Kufa from 1991 to 1994.[25] She was a consultant at the World Bank in 2006, an economic advisor at the State Ministry for Civil Society in 2008 to 2011, and has been the economic advisor for the State Ministry of Governorates Affairs since 2011. Dr. Smesim has published 15 scholarly research articles within economics, in addition to over 40 articles published in various newspapers and magazines. Her scholarly publications topics include budget deficits, investment and globalization, providing economic analysis for key issues within the Arab Homeland.

Jordan

In Jordan, all universities have been co-educational since they were founded and female faculty began working as soon as they were eligible to teach. The University of Jordan was established in 1962,[26] and currently only three of the faculty members within the Department of Economics are female professors with Ph.D.s. Dr. Buthaina Muhtaseb, earned her B.Sc. in Economics and Statistics in 1974 from the University of Jordan and her Ph.D. in Economics in 1995 at Strathclyde University in the UK with her thesis on "The Competitiveness of Jordan's

Manufacturing Industry." She is a current faculty member in the Economics Department at the University of Jordan. Dr. Muhtaseb could potentially be the first female to gain a degree in economics from a Jordanian university. In addition to her success as a professor at the University of Jordan, Dr. Muhtaseb has published 16 research articles and one textbook titled *Competitiveness and Development* in 2010.

Another female faculty member at the University of Jordan is Dr. Dalal Alkadi. Dr. Alkadi has been practicing in the field of economics since the 1980s, and published six scholarly research articles between 1987 and 1990. She first received a B.Sc. in Statistics from the University of Baghdad in 1975 and completed her Ph.D. in Statistics in 1985 at Oklahoma State University in the United States. Due to her background in statistics, her economics contributions emphasize econometrics. She has published four books since 1990. She also published two textbooks: *Statistics for Business and Economics*, 1st and 2nd editions, 2004 and 2005; and *Mathematics and its Application in Business and Economics*, 2006 (listed as first named co-author). Both textbooks are published in Arabic by Al Ahliyya Amman University (the mathematics text is also published in English).

Female ministers of economics in the Arab Homeland

The contributions of Arab women, especially in economics, are not limited to publications, academic careers and advisory roles. Arab female economists have successfully contributed to the workforce in a variety of roles and operations, including the government sector. In addition to the many female economic advisors within the Arab Homeland, including some economists mentioned above, Arab female economists continue to rise to leadership and gain greater influence.

The first female minister within the Arab Homeland was Ms. Naziha Jawdet Ashgah al-Dulaimi as the minister of municipalities in Iraq in 1952. Before her appointment as the first female Arab minister, she co-founded and was the first president of the Iraqi Women League, founded in 1952. Ms. Al-Duhaimi began feminist empowerment in Iraq and set an example of leadership for all other women within the Arab Homeland. The current youngest minister in the world is another Arab woman, Shama Al Mazrui minister of youth in UAE.

Table 21.3 presents 13 women holding ministerships in eight different locations within Arab nations. This list only includes ministry positions that are economics-related:

Table 21.3 Contemporary female ministers in economics within the Arab Homeland[27]

Name	*Location*	*Position*	*Time Period*
Rima Khalaf Hneidi	Jordan	Minister of trade and industry	1993–1995
Dr. Nawal 'Abd al-Moneim al-Tatawi	Egypt	Minister of economy and international cooperation	1996–1997
Dr. Magda Shahin	Egypt	Vice-minister of international economic relations	circa 1999
Dr. Samiha Fawzi Ibrahim	Egypt	Minister of trade and industry	2011–present
Dr. Lubna Bint Khalid Al Qasemi	UAE	1 Minister of economy and planning 2 Minister of foreign trade 3 Minister of development and international cooperation	1 2004–2007 2 2008–2013 3 2013–2016
Leila Solh	Lebanon	Minister of industry	2004–2005
Raya Haffar Al-Hassan	Lebanon	Minister of finance	2009–2011

Dr. Abir Awda	Palestine	Minister of national economics	2009–present
Dr. Lamia Assi	Syria	1 Syrian ambassador in Malaysia 2 Secretary of economy and trade at the Ministry of Economy	1 2004–2010 2 2010
Fatema Marouane	Morocco	Minister of trade and social economy	2013–present
Boutheina Ben Yaghlane	Tunisia	Secretary of State of Finance	2015–2016
Lamia Zeribi	Tunisia	1 Secretary of state of development, investments and international cooperation 2 Minister of finance	1 2015–2016 2 2016–2017

A few additional biographical details are relevant. Dr. Nawal 'Abd al-Moneim al-Tatawi of Egypt was also the first female bank director in the Arab world.[28] Dr. Magda Shahin of Egypt holds a Ph.D. in Economics from the University of Cairo. She was previously an ambassador to Greece, and she is currently a professor and the director of the Prince Alwaleed Center for American Studies and Research, School of Global Affairs and Public Policy at the American University of Cairo.[29] Dr. Samiha Fawzi Ibrahim of Egypt obtained her Ph.D. in Economics at the University of Cairo in 1984.[30] Along with extensive experience teaching as an economics professor at the University of Cairo, she held the role of the Deputy Director of the Egyptian Center for Economics Studies, and served as a board member at the Egyptian Competition Authority, the Bank for Exports Development, the National Council for Women and the General Authority for Investment.

In the UAE, Dr. Lubna Bint Khalid Al Qasemi was also appointed president of Zayed University in 2014.[31] She was rated first in the "top ten most powerful Arabic women in 2013" list and ranked the 42nd most powerful woman in the world by *Forbes* in 2015.[32]

Another Arab female economist to acknowledge is Dr. Nemat Shafik who is the deputy governor of the Bank of England from 2014 to 2019.[33] Although her contributions as an economist are representative of England, she is an Arab woman of Egyptian origin born in Alexandria, Egypt in 1962. She represents the Bank of England on an international level overseeing many reforms and efficiency updates to improve institutional operations. Prior to her current role she was the deputy managing director of the International Monetary Fund from 2011 to 2014. Dr. Shafik was also a vice president of the World Bank, where her implemented improvements are valued at $50 billion. In honor of her vast achievements in economics, she was made a Dame Commander of the British Empire in 2015, in the Queen's Birthday Honours list.

Conclusion

Female economists have been present since the mid-20th century in obtaining advanced economics degrees, in university teaching, in research and publication, and in government service (including at the ministerial level) in the Arab Homeland. The entry of women into studying and teaching of economics at universities in Arab nations began with secular institutions such as the Egyptian National University (now the University of Cairo) and institutions with close ties to the English-speaking academic world such as the American University of Beirut, American University in Cairo, and British University in Cairo. Women's entry into economics in French-speaking universities in Arab countries was slower, paralleling the belated academic participation of women in France, where women did not even win the right to vote until after World War II.

The entry of women into university teaching of economics in the Arab Homeland has paralleled their entry into teaching in other disciplines, but credentials and skills as economists have helped women to rise to ministerial rank in the region. The role of women in liberal economics within Arab nations is similar to the role of women in economics elsewhere in the world. As the field of economics grows, and as economies grow stronger, more women participate in studying economics and in pursuing careers within the field.

Notes

1 We are grateful to participants in the 2016 History of Economics Society conference at Duke University and especially to our discussants, Joseph Persky and Annie Cot, for helpful comments.
2 Culcasi, K. (2012, p.1108).
3 Sayigh, R. (1979, p. 23). On women's economic rights and activity in earlier times, see Janine Sourdel-Thomine and Dominque Sourdel (1973), Abraham Marcus (1983), and Amira al-Azhary Sonbol (2005).
4 Farsoun, S. and Aruri, N. (2006, p. 45).
5 Guinness World Records, retrieved from: www.guinnessworldrecords.com/world-records/oldest-university
6 www.andfaraway.net/blog/2013/12/23/sabat-istanbuly-female-student-at-the-womens-medical-college-of-pennsylvania1885/
7 American University of Beirut Archives.
8 Ibid.
9 Ibid.
10 *The Al-Kulliyah Magazine*. "Through Half a Century: Women Students." June and July 1950. Published by the Alumni Association, American University of Beirut, p. 15.
11 Guity Nashat and Judith E. Tucker (2012, pp. 105, 118–119), and Soha Abdel Kader (1987).
12 Nashat and Tucker (2012) and Kader (1987).
13 University of Jordan Archives.
14 American University of Beirut archive, online.
15 Personal statement via e-mail.
16 University of Cairo website accessed in 2016: http://feps.cu.edu.eg/contacts/fepsfaculty.php
17 Ibid.
18 Curriculum vitae on the University of Cairo faculty website; http://feps.cu.edu.eg/contacts/feps faculty.php
19 https://erf.org.eg/us/
20 www.eces.org.eg/Staff.aspx
21 The Department of Economics at King Abd Al Aziz University in Jedda, Saudi Arabia. See also "Arab universities: The kingdom is king," *The Economist*, April 2, 2016, p. 51, and "First Female Politicians Elected in Saudi Arabia," *Huffington Post*, December 13, 2015.
22 Curriculum vitae, online.
23 Arabic source: University of Baghdad website, www.en.uobaghdad.edu.iq/PageViewer.aspx?id=29
24 Information obtained from http://iraqieconomists.net/en/miss-salam-smesim-ph-d/
25 University of Kufa website, www.uokufa.edu.iq/
26 University of Jordan archives.
27 Rima Khalaf Hneidi, www.un.org/press/en/2010/sga1263.doc.htm; Nawal 'Abd al-Moneim al-Tatawi, http://guide2womenleaders.com/egypt-htm; Magda Shahin, www.ictsd.org/about-us/magda-shahin; Samiha Fawzi Ibrahim, www.eiod.org/uploads/publications/pdf/assessingcgegypt.pdf; Lubna Bint Khalid Al Qasemi, www.arabianbusiness.com/people/sheikha-lubna-al-qasimi-507900.html; Leila Solh, http://whoisshe.lau.edu.lb/expert-profile/leila-solh-hamade; Raya Haffar Al-Hassan, http://whois she.lau.edu.lb/expert-profile/raya-haffar-el-hassan-minister-finance; Abir Awda, www.mne.gov.ps/DesktopDefault.aspx?lng=2; Lamia Assi, www.syrianfinance.gov.sy/arabic/2079.html&pr_docid=2792; Fatem Maroueane, www.artisanat.gov.ma/; Boutheina Ben Yaghlane, www.huffingtonpost.com/author/boutheina-ben-yaghlane; Lamia Zribi, http://siteresources.worldbank.org/WBEUROPEEXTN/Resources/268436-1423672573448/9746237-1475484587168/9917909-1480580082085/Bio_list_of_speakers_EN.pdf; www.abouther.com/node/2336/people/leading-ladies/lamia-zribi-breaks-male-monopoly-heads-tunisian-finance-ministry

28 http://web.archive.org/web/20160816235645/http://www.kenanaonline.net/page/983
29 www.ictsd.org/about-us/magda-shahin
30 Retrieved from Curriculum Vitae, online www.feps.edu.eg/ar/staffpages/samihaelsayed/curiclum/CV.doc
31 https://uaecabinet.ae/en/details/cabinet-members/her-excellency-sheikha-lubna-bint-khalid-al-qasimi
32 www.forbes.com/pictures/mdg45jihh/sheika-lubna-bint-khalid-al-qasimi/
33 www.bankofengland.co.uk/about/people/minouche-shafik/biography.

Bibliography

Abdel Kader, S. (1987). *Egyptian Women in a Changing Society, 1899–1987.* Boulder, CO: Lynne Rienner.

American University of Beirut Quarterly Magazine, Winter 2003, 1(2).

Culcasi, K. (2012). "Mapping the Middle East from within: (counter-) cartographies of an imperialist construction," *Antipode* 44: 4.

Economic Development Board (2013). "Increasing Women's Contribution to Bahrain's Economy. (June 17). Retrieved from www.bna.bh/portal/news/565892?date=2013-07

Egyptian Center for Economic Studies. (2014). Retrieved from www.eces.org.eg/Default.aspx

Faculty of Economics and Political Science, Cairo University. Retrieved from www.feps.edu.eg/en/departments/economics/home.php

Farghali, S. (1966). *Planning under Socialism—and Risk.* University of Southern California Dissertations and Theses. Retrieved from http://digitallibrary.usc.edu/cdm/ref/collection/p15799coll18/id/219299

Farsoun, S. and Aruri, N. (2006). *Palestine and the Palestinians: A Social and Political History.* Boulder, CO: Westview Books.

"First Female Politicians Elected in Saudi Arabia." (2015, December 13). *The Huffington Post.* Retrieved from www.huffingtonpost.com/entry/saudi-arabia-female-politicians_us_566d8368e4b0e292150e3472

Hosseini, H. S. (2003). "Contributions of Medieval Muslim Scholars to the History of Economics and Their Impact: A Refutation of the Schumpeterian Great Gap," in W. J. Samuels, J. E. Biddle, and J. B. Davis, eds., *A Companion to the History of Economic Thought*, Malden, MA: Blackwell, pp. 28–45.

Islahi, A. A. (2015). *Economic Thinking of Arab Muslim Writers during the Nineteenth Century.* Basingstoke, UK, and New York: Palgrave Macmillan.

Marcus, A. (1983). "Men, women and property: dealers in real estate in eighteenth century Aleppo," *Journal of the Economic and Social History of the Orient* 26(2): 137–163.

Minister of Economy and the Moroccan ambassador discuss strengthening cooperation. (2016, March). *Retrieved from Maan News Agency*, https://maannews.net/Content.aspx?id=836880

Ministère de l'Artisanat et de l'Economie Sociale et Solidaire. (2015). Retrieved from www.artisanat.gov.ma/fr

Nashat, G. and Tucker, J. E. (2012). *Women in the Middle East and North Africa.* Bloomington and Indianapolis, IN: Indiana University Press.

Nemat (Minouche) Shafik – Deputy Governor, Markets & Banking. Retrieved from www.bankofengland.co.uk/about/Pages/people/biographies/shafik.aspx

Ristem, A. (2010, February 19). *Minister of Economy holds two meetings regarding the administration and economic activities in Aleppo.* Retrieved from http://syria-news.com/readnews.php?sy_seq=109895

Roba. (2013, December 23). *UPDATED: Sabat Istanbuly, female student at the women's medical college of Pennsylvania, 1885.* Retrieved from www.andfaraway.net/blog/2013/12/23/sabat-istanbuly-female-student-at-the-womens-medical-college-of-pennsylvania1885/

Safa, S. (2016, March 16). *AUB acknowledges achievements and steps forward in gender equity.* Retrieved from www.aub.edu.lb/news/2016/Pages/gender-equity.aspx

Salti, Nisreen. (2015). "Income inequality and the composition of public debt," *Journal of Economics Studies* 42(1): 821–837.

Salti, Nisreen and Ghatta, Hala (2016). "Food insufficiency and food insecurity as risk factors for physical disability among Palestinian refugees in Lebanon: evidence from an observational study," *Disability and Health Journal* 9(4) (October): 655–662.

Salti, Nisreen, Chabaan, Jad, Nakkash, Rima and Alaouie, Hala (2015). "The effect of taxation on tobacco consumption and public revenue in Lebanon," *Tobacco Control* 24(1): 77–81.

Salti, Nisreen, Chabaan, Jad and Raad, Firas (2010). "Health equity in Lebanon: a microeconomic analysis," *International Journal of Equity in Health* 9(1) (January): 1–21.
Sayigh, R. (1979). *Palestinians: From Peasants to Revolutionaries*. London: Zed Press.
Sonbol, A. A. (2005). "How the *Shari'a* Sees Women's Work," in N. Hanna and R. Abbas, eds., *Society and Economy in Egypt and the Eastern Mediterranean 1600–1900: Essays in Honor of André Raymond*, Cairo and New York: The American University in Cairo Press, pp. 159–179.
Sourdel-Thomine, J. and Sourdel, D. (1973). "Biens foncier constitue waqf en Syrie Fatimide pour une famille de Sarifs Damascains," *Journal of the Economic and Social History of the Orient* 15: 269–296.
Souriyati. (2016, February 9). "Thabat Istanbuly: Syrian student studying medicine in America, 1885." Retrieved from www.souriyati.com/2016/02/09/40812.html
UAE Gender Equality Profile 2011. (2011, October). (UNICEF). Retrieved from www.unicef.org/gender/files/UAE-Gender-Eqaulity-Profile-2011.pdf
UAE Women Statistics. Retrieved from www.dwe.gov.ae/stat.aspx
Women and AUB: A Pioneer Spirit. (2003). [*American University of Beirut Quarterly Magazine*]. Retrieved from http://staff.aub.edu.lb/~webmgate/winter02/feature1.html

22

THE INVISIBLE ONES

Women at CEPAL (1948–2017)[1]

Rebeca Gómez Betancourt and Camila Orozco Espinel[2]

Introduction

Inspired by the economic and social trends of the countries of the region, the United Nations Economic Commission for Latin America and the Caribbean, known by the Spanish acronym CEPAL,[3] is the home of "historical structuralism," a well-articulated school of thought. Important work has been done to understand both the CEPAL's role within the 20th-century history of economic thought and its influence on Latin American economic policy.[4] The work of many of its key members—such as Raúl Prebisch and Celso Furtado—has been the subject of important research. The contributions of Maria da Conceição Tavares, one of its central thinkers, have also raised significant discussions within the scientific community.[5] Nevertheless, very little is known about other women whose professional and intellectual careers have been shaped at the CEPAL's forums (journals, seminars, headquarters, etc.) and, more generally, by the CEPAL's ideas; women who contributed significantly to shaping and advancing the development of the Commission's programs and ideas.

Although we cannot compare Maria da Conceição Tavares with Alicia Bárcena Ibarra, the current CEPAL executive secretary, the comparison between Bárcena Ibarra and José Antonio Ocampo, former executive secretary (1998–2003), illustrates the differences in visibility between women and men associated with the Commission. Ocampo has combined an academic career in Colombia and the United States with a highly publicized career as a professional economist, working for the Colombian government and the United Nations. His name is well known to anyone familiar with Latin America's political and economic life. While Bárcena Ibarra's profile is equally as high in academic and governmental spheres, her name and work are less well known to the general public.[6]

Here, we expect to take the first steps toward identifying the women associated directly or indirectly with the CEPAL. The idea is to contribute to rendering their names and work visible beyond their location and fields of work. To the best of our knowledge, there is no register or list of the women who have been professionally or academically connected to the Commission. Our purpose, therefore, is to highlight the importance of their contribution to the CEPAL's research and operational activities and hence to Latin American intellectual, social, and economic life. Our aim is twofold. First, by using the CEPAL's Digital Repository, we will present the academic and professional background of the ten most prolific women who have published via any of the Commission's media (journals, books, reports, etc.), including their fields, sub-fields, and focus areas. The idea is to go beyond the individual evaluation of these ten women's trajectories and contributions, and look for the general trends that connect them as a group. Our goal is not to undertake any evaluations or analyses concerning their work.[7] Our main concern is to identify them individually and then establish their common characteristics. Second, by studying the mechanisms of self-promotion that these women use to make their work visible outside of the Commission (personal website, Academia profile, etc.), we will measure their online visibility.

Our approach demonstrates that a significant number of women have been relatively prolific regarding their participation in CEPAL forums: (1) 35.4% of the total authors are women and 64.6% are men; (2) 28.4% of the total documents identified were published by women and 71.6% by men. Nevertheless, their visibility is poor compared to their male counterparts, particularly their online visibility. Our yardstick throughout this study will be these two groups of men, that is, the group of more prolific male authors at the CEPAL's outlets and the group of male authors with the same number of publications as the ten most prolific women.

This text is divided into five sections. The first will briefly introduce the CEPAL, its history, the international context of its foundation, the specificities of its method of analysis, and some elements to explain its institutional organization. In the second section, we will describe the general course of action we adopted, our data, and the specific empirical procedures used to define and limit our corpus. In the third section, primarily based on the information available at the CEPAL Digital Repository—i.e. the list and content of the publications—we will introduce the trajectory (in terms of fields, sub-fields, and topics of study) of the ten most prolific of the CEPAL's female authors. We will not take into account their activities outside of the CEPAL. In the fourth section we will provide a characterization of their shared features and trends. In the fifth section we study their online visibility. Finally we will provide some concluding remarks.

CEPAL: a brief presentation

The Economic Commission for Latin America was established through a United Nations Economic and Social Council on February 25, 1948 and launched its activities that same year. In 1984 the scope of the Commission's work was broadened to include the countries of the Caribbean. With its headquarters in Santiago, Chile,[8] the CEPAL is one of the five regional commissions of the United Nations. It encompasses 45 member States (20 in Latin America, 13 in the Caribbean, and 12 from outside the region[9]) and reports to the United Nations Economic and Social Council (ECOSOC). Since its creation, the Commission has had ten executive secretaries: nine men and one woman.[10] Three mission statements have structured the Commission from its beginnings: (1) contribute to the economic development of Latin America; (2) coordinate actions directed toward this end; and (3) reinforce economic ties among countries of the region and with other nations of the world. Later, the promotion of the region's social development was included among its primary objectives.

The constitution of the CEPAL falls within a post-World War II period of construction of an appropriate international institutional structure to foster world peace and development (see Ocampo 1998).[11] The main characteristics of the ideas generated and disseminated at the CEPAL are consistent with the fact that the Commission was never an exclusively academic institution and its audience has traditionally been made up of Latin American policy makers. Indeed, the main focus of the people working at the CEPAL is not the development of an academic career, but the pursuit of policy-oriented research. This is particularly relevant to our study. It illustrates that, in contrast to scholars working at universities or research centers, people working at the CEPAL are not necessarily interested in following the norms of academic publication in terms of either the types of publication or the quantity undertaken.

The CEPAL's historic roots date back to the political movements that emerged prior to World War II in Latin America. These movements were responding to the conception, widespread in the northern hemisphere, of the region's economic development as, on the one hand, primarily based on colonial ideology and, on the other hand, linked to the Monroe Doctrine—the idea that the United States was the only foreign power that could intervene in Latin American affairs. At that point, in Latin America, the defensive measures adopted to face the Great Depression and World War II had reinforced a process of industrialization and a tendency to make use of state intervention in a much more extensive way. However, with the exception of the countries of the Southern Cone, Latin American nations remained fundamentally rural societies until the second half of the 20th century. During its early years, the CEPAL's main concern regarding economic policy was thus to give greater rationality to the process of "industrialization by import substitution," generated—with little planning—to soften the successive external shocks associated with the war and the withdrawal of the international markets.[12]

From its earliest years, the Commission has developed a singular method of analysis and a thematic focus that, with some variations, it has maintained to the present day. Likewise, a normative principle has guided the CEPAL's thinking since its creation: the need for the state to contribute to the ordering of economic development under the *specific conditions* of Latin America. The starting point to understanding the CEPAL's contribution to the history of economic ideas must therefore be the recognition of the specificity of its analytical body and its dependence on the historical and economic conditions of the region (Bielschowsky 1998, p. 10). Known as "historical structuralism," the CEPAL's approach focuses on the analysis of the ways in which the Latin American institutional legacy and inherited production structure influence the economic dynamics and generate behaviors that differ from those of "developed nations." Keynesian thought, the historicist school, and the Central European institutionalists had a decisive influence in the early years of the Commission. More recently, the focus has been switched to new theories of international trade and industrial organization, evolutionary theories of enterprises, and New Institutionalism.

Five phases can be identified in the CEPAL's theoretical framework:

1 Origins and the 1950s: industrialization through import substitution (ISI).
2 The 1960s: reforms to facilitate industrialization.
3 The 1970s: reorientation of development "styles" toward social homogeneity and toward diversification as a means of promoting exports.
4 The 1980s: overcoming the external debt crisis through "adjustment with growth."
5 The 1990s: changing production patterns with social equity.

Raúl Prebisch, second executive secretary of the Commission (1950–1963) and former chief of the Banco Central de la República de Argentina, is one of, if not the main figure involved in the constitution of the CEPAL's school of thought.[13] His work was also fundamental for the creation and consolidation of the institutional conditions that would later allow the growth and dissemination of CEPAL thinking. Devised by Raúl Prebisch and first published in 1976, *Revista de la CEPAL* was one of the principal instruments for spreading the ideas and studies of the community of CEPAL thinkers. The main controversies are to be found in it.

During the 1960s and early 1970s, Maria da Conceição Tavares produced important work for the CEPAL pertaining to the development of the Brazilian economy (most can be found in Tavares (1972)). This work established her reputation as one of the main interpreters of *import-substituting industrialization* and, more generally, of structuralism. Today, Tavares is possibly the most visible woman in the CEPAL constellation. Nevertheless, in her single most influential contribution to the literature,[14] her authorship was not attributed, except in a footnote (see Boianovsky 2000, pp. 415–417). From the mid-1960s onwards, Tavares's piece has been regarded as a benchmark reference, the first systematic analysis of the dynamics of the import substitution process in Brazil and Latin America and, particularly, of its exhaustion in the early 1960s (see for example Hirschman, 1968, p. 106).

Today, the CEPAL is organized into ten divisions:

1. Economic Development
2. Social Development
3. Statistics
4. International Division
5. Trade and Integration
6. Economic and Social Planning
7. Production, Productivity and Management
8. Sustainable Development and Human Settlements
9. Natural Resources and Infrastructure
10. Gender Affairs Program

Regarding gender discrimination, important work had been done at CEPAL within the frame of the positive discrimination policies of the United Nations. Since the 1990s, the proactive policy of recruiting more women for different posts, profiles, and departments has been changing at the CEPAL, in line with United Nations recommendations. The model of recruitment policy established from the creation of the CEPAL in 1948 was thus modified, and certain gender equity policies were introduced.

Corpus definition and its limits

From a large corpus of documents, we made a list of the 30 most prolific female authors in the CEPAL's publications. The data used in this analysis come from the CEPAL Digital Repository.[15] This database provides the entire list of publications, from the first CEPAL publication in 1948 to the most recent one. Our sample thus runs from 1948 until April 2017. We kept an index of all of the documents: periodicals, journals, newsletters, annual reports, books, monographs, project documents, studies, investigations, and series (Appendix 22.1).

We defined our corpus in four steps. First, we used R, an open-source programming language and environment software for statistical computing and graphics, to identify the list of authors and their respective publications: 8,938 authors and 42,162 documents published. Second, by using the number of documents published as our criteria, we organized the list of authors into decreasing order. Third, by using the Package "gender"[16] we identified the female authors: 1,734 authors were identified as female, 3,159 as male, and 4,045 were neither identified as female or male. From the 4,893 authors that were identified either as female or male, 64.6% were male and 35.4% female. From the total of 42,162 published documents identified, 9,007 were published by women, 22,739 by men, and the 10,416 remaining correspond to authors whose gender could not be identified with our method. From the 31,746 that were identified as being published either by a man or a woman, 28.4% were published by women and 71.6% were published by men.

The method of assigning gender on the basis of names has significant limitations. The most important of these is the zone of ambiguity that results (associated with the existence of names that are gender neutral, for example). Given that these were the first steps toward the constitution of systematic data taken on women that are directly and indirectly associated with the Commission, we used this method initially even though there was a risk of not being able to identify some of the authors as women.

Fourth, we identified the 30 most prolific female authors and the list of their publications (see Table 22.1). Since the number of authors that were neither identified as female or male was considerable (4,045 authors, or 45.2% from a total of 8,938), from the list of the 100 most prolific authors obtained from the second step of our method, we manually classified (as male or female) the authors that could not be identified automatically by our method. Of the 30 most prolific authors (see Appendix 22.2), the 30th is a woman: Carmen Arretx.[17] Fifth, we focused on the top ten women on the list.

Some limits are associated with our methodological choices. First, our approach excludes all of the women whose job consists less in publishing the results of their work and relates more to both participating in the day-to-day tasks of the Commission and in fieldwork activities. Likewise, it is a well-known fact that women working on teams and doing most of the work on the ground are less visible when results are published.[18] Second, given that a significant part of our corpus comprises institutional publications that are not always signed or are only signed by the leader of the team, some authors are not identified. Third, we do not pinpoint any differentiation between publications, meaning that we give the same weight to all forms of publication. The main point here is that an article in *Revista de la CEPAL* is not the same as the publication of a project report, for example. Likewise, by giving the same weight to all kinds of publications, we could not identify patterns of change within our corpus as a whole, or, in practical terms, the proportion of individual and institutional publications. Fourth, we could not obtain data on other institutions linked to the CEPAL, where the work of women has been particularly important. For instance, the *Centro Latinoamericano de Demografía* (CELADE) is particularly important, as is Carmen Miró's work, the director of this institution. Fifth, our ranking criterion is exclusively based on the number of publications by a given author. This leaves several questions up for debate, such as the differences between being *prolific* and being *influential*. Nevertheless, as shown in the literature, the publication (of various types) became an important indicator for many social sciences from the 1980s onwards, and moreover, a general criterion in evaluating the activity of research workers at all kinds of institutions. For the CEPAL women working before the 1980s, the criterion of counting the publication to measure their intellectual productivity was less valid because their productivity was presented in different forms: more in conferences, seminars, or consulting work than in the publication of CEPAL's articles or books.[19] Sixth, since our corpus is not divided into time periods (by decades, for example) we could not identify changes in the patterns of publication or verify our results by changing the scale of time or reducing the sample. One reason to proceed in the way that we did is to grasp the general tendency of evolution of the publications. We did not want to restrict our period of study to only one decade—the 1990s, for instance, when the number of publications by women grew—but instead took into account all of the contributions from the creation of the CEPAL in 1948 until 2017. Seventh, we did not study co-authored work, either by women or by men.

These limits, we think, are somewhat compensated by the two main advantages of our method. First, we cover the CEPAL's seven decades of existence, from its creation in 1948 to the present. Second, we have started this list from scratch. Our aim is to overcome these limits in future works and thus create a stronger corpus. In so doing, we expect not only to refine the quantitative procedures used but also to build on qualitative methods, such as questionnaires addressed to people working at the CEPAL. The idea is to expand our present results based on both kinds of methods, so that we can best reflect the group of women whose work is central to understanding the evolution of the Commission's thinking and activities.

Who are the most prolific women in CEPAL-associated publications?

The most prolific women

Table 22.1 presents the list of the 30 most prolific female authors from the full period of study, including all publication types.

Using the number of publications as our ranking criteria means that we are comparing authors with different scopes, or periods of time, in which to publish (differing in terms of how long they have been active at CEPAL). Since we are primarily using the number of publications to, first, identify a group of women who have contributed to the CEPAL's ideas and programs and, second, to compare this group to their male peers, this is not a major limitation. In other words, we are interested in the number of publications as a way of identifying them and establishing

Table 22.1 Top 30 most prolific female authors

Author	*Global rank*[1]	*No. of publications*
Arretx, Carmen	23	54
Arriagada, Irma	26	50
Bárcena Ibarra, Alicia	27	49
Rico, María Nieves	31	45
Moguillansky, Graciela	35	41
Schkolnik, Susana	36	40
Huenchuan, Sandra	38	38
Montaño, Sonia	38	38
Griffith-Jones, Stephany	40	36
Ventura Dias, Vivianne	41	35
Dirven, Martine	43	33
Schatan, Claudia	46	28
Del Popolo, Fabiana	46	28
Tavares, Maria da Conceição	47	27
Bucheli, Marisa	49	25
Errázuriz, Margarita María	49	25
Gutman, Graciela E.	52	22
Torrado, Susana	52	22
Moori Koenig, Virginia	52	22
Cordero, Martha	53	21
Herrera, Ligia	53	21
Bustillo, Inés	54	20
Ruedi, Nora	54	20
Manuelito, Sandra	54	20
Oyarce, Ana María	55	19
Pautassi, Laura C.	55	19
Trucco, Daniela	56	18
Guzmán, Virginia	56	18
Gomes, Charmaine	60	13
Romero, Indira	61	12

[1] The position in this list was derived from step number 2 of our method, i.e., our decreasing-ordered list (by number of publications) of all authors (male and female). Authors with the same number of publications (e.g., Carmen Arretx and Willard Philips with 54 publications) share the same position in our "Global Rank".

a comparison and we are not interested for the purposes of this study in how prolific they are *per se*. Nevertheless, we did calculate the number of publications per year of each of the top 30 female authors and their scope of publication. Only half of the ten more prolific CEPAL female authors (e.g., the first ten women listed in Table 22.1) are in the first ten positions of the list of publications per year at CEPAL. The names of five other women appear in the top ten list for publications per year worked at CEPAL: Charmaine Gomes, Ligia Herrera, Susana Torrado, Daniela Trucco, and María Margarita Errázuriz.

An overview of the ten most prolific female authors

This presentation is based on the information that we gathered from the CEPAL's Digital Repository. Concretely, Digital Repository provides the list and the contents of all the publications of each author. Besides this, very little information is available. We expect that by presenting each one of these women, their work will become more visible.

Carmen Arretx (first CEPAL publication 1971; last CEPAL publication 1989)

Carmen Arretx is a Chilean sociologist specializing in demography. Arretx was an active contributor to CEPAL publications during the 1970s and 1980s. Her first publication, a study of the interrelation between economic and demographic variables, provides a good illustration of her interest in statistical questions applied to demographic issues. During the 1970s, Arretx published her work on the series *Documentos de proyecto e investigación* and *Notas de Población*. These works include projections of the population growth for Chile, Brazil, Honduras, and Argentina. She also derived information on births using data from successive censuses to estimate fertility rates in the region. In 1976, she published a document presenting the activities and objectives of the "Programa de Demografía Formal," whose purpose was to determine the structure and dynamics of the population of each country of the region. She also worked on more historical demographic issues such as the estimation of mortality among members of religious orders in Chile in the 18th and 19th centuries. During the 1980s, Arretx's work focused on the application of different methods for demographic estimation (both quantitative and qualitative, based on family histories and, more broadly, on historical demography) and published further methodological contributions on the same theme. Throughout her career Arretx also worked on methodological issues related to the collection and compilation of demographic data in Latin America.

Irma Arriagada (first CEPAL publication 1976; last CEPAL publication 2008)

Irma Arriagada is a Chilean sociologist with expertise in poverty, gender, and family. She has also worked on informal economy and inequalities. She was an active contributor to the CEPAL publications from the mid-1970s to the late 2000s. Arriagada's first publication associated with the Commission, a "*Documento de proyecto e investigación*" on social stratification and mobility in Latin America, was published in 1976. In the late 1970s and throughout the 1980s, Arriagada focused her work on women and inequalities in the job market. In 1990, she published "La participación desigual de la mujer en el mundo del trabajo" in the *Revista de la Cepal*. The article reviews the work performed by Latin American women both in the employment market and in the domestic sphere, while acknowledging the complexity of the interrelationships between the two spaces. During the 1990s, Arriagada focused her research on the changes in the urban female employment market and the links between education, equality, and employment opportunities. At the end of the decade, Arriagada worked on a comparative perspective, on the composition of families and the policies concerning them in Latin America. Throughout the 2000s she alternated her research on gender and families with topics related to poverty, citizen security, drugs trafficking, and consumption. She also did empirical and analytical work on the concept of social capital.

Alicia Bárcena Ibarra (first CEPAL publication 1985; last CEPAL publication 2016)

Alicia Bárcena Ibarra is a Mexican biologist and the current United Nations Executive Secretary of the CEPAL. She works on a wide range of topics relating to environmental issues and their relationship with development, inequality, and gender. Bárcena Ibarra's first contribution to a CEPAL publication analyzes the specific challenges for the countries of the region in terms of environmental and development issues. While Bárcena Ibarra's participation in the CEPAL media in the 1980s and 1990s was not very active (she published two articles during the two decades), during the 2000s she published a total of 20 articles. Issues such as the sources of funding for sustainable development and the debates related to transgenic products in Latin America are recurrent in her work during this period. Throughout the 2010s Bárcena Ibarra's focus moved to the study of the structural restrictions for development in the region. Questions included education, tax policy, gender equality, and the elderly. She published, in particular, in the *Revista de la Cepal*, "Structural constraints to development in Latin America and the Caribbean: a post-crisis reflection." Her latest publication presents her thoughts on CEPAL's specific approach to economic problems. For example, in 2016 she published *Neostructuralism and Heterodox Thinking in Latin America and the Caribbean in the Early Twenty-first Century*, a book co-authored with Antonio Prado.

María Nieves Rico (first CEPAL publication 1992; last CEPAL publication 2016)

María Nieves Rico is an Argentinean social anthropologist and sociologist. She is currently the director of the Gender Affairs Division of the CEPAL. Her topics are public policies with a gender perspective, public policies with an emphasis on rights, the labor market, family life, poverty and economic autonomy, inequality and environmental resources. She began contributing to the activities of CEPAL's outlets in the 1990s. Her first article "Domestic Violence Against Women in Latin America and the Caribbean: Proposals for Discussion" appeared in *Series Mujer y Desarrollo*. Over the course of the decade, she has continued to work on gender-related issues, particularly domestic violence against women and women at work. In early 2010, she published "Privilegiadas y discriminadas: las trabajadoras del sector financiero," a study on the challenges created by economic globalization in terms of improving gender equality in the workplace, in *Cuadernos de la Cepal*. In the 2010s, her research has also focused on the evolution of the social structure of families in Latin America.

Graciela Moguillansky (first CEPAL publication 1986; last CEPAL publication 2011)

Graciela Moguillansky is a Chilean economist specializing in macroeconomic modeling, production, productivity and management, and international trade and division integration. She has been active in the CEPAL's publications since the mid-1980s. During the second half of the 1980s, she concentrated her work on macroeconomic models (Uruguay 1986, Chile 1987, and Venezuela 1988). In the early 1990s she directed her econometric work toward trade policy, inflation, and public deficits. In 1996, she published "The Macroeconomic Context and Investment: Latin America Since 1980" in the *Revista de la Cepal* and focused on the macroeconomic situation of Chile. In 2000, she worked on the impact of privatization and financial volatility as well as on the connections between corporate risk management and exchange rates. She has also worked on public–private alliances and long-term economic strategies.

Susana Schkolnik (first CEPAL publication 1974; last CEPAL publication 2013)

Susana Schkolnik is an Argentinean sociologist specializing in demography, fertility, old age, indigenous peoples, and gender issues. During the late 1980s, Schkolnik published articles on maternal and infant mortality and population aging in various countries of the region.

She continued this line of research during the 1990s and broadened her focus to fertility issues. In the 2000s Schkolnik established a link between demographic trends and social equity. Throughout her period of activity at the CEPAL, Schkolnik paid particular attention to the study of indigenous communities, including an ethnic approach and the study of the demographic trends of different indigenous communities in the region.

Sandra Huenchuan (first CEPAL publication 2003; last CEPAL publication 2016)

Sandra Huenchuan is a Chilean social worker specializing in Latin American studies on aging, human rights, and public policy. She also works on gender, public policies, and methodology. Her publications combine a conceptual and political approach with applications (first in Chile, later in the Dominic Republic) on topics related to support networks and quality of life for older people. Together with Alicia Bárcena Ibarra, she published *Autonomía y dignidad en la vejez: teoría y práctica en políticas de derechos de las personas mayors*, a book based on the work presented at the second Foro Internacional sobre los Derechos Humanos de las Personas Mayores.

Sonia Montaño (first CEPAL publication 2001; last CEPAL publication 2015)

Sonia Montaño is a Bolivian sociologist. During the first decade and a half of the 2000s, she was the officer in charge of the Gender Division at CEPAL. Her main topics of interests are gender, aboriginal women, poverty, and family. She has published articles on the feminist role of the State. She works with Alicia Bárcena Ibarra. Her research focuses on gender and public policy. In the early 2000s, she published articles relating to domestic violence against women and women's empowerment policies as a strategy to overcome poverty. In the latter half of the decade she prepared many handbooks and training manuals on the use and applications of gender indicators, democratic governance, and gender equality. In 2010, she worked on the consequences of the economic and financial crisis on women's work, levels of poverty, and the use of their time. In 2013, she also published "Mujeres indígenas en América Latina: dinámicas demográficas y sociales en el marco de los derechos humanos" with Dirk Jaspers.

Stephany Griffith-Jones (first CEPAL publication 1992; last CEPAL publication 2016)

Stephany Griffith-Jones is a North American economist. In the early 1990s she worked on capital flows, their consequences, and the policy challenges associated with them. During this period, she published on the return of private flows to Latin America and Latin American access to European capital markets. She applied her research to the Chilean case in particular. During the second half of the 1990s she continued to work on the connection between capital flows and development in the region and extended her research to monetary issues (particularly in relation to the Mexican peso). During the 2000s, Griffith-Jones proposed an international financial framework for crisis prevention in Latin America and worked on the stability of emerging economies. She also used the European Investment Bank, and other European financial institutions as examples, in order to identify lessons for Latin America and the Caribbean.

Vivianne Ventura Dias (first CEPAL publication 1986; last CEPAL publication 2003)

Vivianne Ventura Dias is a Brazilian economist specializing in the economics of agriculture and natural resources. She is currently the director of the International Trade and Integration Division of the CEPAL. She has been heavily involved in trade and development issues. In the second half of the 1990s, she examined the integration of Latin America and the Caribbean into the new international economy. Focusing on the Brazilian case, she also worked on the internalization of companies. During the second half of the 1990s, Ventura Dias analyzed the challenge for Latin America and the Caribbean posed by the new multilateral trade negotiations and, more broadly, on the region's situation in the World Economy in 1998. In the year 2000, Ventura Dias worked on Latin American economic indicators and the transformation associated with the structural changes resulting from globalization.

Analysis of the findings of the ten most prolific women in CEPAL: a group picture

1 Diyi Li and Cory Koedel (2017) observe that the number of women's publications is lower than that of men in all disciplines, except in education, psychology, and sociology. We observe the same result at the CEPAL when we compare women's and men's publications (Table 22.2).
2 The number of publications of the ten most prolific women is also lower than for the ten most prolific men (Table 22.3).

Table 22.2 Number and percentage of female and male publications

	Number of publications	*% of the total*[2]
Female	9,007	28.4%
Male	22,739	71.6%

[2] The percentage corresponds to the 31,746 documents that were identified as being published either by a male or female author. As mentioned earlier, from the total of 42,162 published documents identified, 10,416 could not be identified as being published either by a male or female author.

Table 22.3 Number and percentage of publications by the ten most prolific female and male authors

	Number of publications	*% of the total*
Female	426	31%
Male	908	68%

There is a noteworthy difference between the number of men's versus women's publications that seems quite relevant (see Appendix 22.2): the most prolific men published two to three times more often than the most prolific women. In addition, the 29th most prolific man (bottom of list) has the same number of publications as the most prolific woman.

How can this fact be explained? For example, do the men have longer publishing careers at CEPAL? Do they control more labor resources to support their research (e.g., control research departments, have research assistants, etc.)? Do they have fewer administrative responsibilities? Based on our present corpus of materials, we cannot advance a definitive response to these questions. It is nevertheless our intention to develop further research in this direction.

3 In relation to the academic training and professional trajectory of the ten most prolific female authors: one is a biologist (Alicia Bárcena Ibarra, current CEPAL executive secretary), three are economists (Stephany Griffith-Jones, Graciela Moguillansky, and Vivianne Ventura Dias) and six are sociologists. When we compare the professions of the most prolific men, we observe that the majority of the most prolific authors are economists (Nelson 2017).[20]

Alicia Bárcena Ibarra, current CEPAL executive secretary and also one of the most prolific female authors, has an academic background in the natural sciences. The other nine most prolific women are divided mainly into sociologists and economists, with two social scientists. As Dan Hirschman (2017) and many others have shown "the so-called 'demarcation question'—separating science from not-science—is an old and thorny one.[21] Fields (often) want to be labeled as scientific because science is afforded a certain kind of cultural authority along with material resources." We find often a hierarchy among sciences, putting first natural sciences, and then among the social sciences, economics is in a superior category to sociology.[22] At CEPAL women are underrepresented in natural sciences and in economics when compared with men. According to Diyi Li and Cory Koedel (2017) "female underrepresentation is driven predominantly by underrepresentation in science and math intensive fields."

4 When we analyzed the research themes of the top ten women we found the women at CEPAL are mostly working and publishing on topics about social issues and, more specifically, on gender studies and affirmative action, poverty, education, and demographics (Dimand, Dimand and Forget 1995, 2000). One possible explanation for this pattern of publication subjects is that female authors expect to defend their own interests as women through their work, as explained by Michèle Pujol (1992) and Marco (2001).[23] Concomitantly, if we look over the publications of the ten most prolific CEPAL male authors, none of them has gender as a focus. In division 10, "Gender Affairs Program," related to family and gender, men are in the minority (from one to four out of ten).

5 With regard to methodology: given the nature of the institution, as we expected, most CEPAL-associated publications can be classified as applied works.[24] There is a clear link between the research approach that we observe in publications and CEPAL's aims. In the case of the ten most prolific female authors, they all carried out mainly applied research based on fieldwork (this, for a given region or geographical area) rather than theoretical

work. Only the US American economist (Griffith-Jones) is more erudite about general economics. The group of sociologists is very active in applied work. Carmen Arretx's applied works in the field of demography is just one example.

6 The majority of the ten most prolific female authors do field-related work, with the notable exception of the American economist (Griffith-Jones) whose focus is more academic. The evolution of economics over the last 50 years—in particular, to become a more applied discipline—broadens the classification of "scientific articles." This classification can benefit the CEPAL women, who generally work on applied projects.

7 In addition, given that men dominate the theoretical sphere and women are better represented in applied sciences, the rise of empirical methods in economics, and in other social sciences, has opened up opportunities for women. For example, seven out of the ten members of the theoretical section of the American Sociological Association are men.

Even though a large proportion of the work of male authors at CEPAL is also applied, explained by the policy-oriented and pragmatic focus on Latin American/Caribbean economies of the Commission, a higher percentage, compared to their female homologues, is theoretically oriented.

We observe that the ten most prolific female authors publishing from 1971 to the present use the same professional and academic practices for legitimizing the results of their work by publishing, but also utilize conferences, interviews, and fieldwork. We can relate this to a transformation in the criteria of legitimacy and norms of the social sciences disciplines over the last decade, which has shifted in favor of quantity of publications as the best gateway for many jobs.

8 There is a clustering of the women's publications in the period 1990 to 2010. In other words, the group of ten most prolific female authors belongs to the same generation. Based on our current results, the 1990s is a period particularly interesting to study. Two possible explanations can be advanced. First, changes in recruitment policies at the United Nations were oriented toward increasing the number of women hired at the institution, transforming the gender balance at CEPAL and positively affecting women's opportunities to publish. Second, publishing as a criterion of legitimacy pervaded hybrid institutions (academic and policy-oriented) such as the CEPAL.[25]

9 Concerning their nationalities, six are from the Southern Cone (two from Argentina and four from Chile). One woman comes from each of Brazil, Bolivia, Mexico, and North America. Thus, all but one of the most prolific female authors are from relatively high-income countries, the exception being Sandra Huenchuan from Bolivia.

10 Regarding their intellectual position and interests: Susana Schkolnik (economist) works on industrial economics, international trade, and banking microeconomics. Her approach can be classified as heterodox microeconomics. Stephany Griffith-Jones' (also an economist) work can be classified as neo-Keynesian. The group of sociologists works mainly on gender issues and in particular on the situation of the women in the region. Their work is based on both quantitative and qualitative methods, such as ethnography and interviews.

11 The majority of the ten most prolific female authors currently hold a position at the CEPAL and they are (or were) heads of departments. Most of their publications were published while they were working for the CEPAL, but around 15% of the publications already existed before they took up positions at the CEPAL. In the case of Griffith-Jones, however, most of her CEPAL publications were produced while working outside of the CEPAL.[26]

In early 20th-century US academia, women with Ph.D.s were often also given administrative posts—such as deanships—as well as other major service responsibilities. These administrative posts competed for women's time and energy and likely reduced their publication productivity. Female doctoral-level economists who took US federal government work in the early 20th century also often entered women-specific positions (responsible for child welfare, women's issues, etc.).[27]

The CEPAL's fight against gender discrimination continues to reproduce the institutional status quo. For example, if the director of a department used to be a man, more often than not, once he retired, another man would replace him. This pattern was established from the creation of the CEPAL and can only be changed by explicit and active equity policies.[28]

12 What types of publications do the women versus men contribute to? A gender-based study of the frequency of contributions to the newsletters and annual reports compared to more formal research-oriented publications such as books, journal articles, and studies across the CEPAL population from 1948–2017 might yield interesting results. In the case of the most prolific female and male authors in the CEPAL, the list of publications is comparable in terms of the composition of the type of publications. Whether this holds for less prolific authors is unknown. As is well known today, women and men do not contribute to the same kinds of publications.[29] And in 1900–1940, women contributed substantial numbers of book reviews to major economics journals (see Forget 1995; Madden 2002). The question of the different types of publications to which women and men contribute should be kept in mind when assessing careers based on publication counts.

Online visibility

Now we will discuss the inequalities of the online visibility of the CEPAL women. Online visibility can be defined by the presence in professional and social media via Wikipedia, online curriculum vitae (CVs), Twitter, a personal homepage, Academia, LinkedIn, Repec, Research Gate, or professional Facebook pages.[30]

Here, we are presupposing that visibility and self-promotion can be measured by an individual's online presentation. One of the limits of this work is that the use of this method and definition for visibility cannot apply historically, since online technology is very new. This is a contemporary measure of visibility, not a historical measure.

Concerning online visibility: we noted that out of the ten women, only two have a Wikipedia page: Alicia Bárcena Ibarra the current president (a biologist), and Stephany Griffith-Jones, the North American economist. The others do not have their CVs online. In 2017, the women had no personal websites, nor Academia, LinkedIn, Repec, Research Gate, Twitter, or professional Facebook pages.

Concerning the visibility of the ten most prolific men, eight have a personal website, seven have an Academia page, and eight have their CVs online; the men's visibility is broadly apparent. In comparison, the most prolific women authors are still invisible. There is a dramatic difference in online visibility between the most prolific women and men at the CEPAL.

Based on our sample, these women seem less attached to professional self-promotion than men.[31] This may be explained in three ways:

1 The women have less linear and more interdisciplinary trajectories in comparison to men.[32] An interdisciplinary trajectory might make self-promotion hard, because it is more difficult to synthesize and summarize in a few lines their atypical evolution and to present them in short and relatively standard spaces (such as Academia, Twitter or traditional WebPages) in order to obtain greater visibility. The most prolific CEPAL women are more interdisciplinary, so that would mean they have multiple, distinguishable audiences, and often two or more networks with little overlap. Social media might not be helpful in reaching non-overlapping audiences and networks.

2 The women might have less necessity for visibility, communication and promotion of their own work because of the type of work they do: less work in consulting, more teamwork. Providing private/independent services as an expert might be more typical of the men, and online self-promotion is important to attract this type of work. And it is also possible that field-work in teams with other women does not drive the women to self-promotion and visibility.

3 Networking and publications might be mutually reinforcing with a connection between professional and social media. Once some news appears in one online webpage, it is easily transmitted to other pages. Cross-references via online mechanisms can be high. There is a "knock-on" or "magnifier" effect for the number of times works are cited when the number of publications is high among the men with a strong online presence within the institution. The low visibility of women within the institution (at the CEPAL) might be contributing to their low online visibility and activity.

What do we learn from the fact that the top ten most prolific CEPAL women did not self-promote electronically in 2017? Many questions deserve further exploration. The responsibility for less visibility lies with women themselves: so do they desire self-promotion? The issue can be discussed directly with the CEPAL women to see what their position is and evaluate whether self-promotion through a "peacock effect" is desirable. Further, is the online self-promotion gender gap associated with a community- rather than a self-orientation, with different work emphases (studying the economies rather than promoting ideas about the economies), with different primary disciplines (sociology rather than economics), and the positions held in the institutions (the gender department)? Also, are there policies at the CEPAL concerning online visibility? Do certain CEPAL departments have policies and resources devoted to online visibility whereas other departments do not? Do individuals determine what and where to post online, or are these treated as policy decisions made by various groups within the CEPAL? Further institutional and interview-based research strikes us as crucial. Despite limitations with our approach, further exploration of this visibility measure might be appropriate.

Conclusions

Our evidence suggests an imbalance in terms of visibility between the 20 most published female and male authors associated with CEPAL publications. A question arises: why does this matter? In other words, what is the importance of increasing the visibility of women and their work at CEPAL? To answer this question, it is useful to specify the purposes of diversifying the gender representation of "big names" at any institution, particularly for an institution like CEPAL located between the academic and the policy-making spheres. Indeed, representation of a spectrum of viewpoints moves the institution closer to the wide verity of realities of Latin America.

While individual visibility is not the main goal when research and knowledge creation are at stake, here we used online visibility as a proxy variable to underline (in)equality and (non)diversity in relation to researchers' genders. Given the informative and policy-oriented mission of the CEPAL, improving the visibility of women's research appears, to us, to be of primary importance. They are still underrepresented and much less well known outside the close circles surrounding the CEPAL. If we take into account the fact that women's publications emphasize certain areas (e.g. poverty, education, gender, and demographic studies), equilibrating imbalances in visibility seems more urgent. Our identification of the more prolific female authors associated with CEPAL publications is a first step. But this is just that, a first step. Additional efforts must be made to improve the visibility of CEPAL women.

Efforts for improving their visibility can include: (1) implementation of concrete mechanisms to open positions of power to women; (2) intensification in the promotion of women's research through social media such as Academia, LinkedIn, Twitter, and personal websites, both at the individual and institutional levels; (3) taking advantage of the shift from *theoretical* to more *applied* work in social sciences (economics in particular) to render public the results of their work; and (4) encouraging and developing research on the work and role of women in different institutions, geographical areas, professions, and other spheres to recognize their place in society.

We believe that visibility is important in order to increase the decision-making participation and power of women in society. This argument can be applied to the case of women in economics and women within the history of thought as a whole. Our research has shown the importance of continuing the study of women's contributions in economics. The Latin American case is particularly urgent due to the minimal attention received. While many questions remain unanswered, a first steep step toward raising questions about Latin women economists' visibility has been made.

Appendix 22.1 List of CEPAL outlets

	Año Primer N.	*Año Disponible N. De entradas*
Informes Anuales		
Panorama Social de América Latina		1991
La Inversión Extranjera Directa en América Latina y el Caribe		1995
Estudio Económico de América Latina y el Caribe	1948	1949
Balance Preliminar de las Economías de América Latina y el Caribe		1992
Anuario Estadístico de América Latina y El Caribe		1991
Panorama de la Inserción Internacional de América Latina y el Caribe		1996
C olecci one s		
Libros y Monografías		
Libros de la CEPAL		1990
Libros y Documentos Institucionales		1990
Colección "La hora de la Igualdad"	2012	2012
Páginas Selectas de la CEPAL	2015	2015
Manuales de la CEPAL	2015	2015
Coediciones		1995
Copublicaciones		1995
Cuadernos de la CEPAL (A partir de 2014 se fusiona con la colección "Libros de la CEPAL)	1975	1996
Atlas sociodemográfico		2005
Documentos de Proyectos, Estudios e Investigaciones		
Documentos de Proyectos	2002	2002
Sede de la CEPAL en Santiago (Estudios e Investigaciones)	1948	1990
Sede Subregional de la CEPAL en México (Estudios e Investigaciones)	1951	1990
Sede subregional de la CEPAL para el Caribe (Estudios e Investigaciones)	1969	1992

(continued)

	Año Primer N.	*Año Disponible N. De entradas*
Oficina de la CEPAL en Bogotá (Estudios e Investigaciones)	1961	
Oficina de la CEPAL en Brasilia (Estudios e Investigaciones)	1978	1998
Banner Oficina Buenos Aires		
Oficina de la CEPAL en Buenos Aires (Estudios e Investigaciones)	1973	1991
Oficina de la CEPAL en Montevideo (Estudios e Investigaciones)	1960	1990
Oficina de la CEPAL en Washington (Estudios e Investigaciones)	1950	1990
Series de la CEPAL		
Comercio Internacional	1999	1999
Desarrollo Productivo		1995
Estudios Estadísticos	2001	2001
Estudios y Perspectivas – Oficina de la CEPAL en Bogotá	2002	2002
Estudios y Perspectivas – Oficina de la CEPAL en Brasilia	2003	2003
Estudios y Perspectivas – Oficina de la CEPAL en Buenos Aires	2001	2001
Estudios y Perspectivas – Sede Subregional de la CEPAL en México	2001	2001
Estudios y Perspectivas – Oficina de la CEPAL en Montevideo	2004	2004
Studies and Perspectives – ECLAC Subregional Headquarters for The Caribbean	2006	2006
Estudios y Perspectivas – Oficina de la CEPAL en Washington, D.C.	2007	2007
Financiamiento para el Desarrollo		1992
Macroeconomía del Desarrollo	2000	2000
Manuales	1999	1999
Asuntos de Género		1990
Medio Ambiente y Desarrollo	1997	1997
Políticas Sociales	1993	1993
Recursos Naturales e Infraestructura	1999	1999
Seminarios y Conferencias	2000	2000
Población y Desarrollo	1999	1999
Desarrollo Territorial	2007	2007
Gestión Pública	1999	2000
Informe Estadístico – Oficina de la CEPAL en Brasilia	1988	2013
Series Históricas		1975
Documentos de posición del período de sesiones de la Comisión		1948
Publicaciones periódicas, revistas y boletines		
Revista CEPAL	1976	1976
Notas de Población	1973	1973
Observatorio Demografico Observatorio Demográfico de América Latina	2006	2006
Cuadernos Estadísticos de la CEPAL		1991
Textos para Discussão – CEPAL/IPEA	2010	2010

Boletines		
Boletín CEPAL/FAO/IICA	2011	2011
Boletín CEPAL/OIT	2009	2009
Boletín Desafíos	2005	2005
Boletín Envejecimiento y Desarrollo	2005	2005
Boletín Estadístico Comercio Exterior de Bienes en América Latina y El Caribe	2010	2010
Boletín FAL	1992	1992
Boletín Municipalización de los Objetivos de Desarrollo del Milenio	2011	2011
Carta Circular de Recursos Hídricos		
Newsletter eLAC	2005	2005
REDATAM Informa	1990	
Reseñas sobre Población y Desarrollo	2009	2009
Temas de Población y Desarrollo	2005	2005

Appendix 22.2 Top 30 most prolific authors

Authors	*Number of publications*	*Global rank*
Yoguel, Gabriel	124	1
Alleyne, Dillon	104	2
Sánchez, Ricardo	98	3
Kosacoff, Bernardo	96	4
Katz, Jorge	94	5
Durán Lima, José Elías	85	6
De Miguel, Carlos J.	79	7
Padilla, Ramón	77	8
Samaniego, Joseluis	76	9
Cetrángolo, Oscar	75	10
Pérez Caldentey, Esteban	73	11
Hendrickson, Michael	69	12
Behm Rosas, Hugo	68	13
Stumpo, Giovanni	68	13
Franco, Rolando	67	14
Wilmsmeier, Gordon	65	15
Martínez, Rodrigo	64	16
Gatto, Francisco	63	17
Pérez, Gabriel	63	17
Uthoff, Andras	62	18
Mulder, Nanno	58	19
Moreno Brid, Juan Carlos	57	20
León B., Arturo	56	21
Chackiel, Juan	55	22
Ffrench-Davis, Ricardo	55	22
Somoza, Jorge L.	55	22
Titelman Kardonsky, Daniel	55	22
Guzmán, José Miguel	54	23
Phillips, Willard	54	23

Notes

1 This title alludes to the French documentary film *The Invisible Ones*, written and directed by Sébastien Lifshitz. The film presents the lives of a group of homosexual women and men, born in the interwar years in France, who chose to acknowledge their identity at a time when society rejected homosexuality.

2 We are grateful to Kirsten Madden for her comments on previous versions of this chapter and for the encouragement she gave us during every phase of our research. Earlier versions of this chapter were presented at the annual conference of the History of Economic Society (Toronto, June 2017) and at the 6th conference of the *Asociación Latinoamericana de Historia del Pensamiento Económico* ALAHPE (Bogotá, December 2017). The criticism and remarks that we received during these two events were very beneficial to us. We are particularly grateful to Margarita Fajardo. Thanks also to Carole Boulai and Anna Knight for their carefully reading of this chapter.

3 The English acronym is ECLAC.

4 On the economic thought of CEPAL see: Bielschowsky (1998) and Ocampo (1998, 2013) but also Altimir & Lahera (1998). On its influence on Latin American policy see Pérez-Caldentey & Vernengo (2007). Briceño Ruiz et al. (2013) is also a major reference on the CEPAL.

5 See for example: Boianovsky (2000).

6 She previously served as the under-secretary-general for management at the United Nations Headquarters in New York, chef de cabinet and deputy chef de cabinet to the secretary-general.

7 The contribution of these women to CEPAL both in terms of ideas and within the institution will be explored in a future project.

8 In 1951, the Commission established a sub-regional headquarters in Mexico City, which serves the needs of the Central American sub-region. In 1966 a sub-regional headquarters for the Caribbean was founded in Port-of-Spain, Trinidad and Tobago. In addition, CEPAL maintains country offices in Buenos Aires, Brasilia, Montevideo, and Bogotá, as well as a liaison office in Washington, DC.

9 The member states are Antigua and Barbuda, Argentina, Bahamas, Barbados, Belize, Bolivia, Brazil, Canada, Chile, Colombia, Costa Rica, Cuba, Dominica, Dominican Republic, Ecuador, El Salvador, France, Germany, Grenada, Guatemala, Guyana, Haiti, Honduras, Italy, Jamaica, Japan, Mexico, Netherlands, Nicaragua, Norway, Panama, Paraguay, Peru, Portugal, Saint Kitts and Nevis, Saint Lucia, Saint Vincent and the Grenadines, South Korea, Spain, Suriname, Trinidad and Tobago, the United Kingdom of Great Britain and Northern Ireland, the United States of America, Uruguay, and Venezuela. The associate members are Anguilla, Aruba, Bermuda, British Virgin Islands, Cayman Islands, Curaçao, Guadeloupe, Martinique, Montserrat, Puerto Rico, Sint Maarten, Turks and Caicos Islands, and the United States Virgin Islands.

10 The Mexican Gustavo Martínez Cabañas (1948–1950), the Argentinean Raúl Prebisch (1950–1963), the Venezuelan José Antonio Mayobre (1963–1966), the Mexican Carlos Quintana (1967–1972), the Uruguayan Enrique V. Iglesias (1972–1985), the Argentinean Norberto González (1985–1987), the Guatemalan Gert Rosenthal (1988–1997), the Columbian José Antonio Ocampo (1998–2003), the Argentinean José Luis Machinea (2003–2008) and the Mexican Alicia Bárcena Ibarra (2008–present).

11 Several international organizations such as the World Bank and the International Monetary Fund were created during this period.

12 On the CEPAL's history see: CEPAL (1998); Rosenthal (1988); Suarez (1992); and the United Nations (2000).

13 On Prebisch see: Iglesias (1994); Toye & Toye (2003, 2006); Dosman (2006, 2008); Love (1980), Flechsig (1999). On Celso Furtado see: Bielschowsky (1989); Carvalho (2008); Mallorquín (2000); and Vidal (2001).

14 See Tavares (1964).

15 All documents are available in full-text. The CEPAL Digital Repository is a product developed and maintained by the Hernán Santa Cruz Library, located at the CEPAL Headquarters in Santiago, Chile.

16 The Package "gender" encodes gender based on names and dates of birth using historical data sets. By using these data sets instead of lists of male and female names, this package more accurately guesses the gender of a name, and is able to report the probability that a name was male or female. Because of the significant number of people born in the United States during the 20th century with Latin-American ancestors, we used the U.S. Census or Social Security data sets to create our list of male and female names.

17 Arretx has 54 publications, the same number of publications as the 29th male author, Willard Phillips.

18 See Dimand R. (1995) and Groenewegen & King (1994).

19 On the evolution of the practices and outcomes on women working in the social sciences, see Groenewegen & King (1994) and Kahn (1995).

20 On the productivity of economists see: Markoff & Montecinos (1993).
21 The literature on the demarcation problem is vast. For a recent picture on this debate see: Hansson, Sven Ove, "Science and Pseudo-Science", *The Stanford Encyclopedia of Philosophy* (Summer 2017 edition), Edward N. Zalta (ed.), URL: https://plato.stanford.edu/archives/sum2017/entries/pseudo-science/; and in particular Mahner (2007, 2013). See also Renisio (2017) on the evolution of the social sciences.
22 On women in sciences see, for example: Williams & Massinger (2016); Abir-Am & Outram (1987); Zuckerman & Cole (1991); and Kourany (2001). On the superiority of economics among the social science see: Fourcade et al. (2015) and Forget (2011).
23 Accordingly, when we analyzed the research themes of the top ten women we found an emphasis on gender and affirmative actions. Following, for example, Forget's (1995) work on dissertations and also Strober's (1975) article on women's career, aspirations, education, and training in the case of economists we observe that American women were always less important in quantity and in diffusion of knowledge, and were generally less well known than men until the 1970s.
24 Here, by applied work we mean the application of the econometrics and economic theory to address practical issues in diverse fields such as development economics, demographic economics, labor economics, industrial organization, agricultural economics, education economics, health economics, etc., whereas the fieldwork refers more to different methods, that range from short qualitative studies to large-scale surveys, in order to undertake empirical work in economics based on existing data.
25 We wonder if these high-profile administrative positions are appealing to men and women equally. In other words, what is the value of these positions in terms of career advancement at CEPAL? And what is the value of these positions in effecting research productivity? Are these positions resource-returning (e.g. giving the position-holder control to direct a research agenda over more labor resources) so that they can, for example, advance their research? Further qualitative (interviews and ethnography) research is necessary to provide answers to these questions.
26 See Libby (1984 and 1987) on the place of women in the economic profession.
27 Some questions are part of our next research article, such as: (1) We wonder what the average duration of a woman's tenure in a CEPAL department might be. This question is still open, but we consider it crucial to measuring the ratio publication/duration of their position at the CEPAL. (2) We would like to compare the publications of these women at the CEPAL and elsewhere and also study the average tenure for a woman in a CEPAL department.
28 For a recent publication to understand why we know less about women's work than men's see Weetman (2017).
29 See for example RePEc Blog (2017) to see the women present online in this blog.
30 We are aware of some of the limitations of the method we are applying to test the visibility for four of the ten women. This chapter uses December 2017 online self-promotion as the marker of effort to establish "visibility." But this method lacks relevancy for measuring visibility for four of the top ten women whose last CEPAL publications were 1989, 2003, 2008, and 2011.
31 This is why a deeper research is needed to analyze the profile, evolution, and intellectual career of these CEPAL women.
32 See for example RePEc Blog (2017) to see the women present online in this blog.

References

Abir-Am, Pnina G., & Dorinda Outram. (1987). *Uneasy Careers and Intimate Lives: Women in Science, 1789–1979*. New Brunswick, NJ: Rutgers University Press.

Altimir, Oscar, & Eugenio Lahera, eds. (1998). *CEPAL cincuenta años: reflexiones sobre América Latina el Caribe*. Santiago, Chile: Naciones Unidas, CEPAL.

Bielschowsky, Ricardo. (1989). "Formação econômica do Brasil: uma obra-prima do estruturalismo cepalino". *Revista de Economia Política* 9 (4): 38–55.

——. 1998. "Evolución de las ideas de la CEPAL". *Revista de la CEPAL/CEPAL Review*. Nro. Extraordinario: CEPAL cincuenta años.

Boianovsky, Mauro. (2000) "Maria da Conceição Tavares". In *A Biographical Dictionary of Women Economists*, ed. by Robert W. Dimand, Mary Ann Dimand, & Evelyn L. Forget, 415–422. Cheltenham, UK; Northampton, MA: Edward Elgar Publishing Ltd.

Briceño Ruiz, José, Quintero Rizzuto, María Liliana Ruiz, & Dyanna de Benítez (2013). "El pensamiento estructuralista de la CEPAL sobre el desarrollo y la integración latinoamericana: reflexiones sobre su vigencia actual". *Revista Aportes para la Integración Latinoamericana* 19 (28): 1–34.

Carvalho, Fernando J. Cardim de (2008). "Keynes e o Brasil". *Economia e Sociedade* 17 (número especial): 569–574.

CEPAL. (1998). *Cincuenta años del pensamiento de la CEPAL: textos seleccionados*. Vol. 1. Santiago de Chile: CEPAL, Fondo de Cultura Económica.

Dimand, Mary Ann, Robert W. Dimand, & Evelyn L. Forget, eds. (1995). *Women of Value: Feminist Essays on the History of Women in Economics*. Aldershot, Hants, UK; Brookfield, VT, US: Edward Elgar.

Dimand, Robert W. (1995). "The Neglect of Women's Contributions to Economics". In *Women of Value: Feminist Essays on the History of Women in Economics*, ed. by Mary Ann Dimand, Robert W. Dimand, & Evelyn L. Forget, 1–24. Aldershot, UK; Brookfield, VT: Edward Elgar.

Dimand, Robert W., Mary Ann Dimand, & Evelyn L. Forget (2000). *A Biographical Dictionary of Women Economists*. Cheltenham, UK; Northampton, MA: Edward Elgar Publishing Ltd.

Dosman, Edgar J., ed. (2006). *Raúl Prebisch: Power, Principle, and the Ethics of Development*. Buenos Aires: IDB-INTAL.

——. (2008). *The Life and Times of Raúl Prebisch, 1901–1986*. Montreal, Kingston: McGill-Queen's University Press.

Flechsig, Steffen (1999). "Raúl Prebisch's Contribution to a Humane World". In *Global Capitalism, Liberation Theology, and the Social Sciences: An Analysis of the Contradictions of Modernity at the Turn of the Millennium*, ed. by Andreas Mueller, Paul Zulehner, & Arno Tausch, 103–123. Hauppauge, Commack, New York: Nova Science Publishers.

Forget, Evelyn L. (1995). "American Women Economists, 1900–1940: Doctoral Dissertations and Research Specialization". In *Women of Value: Feminist Essays on the History of Women in Economics*, ed. by Mary Ann Dimand, Robert W. Dimand, & Evelyn L. Forget, 25–28. Aldershot, Hants, UK; Brookfield, VT, US: Edward Elgar.

—— (2011). "American Women and the Economics Profession in the Twentieth century". *OEconomia* 1 (1): 19–30.

Fourcade, Marion, Etienne Ollion, & Yann Algan (2015). "The Superiority of Economists". *Journal of Economic Perspectives* 29 (1): 89–114. https://doi.org/10.1257/jep.29.1.89.

Groenewegen, Peter D., & Susan King (1994). "Women as Producers of Economic Articles: A Statistical Assessment of the Nature and the Extent of Female Participation in Five British and North American Journals 1900–39". *Working Papers in Economics*, University of Sidney (201).

Hirschman, Albert O. (1968). "The Political Economy of Import-Substituting Industrialization in Latin America". *The Quarterly Journal of Economics* 82 (1): 1–32.

Hirschman, Dan (2017). "Apparently, economics is a science because men do it". *Scatterplot* (blog). October 10 https://scatter.wordpress.com/2017/10/10/apparently-economics-is-a-science-because-men-do-it/

Iglesias, Enrique V., ed. (1994). *The Legacy of Raúl Prebisch*. Washington, DC: InterAmerican Development Bank.

Kahn, Shulamit (1995). "Women in the Economics Profession". *Journal of Economic Perspectives* 9 (4): 193–206.

Kourany, Janet (2001). *The Gender of Science*. Pearson.

Li, Diyi, & Cory Koedel (2017). "Representation and Salary Gaps by Race-Ethnicity and Gender at Selective Public Universities". *Educational Researcher* 46 (7): 343–354.

Libby, Barbara S. (1984). "Women in Economics before 1940". *Essays in Economic and Business History* 3: 173–190.

—— (1987). "A Statistical Analysis of Women in the Economics Professions, 1900–1940." In *Selected Papers from the Economic and Business Historical Society*, ed. by Edwin J. Perkins, 179–201. University of Southern California, History Department.

Love, Joseph L. (1980). "Raúl Prebisch and the Origins of the Doctrine of Unequal Exchange". *Latin American Research Review* 15: 45–72.

Madden, Kirsten Kara (2002). "Female Contributions to Economic Thought, 1900–1940". *History of Political Economy* 34 (1): 1–30.

Mahner, Martin (2007). "Demarcating Science from Non-Science". In *Handbook of the Philosophy of Science: General Philosophy of Science—Focal Issues*, ed. by Theo Kuipers, 515–575. Amsterdam: Elsevier.

—— (2013). "Science and Pseudoscience: How to Demarcate after the (Alleged) Demise of the Demarcation Problem". In *Philosophy of Pseudoscience: Reconsidering the Demarcation Problem*, ed. by Massimo Pigliucci & Maarten Boudry, 29–43. Chicago: Chicago University Press.

Mallorquín, Carlos (2000). "A Don Celso Furtado, a sus ochenta años: La Sociología Económica Posdesarrollista de Celso Furtado". *Revista de Historia Regional* 5 (1): 69–109.
Marco, Flavia (2001). *Economía género: bibliografía seleccionada*. Serie mujer y desarrollo 37. Santiago, Chile: Naciones Unidas, CEPAL, Unidad Mujer y Desarrollo, Proyecto CEPAL-GTZ "Institucionalización del Enfoque de Género en la CEPAL y Ministerios Sectoriales".
Markoff, John, & Verónica Montecinos (1993). "The Ubiquitous Rise of Economists". *Journal of Public Policy* 13 (1): 37–68.
Nelson, Julie A. (2017). "Yes, Economics Has a Problem with Women". *Economics* (blog). October 10, 2017. http://evonomics.com/yes-economics-problem-women/.
Ocampo, José Antonio (1998). "Cincuenta años de la Cepal". *Revista de la CEPAL/CEPAL Review* (Nro. Extraordinario: CEPAL cincuenta años).
——. (2013). *The History and Challenges of Latin American Development*. Santiago, Chile: ECLAC.
Pérez-Caldentey, Esteban, & Vernengo Matias (2007). *Ideas, Policies and Economic Development in the Americas*. London: Routledge.
Pujol, Michèle (1992). *Feminism and Anti-Feminism in Early Economic Thought*. Aldershot, UK: Edward Elgar.
Renisio, Yann (2017). "Faire science: le 'durcissement' des sciences sociales par la National Science Foundation (États-Unis, 1945–1957)". *Revue d'histoire des sciences humaines*, no. 31, pp. 43–65.
RePEc Blog (2017). "Female representation in RePEc". November 21, 2017. https://blog.repec.org/2017/11/21/female-representation-in-repec/
Rosenthal, Gert (1988). "ECLAC: Forty Years of Continuity with Change". *Revista de La CEPAL/CEPAL Review* (35): 7–12.
Strober, Myra H. (1975). "Women Economists: Career Aspirations, Education, and Training". *American Economic Review*, Papers and Proceedings of the Eighty-seventh Annual Meeting of the American Economic Association (May, 1975), 65 (2): 92–99.
Suarez, Pedro Castro (1992). *Teorías del desarrollo: Crítica a la teoría de la CEPAL*. Lima, Perú: Universidad Nacional Mayor de San Marcos.
Tavares, Maria da Conceição (1964). "Auge y declinación del proceso de sustitución de importaciones en el Brasil", published in CEPAL's *Economic Bulletin for Latin America*.
—— (1972). *Da Substituiçao de Importaçoes ao Capitalismo Financiero: Ensaios sobre Economia Brasileira*. Rio: Zahar.
Toye, John, & Richard Toye (2003). "The Origins and Interpretation of the Prebisch-Singer Thesis". *History of Political Economy* 35 (3): 437–467.
—— (2006). "Raúl Prebisch and the Limits of Industrialization". In *Raúl Prebisch: Power, Principle, and the Ethics of Development*, ed. by E.J. Dosman, 21–30. IDB-INTAL.
United Nations (2000). *La CEPAL en sus 50 años: notas de un Seminario Conmemorativo*. Santiago, Chile: CEPAL. www.cepal.org/es/publicaciones/2244-la-cepal-sus-50-anos-notas-un-seminario-conmemorativo
Vidal, Gregorio (2001). "Celso Furtado y el problema del desarrollo". *Comercio Exterior* 51 (2): 151–158.
Weetman, Frances (2017). "Where are all the women economists?" *New Statesman*, February 3, 2017. www.newstatesman.com/politics/feminism/2017/02/where-are-all-women-economists.
Williams, Joan C., & Kate Massinger (2016). "How Women Are Harassed Out of Science". *The Atlantic*, July 25, 2016.
Zuckerman, Harriet, & Jonathan R. Cole (1991). *The Outer Circle: Women in the Scientific Community*. Ed. by John T. Bruer. New York: W. W. Norton & Co Inc.

23

WOMEN'S EMPLOYMENT IN THE INFORMAL SECTOR IN DEVELOPING COUNTRIES

Contributions of Lourdes Benería and Martha (Marty) Chen

Farida Chowdhury Khan

Introduction

Women's work can be underpaid, invisible, and is often not strictly considered work. This is particularly true in developing countries where the contribution of women to the economy lies mostly outside that which is formally accounted for in national economic statistics. One promise of economic development is to change that situation for women and induct them into good jobs.

In this chapter, I examine the contribution of two women scholars, Lourdes Benería and Martha (Marty) Chen. Both women make the case that economic development creates a disproportionate number of jobs which continue to be unsafe, invisible, underpaid, located within what is considered the "informal economy," and that such jobs have gone primarily to women. And both women believe that it is important to help women workers who do such jobs by providing them intellectual assistance. Such assistance includes the construction of terminology, of theoretical insight, and of empirical evidence to support the struggle to organize via self-representation, improving working conditions.

Both women contribute to the field of economic development by theorizing, collecting data, and discerning patterns on women in the informal economy. Benería made great strides in the field by connecting the expansion of the informal economy to economic liberalization policies, detailing the nature of work and production linkages in the informal sector, and thereby exposing the high representation of women in this sector of the economy. She finds that, contrary to established thinking, development does not provide decent livelihoods to poor women, who predominate in the informal sector and are unable to escape poverty. She is one of the pioneers bringing feminist approaches to development economics, focusing on women's working and living conditions during the process of market-led development. Chen began her work on the ground with non-governmental organizations (NGOs) and was later involved with other international organizations, such as the International Labor Organization (ILO). Chen's concern with giving poor working women voice and control over their work defined the trajectory of her research. This led to the creation of an international organizational network that supports the formation of female worker's collectives in the informal sector and the representation of their concerns to policymakers.

Born in Spain in 1937, Lourdes Benería studied in the very first class of economics undergraduates at the University of Barcelona. She grew up in the Pyrenees in what she describes as pre-modern subsistence conditions and says her life changed when she went to New York City to complete her doctoral degree (Olson and Emami, 2002). Benería's initial pursuit was to understand the implications of development on women. She encountered the informal economy while working on structural adjustment and the debt crisis in Latin America, particularly Mexico. Her work there and in other parts of Latin America resulted in the compilation of detailed information on the effect on women and households of informal work and its increase during crisis periods, as well as during periods of neoliberal transition. She is among the first to note how development policies expanded the informal sector and increased risk and vulnerability among urban poor women who worked in this sector (Benería, 1996).

Martha Chen is third generation of a missionary family working in India. Raised with a concern for people, she was accustomed to most work being informal in the hill town of Mussorie. From petty traders to casual labor or domestic workers, Mussorie's barter and cash economy used labor-intensive technology to produce goods and services. Chen witnessed the transition from rural to urban life for many poor women as India developed. Chen's conceptual formulation of the informal sector strengthened as she became involved in organizing women's work through non-governmental agencies in South Asia. Her major contribution is to provide details of the heterogeneity of work in the informal sector. She does this on a global scale through a vast amount of research and experience on the ground. Another significant aspect of her contribution is the organizing of women informal workers around the globe.

As we will see in this chapter, the informal economy is made up of non-regulated production and work, ranging from homeworking to highly competitive firms using simple technologies and drawing on labor that is abundant in supply. Development economists before Benería and Chen focused on the entrepreneurship present in the informal sector as well as its legality. Benería and Chen shift the discussion to put women's employment and work at the center. The work of these two women provides a feminist focus in framing the informal sector in developing countries.

Historically, most production has been done at home, including the working of raw materials for sale or for wages. This last activity came to be called the "putting out" system. Under industrialization, home production took on a new form enabling the expansion of mercantile capitalism (Finkin, 2015, p. 606). Boxer (1982) describes the importance of women and the "family workshop" in the putting out system that supported expansion of fashion in Paris in the 19th century.[1] Moving beyond the home, by the 19th century in Europe the city streets provided varied types of precarious employment for the urban poor; Mayhew (1851) documents the informal economy for 1840s' London. References to the 20th-century economy of the streets from New York to San Juan are dispersed in many reports (see, for example, Whyte, 1943; Lewis, 1966).

The idea of the informal sector entered the economic development literature in the 1960s. The classic dualistic model of economic development laid out by Lewis (1954) postulated a modern (formal) sector of capitalist accumulation, which drew labor from a "traditional sector." He envisioned a transformation of the traditional sector to the modern sector over time, particularly with increasing capital formation, credit creation, and technical progress. However, this did not happen as Lewis envisioned. Instead, an expansion of the modern formal sector stimulated the development of a new urban traditional sector. This prompted a focus on rural urban migration and the creation of employment in this urban traditional sector (Todaro, 1969).

Keith Hart (1973) studied rural urban migration in Accra, Ghana and coined the term "informal" when referring to the income-generating activities of the urban sub-proletariat who had migrated from Northern Ghana.

Chen and Benería's entry into development economics occurred in the 1970s and their involvement continues even today. It began with an interest in poverty, work, and women and led them to the informal sector. Both of them note that development economists expected this sector to dissolve and merge with the modern sector as development progressed. Contrary to the projections of other development economists, both Chen and Benería find that the informal sector not only persisted, but expanded to include profitable and efficient enterprises as well as marginal activities. While most economists saw the informal and formal sectors as separate spheres with minimal linkages, Benería and Chen provide substantial evidence on the connection and cogeneration between the two sectors.

Women, development, and the informal economy: Lourdes Benería

Early influences on Lourdes Benería

This section examines the early influences on Lourdes Benería's thinking about women and development and her entry into the world of the informal economy. Benería's contributions to understanding the informal sector intersect her interest in the conditions of the poor, the care economy, and other questions that have remained primary for her as a feminist economist. Benería has been reflective about her own experiences in introductions of her work (Benería, 2003; Benería and Roldan, 1987) and in her narration about her life (Olson and Emami, 2002). She has situated herself in feminist economics as an academic and, more specifically, within the field of development.

Benería was born in a rural, mountainous area of the Catalan region in Spain. When she was growing up, there was little modern infrastructure, and she describes life resembling that in the Middle Ages. She began to study economics in the 1950s when economics was first provided as a major or course of study at the University of Barcelona (Olson and Emami, 2002). As she studied history, political economy, and international economics, her formative interests in questions that she would pursue later arose. Traveling to study in France, she realized how intellectually liberating it was to leave Franco's Spain and carried out her graduate studies in New York, first at NYU and then Columbia University. Although Benería found Columbia's economics program to be far less orthodox than that in Spain, there were many economists whom she "respected but did not feel any affinity with" (ibid., p. 235). She found certain categories within economics, such as the idea of a rational man, somewhat perplexing, having grown up in what she describes as an alternative, pre-capitalist system. She had a background that allowed her to cross and borrow from other disciplines when needed, and she kept inquiry as her foremost concern. Around this time, she married and had children, which made her all the more aware of the different standards for men and women in the professions and workplace (ibid.).

After her doctoral work, she became a professor at Rutgers University and also worked for the ILO on rural women in 1977. During this period, she questioned the nature of paid and unpaid work, and theorized about the concept of work. She identified with the branch of feminism considered to be socialist feminism, with class and gender being the main points of analysis. Her work with the ILO "changed her understanding of the world and the orientation of her work" (Benería, 2003, p. x). Esther Boserup's book *Women's Role in Economic Development* (1970) was also influential in the growth of her own approach to development. The field of development had largely ignored women as actors or subjects, and their concerns and interests were absent in both development discourse and policy. Benería sees the 1970s as a decade of "post-Boserup recovery" – the historical processes called development had affected women and men differently, but much more knowledge and detail was necessary to understand why this was the case (ibid.).

At Rutgers, Benería became associate director of the Institute of Research for Women and then moved to Cornell University in 1987. Throughout this time, she associated with heterodox economists, historians, sociologists, and anthropologists, who all influenced her approach to economics, which was already critical and interdisciplinary. In the 1980s she worked with Martha Rodan on Mexico's growing informal sector (ibid.).

Her entry into academe and international organizations occurred during a time when many changes occurred in development policy. The Washington Consensus[2] came through in the 1980s, changing the conditions and patterns of development for most countries. This shift was not well received by economists such as Benería, who, as a feminist economist and interested in distributional issues, found that economic changes were not always benefitting those at the bottom rungs of society.

During this time, women economists were virtually absent from economics panels as the development establishment was male dominated.[3] Benería has been one of the pioneers in bringing a voice to development that was both a female voice and a champion for the cause of women. To do this, she looked at the developments in feminist economics and brought these ideas to study important trends and patterns in developing countries, and in particular, the informal sector.

Redefining the role of women in development

Benería has written extensively about feminist economic thought, showing how it has contributed to economics as a discipline by challenging various fundamental tenets and assumptions. She says that, although not a feminist economist, Boserup recognized that development has operated differently for men and women. Feminists such as Benería followed this by elaborating a critique of modernization theory: Development had differing impacts on men and women because of the asymmetric gender relations and hierarchical structures that were present (Benería and Sen, 1981, Benería, 1995).

With a feminist lens, Benería examines how economic restructuring has led to the informalization of labor markets. Joining other writers such as Sassen (1988) and Joekes (1987) who were skeptical of the effects of globalization, she notes the beginning of this recent process in burgeoning or expanding industries in developed countries, such as high technology and finance. A decentralization of production – vertical and horizontal – changed how jobs are done and moved labor-intensive processes to low-wage regions. In developed countries, stable employment and attachment to one organization of mostly male workers was replaced with less employment security, benefits, hours, and altered job descriptions, and a feminized workforce. The effect of these processes and reduced unionization altered employment contracts, with workers facing individualized and uncertain employment, often holding unrelated jobs, and shifting from job to job. Also, the shift in the location of employment to developing countries was concomitant with the downsizing of large firms, and more outsourcing and subcontracting to smaller firms. Increased trends in informal work, such as part-time or temporary work in the US and EU, contributed to an expansion of the informal sector in developing countries.

During the decades of neoliberal transition that occurred early in Latin America and later in Asia and Africa, Benería, along with other feminists, narrowed in on the effect of structural adjustment for women (Benería, 1995, 1999). With high debt levels and defaults, austerity programs had become common in developing countries. The effects of national austerity programs on households and women were important, especially as it was well recognized by then that poverty was high among lone mothers in developing countries. The decline in incomes and rising poverty led to both the intensification of household work and increased women's participation in the labor force (Benería and Feldman, 1992; Benería, 1999).

Benería extends the historical understanding of the circumstances women face in developing economies with the process of development. Boserup's classic work emphasizes women's participation in agriculture during male migration to urban areas, and the design on women's education to absorb them into the formal labor force in towns. These ideas were based on development patterns and policies in the 1950s and 1960s. However, trends altered in the 1980s and 1990s, when women in developing countries were integrated into the workforce more than ever before. Benería notes that the neoliberal development that began by the late 1970s led to women's participation in export-processing zones, followed by the participation of women in the service sector, including pink collar jobs in financial services, data entry, data processing, and extended to the tourist sector, prostitution and related services, as well as to domestic and daycare workers. Some of this work required migration by women, often by themselves. The deregulation and flexibility of time and contracts in labor markets further facilitated the entry of women and subverted the distinction between paid work and unpaid work (Benería, 2001b).

Empirical evidence of women's work in the informal sector of Latin America

Benería's early empirical work (Benería and Roldán, 1987) focused on the nature of subcontracting and homework in Mexico City during 1981–82. This is a seminal study of women's work in the informal economy and still a source of vital information; key findings are laid out in this section.

The Mexico City study considers two different contexts – one being homework in a putting out system and the other in small enterprises or maquilas. Both of these are vertical subcontracting activities done by larger firms that provide inputs for these activities. These maquilas produce for the domestic market, as opposed to the export-oriented activities near the border. Sectors studied were garments, electronics, consumer durables, cosmetics, plastics, and metal. Benería's particular contribution was to lay out various mechanisms by which the formal and informal sectors articulate. She identifies three or four levels of subcontracting, the number of firms increasing at the very bottom level. The last level hired women, often homeworkers. Here, Benería invokes the Babbage Principle (Braverman, 1974) to understand the principles of operation in the informal sector, where a reduction in labor costs is made through a reorganization of the division of labor. Working conditions are found to deteriorate as one moves down the value chain, with larger firms on the top of the hierarchy dictating the terms of production. The most complex of these subcontracting categories might combine legal and illegal operations. For example, a legal store front pays taxes, minimum wages, and other required benefits, and sells a final product which is produced through subcontracting. At the back of the store an oscillating number of women are hired to do a narrowly proscribed task (such as plastic polishing) as a subcontracting activity at wages below minimum without benefits (Benería and Roldán, 1987).

Studying the trends associated with gender in informal work, Benería found that firms with fewer than 100 workers had greater proportions of women, such feminization being complete for homework. The percentage of women increased as it crossed from legal to illegal. More women were hired in assembly, where more concentration, patience, and physical immobility for long periods of time were required. Within the firms, there were fewer women managers because workers (both men and women, but particularly men) did not take well to women's control of their work. Restructuring of work in these situations involved more supervision by men (ibid.).

In each firm, women had the lowest and men the highest ranges of wages. Lower skills and less physical strength were given as reasons. Women usually worked sitting down in crowded spaces and men were usually given larger spaces and more mobility. Lower wages for women were combined with less certain work and part-time and intermittent or on-call work. Based on information collected through surveys of supervisors, Benería notes the artificiality of skill definition – women were considered more dexterous and patient. Firms reported that women who were hired were able to concentrate better, did careful manual work, were more able to follow orders, were reliable, stable and hence more productive, and therefore less troublesome. Socially, their earnings were considered secondary, allowing them to be paid less. The manual dexterity that had been passed down through generations whereby women did sewing, lace-making, arts and crafts were now adapted for assembling and plastic polishing in electronics, garments, cosmetics, metals, and textiles. They were used to domestic work which is tedious, repetitive, done in crowded spaces, increasing their ability to deal with frustration, and making them more committed and persistent. Assembly work requires these traits. They are less restless and able to sit down for longer periods than men. They also did not have high absenteeism, did not partake widely in alcohol use, and were less active in unions. The women were reportedly hired for their beauty, as opposed to strength and efficiency which were noted as traits for which males were hired. Single mothers were said to be among the most reliable workers (ibid.).

Women who were surveyed gave several reasons for opting for homework – demands of care and domestic chores, husband's opposition to outside work, lack of alternatives, age, and health. Informal work included domestic piece work, jobbers who use family labor at home as well as those that hire wage labor and operate illegally. They were paid per piece/unit, typically with a weekly deadline, with both time and earnings showing high variation. The work included sewing, sorting, assembly, or simple cutting. Often workers were asked to transport the materials themselves. If things were damaged there was no pay. In one example, an amount of five times the value of the merchandise was deducted from the weekly pay through a completely ad hoc calculation (ibid.).

The expansion of the informal sector during crises

Benería returned to Mexico in the late 1980s to learn how households survived a major debt crisis (Benería and Feldman, 1992). It was well known that income distribution had worsened during structural adjustment. The poor had been severely affected and had resorted to working in the informal sector. It was found that both teenagers and women increased their labor force participation significantly in order to cope with the economic hardships. Many teenagers dropped out of school to help generate income for their families. Women had to join the labor force particularly if they were single but even if they were married: two-thirds of her sample began to work to make ends meet. Middle-class women were the only ones able to attain formal sector employment (ibid.).

Benería maintains that the 1990s saw an extending and deepening of these processes which began in the 1980s. Studying Bolivia and Ecuador in 2002 (Benería and Floro, 2006), she found that privatization, market deregulation, and economic restructuring had set the grounds for the expansion of the informal sector. In the 1990s both Ecuador and Bolivia faced trade and financial liberalization policies that brought about a pattern of uneven development, increasing both the concentration of wealth and the deterioration of working conditions for the less fortunate.

The informal sector in Ecuador grew substantially at this time. The open unemployment rates increased to 14.4% (women) and 19.6% (men) while poverty rates rose to 52%. In Bolivia, structural adjustment policies adopted in 1985 led to imposing wage freezes, reducing government spending, and shifting the economy toward export-oriented development, as the public tin mines closed. Displaced populations migrated to urban areas, with the expanding informal economy absorbing much more of the labor.

Benería's conclusions from empirical findings

From these cases in Latin America, Benería concludes and theorizes that the expansion and deepening of markets increased the links between the formal and informal sectors, often blurring the distinction between them. A striking finding was that the size of the informal economy has paralleled women's participation in the labor force, both of them growing during the 1980s and the 1990s.

Building on existing studies and her survey work, Benería outlines the basic characteristics of the informal sector (Benería and Roldán, 1987; Benería and Feldman, 1992; Benería, 2001a, 2001b). While previous literature on economic development had focused on production and the nature of enterprises, Benería emphasizes the condition of labor in defining this sector. In doing so, she notes two types of informal activities – those that are directly linked to formal sector firms and those that are survival activities organized at the home or community level (Benería and Roldán, 1987; Benería, 2003). Both these activities involve temporary work, as well as contingent work lacking benefits and legal protection, and not covered by national legislation. These activities registered more growth in Latin America during and in the aftermath of the debt crises, although they were already high in the region. She also notes that contrary to prior thinking in economics, the informal sector does not vanish with development, but persists, often expanding, with linkages to the formal sector (Benería, 2003).

Benería finds that the feminization of the workforce intensified the reliance on the informal sector in the last four decades (Benería, 2003). With more women available to work, the sector was able to persist and expand. In addition, women's primary involvement in domestic work and childcare continues to be a source of vulnerability for them, leaving women with few options but work in this sector. Despite the increased education of women and increased participation in the labor force, the formal sector does not absorb the increased supply of women in the workforce.

In sum, Benería does not see the increased labor force participation of women in developing countries as having improved their welfare. Large numbers of women, some of whom might have received some education, are stuck in precarious jobs in the informal sector and are constrained by their low mobility, lack of alternatives, and by social norms that reduce their ability to bargain regarding their working conditions and earnings. Benería finds that this increases uncertainty and vulnerability in their living conditions. She distinguishes between poverty and vulnerability, detailing the new vulnerabilities that these urban poor find themselves strapped with – urban life fragmenting family support, no access to health services or health insurance, no protection for old age, and living in unsanitary neighborhoods. Benería and Floro (2006) concluded that even when households were not below the poverty line, they had a high level of vulnerability and therefore responded by moving across multiple jobs, all of which were in the informal sector, and had highly volatile earnings.[4] In all her work on women and the informal sector, Benería calls for a greater universal provisioning and more intervention by the state to address these concerns. Instead of poverty programs, she recommends greater opportunity for work with stable earnings and decent working conditions.

Addressing informal employment: Martha Chen

Martha Chen went to Woodstock school in Mussorie, India and then started at Isabella Thornton College in Lucknow, India, moving to the US to finish her undergraduate studies in English in Connecticut College in 1965. She then spent most of the 1970s and 1980s in Bangladesh and India, working as a field representative of Oxfam and, as discussed in the next section, working with the NGO, Bangladesh Rural Advancement Committee (BRAC). She received her PhD in South Asian Studies from the University of Pennsylvania and worked with the Harvard Institute for International Development, and the Kennedy School of Government, where she continues to hold the position of Lecturer in Public Policy.

Most of Chen's writings are a result of her work with international organizations such as the United Nations and World Bank as well as NGOs. During this time, Chen follows and updates the debates on the informal sector. Like Benería, Chen (2005) notes the dichotomy of informal and formal in the development discourse for over half a century. This duality prevails in the understanding of economy, property rights, social insurance mechanisms, and organizations. And like Benería, Chen recognizes that the globalization of the 1990s contributed to the informalization of the workforce across sectors and countries. Informal firms and small producers lacked the knowledge and technology to compete with formal firms, particularly for export markets, and also faced competition from imported goods in domestic markets (Chen, 2012).

In conceptualizing the informal sector, Chen (2005) recognizes three areas of analysis as necessary. (1) *Segmentation* within the informal economy by employment status, sex and other variables is not understood, including differences in average earnings and risk. (2) The *continuum* of employment relations between formal and informal with many categories in between also needs further analysis.[5] (3) *Linkages* between units and workers along this continuum need to be better understood, as do the costs and benefits of working within this continuum.

The organization of informal sector workers is the prime motivation for Chen's research on informal sector employment. Chen finds that there is new interest in organizing informal workers arising from two trends – the increasing numbers in this sector and the declining numbers in trade unions. Major questions related to the trajectory of her career are: What should member-based organizations for these workers seek? And are there common points across countries, lessons that can be learned, in addition to specific local solutions? In answering these questions, Chen holds major responsibility for the collection of informal sector statistics. She uses empirical information to provide workers a tool to organizing and seeking better working conditions.

Establishing WIEGO

Chen's queries into women's work began early in the 1970s, when she studied food for work aid programs in Bangladesh and went on to consider new forms of income-generating activities for women. She worked with the United Nations World Food Programme at that time and became a founding member of BRAC, which is now the largest non-governmental development organization. Although she initially focused on craft development with micro-credit loans, Chen's interest lay more in practices and policies that would sustain women's employment and help them organize their economic interests within rural power structures. She went with a team from BRAC to study the Self Employed Women's Association (SEWA) in India. Established in 1972, SEWA is the largest trade union of self-employed workers, a subset of informal workers, in the world. This association with SEWA and Ella Bhatt, the founder of SEWA, began in 1979 and continued as Chen worked on women and work in India.

During the 1990s, activists wanted to collect data on homeworking in the informal sector so as to try to improve their lobbying efforts for appropriate policies. Only Morocco, Japan, and some European countries had any statistics. Chen, Bhatt, and others founded a new organization called WIEGO (Women in Informal Employment: Globalizing and Organizing) in 1997 to bring this about.

WIEGO is a network of organizations in 56 countries and it has been registered as a charity/ not for profit in the UK since 2007. WIEGO partners with various national or local informal worker associations – particularly home-based workers, street vendors, and waste pickers. Marty Chen's long experience with informal workers is evident in the many anecdotes that she is able to recount regarding the support that WIEGO provides for informal workers. She relates that while home-based workers are generally harder to organize, such efforts with waste pickers turned out to be easier because of a peculiar history. Compared to other regions in the developing world, Latin American cities modernized early, putting in waste and sanitation systems. With the help of the Jesuits, waste pickers organized around their collective bargaining needs so that future development efforts included their interests (interview, March 10, 2017). The structures they put in place provided a foundation that could be utilized by WIEGO to organize waste pickers in other countries.

WIEGO prepares statistics on the size, composition, wages, and contribution of the informal economy in various countries of the developing world. It also categorizes data on informal employment by gender. In an interview (March 10, 2017), Chen explained that she either does or organizes much of the intellectual work for WIEGO. WIEGO supports informal sector labor organizations through intellectual work, by collecting data, making arguments for favorable policy change, and advocating effectively for the group.

Global statistics on the informal sector

As mentioned above, in her early years, Chen worked with the UN, primarily the ILO, and the World Bank. Over time, Chen's research and writing on the informal sector was done mostly to aid WIEGO with its advocacy and organizing work. A theme of WIEGO is to improve and develop statistics on the informal economy. WIEGO worked closely with ILO, the UN Statistics Division, and the International Expert Group on Informal Sector Statistics, called the Delhi Group.

In her work on the informal sector with ILO in the late 1980s and 1990s, Chen put together a framework to collect statistics on informal workers in both developed and developing countries (Chen et al., 1999; Carr et al., 2000). This is an extremely difficult comparative exercise and relied on surveys carried out in single countries at different points in time that were compiled and extrapolated on a regional basis. Much of the statistical work was done with Jacques Charmes (Chen, interview, March 10, 2017).

Chen notes that in 1991, ICLS (International Conference of Labour Statisticians) adopted an international statistical definition of the informal sector that was put into the 1993 International System of National Accounts. This definition was enterprise based and did not include the many casual workers who were moving in and out of these enterprises. To account for these resources, and provide a fuller picture, Chen advanced an employment-based definition of the informal sector (Carr and Chen, 2002). This definition was arrived at through the close association WIEGO had with ILO STATS.

Expanded definitions put forth in Chen (2012) illustrate that informal employment is a large and heterogeneous category. She first sub-divides informal employment into self-employment and wage employment. Within these broad categories, more homogeneous sub-categories are delineated by status in employment. Informal self-employment is thus categorized into employers in informal enterprises, own-account workers in informal enterprises, contributing family workers (in informal and formal enterprises), and members of informal producers' cooperatives (where these exist).

Informal wage employment consists of employees hired without social protection contributions by formal or informal enterprises or paid domestic workers hired by households. Employees in informal enterprises and casual or day laborers tend to be the largest category in informal wage employment. Status in employment is used to delineate two key aspects of labor contractual arrangements: the allocation of authority over the work process and the outcome of the work done; and the allocation of economic risks involved (Chen, 2012). This employment-centered focus has been accompanied by a significant rethinking of the composition, causes, and consequences of informal employment. The emphasis is on the type and degree of contract and earning risk undertaken by workers as well as the corresponding authority over the establishment and other workers.

Chen also takes care to define what the informal economy is not; it is distinguishable from the formal economy (regular, stable, and protected employment in legally regulated enterprises), criminal economy, and reproductive or care economy. It is both wage and self-employment that is not recognized, regulated, or protected by existing legal or regulatory frameworks (ibid.).

Because few countries directly measured employment in informal enterprises and fewer still measured informal employment outside the informal enterprises, a "residual method" was employed to estimate the data. This indirect approach to estimating total informal employment and its major components outside of agriculture is based on existing published statistical data available for many developing countries, such as a population census, labor force surveys or other types of household surveys that cross-classify industrial sectors (agriculture, mining, manufacturing, trade and services) by employment status (employers, own-account workers, family workers, employees) and by sex. Many countries collect such data but often do not tabulate or publish them. As a result, estimates of the informal economy using the first residual method could be made for only 35 countries, of which fewer than 25 had data disaggregated by sex. A second residual method required additional data on employment in the informal enterprises which was derived from special informal sector surveys or mixed (household and enterprise) surveys. Such surveys were available only in India, Kenya, Mexico, Tunisia, and South Africa (ILO, 2002).[6]

Chen's work with WIEGO to capture the informal sector statistically has been a massive undertaking, the details of which are not possible to summarize here. But in the paragraphs that follow, a series of empirically derived observations are presented to give a sense of the types of insights that result from this body of work. The reader is asked to keep in mind that the breadth of the regional and sectoral scope of her work is wide, and in many cases provides an attempt to detail the nature of both the value chain of products and its relation to informal employment in many countries of Asia, Africa, and Latin America.

Chen notes that the link between working in the informal economy and being poor, especially in the lowest return activities, is stronger for women than for men. She calculates the ratio of self-employment to wage employment in this sector. In Kenya or South Africa, wage employment in the informal sector is more common for women whereas in Benin, Indonesia, or North Africa, it is self-employment that is more typical as a source of women's livelihoods. Another interesting finding from the collected data is that women in Kenya and South Africa are the larger shares of workers in this sector. They make up 79% of all informal sector workers in Kenya and 61% in South Africa. She also finds that, all around the world, self-employment is more important as a source of employment in the informal sector for women than it is for men. However, given the higher labor force participation of men, they constitute the larger share of workers in the informal sector. This is true everywhere globally, except in Latin America where women comprise 51% of the self-employed (ibid.).

Chen estimates the contribution of the informal economy and notes that much work in developed countries has been rendered semi-formal (temporary, part-time, little benefits or protection), contributing to at least half of total employment, with variance depending on region and sector. Women's share in part-time employment is about three or four times as high as that of men (Chen, 2012).

Much of this work is updated in a more recent paper by WIEGO (Vanek et al., 2014). Regional estimates of informal employment reported are more robust because these were made with direct estimates by 40 countries and indirect estimates from 80 countries. The extent to which informal employment accounts for non-agricultural work in developing countries can be quite high – 82% in South Asia, 66% in sub-Saharan Africa, 65% in East and Southeast Asia, though only 51% in Latin America. These important findings show major differences in the developing world in terms of the ability to create decent employment. Despite economic growth in Asia, most jobs are those involving no security or benefits.

Considering specific country cases, she finds that in Costa Rica and El Salvador, average earnings for *informal employers* are at least as high as those in *formal employment*. In Ghana and South Africa, earnings of *informal public wage workers* are comparable with *formal private sector employees* because wages are higher in the public sector. In Tunisia, micro-entrepreneurs who hired others were not poor and had four times the legal minimum salary and more than twice the average salary in the formal sector (ibid.).

Organizing informal workers

The collection of evidence supports the need for workers to organize and make a case for better working conditions and pay. This has been the prime motivation for data collection on the unstable, amorphous informal sector.

Support for organizing informal workers through member-based organizations constitutes the primary work of WIEGO and its network organizations. WIEGO attempts to reorient economic policy to focus on creating more and better work by applying the principle of 3-Vs to the working poor – visibility, voice, and validity. This is done by providing evidence locally and across countries as well as grouping the many member-based organizations of informal workers under the single umbrella of WIEGO. Chen's focus is to provide intellectual support through researching experiences elsewhere and models that could be relevant for specific instances (Chen et al., 2013).

Chen (interview, March 10, 2017) gives the example of Thailand and discusses two involvements by WIEGO in that country. WIEGO worked with the National Statistical Office in Thailand to provide technical capacity. It also helped with bringing issues forward but was careful to ensure that local organizations were empowered, keeping WIEGO in the background. WIEGO also worked with home-based workers, bringing together academics and lawyers with local groups to form a collective to negotiate with the state. In the case of Thailand, these efforts yielded the construction of a footbridge in an important location, as well as more transportation options for home-based workers.

She also describes experiences with organizing informal labor in India. In Delhi, WIEGO worked with vendors, for whom the government had passed an enabling legislation in 2010, but which was not followed. It was SEWA in this case that brought together a Town Vending Committee in 2014. This tripartite committee consisted of the government, the private sector, and vendors and the implementation of the national law is now playing out. Street vendor organizations have more power in each ward and local level.[7]

Chen remains preoccupied with strengthening and expanding WIEGO and talks about the new forms of informality that are emerging (interview, March 10, 2017). Some of these are taking different guises than before and connecting with the new gig economy, such as Uber drivers around the world who are said to be self-employed but unable to determine the manner in which their rates are set. For employees at the lowest ends of the value chain of any sector, such as call workers in information technology, day workers in booming construction industries around the world, head-loaders and informal vans in developing countries that are hired in this manner, the inability to determine pay, hours, or working conditions is routine.

In the interview, Chen also notes that more recently, technology has taken away some informal jobs, such as that of the roving salesperson, in developing countries. She identifies successes by some informal enterprises who have turned their businesses into formal firms. These include a few washer people or *dhobis* who were able to increase the scale of their business and a cheese *wallah* who now has a dairy shop. She alludes to street vendors in Ghana, who now operate even on the highways, underscoring that the highly innovative self-employment sector alters whenever there is a crack to fill to earn a living.

Conclusions

The writings of Benería and Chen trace the advent of the modern informal sector through the dual processes of development and globalization and examine the changes in the nature of work in developing regions. While the body of work of each scholar is broader than their contributions to understanding the informal sector, decades of involvement in development economics with a focus on the poorest female workers led to their converging on informal employment. Benería encountered and exposed scholars to the persistence and expansion of the informal sector through her early work in Latin America and Chen worked with international organizations and with WIEGO to refine and extend this evidence collection to many other parts of the developing world.

Benería's intent was to understand how development affects women, while Chen concerned herself directly with providing the poorest households with occupations that might alleviate their poverty. As a result, Chen has spent most of the last decade organizing workers in unregulated and precarious employment.

Both these authors find that, to understand the new universal trends that global working poor face, it is necessary to gather evidence. Both these scholars amassed quantitative and qualitative information to help us understand the complex nature of production, firms, subcontracting, and work in the contemporary world. They locate women in the center of their studies. They find that the occupations and living condition of women has been determined by the changes brought about through new processes of development.

Benería does a critical theoretical study of the rise of the informal sector, a malaise in the process of development, where work is unregulated and unsafe. She connects this with the evolution of capitalism and the development of nations. In addition, she provides ample empirical substantiation of this phenomenon. She exerts important influence on the manner in which feminist economists understand the process of development.

While both authors have contributed significantly to the empirical study of the expanding informal employment in the world today, Chen has also used the information acquired to rebuild worker organizations across the world in new ways. Despite the reduction in worker organizations in most formal sectors, Chen has persisted in working at the local level to build and strengthen institutions that represent informal workers, and connecting a network of these institutions at the international level. This is a significant achievement in a world of mobile capital, which is able to re-locate where profitable, with a heavily feminized informal workforce serving where needed in the interest of globally integrated firms.

Notes

1 Many of the goods were produced in a multitude of small family workshops, which dotted the city; others, particularly ladies' garments, were fabricated for the most part by women workers in their own homes. While this urban industrial homework received considerable attention from social critics, social workers, and legislators some seventy years ago, and the term "sweatshop" readily evokes an image of the bowed seamstress immortalized in Thomas Hood's poem, "Song of the Shirt," it has received little attention from historians.

Boxer, 1982, pp. 401–402

2 Together, the IMF, World Bank and the US government provided neo-liberal solutions for developing countries which came to be called the Washington Consensus.
3 There are several women such as Alice Amsden, Irma Adelman, Anne Krueger, Nancy Birdsall, and Frances Stewart who were prominent in the field of economic development (Van Der Meulen Rodgers and Cooley, 1999); however, none of these women explicitly made women's issues their focus of study.
4 Because of the economic crisis, most households were in debt, and women were burdened with collateralized debt and under the greatest pressure to make debt payments. This was true in both Bolivia and Ecuador (Benería and Floro, 2006).
5 This point is also made by Benería and Floro (2006).
6 ILO (2002) was written by Chen and her team for the ILO. The second edition of this source is published by ILO and WIEGO.
7 It should be noted that all of WIEGO's activities are initiated and directed by Martha Chen. She works closely with partners and guides the intellectual exercises, and carries out many of them herself with collaborators.

Bibliography

Becker, K. F. (2004). *The Informal Economy: Fact Finding Study*. Stockholm: Swedish International Development Agency.

Benería, L. (1995). Toward a greater integration of gender in economics. *World Development, 23*(11), 1839–1850.

Benería, L. (1996). Thou shalt not live by statistics alone, but it might help. *Feminist Economics, 2*(3), 139–142.

Benería, L. (1999). Globalization, gender and the Davos Man. *Feminist Economics, 5*(3), 61–83.

Benería, L. (2001a). Shifting the risk: New employment patterns, informalization, and women's work. *International Journal of Politics, Culture, and Society, 15*(1), 27–53.

Benería, L. (2001b). "Employment patterns and the informalization of jobs: General trends and gender dimensions," in C. Piras, ed., *Women at Work: A Challenge for Development*. Washington, DC: Inter-American Development Bank, 65–98.

Benería, L. (2003). *Gender, Development and Globalization; Economics as if All People Mattered*. New York: Routledge.

Benería, L. (2007). "Gender and the social construction of markets," in Irene can Staveren, Diane Elson, Caren Grown and Nilüfer Çağatay, eds., *Feminist Economics of Trade*. London and New York: Routledge, 13–32.

Benería, L. and Feldman, S. (1992). *Unequal Burden: Economic Crises, Persistent Poverty and Women's Work*. Boulder, CO: Westview Press.

Benería, L. and Floro, M. (2006). "Labor market informalization, gender and social protection: Reflections on poor urban households in Bolivia, Ecuador and Thailand," in S. Razawi and S. Hassim, eds., *Gender and Social Policy in a Global Context*. London: Palgrave, 193–216.

Benería, L. and Roldán, M. (1987). *The Crossroads of Class & Gender; Industrial Homework, Subcontracting, and Household Dynamics in Mexico City*. The University of Chicago Press.

Benería, L. and Sen, G. (1981). Accumulation, reproduction, and "women's role in economic development": Boserup revisited. *Signs: Journal of Women in Culture and Society*, 7(2), 279–298.

Boserup, E. (1970). *Women's Role in Economic Development*. London: Earthscan.

Boxer, Marilyn J. (1982). Women in industrial homework: The flowermakers of Paris in the Belle Epoque. *French Historical Studies, 12*(3), 401–423.

Braverman, H. (1974). *Labor and Monopoly Capital*. Monthly Review Press.

Carr, M. and Chen, M. A. (2002). *Globalization and the Informal Economy: How Global Trade and Investment Impact on the Working Poor.* Geneva: International Labour Office.
Carr, M., Chen, M. A. and Tate, J. (2000). Globalization and home-based workers. *Feminist Economics, 6*(3), 123–142.
Chen, M. A. (2005). *Rethinking the informal economy: Linkages with the formal economy and the formal regulatory environment* (Vol. *10*, pp. 18–27). United Nations University, World Institute for Development Economics Research.
Chen, M.A. (2012). "The Informal Economy: Definitions, Theories and Policies." WIEGO working paper No. 1. www.wiego.org/sites/wiego.org/files/publications/files/Chen_WIEGO_WP1.pdf. Accessed on February 20, 2017.
Chen, M. A. (2013). Informal workers in the developing world: Organizing in the global economy. *New Labor Forum, 22*(1), 67–73.
Chen, M. A. (2015). *Informal Employment: Theory & Reality.* Unpublished manuscript.
Chen, M., Bonner, C., Chetty, M., Fernandez, L., Pape, K., Parra, F. and Skinner, C. (2013). "Urban Informal Workers: Representative Voice & Economic Rights." Background paper for the WDR.
Chen, M., Jhabvala, R., Kanbur, R. and Richards, C. (2007). *Membership Based Organizations of the Poor.* New York: Routledge.
Chen, M., Sebstad, J. and O'Connell, L. (1999). Counting the invisible workforce: The case of homebased workers. *World Development, 27*(3), 603–610.
Chen, M., Vanek, J. and Heintz, J. (2006). Informality, gender and poverty: A global picture. *Economic and Political Weekly, 41*(21), 2131–2139.
Finkin, M. W. (2015). Beclouded work, beclouded workers in historical perspective. *Comparative Labor Law and Policy Journal, 37*, 603–623.
García Linera, A. (1999). *Reproletarización: nueva clase obrera y desarrollo del capital industrial en Bolivia (1952–1998).* La Paz: Muela del Diablo Editores.
Hart, Keith. (1973). Informal income opportunities and urban employment in Ghana. *Journal of Modern African Studies, 11*(1), 61–89.
Heilbroner, R. L. and Milberg, W. S. (1995). *The Crisis of Vision in Modern Economic Thought.* Cambridge: Cambridge University Press.
International Labor Organization. (2002). *Women and Men in the Informal Economy: A Statistical Picture.* Geneva: ILO.
Joekes, Susan. (1987). *Women in the World Economy.* New York: Oxford University Press.
Lewis, O. (1966). The Culture of Poverty. *Scientific American, 215*(4), 19–25.
Lewis, W. A. (1954). Economic development with unlimited supplies of labour. *The Manchester School, 22*, 139–191.
Mayhew, Henry. (1851). *London Labour and the London Poor.* London: George Woodfall and Son.
Olson, Paulette I. and Emami, Zohreh. (2002). *Engendering Economics: Conversations with Women Economists in the United States.* New York: Routledge.
Sassen, Saskia. (1988). *The Mobility of Labor and Capital: A Study in International Investment and Labor Flow.* Cambridge: Cambridge University Press.
Todaro, Michael, P. (1969). A model of labor migration and urban unemployment in less developed countries. *The American Economic Review, 59*(1), 138–148.
Tronto, Joan. (1987). Beyond gender difference to a theory of care. *Signs: Journal of Women in Culture and Society, 12*(4), 644–663.
Van der Meulen Rodgers, Y. and Cooley, J. C. (1999). Outstanding female economists in the analysis and practice of development economics. *World Development, 27*(8), 1397–1411.
Vanek, J., Chen, M. A., Carré, F., Heintz, J. and Hussmanns, R. (2014). Statistics on the Informal Economy: Definitions, Regional Estimates & Challenges. WIEGO Working Paper No. 2. www.wiego.org/sites/wiego.org/files/publications/files/Vanek-Statistics-WIEGO-WP2.pdf. Accessed on February 20, 2017.
Whyte, W. F. (1943). Social organization in the slums. *American Sociological Review, 8*(1), 34–39.

24

WOMEN'S NEOCLASSICAL MODELS OF MARRIAGE, 1972–2015

Shoshana Grossbard with a comment by Charlotte Phelps

Introduction

In 1972 Charlotte Phelps published "Is the household obsolete?" in the *Papers and Proceedings* of the prestigious *American Economic Review*. This densely written seven-page article presents the foundations of a theory of couple formation and of in-couple individual allocation of resources and distribution of goods. It is a pioneering contribution that predates Gary Becker's (1973) much better known economic theory of marriage. So far Phelps' original ideas on marriage have not been expressed in mathematical terms. Given that such terms became the norm in economic theories of marriage, I am hereby presenting a formalized version of the core ideas in Phelps (1972) in the hope that this formalization might help scholars appreciate this early economic analysis of marriage.

Phelps' theory of marriage is then compared to Becker's and my own. It is thanks to the similarity in our theoretical approaches that I have developed an appreciation for Phelps' pioneering contribution. Some of the major similarities and differences between the three theories of marriage are presented. Two major implications of Phelps' theory are that women's choice to become housewives is not necessarily going to hurt them and that in-couple negotiations about who does what in the household are of great consequence. I also summarize some of my own economic theory of marriage, with emphasis on exchanges of work for money across the members of a couple.

Phelps (1972) was not cited in Becker's writings on marriage (1973, 1981) or in later economic models of marriage such as Manser and Brown (1980), McElroy and Horney (1981), Apps and Rees (1988), or Chiappori (1988). I have not cited her either, as I only recently became acquainted with her contribution to the economic modeling of marriage. The chapter concludes by calling for more recognition for Phelps' status as a pioneer in household economics. In particular, Phelps (1972) deserves credit for being a pioneer in modeling household production as an individual decision in need of coordination with other household members' decisions.

The next section offers relevant background information about Charlotte Phelps and me. The third section offers a more formal version of Phelps' marriage model. The following section compares her theory to that of Becker and to mine. Policy implications can be found in the fifth section, followed by conclusions. In the final section, Phelps summarizes some of her more recent work.

Biographical background

Charlotte De Monte Phelps was born in 1933 and raised in New Jersey.[1] She began her undergraduate training in 1951 at Radcliffe College, shifting from an initial interest in government into economics. Her undergraduate training included a course on economic theory offered by Wassily Leontief. After earning her bachelor's degree, Phelps pursued graduate work in economics at Yale. She studied international trade under the direction of Tom Schelling and monetary policy under James Tobin. Tobin pointed the way to her dissertation topic concerning the impact of tightening credit on municipal capital expenditures and the municipal bond market. She earned her Ph.D. in 1961 and published a paper on her dissertation topic in the *American Economic Review* (Phelps 1969).

At Yale, Charlotte met and married Edmund (Ned) Phelps. As she recalls it, Yale "had an 'unwritten?' rule to prevent nepotism," so when Ned received his instructorship at Yale, she received an appointment to work on the development of an index of economic articles that later became the *Journal of Economic Literature*. She also commuted to teach at Connecticut College for a year during this time, but left because her "idea of what a 'good wife' should do and commuting didn't match." She then received a research appointment from Tjalling Koopmans, Director of the Cowles Foundation for Research in Economics at Yale, and worked with Ned on a paper that was published in the *Review of Economics and Statistics* (Phelps and Phelps 1966).

Ned Phelps received an appointment at the rank of professor with the University of Pennsylvania and the couple moved to Philadelphia in 1966. Limiting her search for positions to the area, Charlotte's research background attracted an offer from Temple University, which appointed her at the rank of instructor. Soon after, the couple divorced. Decades later in 2006, Ned Phelps was awarded the Nobel Prize in economics.

In 1971 Barbara Bergmann invited Phelps to participate in a symposium on women and work at the ASSA meetings in New Orleans, which led to her 1972 article that is at the core of this chapter.

I studied at the University of Chicago in the 1970s, specializing in the economics of marriage. Gary Becker (Nobel Prize in economics 1992) served as the principal advisor on my doctoral thesis about the economics of polygamy in Nigeria. Another Chicago Nobel Prize winner, T. W. Schultz, had consulted in Nigeria and made those data available to me. Before completing my dissertation I published an article in *Current Anthropology* that included a simple version of my theory offering an economic analysis of markets for wife-services and an application to polygamy in Nigeria (Grossbard 1976). Based on consultations with anthropologist Ronald Cohen, a specialist on the Kanuris of Nigeria, it became clear to me that in the city of Maiduguri, Nigeria, wives were mostly employees of their husbands who owned the living quarters and kept custody of children in case of divorce. The idea that husbands employ wives in household production became central to my first theory of marriage. Switching to an application to Western societies where both men and women engage in household production and have property rights to household resources I expanded my theory to include spouses working for each other's benefit in childcare and other household production services. This led to a 1984 article in *Economic Journal*, my 2015 book *The Marriage Motive* and many articles and books on the economics of marriage in-between.

Charlotte and I first met at a 1986 meeting of the Society for the Advancement of Behavioral Economics (SABE). We presented at the same session on family economics and discussed each other's work. Then and later, at the many points where our paths crossed, she was immersed in her work integrating economic analysis with personality tests (see Phelps' comments in the final section of this chapter, and also, Phelps 1988, 1991; Phelps and Ambady 2002). She mentioned her 1972 article, but I did not read it carefully until recently.

Formalizing Phelps' analysis

According to Phelps:

> household formation can be explained by making certain assumptions about human behavior: (1) that each person wants to maximize his or her own happiness [utility], (2) . . . a person's happiness varies directly with own *ability* to give and receive *love* and with own level of self-respect, and (3) that the level of a person's happiness is greater if he or she lives in a household that fulfills the conditions of household equilibrium than if he or she lives alone or in a household that is in a state of disequilibrium.
>
> *Phelps 1972, pp. 168–169; emphasis added*

Utility function and constraints

Phelps does not specify a utility function, but a Phelps-consistent utility function can be obtained based on these and some further assumptions that Phelps makes. She states that a person's happiness varies directly with own ability to give and receive love. If giving love is an activity, not a gift of material goods, giving love (mentioned in assumption 2) can be interpreted as spending time supplying loving care to others, and deriving utility from receiving a partner's love (also mentioned in assumption 2) can be interpreted as deriving satisfaction from the time the partner spends supplying loving care to the individual. In the spirit of Phelps' theory I thus replace the first part of assumption 2 with the following two assumptions: (a) utility varies as a function of *time* spent on giving love and of the loving care that the partner bestows and is received by the individual, and (b) *ability* to love is a parameter that may cause positive shifts in the corresponding utility function:

$$U_i = U_i(love_{ij}, love_{ji}),$$

where individual i is the self, j is a (potential) partner, $Love_{ij}$ is loving and caring time that individual i supplies to partner j and $love_{ji}$ is love that i receives when partner j devotes time to care for the individual. The more the individual and the partner are able to love, the more individual i will be satisfied. Furthermore, Phelps states that utility depends on self-respect, implying that

$$(1)\quad U_i = U_i(love_{ij},\ love_{ji}, selfrespect_i)$$

According to Phelps self-respect is a function of:

> (i) the ability to perform services competently in exchange for payment; i.e., the ability to demonstrate work competence; (ii) the ability to provide oneself with a desired standard of living (food, clothing, shelter, entertainment); (iii) the ability to choose the kinds of work and leisure activities, the timing of these activities, and the linkage to the companionship of other people which will maximize individual satisfaction, and (iv) the belief in own intrinsic worth.
>
> *Phelps 1972, p. 170; Arabic numbers have been replaced with Roman numbers*

It follows from (i) that a person derives self-respect from time working in exchange for payment, presumably in the labor force, implying that $Selfrespect_i = R_i(l)_i$ where l denotes labor, and from (ii) that self-respect can be derived from goods purchased in the commercial sector (x), i.e. function R can be expanded to $Selfrespect_i = R_i(l_i, x_i)$. Furthermore, according to assumption (iii) self-respect is partially based on choice of leisure activities, implying that self-respect is also derived from leisure time which I denote by s and thus:[2]

(2) $Selfrespect_i = R_i\ (l_i, x_i, s_i)$

Using Becker's (1965, 1973) production function terminology, equation 2 can be viewed as the function describing how 'self-respect' is produced. The *ability* to work, to obtain goods that the person values and to optimally choose leisure activities can be modeled as parameters that cause shifts in the production function of self-respect.[3]

Phelps does not explicitly present budget or time constraints, but she specifies that *individuals*, not couples, make decisions regarding time allocation. In contrast, in Becker's (1973) theory of marriage and his (1965) theory of allocation of time he assumes that when individuals are in-couple *couples* make time-allocation decisions. This implies that he assumes a time constraint containing the total time available to both members of a couple.

It can also be inferred from Phelps' (1972) that the budget constraint is an individual constraint. She writes: "In a market economy there are two ways people show they value one another's services: by monetary rewards and by the psychic reward of approval" (p. 170). She thus recognizes monetary rewards, i.e. wages, in the case of labor. More on approval is found on p. 171:

> Approval is a psychic reward itself. It is personal. For approval to be a valuable means of payment it must be given by a person or persons to whom the worker wants to demonstrate competence. It must be given by a person whom the worker thinks is a good judge of the level of performance in the worker's chosen field of work.

Approval from others thus contributes to the utility generated by time at work, l.

According to Phelps the budget constraint will depend on an individual's gender and labor force status. Phelps explicitly writes about women becoming housewives, in which case they get monetary rewards for 'work' in household production of benefit to the spouse (and perhaps other household members). However, on p. 171 Phelps is more gender-neutral:

> If a person fails to achieve his or her targeted goal in terms of money income, and if the person is accustomed to providing the desired standard of living by earning money income, . . . such a person may seek compensation by performing services for others in exchange for approval either inside or outside the household or by lowering the desired standard of living. If one has satisfied the other requirements for self-respect, one will allocate time between the two kinds of work so that the marginal utility per unit of each currency is equal.

This suggests that individuals (presumably men or women) can work part time in loving care and translate approval from their spouse into monetary income.

It can be assumed that Phelps' budget constraint contains all sources of individual income (including earnings from work in the labor force and from supplying loving care) on one side and all uses of that income on the other side (including possible payments to a partner who gives love to the individual).

Optimization and matching

Phelps' third element of self-respect is "the ability to choose the kinds of work and leisure activities, and the timing of these activities, and the linkage to the companionship of other people which will maximize individual satisfaction." "The ability to choose between various kinds of work and leisure" can be interpreted as a process of individual rational choice whereby individuals maximize their own utility function subject to individual budget and time constraints. Phelps does not offer details on this maximization process. She suggests what an individual equilibrium would entail: individual (not household) consumption and "one will allocate time between the two kinds of work so that the marginal utility per unit of each currency is equal" (1972, p. 171).

As for the second part in element (iii), "the linkage to the companionship of other people which will maximize individual satisfaction," it describes a matching process by which individuals match their preferred levels of given and received love.

It is now easier to understand Phelps' assumption (3) stated above and at the onset of her article: "the level of a person's happiness is greater if he or she lives in a household that fulfills the conditions of household equilibrium than if he or she lives alone or in a household that is in a state of disequilibrium" (Phelps 1972, pp. 168–169). Phelps thus has an *individual* allocative *equilibrium*, based on individual maximization and individual willingness to engage in certain activities and purchases, and a household or *couple equilibrium* interpreted as a match by which given and received love correspond and neither of the individuals will want to leave the couple. Furthermore, Phelps also writes about "all households being in equilibrium": "If all people behaved rationally . . . and if all were aware of the conditions necessary for the formation of an equilibrium household, initially all households would be in equilibrium" (p. 169).

Comparing Phelps (1972) to two other economic theories of marriage

Phelps (1972) is now compared to two other economic theories of marriage: Becker (1973) and Grossbard-Shechtman (1984) [hereafter GS]. All three theories aim at explaining both couple formation and allocation of resources within couples.

Comparing Phelps (1972) and Becker (1973)

Phelps' (1972) article innovated research in the economics of marriage in the sense that its publication predates Becker (1973). The two theories both:

1 Assume individual maximization of utility and a comparison of utility if married versus utility while single. Individuals rationally decide to either form a couple or leave one as a function of the relative costs and benefits of marriage and its alternatives.
2 Assume that individuals derive utility from private consumption, including 'goods' produced at home. In Becker's theory these goods are household-produced 'commodities' denoted by Z and individuals compare what they can obtain as singles to the portion of the 'commodities' (potentially) produced in a marriage (as part of a *household* maximization subject to *household* time and budget constraints).
3 Address issues of allocation of time to household production and individual in-couple consumption.
4 View marriage as a contract.
5 Use the concept of equilibrium.

6 Assume that unmeasurable individual utility is a function of something else that is unmeasurable: self-respect in the case of Phelps and individual access to commodities in the case of Becker. In Becker (1973) individual utility is derived from individual access to commodities; in turn commodities are produced with household production functions.

However, the theories also differ on the following points:

1' Becker's theory includes formal models and clearly stated testable predictions.

2' Becker's theory assumes that households produce as if they were one unit. As in his theory of allocation of time (Becker 1965), Becker (1973) assumes that *couples* make time-allocation decisions and that a time constraint contains the total time available to both members of a couple. In that sense Phelps stands out from all the then-available economic literature on time allocation influenced by the *New Home Economics* pioneered by Becker (1960) and Jacob Mincer (1962, 1963):

> The theoretical and empirical literature dealing with labor force participation rates and the allocation of unpaid time among activities uses the terms *household production* and *household consumption*. See Gary Becker [1965], W. G. Bowen and T. A. Finegan [1969], Glen Cain [1966], James Heckman [1971], and John Owen [1969].

And importantly, Phelps continues that she does not use these terms because she believes that "the household is a social organization for individuals who engage in some activities with members inside the group and other activities with members outside the group" (Phelps, p. 172, footnote 13; the dates of the publications have been added to the original).[4] Phelps pioneered by introducing the concept of a household as an institution in which two individuals agree contractually on the allocation of their time. Phelps' individuals make their own decisions regarding production, even if they prefer to be part of a couple and coordinate their decisions with their partner.

3' Time uses central to Phelps' theory are not considered by Becker: loving care given to the partner and received from the partner. In part, the absence of such concept in Becker's theory is a corollary of his assumption that 'households' allocate time.

4' In her theory Phelps also recognizes that there can be exchanges of loving care by one partner for financial benefits offered by the other partner.

5' Even though both theories include the concept of marriage as an *agreement* or contract between two individuals, the need for agreement and coordination in Becker (1973) is not as encompassing as it is in Phelps (1972) since Becker assumes households organize production as a blended decision-making unit, not as separate individuals. In Phelps two individuals continuously remain two independent decision-makers, also at the production stage. Hence the value of agreements regarding household production.

Comparing Phelps (1972) and Grossbard-Shechtman (1984) [GS]

This section first presents the GS model and then compares it with Phelps (1972) and Becker (1973). My theory of marriage was recently tightened in Grossbard (2015).

If a model's goal is to lead to testable implications there is little to gain from modeling unmeasurable utility as a function of unmeasurable *Z*'s.[5] This inspired me to assume instead that individual utility varies with the measurable inputs—time and commercial goods—that enter into the production of what individuals consume. More specifically, in GS individuals maximize the following utility function:

(3) $U_i = U_i(h_{ij}, s_i, l_i, x_i)$

where h denotes time performing activities that benefit a partner and that I call '*Work-in-Household*' (WiHo; Grossbard 2015). WiHo could be any activity that the individual can perform for the partner's benefit. h_{ij} is WiHo time the individual devotes to a partner and h_{ij} is WiHo time that a partner devotes to benefit the individual.[6]

Individual optimization in GS involves maximizing utility function 3 subject to a time and a budget constraint. Starting in Grossbard (1976), well before I first became acquainted with Phelps' work, I have also assumed that when it comes to production at home individuals allocate their own resources even if they are married.[7]

An individual's budget constraint in GS is based on the assumption that there are given prices for own and partner's WiHo. Ignoring non-work income an individual budget constraint is

(4) $wl_i + y_i h_i = px_i + y_i h_j$

where w stands for wage and y stands for the price of Work-in-Household benefiting a partner.[8] This constraint endogenizes the labor force participation decision and the decision to be part of a couple, by recognizing that both men and women could possibly work in the labor force as well as in WiHo (Work-in-Household production for the benefit of their spouse).

Optimization leads to first order conditions from which GS derives individual willingness to allocate time and money to various uses. More specifically, GS obtains individual supplies of WiHo benefiting spouses (and children) and time that can be classified as leisure (benefits the self only) as well as demands for acts of kindness and loving care (WiHo) that a spouse performs for the benefit of the individual.

Couples are formed and remain together if both the amount of WiHo demanded from the other corresponds to the amount of WiHo she or he supplies and the amount of WiHo that the individual supplies corresponds to what the other has a demand for. This implies a variety of possible contracts between partners, married or not. A traditional housewife/husband agreement of the type discussed explicitly by Phelps (1972) and alluded to in Becker (1973) is just one such contract.

The theory shares points 1 to 5 listed above with Becker (1973) and Phelps (1972). As is the case with Becker (1973), but not with Phelps (1972), GS includes a formal model leading to first order equilibrium conditions and testable predictions.

Point 6 shared by Phelps (1972) and Becker (1973) is that they assume that utility (an unmeasurable entity) is a function of a second unmeasurable entity: commodities produced with a household production function in Becker (1973) and a self-respect function in Phelps (1972). This is not the case in GS.

Like Phelps (1972), and in contrast to Becker (1973), GS does not feature '*household* production.' From start to finish individuals are independent decision-makers and allocate their own time (see Grossbard 2011), even if they are in couple and take their partner's preferences and constraints into account.[9] GS replaces Becker's (1973) combined household time constraint with an individual time constraint. For example, I assume that even when in couple a person has a time budget of 24 hours per day (in contrast to Becker's couple's total time of 48 hours per day). Individual time use is restricted to work, WiHo, and leisure.

The following are points that my GS model shares with Phelps (1972) but not with Becker (1973):

- As stated in point 2' above, Phelps assumes that *individuals* make time-allocation decisions, even when in couple. So does GS. In contrast, Becker (1973) assumes *couples* allocate time and other resources toward household production.

- Loving care of the partner is a time use found in Phelps but not in Becker (point 3' above). Phelps' 'love' and my 'WiHo' have a lot in common: they cover many of the same activities and Phelps recognizes that 'love' acts can be work. However, Phelps and GS also differ on this matter: Phelps tends to limit the 'work' aspect of giving love to the case of a housewife aspiring to "provide herself with her desired standard of living" whereas all loving care could possibly be part of WiHo. Phelps differentiates acts of love motivated by altruistic ideals—unconditional love—from those performed with the expectation of a reward in the form of money or approval (Phelps 1972, p. 171). In her view the former contribute to self-respect while the latter are detrimental to it. This difference between the two models can be clarified by some formalization. Consider a utility function that is obtained based on Phelps' assumptions after incorporating her self-respect function 2 into Phelps-based utility function 1, leading to $U_i = U_i(love_{ij}, love_{ji}, s_i, l_i, x_i)$. This Phelps-based function is very similar to equation 3 in GS. What Phelps writes is consistent with her assuming that the partial derivative of this utility equation as a function of loving care is positive in the case of unconditional love but negative in the case of love conditional on a reward. In contrast, I consider all loving care benefiting a spouse as 'work' regardless of gender and whether a person gets 'paid' for it or not. I assume that in equation 3 the partial derivative of utility according to WiHo time supplied is negative and therefore the more an individual engages in WiHo the higher the compensation he or she requires. At the same time some "Work-in-Household" might be motivated out of an idealistic loving disposition, in which case the supply of WiHo starts below the zero axis. This is the case of volunteer work.
- In contrast to Becker (1973), Phelps (1972) considers cases involving the exchange of loving care for financial benefits (point 4' above). GS also models possible exchanges of WiHo, which includes loving care, for financial benefits. However, Phelps limits such exchanges to the case of a housewife whereas GS also models in-couple monetary transfers that incentivize a spouse's supply of loving care/WiHo regardless of gender and employment status. GS does not constrain exchanges the way that Phelps does, for instance, here: "The conditions for household equilibrium can be fulfilled if and only if both members are aware that self-respect and love are complements and that the giving of love is unconditional" (Phelps 1972, p. 171).
- A corollary of point 2' is that according to Phelps (1972) marriage agreements or contracts need to deal not only with consumption and intra-household allocation of commercial goods (as is the case with Becker's theory) but also with coordination of allocation of time and other resources to household production (point 5' above). The same applies to GS. I agree with Phelps that such agreements could be complex and that it might be necessary to renegotiate them regularly: "How can a couple live together without feeling excessively constrained? By negotiating with one another. Life within a household or the experiences of a couple considering household formation may be viewed as a series of negotiations" (Phelps 1972, p. 172).

Policy implications

Becker's (1973) theory of marriage assumes that household production occurs but does not address the question of how households organize production. In contrast, Phelps (1972) and Grossbard-Shechtman (1984) view 'household production' as consisting of the voluntary productive activities of individual members of the household. Since most multi-person households consist of couples, Phelps (1972) emphasizes the need for agreements between the members of a couple regarding both production and distribution of what is produced. Many theories of marriage also recognize the need for in-couple negotiations, including Becker (1973), bargaining theories of marriage (e.g. Manser and Brown 1980, McElroy and Horney

1981, and McElroy 1990), Apps and Rees (1988), and Chiappori (1988). However, what they have in mind are negotiations regarding distribution and consumption in couples.

Negotiations are costly. Family institutions have originated, in part, to reduce negotiation costs and other transaction costs of the kind that are faced by productive firms. Firms and families are similar in that respect, as argued by Ben-Porath (1980) and Pollak (1985). Family institutions, including laws and norms regarding gender roles, often facilitate negotiations by spouses or partners by limiting the range of time-use agreements that are socially acceptable. Such social standards serve as a device to coordinate total work between men and women (Burda et al. 2013). Family formation, including couple formation, can be encouraged by such family institutions. Depending on the social context, societies will opt for different norms about gender roles. Two prominent sets of norms are traditional family norms (often called 'patriarchal', see Lamanna et al. 2014) and egalitarian norms. In societies with traditional family norms, women do more household work than men. These tend to be societies with very limited labor force participation of women. In some pre-industrial societies with almost non-existent labor force participation of women, as among the Kanuris of Nigeria in the 1970s, women assume the entire burden of household production (Cohen 1971).

Norms regarding gender roles may also have influenced economic theories of marriage, especially when it comes to predictions and implications derived from theory. Becker's (1973, 1981) theory of marriage has emphasized the implication that a traditional division of labor is optimal, an implication criticized e.g. by Barbara Bergmann (1995) and Frances Woolley (1996). It is not surprising that a male economist who had reached adulthood at a time when such division of labor prevailed used his theory to rationalize a traditional division of labor. In contrast Phelps, who had reached adulthood around the same time as Becker, never used her theory to offer a rationale for housewives' specialization in household production. However, traditional households with housewives also play an important role in her theory. She takes their existence as given and discusses the Women's Liberation Movement's aspiration to eliminate what she calls the "dependency" of housewives (Phelps 1972, p. 171).

Younger generations, including younger economists of marriage residing in the U.S. such as Betsey Stevenson and Justin Wolfers (2008), have aspired to gender equality in household production (Lachman 2013). This could have influenced their economic theory of couple formation: they do not emphasize the 'firm' side of marriage or cohabitation; they see marriage as an institution that has shifted from being a forum for shared production to becoming one for shared consumption (Stevenson and Wolfers 2008). Instituting more egalitarianism in household production has also been a policy priority in the Nordic countries for many decades. This helps explain why Nordic countries were the first to institute parental leave policies for both mothers and fathers and Nordic scholars have written extensively about the effects of such policies (see Gupta et al. 2008). In societies where most educated women, including mothers, participate in the labor force, egalitarian norms regarding household production seem to encourage couple formation (Sevilla-Sanz 2010), especially in the case of highly educated women (Gimenez-Nadal et al. 2012).

A policy implication regarding household production that I have emphasized is the adoption of laws and norms that consider a wider range of time-use negotiations between spouses than the range considered by Phelps (1972). I find Phelps' rationale for housewives' devotion to household production excessively idealistic. One of the conclusions of Phelps' analysis is that:

> What the members of the Women's Liberation Movement overlook is that many women regard their household activities primarily as acts of love; i.e., leisure activities by my definition. . . . the money income they receive is not conditional on earning approval. They suffer no loss of self-respect for the way they choose to occupy their time.
>
> *p. 171*

While I agree with Phelps' point about the need to negotiate about "who does what" in the household I disagree with her when she writes "No currency, money or approval, can buy love" (p. 172). If she recognizes that housewives supply loving care in return for material benefits, why can't such exchange of love for money be generalized to couples where both spouses participate in the labor force? I would assume that an individual WiHo worker's overall self-respect and satisfaction would depend on how much she/he gets paid for their work. Providing more legal support to exchanges of loving care for money is a key to more fruitful negotiations among partners and potential partners. In turn, if mutually agreeable solutions can be found more easily, this could encourage household formation and lower the number of divorces and separations (Grossbard-Shechtman and Lemennicier 1999; Grossbard-Shechtman 2003b).

Conclusion

In 1972 Charlotte Phelps made an important contribution to the economic analysis of marriage by publishing an article that applies traditional tools of economic analysis to the subject of marriage, couple formation, as well as intra-household production, allocation, and distribution. Gary Becker's (1973) theory of marriage, based on many of the same assumptions, has received considerably more attention. It is hoped that this chapter will encourage scholars interested in the economics of marriage and the family to also read and cite Phelps' pioneering article.

The New Home Economics, under the leadership of Becker and Jacob Mincer, rightfully emphasized the importance of production in the household. However, they conceived such production as 'household production' as if the household is an integrated firm. Phelps (1972) deserves credit in calling for modeling of household production as individual decisions requiring coordination with other household members.

The analysis of production in the household as the result of individual decisions by multiple agents was pursued more systematically in Grossbard-Shechtman (1984) [GS], Grossbard (2015) and a number of my other articles. This approach has led to many testable implications, including predicted effects of fluctuations in sex ratio and compensating differentials in marriage.

Well-functioning families and households need to produce caring and other services for children and other dependants. The approach first presented by Charlotte Phelps and GS could strengthen families by contributing ideas on how to incentivize caring by household members and other forms of non-commercial production. They might help reverse a trend whereby educated young adults are avoiding having children and producing good nutrition and other important goods traditionally produced in households.

It is time to follow Phelps' lead and get away from the black box called 'household production.' Let us make potential producers in the household more aware of the value of their time and other resources and better able to assess what they need to get from their partners in return for their work benefiting partners. Phelps was right to put the emphasis on negotiations by men and women interested in contributing to all that is produced by couples and families. This could lead to better health and cognitive outcomes without the need for intense government intervention that often discourages cooperation between co-parents and between parents and children.

"Is the household obsolete?" A comment on Grossbard by Charlotte D. Phelps

Since many contemporary economists have revealed a preference for formalized models, I am grateful to Shoshana Grossbard for formalizing mine. However, an equally important question for any theory is whether it can be tested against alternative explanations of behavior. My main contribution was to provide empirical tests of Becker's theory with measures of personality to represent 'tastes' that are held constant.

After the *AER* paper, I invested my time in reading literature on personality development and economic behavior. I became convinced that the effects of early childhood learning are revealed in Thematic Apperception Tests (TAT).[10] I used a measure of altruism from the TAT that Becker approved.

I searched the literature on personality for theories and evidence related to my assertion that parents' love to their babies is a foundation for the babies' future happiness. I found a large literature on attachment theory that explains and documents connections between loving care in early childhood and economic outcomes in adulthood (see, for example, Bowlby, 1969, 1973, 1980, 1988).

I found materials that documented connections between early childhood socialization and adult economic outcomes in a thirty-six-year longitudinal study of Boston baby boomers conducted by Harvard psychologists (Sears et al. 1957; McClelland and Pilon 1983; Franz et al. 1991; McClelland and Franz 1992). Social interactions in their families in early childhood influenced their perceptions of opportunities for work and love. Mother-anxiety observed when their children were in kindergarten predicted lower levels of parenting satisfaction and work satisfaction thirty-six years later (Phelps 2005). Mother-infant warmth predicted parenting satisfaction.

I found two nationwide surveys of Americans' mental health (see, for example, Gurin et al. 1975) included TATs. I used data from them to test hypotheses in "A Theory of Social Interactions" (Becker 1974), to study personality differences in fertility (Phelps 1995), effects of parents' divorce on their children's economic outcomes (Phelps 1998), and connections between TAT motives and happiness (Phelps 2001). A finding from the last paper was that altruists tend to marry altruists and are happier than couples who bargain. A point relevant to Grossbard's research is that altruistic husbands reported they helped often with childcare.

Notes

1 The biographical notes for Phelps are based on her personal recollections.

2 The symbol *s* denotes leisure (corresponds roughly to 'time for self' in Grossbard-Shechtman (1984).

3 Some further elements of Phelps' self-respect are discussed below.

4 It is noteworthy that most of the economists that Phelps cites here were associated with the New Home Economics when or soon after it was developed at Columbia by Becker and Jacob Mincer, the two fathers of the New Home Economics (see Becker 2006): Becker was at Columbia while he published his theory of allocation of time; the basic model used by Glen Cain is that of Mincer 1962 (see Haber 1967); Heckman joined the Columbia labor workshop in 1970, the year after Becker left for Chicago; and Owen was a student of Becker and Mincer at Columbia.

5 As I learned from economist Yoram Ben-Porath in the 1970s.

6 WiHo was called '*spousal labor*' in Grossbard-Shechtman (1984).

7 Charlotte Phelps and I first met in 1986. Soon after, she sent me the 1972 article discussed here.

8 In Grossbard-Shechtman (1984) I used the symbol w^* for the 'price' of WiHo (then called spousal labor). More about this price is found in Grossbard (2015).

9 Grossbard-Shechtman (2003a) also includes models with consumption of household public goods that are possibly produced jointly.

10 A Thematic Apperception Test (TAT) is a projective personality test in which a person composes stories about pictures of different situations. Psychologists score the stories for themes of achievement, power, and affiliation. See Smith et al. (1992) for copies of the pictures, the scoring manuals, and essays interpreting the manuals. Themes in the stories reveal motives hidden from conscious awareness. Coombs (1947) found that the TAT captured motives that were excluded from autobiographies, among them being the desire to be accepted and the desire to atone.

References

Apps, Patricia and Ray Rees (1988). "Taxation and the Household." *Journal of Public Economics* 35: 355–369.

Becker, Gary S. (1960). "An Economic Analysis of Fertility." In Demographic and Economic Change in Developed Countries, a Conference of the Universities—National Bureau Committee for Economic Research. Princeton, NJ: Princeton University Press.

——. (1965). "A Theory of the Allocation of Time." *Economic Journal* 75(299): 493–517.

——. (1973). "A Theory of Marriage: Part I." *Journal of Political Economy* 81(4): 813–846.

——. (1974). "A Theory of Social Interactions." *Journal of Political Economy* 70: 1–13.

——. (1981). *A Treatise on the Family.* Cambridge: Harvard University Press (2nd edition: 1991).

——. (2006). "Working with Jacob Mincer: Reminiscences of Columbia's Labor Workshop." In *Jacob Mincer: A Pioneer of Modern Labor Economics*, ed. by Shoshana Grossbard. New York: Springer, 63–105.

Ben-Porath, Yoram (1980). "The F-Connection: Families, Friends, and Firms and the Organization of Exchange." *Population and Development Review* 6(1): 1–30.

Bergmann, Barbara. (1995). "Becker's Theory of the Family: Preposterous Conclusions." *Feminist Economics* 1: 141–150.

Bowen, William G., and T.A. Finegan (1969). *The Economics of Labor Force Participation.* Princeton University Press.

Bowlby, J. (1969, 1973, 1980). *Attachment and Loss: Vols. 1, 2, & 3.* New York: Basic Books.

—— (1988). *A Secure Base: Parent-child Attachment and Healthy Human Development.* New York: Basic Books.

Burda, M., D. Hamermesh, and P. Weil (2013). "Total Work and Gender: Facts and Possible Explanations." *Journal of Population Economics* 26: 239–261.

Cain, Glen G. (1966). *Married Women in the Labor Force: An Economic Analysis.* Chicago: University of Chicago Press.

Chiappori, Pierre-Andre (1988). "Rational Household Labor Supply." *Econometrica* 56: 63–90.

Cohen, Ronald (1971). *Dominance and Defiance.* Washington, DC: American Anthropological Association.

Coombs, A.W. (1947). "A Comparative Study of Motivation as Revealed in Thematic Apperception Stories and Autobiography." *Journal of Clinical Psychology* 3: 65–75.

Franz, C.E., D.C. McClelland, and J. Weinberger (1991). "Childhood Antecedents of Conventional Social Accomplishment in Midlife Adults: A 36 Year Prospective Study." *Journal of Personality and Social Psychology* 60(4): 586–595.

Gimenez-Nadal, Jose Ignacio, Jose Alberto Molina, and Almudena Sevilla-Sanz (2012). "Social Norms, Partnerships, and Children." *Review of Economics of the Household* 10: 215–236.

Grossbard, Amyra (1976). "An Economic Analysis of Polygamy: The Case of Maiduguri." *Current Anthropology* 17: 701–707.

Grossbard, Shoshana (2011). "Independent Individual Decision-makers in Household Models and the New Home Economics." In *Household Economic Behaviors*, ed. by J. Alberto Molina. New York: Springer, 41–56.

—— (2015). *The Marriage Motive.* New York: Springer.

Grossbard-Shechtman, Amyra (1984). "A Theory of Allocation of Time in Markets for Labor and Marriage." *Economic Journal* 94: 863–882.

Grossbard-Shechtman, Shoshana (2003a). "A Consumer Theory with Competitive Markets for Work in Marriage." *Journal of Socio-Economics* 31(6): 609–645.

——. (2003b). "Introduction." In *Marriage and the Economy: Theory and Evidence from Advanced Industrial Societies*, ed. by S Grossbard-Shechtman. New York: Cambridge University Press, 1–37.

Grossbard-Shechtman, Shoshana, and Bertrand Lemennicier (1999). "Marriage Contracts and the Law-and-Economics of Marriage: An Austrian Perspective." *Journal of Socio-Economics* 28: 665–690.

Gupta, Nabanita Datta, Nina Smith, and Mette Verner (2008). "The Impact of Nordic Countries' Family Friendly Policies on Employment, Wages, and Children." *Review of Economics of the Household* 6(1): 65–89.

Gurin, G., J. Veroff, and S. Feld (1975). *Americans View Their Mental Health, 1957.* S.S.A Study no. 3503. Ann Arbor, MI: Survey Research Center, Institute for Social Research.

Haber, Sheldon E. (1967). "Review of '*Married Women in the Labor Force: An Economic Analysis* by Glen G. Cain.'" *Industrial and Labor Relations Review* 21(1): 121–123.

Heckman, James J. (1971). "Three Essays on Household Labor Supply," unpublished doctoral dissertation, Princeton University.

Lachman, Samantha (2013). "Economist Betsey Stevenson: Working Parenthood 'Not Just a Woman's Issue.'" *Salon*. Available from www.salon.com/2013/06/13/economist_betsey_stevenson_working_parenthood_not_just_a_woman%E2%80%99s_issue%E2%80%9D/ (accessed June 23, 2017).

Lamanna, Mary Ann, Agnes Riedmann, and Susan Stewart (2014). *Marriages, Families, and Relationships: Making Choices in a Diverse Society*. Stamford, CT: Cengage Learning, 12th edition.

Manser, Marilyn and M. Brown (1980). "Marriage and Household Decision Making: A Bargaining Analysis." *International Economic Review* 21: 31–44.

McClelland, D.C., and D.A. Pilon (1983). "Sources of Adult Motives in Patterns of Parent Behavior in Early Childhood." *Journal of Personality and Social Psychology* 44(3): 564–574.

McClelland, D.C., and C.E. Franz (1992). "Motivational and Other Sources of Work Accomplishments in Mid-Life: A Longitudinal Study." *Journal of Personality* 60(4): 679–707.

McElroy, Marjorie B. (1990). "The Empirical Content of Nash-Bargained Household Behavior." *Journal of Human Resources* 25: 559–583.

McElroy, Marjorie B., and M.J. Horney (1981). "Nash Bargained Household Decisions: Toward a Generalization of the Theory of Demand." *International Economic Review* 22: 333–349.

Mincer, Jacob (1962). "Labor Force Participation of Married Women: A Study of Labor Supply." In *Aspects of Labor Economics*, ed. by H. Gregg Lewis. Princeton, NJ: Princeton University Press, 63–105.

—— (1963). "Market Prices, Opportunity Costs, and Income Effects." In *Measurement in Economics*, ed. by C. Christ. Stanford, CA: Stanford University Press, 67–82.

Owen, John D. (1969). *The Price of Leisure*. Rotterdam: Rotterdam University Press.

Phelps, Charlotte D. (1969). "Real and Monetary Determinants of State and Local Highway Investment, 1951–1966." *American Economic Review* 59: 507–521.

—— (1972). "Is the Household Obsolete?" *The American Economic Review Papers and Proceedings* 62(1/2): 167–174.

—— (1988). "Caring and Family Income." *Journal of Economic Behavior and Organization* 10: 83–98.

—— (1991). "The Disappearance of Polarized Altruism." *Journal of Economic Behavior and Organization* 15: 91–113.

—— (1995). "Wives' Motives and Fertility." *Journal of Economic Behavior and Organization* 27: 49–67.

—— (1998). "Gender Differences in the Long-term Economic Consequences of Parental Divorce." *Journal of Economic Behavior and Organization* 37: 151–168.

—— (2001). "A Clue to the Paradox of Happiness." *Journal of Economic Behavior and Organization* 45: 293–300.

—— (2005). "The Evolution of Caring." In *Economics and Happiness: Framing the Analysis*, ed. by L. Bruni and P. Porta. Oxford: Oxford University Press, Chapter 11.

Phelps, C.D., and N. Ambady (2002). "The Mother's Voice: A Predictor of the Father's Impact on their Child's Adult Economic Outcomes." *Proceedings of IAREP/SABE Conference on Behavioral Economics* 308–312.

Phelps, Edmund S., and Charlotte D. Phelps (1966). "Factor-Price Frontier Estimation of the U.S. Non-farm Business Sector." *Review of Economics and Statistics* 48: 251–265.

Pollak, Robert A. (1985). "A Transaction Cost Approach to Families and Households." *Journal of Economic Literature* 23(2): 581–608.

Sears, R.R., E.E. Maccoby, and H. Levin (1957). *Patterns of Child Rearing*. Evanston, IL: Row, Peterson.

Sevilla-Sanz, Almudena (2010). "Household Division of Labor and Cross-country Differences in Household Formation Rates." *Journal of Population Economics* 23: 225–249.

Smith, Charles P., John W. Atkinson, David C. McClelland, and Joseph Veroff (1992). *Motivation and Personality: Handbook of Thematic Content Analysis*. Cambridge: Cambridge University Press.

Stevenson, Betsey, and Justin Wolfers (2008). "Marriage and the Market." *Cato Unbound*, January 18. Available at: www.cato-unbound.org/2008/01/18/betsey-stevenson-justin-wolfers/marriage-market (accessed June 23, 2018).

Woolley, Frances (1996). "Getting the Better of Becker." *Feminist Economics* 2: 114–120.

INDEX

References to notes are indicated by n, references to tables are in **bold**.

For Product Safety Concerns and Information please contact our EU
representative GPSR@taylorandfrancis.com
Taylor & Francis Verlag GmbH, Kaufingerstraße 24, 80331 München, Germany

www.ingramcontent.com/pod-product-compliance
Ingram Content Group UK Ltd.
Pitfield, Milton Keynes, MK11 3LW, UK
UKHW050232200926
475702UK00020B/2978
* 9 7 8 0 3 6 7 6 5 9 7 8 3 *